Women's Movements
in the Global Era

Women's Movements in the Global Era

The Power of Local Feminisms

Amrita Basu

Editor

WESTVIEW PRESS

A Member of the Perseus Books Group

Designed by Brent Wilcox

Library of Congress Cataloging-in-Publication Data
  Women's movements in the global era : the power of local feminisms / Amrita Basu,
editor.—1st ed.
    p.   cm.
  ISBN 978-0-8133-4444-7 (alk. paper)
  1. Feminism—History—21st century.   I. Basu, Amrita, 1953–
  HQ1155.W686 2010
  305.4209'0511—dc22

                                                              2009035873

For my mother,
Rasil Basu

Contents

Acknowledgments

This book, like its predecessor, *The Challenge of Local Feminisms*, received generous support from the Ford Foundation, which has demonstrated extraordinary commitment to women's studies and women's movements. When I spoke to Alison Bernstein about this book, she responded with characteristic enthusiasm and generosity. I am deeply grateful to her and to Sheila Devaney for shepherding this project to completion. I am also thankful to Amherst College for providing the resources and environment that have made this book—and all my work—possible.

Alex Masulis encouraged me to consider this book and he and Sandra Beris made it happen. Julie Ajinkya provided enormous help in the early stages, Nora Lawrence and Amy A. Ford as the project continued. I could not have completed the book on time without Andrew Halterman's energetic and responsible assistance.

My feminist political scientist friends and fellow travelers, Martha Ackelsburg, Cynthia Enloe, Mary Katzenstein, Eileen McDonagh, and Molly Shanley, offered helpful comments on the Introduction. Sonia Alvarez, Elisabeth Jay Friedman, Mark Kesselman, Sayres Rudy, and Lisa McIntosh Sundstrom also provided valuable advice.

The fifteen years since *The Challenge of Local Feminisms* was published have been a period of enormous personal change. My sons, Ishan and Javed, have grown into impressive young men. I have lost my remarkable brother-in-law, Rob Borsellino; inspiring uncle, Patwant Singh; and extraordinary father, Romen Basu. My sister Rekha has provided levity and solace in the hardest of times. Other family members, Romen, Raj, Meher, Judy, Rebecca, Jonathan, Saida, and Elijah have made life meaningful and fun. Mark graces my life and work with his vitality, intelligence, and devotion. My mother Rasil introduced me to global feminism through her work at the United Nations and deepened my understanding of local feminism through her work with Ekatra. She has taught me about the importance of sustaining feminist commitments over time and space. This book is inspired by her example and dedicated to her with love and gratitude.

Boxed Information

Indices

Human Development Index Ranking: This index measures factors relating to life expectancy, educational opportunities and achievement, and income. This index, which ranks each country between 0 and 1, is meant to serve as a frame of reference for both social and economic development.

Gender Empowerment Measure Value: This index measures the level of economic and political activity of women in a given country and is typically used as a measure of progress. The index is particularly concerned with measuring the effectiveness and utilization of institutions designed to support women's empowerment. Measures of empowerment include political representation and participation and economic activity.

Gender-Related Development Index Value: This index measures the same factors as the Human Development Index but takes into account the inequalities that exist between men and women in a given country. Measures of inequality include (but are not limited to) access to education and income disparity. A country's Gender-Related Development Index value is usually lower than its HDI value.

Key Terms

Condom use at last high risk sex: The percentage of men and women who have had sex with a nonmarital, noncohabiting partner in the last twelve months and who say they used a condom the last time they did so.

Contraceptive prevalence rate: The percentage of married women of reproductive age (15–49) who are using, or whose partners are using, any form of contraception, whether modern or traditional.

Enrollment ratio, gross: Total number of pupils or students enrolled in a given level of education, regardless of age, expressed as a percentage of the population in the theoretical age group for the same level of education. Gross enrollment ratios in excess of 100% indicate that there are pupils or students outside the theoretical age groups who are enrolled in that level of education.

Estimated earned income: Derived on the basis of the ratio of the female nonagricultural wage to the male nonagricultural wage, the female and male shares of the economically active population, total female and male population, and GDP per capita; given in purchasing power parity terms in U.S. dollars.

Fertility rate, total: The number of children that would be born to each woman if she were to live to the end of her child-bearing years and bear children at each age in accordance with prevailing age-specific fertility rates in a given year/period, for a given country, territory, or geographical area.

Labor force participation rate, female: The number of women in the labor force expressed as a percentage of the female working-age population.

Mortality ratio, maternal, adjusted: Maternal mortality ratio adjusted to account for well-documented problems of underreporting and misclassification of maternal deaths, as well as estimates for countries with no data.

Professional and technical workers, female: Women's share of positions defined according to the International Standard Classification of Occupations to include physical, mathematical, and engineering science professionals; life science and health professionals; teaching professionals; and other professionals and associate professionals.

Women in government at ministerial level: Includes deputy prime ministers and ministers. Prime ministers were included when they held ministerial portfolios. Vice presidents and heads of ministerial-level departments or agencies were also included when exercising a ministerial function in the government structure.

Sources

BBC country profiles: http://news.bbc.co.uk/2/hi/middle_east/country_profiles/803257.stm#facts

CEDAW Statistical Database: http://unstats.un.org/unsd/demographic/products/indwm/statistics.htm

United Nations Human Development Reports: http://hdrstats.undp.org/countries/

U.S. Department of State: http://www.state.gov/r/pa/ei/bgn/

Introduction

AMRITA BASU

In the past fifteen years, women's activism has become more extensive and more contentious. Global networks that address women's rights have flourished. So too have women's policy bureaus in governments and the femocrats (feminist bureaucrats) who staff them. Women's organizations have been active in designing constitutions, collaborating with political parties, and pushing for new legislation. However, feminism remains deeply contested, particularly by conservative religious groups. Wars within and between nations have increased women's vulnerability and weakened women's movements. The spread of neoliberalism has created new economic opportunities for some women and increased hardship for many more. Moreover, the very advances that women have made—in the nation and the world—have given rise to new divisions among feminists.

My earlier book, *The Challenge of Local Feminisms,* was written in anticipation of the UN-sponsored women's conference in Beijing in 1995, the culmination of a series of conferences that began in Mexico City two decades earlier. It analyzed the strengths and weaknesses of women's movements from seventeen regions, across North-South and East-West divides. It identified women's movements' varied responses to domestic and international constraints. *Women's Movements in the Global Era* explores the lessons that the past fifteen years hold for women's movements. How, since the Beijing conference, do activists and scholars regard feminism and its relationship to women's movements? How has the collapse or emergence of democracy influenced them? What is the relative significance of domestic and global influences on local women's movements?

The volumes that have been published on women's networks, activism, and movements over the past fifteen years illuminate the diversity among women's

1

movements. A number of books are thematically organized around timely issues such as the impact of globalization and religious nationalism on women (see, for example, Naples and Desai 2002). Much has been written on transnational and international networks, issues, and arenas.[1] There has been extensive work on state feminism and women's governance.[2] Some studies have fruitfully compared women's movements in similar settings. The Comparative State Feminism series, for example, focuses on women's movements in democratic, advanced industrial societies in order to develop testable hypotheses about their achievements.[3] These writings not only address a variety of themes but also illustrate varied approaches to studying women's movements. Some studies focus on a particular issue, others on a range of issues, some on the origins, others on the outcomes, some on the global, and others on the national context.

Women's Movements in the Global Era comprises thirteen chapters with cases studies of sixteen countries from the major regions of the world. Three of them are on Asia (Farida Shaheed on Pakistan, Naihua Zhang and Ping-Chun Hsiung on China, and Kalpana Kannabiran on India), two on Africa (Elaine Salo on South Africa and Shereen Essof on Zimbabwe), two on the Middle East (Islah Jad on Palestine and Nayereh Tohidi on Iran), three on Latin America (Cecelia M. B. Sardenberg and Ana Alice Alcantara Costa on Brazil, R. Aída Hernández Castillo on Mexico, and Elisabeth Jay Friedman on Brazil, Chile, Venezuela, and Bolivia), two on Europe (Lisa McIntosh Sundstrom on Russia and Elzbieta Matynia on Poland), and one, by Julie Ajinkya, on the United States. Accounts of at least two countries from the same region enable readers to compare countries within and across regions.

Analyzing women's movements in countries that differ with respect to their political systems, degrees of stability, and levels of economic development reveals the conditions under which women's movements are most likely to be successful. It also suggests, for reasons explored later in the chapter, that women's movements under widely different conditions have been most successful in addressing violence against women and least successful in challenging class inequalities.

The authors' principal focus is on women's movements that are national in scale, influence, or structure but are also active at the local level. However, to depict the range of issues that women's movements address, some of the chapters explore struggles by women who have been historically marginalized by mainstream women's movements: Rosalva Aída Hernández Castillo analyzes indigenous women in Mexico; Elisabeth Jay Friedman explores, among other issues, lesbian, gay, bisexual, transgender, and intersex (LGBTI) organizing in

Venezuela, Chile, Bolivia, and Brazil; and Islah Jad describes Palestinian women's struggles in what has yet to become a sovereign state.

The authors were asked to address a common set of questions:

- How do they define feminism and women's movements, and how are their understandings influenced by the contexts they examine?
- What impact do international and transnational influences have on the women's movements they analyze?
- How has the state influenced the emergence, growth, and decline of women's movements? To what extent and why have women's movements sought both to challenge the state and to work within it?
- What is the relationship between women's movements and broader movements against colonialism, authoritarianism, and secularism, among others?
- What impact do key groups and organizations within civil society have on women's movements? What is the relationship between women's movements and nongovernmental organizations (NGOs)?
- To what extent and how have women's movements addressed domestic violence, women's political representation, the rights of sexual minorities, and poverty and class inequality?

In elaborating on these key themes, I draw on the authors' chapters as well as other relevant literature. I argue that the challenge women's movements encounter is achieving a productive balance between alliance and autonomy in several spheres. This entails, first, attaining strong foundations within the national context while forging links with international and transnational forces. A second challenge concerns the state. Women's movements have been most successful when they have engaged the state, through contestation and collaboration, without abdicating their own identities and constituencies. Third, women's movements have been best served by forging strong linkages with other social movements and groups within civil society without relinquishing their own objectives and identities. The last section of this chapter analyzes the relative success of women's movements in addressing key issues.

Feminism and Women's Movements

The authors in this volume use the terms *feminism* and *women's movements* in different ways, and some employ other terms than these, but all of them contend with the desirable balance between breadth and specificity. A broad definition of women's movements calls attention to the far-reaching expressions of women's agency and activism. However, if women's movements are simply considered compendiums of multiple forms of women's activism without specification of their characteristics, the term becomes devoid of analytic and political precision. One particular challenge is to differentiate women's struggles for gender equality from the many struggles that ignore or accept gender hierarchies. Maxine Molyneux's seminal distinction between women's practical and strategic interests provides one such attempt (1985b). Strategic interests, which are commonly identified as feminist, emerge from and contest women's experiences of gender subordination. Practical interests, by contrast, emerge from women's immediate and perceived needs. A number of essays in this volume draw on Molyneux's distinction to differentiate among women's struggles that have variable relations to feminism. However, some question whether struggles around strategic and practical interests are mutually exclusive. Elaine Salo argues that Sikhula Sonke, a South African union of farmworkers, combines reformist and radical approaches that are both strategic and practical. Furthermore, movements are dynamic entities. What begin as struggles to achieve women's practical interests can turn into struggles to defend their strategic interests, and vice versa.

It is tempting to shy away from identifying oneself as a feminist because it is so contentious. Shereen Essof comments that women activists in Zimbabwe dropped the term *feminism* because it was considered inflammatory. Elzbieta Matynia notes that the word *feminism* had such pejorative connotations in Poland that until recently it was considered political suicide for a woman who was active in public life to identify herself with feminism. However, certain acts can be deemed feminist by virtue of their impact, regardless of the ways activists vew them. Moreover, many activists describe themselves as feminists precisely because of the term's normative, political connotations.

I continue to employ the distinction between feminism and women's movements, as I did in *The Challenge of Local Feminisms*, and to define women's movements expansively. Myra Max Ferree suggests that whereas feminism is activism to challenge and change women's gender subordination, women's movements entail women organizing to achieve social change (Ferree and Tripp 2006, 9). Women's movements are defined by their constituencies, namely, women, but can address a variety of goals, whereas feminism has specified goals, of challenging gender inequality, but its constituencies can be male or female.

Feminism, unlike women's movements, can occur in a variety of arenas and assume a variety of forms. Feminism connotes both ideas and their enactments but does not specify who will enact these ideas or what forms these enactments will take. Feminist discourses influence the character of speech, thought, and expression in the home and the workplace, among individuals and groups, in everyday life, and, episodically, in politics, culture, and the arts.[4] Feminists have created new epistemologies and subjects of research concerning the politics of daily life.[5] Black, lesbian, third world, and intersectional feminisms question the coherence of women's identities by exploring the intersections of gender and other forms of inequality. Feminism may have a greater impact on individuals than on groups, on family relations than on state policy, and on the arts than on politics. These expressions of feminism may have a cumulative impact on the society, the polity, and the economy.

As many of the chapters in this book demonstrate, feminist cultural interventions through feminist magazines, bookstores, publishers, novels, poetry, plays, and performances have had a far-reaching impact on women's movements. Often feminist cultural expression precedes the emergence of women's movements. Matynia argues that feminism emerged in Poland in culturally specific forms at the local level. These "microinterventions" were primarily cultural and performative and fell under the radar of state control. Julie Ajinkya notes that in the United States, women poets, playwrights, and novelists such as Audre Lorde, Cherrie Moraga, bell hooks, Barbara Smith, Beverly Smith, and Merle Woo posed some of the first and most powerful critiques of the predominantly white middle-class women's movement in the 1960s and 1970s. Women of color subsequently formed organizations to advance their own interests. But the significance of feminism rests not solely on its impact on societal structures and institutions but also in its influence on language, consciousness, and women's self-expression.

The Global Context

One of the most significant changes in women's movements over the past fifteen years has been the increased influence of global forces. Transnational advocacy networks, international funding for NGOs, and global discourses of women's rights have grown. But the impact of transnational forces is mediated by national ones.

Both enthusiasts and critics of globalization tend to use the term *global women's movements* to describe many different phenomena. Thus, it is important to differentiate between three different aspects of international and transnational influences. The first is the growth of transnational networks and advocacy groups; the second, the growth of international funding for nongovernmental organizations; and third, international conferences, particularly under the aegis of the United Nations. None of these transnational entities are the same as movements, though they have important implications for movements.

All three forms of transnational and international influence have increased. All three have brought about the circulation of new discourses, particularly by introducing or increasing a focus on women's rights. Violence against women has come to refer to a range of practices that violate women's human rights. All three global influences have entailed the increased institutionalization of women's movements by strengthening nongovernmental organizations and collaboration between the state and women's movements. However, none of these global activities can be equated with global or transnational women's movements, in part because of the enormous challenges of organizing them. Sidney Tarrow notes, "For one thing, sustaining collective action across borders on the part of people who seldom see one another and who lack embedded relations of trust is difficult. For another, local repertoires of contention grow out of and are lodged in local and national contexts. Even more difficult is developing a common collective identity among people from different cultural backgrounds whose governments are not inclined to encourage them to do so" (2005, 7).

As many scholars have suggested, transnational networks differ in important respects from international organizations. Whereas international organizations typically consist of a coordinating umbrella organization composed of representatives from multiple national member organizations, transnational organizations consist of loosely affiliated, decentralized coordinating bodies. Transnational organizations tend to form and disband more quickly than international organizations. The growth of market forces and communication technologies has influenced both the growth and the structure of transnational organizations.

There are some important differences between transnational advocacy networks and women's movements. Transnational advocacy networks, as Keck and Sikkink define them, include governmental and nongovernmental actors, foundations, the media, and parts of regional and international bodies (1998, 9). Although movement activists may participate in transnational networks, the networks themselves are not movements but broadly affiliated groups. By contrast, although women's movements might have close links with the state and feminists may be active within it, women's movements are primarily located within civil society.

Furthermore, whereas transnational advocacy networks are primarily issue based and policy oriented, the agendas of women's movements are broader and more diverse. They often shift their attention from one set of issues to another as political circumstances change. They are committed to solidarity building, consciousness raising, and negotiating the different interests and identities of their members. They may appear to be less efficient than transnational advocacy networks in influencing policy outcomes. However, their diffuse activities have far-reaching influences on politics. In exploring the major determinants of states' decisions to adopt measures to prevent violence against women in thirty-six countries, Laurel Weldon (2002) identifies the roles of women's movements as paramount. She further suggests that women's movements are far more effective than women's lobbies and interest groups because they engage in broad-based activities.

The second dimension of transnational linkages concerns increased international funding for nationally based NGOs. Funding for women's organizations that engage in service provision, income generation, and research and documentation has grown significantly. It has sustained impoverished activists and enabled them to increase their expertise, expand their reach, and gain leverage with the state. However, international funding has also created new challenges. The extent to which women's organizations can avail themselves of funding is limited by geopolitical realities. In Iran, Nayereh Tohidi points out, women's rights activists have refused grants and donations from international donors because of government repression against civil society organizations that do so. Iranian women's organizations thus have the unsatisfactory alternatives of either being branded foreign agents and incurring government repression or lacking resources to engage in a range of activities that require material support.

The chapters in this volume suggest that foreign funding has been double-edged for many women's movements. Lisa McIntosh Sundstrom argues that foreign funding for civil society organizations was a major impetus for the development of the women's movement in Russia in the early 1990s. Conversely, donors' decisions to shift funding from Russia to Afghanistan and Iraq after 2001 seriously undermined women's organizations. She suggests that foreign funding not only failed to bring about the institutionalization of the women's movement but also discouraged women's groups from seeking wider public support and building domestic constituencies. She argues that women's organizations have focused narrowly on donors' agendas and have emphasized technical expertise in project execution and grant management at the expense of broader goals.

Naihua Zhang and Ping-Chun Hsiung argue that given the dearth of domestic funding, the independent Chinese women's movement has relied on external funding. However, they argue that Chinese women's organizations have been so eager to overcome decades of isolation that they have sometimes failed to critically examine the sources and purposes of external funding. Chinese women's groups have collaborated with right-wing religious groups in the United States that have promoted chastity education and opposed safe-sex education in the name of stopping the spread of HIV/AIDS. Farida Shaheed worries that many women's groups have become donor driven, adapting their programs to the latest "flavor of the month."

> Quite apart from the question of whether the groups have the requisite technical expertise for some of these activities, there is a danger of organizations' losing their self-determined purpose. The creation of jacks—or janes—of-all-trades and masters of none is likely to produce a multitude of groups attempting to deliver on too many fronts, therefore doing everything rather superficially instead of intervening in a focused manner. Uniform imposed agendas and the need to deliver "SMART outputs" (specific, measurable, achievable, reliable, and time-bound) undermine the scope for innovation.

The Women's Action Forum (WAF), which is at the forefront of the women's movement in Pakistan, does not accept funding from any sources other than personal donations, as a matter of principle. Shaheed argues that although WAF's financial autonomy enabled it to launch a mass movement against the Zia dictatorship in the late 1970s, it has been hampered by a lack of resources and effective fund-raising strategy.

The third and in my view most productive global influence on women's movements have been the United Nations' support for women's rights and women's conferences, particularly since 1985. Although women's movements have always been among the most international movements in the world, global interactions among movements have significantly increased. The UN world conferences on women in Mexico City (1975), Copenhagen (1980), Nairobi (1985), and Beijing (1995), as well as interim conferences on other related issues, have been key sites of these interactions. These conferences created opportunities for negotiations between states and women's movements. In preparing for the fourth global women's conference in Beijing, between 1993 and 1995, governments discussed draft plans with women's groups at numerous regional and international preparatory meetings. In some countries women's movements, NGOs, and governments collaborated extensively in preparing the final document.

The Platform for Action, which resulted from the Beijing women's conference, is a manifesto of global women's movements. It calls primarily on governments but also on NGOs to mainstream gender by integrating a gender perspective into the design, implementation, monitoring, and evaluation of legislation, policies, and programs. It encourages a closer relationship between women's movements and the state. The Platform for Action supports the creation of women's machineries and asks states to ensure that women hold at least 30 percent of elected positions.

States have created women's agencies, commissions, ministries, committees, secretaries, and advisers to work toward gender equality and challenge discriminatory practices. In Brazil and Chile, the state created full-fledged ministries of women's affairs, the National Council on the Rights of Women and the National Women's Service, respectively. The South African government's support for gender equality has been especially far-reaching. The Mandela government created the Office on the Status of Women and developed the National Framework for Women's Empowerment to oversee gender mainstreaming in state departments and policies. The government also created the Joint Standing Committee on Improving the Quality of Life and Status of Women, which supported the gender mainstreaming process in the state. In addition, an independent body, the Commission on Gender Equality, was established to monitor the implementation of gender equality in the state and the private sector. Although women's movements continue to debate the line between productive and demobilizing forms of institutionalization, they have ceased to view the state as either enemy or ally and have supported the creation of women's bureaus that will mainstream women's concerns.

Less recognized but no less important, international women's conferences have enabled women's movements in the global South to influence international discourses and agendas and provided women's movements with recognition and support from states and international actors. Although human rights discourses are often assumed to emanate from the global North, Elisabeth Jay Friedman points out that Latin American women advocated human rights because of their experiences of fighting authoritarian rule. They were thus at the forefront of the UN-sponsored conference in Vienna that named women's rights human rights. Naihua Zhang and Ping-Chun Hsiung note that the Chinese government decided to hold the international women's conference in Beijing in 1995 in part because it was pressured by a burgeoning women's movement to do so. The movement became stronger as a result of the opportunities the conference provided to network with international groups and the domestic legitimacy it thereby gained. International conferences have also increased opportunities for national and regional interactions. Since 1981, Latin American and Caribbean feminists have been organizing *encuentros*, gatherings for sharing ideas, developing strategies, and fostering closer links between women's movements in the region. Encuentros have taken place every two to three years in Argentina, Brazil, Chile, Colombia, Costa Rica, the Dominican Republic, El Salvador, and Peru; the last one was held in Mexico in March 2009. The encuentros have generated a number of thematic regional networks. These include the 28 September Campaign for the Decriminalization of Abortion in Latin America and the Caribbean, the Network of Latin American and Caribbean Women's Health, the Network of Afrolatinamerican and Afrocaribbean women, and the Latin American and the Caribbean Feminist Network Against Domestic and Sexual Violence. Some of these, like the Indigenous Women's Continental Alliance, grew out of indigenous movements that then engaged with regional feminists.

Sonia Alvarez argues that "in the case of Latin America, the peculiarities of the regional and national political contexts in which feminisms unfolded also impelled local movement actors to build trans-border connections from the bottom up." She suggests that the logic informing intraregional and intergovernmental organization (IGO) transnational advocacy differed significantly. "An internationalist identity-solidarity logic prevailed in the 'encuentro-like' intraregional feminist activism of the 1980s and 1990s, whereas a transnational IGO-advocacy logic came to predominate in region-wide feminist organizing around the Rio, Vienna, Cairo and Beijing Summits of the 1990s" (2000, 30–31). The encuentros have enabled certain groups of women who are marginalized within the national context—indigenous women, lesbians, Afro–Latin American and Afro-Caribbean women—to achieve greater visibility. They have also enabled local actors to enhance their leverage vis-à-vis governments. However, these two forms of transnationalism have sometimes collided. Whereas locally and nationally based feminists often seek radical transformation and broad-based cultural change, intergovernmental organizations have been more committed to influencing policy around particular issues. The encuentros have witnessed fierce debates over the costs to women's movements of relinquishing their autonomy to the state and foreign donors.

A large number of regional women's networks emerged in Africa in the mid-1980s, including the African Women's Development and Communication Network, the Forum for African Women Educationalists, Women in Law and Development in Africa, Gender in Africa Information Network, the Association of African Women for Research and Development, ABANTU for Development, the Association for Women in Development, Akina Mama wa Afrika, and Femmes Africa Solidarite. These African networks of activists, scholars, and policy makers have been influenced by international, regional, and domestic forces. Peace building and conflict resolution, women's political representation, and the HIV/AIDS pandemic have been especially significant concerns. Melinda Adams notes that African women's networks have been effective in challenging state abuses within the continent and influencing regional bodies like the African Union and international organizations like the United Nations (Ferree and Tripp 2006, 193–194).

It has been difficult to organize regional gatherings as effectively in the Middle East and Asia because of the enormous diversities within these regions. However, there have been extensive exchanges between feminists in South Asia and the Middle East. Farida Shaheed argues that the Indian women's movement led the Pakistani women's movement to demand quotas for women's representation in local-level governing bodies (the *panchayats*). In Iran, Tohidi writes, one of the major feminist campaigns, the collection of a million signatures demanding a reform of family law in 2006, was influenced by a similar campaign that Moroccan women had launched many years earlier.

The most valuable impact of the UN-sponsored International Women's Year conferences has been to strengthen women's movements and enable them to influence state policies. National governments have needed help from women's organizations in writing the reports they must submit to the United Nations. In gathering data, women's organizations have acquired familiarity with women's conditions across regional and class lines. In Pakistan, for example, in preparing a joint report by the government and nongovernmental organizations for the 1995 conference in Beijing, women's organizations worked closely with labor, human rights, and peasant movements. This amplified their own conceptions of women's rights and encouraged other movements to adopt a women's rights agenda. Women's movements have then used their influence and the UN Platform for Action to negotiate with their governments.

The UN conferences have played a particularly important role in increasing the legitimacy of nationally based women's organizations in nondemocratic settings. Although the Brazilian military government had suppressed civil society groups, it conceded to UN pressure and designated 1975 International Women's Year. The UN-sponsored conference in Rio that year resulted in extensive women's organizing and the creation of the Centre for the Development of the Brazilian Woman. In Iran, President Ayatollah Hashemi Rafsanjani created an Office of Women's Affairs to advise him on gender policies and plans. Under Khatami's presidency, this office, renamed the Office of Women's Participation, further expanded and emphasized women's participation in politics and civil society.

Naihua Zhang and Ping-Chun Hsiung argue that the Beijing conference was a reflection of the strength and influence of the Chinese women's movement. Contrary to the assumptions of Western observers, it was the driving force behind China's decision to host the conference. A host of women's organizations that emerged at the local level in the early 1980s played an active role in the NGO Forum. The conferences increased opportunities for collaboration between diasporic and mainland women's groups, allowed international ideas to be debated, and enhanced opportunities for travel to and from China. The Chinese government's endorsement of the Beijing Platform for Action further strengthened the Chinese women's movement.

National women's movements have responded to international conferences in ways that best enable them to achieve national objectives. Dongxiao Liu (2006) argues that women's movements in China and India responded to the Platform for Action in Beijing in different ways because they appreciated differences in the character of the state and its relationship to social movements in the two countries. Women's movements could best defend their interests by supporting the Platform for Action in China's authoritarian state and by rejecting it in India's democratic context. She argues that movements must provide official justification for articulating policy demands in authoritarian contexts. Thus, the Chinese women's movement has become "discursively adept" in finding official justification for their claims. By contrast, some democracies enable certain movements to articulate policy demands. Thus, the Indian women's movement has been able to draw directly on women's experiences to criticize national policies. While the Chinese government could have ignored the women's movement, the Indian government could not.

To summarize this section, women's movements are primarily national rather than global but are more influenced by global forces than they were in the past. The influences on women's movements of the three international and transnational forces I have described have varied widely. The most productive form, UN-sponsored international conferences, has strengthened rather than displaced politically engaged women's movements and increased opportunities for regional exchange. The most significant benefit for women's movements has been an increased ability to develop new competencies and influence states.

Women's movements, as Raka Ray (1999) argues, are shaped and influenced by political fields, which include such actors as the state, political parties, and social movements. She argues that, at any given point, women's movements must recognize the relative strength of different actors within the field of power and negotiate with forces that are both sympathetic and hostile to their demands. In the section that follows, I argue that three factors have been especially important to understanding the strength and character of women's movements cross-nationally: their relationship to the state, to other social movements, and to broader actors within civil society.

Women's Movements and the State

Women's movements cannot escape the state. Whether they reject, oppose, ignore, or support it, they must reckon with it. What kinds of state policies are most commonly associated with the emergence of women's movements? Why have women's movements made the state the focus of so many of their demands? Why have they been so divided about how closely they should work with the state? What are the characteristics of states in countries with strong women's movements?

Several of the chapters demonstrate that extensive women's activism has often occurred during periods of authoritarian rule. In Poland, Matynia notes, women mobilized on the largest scale when freedom was most drastically curtailed: under the Nazi occupation in the 1940s and during the period of martial law in the 1980s. As Friedman points out, women played critical roles in motherist movements against authoritarian regimes in Latin America. Women have been at the forefront of struggles against state repression in Iran in the post-Khomeini years when the failures of Islamic extremists became evident. Women were extremely active in anti-colonial nationalist movements in India, Zimbabwe, and South Africa. State repression, particularly when it transcends the political domain and permeates civil society, has often been a catalyst to women's activism. Nationalist, revolutionary, and democratic movements have employed gendered images, and women's participation has been vital to the success of mass movements.

Women's movements are also likely to emerge when there is a chasm between official pronouncements and actual policies. Examples include states that recognize some but not other women's citizenship rights, recognize the rights of racial or religious minorities but not those of women, break their promises to adopt policies around gender inequality, recognize and then retract women's rights, and violate international conventions and constitutional guarantees prohibiting gender discrimination. States that have benefited from women's support are most vulnerable to women's subsequent opposition. The first wave of feminist demands for suffrage in the United States and Western Europe followed from states' recognizing the rights of some but not all citizens to vote. The aftermath of colonial struggles witnessed the emergence of women's movements where states prohibited gender discrimination, as in India, and discrimination against women and gays and lesbians, as in South Africa.

Social movements emerge, Charles Tilly (1995) argues, alongside the creation of modern states, to contest states' authoritative control over resources, power, and force. States constitute the citizens who are claimants and the objects of their claims. Women's movements, historically and cross-nationally, are overwhelmingly directed at the state. Their demands include suffrage, increasing women's political representation, prohibiting violence against women, expanding social welfare provisions, curtailing discrimination based on gender and sexual orientation, ensuring equal pay, making abortion legal and accessible, and creating shelters for battered women. At the same time, the relationship between women's movements and states is double-edged. Excessive reliance on the state to enact public measures supporting gender equality in Poland and Russia during the communist era in many ways suppressed public deliberation and consciousness of inequality within the home and family.

Given the extent to which women's movements have made demands on the state, their ambivalent responses to state concessions and to working with the state may seem surprising. There are three important reasons for their wariness about the state. The first is that the terms of collaboration are set by the state and states generally concede much less than women's movements demand of them. Second, there is always a danger that the institutionalization of women's movements will deplete the strength and radicalism of autonomous women's movements. Feminists within the state are likely to be most successful when they are pressured and supported by autonomous women's movements outside the state. Third, the heterogeneous composition of women's movements is often starkly evident with respect to their access to state power. Educated, urban, elite women are more likely to be drawn into women's policy machineries and to run for office than poorer, less educated, minority women. These divisions within women's movements are heightened over the question of what stance women's movements should adopt in relation to the state.

Women's Movements and Other Social Movements

Women's movements have often grown out of other social movements—for independence, democracy, socialism, and ethnic autonomy. Women who have been active in anticolonial nationalist movements have voiced feminist demands and subsequently created independent women's organizations. Women's activism in movements against dictatorships in Latin America in the 1970s brought about the creation of strong women's movements. The catalyst for women's movements is both the positive experiences and social validation that women's activism entails as well as the disappointing outcomes of these struggles. Movements often gain more from women than women gain from movements. The democratic governments that have emerged from struggles against colonialism and authoritarianism have often failed to provide women the rights and freedoms that they had sought. In Poland, Matynia argues, women mobilized on a large scale on behalf of their rights as women during the mid-1990s when they found that their earlier struggles had placed them in "fenced playgrounds," divorced from political power.

Social movements are influenced by the achievements and failures of prior movements and frequently give rise to movements that either challenge or further refine their goals. Women's movements have an especially synergistic relationship with other movements. They often grow out of other social movements and periodically reestablish links with them to address the multiple inequalities women face. Rosalva Aída Hernández Castillo attributes the growth of the indigenous women's movement to the Zapatista movement in Mexico, in which indigenous communities challenged the dominant mestizo community and fought for self-determination. By confronting racism against their communities, indigenous women came to confront sexism within it. But they continued to identify with the indigenous movement and to participate in it.

Farida Shaheed describes a peasant movement in the Punjab in 2002 in which women organized a *"thappa* brigade" (a *thappa* is a long wooden stick used by women for washing clothes and harvesting). The movement's central objective was the attainment of land rights. As the movement gained momentum, it incurred repression by landlords and the state. In response, women formed thappa brigades that prevented state officials from removing timber from their lands and prevented the confiscation of their harvests. The public recognition and self-assurance that women achieved through their activism resulted in their addressing feminist issues like domestic violence. They formed the Women's Peasant Association so that women could gain access to a government scheme for land. However, despite urging from the women's movement, these women did not claim inheritance from their families for fear of dividing the struggle.

Women's Movements and Civil Society

Scholars have debated the extent to which burgeoning civil societies are characterized by conservative or democratic features. While enthusiasts praise their democratic character and potential, critics point to their conservative features.

Less attention has been devoted to the links between women's movements and the civil societies in which they are located. As a broader terrain than women's movements, civil societies create spaces for multiple forms of collective action that influence women's movements in diverse ways. Jude Howell notes that "civil society is a double edged sword for feminists. It can provide a site for organizing around feminist issues, for articulating counter-hegemonic discourses, for experimenting with alternative life styles and for envisioning other less sexist and more just worlds. . . . Yet it can also be an arena where gendered behaviour, norms and practices are acted out and reproduced" (Howell and Mulligan 2005, 6). Anne Phillips (2002) points out that compared to the state, civil society is less regulated and therefore more susceptible to discriminatory practices.

Women's movements often grow amid the expansion of civil society that occurs during democratization. But the implications of democratization for women's movements are complex and multidirectional. International support for democratization has strengthened NGOs that can either rival or complement women's movements. Democratization in the current era has also been associated with the growth of nationalist and religious institutions that have promoted traditional family structures and opposed women's rights in the family. Nationalist appeals have found strong support within civil society when they challenge the state and Western cultural or economic domination.

Ethnic and religious nationalisms—in India, Iran, and South Africa, among other countries in this volume—have vexed women's movements. Conservative community leaders have often opposed women's rights within the family and upheld customary or religious laws. In South Africa, rural women have been subject to extensive discrimination, particularly with respect to landownership and inheritance. Reforms of the Customary Marriages Act made women equal partners in customary marriages. However, chiefs continue to exercise enormous power over traditional courts and communal land and oppose women's inheritance rights. The African National Congress has been loath to undermine the power of chiefs, who provide it with electoral support. Islah Jad notes that the Islamist movements in Palestine have weakened the secular women's movement and its attempts to strengthen secular over religious law.

With democratization, there has been an extensive growth of NGOs that concern women and gender. In some respects they have strengthened and complimented women's movements. However, NGOs are neither movements nor surrogates for them. NGOs are generally much less active than women's movements in political contestation and mobilization and more active in service delivery and issue-specific activities. Several authors worry that NGO-ization may undermine movements' transformational character.

Matynia argues that civil society, unlike the NGO sector, neither prescribes one best way of action nor enforces any one agenda. Rather, it provides an inclusive space for diverse, indigenously inspired initiatives to conduct public dialogue with the state, which in the case of women's organizations means negotiating matters of gender justice. She describes the vacuum caused by the collapse of communism: "The resulting civic vacuum is only partially filled by the existing NGOs, with their separate niches of expertise, often performing auxiliary functions for the various governmental agencies. Even though they greatly enhance the institutional landscape of democracy, the public debate that they generate is fragmented and limited to their specific concerns."

Islah Jad questions a tendency to use the terms social movements and NGOs interchangeably in Palestine and the Middle East more broadly. She argues that the grassroots women's organizations that emerged during the first intifada engaged with women across the class spectrum. The availability of new funding sources transformed women's organizations into NGOs that collaborated closely with the Palestinian Authority. The growth of NGOs in the absence of a state contributed to the depoliticization of the women's movement and strengthened conservative Islamic forces.

Democratization has also affected relations between groups that jointly opposed authoritarian regimes. Many countries found the church an important ally in struggles against authoritarian states but a liability once democracy was achieved. Friedman notes that poor women organized extensively during the period of authoritarian rule in Chile, Brazil, and elsewhere. Given repression against left-wing parties and trade unions, the Catholic Church provided a safer venue for political organizing. In Mexico, R. Aída Hernández Castillo argues, Liberation Theology supported radical grassroots movements that encouraged indigenous women's activism. She attributes the creation of a national network in 1997 in part to its influence.

However, the Catholic Church became the major opponent of reproductive rights once democracy was achieved in Latin America and East and Central Europe. Thus, even with state support, women's movements have been unsuccessful in securing women's rights to legal first-trimester abortions in Brazil, Venezuela, Chile, and Bolivia. They have been similarly unsuccessful in Poland and Russia. In Brazil, pastors with the consent of bishops participated in a grassroots campaign against abortion. They distributed plastic models of aborted fetuses to people who attended Sunday mass in Rio de Janeiro's parishes in December 2008. The church has also supported legislation prohibiting public systems from distributing the "morning-after pill" through the public health system in several cities.

Women's movements have responded to these conservative forces within civil society in a variety of ways. They have tried to influence state policies, relatively unsuccessfully with respect to reproductive rights in Eastern Europe and Latin America. They have sought to legitimate their claims by using international instruments, with varying degrees of success, sometimes promoting a backlash. They have forged alliances within civil society, particularly with religiously observant women who share some of their objectives, with some success in Iran, among other places.

The emergence and growth of women's movements, and particularly their success in achieving increased political representation and securing measures to prevent violence against women, have rested on their attaining support from the state, civil society, and international forces. Women's movements have been much less successful in addressing poverty and class inequality because of a lack of domestic and international support. Religious forces have also placed obstacles in the way of women's attaining certain rights within the family, including property ownership, legalized abortion, and sexual freedom.

Violence Against Women

Women's movements in most countries have addressed violence against women in private and public domains. In Iran the "Stop Stoning Forever Campaign" opposed the stoning of women who are accused of adultery. The Indian women's movement's earliest campaigns exposed and confronted "dowry deaths," that is, the murder of brides by their husbands and in-laws who sought a larger dowry from the brides' families, and police rape of women in custody. It has been active in contesting violence against *dalits* (untouchables), minorities, and poor women. Feminists have fought for expanded understandings of what constitutes violence. In South Africa they fought for a definition of rape as any act of coercive penetration in which men, women, and children are potential victims. Under pressure from the women's movement, the Bolivian constitution recognizes that women have a right to be protected from not only physical and sexual but also psychological violence.

Feminists have adopted a variety of approaches to addressing violence against women in both public and private spheres. They have demonstrated the difficulties of determining what constitutes free choice for women who experience marital and date rape. Women's movements have proposed multiple forms of intervention including legislation and public policies, the creation of shelters, family courts, walk-in assistance, and counseling centers for battered women. They have engaged psychologists, social workers, lawyers, and doctors to work with survivors. They have developed education and job-creation programs so that women do not have to return to abusive situations.

There are several explanations for the importance that women's movements have accorded to violence against women cross-nationally. Kannabiran poignantly argues that violence against women is a foundational issue that all feminisms must confront.

> Violence against women . . . has locked women of different classes, castes, and communities into multiple intersecting axes of inequality and discrimination that spread out over a wide range—from social and economic life to political inequality—tying women of different classes together through the similarity of their experiences as women and holding them apart in almost unbridgeable ways through the differences in their experiences as members of different social classes. The conditioning and determining environment for feminist struggle, then, is marked by "violence," which straddles the lawful and unlawful, the legitimate and the "illegitimate," domination and resistance, injustice and justice, order and chaos, and takes many forms.

International organizations have encouraged women's movements to confront violence against women and the international women's conferences have pressured their governments to do so. The global human rights movement has addressed violence by multiple actors in multiple sites. Opposing violence has large-scale societal support, however deep-seated the challenges to ending it may be. Moreover, opposition to violence against women has generated productive debates within women's movements about the intersection of gender, race, and class. The more serious challenge, as Elaine Salo (2005) notes, is to identify and rectify the structural causes of violence against women. She notes that few shelters in South Africa, especially in the rural areas, have helped women attain independence in the long run.

Political Rights and Representation

Women have played important roles in drafting new constitutions in countries in which they were active in struggles for the creation of multiparty democracies. Thanks to feminist pressures, the Polish constitution includes an article decreeing equal rights for women and men. In South Africa, the Women's

National Coalition waged a successful struggle to ensure that the constitution guarantees equality and freedom from discrimination for all, regardless of race, gender, religion, sexual orientation, and disability.

Not all of these attempts have been successful. As Shereen Essof shows, the women's movement in Zimbabwe formed the "Women's Coalition (WC) on the Constitution" in 1999. Through a process of broad-based mobilization and education, it drafted the Women's Charter. When the president ignored most of the charter's provisions, the coalition successfully mobilized against the constitutional referendum. However, the coalition's victory was short lived. Against the backdrop of spiraling violence and a deepening socioeconomic and political crisis, the government sidelined the constitutional debate and engaged in repression against women.

Women's movements have also mobilized on behalf of electoral candidates who support their demands. With the formation of the National Women's Political Caucus in 1971, Ajinkya argues, the U.S. women's movement sought to increase women's representation in elected and appointed office at local, state, and national levels. It provided pro-choice candidates with financial support and helped them improve their skills. In the 1980s other organizations were formed to promote women's political representation, including women-of-color organizations like the National Political Congress of Black Women. Similarly, women's organizations were extremely active during the 2009 presidential elections in the United States, though they were divided between support for Hillary Clinton and Barack Obama.

The women's movement in Iran organized on a massive scale during the 2005 national elections. Discontent with the Khatami regime, it challenged candidates to come up with specific plans for addressing gender inequality. About 90 NGOs, many of them concerned with women's issues, joined 350 prominent female writers, academics, lawyers, artists, activists, and journalists and 130 bloggers to organize a public protest against the breaches of women's rights in Iran. In spite of intimidation, about 3,000 women gathered at the University of Tehran in June 2005, weeks before the elections, and demanded changes in the constitution and the legal system. They identified the present laws, based on sharia, as the main obstacle to achieving gender equality and women's empowerment.

Women's movements have also fought for increased women's political representation at all levels of government. This has been one of the main demands of the South African women's movement. In Poland, Matynia notes, women's organizations worked closely with the Parliamentary Women's Group to establish the Pre-Electoral Women's Coalition and launched public debate on the small number of women in legislative and executive bodies. Their concerted action prompted the three political parties to come up with quotas for women in the 2001 elections.

Quotas constitute an important demand of women's movements in many countries. In Brazil feminists worked closely with Congress to create a quota law that guarantees that 20 percent of all candidates in proportional elections (town councilors, as well as state and federal deputies) would be women. In 1997 another law was passed, raising this percentage to 25 percent for the 1998 elections and to 30 percent for subsequent elections. In Pakistan post–martial law, the women's movements pressured the government to introduce quotas for women in the national and provincial assemblies and the Senate in 2002. In India the women's movement successfully lobbied for the creation of 30 percent quotas for women in the local-level *panchayats*. It has not yet been successful in attaining quotas for women at the national level, in part because caste-based political parties believe that quotas for women should take caste into account.

Struggles to increase women's political representation have had mixed results. Where party-based quotas exist, political parties have often acted as gatekeepers and failed to nominate and support female candidates. In all situations, women encounter innumerable barriers and prejudices that have impeded electoral success. The higher the political office, the greater the challenges women confront. Thus, women in Russia, Brazil, the United States, and India have achieved greater electoral success in local than in national elections. Nonetheless, women's movements have had considerable success in increasing women's political representation as a result of women's participation in prior movements and extensive international and some state support.

Sexual Minorities

Some of the broad factors that influence the strength of women's movements and lesbian, bisexual, gay, transgender, and intersex movements are the same. Strong and effective LGBTI activism has occurred when it has found transnational and international support, when gays and lesbians have participated in broader social movements, and when states have prohibited discrimination on grounds of sexual orientation. Furthermore, conservative religious forces have sometimes but not always obstructed gay and lesbian rights. Friedman points out that the church has more vehemently opposed abortion than same-sex relations in many Latin American countries; the recently proposed changes to the Venezuelan and Bolivian constitutions prohibit discrimination on grounds of sexual orientation.

In Brazil and South Africa, gays and lesbians have been active in a variety of social movements. The South African constitution provides far-reaching protections to gays and lesbians. Same-sex relations and marriage are legal, and antigay discrimination is banned. Activist organizations like the Treatment Action Campaign, which has engaged in AIDS activism, have confronted homophobic violence. The Brazilian government has also organized a variety of civil society initiatives to combat homophobia and been at the forefront of international and regional action on sexual rights. The Brazilian delegation to the UN Commission on Human Rights proposed the 2003 resolution "Human Rights and Sexual Orientation" that called on member states and the UN itself to promote and protect the human rights of all persons regardless of their sexual orientation.

Contrast this with the numerous countries in which the state has been overtly repressive toward LGBTI groups. Sexual relations between same-sex couples are a criminal offense, potentially subject to the death penalty, in Iran and Pakistan. Homosexuality is a crime in India, carrying sentences often years to life imprisonment, though convictions are rare. Male, but not female, homosexuality is illegal in Palestine, and carries convictions of up to ten years.

The most serious assaults on gay-rights activists have occurred when the state has coupled its opposition to homosexuality with appeals to nationalist and religious values. Laws passed in Zimbabwe in 2006 criminalize homosexuality. President Mugabe has described homosexuality as un-African and blamed gay men for Zimbabwe's problems. The government attacked, detained, and tortured activists in the Association of Gays and Lesbians in Zimbabwe and made it very difficult for people infected with the AIDS virus to receive medical attention. The Iranian government has similarly depicted homosexuality as anti-Islamic and has ordered the execution of 4,000 people who were charged with engaging in homosexual relations since the 1979 revolution.

By contrast, in India, where homosexuality is illegal but the state and political parties have not depicted gays and lesbians as anti-Indian or antireligious, gay-rights activism within civil society has grown. As Kannabiran shows, queer activists have documented lesbians' susceptibility to physical and verbal abuse, battery, house arrest, coercion into heterosexual marriage, and expulsion from the family home. An early resolution by a group of lesbians at the National Conference on Women's Movements in India in 1994 endorsed women's rights to choose their sexual orientation. Eleven years later, the National Conference on Women's Studies unanimously adopted a resolution demanding the repeal of Section 377 of the Indian Penal Code that criminalizes homosexuality.

In the United States, the so-called culture wars have been fought in part around gay rights. The military's "don't ask, don't tell" policy means that homosexuality is still a cause for dismissal. President Obama has opposed gay marriage but also opposed a federal ban on gay marriage, allowing states to decide on the legality of gay marriage. Gay, lesbian, and transgender activism is strong in the realm of civil society. Thus, in both India and the United States, the fact that the state has not openly allied with conservative forces in civil society to attack same-sex relations has prevented large-scale repression of gays and lesbians and allowed civil society activism around sexual orientation to occur outside the realm of state control.

Poverty and Class Inequality

Innumerable women are subject to grinding poverty and class inequality. R. Aída Hernández Castillo describes the malnutrition and disease that afflict indigenous women in Mexico. Sardenberg and Costa point to the significant growth of female-headed households, particularly among poor black women in Brazil. Kannabiran notes that in India, while the phenomenon of male farmers committing suicide to escape their horrendous debts is well known, the impact of these suicides on their wives and women's suicides are largely undocumented. Elaine Salo describes the conditions of women in urban and rural informal settlements in South Africa where water, sanitation, housing, and jobs are inadequate or nonexistent.

Women's movements have forged alliances with poor rural and urban women around particular issues, but have generally failed to systematically tackle poverty and class inequality. Ajinkya notes that while liberal feminists have addressed equal pay largely for middle-class women and women-of-color organizations have addressed the problems of black and Hispanic women on welfare, neither of these groups or others have focused explicitly on poverty. The women's human rights framework that women's movements have fruitfully employed to address violence against women has been less productive in addressing economic inequality. What explains this?

Women's movements in nondemocratic regimes have generally prioritized demands for civil and political rights over socioeconomic equality. In Iran, Palestine, and Zimbabwe, the climate of political repression has narrowed the agendas of women's movements to confronting overt physical violence rather than systemic or structural violence. In democratic contexts, there has been a schism between movements that are concerned with economic redistribution and inequality and movements that are primarily concerned with social and political matters.

In the past Keynesian welfare states in the North and developmental states in the South addressed poverty and economic inequality. Most states today fail to do so. What Banaszak, Beckwith, and Rucht describe as reconfigured states (2003, 6–7) have downloaded power and responsibility to lower state levels, uploaded power and responsibility to higher state levels, laterally delegated responsibility to nonelected state bodies, and off-loaded responsibilities to nonstate actors. All of these shifts have made it harder for women's movements to address poverty and class inequality.

States' uploading of authority onto institutions like the International Monetary Fund, the World Trade Organization, and the World Bank have reduced states' accountability to women's movements. States' off-loading of responsibilities has strengthened NGOs over social movements. The NGO sector consists primarily of professional skilled women whose lives are far removed from those of impoverished women. Moreover, NGOs have generally engaged in microlevel projects to provide women with greater skills and incomes rather than engaging in more systemic challenges to inequality. Poverty has not featured centrally among femocrats' concerns.

The most significant gains of women's movements have resulted from state concessions. They have faced an uphill battle in getting neoliberal states to address class inequality. To the extent that women's movements have had some success in this realm, it has been in the minority of countries in which left-of-center governments occupy power. Governments in Venezuela, Bolivia, Brazil, and Chile have introduced policies that increase social welfare provisions for women with respect to health care, education, and employment.

The UN conferences and the Platform for Action have not provided women's movements with as much support in fighting poverty and class inequality as in addressing violence against women and women's political participation. The extensive commitments that governments made to eight Millennial Development goals in the 1990s have shrunk. Gender figures in only one of the eight goals, and the solutions proposed for reducing poverty and guaranteeing basic health and primary education are inadequate.

Many women's movements have sought out other international settings like the World Social Forums in Brazil in 2002 and India in 2004 that focus primarily on social justice and economic inequality. At the 2002 World Social Forum, feminists launched the Campaign Against Fundamentalisms, a network of Latin American Southern Cone feminist organizations committed to challenging neoliberalism and religious fundamentalism. In preparation for the 2004 World Social Forum, women's organizations planned a series of events that linked a critique of neoliberalism to demands for economic, sexual, and reproductive rights. The Women's International Coalition for Economic Justice, which emerged during the UN five-year review of Beijing, claimed economic rights as part of the women's human rights agenda.

A number of transnational advocacy networks have challenged the gendered consequences of globalization. Development Alternatives with Women for a New Era, Women in Development Europe, and the Women, Environment, and Development Organization have all explored the negative consequences of economic restructuring for women. Consumer groups have addressed the effects of trade liberalization on women workers and organized campaigns against sweatshops. A network of organizations in Central and Eastern Europe formed La Strada to investigate and challenge the links between the devastation of national economies and the emergence of the profit-making industry around trafficking in women.

Certain transnational advocacy networks have effectively challenged economic inequalities that result from the actions of multinational corporations and certain multilateral organizations. The challenge has been forging closer links between national women's movements and these transnational advocacy organizations. Women's movements have not generally pressured their national governments to redesign economic policies to address the gendered character of poverty and class inequality.

Comparative Perspectives

As the chapters in this book demonstrate, women's movements exist in the most diverse political environments. As politically savvy, strategic actors, they identify opportunities to effect change in the most challenging circumstances. However, there is enormous variation in the strength and success of women's movements in the contexts the authors describe. At one end of the spectrum is the Russian women's movement that McIntosh Sundstrom argues barely exists. At the other end is the Brazilian women's movement that Sardenberg and Costa describe as strong and flourishing. What explains the differences between the strength of women's movements in these two countries and in others?

All of the authors place women's movements within the national context from which they emerge and which they seek to influence. Indeed, the achievements of women's movements must be judged primarily by their impact on the nation and particular groups within it. One important challenge has been negotiating the value of international support and collaboration. The United States is the only country in this volume in which the women's movement does not need international funding or political support. Elsewhere, at one end of the spectrum, women's movements have suffered from a dearth of international support. Russian women's organizations, for example, have been weakened by the decline of international funding. At the other end of the spectrum are Palestine, Pakistan, and Poland, where substantial international support has threatened to displace local priorities with donor-driven agendas. Some countries like South Africa, India, and Brazil have been able to achieve a better balance between autonomy and collaboration with international groups. How nations are situated within the global political economy has important implications for the choices women's movements make.

Political conditions have hindered certain collaborations and permitted others. Whereas Latin American women's movements have not experienced geopolitical constraints on organizing, women's movements in other regions have found it difficult to engage in similar forms of collaboration. Wars within and across national borders in Africa, the Middle East, and South Asia have impeded the free exchanges of people and ideas across borders. At times this has brought women's groups together around peacekeeping initiatives in the Middle East and South Asia. But it has made collaboration among women's movements less likely.

If women's movements have engaged the state in all the countries described in this volume, their success in doing so has varied enormously. At one end of the spectrum are undemocratic states that have engaged in repression against women's movements. Zimbabwe is a prime example. The Palestinian women's movement has been weakened by the Israeli state's aggressive, expansionist policies. Then there is Russia, where the women's movement has refrained from making demands on the state, in part because the state's historic commitments to gender equality in the public domain have discouraged it from doing so. At the other end of the spectrum are left-of-center governments in Brazil, Venezuela, Bolivia, and Chile that have been receptive to the demands of women's movements. But in democratic contexts like the United States, Brazil, India, and South Africa, the temptations of abdicating movement activism for participation in the state are great. Women's movements have been strongest when they have combined a strategy of collaborating with the state with maintaining strong links to sympathetic forces within civil society.

The relationship between women's movements and other social movements is another key determinant of their success. Women's movements have often grown out of broader political struggles: the civil rights and antiwar movements in the United States; nationalist movements in Zimbabwe, Palestine, South Africa, India, and Pakistan; and movements against authoritarianism in Latin America. Links between the women's movement and other popular democratic movements often broaden the class base of women's movements. By contrast, one possible explanation for the weakness of women's movements in contemporary Poland and Russia is the relatively small role they played in democracy movements that challenged communist regimes. However, women's movements and feminist movements in particular differ greatly in the extent to which they have continued to collaborate with broader democratic movements. Shaheed notes the importance but also the difficulties of sustaining linkages between the Women's Action Forum and peasant and working-class movements in Pakistan. Ajinkya identifies the chasms between women's movements based on class and race in the United States. Set against this are accounts of linkages that women's movements have formed with AIDS activists and labor organizations in South Africa, with popular movements and women's movements in Brazil, and with movements for human rights and civil liberties in Pakistan and India.

The extent to which women's movements are able to withstand opposition and forge productive alliances with civil society organizations is also vital to their success. Women's movements in Palestine, Pakistan, and Iran have been threatened by the growth of conservative Islamic groups. The increased power of the Catholic Church has undermined many of their achievements in Latin America and central Europe. A critical question concerns the strength and diversity of civil society. In Iran, for example, many moderate Islamic groups have challenged orthodox groups and supported women's movements. In South Africa, women's movements have been strong enough to challenge the surge of Zulu cultural nationalism in recent years.

Women's movements in most regions of the world have addressed the question of violence against women. Most states at least in principle support their efforts, and international agencies have pressured them to adopt measures to prevent and redress violence and provide support for victims. Sometimes, as in India, women's organizations have simultaneously addressed state violence and domestic violence. At other times, as in the United States, as Ajinkya demonstrates, their approach to violence against women diverges along race and class lines. Nonetheless, women's movements have found large-scale civil society support in addressing violence against women.

At the other end of the continuum are struggles to challenge class inequality and poverty. Given the extent to which women's movements are encouraged by state concessions, the difficulties they have faced in influencing states' economic policies have been a serious liability. Most states are less responsive to women's movements—or any social movements—on matters of economic policy than around a range of social issues. Although transnational advocacy organizations have challenged the destructive consequences of neoliberalism for women, powerful international financial and multilateral institutions have influenced states in the opposite direction. Moreover, transnational advocacy organizations have found it difficult to engage in the kind of locally based, solidarity-building, consciousness-raising activities that women's movements have undertaken in addressing violence against women. How macroeconomic arrangements affect women differs according to women's class backgrounds so that women's movements have not adopted a unified position on the issue.

This comparative analysis also points to the dynamism of movements and the feminists who study and participate in them. Activists who are principally committed to a single set of issues and a single set of strategies increasingly work in a highly interconnected world in which they confront and respond to alternative approaches. Secular feminists have formed alliances with religious groups. Activists who were exclusively concerned with gender inequality have expanded their focus to address racism and indigenous rights. Movements that refused to work with the state at certain moments have later done so. The authors in this volume illuminate in word and deed the resilience and power of feminism and women's movements then, now, and in the years to come.

Notes

1. One of the most important studies of women's transnational advocacy networks is Moghadam 2005. On transnational women's movements, see Eschle 2001; Molyneux 2001; and Ferree and Tripp 2006.

2. Some samples of the vast literature include: Lycklama à Nijeholt, Vargas, and Wieringa 1998; Haussman and Sauer 2007; and Outsjhoorn and Kantola 2007.

3. The Research Network on Gender Politics and the State has published a number of edited volumes, including Mazur 2001; Stetson and Mazur 1995; and Stetson 2001.

4. For an insightful discussion of the impact of feminism on institutions, see Katzenstein 1998.

5. Cynthia Enloe's work on the gendered militarization of daily life is seminal in this regard. See, for example, *Maneuvers: The International Politics of Militarizing Women's Lives* (2000) and *The Curious Feminist: Searching for Women in an Age of Empire* (2004).

South African Feminisms—
A Coming of Age?

ELAINE SALO

Fifteen years ago, in 1994, we wondered what the onset of formal democracy in South Africa would mean for South African women, in particular black South African women. The Women's National Coalition, a strategic alliance of women formed across the divides of race, class, the urban-rural divide, and religious beliefs, waged a successful struggle to ensure women's representation at the national negotiations between 1990 and 1994. The WNC's major gains, which marked the high point of the South African women's struggle at the time, guaranteed that the rights of women and other gender minorities would be enshrined in the national constitution and that women would be ensured representation at every level of government, as gender was taken up in the nation-building project (Hassim 2003; Lewis 2007). These gains arose from a strategic feminist alliance, a rare moment of solidarity, sutured across South African women's multiple identities and differences. Such feminist solidarity arose from two processes. First, the convergence of women's critical gender consciousness in their diverse struggles for social and gender justice in various cultural, socioeconomic, and political sites helped forge this new unity. Second, as women asserted their claim to political representation in the transitional moment when old patriarchal alliances were being unbundled and new alignments created, they enabled this feminist alliance.

The dawn of that new day in South Africa in 1994 did indeed mark a victory for the recognition of women's and queer people's rights, but it also marked another phase in the development of South African feminisms. In this contemporary phase of feminist development, South Africa's constitutional commitment to gender equality and its official obligation to gender mainstreaming marked

SOUTH AFRICA

Human Development Index ranking: .674
Gender-Related Development Index value: .667
Gender Empowerment Measure value: not available

General

Type of government: Democratic Republic
Major ethnic groups: Black (79.7%); White (9.1%); Colored (8.8%); Indian/Asian (2.5%)
Languages: eleven official languages, including Afrikaans, English, isiNdebele, Sepedi or Northern Sotho, Sesotho, Seswati, Setswana, Tshivenda, isiXhosa, Xitsonga, and isiZulu
Religions: Predominantly Christian; traditional African; Hindu; Muslim; Jewish
Date of independence: 1961; majority government, 1994
Former colonial power: Holland, England

Demographics

Population, total (millions), 2005: 47.9
Annual growth rate (%), 2005–2015: .5
Total fertility (average number of births per woman): 2.8
Contraceptive prevalence (% of married women aged 15–49): 60
Maternal mortality ratio, adjusted (per 100,000 live births), 2000: 400

Women's Status

Date of women's suffrage: 1994
Life expectancy: M 49.5; F 52
Combined gross enrollment ratio for primary, secondary, and tertiary education (female %), 2005: 77
Gross primary enrollment ratio: 102*
Gross secondary enrollment ratio: 97
Gross tertiary enrollment ratio: 17
Literacy (% age 15 and older): M 84.9; F 80.9

Political Representation of Women

Seats in parliament (% held by women): 32.8
Women in government at ministerial level (% total): 41.4

Economics

Estimated earned income (PPP US$): M 15,446; F 6,927
Ratio of estimated female to male earned income: .45
Economic activity rate (% female): 45.9
Women in adult labor force (% total): 38 (this figure obtained at the CEDAW Statistical Database)

*Gross enrollment ratios in excess of 100% indicate that there are pupils or students outside the theoretical age groups who are enrolled in that level of education.

the end of the antiapartheid feminist "triumphs" and the onset of a period in which gender struggles for the realization of substantive gendered citizenship have been redefined. In this essay I attempt to sketch the broad characteristics of these emergent multiple gender struggles, as they are informed by the new forms of postapartheid patriarchal nationalism and shaped both by South African women's and gender minorities' multiple identities of class, ethnicity, location, and sexual orientation and their modes of agency and activism as well as by men who find themselves on the periphery of a new hegemonic masculinity. At the same time, South Africans' transnational engagements also inform the trajectories of these new struggles.

In this postapartheid moment we are witnessing the complex, varied forms of feminist and gender activism emerging as the culture of human rights has deepened and diversified. Women's diverse identities are now expressed in social activism that has become issue based in the new South Africa. In addition, feminist gains made during the apartheid struggle as well as women's rights won in regional and global forums of governance such as the Convention on the Elimination of All Forms of Discrimination Against Women (CEDAW), African Union (AU), and Beijing Platform for Action have created significant space of agency for femocrats in the South African state.[1] However, this official space is severely circumscribed by the limitations of a neoliberal economic climate and a reinvocation of unequal religio-cultural gender practices in support of the dominant new forms of political patriarchy. While official state discourse resonates powerfully with the fundamental values of a gendered democracy (houses, safety and security for all, the people shall govern, the doors of learning shall be opened), the ability of policy makers to deliver on these promises is severely curtailed by the brute realities of neoliberalism.

Women and gender minorities in civil society have sought to respond to these structural and cultural limitations through conventional nongovernmental organizations (NGOs) and new social movements in the local context. Their participation in creative transnational and continental social movements has created new solidarities but also informed local class-based tensions. Many feminists have sought to influence state policy from locations within the nongovernmental organization sector, and thereby face a new set of opportunities and challenges. This sector has become increasingly professionalized, as it requires more complex, nuanced mediations among a politicized, impoverished support base, a bureaucratic state, and donor funders' agendas. Yet other women's rights activists have chosen to align themselves with grassroots social movements that support a more transformative socioeconomic agenda in the national, regional, and global contexts, while nurturing organic feminist agendas within these forums. These diverse forms of feminist practices are informed by local and, increasingly, transnational exchanges, as South Africans regularly participate in diverse international arenas of policy making, research, and activism, be it as members of the state in forums such as the United Nations, as members of the antiglobalization movement such as Jubilee 2000 and the World Social Forum, or as members of the nongovernmental sector that is called upon to inform and fulfill donor agendas. At the same time, newer forms of nationalism are emerging, accompanied by the public performance of hypermasculinity that draws upon a rich imagery of a romanticized traditional culture in which politically reempowered men can take care of their multiple women and transform them from tattered and impoverished into cosseted and glamorous dependents. These powerful though superficial invocations of culture and tradition, however, threaten other women's and sexual minorities' human rights. This hypermasculinity and the growing conservatism of many femocrats have made it imperative for the women's and gender-justice movements to engage the state in collaborative and confrontational ways in order to ensure its responsibility in realizing social justice in this new era.[2]

In this chapter I set out the key features of these developments in feminist and gender movements. I have divided this chapter into two parts. In the first part I indicate that, in the postapartheid and postcolonial moment, the South African feminist alliance identified the state and its national gender machinery as the key sites through which constitutionally enshrined gender rights would be delivered. Now, in the more sobering aftermath, feminists have begun mapping out the limitations and challenges of such an approach in achieving social and economic justice in various spheres. In the second part, I demonstrate that in the contemporary moment we have to take into account the complex, multiple terrains of women's gendered struggles in the context of the local neoliberal economic climate, dominant new forms of nationalist masculinity, and globalization and determine how these struggles are expressed in relation to women's hitherto muted identities and differences. I also ask what challenges the growing lesbian, gay, bisexual, transgender, and intersex (LGBTI) movement poses to feminists in the more conventional women's movement. These issues also inform a new agenda for feminist activist-scholars.

I contend that in the contemporary period, South African women's struggles have merged with issue-based activism, as claims for gender justice coalesce around the substantive realization of socioeconomic rights in the everyday practices of citizenship in diverse socioeconomic and cultural sites. These struggles also reveal the need to review, rework, and expand religio-cultural practices that are complexly intertwined with women's and gender minorities' identities, without requiring that we completely jettison our communal affiliations or associated identities.

These multifaceted struggles reflect South African women's and gender minorities' heterogeneous intersectional identities. At the same time, women and gender minorities must unite in momentary, essentialist alliances to defend their hard-won constitutional and political gains. The gendered engagements in these diverse arenas have created numerous challenges. How are these gendered needs being asserted in relation to other aspects of cultural and economic inequalities, and are these expressions mutually reinforcing or contradictory? How effectively are class- and race-based tensions between NGO staff and the women they represent mediated as South African women's and gender NGOs become increasingly reliant upon professional staff? Have feminists been cognizant of the diversity of gender movements (such as LGBTI and critical men's organizations) and other movements for social and economic justice in the country? How, if at all, has the critical men's movement addressed issues of homophobia? Do these strategies sufficiently represent the rich diversities and highly contingent nature of gendered struggles? How do we translate these claims for more complex forms of social, cultural, and economic rights into nuanced, effective policy?

If we are to support a radical realization of women's gender rights as they intersect with other aspects of inequality, we need to build alliances across diversity rather than assume shared solidarity. We also need to renovate the theoretical concepts to talk about these developments. Ultimately, the alignments of patriarchal power in the contemporary postapartheid moment have begun to harden and are expressed in novel ways that reshape the conventional meanings of femininities and masculinities to produce new forms of gender inequalities. South African feminists must heed these new gender inequalities in order to map out strategies of struggle and alliance building across the social and political spectrum.

Femocrats, the State, and the National Gender Machinery

Women's activism during the transitional negotiations helped enshrine gender equality as a central aspect of the new South African constitution. The equality clause in Section 9 of the constitution guarantees equality and freedom from discrimination for all, regardless of race, gender, religion, sexual orientation, and disability. The constitution framed the vision of gender equality in the newfound democracy; however, the substantive realization of this right had to be propelled by other means.

Women's gendered gains in the new state were reinforced in two ways. First, citizens recognized that the skewed economy, which mainly privileged white South Africans, needed to change. Consequently, the Reconstruction and Development Program (RDP), implemented between 1994 and 1996, focused on a people-centered transformation of the economy. Gender was poorly conceived in the program; nevertheless, the RDP set the basis, in the local context, for the formulation and implementation of gender mainstreaming and for the gender budgeting project in the Ministry of Finance. Second, South Africa became a signatory to key international and continental conventions formulated by international and continental institutions such as the United Nations and the African Union. South Africa became a signatory to CEDAW in 1994 and ratified the Beijing Platform for Action as well as the AU protocols on human rights, which recognize women's human rights. (The need to expand the AU protocols to include LGBTI rights was and remains barely recognized.)

• • •

Women's representation at various levels of the government and the institutionalization of gender machinery are the key gains of the South African women's movement in the postapartheid era. After the 1994 election, the demands that the Women's National Coalition (WNC) made in the Women's Charter for Effective Equality laid the basis for women's representation in all levels of government and for the founding of the gender machinery. Women constituted 27 percent of the members of parliament, including a number of key feminists, but secured only 7 percent of the cabinet posts in the Mandela government. The number of women cabinet ministers increased to 45 percent in 2004, during President Thabo Mbeki's tenure (1999 to 2008), including South Africa's first woman deputy state president, Phumzile Hlambo-Ngcuka.

Between 1994 and 2002 the South African government committed itself to mainstreaming gender representation throughout the various levels of the state and in policy formulation and implementation. The Mandela government established the Office on the Status of Women and conceived the National Framework for Women's Empowerment, a policy designed to oversee gender mainstreaming in state departments and policies. Another key outcome of South Africa's commitment to CEDAW was the Joint Standing Committee on Improvement of Quality of Life and Status of Women (JSCLSW), together with the Reproductive Alliance, gave impetus to the gender-mainstreaming processes in the state and international recognition to South Africa's commitment to gender equality (Hassim 2006). In addition, the Commission on Gender Equality was established as an independent body to monitor the implementation of gender equality in the state and the private sector.

The feminist parliamentarians' activism in the early days of the Mandela presidency and the formation of the national gender machinery saw a number of policy gains for women. The porous boundaries between femocrats and activists in civil society also strengthened the fight to formulate new gender-sensitive legislation and to transform key legislation to take into account men's and women's gendered needs. These changes included the revision of a slew of legislation to remove the most egregious aspects of gender discrimination. Consequently, the Domestic Violence Act, Child Maintenance Act, Customary Law on Marriages Act, and changes in labor legislation acknowledged sexual harassment and made improvements in women's employment conditions.

Feminist activism in population, social development, and financial policies brought about important gendered changes as well. Individual femocrats, such as Noziziwe Madlala Routledge, Pregs Govender, and, for a time, Frene Ginwala played key roles in parliament in formulating gender-sensitive legislation and challenging the state's budgetary priorities, especially for military defense. In 1996 Statistics South Africa, the office responsible for gathering demographic data, began collecting gender-disaggregated data. These statistics have revealed the extent of reported rapes, raised the general population's awareness of gender-based violence, and galvanized civil society. At the same time, a number of well-known women announced publicly that they had been subjected to sexual assault, and some famous male sports personalities were exposed as violent abusers.[3] As I show below, most of the NGOs concerned with gender-based violence were founded between 1995 and 1997, in response to the heightened awareness of the extent of the problem.

In addition, femocrats' actions on the government Finance Committee, buttressed by the commitments made in the Reconstruction and Development Program, saw the formulation of the Women's Budget Initiative, begun by Pregs Govender, ANC member of parliament, and Debbie Budlender, feminist economist, in 1995.[4] This budget initiative sought to disaggregate the national budget in terms of its impact on men and women while taking into account their different social locations across race, generation, ethnicity, and the rural-urban divide. The Women's Budget Initiative was, initially, well received by the new finance minister, Trevor Manuel, who committed to integrating gender into the macroeconomic policy (Govender 2007). At the time, feminists in parliament were also fairly accessible to their activist colleagues in civil-society organizations. Consequently, the JSCLSW together with the Reproductive Rights Alliance, a feminist forum, set out to formulate and lobby support for the Termination of Pregnancy Act. This act, which guarantees all women the right to reproductive choice, was passed in 1996, two years after feminist activism in support of it was initiated. Likewise, the Domestic Violence Act of 1998 gave victims the right to seek police protection from assault and assistance in finding temporary shelter. The review of other key legislation, such as the Sexual Offenses Act and various bills governing women's rights under customary law, was protracted, however. When the Sexual Offenses Act was finally changed in 2003, rape was more broadly defined to recognize that men, women, and children are potential victims and incorporated any coercive act of penetration of the anus or genital organs.

Femocrats met uneven success in bringing about gendered transformation in customary laws. Initially, the changes in the Customary Marriages Act were made relatively swiftly and elevated women, especially black women, to equal partnership in customary marriages, while still recognizing the status of African and other legal traditions. However, the ruling African National Congress party has been loath to challenge the traditional chiefs' sole powers over the traditional courts and control over communal land in rural areas, because these chiefs are called upon to deliver votes to the ruling party during national elections. Subsequently, proposed changes to customary laws that infringe on women's rights have proved to be the most difficult to change (personal conversation with Pregs Govender, November 2008). During the 1990s the Rural Women's Movement (RWM) drew attention to the gendered discrimination that in particular black rural women faced under customary laws, especially in relation to landownership and inheritance.

The RWM, supported by feminists in the WNC and parliament, protested the traditional chiefs' sole rights to allocate access to communal lands, since women formed the majority of the rural population and they especially required guaranteed access to land for their own and their households' survival. Despite women's activism, the call to gender the Communal Land Rights Bill was defeated, and the legislation was passed in 2004. Traditional leaders were given autocratic power over access to and use of land in rural areas, where the population is overwhelmingly feminine. The constitutionality of the act is currently being challenged (Groenewald 2008). Similarly, the Bill on Customary Inheritance and Succession and the Traditional Courts Bill are currently being debated in parliament; they place rural women in a vulnerable position as regards their right to inheritance and to justice. The traditional male chiefs' legally entrenched powers over rural resources in these impoverished feminized contexts, and the associated defeat of a feminist agenda, has meant that an exaggerated form of culturally inscribed respectable femininity has become the only means to assert some claims to resources.

Women's physical presence in the state has increased, but while they have diversified the gendered makeup of the state, they have not necessarily acted to realize the citizenship rights of the poorest sector of our population, namely, poor women and their dependents, located in the vast urban informal settlements and the rural periphery. All of the women cabinet ministers in government are members of the erstwhile liberation movement, the African National Congress. However, they are by no means feminists, nor can they be trusted to act in women's gendered interests. Femocrats, such as Frene Ginwala, Pregs Govender, Phumzile Hlambo-Ngcuka, and Noziziwe Madlala Routledge, who were vociferous lobbyists for gender-sensitive policies, have been silenced, as their energies are channeled into other arenas of governance or as they have been marginalized. Other femocrats, especially those who are members of the ruling African National Congress Women's League, have jettisoned the gender agenda, as they assert their primary loyalty to the male leaders in the African National Congress and depend on these men's patronage. Their presence in the state exemplifies how women's presence in the state does not guarantee their support for the substantive realization of gender justice.

For instance, President Mbeki's cabinet has had the highest number of women ministers in history; however, their policies have undermined women's gendered socioeconomic and health interests. Geraldine Fraser Moleketi extended access to the child welfare grant to all racial groups but cut the value of the grant to a minimum amount during her tenure as minister of social development. The New Women's Movement in the Western Cape protested her actions but was dismissed as a minority group because most of the members happened to be poor colored women. When she became minister of public service and administration, her policy actions initiated the biggest civil servant strike in postapartheid South Africa, in 2007. This sector consists of a feminized workforce and incorporates public school teachers and nurses. Mbeki's minister of health, Manto Tshabalala-Msimang, is an AIDS denialist, and refused to provide affordable access to antiretroviral (ARVs) drugs to poor people living with HIV/AIDS. Women, who are the most vulnerable to infection and constitute the majority of caregivers, have borne the brunt of the minister's decision. When health deputy minister Noziziwe Madlala Routledge challenged these decisions, she was dismissed from the cabinet.

Fourteen years on, it is clear that the equality clauses enshrined in the constitution and the national gender machinery have provided women with access to state power. Many feminists have chosen to focus their energies working as women's rights advocates at diverse levels in the state, to ensure that state resources are used to deliver on policy changes. These advocates, such as the

Gender Advocacy Project in the Western Cape and the Center for Applied Legal Studies at the University of the Witwatersrand, have been able to influence policy makers because of their close alliance with women in the state. And as noted in 1995, "If the gains women have made at the constitutional, legal, and parliamentary levels are to be meaningful, the legacy of gender, race and class exploitation and oppression handed down mainly to black women, particularly black working class and rural women will have to be aggressively addressed by both the government and society as a whole" (Kemp et al. 1995, 157). Subsequently, the women's and gender movements have been articulated as rights-based approaches that have informed the growth and institutionalization of NGOs. And the gendered identities through which these claims to rights are expressed have grown exponentially, challenging and reinforcing the socioeconomic and religio-cultural status quo. There has been an increase in NGOs addressing information, education, and support networks on gender-based violence, shelter, and sexualities, especially on LGBTI issues. At the same time, the complex global donor-funding environment and the technocratic approach to gender mainstreaming have necessitated the professionalization of the NGO sector. Consequently, more skilled women and men, often with tertiary-level education, are employed to do the work, thereby initiating class-infused tensions. These workers share class identities with state representatives, and they often tend to expend their energies on strengthening alliances with the former, at the cost of their poorer, less skilled constituencies. In addition, NGO workers are also required to travel abroad, live in hotels, and engage in regional and global-funding and agenda-setting forums such as African Women in Development. Poor women in the local context read these increased travel opportunities for NGO workers as a sign of their growing alienation from the more immediate concerns for survival. These tensions are expressed in the everyday work context as suspicion and distrust and have delayed or threatened many well-intended work agendas.

A shift has occurred in poor women's activism and the actions of feminists who support them, sparked by the growth in socioeconomic inequality in recent years and the sea change in government's economic strategies since 1996. The plight of women farmworkers, rural women, and poor women living in urban informal settlements has accentuated the sharp contradictions between the formal rights-based discourse of the South African constitution and the growing socioeconomic inequalities brought on by neoliberal economic policies. These women have thrown their lot in with issue-based movements, focused on the demands for the realization of socioeconomic rights. Also, those feminists interested in emancipatory politics have begun to question femocrats' ability to influence policy necessary to bring about much-needed structural transformation so that substantive gender equality is realized. In fact, some of our hard-won feminist gains in the state, such as the Women's Budget Initiative, have been rolled back, especially after the state embraced the conservative neoliberal macroeconomic policy, Growth, Employment, and Redistribution Strategy (GEAR), in 1996.

This new economic policy was implemented in consultation with the International Monetary Fund and the World Bank (Govender 2007) and in keeping with global economic shifts (Salo 2005). GEAR is South Africa's own homegrown structural adjustment program that required cuts in social spending and trade liberalization. At the same time, the South African state's approach to the HIV/AIDS pandemic was also set back by President Thabo Mbeki's muchpublicized AIDS denialism. The economic policy shift, and the state's reluctance to actively promote antiretroviral medication as one of the primary means to assist people living with AIDS, marked a new era for all social movements in South Africa, including the women's movement. Women's rights activists had come to realize that, while necessary, the gender transformation in legislation has proved to be insufficient in improving the lives of the majority of South African women and of sexual minorities. By the late 1990s, feminists, like other post-apartheid social movements, had grasped that the transformation in women's gendered rights could not be entirely entrusted to the state, even one run by an erstwhile progressive liberation movement in a new democracy (Hassim 2005).

Feminist activism institutionalized in tertiary education and NGOs, is issue based and more closely aligned with women's diverse ethnic, religious, and class identities as well as diverse sexual orientations. At the same time, a critical men's movement has also surfaced, as feminist men have begun to interrogate the link between masculinities and women's oppression. The diversification and professionalization of feminist activism have also raised questions about the possibilities and challenges of alliance building between the various sectors of the women's movement across the divides of class, urban and rural locations, and sexual orientation, as well as between women and the critical men's movement.

Activism in the Academy:
Skilling for the Femocratic Dictatorship?

Women's activism in the antiapartheid movement between 1980 and the 1990s has contributed much to the institutionalization of women and gender studies

(WGS) departments and courses in the South African academies. These courses and programs grew exponentially in the postapartheid transition, assisted by the new democratic era and the international institutionalization of gender mainstreaming in the United Nations and other global bodies, as well as the Beijing Platform for Action in 1995.

Many women[5] who were active in the antiapartheid women's movement of the 1980s were also employed in the academy as researchers and lecturers. Most of these courses and programs were first offered at universities that were considered to be antagonistic to the South African state, such as the Universities of the Western Cape, Cape Town, Witwatersrand, and (then) Natal. These women identified the need to include gender as a key analytical tool alongside class and race, as part of the progressive social science tool kit at the time. Consequently, many of the women and gender studies courses were of the socialist feminist (see, for example, Volbrecht 1986) or Africanist (see, for example, Qunta 1987) variety, examining the relationship between women's gender interests and working-class movements or recuperating African notions of gendered personhood. These women mediated the institutional bureaucratic structures to establish women and gender studies courses across the various disciplines or grow fully fledged women and gender studies departments that offered undergraduate and postgraduate programs.

In addition, they also tackled the masculinist institutional culture and associated employment policies at these institutions, pushing for changes in the policies governing parental leave and establishing sexual harassment policies where none existed. So, for example, Rhoda Kadalie, a prominent women's rights scholar at the University of the Western Cape, formulated the first sexual harassment policy at a South African tertiary institution, in 1992. Since then, women and gender studies courses and full programs are available at nine out of twenty-seven tertiary institutions—the highest number of WGS sites on the continent (Boswell 2003).[6] While most of the courses tend to be informed by Western-based feminist thought and writers, women and gender studies at the University of the Western Cape and the University of Cape Town have begun to focus their curricula on African feminist thinkers and women's movements on the African continent. Feminist scholars' establishment of and contribution to two feminist journals, namely, *Agenda*, located at the Agenda Feminist Project in Kwa Zulu Natal, and *Feminist Africa*, based at the African Gender Institute at the University of Cape Town, have provided much-needed material to enrich WGS curricula. These journals have also assisted in sustaining WGS as a viable project within the academy, while informing research and policy agendas.

Many WGS graduates form the labor pool that provides skilled employees for the NGO sector. In this manner, organic alliances are built and sustained across the academy–civil society divide. However, these alliances tend to be exclusive to women from the educated classes and, in most cases, unwittingly inform the growing divide between the NGO sector and poor, nonliterate, and rural women. Feminist scholars also straddle the academy-activist divide with a fair degree of discomfort. The pressure to adhere to the strict professional publish-or-perish requirements has increased as the South African academy has become managerial in character, and the boundaries of "legitimate" knowledge are more closely policed through the expectation of publication in peer-reviewed international journals. The latter requirement leaves little room for more experimental, innovative modes of knowledge production because these will not be considered as fitting the institutional requirements of accredited publications.

We debate quietly whether it is best to leave our activism at the doors of higher learning, to limit ourselves to the publication and research requirements of the academy, or to continue collaboration with the NGO and grassroots women's organizations as scholar-activists but risk institutional disparagement about our claims to being bona fide scholars. Yet the success of feminist scholarship and mentoring is reflected in the increasing numbers of graduates in women and gender studies who are employed in the gender-NGO sector. Their increasing numbers in this sector have changed the organizational culture and introduced new power dynamics even as their skills have facilitated access to much-needed donor-funded resources.

NGOs and the Professionalization of Feminist Organizations in Civil Society

As stated above, the NGO environment has shifted as the funding environment has become more complex and the need for professionally trained NGO staff has increased. This is especially so in the field of gender-based violence as individual women seek assistance with shelter and litigation. However, the movement against the violation[7] to women's bodies has met with mixed success. The numbers of NGOs offering services in this field has grown extensively, and now these services are offered to women living in informal urban settlements and rural areas. However, the tendency to ignore poor women's embeddedness in social relations especially in impoverished areas, and the antiviolation activists' focus on women's rights as supposed autonomous individuals, has hindered this struggle. Most women don't bring formal charges against abusive partners, and those who do initiate litigation against their abusive partners tend to withdraw the charges later. These NGOs and shelters cannot offer the women long-term solutions, and they risk social sanction from their families and social networks when they seek assistance. As a result, some NGOs have begun to use a more holistic approach and target men and the elders in communities in their efforts to combat bodily and emotional violation of women.

General public awareness about the extent of these physical and emotional violations in general and rape in particular grew as collection of rape statistics improved and the police department was pushed to improve its victim-support services. General public support for women's struggles against gender-based violence has also strengthened, particularly among some men because the issue is so closely linked with widespread concern about safety and security in South African society. Mention has already been made of prominent women who spoke out publicly about their experiences as rape victims. These rape incidents drew attention to the intimate nature of rape as a sexual crime. The systemic socioeconomic roots of gendered violation and of rape in particular were highlighted by the heinous rape of Baby Tshepang in 2002 and by the shelter movement.

Most of the NGOs concerned with the protection and delivery of women's rights have mainly been concerned about gender-based violence. A few, such as the Gender Advocacy Project (in Cape Town) and Gender Links (based in Johannesburg), tend to monitor gender mainstreaming in more than one area, such as the media, local and national government, and health delivery services.

Most NGOs that provide services in education, legal support, and psychological counseling for victims of gender-based violence were founded in the mid-1990s and tend to be based in the urban areas. The NGOs concerned with this issue include the Network Against Violence Against Women and the Rape Crisis Center as well as the St. Anne's Home and Saartjie Baartman Center for women and children, based in Cape Town; Masimanyane Women's Support Center, based in East London; and the NISAA Institute for Women's Development, Agisanang Domestic Abuse and Training (ADAPT), and Tshwaranang Legal Advocacy Center, all based in Guateng. The services that these NGOs offer require a diverse set of skilled personnel, ranging from lawyers and medical practitioners to psychological counselors and social workers. Their clients tend to be mainly black[8] working-class women living in urban townships and informal settlements or who are homeless and living on the city streets.

At NGOs such as Saartjie Baartman and St. Anne's Home, shelter is offered to women and children for a period ranging from one month to two years, and some empowerment skills are offered to the women, including computer skills and arts and crafts. However, few of these shelters have instituted a tracking system to establish whether the counseling and training offered to the women have assisted them in becoming relatively independent in the long term (Maharaj 2008). Even though some NGOs such as Tshwaranang and Masimanyane extend their services to remote rural areas, there is a lack of services for victims of gender-based violence in rural areas. Shelter services offered by organizations such as NISAA, St. Anne's Home, Saartjie Baartman, and ADAPT experience an overwhelming need for shelter from domestic abuse in urban contexts where housing shortages are critical. Their inability to meet poor women's and children's demands for safe shelter, security, and skills to obtain employment in the long term points to the limitations of the individual rights–based approach to ending gendered abuse. NGOs such as NISAA and ADAPT acknowledge the deeper socioeconomic aspects of gender violation that require a transformative approach and partnership with the state, but to which the latter turns a blind eye.

ADAPT: Men as Part of a More Effective End to Gender Violation?

Agisanang Domestic Abuse and Training (ADAPT) is a nongovernmental organization that was founded in Alexandra township by Mmatshilo Motsei, in 1992. Motsei says that she became aware of women's and children's experiences of violence while working as a researcher for a health policy center at Wits University. ADAPT defines gender-based violence as a symptom of wider structural economic violence. Motsei argues that women in Alex experience abuse "not only from men, but from the state." She says that "homelessness, joblessness, high levels of crime in a culturally conservative, patriarchal society are some of the challenges that women in Alex had to, and continue to contend with." In an attempt to raise awareness of the multiple, gendered, and socioeconomic roots of women's abuse, and the social costs of gender-based violence, ADAPT has used a holistic approach to end gender-based violence and incorporated men, women, young people, and the elderly in "a community empowerment model that emphasises the influence and responsibility of the whole community in the prevention" of women's violation.[9]

More than other NGOs and shelters, ADAPT acknowledges that poor black women are subjected to interlinked forms of structural and interpersonal violence. The organization attempts to address the causes of gender violation at multiple social and psychological levels by targeting men and women in their programs. The organization offers counseling and support services and gender-sensitivity training for men and mentoring for young boys in an attempt to prevent abuse. Motsei argues that "ADAPT aims to achieve a society free from domestic and sexual violence against women, through the creative participation of both men and women." ADAPT's prevention strategy focuses on transforming the meanings and practices of masculinities in the local context. This inclusive approach marks the shift in a local feminist approach to engage with and interrogate practices of masculinities and that targets men primarily as means to end the violence. However, more radical feminists are critical of such an approach because men become the primary focus and are the recipients of services and other precious resources. ADAPT's engagement with women and their relationships with men and children have brought to the surface the limitations in the palliative approach termed *gender-based violence* that regards the woman as an autonomous actor who is not embedded in a web of social relationships. Our failure to recognize the interlinkages between structural and more personal forms of violation, as well as the turn to "culture" as a means to manage these violations and to respond accordingly, has informed the contradictions between the demands for gender rights, on the one hand, and religio-cultural rights, on the other. These contradictions have found expression in the heady rise of ethnonationalist masculinity, exemplified by the Jacob Zuma rape trial.

The Jacob Zuma Rape Trial: Gender Rights, Cultural Rights, Masculinities, and the Challenges of Common Sisterhood

The rape charges brought against erstwhile South African deputy vice president Jacob Zuma and the subsequent trial in November 2006 became the lodestone for unified women's activism against gender-based violence and the debate on women's rights, masculinities, and cultural rights. Briefly, here is the background of the story. In November 2005 a thirty-one-year-old woman, "Kwezi," who was a family friend of Jacob Zuma, and who considered Zuma her "uncle," claimed that Zuma had raped her at his home, where she was staying for the night.

The trial itself became the stage on which issues that lay at the heart of the debate about gender rights and cultural rights played themselves out. By then Jacob Zuma had been fired by President Mbeki, ostensibly because he was involved in corrupt dealings related to the notorious armaments deal. Many already considered Zuma to be the innocent victim of Mbeki's attempts to sabotage the former's presidential hopes. The rape charges were added to this heady mix. The arguments about the gendered propriety expected of Zulu persons were central to the trial. Throughout the trial, Zuma deliberately marked himself as the traditional Zulu man-warrior. He wore traditional Zulu dress and testified in isi-Zulu, despite being fluent in English, the language of the justice system. In his testimony Zuma argued that he had understood that Kwezi had "consented to sex within the context of Zulu norms around sexual relations" because she was wearing a kanga (sarong) and no underwear and sat in a particular way (Vetten 2007, 438). He also argued that he had aroused her sexually, and he could not stop because, in Zulu culture, this was tantamount to rape. The defense also used her sexual history to portray the young woman as a cunning seductress, who did not behave in the appropriate manner expected of a respectful Zulu woman.

Outside the court, many Zuma supporters appeared, men and women, old and young, wearing T-shirts bearing his image and the words "100% Zulu Boy." At the end of the first day of the trial, Zuma appeared singing "Umshini Wami" (Bring Me My Machine Gun) to an adoring crowd of supporters. This song resonated both with the notions of masculinities tied up with warfare (in this case "a war" against Mbeki's alleged victimization of Zuma) and with the symbolized male power defiant in the face of the rape trial by a court system based on colonial legal traditions (see Vetten 2007).

In opposition to the performance of Zulu cultural identity, women's activists, mainly from urban-based women's organizations such as People Opposed to Women's Abuse, appeared wearing *kangas* and placards protesting the gender stereotypes used in the trial in defense of Zuma. Often the two opposing sides became embroiled in verbal slinging matches, and in at least one incident, a woman thought to be the defendant was stoned. At the same time, women's organizations who supported the protests against gender-based violence outside the court founded the One in Nine Campaign, launched as an advocacy campaign to provide support for Kwezi, the complainant.

Three of the gender-violence advocacy organizations tried to assist as amici curiae and to highlight the problems surrounding criminal law in relation to rape charges that put the plaintiff at an inherent disadvantage. Race became another complicating factor, even as these women's organizations sought to support the complainant in sisterly solidarity. The complainant rejected the offer for legal support from the women's organizations, but they intervened anyway, possibly "in the interests of the wider cause" (Suttner 2007). The legal experts from the organizations were white, the complainant black, thus raising the ever-thorny racial and class divide between the leadership in women's organizations and their clientele. The decision to override the complainant's request also emphasized black women's constant complaint that their voices and decisions are often silenced by white women's actions. Suttner asks whether "these intentions had to be implemented against the will of the person affected most. . . . Should one not ask whether the complainant would not have been undermined and overridden again, thus further disempowering her as a human being?" (ibid., 16).

Yet despite all these fractures that marked the solidarity of the women's rape protests at the trial, the One in Nine Campaign successfully extended its campaign to launch ongoing protests outside courtrooms, in solidarity with rape survivors who have brought charges against their assailants. In addition, they continue to emphasize the secondary victimization that rape survivors are subjected to when they are faced with insensitive police and discriminatory rules of evidence in the legal process. Their campaign calls for a reformulation of criminal evidence permitted in rape trials that correct the inherent gender bias. Most of the participants in the actual protests are black, mainly urban-based women, reflecting the campaign's increasing ability to reach over and cross the racial divide in solidarity against gender-based violence.

The Zuma trial also surfaced responses from members of the critical men's movement, such as the Sonke Gender Justice Network and Men as Partners Network. These men draw attention to the egregious practices of dominant masculinities in South Africa through their campaigns such as the Annual Men's March Against Gender-Based Violence held in December, during the Sixteen Days of Activism Against Violence Against Women. They were critical of the militaristic, ethnonationalist meanings of masculinity that were exhibited during the Zuma trial. In their report on the status of women, the *South Africa Country Report*, they remark that Zuma's failure to restrain misogynistic protests at his trial represented the "potential for senior leaders to undermine gender transformation" (Sonke Gender Justice Network 2007). However, these critical men's movements confine their concerns to misogyny, their membership remains exclusively heterosexual, and they have yet to begin to address issues such as homophobia.

NGOs and the Limitations of the Professional Feminist Movement

Like the nongovernmental organizations discussed earlier, the One in Nine Campaign's advocacy in the aftermath of the Zuma trial remains focused on an individual rights–based approach to women's rights for gender justice. Such rights-based approaches assist all women by addressing the gender biases, regardless of race or class, that we face when seeking state services. Rights-based approaches come up against the limitations of socioeconomic constraint when the solution to poor women's gendered issues cannot be successfully addressed without meaningful change in their economic statuses. It is not surprising that many women seek alternative solutions in men's crude expressions of tradition and a reified cultural identity. Individualist approaches to gendered problems do not address different cultural notions of gendered personhood that are relational.

Ordinary women, especially the poor based in the urban informal settlements and rural areas, want the gendered aspect of socioeconomic inequalities addressed, particularly in relation to health care and access to basic services such as water, sanitation, housing, and employment. In addition, they may want a transformation in religio-cultural practices that are more equitable without necessarily denigrating or leaving their communities or repudiating their relational identities. In some cases where rights-based NGOs have worked with poor women to address their issues, these erstwhile "clients" develop a radical gender consciousness and often push these organizations to assume a more radical position in relation to agency, the demand for socioeconomic rights, and a radical expansion of cultural practices to incorporate gender equality.

In the next section I look at two rights-based NGOs where the concerns of the poor women have given rise to tensions within the organization about agenda priorities or transformed the organizational agenda. Women activists' growing awareness of the interrelatedness between local conditions and global politics and trade has led them to adopt a more multipronged strategy in their struggles for gender justice. This has required these organizations to engage in local campaigns and to participate in international campaigns in partnership with like-minded international NGOs such as ActionAid International and Oxfam. First I examine the relationship between the Women on Farms Project (WFP) and Sikhula Sonke. I then look at the status of women in the renowned HIV/AIDS rights organization Treatment Action Campaign (TAC).

Thinking Global, Acting Local:
Women on Farms and the Sikhula Sonke Trade Union

The Women on Farms Project developed in 1992 to address the rights of women farmworkers, particularly in the Western Cape. The NGO workers, who mainly consist of professionally trained women, traditionally gained access to the women farmworkers via a grassroots organization, Vroue Regte Groepe

(Women's Rights Organizations on Farms). Commissioned research on workers' living conditions on farms revealed the bleak reality of poverty among farmworkers and the increasingly harsh levels of labor exploitation.

In a 2003 study researchers found that most farmworkers were now employed mainly as informal, casual workers with an increase in the feminization of work in the deciduous fruit and wine industry (SANPERI 2008). These findings led the NGO to conclude that the globalization of the South African deciduous fruit and wine industry, the increased vulnerabilities of farmworkers, their socioeconomic rights, and their conditions of employment were interconnected. So despite the celebration of the rights-based discourse in South Africa, these farmworkers' activism indicated that local women's claims for rights, via NGOs such as Women on Farms, was limited if the conditions of the global trade system were not addressed. At the same time that the WFP was uncovering the extent of women farmworkers' vulnerabilities, donor funding in the postapartheid context was declining. The WFP grew increasingly critical about its dependency on donor agencies for funding and worried about the implications of potential closure for its primary constituency, the extremely vulnerable farmworkers. The WFP met with farm women and decided to establish "a membership organization of women, led by women."[10]

Sikhula Sonke[11] was constituted on South African Women's Day, August 9, 2004, and registered as a trade union for women farmworkers later that year. The trade union has thirty-three hundred members living on farms in the scenic fruit- and wine-producing valleys of the Western Cape. Sikhula Sonke calls itself a social movement labor union, fighting for the rights of marginalized women workers. Sikhula Sonke's local campaigns have raised awareness about farmworkers' and women farmworkers' particular gendered vulnerabilities to poor employment conditions, evictions from farms, alcoholism, HIV/AIDS, gender-based violence, and dependence upon men.

On the international front, Sikhula Sonke has collaborated with ActionAid International to raise awareness of women farmworkers' impoverishment among the shoppers and shareholders of transnational companies, such as the Tesco supermarket chain in the United Kingdom, which purchase South African produce. At their presentation to the Tesco annual meeting in the UK, in 2006, Sikhula Sonke member and farmworker Gertruida Baartman said that "TESCO can say good things, but the truth is the people are not treated well here" (on South African farms).

The general secretary, Wendy Pekeur, acknowledges that the process of farm women's empowerment is a long and difficult road, but she argues that this model of unionizing focused on women's rights and leadership in the labor movement will benefit everyone in the long run.[12] Sikhula Sonke's relative success is the outcome of collaborative partnerships between grassroots women's organizations, nongovernmental organizations in the local context, on one hand, and international collaboration with social movements' NGOs, on the other. The organization's simultaneous practical engagements at the local and global levels challenge Maxine Molyneux's (1985) classic distinction between women's practical and strategic gender needs to categorize women's movements as reformist or transformational. These practices are considered both reformist and transformational in Molyneux's schema, and call for "feminists to take [conceptual] account of the multiple levels at which the struggle for women's substantive rights [are being] waged" (Salo 2005, 66). Also, the trade unionists from Sikhula Sonke engage as equals with scholar-activists who straddle the divide between these organizations and the academy, often challenging incorrect or ineffective conceptual descriptions of their realities. Consequently, the apparently class-inflected knowledge and power boundaries between the women in the academy and women workers have become exceedingly porous. Conceptual hierarchies such as those posed by Molyneux appear to be false binaries that fail to capture the complex simultaneous strategies that the organization employs.

Sexual Rights: Gendered Alliances on the Margins of Heteropatriarchy

The close relationship between gender justice and broader social justice is also represented in poor women's choice to support broader social justice movements that are often led by males. These women's membership raises questions about the possibilities of negotiating gender inequities within mass-based social movements. The HIV/AIDS pandemic and the social movement it birthed, the Treatment Action Campaign, is the keystone for key debates on the intersection of gender, sexuality, and socioeconomic justice in South Africa. The Treatment Action Campaign is a mass-based organization led by a black homosexual middle-class man and consisting primarily of women who are heterosexual, black, and poor. Both these groups are on the margins of heteropatriarchy. TAC is a social movement founded to demand poor people's right to access antiretroviral medications. TAC was established in 1998 when a small number of protesters in Cape Town demanded antiretroviral treatment for pregnant women to reduce the risks of transmission to their unborn children. Since then the organization's membership has grown into a popular social movement of approximately 20,000 members, most of whom are black, poor, working-class women. However, TAC's most recognizable, celebrated image is embodied in its founder, the openly gay, charismatic Zackie Achmat. The tensions that emerge about gay, educated, middle-class men leading an overwhelmingly heterosexual women's organization pose novel debates about intersectionality, power, and alliance between gendered identities on the margins of heteropatriarchy.

The structural determinants of HIV/AIDS such as mobility, poverty, and gender inequalities in South Africa place black heterosexual women most at risk of contracting the infection. Almost 60 percent of adults living with HIV are women (Medical Research Council 2005) while young women aged between fifteen years and twenty-four years have an HIV incidence that is eight times higher than for men of the same age (Shisana 2005). Women bear the brunt of care associated with the epidemic because they are the primary caregivers in more than two-thirds of the households in this region (VSO 2006, cited in Meintjies-Moakes 2008). Lesbian women have been at risk of infection through a unique form of gender-based violence termed *corrective rape*.[13] Heterosexual men who feel threatened by lesbian women's apparent independent sexual choices and fear the stigma attached to HIV/AIDS have targeted lesbian women HIV/AIDS activists who have disclosed their sexual preference. Similarly, though, the stigma attached to homosexuality, the widespread and deep-rooted homophobia in South African society, and the relative anonymity of the lifestyle have also placed these men at risk of infection, too.

Initially in South Africa, as in the United States, HIV/AIDS was first identified in another gender minority, namely, homosexual men. As a result, AIDS activism is historically rooted in the gay-rights campaigns that were part of the broad antiapartheid movement. The antiracist, antihomophobia AIDS-rights struggle was simultaneously embodied in personalities such as Zackie Achmat, Simon Nkoli,[14] and Edwin Cameron, who were all fierce adversaries of the apartheid state, openly gay, and also infected with HIV. Achmat and others applied the political lessons learned in the antiapartheid struggle in TAC to demand dignity, equality, and affordable treatment for people living with HIV/AIDS. TAC has used a mix of strategies to great effect to promote the rights of people living with HIV/AIDS. They have, at times, collaborated with the South African state and protested the actions of the international biomedical industry and the state, while educating people about coping with HIV/AIDS and antiretrovirals in communities. They have also gendered their campaign by focusing on pregnant women's rights to affordable medication.

Initially, TAC's adversarial approach was aimed at the transnational pharmaceutical industry to protest their monopoly over the production of antiretroviral medication and the block on wider access to generic drugs. Later, TAC's opposition vis-à-vis the South African state increased when the latter failed to implement the national AIDS Plan[15] or to make good on its legal victory against a major pharmaceutical company to make medication more affordable. The animosity reached the breaking point when President Mbeki, supported by his health minister, publicly announced his doubts that HIV caused AIDS and questioned the efficacy of ARVs. The health ministry balked at providing ARVs through the public health system. In 2002 TAC successfully challenged the state at the Constitutional Court to ensure pregnant women's access to ARVs to prevent mother-to-child transmission. Yet despite this court decision, the ministry steadfastly refused to provide ARVs. Zackie Achmat protested the state's refusal by deciding to forgo his ARV regime and became seriously ill as a result. After Nelson Mandela intervened, the health minister agreed to provide ARVs freely to people living with HIV/AIDS, and TAC ordered Achmat to end his ARV "fast." However, the minister's steadfast AIDS denialism, coupled with the stigma associated with HIV/AIDS, continues to obstruct efficient access to ARVs. This situation has required that TAC and other civil society organizations monitor access to ARVs through the various public health sites and educate people about the ARV regime.

TAC relies on the women who constitute the majority of its members to educate people living with HIV/AIDS about their right to ARVs, about the etiology of the disease, and about healthy lifestyles. Women also mobilize the membership to participate in public protests. Consequently, women have become increasingly empowered within the organization and have demanded that TAC develop a special focus on women's health, leadership, and violence and provide gender training for men (TAC 2007a). The implementation of these demands has created tensions within the organization, especially about the recognition of women's contribution to the organization and the sensitivity to gender within the organizational culture. Debates have also surfaced about the meaning of gendered leadership in an organization that represents heterosexual and homosexual men and women affected by HIV/AIDS and the extent to which women are part of TAC's public face (see Meintjies-Moakes 2008). Until recently, women have mainly been active as volunteers in TAC or employed in its literacy programs. Women were subsequently elected to the National Executive Committee, and a woman, Sipho Mathi, was elected as the general secretary in 2006. However, key women have also resigned from the organization, indicating the difficulties TAC faces as it attempts to be a truly representative organization, fighting for the rights of an extremely marginalized sector of society, namely, homosexual and hetero-sexual men and women living with HIV/AIDS.

These internal struggles also raise the question of whether an organization that consists mainly of heterosexual, poor, black, working-class women should also be led by women, and if so, would these women necessarily possess a crit-ical feminist consciousness? And what of a black gay male leadership who is known to be progressive, who acts in the material interests of its members? Is such leadership necessarily unrepresentative? The gender dynamics in TAC raise questions about representation, leadership, and gender essentialism such as whether marginal men can develop a critical feminist consciousness and whether they can legitimately lead an organization that consists mainly of women. Furthermore, they also raise innovative questions about the fractures of gender and power associated with marginal, intersectional identities. For ex-ample, how do mainly heterosexual women's organizations build strategic al-liances with gay and lesbian organizations? What relations of power are expressed in these alliances?

HIV and the Homophobia Campaign

South Africa's constitution is lauded as one of the most progressive, ensuring its citizens' freedom from discrimination on the basis of sexual preference. In so doing the state enshrined the human rights of lesbian, gay, bisexual, trans-gender, and intersex people. However, despite this progressive constitutional protection, homophobia remains an embedded, widespread problem in South African society. Between 2006 and 2008, six "out" black lesbian women and one "out" black gay man were murdered. LGBTI activists suspect that these people were the victims of homophobic attacks (Lee 2008).

Our experience with the HIV/AIDS pandemic has raised difficult questions about the relationship between heterosexual women in the women's movement and the LGBTI community. However, the campaign against the HIV/AIDS pandemic has also created an opportunity for gay and lesbian organizations and HIV/AIDS rights organizations such as the Treatment Action Campaign to form a strategic alliance to raise public awareness of gay and lesbian people's rights, as well as the threat of homophobia. The case of Zoliswa Nkonyane, a young lesbian HIV activist, is illustrative of this. Zoliswa, who was open about her pos-itive status and her sexual preference, was murdered in Cape Town in 2006. The attack on her took place when she and a friend were confronted by a girl who called them "tom boys who wanted to be raped" (ibid., 5). The girl sum-moned a gang of men to assault Zoliswa and her friend. Her friend managed to escape the attack, but Zoliswa was stoned, stabbed, and beaten to death. Her killers were arrested; however, their trial has been postponed on numerous occasions and remains unresolved. The Triangle Project, a lesbian- and gay-rights organization, and the Treatment Action Campaign have campaigned jointly in the media and led public protests against delays in the justice system. In so doing, they have drawn attention to the deadly threat of homophobia as gay and lesbian people courageously step out of the closet. The eradication of homophobia within mainstream women's organizations and alliance building between the latter and the LGBTI rights movement still need to be addressed in an effective manner.

Conclusion

The flowering of a human rights culture in the early postapartheid era has provided the context in which the struggle for women's and gender minorities' human rights have diversified and deepened in South Africa. The increased representation of women in the state and associated feminist activism have ensured the enactment of progressive legislation advancing women's rights for physical, cultural, and economic autonomy. The slew of progressive gender legislation solidified the gains of the women's movement; however, it also mapped out a new phase of struggle for the meaningful realization of these rights for women and gender minorities, especially among the poorer sectors of the population. This new phase has been marked by the claims for women's and gender minorities' sexual health and reproductive rights in the context of HIV/AIDS.

The implementation of a neoliberal economic policy, GEAR, in 1996, deepened the economic divide between the elite, well-resourced, urban-based sectors of the population and the poor, located in the urban and rural peripheries. Women formed the majority of the poor and rural populations and so suffered the brunt of these economic changes. At the same time, the women's movement has become increasingly concentrated in the urban-based NGO sector where staff consists of professional, skilled women. Consequently, the socioeconomic divide between poor and rural women and the more educated NGO sector has widened, forcing poor women to struggle for socioeconomic rights in the male-led broader social movements. The campaigns against gender-based violence, especially against rape, remain among the most prominent campaigns that seem to unite women across the racial and class divides. In addition, a critical men's movement has also emerged in response to women's sustained critiques of destructive masculinities that fuel gender-based violence.

The need to target women's claims for gendered rights, simultaneously at the local and global level, is also becoming increasingly prominent. This multipronged strategy is being adopted by the women's trade union Sikhula Sonke, which emerged from the NGO Women on Farms, and the Treatment Action Campaign against HIV/AIDS. The HIV/AIDS pandemic has exacerbated the socioeconomic divide within the women's movement; however, it has also provided new opportunities for alliance building in the global and local campaigns to claim women's and LGBTI people's sexual health and reproductive rights. It is clear that as the movement for women's and LGBTI people's gendered and sexual rights grows, and as a critical men's movement gains momentum, the debates about how and when alliances are built across the divides of gender, sexual preference, and class will become more prominent in the future.

Notes

1. I use *femocrats* in the original Australian feminists' use of the term to refer to women who have entered the state because they are (1) biologically female and meet the state's gender quota but do not necessarily support a feminist agenda or (2) feminist activists, who have been awkwardly assimilated into the state under conditions of an untransformed patriarchal culture. They may define the state bureaucracy as a site of struggle in which they seek to gender state policies.

2. The same situation has arisen in Australia, although for different reasons. See Sawer 2007.

3. In 1997 Nomboniso Gasa, a prominent feminist, was raped, and she decided to go public about the assault. Journalist Charlene Smith did the same in 1999, after she had been raped and stabbed in her home. She wrote an article for the *Washington Post* in June 2000 in which she claimed that rape had become endemic in South Africa. This initiated a bitter debate between Smith and President Mbeki, in which he argued that Smith was maligning black men as HIV-infected rapists with uncontrollable sexual appetites. Both women are well known in feminist circles in the state, and their stories gave further impetus to the struggle against gender-based violence. Cricketer Makhaya Ntini was tried for rape when a young woman, Nomegezi Matokazi, alleged he had raped her in a public bathroom. He was found guilty but acquitted on appeal. The partner of James Small, a popular rugby player, revealed that he subjected her to violent abuse.

4. Debbie Budlender and Pregs Govender were initiators of the Women's Budget Initiative at the time.

5. These women included inter alia Fatima Meer, Shamim Meer, Vivienne Taylor, Belinda Bazzoli, Rehebohile Moletsane, Hloni Kwenaite, Xoliswa Sibeko, Cheryl de la Rey, Allison Lazarus, Mrs. Kwenaite, Jacklyn Cock, Denise Ackerman, Rhoda Kadalie, Michelle Friedman, Amanda Gouws, Christelle Stander, Isabel Hofmeyer, Sheila Meintjies, Annette Seegers, Cathi Albertyn, Jane Bennett, Shireen Hassim, Terri Barnes, Karen Chubb, Marie Mac Donald, Mickey Flockemann, Cheryl Ann Michael, Zoe Wicomb, Gertrude Fester, Cheryl Potgieter, Sheila Meintjies, Barbara Klugman, Mamphele Ramphele, Mary Simons, Ginny Volbrecht, Anne Mager, Helen Bradford, Desiree Lewis, Cheryl Hendricks, Elaine Salo, Lynn Denney, Debbie Budlender, Pat Horn, Shirley Walters, Di Cooper, Salma Mohammed, and others.

6. University of the Western Cape, University of Cape Town, University of Stellenbosch, Rhodes University, University of Fort Hare, University of Pretoria, University of Johannesburg, University of Kwa Zulu-Natal, and University of South Africa.

7. Thanks to Pat McFadden for insisting on the use of term *violation* rather than the phrase *gender-based violence* as a means to instantiate these complex links between physical and emotional violence and structural, systemic violence.

8. I use *black* here in the comprehensive sense, to refer to people previously classified as African, colored, and Asian under old apartheid classificatory categories.

9. www.comminit.com/en/node/1822.

10. www.wfp.org.za/content/XID10-history.html.

11. Isi-Xhosa, meaning "We grow together."

12. Wendy Pekeur interviewed by Koni Benson, October 24, 2006.

13. Interview with Vanessa Ludwig, director, Triangle Project, November 3, 2008.

14. Nkoli died of an AIDS-related illness in 1998.

15. Formulated during the Mandela presidency.

2

Ramagwana Rakajeka: Opportunities and Challenges of the Zimbabwean Women's Movement

SHEREEN ESSOF

On February 8, 2001, representatives of the Zimbabwean women's movement streamed up the stairs to one of the epicenters of Harare's alternative culture, the popular leftist venue the Book Café.[1] As I walked up the stairs to the café, the energy was palpable as women said their hellos and sat in clusters at tables on the deck of the café, catching up, getting refreshment, and browsing the notices for upcoming poetry readings, music gigs, and political debates, but all the while aware and alert to the question of the day: "Does Zimbabwe have a women's movement?" This was an intriguing question. The individual women activists, the range of women's organizations present, from those orientated to technical gender and development frameworks to those advocating for women's human rights to those naming themselves overtly feminist: all self-identified as a movement, and the question flew in the face of the wide range of robust activity individual activists and women's organizations had engaged in during the intervening years since Zimbabwe's independence in 1980.

As the meeting progressed, I became amazed by the spectrum of views generated in the debate. Some questioned whether the activities of Zimbabwean women's organizations indeed constituted a movement and called for taking stock of its concrete achievements. Others argued that there was a movement, even though it had an organizational face, and that this movement

ZIMBABWE

Human Development Index ranking: .513
Gender-Related Development Index value: .505
Gender Empowerment Measure value: not available

General

Type of government: Parliamentary
Major ethnic groups: Shona (71%); Ndebele (16%); other African (11%); white (1%); mixed and Asian (1%)
Languages: English (official); Shona; Sindebele
Religions: syncretic; Christian (75%); Christian sects; animist; Muslim

Demographics

Population, total (millions), 2005: 13.1
Annual growth rate (%), 2005–2015: 1.0
Total fertility (average number of births per woman): 3.6
Contraceptive prevalence (% of married women aged 15–49): 54
Maternal mortality ratio, adjusted (per 100,000 live births), 2000: 880

Women's Status

Date of women's suffrage: 1919
Life expectancy: M 41.4; F 40.2
Combined gross enrollment ratio for primary, secondary, and tertiary education (female %), 2005: 51
Gross primary enrollment ratio: 95
Gross secondary enrollment ratio: 35
Gross tertiary enrollment ratio: 3
Literacy (% age 15 and older): M 92.7; F 86.2

Political Representation of Women

Seats in parliament (% held by women): 22.2
Legislators, senior officials, and managers (% female): unavailable
Professional and technical workers (% female): unavailable
Women in government at ministerial level (% total): 14.7

Economics

Estimated earned income (PPP US$), 2005: M 2,585; F 1,499
Ratio of estimated female to male earned income: .58
Economic activity rate (% female): 64.0
Women in adult labor force (% total): 44 (this figure obtained at the CEDAW Statistical Database)

was in a constant state of flux and evolution. As one participant in the debate argued,

> If we look at the sixties into the eighties, it is clear that women of Zimbabwe have come a long way. We began with a heavy focus on domestic skills, being able to cook, knit, sew, craft, etc., but that was part of the creating—those women's clubs were fundamental to the women's movement because in the eighties and nineties we could say, "Fine, we've come this far; we need to move a stage further," and then we went into the women's rights phase of the movement with added vigor. . . . The problem that I have when people say that we don't have a movement is I think they are taking a very narrow definition. They have looked at what is going on in someone else's territory and then decided that because that is not going on here we cannot have a movement. A movement has its roots in its own particular context.

The debate continued as women argued that the movement had been so ideologically weakened that it was reduced to perpetuating the patriarchal status quo. Some felt that women activists in Zimbabwe were at a watershed, being challenged to step out of the box of the predetermined and prescribed solutions and organizational forms of the past and "take a much more grounded and radical stance, rooted in feminist discourse, to confront patriarchy inside and outside our organizational bases." Muted voices recognized a movement, but described it as "weak" and "disarrayed." One commentator later was to refer to the movement as "paralyzed."

The feelings expressed at the Book Café meeting discounted my experience of witnessing creative and assertive organizing by women while working for the Zimbabwean Women's Resource Centre and Network (ZWRCN) during 1995–2000. I knew that the terrain of women's mobilizing in Zimbabwe was both rich and deep (Barnes 1991; Schmidt 1992; Barnes 1999) and that women's participation in the nationalist struggle for independence (Staunton 1990) provided the impetus for postindependence demands that sought gender equity and disrupted preexisting gender relations and cultural norms. However, I also knew from my experience that the ensuing years saw patriarchy reassert itself as the political will to address gender inequality in Zimbabwe diminished rapidly and was replaced by intensified regulation of women in both the private and the public spheres. This was done through the powerful invocation of counterrevolutionary cultural-nationalist discourses that portrayed women's organizing as feminist, and feminism as antinationalist and proimperialist, which went a long way toward destabilizing and weakening the movement.

Feminism Submerged?

The Book Café meeting obliquely raised the lack of "a clearly articulated ideological position in the movement" as one part of the problem. Just what happened to feminism as a grounded base for women's organizing in Zimbabwe?

The early postindependence years saw clearly articulated feminist discourses and the birth of a set of organizations that were rooted in a feminist politics and agenda. These discourses were based on the recognition of patriarchy as a system of male oppression and domination, which sought a holistic and structural transformation of society and relationships, a vision embodied by women who were, at the time, self-proclaimed, "outed" feminists. However, in the face of an increasingly hostile state, where the assault on women gradually meant that even past gains seemed precarious, the movement quickly began to distance itself from an "overt" feminist politics. As one activist noted, "Feminism in this country died—because Zimbabwean women were not ready to defend feminism. They did not realize how critical feminist thinking and energies were for the bigger movement; they backed off. I remember a leader of a key women's organization telling me, 'It's too hot an issue.'"

Thus, by the latter 1990s one saw the disappearance of the words *oppression*, *exploitation*, *patriarchy*, and *feminism* from the movement's lexicon, and it is revealing when one considers the terms that seemed to have replaced them: *gender* and *mainstreaming*. These moves to "disappear" feminism as an articulated discourse framing women's activism and actions could have, on the part of women activists, been presented as "strategic" to ensure that the spaces for organizing remained open. This is debatable, however, and the move has not been articulated as such. Feminism was constructed as too inflammatory. It required naming oneself in a way that could not be easily accommodated by the state and the collective national psyche, or indeed by some women within the movement.

And so, a decade later, it is not surprising that clearly articulated feminist voices were muted, overtaken by gender and development and women's human rights discourses. The availability of donor aid[2] in support for this work fueled a bevy of women's organizations with wide national rural and urban networks and linkages. These organizations and their networks formed the face and operating base of a somewhat syncretic movement that over time waxed and waned depending on the operating context.

These organizations found the articulation of gender and development discourses under the rubric of the United Nations and a series of global international instruments, including the Convention on the Elimination of All Forms of Discrimination Against Women, a relatively safer discursive haven for furthering women's equality as well as a means of providing more leverage for a women's agenda. In this way, a developmental gendered politics emerged and gained ascendance over more radical feminist voices.

Gender was increasingly being promoted and used by the World Bank, the United Nations, bilateral agencies, civil society, and the Zimbabwean government, all of whom were linking the concept to development assistance. At this time the movement saw many women take up a more technocratic gendered discourse in servicing these sites, as consultants. One needs to guard against the language of development agencies taking over the voices of political struggle in this way as it obscures power relations and waters down the critical political edge.

Be that as it may, women within organizations forged links with donors, the state, and civil society, and these links were used to further women's collective action agendas if the situation demanded it.

Critical Considerations

But the lingering question for me at that February meeting was not whether Zimbabwe had a women's movement. Instead, I found myself asking: What kind of movement develops in this kind of context, under these pressures? What form and shape does it have to take in order to survive while seizing the opportunities and confronting the challenges to further the struggle for equality for all?

I argue that the strategy that evolved over time, from the birth and growth of somewhat disparate sectoral women's nongovernmental organizations including community-based organizations and their constituencies, came to comprise the base of the movement. Over time, this base formed strategic coalitions in pursuit of a women's human rights–based agenda. These coalitions saw organizations, their urban and rural networks, and concerned individual activists coming together in various issue-driven configurations, forming and disbanding and reforming again as needed. After years of organizing in this way, with somewhat fragile gains, women activists turned to the constitutional reform process as the ultimate forum for enshrining gender equality and entrenching Zimbabwean women's rights via the vehicle of building a national coalition.

This decision grew out of the belief that "together we would make a bigger difference,"[3] that coalitions and networks were based on notions of solidarity, mutual support, and information sharing. This was thought to bolster advocacy by bringing together the strength and resources of diverse groups to create a more powerful voice for change (VeneKlasen and Miller 2002). The women's movement believed that it was possible to develop a united women-centered and women-driven agenda as a means to corral forces, consolidate a plan of action, and move forward as a political force and constituency.

I further argue that during this process the power of collective organizing was recognized and strategically refined. But this also presented challenges to the women's movement in Zimbabwe. Until the birth of the Women's Coalition (WC) on the Constitution in 1999, very few divisive issues were apparent within the movement. Diversity was evident around personal identities, but political or ideological differences were concealed, the invisibility assisted by the language of gender and development, with its depoliticized messages associated with national development, such as "Women are here to complement the efforts of the government," "Everyone is a stakeholder," and "Women must be given their rights because it is good for development." This kind of discourse masked the huge ideological divides that lie beneath debates on national questions.

The Zimbabwean experience confirms that the state has been the central focus of women's organizing, as has been characteristic of women's movements in other African contexts. Similar conclusions have been drawn by Manuh, in her analysis of relations between women, society, and the state under the People's National Defense Committee rule in Ghana (1993), Tsikata's work on women's political organizations in Ghana (1999), Mama, writing on Nigeria (1999), and Tamale, writing on Uganda (1999). These studies raise critical and relevant questions concerning the strategies that women's movements have taken in effecting meaningful and sustainable change and the "likelihood of existing organizational forms challenging women's oppression or advancing women's political, social or economic interests" (Mama 1999, 19).

Whether women should organize within the state or stay outside of it has been the subject of much debate internationally. Some commentators believe that effective reform can come only via state instruments, while others argue that the state co-opts women's issues. Skeptics point to ways in which new legislation that seemingly favors women has afforded the state, not women, more power (Gandhi and Shah 1991). S. Alvarez (1990) and Jaquette (1989) take both perspectives into account when they argue for more pragmatism, working selectively with the state while maintaining an awareness of its limitations.

Citizenship is an important way in which the relationship between women and the nation-state has been theorized. It is not gender neutral. Men and women have been incorporated into citizenship in Zimbabwe in very different ways. Nationalism has not been constructed in a gender-neutral fashion, either. The control of Zimbabwean women, be it in the private or public sphere, is central to the nationalist agenda, and the identification of women as bearers of cultural identity affects their emergence as full-fledged citizens. While in post-colonial contexts many nationalist projects have equated the emancipation of women with "modernity," many states, Zimbabwe included, have been quick to abrogate reforms where they have felt that women are being a threat to nationalist ideals.

What is clear is that in the process of negotiation with the state, not only are women's agendas often ignored, blocked, or watered down, but women themselves are co-opted into state machinations through personal, professional, or political allegiances and interests. In this way, the state allows a certain amount of leverage, an allotted space for radical dissenting voices, but tolerates it only up to a point. The example of the debate on constitutional reform in Zimbabwe, discussed below, demonstrates just this, that the state does not allow for the consolidation of radical voices.

The varied political identities of women and the failure of the Zimbabwean women's movement to have sustained conversations around the building of a common vision, issues of difference, and power, meant that diversity became a weakness rather than a strength. The fragmentation caused as a result of political differences and an increasingly partisan politics further weakened the movement at a time when an authoritarian state was consolidating its stranglehold. But despite this polarization, the chance of the women's movement's being a radical space for change still exists. The challenge lies in how it is that we organize, what it is that we learn from our experience, and how we move forward in facing challenges. But before we march into the future, let me take a step back into the past.

Riding the Nationalist Wave

With considerable numbers of women participating in the liberation struggle in the late 1960s and 1970s, the image of the subservient mother or daughter came to be challenged by the female combatant (Gaidzanwa 1992). Women had multiple roles during the war of liberation. Many fought on the front line as female combatants under difficult conditions. Margaret Viki, a runner during the war, recounts:

I think if the women had not been there the freedom fighters would not have won the war. Women did a great job. Cooking and providing food for the freedom fighters was a way of fighting on its own. . . . The fact is we fought a war. Carrying pots of food up the mountains is no joke. I do not think that the men would have managed if the women had not been there to do all this. I think they would have ended up being killed by the freedom fighters after they had refused to cook and carry food for them. The men were around, but they only used to tell the women to "Hurry, before the soldiers come and beat you up!"

Despite an unreconstructed gender politics, women retained their courage and their strength, and they kept going and hoped for a new society in which women would be men's equals. As Meggi Zingani, a former combatant, recounts, "They said that after independence everyone would be free from colonialism. No one would be forced to dig contour ridges; we would have as many cattle as we wanted; a married woman without a marriage certificate would have the right to be treated as legally married; and that we would be treated like human beings."

Women proved to be just as able and dedicated to the cause for national liberation as their male counterparts, and the socialist principles that underpinned the struggle left little justification for continued discrimination. As more opportunities to study abroad opened up, women in exile made use of knowledge gathered from their own experiences in different educational institutions, societies, and the international feminist movement to develop critiques and to challenge gender subordination.

Thus, the foundations for the subsequent emergence of a women's movement and demands for compensation and rights were laid. The compensation came in the form of demobilization money for some. But this was not enough, and women agitated for more meaningful change.

The move by the state in the first decade of independence to afford women access to state structures and policies arose out of a need to placate women who had participated in the nationalist struggle for independence. Prior to independence, black women were considered minors under the colonial administration's codified customary law (Zuidberg, McFadden, and Chigudu 2004). This had to be righted. This was done through the plethora of gender-sensitive legislative changes in the early 1980s. The Sex Disqualification Act (1980) allowed women to hold public office. New labor regulations required equal pay for equal work and created the possibility for maternity leave.[4] The passing of the Legal Age of Majority Act in December 1982 afforded all Zimbabweans legal majority status at the age of eighteen. But LAMA provoked outrage in traditional quarters, as men, accustomed to exercising full control over their daughters and wives, suddenly found that they could no longer be assured of this. Under LAMA, women could, at least in theory, choose their sexual partners, inherit property, and engage in economic and political life. LAMA was complemented by a series of laws that provided maintenance claims for women in unregistered customary marriages[5] and a provision for the equitable distribution of matrimonial assets on divorce,[6] making property grabbing by relatives of the deceased and dispossession of the surviving spouse and children illegal.[7]

The Ministry for Community Development and Women's Affairs was established in 1981, and women who felt that the national structure would enable them to advance their interests enthusiastically welcomed it.[8] Organizations like the Association of Women's Clubs (AWC) and Zimbabwe Women's Bureau (ZWB)[9] threw their weight behind the ministry and like many other civil society organizations were committed to national reconstruction and development. The ministry was never particularly powerful within the government, but in its early days it did provide a valuable platform for the building of a gender consciousness and the exploration of feminist issues. But for the women who were exploring feminism and who participated in these structures, realization that discrimination against women was as much about the personal as the political resulted in frustration. Women soon realized that the state was not interested in taking the necessary steps to overcome women's subordination in Zimbabwean society.

Women activists soon found themselves criticizing the ministry's programs that had been conceptualized within the women in development paradigm, seeking to add women onto mainstream development programs without attending to the evidence that these programs were themselves part of the problem.[10] The ministry, in line with party dictates, limited its activities to supporting women within highly circumscribed notions of their place in society, consistently refraining from challenging an oppressive and exploitative status quo; the programs they were committed to were reflective of an unreconstructed gender politics.

The Growth of Postindependence Mobilization

Patriarchy slowly reconfigured itself, and the political will to meaningfully address gender inequality in Zimbabwe diminished rapidly. It was replaced instead by the desire to regulate and control women in both the private and the public sphere. It was against this backdrop of moral panic that Operation Clean-Up took place over a weekend in October 1983. Soldiers and police swept through the major city centers of Zimbabwe, arbitrarily arresting unaccompanied women and charging them with prostitution. Its purpose was to harass and control single women, many of whom had returned home after fighting for independence only to experience unemployment and marginalization. The clash between customary and common law meant that there were repeated attempts to undermine LAMA and to deny property and inheritance rights to women. These outrages were met with direct and concerted action by women from all walks of life. Operation Clean-Up was dramatic enough to provoke a change in Zimbabwean women's consciousness. As activists realized how little room state patronage allowed for the advancement of women's rights, a different kind of women's mobilizing began to take shape.

This "new" activism now took place outside of state mechanisms (although still engaging with them), bringing together women from all sectors of Zimbabwe's still-divided society around gender interests for the first time. The Women's Action Group (WAG) evolved out of a series of public meetings held during the latter part of 1983 to discuss the abuses of Operation Clean-Up. Out of these meetings, a pressure group was constituted. This core group of forty to fifty Harare-based women[11] took up the fight for women's human rights via three subcommittees: "a case study group responsible for the compiling of a dossier of individual arrests and detentions with a view to taking legal action against the government . . . a publicity group responsible for publishing articles of protest on behalf of the arrested women . . . a delegation group which sought audience with the state" (P. Watson 1998, 13). Over a period of three years, WAG evolved into a community-based organization with a national membership committed to building a movement of women fighting for the rights of women.

Growing consciousness and recognition of the continuing injustices faced by women meant that WAG was joined by a plethora of organizations over the next decade. These, at least initially, saw Zimbabwean women of all races working together to challenge the patriarchal precepts of a society that tolerated the abuse of women by men and the increasing invocation of tradition to validate discriminatory behavior. By 1995 there were more than twenty-five registered women's organizations addressing various aspects of Zimbabwean women's lives in urban and rural areas and spanning a range of practical and strategic gender interests (Molyneux 1985).

They reflected a conceptual unevenness in understandings and articulations of gender as a political struggle: some were overtly feminist in orientation, fight-

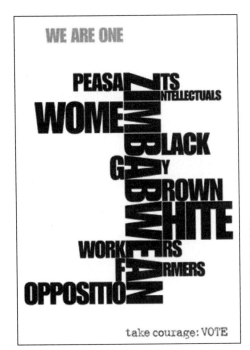

FIGURE 2.1
Poster from the Portal of Truth
series: a month of graphic
activism in the lead up to the
2002 elections. Designed by Chaz
Maviyane-Davies.

ing for structural change, while others sought to secure women's human rights within the status quo, still others working to give women the necessary skills in order to survive. Nevertheless, by the 1990s, they were all contributing toward redefining the private and public sphere and demanding full citizens' rights for women. They invoked international instruments and channeled energy into both claiming and protecting women's rights with regard to land, marriage, sexual harassment, gender-based violence, property and inheritance rights, and full political and economic participation.

During the 1990s these organizations came to constitute a loose network, each complementing the work of sister organizations in the struggle for gender justice. However, as Zimbabwe plunged into socioeconomic and political upheaval in the latter part of the 1990s, conditions for women's activism became increasingly difficult. As previously mentioned, a clear feminist discourse disappeared, and the state's now open hostility meant that women activists were targets of state-sponsored violence. Meanwhile, the deeply uncivil nature of civil society (Mama 1999) with regard to gender meant that alliances formed to further women's rights had to be carefully negotiated and remained tenuous.

Zimbabwe in the latter half of the 1990s was a potent cocktail of dashed hopes around land reform, anger over the strangling effects of economic structural adjustment programs, and a sense of betrayal regarding the corruption and flouting of the rule of law seen in the government led by the Zimbabwe African National Union–Patriotic Front (ZANU-PF). With Zimbabwe at its most politicized level in two decades, the moment was ripe for organized resistance. In 1996 this came from within the ranks of civil society through the birth of the National Constitutional Assembly (NCA).[12]

Constitutional Reform

It was patently clear by 1997 that the biggest problem underlying the Zimbabwean polity was the governance framework, that is, the constitution. At that stage the Zimbabwean constitution had been amended more than fifteen times since 1980, and was not, and has never been, a document negotiated and owned by the general population. Thus, civil society groups contended that unless the governance framework protected the fundamental rights of citizens, as well as providing the necessary checks against executive and state excesses, the social and economic problems of the nation would not be solved.

The NCA was a civil society coalition that sought to build a broad alliance of civic organizations[13] in Zimbabwe, interested in matters of governance and human rights. The objectives of the NCA were to raise the level of national consciousness concerning the need for a new constitution, review the Lancaster House Constitution,[14] and draft a new "home-grown Zimbabwean constitution" through a process that involved real national debate.

The NCA posed a direct challenge to ZANU-PF by bringing the constitutional debate onto the streets and to rural communities. Its impact on the political scene exceeded all expectations, with the NCA becoming the largest civil society coalition of the postindependence period.[15] The coalition worked through an executive committee and task forces initially headed by Morgan Tsvangirai, the trade-union leader. This move cemented the alliance between the union movement and other civil society organizations.

Fearing civic unrest, the state desperately needed to seem responsive, and sought to derail the NCA by launching its own parallel process. It established the Constitutional Commission (CC) of Zimbabwe and appointed approximately four hundred commissioners, some of whom were co-opted from the NCA, to gather people's submissions. These submissions were, once again, to be used as a basis for drafting a new constitution. The CC was problematic not only in terms of transparency and accountability but also in that it showed no particular commitment to gender equity.[16]

Coalition Building as a Strategy

With two parallel processes under way, neither of which made "real" room for women to explore their own concerns and consolidate their demands, women's organizations came together to carve out their own space. In so doing, they were informed by a decade of experience of coalition advocacy during which various networks formed nationally and regionally.

I could cite the Working Group on Gender Politics, a network established in 1996 to support women parliamentarians and a women's position in parliament, and the Women and Land Lobby Group, established in 1995 as a network to further women's land rights, as national examples. Women and Law in Southern Africa (WLSA), established in 1993 as a research network, which sought to "contribute to the sustained well being of women within families and societies, specifically within the Southern Africa . . . achieved through (a) collaborative strategic and action research in the socio-legal field and (b) lobbying for legal reforms and policy changes on laws and practices that disadvantage women," and Women in Law and Development in Africa (WILDAF), established in 1990 as "a pan-African network of organizations and individuals who work in the area of law and development to promote and strengthen strategies which link law and development to increase women's capacity to claim and enjoy all their human rights," are regional examples of networks and coalition building.[17]

But despite the forming of various national and regional coalitions and lobbying and advocacy initiatives, the activity of the period did not translate into a meaningful transformation of gender relations in Zimbabwe. In fact, substantive and sustainable progress was somewhat illusory and circumscribed. It was the *Magaya*[18] ruling of the Supreme Court of Zimbabwe that proved this. The case illustrated how gains can be abrogated; it brought to center stage the relationship and tensions between customary and general law, culture, and tradition, and how those debates affect women's rights.

Hitting Up Against Customary Law

In 1999 Venia Magaya became a symbol of resistance to the negative interpretations of customary law in Zimbabwe when the Supreme Court ruled that LAMA does not, in fact, provide for women to be treated as adults under customary law. Through its ruling in the inheritance case *Magaya v. Magaya*, the court overruled prior cases confirming women's right to inherit under customary law[19] and indicated that cases allowing women to pursue legal proceedings in their own right had in fact been wrongly decided. Thus, the court underscored the injustices suffered by women under customary law, stating that the inequities were justified by the patriarchal nature of the society and the necessity of maintaining a patrilineal tradition.

The case was instrumental in bolstering the argument that most of the discrimination Zimbabwean women faced was rooted in customary law and a static culture in collusion with patriarchy. It was therefore not surprising that women activists turned to the constitutional review process as the ultimate forum for enshrining gender equality and entrenching Zimbabwean women's rights.

The Birth of the Women's Coalition

Thus, the Women's Coalition on the Constitution was born. The coalition was a network of about sixty-six women activists, researchers, academics, and representatives from thirty women's and other human rights organizations.[20] Launching itself in June 1999, the coalition aimed to "unite women around the constitution, provide information to women on the constitution reform process and gender issues therein which would constitute a critical mass for lobby and advocacy to engender the constitutional making process and ensure the adoption of a constitution which protects women's political, social, economic and cultural rights." The understanding was that "the coalition will be inclusive, consisting of women of all possible races, linguistic and ethnic groups, classes, religions, occupations (including students), political parties, geographical locations, marital status and disabilities."[21] In setting out to realize its aim, the coalition was organized through a management structure comprising a chairperson, core group and secretariat, subcommittees, and general membership.

The goals of the coalition were fulfilled through intense and rigorous programming that included a series of national and provincial consultative workshops and conferences to formulate a women's agenda. These consultations were held in both rural and urban areas. The coalition embarked on an aggressive media campaign using radio and television and the production of posters, T-shirts, and flyers in the three national languages, as well as scarves and pins, which all collectively sought to educate and share information about the draft constitution referendum.

The coalition faced a mammoth task. From the outset, members pooled skills and resources and complemented each other in order to sustain a process that did not necessarily fall within their particular organizational ambits. However, the participants were united in their understanding of the coalition as a space in which a women's agenda could be developed and pursued, and this fueled the dynamism and vibrancy that drove the coalition and its activities.

The Women's Charter

The WC, through its institutional membership and networks, had embarked on a broad-based civic education campaign and a mass mobilization of women. This created opportunity and space for ordinary Zimbabwean women from all walks of life to engage in the debate on constitutional reform and its implications for women. For most women, this was the first time they saw and understood the constitution and how it affected them. This political education and mobilization process led to the historic Women's Charter (2001). McFadden refers to the Women's Charter as "women articulating a consciousness about themselves as autonomous individuals who claimed their rights from a position of understanding that naming themselves differently would mean a qualitative different political and social agenda for the [women's] movement as a whole" (2002, 2). The resolutions in the women's charter were used by women throughout the country as a framework to make inputs into both CC and NCA processes.

The Women's Charter would also form the basis of future advocacy efforts, an optimistic attitude clearly expressed by one coalition member: "Perhaps we were naïve to think we could continue to experience this utopia where we weren't targeted. We were happy, we organized, we knew that women and a women centered agenda could be a powerful rallying point."[22]

While the state monitored and policed civil society groups like the NCA (to the extent that the state-controlled media were instructed not to carry any NCA material), it did not seem to notice the WC. The strong women's outreach program, strategic civil society alliances, and a vocal group of women within state processes meant that the WC had a constituency and multiple bases from which to push for change. It thus constituted a powerful force that could direct action.

The Challenges Presented by Partisan Politics

But there was a silent crisis occurring within the WC and the wider women's movement. Several questions arose within the WC at the time when the CC was formed, including: Shouldn't the NCA fold up, now that the CC had been formed? Wasn't the CC a better platform for advancing women's rights and interests, since it was government engineered, and therefore more likely to be taken seriously? Didn't all women want a new constitution that guaranteed their rights, regardless of how this was arrived at and by whom? How much of a voice were civil society and the women's movement going to have in the CC? Was joining the CC co-optation or critical co-operation? A metaphor used by some at the time was that Zimbabwe was like a bus, badly in need of help in order to put it back on the road. Should those who wanted to do this be inside the bus (like the CC)? Or should they be outside the bus (like the NCA)? These questions reflected varying degrees of belief in the state and its role in furthering women's interests and rights. In 1999 these questions became much harder to answer with the birth of the Movement for Democratic Change (MDC).

In September 1999 Morgan Tsvangirai announced the establishment of the "political formation" that would be led by labor movements, with support from allied progressive social forces, some of which constituted the NCA. The MDC was seen as "the biggest ever opposition party in Zimbabwe with the necessary national support" ("MDC Launch" 1999). NCA chair-elect Tsvangirai stepped down to concentrate on the formation of the new party, and NCA deputy chairperson Thoko Matshe, a self-proclaimed feminist and then director of the ZWRCN, was unanimously chosen to lead the NCA. This was partly because of her strong personality and partly because the NCA sought to project itself as an alternative democratic space.

Matshe's election signaled an important new stage: having a women's movement leader chairing a civic alliance propelled the women's movement into a prominent role within the broader civic society mobilization. As one coalition member noted, "To a large extent during the latter 1990s, the whole civic process was in the hands of the women's movement, through the Coalition and our presence in the NCA. The media would call us the group of thirteen because we were the thirteen biggest women's organizations leading things." This meant that women were involved in both democratic and women's struggles, and this "double militancy" (Hellman 1992) meant that "it felt schizophrenic, we were all juggling so many hats, but we were clear that when it came to the Coalition it was about women, women, women first."[23]

The WC, already smarting from unstated internal divisions, was thrown into more confusion by these developments. A new set of questions emerged: Would continuing to support the NCA be tantamount to being antigovernment? What were the implications, personally and collectively, of seeming to be pro-opposition? What was the best way to frame the women's rights questions, and what was the best platform to promote these?

When members of the WC, of their own volition, joined the CC, the resulting crisis brought into question the underlying principles on which the

Women's Coalition was founded. These principles had not been put on the table explicitly, debated and agreed to by members of the coalition. One can surmise that the unspoken assumption until then was that a general agreement on the rights of women and what women wanted in a new constitution was enough. But this assumption was severely tested in the months that followed.

The Women's Coalition, now an umbrella body for women's movement organizations, claimed for a while that they were not going to align with the government constitutional commission process. Neither were they going to align with the civic National Constitutional Assembly process. The women's coalition was determined to focus on a women's articulated and centered agenda, even though it acknowledged that individual Women's Coalition members had the right to be a part of the two parallel processes. But tensions began to surface against the backdrop of a nationwide intensification of political, social, and economic crisis in the country that translated into a polarized politics.[24] The point is that in this period the entire country was locked in this polarity, and the women's movement was not exempt from these politics. It is then not surprising that women's groups fractured along the lines of political identity and allegiance.

While the Women's Coalition had resolved early on that as an entity it would not form an alliance with either the NCA process or the CC process, individuals and organizations within the coalition were free to do so. It was further agreed that the coalition would lobby both the NCA and the CC on gender issues. But while women identified the struggle for the entrenchment of women's rights as a common goal, there were multiple views on what strategies to follow to achieve this. Again, this rhetoric could only go so far in masking the deepening political polarization within the country and its resulting tension within the WC.

Women who pursued the strategy of engagement with the state were often frustrated by the cumbersome state-sponsored process. When a female commissioner was assaulted by a fellow (male) commissioner, it confirmed the patriarchal power differential in a very real way: "It became obvious working for the CC that we underestimated the degree of patriarchy in our society. Every single item concerning women in the CC was contested and had to be struggled for; it was not easy."[25]

Women aligned with the more democratic NCA were somewhat more successful. They seemingly had more space to challenge and were vocal about gender imbalances within the NCA and campaigned vigorously and successfully for increased female representation on task forces. As a result, at the NCA general assembly held in June 1999, eight women were elected onto the eighteen-member governing structure.

The February 2000 Referendum

By December 1999 the CC had completed its consultations and handed over to the president of Zimbabwe a draft constitution. The next step in the process was putting the draft to a national referendum that was held on February 12–13, 2000. The Women's Charter was used as a yardstick to gauge the extent to which women's demands had been incorporated into the draft constitution.

The findings were disappointing and showed only minor improvements on women's rights. This was obviously deemed unacceptable by the Women's Coalition, which saw the draft constitution as a compromise, as "half a loaf,"[26] and decided that what the CC's draft constitution had to offer was insufficient for what was at that time 52 percent of Zimbabwe's population.

The draft constitution also received criticism from the NCA, opposition parties, academics, and, more surprisingly, from some of the CC commissioners, who accused the chairperson of the commission of "doctoring" the submissions made by the people and instead conforming to the wishes of Mugabe and his henchmen. The very public failure of the draft constitution to reflect the content of people's submissions to the commission led to particularly dramatic rejections of the draft from the opposition.

But more damagingly, it was also criticized from within, a government-appointed body criticizing government manipulation and the orchestration of the process. Some commissioners were particularly critical of the undemocratic way in which the draft had been rushed through their final session.[27] Twenty-four commissioners, led by the vocal woman journalist Lupi Mushayakarara, signed a petition against the draft and subsequently led an unsuccessful legal battle to have the draft reconsidered and the referendum postponed. In the weeks that followed, several commissioners switched sides or even resigned, and urged a no vote against the draft,[28] stating it did not reflect the views of the people, that the commissioners had had no time to study or debate the draft, and that "there was no democracy in the manner in which the chairman . . . processed both the Draft Constitution and the Final Report of the commission."[29]

The understandings and effects of the strategic decisions made by coalition members had a lasting impact. Some member organizations felt the need to remain "neutral" and not align in terms of party politics; others knew that the push for a transformative agenda demanded that women vote no in the referendum. Members spoke of a "backlash" of infiltration and destabilization within the Women's Coalition. But this was just evidence of the already existing tensions and failure to have the necessary conversations about differing political positions. After much political jockeying, the coalition eventually made a call for a no vote in the referendum on the constitution and went on to mobilize its constituency. Twenty-six percent of eligible voters voted, and the majority of them rejected the draft constitution. The victory of the "Vote No" campaign did not mean contentment with the dysfunctional Lancaster House Constitution but was a political victory and infused hope into Zimbabwe's democratic system.

The result shocked and galvanized the state: for the first time in twenty years the referendum showed the ruling party faced an opposition and discontent. The state quickly sidelined the constitutional process and harnessed rising discontent over its own failure to implement a timely and meaningful land-redistribution program. It did this by mobilizing scores of so-called war veterans to invade white-owned commercial farms.

Hundreds of farms were occupied, and land was ostensibly distributed to needy landless people. In the process, some farmers and farmworkers were killed, and thousands of people were physically abused. Besides the farm invasions, war was also waged in rural and urban areas to rid them of opposition leaders and supporters. This was all done under the guise of land reform, when in fact it resulted in violations of black people's rights and had very little to do with the land question. Women bore the brunt of these human rights violations. Hundreds of cases of rape, gang rapes, forced concubinage, murder, torture, and the physical abuse of women were recorded in the 2000–2001 period (Crisis in Zimbabwe Coalition 2003).

The Politics of the Lowest Common Denominator

This political destabilization, which set the tone for things to come, left the women's movement in disarray. The most affected were the coalitions and networks based on what I call the lowest common denominator: an idea of shared female identity, which had not yet been exposed as inadequate during the earlier era of the depoliticized discourses of national development. It was at this time and on this basis that some coalition members could say "There are cracks in the movement" and "We have 'fragmented' and 'fallen apart.'"

As I have already mentioned, the women's movement up until this moment had operated with a particular understanding of and way of relating to the state. For the most part, the movement viewed the state as an arbiter of development and a bestower of rights. This is evidenced through the movement's fixation on asking, challenging, and appealing to the state to enshrine rights. Advocacy up until this point had demanded an expansion in the roles of the state through the provision of services and the establishment of frameworks that mitigate gendered impacts and ensure gender equality. In this way the state has always been seen as integral to the securing of women's rights.

Of course, this is in contradiction to a movement that at the same time increasingly saw itself in opposition to a state that was a patriarchal, hostile, conservative, totalitarian structure. Be that as it may, the women's movement was in a strong position to determine and move forward and make a women's agenda a national agenda. This cannot be discounted, no matter its successes or failures.

But the Women's Coalition lacked a clear set of nonnegotiable guiding principles, as did the women's movement as a whole in Zimbabwe. This lack of unity contributed in large measure to the feelings of "paralysis," "fragmentation," and "dissolution" in the women's movement. Three major lessons stand out.

The political crisis in Zimbabwe demonstrated the need for the women's movement, for its coalitions and networks, to have strong foundations, shared values and principles, and a grounding body of ideas reflecting its needs, aspirations, and vision. This is necessary whether it is named as feminist or not. By their very nature, coalitions and networks are based on a commonly identified issue and set of objectives. Bobo, Kendall, and Max define a coalition as "an organization of organizations working together for a goal" (2001, 12).

Coalitions are not built because it is good, moral, or nice to get everyone working together. The only reason to spend the time and energy building a coalition is to amass the power necessary to do something that cannot be done through one organization (ibid., 70). Similarly, VeneKlasen and Miller also caution that the very reasons for forming coalitions or alliances are often the reasons why they are difficult to manage: "[Coalitions] sometimes suffer from unrealistic expectations, such as the notion that people who share a common cause will agree on everything" (2002, 311).

While the members of the WC were united in demanding that women's rights be enshrined in a new constitution, the WC was less united on how this was to be arrived at:[30] Was confronting the state a desirable tactic? What kind of alliance would the women's movement have, if any, with the opposition political parties in this process? Was a good constitutional document all the women wanted, or was it critical that this should emerge from an inclusive process? What exactly would constitute good-enough participation, by and for women? How would the question of race and racism be tackled both within the ranks of the WC and in the wider political discourse?

The WC had been formed in what appeared to be an uncontested political terrain, a time of fair weather. Come hail and thunderstorms, though, and questions began to emerge about how far the unity of the coalition would go. For example, until 2003, the WC and the women's movement more broadly had not been able to mobilize their memberships around the issue of political violence against women. On the surface, it would appear that violence is an issue against which all women are united. In reality, this is an issue that tears the movement apart because of its partisan nature.

2000 Parliamentary Elections

Against the backdrop of this spiraling violence and the deepening of the socioeconomic and political crisis, the government rapidly sidelined the constitutional debate in preparation for the impending parliamentary elections, which had been delayed until June 2000. Meanwhile, still riding high on the referendum victory, the WC still recognized the potential strength of bringing women together across political divides and sought to consolidate this by supporting and voting women candidates into parliament. Of course, we know that it is not enough to have women in parliament as a form of window dressing, as numbers do not necessarily translate into gender equality. And just as being in a woman's body does not mean you carry a gender politics or have an interest in social transformation, neither does it mean that parliament will be accommodating and receptive to women's interests. The coalition nonetheless began to facilitate a women's political agenda by endorsing and supporting the fifty-five women candidates who were standing for parliamentary elections. As one woman parliamentary candidate noted: "The powers that be started to see women could be a force to be reckoned with politically. Unlike male politicians, women began talking across political parties."

This was the first time in the history of Zimbabwe that a women's agenda had been articulated in this way and that the possibilities of cross-party alliances around a women's agenda were recognized. The coalition was in some senses swept away by the tide of events with an unreconstructed politics around difference, diversity, and power within its own ranks. At a meeting in May 2000, women from different political parties sat together to brainstorm about how to beat their male counterparts at their own game. As one participant described the meeting: "Women buried their political differences—every political party has been guilty of suppressing the rise of women within the ranks, but women are not out of this highly contested political race. We have another battle of our own: challenging men's dominance in politics."

The Costs of Mobilizing for Women

But the coalition was only as strong as its constituent parts, and these constituent parts were individuals and organizations. These organizations had commitments to their structures, systems, and areas of operation, and these structures were already buckling under the pressures of intense political organizing around the constitution. They also had responsibilities to donors, and this set of circumstances did not readily allow the flexibility to engage with the rapidly changing national political landscape.

Internally, there still remained a general anxiety concerning the meaning of "politicized action." This nervousness manifested itself through the stance taken by numerous boards of established organizations, which were in structural positions of power and suddenly found themselves vulnerable to charges of political activism and even subversion. Board members began calling for a more circumscribed approach to coalition activities, curtailing affiliation with and contributions to the coalition for a variety of reasons, including ZANU-PF allegiance, commitments to donors, or security risks to staff.

State-sponsored violence against all political opponents, real and imagined, presented a very real threat at this time as well. Members of ZANU-PF and the MDC entered into retaliatory battles, and the police generally ignored the resulting property destruction, assaults, torture, and deaths.[31] Women did not go unscathed; many were assaulted and beaten for their political affiliations ("Women Brave Violence" 2000). Both MDC and ZANU-PF women supporters were targeted. Women who identified with the Women's Coalition by wearing coalition head scarves were also vulnerable, as were women contesting seats in the upcoming elections. Nyasha Chikwinya, a ZANU-PF candidate, was beaten so severely that she had to wear a neck brace. Sekai Holland, an MDC candidate, also survived an assault. Women also became victims of violence within their own political parties. One parliamentary candidate stated, "Yes, there was violence, even within political parties women were exposed to violence. It was a fight for survival, so there was violence from without, the violence that seized the nation, but also violence from within."

The WC encouraged women to stand for election, campaign, and vote, but when women became vulnerable as a result, it could offer very little by way of support or protection. Many key organizations lost staff members during this period. The reasons for this included the disjunctures between the perspectives of board members and staff, as well as the deepening national and socioeconomic strife, which compelled many women to prioritize their personal and financial security. In the words of one woman activist, "Women activists have been exposed, we've had threats, some implied, some direct. We are doing some serious thinking, counting the costs. I may be prepared to sacrifice myself, but what about those I am responsible to?" This period of intense organizing also left many women activists exhausted and in need of space and time to regroup. This "burnout" led to resignations, immigration, and withdrawal. A stalwart feminist organizer observed in 2001, "As you can see, all those strong organizations are without staff—a top layer of leadership has gone."

Revisiting the Debate at the Book Café

This is the context into which we can place the Book Café debate. There was a collective pause after the 2000 elections and the intense activity and expectations that preceded it. Some women at the Book Café described a need to "lie low" or to "go underground" in the face of what was an even more violent presidential election in 2001. If the women's movement had found itself in a cul-de-sac, the Book Café meeting was perhaps the first step toward a period of necessary reflection on the women's movement in Zimbabwe, its underlying principles and vision, its form, and its strategies.

This scrutiny of women's organizing in Zimbabwe, and the repercussions of women's engagement with the constitutional reform process, raises some pertinent questions. What insights can we gain from the particular features of the Zimbabwe women's movement in the latter 1990s?

Lessons Moving Forward

Over the past two decades, there has been a significant transformation of women's organizing in Zimbabwe, a transformation that runs parallel to the realization of the power of political consciousness within the movement. The question is, under what conditions does a conservative state, together with a hostile political, social, and economic environment, give rise to this particular type of coalition politics?

To answer this question fully would require comparative research on other authoritarian or militarized environments. In the Zimbabwean context, one can argue that due to state antagonism and the rapidly shrinking space for organizing by civil society, there were opportunities for quiet, yet strategic, coalition building. It enabled women for a considerable period of time to operate "below the radar," to continue working within bounded organizational entities while simultaneously organizing more effectively around common women's human rights interests. For much of the 1990s, this mode of organizing enabled the women's movement to continue its activities precisely because it was not perceived as a threat or a consolidated site of power.

When women did come under attack, it was not solely because they were women advocating a certain agenda but because they were perceived primarily as political players with the ability to influence and direct the course of action while maintaining a clearly articulated "women's agenda." More significantly, women began to see themselves as a political force. This signified a radical change, because women had not presented a political challenge to the state in this way before.

This leads me to reflect on women vis-à-vis the state. The Zimbabwean case demonstrates the emergence of an evolving political strategy. The conceptualization of the state as a multiplicity of sites demands a variety of strategies and actions to take an agenda forward. These strategies and actions cannot be prescribed but must be developed out of, among other things, a close reading of the context and its power differentials.

The extent to which the Zimbabwean women's movement has understood and fully exploited this conceptualization of the state is debatable. The wisdom of fixating solely on rights and legal reform is called into question. As one feminist activist pointed out, "It seems a pity that fifteen to twenty years after the existence of some of these organizations, we still peddle the falsity that the answer lies in the law. You can demand from the state laws from A to Z but it will not work—we've seen it. Our battle is in fact not with the law per se; our struggle is with patriarchy."

Just as the women's movement in Zimbabwe has made demands on the state, it has also sought alliances from broader civil society. In the period leading up to the 2000 parliamentary elections, civil society became an important force in the push for a democratic dispensation. Civil society has generated the National Constitutional Assembly, and the NCA was the space out of which the opposition party, the Movement for Democratic Change, emerged.

Civil society in Zimbabwe is an umbrella term that includes the trade union movement, student activists, churches, academics, political commentators, the media, development activists, and anticapitalist, socialist, human rights, and women's movements. By its very nature, it is heterogeneous and includes competing agendas. Within an authoritarian national context, the harsh reality is that civil society structures are fragile and have limited reach and capacity.

One might think that civil society would be a more receptive recipient and conduit of a gender agenda than the state. But it is something of a political tragedy that broader civil society in Zimbabwe, increasingly assumed to be the voice of democracy and progressive principles, did not at any time sponta-

FIGURE 2.2 Women protesters gather outside Zimbabwe House to voice their opposition to Zimbabwean president Robert Mugabe in September 2007, London.

neously protest blatant violations of women's rights. It was only around the issue of constitutional reform that the brief alliance between women and broader civil society was cemented.

This could be explained bluntly as being borne of instrumentalism: the NCA needed women to legitimate their agenda, draw in their constituency, and secure donor funding. Women then found themselves having to wage a struggle within the NCA for gender concerns to be addressed in a meaningful way. It could be argued that women would have been unable to organize on such a massive scale without this kind of political opening. However, freedom will arrive only when the struggle for change is total and not based on a nationalist understanding of a two-tier model of liberation that puts women's (or other so-called sectoral groupings') struggles to overthrow patriarchy on hold for the "bigger" issue of national liberation, or in this case the overthrowing of Mugabe and the ZANU-PF regime. True emancipation, like a true movement for democratic change, has to embody and live a different political culture and vision from the outset. It is with this put into practice that the struggle must be waged.

The 2000 elections was a different political moment in the history of Zimbabwe, and the overarching political context had so dramatically shifted that the women's movement needed to look again at how they commonly defined issues, as well as at the strategies they should adopt in the changed circumstances. These issues and strategies include defining internal relationships and structures and figuring out how to manage relations with external forces, including the state and broader civil society.

The formulation of strategy and action based on a close reading of context is vital given the complexity of the period. For example, the movement has been united in its calls for gender-equitable land redistribution in Zimbabwe, but the wider political context necessitated a recasting of those demands and the values that underlay them. Could it be tenable, for example, for the Women's Coalition to applaud the violent land seizures based on a nationalist understanding of the need for indigenization and the long-overdue land reform that some members of the WC upheld? If women were given some of that land, knowing that other women had been killed or raped in the process, what position would the WC take?

The women's movement has the potential to be one of the most potent forces for claiming women's rights but also social transformation more broadly. If they are based on commonly agreed-upon values and principles, coalitions are more able to manage their own diversity in changing political circumstances. But if they merely work on common issues and do not recognize the diversity of values and principles that exists within them, coalitions will immobilize themselves. Affirming difference, particularly fundamental difference, is a critical part of effective strategizing. It allows groups to negotiate and renegotiate the terms of coalition, and how far they will go with one another. In cases where huge differences lie underneath a surface of unity, it may be necessary to let go of the coalition. The case of the WC in Zimbabwe illustrates the political nature of coalitions. Rather than seeing coalitions as mere functional organizational formations, they should be seen as political institutions with political issues to deal with, both internally and externally. How well a coalition navigates the political terrain will determine whether it survives.

Molyneux (1985b) argues that whatever forms female mobilization has taken, it has always expressed demands for full citizenship and rights, while highlighting women's everyday strength and ability to pursue their interests in the public sphere. She goes on to suggest that this formulation of interests, whether they are practical or strategic, is intrinsically linked to identity formation. The concept of women's interests as informing political identity leads me to consider how women become motivated to act and make certain demands at particular points in time. As I have illustrated, it is erroneous to assume that the terrain of the Zimbabwean women's movement is all-encompassing or that women's interests are uniform.

While a clearly articulated feminist discourse remains largely suppressed, the strategies employed by the movement have continued to suggest a femi-

FIGURE 2.3 An activist billboard dominates the main road into Zimbabwe as people drive and walk past it in Musina, South Africa, April 2008.

nist consciousness. The Zimbabwean Women's Charter best exemplifies this consciousness. Women's persistent challenge to patriarchy through demands for entitlement, the formulation of a women's agenda, and the need to advance this through women's political representation evidence a transformational agenda informed by a feminist vision.

The Zimbabwean women's movement, operating in an increasingly hostile political environment and traversing similar terrain as other continental women's movements, has not only worked to change the relationship between women and civil society but also challenged women's relations with the state. As one coalition member noted, "The African women's movement is not only the most exciting movement to emerge from the twentieth century as a century of nationalism and nationalist resistance, but it is also really at the cutting edge of a new politics. The women's movement is very central to crafting a new politics, a postcolonial politics, and this is very central to the vibrancy of the women's movement, because we are overturning everything."

This has major implications for theory; indeed, this article demonstrates the ways in which reflection on activism can pose useful questions for the development of new theories and radical activism for change. Activist scholarship is about critique, not just advocacy. It is part of a project of producing new knowledge, of integrating more abstract and universal sorts of knowledge with more concrete and particular sorts of knowledge, and of keeping action and its possibilities at the center of attention. One reason for activist scholarship is obvious but worth restating: the world is in considerable need of improvement, and improvement comes in large part by means of social movements, struggles, and campaigns to change public agendas, not merely by the provision of technical expertise to those already in power. Activist scholarship can help inform thinking and strategies, thereby supporting movements in their agenda of transforming the world.

Postscript

Harare, Zimbabwe. Shereen Essof. Diary entry, October 17, 2008

There is a war in Zimbabwe! It has a name. It has a face! It is being fought across the bodies of women, men and children who live like prisoners in a country that is no longer theirs. Even as they hold Zimbabwean passports. Even as they were born and bred in Zimbabwe. They have nowhere to go. Nothing to eat. No means to speak their suffering because when they do, they are beaten up, abducted, tortured and thrown in deathly prison cells. Each day leaders of the world allow it, it takes away a limb, a child's future, a woman's life as she has no health care. Each day the casualties multiply. What we are doing is not enough. As feminist activists we witness this wave of military terror and suppression of the people of Zimbabwe. This is an intensification of the ZANU-PF threatened campaign of "Ngatipedzenavo," "let's finish them off." Nothing short of sustained mobilization and mass action led by Zimbabweans and supported by all who care about justice across the world will shift things.

Against such a backdrop what organizing is possible? The women's movement is weak but alive, and many organizations continue to just tread water in order to survive. Often telephones do not work and there is no electricity and water. But despite this, many organizations provide safety to women from rural areas who are escaping the politically motivated violence. Those women activists working in organizations and structures outside of the country use their positioning in big and small ways to contribute to the struggle for change. It is difficult to organize in a country where women are engaged in the daily struggle for survival and where there is no respect for the rule of law. Difficult but not impossible. Resistance comes in many forms, from the daily resistances of women who fight to live despite great deprivation, to women's mobilizations and articulations of the need for change despite the possibility of detention, arrest and torture.

• • •

Feminist Political Education Project.
Calls for Immediate Conclusion of
the Cabinet Formation Talks.
October 17, 2008.

The Feminist Political Education Project (FePEP), an autonomous grouping of feminists, operating from within and outside of Zimbabwe, creating spaces for Zimbabwean women to come together in solidarity, to share information and strategies to inform political processes, undertook an intensive lobby to place the feminist agenda in the political agenda. In the wake of the March 2008 stolen election and the negotiations facilitated by the Southern African Development Community, which resulted in a protracted deadlock among the political parties, FePEP held a women's conference on the October 16, 2008. The conference was primarily aimed at providing women from Zimbabwe with an opportunity to familiarize themselves with the current political developments as well as provide an opportunity for Zimbabwean women to have direct interaction and dialogue with chief negotiators from the political parties. Women at the conference were able to receive firsthand information from the chief negotiators and the facilitator on the ongoing political process in the country. The women present agreed to issue a communiqué to the heads of political parties and the Thabo Mbeki–led facilitation team, expressing their grave concerns on the undue delay in finalizing the issue of cabinet formation. The communiqué also highlighted some of the major issues facing Zimbabwean women today.

As women of Zimbabwe we are alarmed by the continuous and undue stalling in the cabinet formation talks. We note with concern that this has consequently delayed the implementation of the Global Political Agreement (GPA) which came into force on the 15th of September 2008 providing for immediate implementation upon signature.

We are alarmed that the delay in forming a Cabinet has prolonged the suffering of Zimbabweans, in particular women. As women, we are calling upon the Principals [Heads of Political Parties] to immediately form a Cabinet so that the New Government can urgently begin to address the pressing issues we face on a daily basis that is access to food, clean water, electricity, health facilities and sanitation among others.

There must be the immediate formation of Cabinet and setting up of the New Government that takes seriously the commitments made in the GPA to gender parity.

We re-iterate our continuous call on the leaders of the political parties to stop political posturing and advancing selfish individual interests. This is not about specific party agendas nor is it about individual glory; rather, this is about the country and the people of Zimbabwe. As the GPA says, we must put Zimbabwe first.

We believe that the GPA provides an adequate framework to begin to meaningfully deliver results to address the needs of the people of Zimbabwe. Therefore, the political parties must recognize the need to work together. Thus a "re-orientation of attitudes" is imperative if sustainable progress is to be attained. We further demand the following urgent needs to be met immediately:

- availability of affordable and accessible food
- provision of accessible clean water and electricity
- provision of affordable and accessible health services including ARVs [antiretrovirals]
- restoration of a functional education system
- easy access to our cash in the banks

The people of Zimbabwe have suffered enough. The suffering must stop now! We demand an environment where freedom of expression as a basic human right is possible. This should include an immediate end to all politically motivated violence, harassment, imprisonment and torture.

"Enough, a new Zimbabwe now!"

I have been involved in documenting and researching the women's movement in Zimbabwe for the past fourteen years. Much of the interview material used in this chapter is drawn from research work undertaken in the period 2000–2004, during which I conducted in-depth one-on-one interviews with key women in the women's movement and within state-led and civil society processes. For the purpose of individual safety and security I have not included the names of the people I have interviewed.

Notes

1. The title of this chapter comes from the words of a woman from Mashonaland East, uttered by way of reflection on her life, which had been ripped apart by politically motivated violence during the 2000 parliamentary elections. "Ramagwana Rakajeka in Shona" literally translates as, "The future will be better next time."

2. It is important to note that not all donors are alike and that donor funding of nongovernmental organizations (NGOs) in Zimbabwe does not necessarily imply a totalitarian hold over the activities therein. External interventions through funding are not always imperial, and not always counterproductive. Sometimes insubordination by both donors and recipients is behind much of the creativity in women's NGOs and Zimbabwean civil society more generally.

3. Head of the education task force of the Women's Coalition on the constitution.

4. Minimum wage, 1980; equal pay regulations, 1980; Labor Relations Act, 1984; public service pensions (amendment) regulations, 1985.

5. Customary Law and Primary Courts Act, 1981.

6. Matrimonial Causes Act no. 33, 1985.

7. Deceased Person's Family Maintenance (amendment) Act, 1987.

8. The official philosophy of Marxist-Leninism was thought to be more progressive.

9. Established in 1938 and 1978, respectively.

10. Little attention was paid to the growing body of evidence that "development" has often upheld male interests to the detriment of women's.

11. Including among others Devi Pakkiri, Peggy Watson, Mary Tandon, Rudo Gaidzanwa, Zine Chicopee, Petronella Maramba, Elizabeth Rider, Ann Forder, Eunice Kapuwa, Kate Truscott, and Sheila Chikoore.

12. Formed by five young activists, two of whom were feminists.

13. The organizations came to include trade unions, students' movements, the mainstream churches, human rights organizations, media houses, and women's groups.

14. The Lancaster House Conference of 1979 marked the end of Zimbabwe's war of liberation. The conference brought together the Rhodesian government and the black liberation movements, and adopted the Lancaster House Agreement and the Lancaster House Constitution that paved the way for the elections held in 1980.

15. By September 2000 the NCA had more than 30,000 registered individual members and 200 institutional members countrywide.

16. Women constituted 13 percent of those on the commission, and despite the outcry concerning the low level of representation, no redress was forthcoming.

17. See http://www.wlsa.org.zw and http://www.wildaf.org.zw, respectively.

18. *Magaya v. Magaya*, SC 210/98.

19. The Administration of Estates Act, 1997.

20. Member organizations included AWC, Dorothy Duncan Centre for the Blind, Family Support Trust, FAMWZ, Harare Legal Projects Centre, Jekesa Pfungwa, Musasa Project, Mwengo, NCA, SAFAIDS, SAPES Trust, UZ-Law Faculty, WILDAF, WASN, WLSA, Women in Politics and Decision Making, WLLG, Women, Leadership and Governance Institute, WAG, Working Group on Gender Politics, Young Women's Christian Association, ZAUW Residents Association, Zimbabwe Association of University Women, ZCC, ZWLA, ZWW, ZWB, and ZWRCN.

21. Minutes of the meeting of the Women's Coalition for the Constitution, June 7, 1999.

22. WC member.

23. Feminist activist, NCA member, and Women's Coalition member.

24. At this time either you were for the MDC's slogan for change, "Chinja Maitiro, Maitiro Chinja / Guqula Izenzo, Izenzo Guqula" (Now is the time, fight for change, support the movement), or you were "reclaiming the land," as ZANU-PF advocated.

25. Women's commissioner.

26. And there were substantial debates within the coalition as to whether half a loaf was better than no loaf at all!

27. *Financial Gazette*, December 2, 1999.

28. *Chronicle*, January 27, 2000.

29. *Chronicle*, February 8, 2000.

30. And dare I say what actually constituted women's rights. So, for example, in a conservative and fairly religious context like Zimbabwe, the rights of lesbian women were never discussed openly, and we know what the state's response to LGBTI rights was.

31. See Statement of the National Democratic Institute Pre-Election Delegation to Zimbabwe, issued in Harare, May 22, 2000; Who is Responsible? A Preliminary Analysis of Pre-election Violence, Zimbabwe Human Rights Forum report, June 2000; and Zimbabwe: Terror Tactics in the Run-up to Parliamentary Elections, Amnesty International report, July 2000.

3

The Women's Movement in Pakistan: Challenges and Achievements

FARIDA SHAHEED

The lively debate in feminist circles involving naming, identifying, locating, and evaluating the changing character of women's activism that this volume sets out to examine is largely muted in Pakistan, due partially to the paucity of academic institutions and journals that would provide venues for such debates. In the absence of such forums, the debate, such as it is, runs largely in a subterranean manner confined to drawing rooms and the "interior" spaces of fairly limited circles of activists and civil society organizations, especially those focusing on women rights and human rights in general. Considered reflection and rigorous debate are rare luxuries for civil society actors with a rights agenda in Pakistan, where, since 1977, unfolding events have required constant vigilance and prompt responses. With reflection and debate carried out on the run, between urgent campaigns, protests, and picket lines, my examination of women's movements and their linkages with other social movements draws on my own personal engagements with the women's movement and mostly undocumented debates within the women's movement and its affiliated groups.

In this chapter I provide a brief review of some of the conceptual issues surrounding concepts of feminism and suggest the need to differentiate women's rights movements from women's movements from the perspective of Pakistan, where the term *feminism* does not exist. A historical review illustrates the factors that influenced the movement's understanding, strategies, and outcomes, taking the example of activism on political rights and sexual violence. A third

PAKISTAN

Human Development Index ranking: .551
Gender-Related Development Index value: .525
Gender Empowerment Measure value: .3777

General

Type of government: Parliamentary Democracy
Major ethnic groups: Punjabi; Sindhi; Pashtun; Baloch; Muhajir; Saraiki; Hazara
Languages: Urdu (national and official); Sindhi; Siraiki; Pashtu; English and others
Religions: Muslim (97%) (Sunni 77%, Shi'a 20%); small minorities of Christian, Hindu,
    and others

Demographics

Population, total (millions), 2005: 158.1
Annual growth rate (%), 2005–2015: 1.9
Total fertility (average number of births per woman): 4.0
Contraceptive prevalence (% of married women aged 15–49): 28
Maternal mortality ratio, adjusted (per 100,000 live births), 2000: 320

Women's Status

Date of women's suffrage: 1947
Life expectancy: M 64.3; F 64.8
Combined gross enrollment ratio for primary, secondary, and tertiary education
    (female %), 2005: 34
Gross primary enrollment ratio: 75
Gross secondary enrollment ratio: 23
Gross tertiary enrollment ratio: 4
Literacy (% age 15 and older): M 64.1; F 35.4

Political Representation of Women

Seats in parliament (% held by women): 20.4
Legislators, senior officials, and managers (% female): 2
Professional and technical workers (% female): 26
Women in government at ministerial level (% total): 5.6

Economics

Estimated earned income (PPP US$): M 3,607; F 1,059
Ratio of estimated female to male earned income: .29
Economic activity rate (% female): 32.7
Women in adult labor force (% total): 27 (this figure obtained at the CEDAW Statis-
    tical Database)

section examines the relationship of the women's movement to other social movements and the issues of collaboration. The final section explores the challenges faced by the women's movement in contesting political Islamist groups from within a human rights framework.

Of Feminisms and Movements

The relationship between women's activism and other social movements raises a number of questions: Where should the lines be drawn between feminism and other "isms"? What qualifies as feminist activity, and how does this differ from women's activism in other spaces and movements? Concomitantly, what defines a movement, as distinct from a trend? At what point can moments of activism be said to have transmuted into a movement?

In contemporary usage there has been a blurring of terminology such that *feminist movement* is used interchangeably with *women's rights movement* or, simply and more broadly still, *women's movement*. Meanings have shifted over time and, depending on the ideological positioning and understanding of the user, the term *feminist* can refer to any and all actions ranging from improving "women's lives in some way" (Krook 2008) to a concept of pluralistic feminisms that, based on experiential differences, have led to distinctive "black" or "third" world feminisms (Phillips 2002). That there is lack of consensus on what constitutes "feminism" was evident in the heated debate recently provoked by my use of the term *indigenous feminisms* in a coauthored paper (Wee and Shaheed 2007).[1]

The paper posited indigenous feminisms not as a reference to linkages between indigenousness and feminism but as describing women's endeavors to assert their rights within their own sociocultural contexts. The reactions were unexpected given the considerable efforts of feminists to emphasize the diversity of differently located women, especially those from the third world, or what is called the global South. Most, if not all, of those present would have identified themselves as feminists, and many were from the global South. In the ensuing discussion, a number of those present took exception to this use of the term, questioning how actions not emerging from and grounded in feminist theory could be termed *feminist*. While there are indeed important questions concerning what feminism is, should be, and can cover, the dispute indicates an assumption that only those with a theoretical grounding in a presumably "authentic" feminist body of textual knowledge should be deemed feminist.

A first point of disagreement around the term *indigenous feminisms* related to the degree of inclusiveness: should all women actively engaged in social and political fields be included within the women's movement regardless of whether they specifically address gender relations? Should, for instance, any women organizing in public spaces be included in the women's movement by virtue of their gendered presence in the public political arena? Specifically referring to the case of the Madres de los Desaparecidos (Mothers of the Disappeared), some feminist seminar participants said no, because it is "just a movement of mothers that does not try to change the system," and is thus outside the parameters of "feminist" actions. Others felt that in a context in which women are supposed to remain confined to the domestic sphere, the defiance of prescribed female roles by such women constitutes a feminist move, regardless of any intent to change the system.

There is no doubt that through their actions and organizing, women involved in such initiatives enhance their own personal autonomy as individuals. It is also true that, by increasing women's public visibility, such initiatives may help to reconfigure public arenas and thereby enhance the space for other women as well. Nevertheless, in the absence of any articulation and actions supportive of women as a group with a modicum of common interests, the basis for including these women—active as they may be—as part of the women's movement is unclear. Women's agency may be critical to women's empowerment, but it does not automatically translate into demands for gender justice and equality, as is vividly evident in studies on Rwanda and other places of violent conflict (see, for example, Blizzard 2006; and C. Sperling 2006). The suggestion that all women, regardless of class, ethnic, religious, or other identity, automatically constitute a coherent group with similar interests is, of course, invalid and has been written about extensively. Quite separate is the question of who determines whether someone is a feminist. Would women engaged in initiatives such as the Mothers of the Disappeared consider themselves to be part of the women's movement? These conflicting views suggest a need to distinguish between the unintended impact of actions that alter women's prescribed roles and the self-perceptions from those undertaken as consciously "feminist," that is, with the specific intention of changing gender relations. For instance, women's participation in the peasant movement in Punjab, briefly discussed later, had no feminist aim when it started. Yet activism within the movement did change women's perceptions and some of the gender rules in their communities and families. Today, some five years after the height of activism, women involved in the movement have started articulating demands for greater rights as women, rather than as an undifferentiated "landless peasantry." I posit that women's engagement in movements that do not explicitly aim to change gender relations may have the unintended result of increasing autonomy for women but that a minimum criterion for inclusion in a movement for women's rights is that the women themselves must reject the current arrangements of gendered relations.

A second point of divergence concerned the conceptual and historical location of feminism. Some of those present rejected the notion of "indigenous feminisms" because this did not fit the "modernist liberal project." Contrasting views were that indigenous feminists include women who fought against the gendered oppressions of the colonialists and that there are long historical traditions of women's struggles in their country predating the advent of Western feminists, who, in any case, tend to talk down to the women at the grass-roots level. The proposition that there is a singular origin of women's rights activism is one I have contested as both ethnocentric and unhelpful. My concern is less with arriving at conceptual clarity in theoretical debates than with addressing and overcoming the immobilization of women resulting from the acceptance of such a premise. The deliberately promoted myth that women who engage in struggles for women's rights are, ipso facto, Westernized and alien to their own societies ought to be robustly contested. The fear of being cast beyond the pale, of losing what little social networks or social capital women can harness within their own communities, has a seriously detrimental impact on women's activism for their own rights, as I have argued elsewhere (Shaheed 1994, 1999). Moreover, having uncovered a rich legacy of women's assertions for rights as women and for social justice across space and time in Muslim contexts, I have no doubt that women's struggles for more gender equitable and more just societies precede the "modernist liberal project" (Shaheed and Shaheed 2005). While the language of gender equality is recent and tied to specific developments, "justice" and "injustice" are powerful concepts that resonate deeply in most cultural and historical contexts. Indeed, it was discussions about retrieving women's struggles for rights from the margins and footnotes of history and how to bring these to the center that led Vivienne Wee and myself to coin the term *indigenous feminisms*. That the history of women's activism has so thoroughly disappeared from everyday social consciousness is itself a problem meriting further examination.

Additionally, as someone engaged in human rights and feminist activism, it seems to me that viewing feminism exclusively in terms of a "modernist liberal project" falls into the trap of narrowly confining the women's movement for rights within the parameters of human rights discourse. While much of women's activism since the middle of the twentieth century has taken place within the human rights discourse that is, indeed, located within the modern liberal project of nation-states, we do women a great injustice if we simply disregard or actually discard women's activism for rights for women that preceded nation-states as either irrelevant or "something else." If *feminism* is defined as "a discourse centrally concerned with gender inequality and women's empowerment" (Basu 2005b), then feminism is far older than the liberal modernist project.

In Pakistan's context, regardless of contested meanings, the absence of an equivalent term for *feminism* in any of the local languages, apart from limiting its usage, raises its own challenges. The absence of vernacular terms facilitates the suggestion—aggressively promoted by opponents of women's rights and gender—that "feminism" is a North American and European agenda, if not an outright conspiracy, and its local "Westernized" proponents are, at best, out of touch with the grounded reality of "local women" and unrepresentative of their needs and, at worst, agents of Western imperialist agendas. Aided by such propaganda, feminists are popularly projected as aggressive antimen women. The net result is a discomfort with and lack of ownership of the feminist label even among women actively demanding greater rights and opportunities for women.[2]

Although the numbers are increasing, relatively few women in Pakistan self-identify as feminists. Most of those who do are urban, educated women with access to English; many had some association with leftist movements prior to activism for women's rights. Those who have identified as feminists since the 1980s have been inclined to differentiate between a women's movement, even a women's rights movement, and a feminist one. The women's movement would include all those actively seeking to bring about more gender equal rights and greater autonomy for women within the operative structures of state and society. Avoiding the term *patriarchy*, such women commonly articulate the problem as one of "male domination," without addressing underlying questions of power. (Unlike feminism, patriarchy does exist in local language, so the use of *male dominated* does not reflect a lack of choice in local idiom.) Feminists, in contrast, see the essential problem as that of patriarchy as a system privileging males over females manifest in the structures of both state and society within and beyond national boundaries. Their concern is how to challenge patriarchy as a system that actively disempowers women, regardless of other sociopolitical differences. For feminists, therefore, providing women with greater opportunities and representation in decision-making forums, improved health, and better laws is not an end. At best, these can serve as stepping-stones to a restructuring of power relations, structures, and systems.

In the 1980s a more nuanced understanding of feminism evolved among Pakistani activists from the experience of activism, rather than a study of and conceptual engagement with feminist theory. The experience of working with differently situated women brought to light how untenable it was for the women's movement to demand rights for women exclusively in terms of the narrow yardstick of whether discrimination is based on "sex alone," ignoring the differences in women's lived realities. (*Sex alone* is the term qualifying the constitutional provision prohibiting gender discrimination that is now contested by women's rights and more general human rights activists as inadequate.) The women's movement expanded to embrace the voices and causes of differently situated women, especially with respect to class but other identities as well, developing an understanding of that cumbersome term *intersectionality* (a term still not used in Pakistan). The process of learning and accepting women's diversities and the need to address them comprehensively was neither instant nor smooth and entailed learning from past mistakes, sometimes at the cost of losing ground with differently situated women. Initial hesitation points to the relatively privileged background of those leading the women's movement who enjoyed other privileges because of class, urban location, education, and other such factors.

In the Pakistani context it seems more appropriate to speak of a women's movement that has some feminist underpinnings or, to use phraseology suggested by Amrita Basu (2005b), a women's movement with feminist demands. Terms for the women's movement and the women's rights movement exist and are commonly used in local languages. Further, although the dividing line may not always be easily distinguishable in practical terms, there is some value in trying to distinguish between a wider, more generalized women's movement and a women's rights movement, according to the primacy placed on gender equality and institutional base in activism. In this, a women's rights movement would be characterized by the gendered perspective on issues adopted by adherents or activists, by the primacy placed on achieving greater gender equal rights, and by the consistency of conscious actions from institutional bases identified with the movement. The broader and more fluid women's movement would encompass institutions and individuals who, in the course of their engagements in other arenas and fields, take up women's rights issues but whose principal concern is not gender equality or inequality. This distinction enables a consideration of the interstices of the women's movement with other social movements for change, making it possible to account for and include the activism of individuals within nonfeminist or nonwomen's organizations and institutions for women's rights as part of the movement. These imprecise intersections with their smudged boundaries are where opportunities for interactions and engagements across movements occur, providing considerable scope for mutual learning through a cross-fertilization of ideas, analyses, and modes of activism. Equally, these spaces provide important openings for interchange with and the participation of those who are not, or not squarely, inside the women's rights movement on a daily basis. In addition to the overlap of different social movements, these ill-defined spaces, I would suggest, are where engagements with "femocrats" and other state representatives—male and female—occur in the pursuit of more gender-equitable development plans and policies. This interaction is essential for helping to institutionalize changes and for broadening the support base for the women's movement.

A related question is what elements distinguish a movement from trends, campaigns, or even a "nonmovement"—a term used with reference to women's activism in Iran (Bayat 2007). To what extent do social actions require a focused leadership, a clear-cut strategy for change, and organizational underpinnings to qualify as a movement? As in the case of "feminism," no clear consensus emerges. Hence, in Pakistan, people question whether the robust activism of women through the 1980s, acknowledged locally and internationally as a women's movement, can be called a movement given the limited number of activists and groups in a struggle that, for many years, remained state oriented. The answer, of course, depends on one's understanding of social movements. My understanding is that the 1980s activism was definitely a movement and that today's activism constitutes a different phase of the same movement. If the contemporary phase is less street oriented and more diffused than the 1980s phase, many groups and individuals are the same; while the movement has lost its intensity and become more institution based, there is a greater range of actors than before.

The Pakistani Women's Movement

Political developments have not favored a sustained women's movement in Pakistan. Soon after independence the political process, a crucial vehicle for activism in the anticolonial period, became derailed, starting with a ten-year martial law in 1957. Activists dispersed, women's issues dropped off the sociopolitical radar screen, and in the decade 1957–1968 the struggle for women's rights ceased to be visible as a movement. To the extent that it existed, lobbying for women's rights was carried out via informal social networks by women connected to and therefore able to access the corridors of power. Gender inequality was altogether absent from the agenda of socialist groups active in the 1960s and 1970s despite the presence of some women. Nor did women within these groups take up women's issues. Indeed, the exceptional feminist groups formed around this period were viewed by those engaged in the socialist movement(s) for change as deviations, counterproductively diverting focus and energy from the main class struggle.[3]

The current women's movement in Pakistan is divided into two phases: a period of intense, publicly visible activism inwardly focused on national issues in the 1980s and a more diffused movement since the 1990s. The differing nature of activism points to the dialectic relationship between movements and the historical period in which they are embedded, with movements influenced and shaped by the specific configurations of power they confront. The earlier phase originated in the context of a military dictatorship that, having "arrogated to itself the task of Islamizing the country's institutions in their entirety" (Khan 1985, 127), sought to reshape society in ways that systematically rescinded women's rights and narrowed their spaces (for a detailed account, see Mumtaz and Shaheed 1987). Forced by circumstances to focus entirely on resisting immensely problematic legal changes and policy initiatives, this earlier activism largely ignored international arenas. While some personal connections with feminists and women's rights groups abroad continued, activists did not use the UN system and processes around the women's conferences. These arenas assumed far greater importance as sites for negotiating demands and inserting feminist demands in the 1990s, after the restoration of democratic processes. Earlier activists did not think of the UN framework as relevant to the issues being faced within the country. Moreover, they felt unable to spare the time to engage more fully with transnational women's movements. Subsequently, a combination of factors, not all of them directly linked to women's activism within the country, enabled the demands for gender equality to be sustained.

Under the military and quasi-military rule of Gen. Zia-ul-Haq (1977–1988), the women's movement emerged in direct opposition to state repression. Counterintuitively, the movement born in opposition managed to put women permanently on the national agenda of diverse political actors, the state apparatus, and even its opponents in the politico-religious parties, such as the Jamaat-i-Islami. The intense activism of the 1980s emerged in a period characterized by an almost casual snuffing out of rights, the installation of barbaric punishments, and religiously wrapped rhetoric intended to stifle democratic voices and any form of dissent. All citizens felt the impact, but, as the least powerful segments of society, women and minorities became special victims. Concerted efforts sought to push women back within the strict confines of "home and hearth" or *chador aur chardiwari* (veil and the four walls of a homestead), rescind their rights, and curtail their liberties. The unprecedented convergence of military and religion in state power had a devastating and lasting impact.

Social movements such as existed were all in retreat; the labor movement had still not recovered from the early and brutal suppression of workers' strikes. The elected prime minister Z. A. Bhutto, deposed by Zia, had been hanged, and the sometimes despairing protests (there were dozens of self-immolations) to save Bhutto's life had given way to depression and despondency. All political activities had been banned, and there was no parliament with which to engage. Becoming attached to an existing movement, even if it had been desired, was simply not an option.

The actual spark igniting activism was provided in September 1981 by the case of a couple who became victims of the soon-to-be-infamous Hudood laws newly promulgated by the military regime as part of its so-called Islamization. The new provisions covered rape, abduction, and other sexual crimes and additionally criminalized all forms of consensual sex outside marriage. The law led to incredible injustice, as evidenced even in this first case (for details, see Mumtaz and Shaheed 1987; and Jahangir and Jilani 1990). In a nutshell, Fehmida, a college student, had eloped with the driver of her college bus. Attempting to annul the marriage, Fehmida's parents registered a case of abduction without realizing that the new legal provisions empowered the police to register a case of "illicit relations" (*zina*) when they found no evidence of abduction and insufficient documentary proof of marriage. A lower court sentenced the two to the maximum possible sentences: death by stoning for the already married Allah Bux and a hundred lashes of the whip for Fehmida.[4] Ironically enough, on reading the news, the original intention of the small feminist collective was not to start a women's movement but to mobilize as much opposition to the horrifying possibility that someone could be legally stoned to death and whipped a hundred times. That it became a women's movement was due to the response of men who were either dismissive ("This is Pakistan—it'll never happen") or defeatist ("This is martial law, and there is nothing you can do about it").[5] The collective, Shirkat Gah—Women's Resource Center—was a voluntary group formed in 1975 by young professional women for the purpose of raising consciousness and integrating women's rights and development. One of its activities was collecting information on women, including through regular press clippings, hence the attention to the small news item of the Fehmida and Allah Bux case and consequent outrage. Conscious of the limited impact a ten-member collective was likely to have, Shirkat Gah called a meeting of various women likely to be equally concerned and ready to act collectively against the growing negative repercussions on women of the regime's so-called Islamization. This led to the creation of the Khawateen-Mahaz-e-Amal, better known by its English name, Women's Action Forum, as a platform for women and women's organizations to oppose the regime's agenda and to defend women's rights. Formed as a lobby-cum–pressure group for women's rights, WAF brought together individual women and women's groups across political spectrums on a minimal agenda. To galvanize the broadest possible consensus, the platform allowed groups to participate or dissociate from specific actions.

Angered by the increased harassment in the streets and, for many, a questioning of their status both in workplaces and at home, women felt they were at a crossroads and had no option but to stand up for their rights regardless of the magnitude of opposition. This was most acutely felt by middle-class urban women, especially those from the professional and upper-middle classes who, having gained the most, also stood to lose the most from changed circumstances and policies.

During the 1980s the women's movement was intensely focused on the state apparatus, seeking to counter the state's proposals to rescind women's legal rights and reduce their presence in public arenas. Virtually every day brought new measures that needed to be responded to: proposals to ban the coverage of women by the media; directives making chadors compulsory for all government students, teachers, and employees; new laws that reduced the status of Muslim women and non-Muslim men to legal minors; and so on (see Mumtaz and Shaheed 1987 for details). Ironically enough, despite their rejection of the regime, activists were still dependent on those in power to reconsider or amend the measures being proposed. In their internal discussions, activists recognized that bringing about social change required working with women and reaching out to women at the grassroots level but concluded that the constant barrage of negative laws and policies being promulgated or proposed made it imperative to focus all attention on preventing further retrogressive steps (WAF Convention Report 1982).

Activism started in the absence of a preexisting women's movement that would have provided an institutional base and networks. Before WAF, women's organizations tended to be welfare oriented. A few, such as the socialist-oriented Democratic Women's Association, focused on class rights and articulated demands in terms of better life conditions for women of the oppressed classes without, however, addressing gendered differences within that class.

In contrast to movements seeking to expand existing rights and liberties in a refashioning of women's roles and "womanhood," the 1980s activism was reactive in nature, concerned with resisting the encroachment and erosion of personal freedoms and rights. Significantly, the expanded spaces and freedom enjoyed by at least some women had not emerged as a consequence of social movement activism. Instead, evolutionary processes had slowly enlarged the circles of self-determination for women, particularly for those from the middle and upper-middle classes. The reactive activism resulted from the cumulative felt impact of state moves to rescind women's rights and to formalize official policies of segregation across the board; it emerged from experiencing increasing harassment in public spaces and, for many, also within their own households. A few of those leading the movement came from the elite as well as the lower-middle and working classes, but most were gainfully employed professional middle-class women. A substantial number who self-identified as feminists had links with either the transnational women's movement or with leftist ideology, if not groups.

Post-1988, the arena for activism shifted from the streets to the courts and other state institutions. Having honed their skills in oppositional tactics through years of street-oriented protest, activists discovered that the new parameters of governance required different skills to lobby effectively for legislative change and improved policies. These had to be developed. It no longer sufficed to air outrage, condemn events, and highlight the negative impact of proposed or passed legislation and polices. The new circumstances required more nuanced, detailed responses that included analyses not only of proposed measures but also research on potential alternatives, including adaptations of measures in other countries; concrete proposals for measures had to be formulated, discussed, amended, and rediscussed among the activists and with potential allies before being proposed and negotiated with decision makers.

By 1995 activists had developed some aptitude. New lobbying skills became evident in the first government-nongovernment partnership in preparing the Pakistan report for the 1995 UN Fourth Conference on Women, held in Beijing. In the meantime, more systematic reaching out to women outside main urban centers by women's organizations (a number growing out of WAF) helped to widen the base of the movement. Enhanced interaction and linkages with other social movements led to the adoption of at least part of the women's movement agenda by actors outside the movement, amplifying the voices for women's rights. This was especially visible among some groups engaged in labor, the human rights organizations, and the rights-oriented civil society groups in general. In turn, these linkages helped activists in the women's rights movement develop a more nuanced and deeper understanding of how intersectionality plays out in women's lives and issues. The different nature of activism in the 1980s and subsequently is illustrated by two issues: political representation and violence against women.

Political Rights and Representation

The practice of reserving seats for women in legislatures predates independence, so it has never been a particularly controversial subject. The means for filling these seats in Pakistan since the 1962 constitution has been problematic, however. It is assembly members (themselves returned on the basis of popular franchise) who elect the candidates to reserved seats. This modality has been criticized on a number of counts: for delinking women from the political power base, for making women so elected accountable not to a female electorate but to the predominantly male politicians who bring them into office, and for depriving women of a political training ground. Furthermore, political parties have used the existence of such seats as an excuse not to field women from general seats. Alternative suggestions include reserving constituencies rather than seats in the manner of the Panchayati Raj system of local government in India, or amending Pakistan's Political Party and Public Representation Acts to make it obligatory for parties to field a percentage of female candidates.

During the Zia era political rights were a matter of general concern. For both the women's movement and other anti-martial-law activists, a principal demand was the restoration of democracy. Yet operating under a strict martial-law regime, WAF worked to lever open the rather narrow wedge separating "women's issues" from "politics" and deliberately called itself nonpolitical until 1991, when it amended this to "politically nonaligned." Apart from avoiding state repression, the label was intended to allay concerns among potential women activists about getting involved in "politics." Separately, women's rights activists sought to insert women's rights into the agenda of political parties. Direct interaction with political actors was limited. The strategy adopted was to prepare a general agenda on women's rights and to circulate it to all parties. Although relatively little follow-up was done to ensure the adoption, a number of parties did adopt some of the WAF points. By the early 1990s all political parties, including the Jamaat-i-Islami, had started to address women in their manifestos.[6]

More problematic was trying to seek a calibrated engagement with the anti-martial-law movement while remaining a nonpolitical women's movement. Initial hesitation about whether to support the women brutalized by the regime in the 1983 Movement for the Restoration of Democracy was quickly overcome. The bigger challenge was how to reconcile the activism within the prodemocracy movement with the WAF stance of being nonpolitical. Many WAF activists regularly participated in anti-martial-law and prodemocracy demonstrations. Asserting that such participation was in the capacity of individual citizens and not as part of, or as representatives of, WAF, activists argued that membership in a women's rights platform could not take away their rights as citizens to engage in political activities. While dividing activism carried out within the women's movement from that in the anti-martial-law movement may have made sense in conceptual terms, it was practically untenable. Newspapers regularly reported the presence of WAF in such demonstrations and meetings, regardless of the official position of its adherents. The conflicted positions regarding this engagement were never fully resolved. In retrospect, however, this engagement may have contributed to women's rights activists' gaining a measure of respect from political actors that, in turn, may have subsequently helped women lobby within democratic setups, hobbled as these may have been.

Post–martial law, campaigns around political rights maintained a focus on having political-party manifestos address women's concerns, but a new focus became women's political representation. The initial impetus for the demand to restore women's reserved seats in the national and provincial assemblies was the lapse of the 1973 constitution's provision for women's seats following the 1988 general elections. Without this measure, the number of women in parliament dropped from twenty-four in the 1988 assembly (the highest number until then) to two in the following assembly. Possibly women in Pakistan feel the need for political representation even more keenly because frequent military rule has meant the wholesale elimination of women from the ranks of policy decision makers. The nature and modality for such affirmative action have been hotly debated, leading women activists to engage with political parties more systematically in the later phase.

By 1996 the second phase of the women's movement had run enough campaigns and done enough lobbying to have a number of proposed measures included in the National Plan of Action for Women, Pakistan's domestic policy for the implementation of the Beijing Platform for Action that was launched in 1998. WAF continued to be the main vehicle for articulating a collective demand, but the groundwork and organizing were carried out by specific women's groups, such as Shirkat Gah—Women's Resource Center and Aurat Publication and Information Services Foundation. These groups undertook research, formulated possible measures, and organized discussion forums bringing together a diverse set of actors that included political-party representatives and bureaucrats but also other civil society groups to build a consensus. WAF and these groups are not mutually exclusive, however. Many women bridge the two, and many activists chose to lobby as WAF, rather than as separate organizations. The campaign was picked up and supported by other human rights–oriented civil society groups and actors.

Efforts to increase the number of women in local government were inspired by the example of the Panchayati Raj in neighboring India. Like their counterparts in India, women's organizations in Pakistan tried unsuccessfully to suggest the same principle for the parliament. The government's decision to introduce a 33 percent quota for women in the new local government system on the basis of direct elections in 2000 was primarily the result of intensive lobbying by women activists within the country, but the UN endorsement for one-third female representation in political decision-making forums around the time of the Beijing conference is likely to have encouraged the government to take concrete action. The first round of elections inducted close to 40,000 women into the political process. In 2002 new quotas were introduced in the national and provincial assemblies as well as, for the first time, in the Senate, responding to the movement's long-standing demands.[7]

Domestic Violence

At what point activists took up the issue of domestic violence depends on the definition of *domestic violence* used. Does the rubric include the violence visited upon family women in the name of honor? What about issues like forced marriages and child marriages? These and many related subjects have been campaign topics, and activists in Pakistan have never understood domestic violence as being limited to spousal violence. Early on, activists took up individual cases of domestic violence brought to them by the concerned women or their supporters. They visited hospitals and jails to consult with and provide relief and help to survivors of violence upon learning of cases through the media. (This part of activism remained largely unpublicized.) The activism of the 1980s, galvanized by the infamous zina section of the Hudood Ordinances of 1979 relating to sexual relations, rape, and other criminal acts of a sexual nature, ensured that gender-based violence was on the agenda from the start. From state violence, that is, corporal punishments, incarceration, and the torture of women political workers, activists quickly picked up other facets. Within its first year, WAF organized two seminars on "crimes against women" (first in Karachi and then in Lahore). WAF newsletters indicate that activists used *crimes against women* in much the same way as *violence against women* or *gender-based violence* is currently used, including systemic and structural violence in addition to interpersonal forms of violence. Seminars, pamphlets, public protests, press conferences, and press releases regularly highlighted "crimes against women." Some campaigns took up specific forms of violence.

In 1989 growing media reports of women burned in their kitchens as a result of supposed accidents resulting from stove bursts led to an intensive, albeit short-lived, campaign. Activists met with survivors or their relatives, confirming that, as suspected, most were not accidents resulting from faulty technology but intended homicides by husbands or in-laws, or both. The demand for an independent inquiry into the production of gas stoves was fulfilled, and such reports ceased to appear after a year. It remains unclear, however, whether there was a real drop in cases or merely a drop in reporting. In any case, with the demand fulfilled, activists were unclear about how to take further action on the issue.

Activists did not use the term *violence against women* until the early 1990s. The change reflects the greater engagement of local activists with the international arena and the adoption of language made popular not just by feminists but, to a large extent, by the United Nations. The demand for legislation on domestic violence was articulated only in the second phase. Demanding progressive legislation earlier from a government bent on rescinding rights had seemed pointless. To be effective, however, activists had to widen their support base and overcome their own lack of lobbying skills. After 1990 women's organizations and individuals from within the movement functioning as gender experts in development forums used their respective institutional bases to raise public concern around domestic violence. Simultaneously, they started addressing related aspects of domestic violence such as legal aid, shelters, and spreading legal awareness. The acute need for these activities was a lesson from the Zia era when women learned just how quickly rights can be overturned when so few women know about their legal entitlements, much less enjoy them. A diversified institutional base has helped activists to address the myriad facets of domestic violence beyond just naming and shaming to interventions directly addressing the needs of women facing violence.

Violence against women is one issue that has been widely taken up by women's groups as well as rights-oriented groups in smaller towns and fairly remote areas. For example, research into so-called honor crimes has been conducted by a group in remote South Punjab, Sangtani. Others have taken up issues of violence against women, from forcible marriages to police failure to register rape cases. In many instances, action has followed capacity being built through linkages, training, and support extended by urban-based women's groups. Increased capacity has bolstered the ability of such groups to directly intervene with the police and administration. A few, such as the urban-based

Behbud-e-Niswan Network (Women's Welfare Network) in Faisalabad, have set up alternative dispute resolution forums to directly address issues of gender-based violence in their communities. Additionally, the issue has elicited the support of others outside the women's rights movement, such as retired members of the judiciary and, importantly, doctors.

Nationally, civil society groups and individual experts used their collaboration with the government on the National Report for Beijing in 1995 to highlight different forms of violence and to insert recommended measures in the relevant chapter. In 1996 this was followed up by preparing new guidelines for the government-run shelters for women. Simultaneously, wearing their "expert" hats, activists contributed to the National Plan of Action for Women as the domestic policy for implementing the Beijing Platform for Action. Despite being adopted by the government in power, the new guidelines had little visible impact and remained on the shelves of bureaucrats' offices, collecting dust. Meanwhile, constantly dealing with legal cases where the women required shelter and dissatisfied with the jail-like conditions of the government-run shelters, Hina Jilani, an internationally renowned lawyer and human rights activist, set up the first autonomous women's shelter. Subsequently, others, including a few former judges, galvanized and sensitized by activists to the issue of violence against women, including domestic violence, helped to establish additional new shelters.

Separately, organizations with a focus on gender-based violence have researched and highlighted the procedural problems women confront in reporting and registering cases of domestic violence. The more activists engaged with the issue, the more they found new facets requiring attention. With respect to shelters, for instance, it was not enough to have guidelines issued; far greater efforts were required for effective implementation to make these meaningful. Another lesson was that state institutions, with their ponderous bureaucracy and intricate protocol and departmental divisions, cannot merely duplicate the initiatives of unencumbered civil society institutions. To move from policy statements to actual implementation, recommendations need to be grounded in bureaucratic reality rather than activist idealism. Hence, with respect to shelters, it was only in 2007 that the Punjab government was persuaded to formulate and notify new more detailed human rights–oriented guidelines. Prior to this, activists worked with the government officials to change their perspective on the issue. In 2008, grappling with how to ensure effective implementation, a women's rights organization undertook a series of activities: first, a rapid assessment of issues confronting staff; second, translating the English-language guidelines into the vernacular; third, persuading the top concerned bureaucrat to issue a directive for all departments to cooperate; fourth, writing a manual of operations for shelter; and fifth, preparing training modules and running orientation sessions for staff, local government officials, and local activists. This is a far cry from the press releases and broad policy demands formulated earlier.[8]

Similar developments are visible with respect to the police. Inspired by the newly established Brazilian women's police stations, WAF had successfully lobbied to strengthen the number and position of women in the police force and the establishment of women's police stations, only to discover that this measure was far from adequate. Apart from the grossly inadequate number of women's police stations and the lack of clear jurisdiction and authority as well as expertise, increasing the number of women police and women's police stations left untouched the hugely problematic legal definitions and medico-legal procedures. Also untouched was the general attitude of male police, leading some women's groups to engage with the main male police force in gender-sensitization programs.[9]

Consistent efforts to mobilize women across class and location contributed to a groundswell of public opinion and lobbying policy makers led women members of the Punjab provincial assembly to table a domestic violence bill in 2002. Vehemently opposed by members of politico-religious parties, the bill got stuck in committees, making little progress. Nevertheless, the momentum built eventually led to the Domestic Violence Bill passed by the national assembly in August 2009 and sent to the Senate for approval.

One final change between the activism of the 1980s and the present relates to the presence of many more funded institutions than ever before and what this implies for the women's rights movement. In Pakistan, as elsewhere, there is considerable debate about the negative impact of what is called the NGO-ization of the women's movement. Yet there can be little doubt that the emergence of such groups has helped to sustain the movement in ways that were not possible on the strength of purely voluntary activism, after working hours and on weekends. Growth has been aided by the resources made available through international donor agencies (mainly through UN agencies and multinational and bilateral assistance programs). Financial assistance has had both positive and negative impacts. Support has allowed organizations to expand their work beyond the larger cities to smaller towns and villages across the country, something that had not been possible before. This has created or strengthened linkages with existing community-based organizations and catalyzed new groups, producing a ripple effect.

However, a number of groups have become not only donor dependent but donor driven, adapting programs to the latest flavor-of-the-month activity in vogue, be it health initiatives or income generation, legal aid or gender-responsive budgeting, or environmental preservation. Quite apart from the question of whether the groups have the requisite technical expertise for some of these activities, there is a danger of organizations' losing their self-determined purpose. The creation of jacks—or janes—of-all-trades and masters of none is likely to produce a multitude of groups attempting to deliver on too many fronts, therefore doing everything rather superficially instead of intervening in a focused manner. Uniform imposed agendas and the need to deliver SMART outputs (specific, measurable, achievable, reliable, and time-bound) undermine the scope for innovation. Movements would rarely, if ever, have achieved change had they restricted themselves to what was "achievable" and "measurable," for instance, or been constrained by the fear of failure. The mushroom growth of nongovernmental organizations is by no means confined to women's groups, and all NGOs confront similar problems. Yet the sheer intensity of almost a decade of nonstop public interventions by the women's movement in the 1980s combined with the increased focus on gender within the international community as well as the boost to women's concerns provided by the 1995 Beijing conference means that few civil society organizations concerned with promoting rights ignore gender. The real challenge for civil society organizations, even if they are donor supported, is to avoid being donor driven so they can maintain their own agenda and perspective.

Exceptionally, conscious of the potential dangers of the pull of purse strings, WAF as a matter of principle does not accept funding from any sources other than personal donations, although its work is supported by women's organizations dependent for the most part on mobilizing external financial support. The existence of WAF as an independent forum during the Zia years was critical to launching a movement, and there is considerable merit in having at least some forum for women's rights that is independent of external funding. But two concerns need to be underlined: first, the WAF experience indicates that relentless activism leads to burnout, and, second, unsupported activism may not be sustainable over a longer period of time. The two are not necessarily interconnected. WAF became far less active between 1991 and 2005 for a number of reasons. Burnout was one. Another was that different political orientations, submerged in the face of an obvious and devastating opponent in the martial-law regime, resurfaced following the return of democracy. A third was that the sense of urgency had dissipated. Recently, WAF has become more active once again. An encouraging development has been the opening of new chapters in smaller towns and the expressed desire for more chapters to be opened. Yet funds are bound to remain an issue since the absence of funds may marginalize those with fewer resources who cannot, for example, afford to travel and interact with other women. If activism is to include women outside the small group of well-resourced women, the movement needs a more effective fund-raising strategy. Eventually, the solution may be a mass-based membership group with access to its own funding.

Finally, historic specificity influences which issues a movement addresses, the demands it articulates, and the arenas it utilizes for contestation and negotiation as well as who is considered to be an ally and the choice and nature of the relationships forged—or not—with other movements. Movements are shaped not only by the alliances they build but also by the preexisting networks of communication activists can mobilize and rely on (Freeman 1999). The choices made by any movement are driven by an assessment of the strategic value of possible options, however unconscious or informal such an assessment may be. In Pakistan the experiential knowledge of activists in the 1980s, their class, and their ideological background influenced such decisions, as did the circumstances in which they became active.

Linkages with Social Movements

As a women's rights platform, WAF did seek to engage with and to influence diverse actors, but it was not always clear about the terms of such engagements. It was also fiercely conscious of a need to remain impervious to all external influences that could either detract it from its main purpose or co-opt it into another agenda.[10] I will review here the women's movement's linkages with the human rights movement and two particularly important social movements: the labor and peasant movements.

Women's activism preceded other forms of sustained social activism in the 1980s, and those in the women's rights movement helped to catalyze and develop Pakistan's human rights movement. Today, the Human Rights Commission of Pakistan, an independent civil society organization unconnected to the government in any way, is seen to lead the movement. But by the time the first meeting was called to launch the HRCP in 1986, women activists had already been waging their battle to defend women's rights for five years, and the most vociferous opposition to Islamization came from women's groups (Toor 1997). Women activists were therefore present in large numbers at the HRCP inaugural meeting; they were among its founding members and continue to figure prominently in its council and all its activities.

A number of issues that WAF took up were not women specific but broadly concerned with human rights. In 1986 WAF had formed the Women's Joint

Action Committee to oppose the Shariat Ordinance, comprising six organizations and WAF.[11] On July 13, 1990, mobilizing beyond women's groups, it was WAF rather than the HRCP that called for joint action to challenge the Shariat Bill, recently passed by the Senate and awaiting hearing in the national assembly (Shaheed and Hussain 2007). Half of some forty organizations responding to the call then formed the Joint Action Committee for People's Rights as a civil society coalition. While still confined to a few urban centers, JAC continues to function as an important platform for human rights campaigns and activities that bring together groups with diverse institutional agendas. Sharing a common goal and human rights perspective, some member organizations concentrate on the rights of specific groups, such as minorities, women, or labor, or an area of work, such as education or legal assistance. Some engage in development-oriented work and service delivery, while others, such as theater groups, concentrate on raising awareness.

Linkages with the labor movement had two separate drivers. In 1984 a woman trade unionist approached women's rights activists in WAF for support in dealing with the harassment of female union members by the management of a local pharmaceutical company. Because union activities rather than gender identity were the immediate cause of conflict, this did not fall within the ambit of what at the time was considered a gender-specific issue. It took years for the issues arising from power differentials due to intersectionality to become an unquestioned principle in the movement. In this first instance, for example, WAF supported the women in terms of the harassment being faced but did not extend support subsequently when the union women were fired from their jobs. Initial support was probably propelled by the fact that management intimidation included sexual harassment—an unambiguously gendered issue (Mumtaz and Shaheed 1987).

In the meantime, to further the women's agenda within the trade union movement, WAF engaged with trade unions by participating in May Day events and other union gatherings as well as working with female trade unionists. The aim was twofold: first, to encourage labor leaders to pay greater attention to the specific problems of women workers who are grossly underrepresented in union activities (Zia and Bari 1999) and, second, to catalyze a broader definition of the labor movement from the "worker in the workplace" to encompass the worker's entire family, for which WAF organized several events for unionists, workers, and their families.

The far greater, if still insufficient, attention paid to women workers by trade unions today is only partly attributable to the women's movement. This reorientation has been propelled by the stress placed on women's rights by the

International Labor Organization (ILO). The greater emphasis on women in the international community and closer linkages and involvement of women trade union leaders in the women's movement have combined to catalyze women workers' groups, such as the Women Workers Organization and Women Workers Helpline. In addition, collaboration between the women's movement and the labor movement has increased focus on women in labor-focused organizations such the Pakistan Institute of Labor Education and Research, which has established centers for women workers, researched the conditions and issues of women workers in collaboration with feminist-oriented organizations,[12] and includes gender in its training programs for (mainly male) labor activists. These civil society groups bridge the labor and women's movements. Identifying as part of a broader social movement seems critical, however. Hence, WAF attempts to forge closer links with professional associations, such as those of telephone operators and nurses, for example, produced neither lasting ties nor new initiatives. Momentary linkages occurred usually when women in these professions confronted a specific problem, commonly that of sexual harassment, or when they were actively demanding rights such as better salaries or work conditions. In retrospect, these associations were perhaps too narrowly focused on improving and safeguarding the rights of women workers within their particular institutions; the concerned women may not have seen themselves as part of the wider labor movement, and they certainly never joined the women's movement. The dissimilar outcomes of engaging with different types of labor organizations suggest that effective linkages across movements can be sustained only when each considers itself to be part of a movement for social change with some commonality of purpose.

A different example relates to interlinkages with a peasant movement for land rights. In 2001 the peasant movement in Punjab became famous for the women's "*thappa* brigade," the *thappa* being a long wooden stick used by women for washing clothes and threshing harvests.[13] The catalyst for the movement was a 1998 government announcement that the state was considering granting peasants the right of ownership over their homes. It was in the pursuit of this smaller claim that peasants coincidentally discovered that, under the original agreements formulated by the British colonial rulers, they may actually be entitled to ownership of the lands they had been tilling for generations. They also discovered that the leases for the farms being run by the military and other state institutions such as the Punjab Seed Corporation had not been renewed, in many cases since before independence, as confirmed by the revenue department (for details, see Mumtaz and Mumtaz forthcoming). With the slogan *Malkiaat ya maut* (Ownership or death), land rights became the movement's main demand. As the movement gained momentum, peasants stopped paying any share of the produce to farm management and resisted attempts to convert them from tenant farmers (with rights) to contract laborers who could be evicted without notice. In the absence of firm legal ground, management resorted to strong-arm tactics supported by the full weight of the state: the police and the paramilitary Rangers. Employing increasing violence, authorities laid siege to the troubled areas, cordoning off entire villages, cutting off water and other supplies from reaching villagers, blocking the sale of any produce, and preventing access to facilities. Unable to reach medical help in time, at least two pregnant women died in Okara. Peasants were arrested, several were shot and killed, and many others, including women, were injured.

Women came to the foreground around 2001. Stories differ on when and how women became involved, but the most plausible account seems to be the one related by an old man who recalls that in one Okara village, upon hearing that two children had been killed, women did not stop to inquire whose children and ran to their rescue, picking up whatever came to hand, including thappas. Furious, they destroyed the police van and attacked policemen who, unwilling to fight the women, ran away. This initial success galvanized further and more prominent and systematic activism on the part of the women with the full support of male activists, mostly immediate relatives. In different villages, thappa brigades were formed, and women successfully intervened on several occasions in direct confrontation with the authorities. They prevented state officials from removing wood from their lands, and on two occasions foiled attempts to confiscate their harvests. The women's thappa brigade caught the public imagination so that the thappa metamorphosed from a symbol of women's domesticated roles to a signifier of their activism and, as the only "weapon" ever wielded by the peasants, a symbol for the entire movement.

The peasant struggle received support from across the spectrum of human rights groups and small parties such as the Pakistan Labor Party and the minuscule but enthusiastic Communist Party. Women's rights groups extended their full support. They visited the affected villages, were part of the delegations interceding with the authorities, and helped provide legal assistance to fight the cases registered against the peasants. They also arranged accommodation and shelter for women activists of the movement. At the height of the struggle, addressing a gathering of peasants, Asma Jahangir, an internationally renowned human rights leader, jokingly told the women that now that they had taken up their thappas as weapons of self-defense, they should use them to correct matters within their homes as well. At the time, the women's response was that this was a joint struggle and not the time to fight with their men, who needed their support. This is the only recorded instance of activists from the women's movement bringing up the issue of gender. Otherwise, activists simply supported the peasant movement—both women and men—in whatever manner seemed appropriate at the time. Yet as matters settled into a stalemate with the cessation of police and army action, women activists lost regular contact with the peasant women. More recently, a research project seeking to understand women's organizing in different spaces—as women-specific organizations, in general organizations, as part of networks, and as part of social movements—has renewed contact.[14]

Activism in the peasant movement has altered women's lives. At the very least, it has changed women's self-perceptions (Mumtaz and Mumtaz forthcoming). The exhilaration of successfully confronting the police and Rangers, evident in interviews, has left women with newfound self-confidence. Attesting to this greater self-assurance, women have broken their previous silence around the sexual harassment they confronted during the struggle. Importantly, especially in those areas that experienced the most intense and violent confrontation, women report a reduction in domestic violence. And, of course, the families as a whole are financially far better off because without sharecropping, they now benefit from the sale of all their produce. In Okara peasant women are creating new options for their daughters, sending them to nursing schools and other technical institutions that will not bind their livelihood to access to land. Newfound self-confidence has enabled a number of women to renegotiate the parameters of their family lives and spousal relations, and some boast of telling their husbands wanting to create trouble to leave the home, or "go get divorced if you want to." Nevertheless, women still do not want to claim their right of inheritance from the family. They are however, eager to access land being granted by the government (as well as other women-specific financial support schemes). To facilitate access to such government schemes, in 2009, women supported by male relatives formed the Peasant Women Welfare Foundation in Okara, covering six villages, and the Peasant Women Welfare Society in Khanewal.

It is unlikely that these changed circumstances would have come about had so many groups, including women's rights organizations, not extended unqualified support. From today's perspective, however, perhaps the most important lesson to be drawn from this experience is that while instant, largely spontaneous, solidarity actions by the women's movement with and for women involved in different struggles are necessary and welcome, they are far from sufficient. If the women's movement is to widen its base in a sustainable manner, activists in the women's rights movement need to build and maintain consistent and long-term linkages. While efforts to ensure more appropriate and women-responsive policies and laws are necessary, equal attention and energies need to be devoted to supporting women's access to them. To build an effective alliance with women in other social movements, the women's rights movement needs to integrate the concerns of other movements squarely within the women's agenda. Economic rights have not been addressed sufficiently or adequately by the women's movement in Pakistan. In the 1980s the movement addressed women's economic rights only as generic concerns. Individual activists did take up economic issues in their capacity as development or gender experts with the Women's Division of the cabinet,[15] and UN bodies, especially the ILO, but such individual actions did not produce a concrete agenda for change within the women's movement.

The Framework for Rights and Identity

Literature distinguishes between movements whose principal agenda is redistribution, sometimes called instrumentalist movements, and movements that seek recognition, as Nancy Fraser (2003) argued, based on the formation or preservation of identity. Redistributive or instrumental demands include the benefits of education and health as well as employment opportunities. But they also revolve around the right to be included in decision making or advocate for a reworked basis for decision-making processes, such as movements demanding the right to vote. Movements can also arise in defense of the status quo against real or perceived threats either to collective identity and autonomy or to previously held rights or privileges. Although specific movements may place greater emphasis on one or the other aspect, I would agree with the contention that most have dual faces that "dialectally combine demands with an expressive dimension" (Stammers 1991). For example, demands for quotas in jobs and in political processes are often made on the basis of creating, strengthening, or redefining a collective identity (e.g., in movements demanding regional autonomy in Pakistan or the *dalit* [untouchables] movement in India). The absence of proactive expressive dimensions within the Pakistan women's movement, I believe, poses a challenge, especially in view of the concentrated attention on this aspect of movement building so very visible in movements of political Islamists.

In the 1980s the women's rights movement was obliged to engage with identity. It did so in resistance against the new identity being formulated and promoted by the military regime and its politico-religious cabinet allies, using a hegemonic "Islamization" and "Islamizing" discourse (Toor 1997) backed by brute military force. The regime sought to eliminate the diversified norms adopted by the upper to middle classes by re-creating a straitjacketed Pakistani womanhood defined, among other things, by new dress codes. Notions of the good "Muslim" or "Islamic" and occasionally "Eastern" woman were forwarded and frequently counterposed to professionally working women. This reconceptualization was aggressively promoted by the state through its monopoly over electronic media, but equally through directives and at state functions where, for example, women were regularly presented chadors as gifts. Discourse and tactics found resonance among conservative and traditional elements within society who replicated and amplified both the discourse and the message. In a sense, the very defiance of such impositions can be taken as defining the expressive dimension of the movement. The Pakistan experience thus suggests that when movements are concerned with defending rights and resisting change, their engagement with identity is likely to be one of defending expressive dimensions rather than seeking to institute new signifiers in the daily interpretation of identity.

The preservation and defense of identity should not be confused with the promotion of identity by contemporary movements defined as political Islamists most obviously through the imposition of various forms of dress code and the veil. These are not a preservation of tradition; the nature of the veil bears little or no connection with traditional forms of dress. The aggressive promotion of new forms of outward appearances and social behavior must be seen as integral symbols of belonging to these new movements. No similarly obvious signifiers mark the collective identity of women's rights activists. Moreover, even if this focus on identity stems from the absence of any coherence of a political economy agenda, as insightfully suggested by Samir Amin (1989, especially chap. 4), these expressive dimensions appeal to, make use of, and find resonance with what people view as their own culture. No such resonance exists for human rights as a framework for gender equality.

Between 1981 and 1991 WAF selectively used an Islamic framework for countering measures proposed in the name of Islam. The use of the Islamic framework, always a contentious issue within WAF (see Mumtaz and Shaheed 1987), was propelled by an understanding that the human rights framework would not suffice to galvanize popular support against the regime's propositions and ordinances. People, especially potential women activists, required reassurance that they were not being asked to speak out against their religion, only against the proposed measures of a fallible and dictatorial regime. While "buying into the terms of the debate set by the Islamicists" may have affirmed the Islamicists' hegemony, it is also true that by linking up with other anti-martial-law groups and those opposed to the imposition of supposedly religious laws, WAF successfully "built up an effective counter-hegemony" (Toor 1997, 113, 121–122). At its 1991 convention WAF unequivocally declared it was secular. Subsequently, referencing Islam was dropped. In its place a "compromised citizenship" became the preferred framework (Jamal 2005), regardless of the issue, which referred more exclusively to the human rights framework.

Human rights and constitutional provisions were always a reference point. The early formulation of the "crimes against women" terminology carries an implicit demand that such acts be criminalized and prosecuted by the state. The use of the human rights framework may be inadequate, however. The human rights framework is located squarely within the parameters of nation-states and presumes that the state as the principal guarantor of rights has, or can be persuaded to have, the best interests of all its citizens at heart. The fallacy of this assumption is patently obvious in Pakistan's history. When the state is the, or one of the, main adversaries, such presumptions are counterproductive.

The adoption of a human rights framework tends to focus the attention of movement activists on achieving citizens' rights as entitlements granted by the state, propelling them to devote maximum energies and resources to "upward rather than downward linkages" (Basu 2005b). Equally, although this is now starting to change, the human rights framework tends to focus on the entitlements of individual citizens, ignoring underlying equations of power and attendant structures that need to be addressed and, in the case of women, fundamentally altered. Institutions adopting a human rights framework have a propensity to focus on the state in ways that takes activism away from changing ground realities through direct actions. Finally, the human rights framework seems inadequate as a response to the immense challenges being posed by nonstate actors. This includes militarized groups that seem to be challenging the very legitimacy of the nation-state as a framework, such as the fanatical Pan-Islamicists, but equally challenges are posed by transnational corporations that do not fit and are therefore not accountable within the current governance structures predicated on nation-states, including all international institutions.

That said, I do not mean to suggest that the human rights discourse or framework should be discarded. The human rights framework still provides a counterpoint, however inadequate, to the use of culture and religion to justify the structures of patriarchy. What I am suggesting is that the women's movement needs to consider more strategic ways of developing the expressive dimensions of its activities, by appropriating and refashioning the cultural contexts in which it operates. I believe this is necessary for the movement to be able to counter the incursions of the religious Right. The expressive dimensions need not be religious. While rights activists need to spell out more concretely their political economy, to use Amin's language, they must simultaneously seek to ground themselves in a dynamic indigenous culture. That this may be difficult does not make it any less important.

Conclusion

I have argued that there is a case to be made for distinguishing a general women's movement from a women's rights movement in order to take into account the contributions of individuals who may be active but may not as such be activists of the women's movement. I have proposed that, far from being peripheral, ill-defined gray areas of activism within a larger, more fluid women's movement are important contributors to the growth and sustainability of the women's rights movement that buttress the more identifiable rights-focused movement. The concept of indigenous feminisms may be one way of exploring and taking into account the varied conceptualizations and activism of differently located women. In any case, the overlaps and intersections between movements are vital for any movement's development both in terms of expanding the number of actors taking forward a movement's agenda and for creating the ripple effect necessary to effect desired social change. Contentious and vexatious though they may be, linkages with other social movements are critical for women's movements (as any other), for they facilitate and deepen understanding and promote a consciousness among activists about the complex interconnections of people's lives. For this to happen, women's rights activists must adopt the immediate concerns of differently situated women as integral components of the women's agenda, such as the property rights of peasants as well as others, labor rights, and so forth. The experience of Pakistan suggests that a shared understanding and commitment to social change on the part of those seeking alliances are preconditions to effective relationships across movements. Without such a shared orientation, bridging efforts are unlikely to amount to much, as exemplified by the lack of sustained relationships with associations of telephone operators or nurses. A further area for investigation and action is how to build effective bridges and overcome the presence of contentiously engaged partners from within the same movement.

The salience of the culturally expressive dimensions of movements for women's activism is usually neglected. The interweaving of culture, economics, and the political domain, I believe, deserves greater attention from both academics and activists. Though usually neglected, this interweaving may constitute a key challenge for activists in contemporary women's movements. In Pakistan there seems to be a need for the women's movement and more generally for human rights groups to develop a more conscious cultural aspect. It is especially important to provide a counterpoint to the rewriting of history and culture by those seeking to build political constituencies on the basis of a self-serving political use of religious identity. The human rights framework needs to be complemented by a more effective use of the creative arts combined with retrieving historical and cultural traditions that resonate with people's everyday lives.

While the human rights framework is an important and necessary counterweight to hegemonic discourses of tradition and religion, without an indigenous cultural base, it may simply be insufficient to meet the challenges of changing gender relations that are deeply embedded in cultural notions of people's perceptions of self and others. Antonio Gramsci's argument about class struggle bears consideration: the class (or alliance of classes) that emerges in dominant or "hegemonic" positions "will always attempt to secure a hegemonic position by weaving its own cultural outlook deep into the social fabric" (cited in Toor 1997, 111). This is true with respect to gendered relations of power that are reproduced in all aspects of social interaction and are justified by and internalized as the given culture. Ultimately, rights can be enjoyed only if and when they have become an integral part of people's culture, however this is defined.

Notes

1. This section draws on feedback and continued discussions with Vivienne Wee.

2. Negative stereotyping is neither new nor unique to Pakistan, South Asia, or third world countries (see, for example, Freeman 1999). Today this may be somewhat less of an issue in the West, but calling oneself a feminist tends to assume more overtly political dimensions in contexts such as South Asia (Forbes 2003).

3. Personal communication by Aban Marker, founding member of Shirkat Gah—Women's Resource Centre, which was if not the first feminist women's organization, then certainly one of the very first, formed in 1974.

4. The case was later overturned. The maximum punishments have never been implemented in Pakistan.

5. The collective was Shirkat Gah—Women's Resource Centre, of which I have been a long-standing member. These were the responses we all seemed to have received when we approached men with the idea that we had to do something to prevent this sentence from being executed. Shirkat Gah then called the first meeting that led to the creation of the Women's Action Forum as a platform for women and women's organizations to oppose the actions of the regime.

6. WAF also wrote and circulated "position papers" on various aspects and produced "women's agendas" before general elections and other major events such as the UN Conference on Human Rights in 1993 and Conference on Women in 1995.

7. Out of a total of 342 seats in the national assembly, 60 seats were reserved for women and 10 for minorities. These seats were to be allocated on the basis of proportional representation to

parties garnering at least 5 percent of the total general seats. In the provincial assemblies, out of the full 371-seat Punjab Assembly, 66 were reserved for women and 8 for minorities; in the 168-seat Sindh Assembly, 29 were for women and 9 for minorities; in the 124-seat North West Frontier Province Assembly, 22 were for women and 3 for minorities; and in the 65-seat Baluchistan Assembly, 11 were for women and 3 for minorities.

8. These current activities are being carried out by Shirkat Gah as part of its work in the five-year action research project Women's Empowerment in Muslim Contexts: Gender, Poverty, and Democratization from the Inside Out, supported by the UK development agency DFID. This project takes forward earlier Shirkat Gah work, and other aspects of shelter-related work are being addressed by Shirkat Gah's main Women's Empowerment and Social Justice Programme. The GTZ development agency has been the catalyst for change with the Department of Social Welfare, which is responsible for shelters (*Survey Report: Issues Requiring Guidance/Instructions "Dar-ul-Amans"* [Punjab, March–April 2008], prepared by Khalida Ahson for the Shirkat Gah WEMC project).

9. Based in Islamabad, Rozan, which has always had a focus on gender-based violence and violence in general, has been particularly active, working with the police training academy to institute self-awareness and changed attitudes.

10. For a more complete discussion, see Mumtaz and Shaheed 1987, chap. 9.

11. The six organizations were the Democratic Women's Association, Punjab Women Lawyers, Shirkat Gah—Women's Resource Centre, Simorgh Women's Resource and Publication Centre, ASR, and Aurat Publication and Information Services Foundation.

12. Some, like the Social Development Policy Institute, are not women's organizations but have feminists on staff.

13. This section draws on research conducted by Fareha Arshad and Mohammad Ahmed for the Punjab team of the Shirkat Gah–WEMC project, still under way, and Fareha Ahsan's paper "Women in the Movement (AMP): A Question of Sustainable Empowerment," presented at the Shirkat Gah–WEMC Seminar, December 2008, in Lahore.

14. Shirkat Gah Women's Resource Centre as part of its WEMC research.

15. A separate government machinery for women was recommended by the 1976 Commission on Women, and all the preparation had been done under the government of Z. A. Bhutto, although it came into existence after Zia's coup, in 1978.

Feminist Deliberative Politics in India

KALPANA KANNABIRAN

Feminist organizing in India can, in the first instance, be traced back to the late 1970s, which witnessed the emergence of autonomous women's groups in different parts of the country. A few years after the formation of these groups, in the very early 1980s, feminists had already begun to look back at where the roots of their activism lay, drawing strength from women raising similar questions in the context of colonialism in the early part of the twentieth century (Kannabiran 2006; Kannabiran and Kannabiran 1997). Simultaneously, these groups had also begun to build bridges with feminists abroad, forging a broad-based alliance that transcended national boundaries and historical periods. Clearly, however, this effort raised a series of questions, on the one hand, in relation to the glorification of the past and, on the other, with respect to the limits of solidarity and identity of interest in an unequal world order.

The delineation of feminist struggles provided by Jacqui Alexander and Chandra Mohanty (1991) offers a useful point of departure in the second respect. They suggest that it would be more theoretically productive to think in terms of transnational feminism, rather than international feminism. This would include at least three elements: (1) a way of thinking about women in similar contexts, but different geographical spaces, across the world rather than as all women across the world; (2) an understanding of a set of unequal relationships between peoples; and (3) a consideration of the term *international* in relation to an analysis of economic, political, and ideological processes that are underwritten by the operations of race and capitalism—for instance, when we argue that antiracist, anticapitalist positions are necessary for feminist solidarity. Mohanty's work especially draws from the fact that feminism in the third world

INDIA

Human Development Index ranking: .619
Gender-Related Development Index value: .600
Gender Empowerment Measure value: not available

General

Type of government: Federal Republic
Major ethnic groups: Indo Aryan (72%); Dravidian (25%); other (3%)
Languages: Hindi, English; 16 other official languages and more than 1,000 others
Religions: Hindu (81.4%); Muslim (12.4%); Christian (2.3%); Sikh (1.9%); others (1%)
Date of independence: 1947; republic declared, 1950
Former colonial power: Britain

Demographics

Population, total (millions), 2005: 1,134.4
Annual growth rate (%), 2005–2015: 1.4
Total fertility (average number of births per woman): 3.1
Contraceptive prevalence (% of married women aged 15–49): 47
Maternal mortality ratio, adjusted (per 100,000 live births), 2000: 450

Women's Status

Date of women's suffrage: 1950
Life expectancy: M 62.3; F 65.3
Combined gross enrollment ratio for primary, secondary, and tertiary education
    (female %), 2005: 60
Gross primary enrollment ratio: 116*
Gross secondary enrollment ratio: 50
Gross tertiary enrollment ratio: 9
Literacy (% age 15 and older): M 73.4; F 47.8

Political Representation of Women

Seats in parliament (% held by women): 9
Women in government at ministerial level (% total): 3.4
Seats in lower house or single house (% held by women): 8.3
Seats in upper house or senate (% held by women); 10.7

Economics

Estimated earned income (PPP US$): M 5,194; F 1,620
Ratio of estimated female to male earned income: .31
Economic activity rate (% female): 34.0
Women in adult labor force (% total): 28 (this figure obtained at the CEDAW Statistical Database)

*Gross enrollment ratios in excess of 100% indicate that there are pupils or students outside the theoretical age groups who are enrolled in that level of education.

is shaped also by histories of colonialism and the resistance to colonialism and neocolonialism.

In relation to the first point, that is, the need to retain a sense of history without glorifying every aspect of it, movements for social reform and radical transformation, whether communist, non-Brahmin or anticaste, or movements of *adivasis* (original inhabitants or tribals), during the colonial era, contain the first articulations of the need to legislate protections for women against discrimination and more centrally against violence; it is also in these movements that one finds the complex debates—in legislative bodies, governments, and civil society—between groups differently positioned on a particular issue. These movements also make the connection for us between people's aspirations and laws, which were in the first instance devised as means to deliver the broader goals of social justice, of which "women's emancipation" was a part. Throughout this "prehistory" of constitutional rights for women, one catches glimpses of the recognition of the need for special treatment as well as the acknowledgment that women inhabited an intersectional space, as part of communities, castes, tribes, and regions, and acted from that complex location. This prehistory keeps throwing up ways in which women from different backgrounds interrogated the monolithic notion of a universal "Indian womanhood" that the courts seem to cling to well into our time.

Violence against women, from these early articulations of women's rights in India through the present, has locked women of different classes, castes, and communities into multiple intersecting axes of inequality and discrimination that spread out over a wide range—from social and economic life to political inequality—tying women of different classes together through the similarity of their experiences as women and holding them apart in almost unbridgeable ways through the differences in their experiences as members of different social classes. The conditioning and determining environment for feminist struggle, then, is marked by "violence," which straddles the lawful and unlawful, the legitimate and the "illegitimate," domination and resistance, injustice and justice, order and chaos, and takes many forms—holocaust, war, peacekeeping, on the one hand, and the range of violence of normal times, on the other—against sexual minorities, persons convicted of crime, political suspects, all persons who are not men, and down the scale of graded inequality in the caste system, to name a few.

There is, especially in structural violence, a deep foundational basis in systems of patriarchy. And because practices of violence are written on bodies, because the physical body bears the burden of the violence, as much as the mind retains a memory of it, there is an intimate, inverse connection between violence and well-being.[1] This connection also comes into play from the other end: there are legitimate and illegitimate, acceptable and unacceptable, forms of illness and infirmity. There is also the question of the ways in which the normal is constructed, especially in relation to "ability" in an able-normative society. What are the ways in which denial of recognition and legitimacy ties in with the experience of violence by groups so denied?

Looking at this entire range, therefore, violence is both objective fact and subjective experience; it is overt and physical, and subterranean, embedded in consciousness at the same time. Violence structures consciousness in multitudinous ways, depending on social location. The law treats violence in multitudinous ways, depending on who the perpetrator is, who the victim is, and what the circumstances are. Is violence an exception? What is the relationship between violence and sovereignty? And violence and democracy?

I have argued elsewhere (Kannabiran 2005) that violence against women is perhaps more appropriately described by the phrase "violence of normal times"—it extends quite literally from the womb into and through the life worlds of women within families, between families, within communities, between communities, and in relation to the state, for instance. Where groups are unequally placed in relation to each other or in relation to the state—*dalit* and adivasi communities—the women of these groups bear the consequence of that inequality in ways that are specific and distinct from the ways in which men of the same groups might be affected. To speak to the problem of violence against women is perhaps the only way of addressing the problem of discrimination against women effectively, because the systemic and systematic violence that women are subjected to is inextricably tied to the deeply entrenched practices of discrimination that guarantee impunity to perpetrators of violence against women.

What is the relationship between neglect and violence? Ted Honderich's argument (1989), that the scale of human suffering, the inequality of its spread, the persistence in the patterns of inequality, and the refusal to address it effectively make redundant the distinction between omissions and acts, is very pertinent to our consideration of this connection. Where the consequences of overt violence and persistent negligence match each other in scale and effect—number of lives lost and number of years lost in each lifetime—and enjoy the same guarantee of impunity, does this scale of neglect not amount to collective violence? These are concerns that have provided the common ground for struggles around women's rights, human rights, civil liberties, adivasi rights, dalit rights, the rights of sexual minorities, and disability rights in India.

Women's participation in public and political life has been actively obstructed despite vociferous demands for representation. This extends from legislative bodies to the executive and judiciary, locking discrimination and civic disability firmly in place. It is useful to look at the figures to get an idea of the extent of the problem (Kannabiran and Ekta 2006, 53–60; Rai 2002).[2] Immediately after the enactment of the Seventy-third and Seventy-fourth Constitutional Amendments, 800,000 women entered the political process in rural and urban areas through the *panchayats* (elected local level bodies) in 1993–1994 through a single election. In the state legislatures and Parliament, on the other hand, the percentage of elected women representatives is very low. From the records available of the past fifty years, since independence, the strength of women in the political field as reflected in state legislatures remained at an average of 3 to 5 percent of those elected. At the level of Parliament, the position of women members has varied between 5 and 8 percent. What is even more cause for concern is the sharp decline in the percentage of women who are successful in elections at the national level.[3]

Women have entered politics at the national, state, and district levels. It is useful to look at the issues elected women representatives face at these different levels and the ways in which they have addressed these issues. It is also possible then to formulate mechanisms through which these obstacles can be circumvented.

Elected women in the Indian Parliament are predominantly from educated, elite backgrounds with a history of political leadership in the family. None of the women in Parliament has been part of the movement for women's rights in the country. Once elected, there is a tendency to give women in ministerial positions "soft portfolios," and women are rarely found in leadership positions in their parties. There is a complex process through which any effective advocacy on women's issues is disabled in political spaces at the national level.

Women in local self-government, on the other hand, have had diverse experiences—all necessary for the development of political consciousness. Some women have been put up as puppet candidates, have never visited their office, and have signed or put a thumb impression where the village leader has ordered them to: "Our men come with the papers and we merely put our thumb impressions on them. We sit apart away covering our faces and feel shy saying anything . . ." (Bedi 2003). There are several who have entered this way, but have undergone training by different agencies and taken charge. Women *sarpanches* (panchayat heads) who underwent training under the *gramsat* program in Karnataka were taken to visit the state legislature—the Vidhana Soudha. Later, in meetings in their panchayats, this became the validation of their authority: "They often ended an argument, especially with men, with 'What do you know? Have you seen the Vidhana Soudha? I have!'" (Vyasulu and Vyasulu 1999).

In Haryana women sarpanches have struggled to regain grazing lands back for the village and had liquor vendors closed down. When schoolteachers have been recalcitrant, they have taken the matter up with the school principals. To address women's reproductive health needs, they have made sure that mid-wives are accessible at all times in the village—a concern that would rarely occur to a male sarpanch (R. Das 2003).

Women belonging to the Scheduled Castes and Scheduled Tribes, however, face enormous hurdles in the course of performance of work. The widespread discrimination based on caste can take overt forms—where women are physi-cally obstructed from performing their duties and assaulted if they persist—as was the case with Dubbaka Manjula in Andhra, who was stripped and paraded in the village by dominant-caste men. This discrimination can take covert forms where non-dalit members of the panchayat abstain from meetings and do not let a quorum gather, thus rendering the panchayat ineffective.

The sharp asymmetry between women leaders in local bodies, on the one hand, and women in state legislatures, on the other, points to the fact that the responsibility for the "missing women" in politics cannot be completely ac-counted for by recourse to cultural stereotypes, but rather the responsibility lies in the abject failure of the state to create enabling conditions for women to enter the political field in any meaningful way. If it were true that stereo-types impede entry, we would not have 800,000 women entering the panchayat system and urban local bodies. Feminist collectives have campaigned for women's reservation in Parliament and state legislatures, positions among fem-inists varying between whether there should be proportionate representation for women to ensure the presence of women belonging to dalit and adivasi communities or whether there should be a flat 33 percent, which might mean that women from dominant and economically powerful groups alone will get elected. Women's groups have also worked on the ground to strengthen women who have been elected to local bodies, providing them with the information and tools necessary for effective governance. The problem of violence and the threat of violence, however, continue to impede effective political participation by women, as Bhanwari's case, discussed later in this essay, demonstrates.

Feminist politics enables a fuller engagement with these questions. The Na-tional Alliance of Women engaged in detailed deliberations in every state between 2003 and 2007, on the relationship between poverty, discrimination, well-being, and violence, as part of the process of documenting the situation on the ground, contesting the position of the Indian government before the UN Committee on the Elimination of Discrimination Against Women, and wresting recognition for the Indian feminist position on a range of critical concerns (CEDAW 2007).[4]

In looking at the contemporary history of feminist politics, my attempt will be to broaden the canvas, to map the common ground as it were, in order to

FIGURE 4.1 International Women's Day demonstration, Women's Rights Federation, Mangalagiri. Andhra Pracesh, 1996. Photo from Asmita Archives.

draw in the articulations of women's entitlements and the identification of discrimination against women in different struggles. Although these struggles might not call themselves "feminist," it is my argument that the articulation of feminism takes place at multiple sites, in multitudinous ways, not in women's groups and feminist collectives alone. While the latter have undoubtedly catalyzed change and provided the theoretical tools for the delineation of women's rights, the struggles around these rights spread far beyond the space of women's collectives.

This essay looks at the diversity of feminist politics in India at different moments, mapping the methods, contexts, and specific struggles that women have engaged in. The idea is not to present "feminist victories" but to point to the significant shifts and ruptures that have been effected both in the public and in the private domains, in consciousness and institutional structures as a result of feminist politics—and also the patriarchal encrustations that remain embedded, unshaken by the torrent of feminist fervor. Most important, it attempts to map the locations of feminist politics in contemporary India.[5]

The Idea of Feminist Insurgency

Looking at the ways in which women have turned our world upside down; trying to make sense of wave upon wave of changes, questions, and struggles by women; and trying to come to terms with the ruthless censorship that has silenced generation after generation, I began to wonder whether it is apt to frame the issue of politics in terms of insurgency.[6] The idea of feminist insurgency opens up exciting possibilities for comprehending women's resistance and helps us grasp the totality, continuity, and turbulence of women's resistance.

Besides describing the past, speaking of an insurgency that is feminist conjures up exciting future possibilities of fashioning a revolution built on feminist critiques of masculinity in the revolutionary praxis that has emerged in different postrevolution societies across the world. In this last sense, however, the feminist revolution is an idea, ever in the making, a vision—a utopia. What are the praxeological foundations of this utopia?

It is productive, for a beginning, to construct a three-layered approach to revolution (of which insurgency is part). In its first sense, the notion of revolution as political upheaval carries forward the idea of crisis and a new beginning, the emergence of life through freedom. In this scheme, then, the revolution is the terrain of severance between what was and what will be— also between what was and what ought to be. The popular idea of the revolution contains the revolt as a defining moment—the uprising—that can either be one single wave or a series of waves that in small, continuous, contiguous movements wash new ideas ashore and offer new ways of being. Even as the revolution is being crafted, the second definition begins to take root— changes in consciousness, in economic relations, and in living conditions of large numbers of people being continuous, cumulative outcomes of revolutionary processes. Ranajit Guha's analysis (1983, 335–336) of insurgency and peasant revolt in early colonial India draws in for us the third element, that of a cyclicity inherent in the idea of insurgency—the uprising not any more the culmination of a linear progression toward a single goal but rather a paradigm that was rooted in the relationship of dominance and subordination characteristic of Indian society, where the inherent tradition of oppression and exploitation was as pervasive as the countertradition of defiance and revolt, which were reciprocal terms that conditioned and reproduced each other cyclically over the centuries. This approach to revolution offers a way of reflecting on the past and mapping the present while on the road to a meaningful future for women.

How does this carry forward the idea of the feminist insurgency? Women have turned our world upside down ceaselessly. And it is a constant struggle for each new generation grappling with concerns that are constantly emerging, shifting, changing, and taking new shape. It can scarcely be forgotten that difference, diversity, and pluralism provide the context for this struggle just as power, hegemony, and violence in multifarious forms are pitted against the context and undermining it in a deep-rooted antagonism.

The traditions of the heterodox sects and devotional movements like the Bhakti movement allowed women to transcend the physical constraints imposed on them by institutions of caste, marriage, and female seclusion. The pursuit of a larger devotion by definition meant they would inhabit a public space and not be subject to normal restrictions of caste or patriarchy. Recalling to memory the creative resistance to systems of oppression, and the articulation of utopian visions by dalit intellectuals and women who have a history that dates back further than the European Enlightenment, Gail Omvedt (2008) points us to a different way of thinking about the genealogy of the present.

Through the nineteenth and twentieth centuries, women in the Indian subcontinent resisted forced widowhood, unequal inheritance rights, the denial of education, forced marriage, sexual violence within and outside the family, and moralistic definitions of the private and public that disabled possibilities for building solidarity and fragmented common concerns. Tarabai Shinde, writing in fury over the death sentence (later reduced to transportation to a penal settlement outside the state), of a young widow for the murder of her infant, in 1882, strikes one of the earliest notes of revolt, a defining moment in the paradigm of feminist insurgency, if we can call it that: "God brought this amazing universe into being, and he it was also who created men and women both. So is it true that only women's bodies are home to all kinds of wicked vices? Or have men got just the same faults as we find in women? I wanted this to be shown absolutely clearly, and that's the reason I've written this small book, to defend the honour of all my sister countrywomen. I'm not looking at particular castes or families here. It's a comparison just between women and men" ([1882] 1994, 75).

It was not one but countless revolts, insurgencies, and revolutions—against husbands, fathers, families, communities, castes, and parties: Rukmabai, married in her minority, who repudiated the marriage when she attained adulthood and resisted a court order to return to her husband, courting arrest instead; Kandukuri Rajyalakshmi, who offered shelter to widows, arranged their remarriages, and assisted in childbirth when sexually abused widows arrived at her door pregnant; Duvvuri Subbamma, who turned widowhood around and used the release from conjugality to spread the word of freedom and self-rule, going to jail several times, and when she was free, traveling on foot from one village to another carrying bundles of *khadi* on her head; Chityala Ailamma, poor with no formal education, a legend in the Telangana armed struggle in the 1940s, who resisted the usurpation of her land by landlords and violence by the police and declared: "There is nothing of my husband. Nothing of my son. It is my name that has stood. Wherever I go the [party] folk come and say, 'one should be like Ailamma'"; or Sugra Humayun Mirza, a gifted poet who set up schools for girls, started an organization of Muslim women, Anjuman-e-Khawateen, and was the only non-Hindu woman in the Hindu Women's Association:

> *Who will care to visit my grave when I am gone?*
> *Only the wind will raise its dust when I am gone*
> *No one knew my worth while I was alive;*
> *No one will shed tears for me when I am gone.*
> *The regret remains that my people ignored me,*
> *But a voice will rise in protest from my grave, when I am gone.*[7]

This struggle was far from easy and often met with violent opposition from the conservatives, but they survived in their own lifetime and through their work for posterity. These women and others like them opened up a whole new world to women of their times and later, a world that they were free to inhabit on their own terms.

The articulation of feminism on the Indian subcontinent today draws on these and similar genealogies that have formed the basis of the practice of transnational and transversal feminist politics (Yuval-Davis 2006). Women's struggles to craft feminist revolutions have been marked by the fact that there is no one government, no single target, no elaborate planning or strategy, no spontaneity, no overtly violent overthrow. Yet revolutions there have been. Not war and peace, and hence no victors and vanquished, but revolutions that held the promise of life and freedom, so rare and precious for women. In Ratnamala's words:

> *My daughters shall not*
> *Grow up beautiful*
> *But they will inherit*
> *The wealth of my story*
> *Neither will they be happy*
> *For the hour of their days*
> *Shall be counted*
> *By ten times the troubles I now bear*
> *But they will not weep*
> *Nay, theirs shall be a countenance*
> *Of firm defiance.*[8]

What grew out of these various movements across the country were trenchant critiques of the established order—dalit women rising in one voice against the state's liquor policy that flooded rural poor communities with cheap liquor while divesting them of land, fair wages, and food subsidies; middle-class women taking to the streets to protest against the rise in prices of essential commodities; Muslim women forming a women's *jamaat* (collective) and deciding on cases of domestic violence; Christian women demanding, deliberating on, and securing a more equitable right to divorce; adivasi women fighting and winning struggles for effective control over land; queer women campaigning successfully for the decriminalization of homosexuality and the right to same-sex relationships; women with disabilities fighting for recognition of their specific situations and rights; women struggling to conquer the night; and so many more. There is also in this field no distinction between the archetypal private and public realms. The ways in which the sexual division of labor travels between conjugality and the home to work and struggle demonstrate the impossibility of containing women within boundaries, because the boundaries are constantly shifting back and forth with the women. But even though this is true—rather, because it is true—there is a deep disturbance, a rage at the "displacements" that seemingly unobtrusive inversions and subversions, or insurgencies by women in generation after generation, across caste, class, and community, push forward relentlessly.

What is the place of violence in the feminist revolution? What are the ways in which "justice" may be or has been imagined and realized? What are its paradoxes? How do the daily lives of individual women and the shared lives of collectivities in an era fractured by conflict and global wars of armies and capitalist production shape the idea of the feminist revolution itself?

Contexts of Feminist Organizing in Contemporary India

Historically, women's movements on the subcontinent have often emerged in response to grave violence and injustice against women—by communities, families, and the state. Although the term *feminist* came to be adopted in metropolitan India only in the late 1970s, a glance at the history of women's struggles around entitlements and life reveals the broad overlaps in the contours of struggles labeled "women's movements" and those that call themselves "feminist." Challenging the patriarchal basis of institutions and social spaces, presenting a cogent argument for why freedom is indispensable to women, and identifying and interrogating the foundations of unfreedom are the signposts of feminist movements. If women's movements in the times before feminism carry forward traditions of resistance that bear these signposts, the distinction between the terms *feminism* and *women's movements* becomes one of chronology, not necessarily of political agenda.

The articulation of women's rights in India in the mid-1970s—the second phase of feminism, in a manner of speaking—focused on questions of civil and political rights in relation to the state and, more important, within collectivities—communities, movements, families—forcing the state to resolve contending claims. The discourse of women's rights in India first focused on issues of violence: state violence in the form of custodial rape in the aftermath of the Emergency in 1975, later moving on to raise the issue of domestic violence, particularly dowry-related violence.[9] Gradually, over the decades of the 1980s and 1990s, Indian feminist writing presented a more nuanced understanding of violence in the context of religious fundamentalism and identity politics, economic liberalization, and caste violence and displacement, especially of adivasi communities.

This process interlocked with human rights discourses that too began to focus increasingly on violence against women as a human rights issue, culminating in, but not stopping with, the "Women's Rights as Human Rights" formulation in Vienna in 1993 and the appointment of the UN special rapporteur on violence against women. By 1995 the movement for "women's rights as human rights" had forced public attention worldwide on the question of women's rights against violence both in the context of debates in the World Conference on Human Rights in Vienna in 1993 and in Beijing at the Fourth World Conference on Women in 1995. Several feminist groups in the early nineties began to use international conventions as a rallying point for mobilization on the ground—popularizing the Beijing Platform for Action and preparing alternative reports for CEDAW, for instance. These conventions also became the medium through which women's collectives negotiated firmer commitments and concrete measures from the state and policy-making bodies like the Planning Commission. This two-way translation of international conventions has drawn in women's groups from across the country and raised several concerns with respect to the blunting of the radical edge of feminist politics, an ongoing debate. Yet the positive policy and judicial implications of this strategy must enter any account of contemporary feminist politics in India.

This section will examine a few specific locations of feminist politics since the late 1970s and will attempt to draw the connections between social and political movements and feminist articulation.[10] The issues discussed in this section broadly represent core Indian feminist concerns since the 1970s. Although the way in which they are clustered in this discussion might not mirror the chronology or specific trajectory of the debates, the attempt is to capture the richness of the debates across time and the boundaries of struggles.

The Meanings of Custody

Custodial violence was the bridge between the women's movement, the civil liberties movement, and legal scholarship in India in the late 1970s—custodial rape the critical issue—first with Mathura in Maharashtra[11] and soon thereafter with Rameeza Bee in Andhra. These two cases illustrate the early convergence between women's rights and human rights.[12] At the time that Rameeza was assaulted, the civil liberties movement was at its peak in Andhra Pradesh. The Tarkunde Committee had just submitted its findings on encounter killings of Naxalites during the Emergency. A group of women who had been in jail or underground during the Emergency had already raised questions related to women's rights within their parties and testified about police excesses (Kannabiran and Kannabiran 1997). These women formed a critical part of the first feminist groups in the state, and perhaps the country.

Very soon thereafter, it became clear to feminists that for women, "custody" has many faces.[13] Case law around writ jurisdiction, especially habeas corpus, demonstrates the convergence between domestic violence and custodial violence, where the threat of detention and custodial violence marks the alliance between policing practices of the family and the state and raises issues of citizenship in the domestic sphere (P. Baxi, Rai, and Ali 2006). It has been argued that the writ of habeas corpus, although discussed widely in relation to custodial violence and state repression in human rights discourse, has not received adequate attention in terms of its routine use in courts in cases of "choice marriages" (as opposed to arranged marriages). Adult women have used it to challenge their own detention in state facilities, parents have used it to "recover" adult daughters who have married by choice, husbands of newly married girls have used it to claim them from their natal families that refuse to recognize the marriage, and couples seek protection against possible arrest and detention on charges of abduction or rape. Writ jurisdiction, Pratiksha Baxi observes, "comes to detail contestation over the legality of the detention of a woman who is described by her family as a subject who has been *abducted* for the purpose of illicit sex or forcible marriage, and by the affinal family as a *consenting* subject" (2006, 62).

Section 376 of the Indian Penal Code sets out one field of custody—the public face of custody, in a manner of speaking, that Rameeza Bee and Mathura illustrate. However, in the course of their work over the past three decades, women's groups have had to contend not merely with this public face of custody but also with the multiple axes along which women are subjugated through interacting regulatory techniques that travel back and forth between state and community—between courts and panchayats, between statutory village panchayats and caste panchayats—most evident in the case of marriages by choice (P. Baxi, Rai, and Ali 2006; see also Chowdhry 2007).[14] Given the complexity of the context, the impact of feminist mobilizing has been uneven. Although women's groups in the country have been able to address questions of domestic violence and dowry effectively, the impact of feminist mobilizing on marriage by choice has been weak, with "honour crimes" and forced marriage continuing to hold especially young women in captivity in their families.[15]

The Dilemma of Choice

A major issue foregrounded by the women's movement that resonates through marriage reproductive rights and sexual orientation is the complex issue of choice. Traditionally, this issue has been posed in feminist discourse, in the United States, for instance, in terms of its relevance to reproductive choice, specifically abortion rights and the right to procreative autonomy. This limited application of "choice" in the Indian context does not enable an understanding of the multiple articulations of the right to choice by women on the subcontinent, beginning with Rukmabai's historic repudiation on attainment of majority of a marriage contracted when she was a child, risking arrest by the British government for noncompliance with a court order that required her to return to her husband (see Chakravarti 1989, 74). At the core of the problem of choice is the question of culture and the collective conscience that does not militate against violent misogyny and social exclusion in our societies.

If marriage by choice presents a major obstruction to women's exercise of the right to personal liberty, the problems around the exercise of the right to reproductive choice highlights for women's groups across the country the dilemma of criminalizing a systemic practice while recognizing the vulnerability of the "agents."[16] How is female infanticide (and now sex-selective abortions of female fetuses) related to other practices classified as "social evils"?

In a context where "son preference" and the abhorrence of female children are deeply entrenched, practices of eliminating girls have been described as gender cleansing, and women, particularly female children, have been described as the "endangered sex" (Harriss-White 1999). The situation that women find themselves in, however, is far from easy. Proactive responses from the state can result in holding mothers across generations complicit, while fathers and sons are liberated from the circle of complicit—the patriarchal guarantee of impunity that simultaneously ties women in a double bind. The mother who bears daughters risks death or desertion at the hands of her affinal family, and the mother who ensures the birth of sons, which is the one precondition for her enjoyment of liberty in the home, faces the possibility of the loss of liberty at the hands of the state. Stepped-up population-control programs likewise inevitably pose grave survival risks to girls. The central question that remains somewhat unresolved in debates on reproductive choice is how one reconciles an opposition to "sex-selective abortion" with the absolute right to choice. Feminist disability rights activist Anita Ghai (2008, 405), currently president of the Indian Association for Women's Studies, argues that abortion is a central issue for both the disability movement and feminism—with both movements holding contradictory standpoints. Any prenatal screening or selective abortion, from a disability-rights standpoint, is locked in with strategies of eugenics—disability being viewed as deficit rather than as a measure of human diversity. The context in which the choice on abortion is made, according to her, is critical to an understanding of the politics of abortion.

While the Prenatal Diagnostic Testing Act is seen as a solution to this problem, the magnitude of the problem urges a reorientation to the problem itself. Juxtaposed to this is the need to make a clear distinction between the woman's right to abortion and the right of the female fetus against abortion. This question is further complicated by the fact that there is no clear gender line between those who demand "female feticide services" and those who do not. It is women—often older women—in the family who make the most vociferous demands, and it is predominantly women in the medical profession who provide the services. The standpoint of most doctors on this issue echoes the argument of procreative autonomy that has been developed in U.S. courts (Dworkin 1996, 72–116). This right is one that developed with respect to the right to contraception and was extended to argue that whether or when to have a child was part of the right to privacy and that mothers especially had a right to procreative autonomy. The relevance of the principle of procreative autonomy (and more generally the right to privacy) to the Indian context is twofold to begin with. First, with respect to coercive family planning or population-control programs of the state, this right includes the right to refuse family planning without detriment to the entitlement to state welfare; it also includes the right to free, full, and informed consent with respect to the use of contraceptives. There is, in this sense, an immediate link between the right to procreative autonomy and the right to life and livelihood of the mother with respect to the conditions for receipt of welfare or participation in government (loans or limiting the right to run for political office to those with two children or less, for instance) and with respect to the dumping of hazardous contraceptives on masses of poor women, a direct human rights injury.

On a second level the relevance is negative. While procreative autonomy must certainly include the right to abortion, this right must be mediated by the state's commitment to women's right against discrimination. The selective abortion of female fetuses, in this context, cannot be interpreted as part of the right to procreative autonomy, since it is a practice of discrimination. Yet this is not an issue that is simple and subject to a linear interpretation. The very use of the term *feticide* implies the acceptance of fetal rights and of the status of the fetus as a person, veering dangerously close to the position of antiabortionists who raise the issue of fetal rights as a limitation on the right to procreative autonomy. The problem in tackling the issue of female feticide arises precisely on this score. Doctors and medical professionals tend to read this demand as a matter related to procreative autonomy and encourage that autonomy in female-feticide service seekers. Further, if fetal rights are granted to female fetuses, they must also be granted to other classes that are silently exterminated as well. The specific case of disability may be raised here. It is accepted practice, medically, legally, and socially, to demand and provide abortions if fetal abnormalities are detected. The effect is the same and pushes us dangerously close to the eugenic standpoint. The rights of persons with disability must include the right to be born. The issue of abortion forces a synthesis of jurisprudential reasoning with a political reading of rights as they have been articulated in movements. Abortion, as a decision of whether or not to have *a* child, is a matter of procreative autonomy for the mother. Sex-selective abortion (and disability-selective abortion) and the more recently discovered practice of sex-selective conception, however, invoke the right to life of women (and persons with disabilities) as a class, which includes the right to be born.

By this argument sex-selective abortions must be seen as part of the practice of killing female children. Sex-selective abortions alone already match, even surpass, the worst episodes of crimes against humanity in scale. There are clear correlations between the proliferation of sex-determination tests, increase in sex-selective abortions (female feticide), and the decline in sex ratio, with urban areas showing a sharper drop in the sex ratio than rural areas. And not only do the numbers increase each year, but techniques for eliminating the birth of girl children proliferate. The most recent method of exterminating girls that is on offer is sex-selective conception. Nussbaum provides a very useful and nuanced reading of the intersection of privacy jurisprudence with questions of culture, difference, equality, and rights, arguing among other things that there must be "a reliance on equality and equal protection where the relevant issue involves systematic hierarchy and subordination" (2004, 273).

Choice in matters of contraception and sexual relationship is overwritten by sexual violence and fear for women affected by HIV/AIDS in high-prevalence settings, affecting significantly their right to negotiate condom use or choosing to leave risky relationships. As the Positive Women's Network says, "Being diagnosed with HIV/AIDS rewrites women's lives. Fear of rejection, stigma, discrimination and harassment prevents them from disclosing their status (*Second and Third Alternative Report* 2006, 89).

The question of choice is also critical to the articulation of the right to sexual orientation. Queer activists have demonstrated through painstaking research the ways in which heteronormativity is established through the violent exclusion of all queer people, violence being used along different dimensions—interpersonal, intrapersonal, and collective. Queer women especially, more vulnerable in comparison to queer men, face physical and verbal abuse, battery, house arrest, coercion into heterosexual marriage, and expulsion from the family home. There has also been an increasing trend toward suicide pacts among queer couples unable to cope with violently hostile environments and the absence of legal protection (Fernandez and Gomathy 2005).

An early resolution by a group of lesbian women at the National Conference on Women's Movements in India in 1994 underscores the importance of choice, freedom, and sexuality: "Women are not given a real choice to explore and choose their own sexuality. We believe that every woman should have individual freedom to explore and choose her sexuality." This resolution was met with hostility and "hate-filled, violent opposition by a vocal minority" that asserted that lesbianism was "'unnatural,' 'a psychological disorder' and something that 'needed explanation'" ("Report on Lesbian Meeting" 2007, 299). Eleven years later, the National Conference on Women's Studies organized by the Indian Association for Women's Studies in Goa in 2005 adopted a unanimous resolution demanding the repeal of Section 377 of the Indian Penal Code that criminalizes homosexuality, delineating for the first time an organizational standpoint on diversity at the national level that moved beyond caste, class, and community:

> We in the women's movement have long recognized that constructions of what is "natural" and "normal" have been used to define and control us as women. We also recognize that rigid binaries of "man" and "woman," notions of what constitutes a "normal" body and notions of what constitutes "acceptable" sexual

FIGURE 4.2 Women at a human rights *jatama* (fair), Vikarabad. Andhra Pracesh, 1998. Photo from Asmita Archives.

behaviour limit possibilities for all of us. They also stigmatise and deny citizenship rights to individuals and communities perceived to deviate from the "normal." These include, for example, people with disabilities, those who are same-sex desiring, lesbian and bisexual women, transgender people, hijras and sex workers. ("Resolution on Section 377" 2007, 316)

While able-bodied women are disabled through violence and sexual assault, a woman with a disability is, to use Andalamma's words, "like a kite, going whichever way the wind blows it," veering between the mercy and goodwill of parents, brothers, sisters, husband, and in-laws, on the one hand, and complete destitution, on the other.[17] Yet we know from several such testimonies that it is not physical impairment that is the problem. Anita Ghai argues that in order to understand the specific situation of disabled women, feminism must "deal with the twofold but separate oppressions of being a woman in a sexist society and being disabled in an able-normative society" (2008, 402). On another track, if the creation of barrier-free access and communication in multiple nonverbal languages is a precondition for the exercise of personal liberty in its fullest sense for differently abled people, how does the refusal to create barrier-free environments as a norm in the entire public domain (to begin with) inform our understanding of liberty and choice? In a cultural environment that is structured around the violent policing of women, what are the specific implications of this general denial of liberty for differently abled women?

The Persistent Problem of Sexual Assault

The current debates on sexual assault have a history that dates back to the Emergency of 1975. While the problem to begin with was in the way in which the offense of rape was constructed in the Penal Code, the more difficult problem had to do with the place of rape and the woman's sexualized body in the social imagination of India. The early experiences of Mathura (a working-class adivasi girl) and Rameeza Bee (a working-class Muslim girl) marked the beginnings of civil liberty debates on criminal law, particularly the issue of custodial violence and custodial rape. These two cases demonstrate the ways in which sexual integrity is tied even within domains of criminal justice to the hierarchies of community in a plural society.[18] The trapping of women's bodies in discourses of honor, community, and "Indian Womanhood" is a very complex reality that must be unpacked in order to restore to women across class, caste, community, and region a sense of integrity and justice.

The early history of Indian feminist campaigns on reform in rape laws is well documented. There have been significant shifts inaugurated in the second phase of feminist discourse on sexual assault, which figures in multiple sites, not just within women's groups: for instance, the shift from looking at rape within a framework of "women's rights" to looking at it as a "human rights" issue, the broadening of the category of sexual assault to child sexual abuse and homosexual assault as well, the shift in the understanding of assault away from the restrictive terms of penile penetration, and the reflection on the meaning of sexual assault in times of collective violence.

Clearly, debates around international conventions had a perceptible impact on jurisprudence of sexual violence in India, particularly in the Supreme Court.[19] Women's groups in Delhi approached the Supreme Court of India in 1997 for directions concerning the definition of the expression "sexual intercourse" as contained in Section 375 of the Indian Penal Code.[20] The key elements of the petition provided by the women's groups may be summarized as follows: child sexual abuse, largely neglected by law, was sought to be brought within the definition of sexual assault; penetration, hitherto confined to penile-vaginal penetration, resulting in acquittal or mitigation of sentences to attempted rape, it was argued, must be redefined to mean penetration whether anal, with objects, or any other method to encompass the range of assaults women and children were subjected to; and women's consent should be defined to mean "unequivocal voluntary agreement." The entire effort aimed at bringing boys under the age of sixteen and women of all ages within the ambit of a comprehensive law on sexual assault. Further, two sections in the Evidence Act (146 and 155) that refer to past sexual history were recommended to be deleted.

It may be recalled that these sections first came into question in the cases of Mathura and of Rameeza Bee, where past sexual history was used, not to disprove the assault but to exonerate the accused. These provisions in the law, therefore, were first problematized by feminist groups and were subjected to a larger critique of the patriarchal basis of criminal law, especially that dealing with sexual assault on women—whether "outraging modesty" or rape. The accusation of rape hitherto relied heavily on medical and forensic reports, and it was physically impossible for assaulted women and children to ensure medical examination in the stipulated time. The Law Commission, recognizing the difficulties arising from this requirement, recommended that the "absence of a medical report in the case of a sexual assault shall not be a factor against the complainant/person assaulted." While providing additional safeguards against further trauma in the case of children who have been subjected to abuse, the recommendations urge that all officers in every part of the criminal justice system dealing with cases of sexual assault must be trained and sensitized in dealing with these issues.

The definition of rape, the Law Commission recommended, should be replaced by a definition of sexual assault, which would mean penetration by any part of the body or by an object into either the vagina, anus, or urethra of a person or performing oral sex against the other person's will, without consent, with consent obtained through coercive means, with consent through impersonation or deceit, when the person is not in a frame of mind to give informed consent, and when the consenting person is below the age of sixteen. The explanation to the definitional section states that "penetration to any extent is penetration for the purposes of this section," removing the rupture of the hymen as the critical marker of rape or sexual assault. In an attempt to introduce protection against child sexual abuse, a new section, 376E, was sought to be introduced, which spoke of touching the body of another person with sexual intent or inviting the other person to do the same, without that person's express consent, bringing into the ambit of the definition persons who are in the position of trust or authority toward a young person.

After decades of finding that patriarchal predispositions and biases hindered a basic understanding of women's experience of sexual assault, with the norm being defined by the male experience, groups across the country found their work adversely impacted by the lack of judicial and other officers who have an understanding of and empathy for women's experience of violence and discrimination under patriarchy. Within the judiciary, even long after Mathura, while judges did say that a greater number of women in the judiciary would make a difference in the judicial view of women's experience, especially of sexual assault, representation continues to be a silent issue with the judiciary, particularly at the High Courts and Supreme Court. As one judge wondered, notwithstanding the paucity of women judges, perhaps women judges trying cases of sexual assault on women would put the survivor at greater ease "without allowing the truth to be sacrificed."[21] Yet even the Law Commission report only speaks of greater sensitivity and understanding, not of greater representation.

In the same year, the Supreme Court delivered the *Vishakha* judgment in a petition filed by women's groups in Rajasthan. The term *hostile environment* was first used here in the context of sexual harassment in the workplace,[22] more specifically in relation to the sexual assault on Bhanwari Devi, a dalit woman working on a government program in Rajasthan. Drawing as it does on more than three decades of feminist campaigns across the country, the idea of "hostile environments" has very far-reaching possibilities in articulating the vulnerability of women to violence and the entrenchment of cultures of impunity. This hostility is, of course, aggravated in the case of women who belong to marginalized groups and communities. The relevance of this idea does not stop here. "Hostile environment," far from describing merely the situation of women in the workplace, can equally effectively be used to describe the multiple domains where marginality and dispossession are produced and consolidated through the interlocking of discrimination and violence.

The Prostitution Question

The debates on prostitution in India and the problems with the application of criminal law began in the late nineteenth century with the use of Sections 372 and 373 of the Indian Penal Code, which sought to imprison women for procuring minor girls for prostitution using the ceremony of adoption and dedication. The practice at the center of these debates was the dedication of *devadasis* to temple service. We can trace the trajectory of contemporary debates on prostitution in India to earlier debates in colonial courts and outside on the use of criminal law, property law, and citizenship rights.

The question of prostitution, when it came up for debate in the context of social reform and devadasi abolition in colonial India, was already connected to Josephine Butler's campaign around the Contagious Diseases Act and to the

Social Purity Movement. Indian reformers, proabolitionists and antiabolitionists, set forth complex arguments on the place of prostitution in an emergent social order, especially on whether it was coeval with progress and modernity and whether it was consistent with the goals of nationalism and freedom. The question of rights to citizenship and civil rights came more sharply into focus in the context of the freedom struggle (see Ramamirthammal 2003). Consequent on participation in the struggle, questions arose about the extent of segregation that was necessary in order to ensure that "respectable" people would not be sullied by contact. Could children of prostitutes be together in the same schools with children from "respectable" families?[23] Should prostitutes be seated separately in meetings that demanded freedom from colonial rule? If they courted arrest, could they lay legitimate claim to the privileges of political prisoners, or were they to be treated as prostitutes?[24] Later still in the mid-twentieth century, women in the Telangana Armed Struggle were campaigning against the devadasi system as a form of bondage and feudal servitude that was sexually exploitative of dalit women (Sanghatana 1989). The multiple resonances of the debates on prostitution are echoed in the recent debates in 2005 around the banning of dance bars in Mumbai, which have drawn women from communities of traditional entertainers and performers—like the Bhedia, Chari, Bhatu, Rajnat, Dhanawat, and Gandharva ("Women's Groups Oppose Ban" 2005).

Clearly, the question of prostitution is not one that can be looked at in isolation in one country or region alone. Especially today, the connections between prostitution and international trafficking in women and children are central to human rights debates and activism (Jeffreys 2002). The World Charter for Prostitutes' Rights speaks of decriminalization, the granting of full citizenship rights, and recognition, humane conditions of work, freedom of association and the right to access health care and services.[25] There has been considerable work in India on various aspects of the prostitution debate that have examined decriminalization, partial decriminalization, sex work, legalization, trafficking, and rights of women in prostitution, to name a few.[26] Cases that have forced scrutiny of custodial facilities for women, especially in the matter of protective homes for women and girls under the Suppression of Immoral Traffic in Women and Girls Act of 1956, point to chronic sickness, mental illness, communicable diseases, and inhuman conditions in these homes as well as the complete absence of other livelihood options for women and girls taken into custody, all manifestations of the recriminalization and revictimization of women in prostitution by the state.[27] Prajwala, a women's group in Andhra Pradesh, has filed a public-interest litigation in the

Supreme Court of India seeking victim-protection protocols that will ensure that women are not retrafficked.[28]

The debates on prostitution in India range from seeing it as sex work—another form of labor—to a systemic victimization of women (and children) that must be eliminated, by stages if necessary. Across these widely divergent positions, however, there is unanimity about the need to protect women in prostitution from a repressive state that uses a range of laws—not just the Immoral Traffic Prevention Act—bolstered by raw police arbitrariness and custodial abuse in order to subjugate these women.

Globalization-Fundamentalism-Conflict

A study by the North East Network, a feminist collective that has a presence in the entire North East region, discusses several cases between 1966 and 2004 from Manipur, Nagaland, Mizoram, and Assam, arguing that the trauma of assault in each of these cases is aggravated by the taboo on disclosure in communities, tied as rape is to ideologies of honor and shame; apathetic governments that guarantee impunity to perpetrators of sexual assault; and skewed peace processes, like the Mizoram Peace Accord, that contain no special provisions for women survivors of conflict. While most cases have gone completely unacknowledged by the government, a few cases of gruesome assault have been difficult to ignore. However, in these cases, where compensation has followed acknowledgment, the harm has been far beyond redress or remedy.

The scale and gravity of the assault on Kashmiri women, women of northeastern India over the past two decades, Muslim women in Gujarat in 2002, and adivasi women of Vakapalli in Andhra Pradesh in 2007 can be understood only within the larger framework of collective violence that has included the disappearance and mass killings of men of these communities and the collective sexual assault on women. In the case of the northeastern states and Kashmir, the primary distinction that has been drawn in the context of the political situation in these regions is between force (legitimate) and violence (illegitimate) (ibid.). While this is a distinction states and governments make all too easily, as Charles Tilly (2003) points out, the distinction itself is fraught with insurmountable obstacles. What is the precise boundary between the two?

With respect to Kashmir, in the context of increased disappearances, rape, and abduction and a heightened presence of the army, Zamrooda Khanday speaks of the "terror of the night" that curtails women's mobility and has resulted in a sharp rise in stress-related morbidity among Kashmiri women

(Khanday 2005). In Gujarat, the targeted attack on Muslim women by Hindu men, supported by Hindu women, has been documented by several human rights missions that visited survivors in the aftermath of the carnage in Gujarat in February and March 2002. Syeda Hameed reports that testimonies of the aggravated sexual assault on Muslim women in February and March 2002 ranged from rape and gang rape to insertion of objects into the body and stripping, followed in a majority of cases by gruesome murder. Several witnesses from Baroda reported to the International Initiative on Justice that the police often hit the stomachs of pregnant Muslim women in "combing operations" (house-to-house searches for Muslims) while shouting, "Kill them before they are born!" (International Initiative for Justice 2003, 2). The violence was preplanned, organized, and targeted, and sexual violence was part of the strategy. The scale of harm put the experience within the frameworks of genocide and political pogroms—it was not merely another form of criminal violence (Upendra Baxi makes this distinction in 2005, 335). Public and mass acts of sexual violence and gender-based crimes such as cutting of breasts and uteruses, forced nudity, stripping and parading women naked, forcible pregnancy, exhibiting sexual organs in the presence of women, and mutilation of women's genital organs are no longer adequately expressed through the definition of rape in the Indian Penal Code, in these contexts. In Tanika Sarkar's words: "The pattern of cruelty suggests three things. One, the woman's body was a site of almost inexhaustible violence, with infinitely plural and innovative forms of torture. Second, their sexual and reproductive organs were attacked with a special savagery. Third, their children, born and unborn, shared the attacks and were killed before their eyes" (2002, 2875).

The escalation of conflict and collective sexual violence against women of targeted communities and regions has forced women's collectives across the country to examine the underlying causes and grave implications of this violence for women within communities, between communities, and between women and the state. The effects of globalization are disastrous, especially for poor and underprivileged peoples and nations across the world. It is by now clearly established that globalization creates economic volatility, instability, and sharp disparities; that it forces a decline of social security; that it increases the vulnerability of migrant labor through the entrenchment of unfair contracts even while expanding the scope and possibilities of migration and enhancing the mobility of labor; and that it has eroded all forms of mobilization around labor rights across the world and, most important, has resulted directly in the exacerbation of ethnic conflict and practices of social exclusion. While the state "recedes" in the economic realm, it becomes increasingly authoritarian, systematically negating all democratic processes and entrenching repression as the only method of governance, again a fact that severely undermines the position of those already at a disadvantage.

The globalization of culture is part of this process and cannot be seen as separate from it. The imperative for cultural globalization is hegemonic and fundamentalist, and the effects of that hegemony and fundamentalism (or religious nationalism) lie strewn before us: in the cultural realm by conflating nationalism with religion; in the political realm by defining only one form of religious nationalism as intrinsically patriotic and all else as terrorist—and then moving on to use adherence to a religion interchangeably with propagating the politics of religious nationalism and fundamentalism; and in the politicocultural realm by making religious membership the basis for citizenship claims ("India is for Hindus, Muslims go back to Pakistan" was a slogan on many walls in Gujarat). This hegemonic fundamentalist culture is strengthened by global capital, by the proliferation of this politics across national boundaries, and by the strengthening of diasporas along fundamentalist religious and ethnic lines, providing economic support to the politics of hate in the countries of origin.

Women's vulnerability is embedded within larger arenas of culture as ideology and practice that shape the ways in which communities act on women prior to, during, and after conflict. Questions of culture in turn are tied to the larger politico-economic forces of globalization and neoliberalization that condition and select specific articulations of "tradition," tying wars of imperialism to wars of faith, so that it is no longer possible to distinguish between the two. Within this larger context, culture makes women's lives intelligible within patriarchal moorings, seeking to entrench them further in times of disturbance. The more one looks at women's engagement with fundamentalism, therefore, the more necessary it becomes to look at ideas and ideologies of culture and belonging that undergird these responses.

The assertion of dominance of those engaged in fundamentalist mobilizations is often offset by increasing conflict and violence in the home—virtually the only space where the men in these groups are certain of their authority and control. This could, of course, be extended to argue that fundamentalism, militarization, and militancy interlock in situations of conflict and rely on the use of the weapons of war, which are essentially also symbols of masculinity and domination. For women in fundamentalist movements—and women's agency is a critical question that we need to contend with—the test is inevitably about how well they are able to master masculinist discourses and strategies and how well they are able to reconcile their "femininity" with aggression. For those who nurture men in combat, part of that nurturance is complete acquiescence and submergence under the larger goals of combat, personal liberty in the home being but a small casualty—the chaste, compliant wife and the selfless devoted mother being the ideal supporters of men out at wars of "faith." To the extent that fundamentalist mobilizations perpetuate and rationalize inequality and discrimination, they are antithetical to feminist politics.

In addressing these issues, women's groups have had to move beyond the boundaries of "civil and political rights" to straddle the "private," "nonstate" spaces of communities and movements and the public space of engagement with state actors. While this effort inevitably carries with it the risk of alienation from both sides, such critical engagement often being read in terms of legitimacy, complicity, and co-optation, groups that have engaged in deliberation, especially in Gujarat, Kashmir, the North East, and Andhra, continue to interrogate the foundations of politics and solidarity.[29]

Well-Being in Violent Environments

From looking at instances of overt "gender-based" violence, feminist organizing has moved to asking questions that pry open the different intersections between sectoral movements. As a result, feminist politics is no longer separate and discrete but has restructured the political agendas of diverse struggles.

Development projects across the country (Sardar Sarovar, Nandigram, Singur, and Polavaram, to name a few) have paid scant attention to the needs of people from entirely displaced villages—inevitably dalit and adivasi communities. Coal mining, the construction of dams, the building of wildlife sanctuaries, industries, and now special economic zones have posed the biggest threat to survival and livelihood, especially of indigenous adivasi and dalit communities. Displacement has meant not merely the loss of house or homestead but land and natural resources that formed the basis of the economic survival of these communities as well. It has also meant a more deep-rooted dispossession in terms of the loss of community assets—schools and local institutions and infrastructure around which these communities have built their lives. The quantification of relief and rehabilitation always weighs the benefit in favor of the state or the multinational corporation (or both) that is the prime mover. The process of displacement is often traumatic, with entire communities being asked to leave their villages in the middle of the monsoon or asked to demolish their homes themselves. The practice of uprooting people and tearing them apart from their contexts is in itself a process fraught with force and violence. In feminist revolutionary poet Ratnamala's words:

The roots of the tree go far below the earth. It can't just be plucked out from one place and put into another. There is an environment, a climate, and the quality of the earth itself that is specific to every region. People similarly built their lives around the conditions that are specific to a particular region, and in relation to their environment. When they uproot themselves from these surroundings and resettle somewhere else . . . village communities are flung apart. . . . As a result of this women lose their entire communities of support—communities that they depend on in times of crisis, and in times of celebration. (2008, n.p.)

Further, the policy, as displaced women in the Narmada Bachao Andolan argue, is biased against women, because single women are not seen as independent entities, while single men are. This difference is especially evident in the case of widowed and divorced women, who were seen as part of the extended family, while widowed or single adult men were treated on par with families ("M.P. Government" 2004).

Even in instances where there is a land-based rehabilitation policy, as with the Sardar Sarovar Project, there is a disbursement of cash compensation, which has undermined family survival and affected women's position adversely. The cash, in itself grossly inadequate, is given to men, who, unable to purchase land with it, buy motorcycles or liquor instead. Therefore, in cases where displacement has already taken place, it is in women's interest to receive irrigated land with a minimum of two hectares per family, as that is the minimum that would be required to sustain the family.

Underscoring the interconnections between different fields of violence that congeal in contexts of displacement, Ratnamala echoes Minow's view when she argues that even overt manifestations of family violence are triggered and exacerbated by forced displacement and the loss of livelihoods. In these times of loss and crisis, placing money in the hands of men destroys entire communities: "When there is land, there is work around cultivation, and there is a mutual interdependence both at the family and community level leading to a certain degree of stability in these communities. The moment money enters the picture the instability that typifies money begins to typify people's behavior as well. . . . Women bear the brunt of the violence that results from this anarchy" (2008, n.p.).

If displacement foregrounds one set of crises faced by agricultural communities, mass suicides by farmers push another set of crises to the fore. Andhra Pradesh and Maharashtra have seen a spate of suicides by farmers in the past few years. By December 2004, 644 farmers from different castes had committed suicide in the Vidharbha, Marathwada, and Khandesh regions. A majority of the farmers who died in Maharashtra were married and left families behind to cope with the debt (*Causes of Farmer Suicides* 2005). The fact of having to care for families, pay off debts, and deal with moneylenders makes women survivors extremely vulnerable to exploitation and assault. The shouldering of the entire responsibility of family, where men have migrated out in search of work or have ended their lives, coupled with very scarce survival and livelihood options, has a negative impact on women's physical and mental health as well (R. K. Das and Das 2005).

Women figure in another important way. Among the thousands of farmers who have taken their lives in the state of Andhra Pradesh, women farmers figure in large numbers. Their figures do not enter the official accounting because in the official reckoning, a farmer is a landed male with a title to land and women do not fit this description. There are women who have taken charge of entire families after the distress migration of adult men in the family to cities. There are others who are the heads of households despite the presence of adult men. The reason for the suicides by these women is the same: mounting debts.

In a single year, from August 2001 to August 2002, there were 311 women's suicides in just Anantapur district alone. And these were only the recorded ones. There must have been a lot more that went unreported. Close to 80 percent of these 311 were from villages. And most of the women were from a farming background (Sainath 2002).

Different parts of the country have witnessed the spiraling of starvation deaths over the past five years, which is particularly acute in rural and forest areas. Mahabubnagar district in Andhra Pradesh, Kashipur in Orissa, and Wyanad in Kerala are but a few instances. The reasons for chronic malnutrition, hunger, and starvation are closely tied to the breakdown of traditional livelihoods because of trade liberalization policies, landlessness, the decline in real agricultural wages, and the curtailment of adivasi communities' access to forests (Orissa 2002). Caught in the trap of debt bondage, surveys have found that in the best situations, families "rotate" hunger, with one person going hungry each day. Children drop out of school in order to find work that will feed them. The pressure on women in rural households becomes more acute in this situation: "The time and energy they spend in fetching water, firewood and fodder shoots up. But their food intake goes down. The women eat last, after feeding the rest of the family. They then have to worry about feeding the livestock. That mix of rising exertion and falling nutrition will devastate many" (Sainath 2002, n.p.).

The third National Family Health Survey conducted in 2005–2006 in all twenty-nine states shows that the percentage of children in the age group six to thirty-five months who are anemic is as high as 80 percent or more in Chhattisgarh, Gujarat, and Punjab. It is only slightly lower—around 72–74 percent—in Orissa and Maharashtra. For adults, while anemia is high between both sexes, it is very high among women, with the prevalence of anemia among women more than double that among men in all states (Ghosh 2006a). A close look at statistics reveals a correlation between poverty and poor access to basic health care, with mortality and morbidity rates being far higher for dalit and adivasi people than for other sections.

Where livelihood choices are completely undermined in rural areas, the exacerbation of poverty and the total absence of reasonable health care increase vulnerability of communities to illness and premature death. This has been a concern with community health collectives in different parts of the country, which have persistently voiced the need to inflect public health policy with feminist consciousness (Qadeer 1998).

Issues of reproductive health are especially critical to an understanding of women's well-being in violent contexts. As a result of the gas disaster in Bhopal, the Sambhavna Clinic found high rates of gynecological problems such as leucorrhea (white discharge from vagina), menstrual irregularities, amenorrhea, and sterility. Sambhavna records also indicate that in some neighborhoods near the Union Carbide factory, the average age of menarche is 13.75, more than a year later than the national average for India. Maternal mortality and morbidity for India as a whole are unacceptably high, with 130,000 women dying each year due to preventable causes related to maternal health, or one woman dying every five minutes (*Second and Third Alternative Report* 2006, chap. 8). Offsetting this is the fact that the market for womb space (in the form of surrogate motherhood or "reproductive tourism") has emerged as the new capitalistic enterprise that is recommended to poor states, and the Indian Council for Medical Research estimates that it could earn $6 billion in a few years (Ghosh 2006b).

Women's alienation from informed reproductive choice has far-reaching consequences on their well-being and health. Research on contraception lacks transparency and accountability, and women's reproductive rights are compromised by the lack of follow-up and informed consent. Saheli attributes this to biases in scientific and technological research and the absence of women in policy making (Bal, Subramanian, and Murthy n.d.). One recent study has found that while even the poorest communities have internalized the ideologies of family planning propagated by the state, this did not lead to informed and planned reproductive choice but led instead to the use of abortions and terminal contraceptive methods that impacted adversely on mental health (R. K. Das and Das 2005).

FIGURE 4.3 Anti-liquor meeting organized by the National Alliance of Women, Hyderabad, 1996.

There is an immediate relationship between the increasing ill health of India's impoverished and the increase in superstitions and dependence on traditional healers and practitioners of witchcraft. The collapse of the public health system and inaccessibility of private health care have increased the incidence of diseases, unnatural deaths (e.g. death due to cholera, smallpox, drowning, lightning strikes), and ill health. Women's groups in Chhattisgarh have found that the impoverishment of communities has simultaneously led to the destruction of domestic animals and crops (*Second and Third Alternative Report* 2006, chap. 8). Witchcraft accusations and witch hunting—where women, primarily, are targets—then become the only tools available to communities, in remote areas especially, to make sense of their life worlds.

The Possibilities of Feminist Deliberative Politics: Bhanwari's Struggle

In this section I attempt to map the trajectory of feminist politics and its possibilities by examining the work and struggle of Bhanwari Devi, a working-class dalit woman, which have ushered in far-reaching transformations in judicial reasoning on violence against women.[30] At the local level and for feminist struggles generally, looking at this case serves a pedagogic purpose in that it helps us understand how women craft multiple resolutions in contexts of graded and multiple patriarchies and graded inequality of the caste system.

In 1984 the government of India set up the Women's Development Program (WDP) in Rajasthan with the primary objective of empowering rural women to play an active role in development. Bhanwari Devi from the village Bhateri was recruited as a *saathin* (a community worker) in the program in 1985. The program took up issues related to local government, land, water, the public distribution system, minimum wages, health, literacy, and child marriage—all issues relevant to the area and immediately relevant to the lives of the saathins themselves. Child marriage was, for instance, discussed for the first time in Bhateri as part of the program in 1986. Bhanwari and the other saathins had married their daughters off before they attained puberty, prior to their joining the program. Discussing this issue and mobilizing around it as part of the program led to an agreement among the saathins to postpone the *gauna* (postpubertal ritual signaling cohabitation) of their daughters. Bhanwari began to educate her daughter, and by 1989 she had established her presence as a fearless and dynamic activist. She was also now a full-time trainer in the WDP.

In April and May 1992, seven years after Bhanwari had joined the program, the government decided to observe the anti–child marriage fortnight. Rather than be part of a meaningless ritual protest, Bhanwari set about identifying families that were planning to marry off their young daughters during *Akha Teej*. Despite facing hostility from the village elders, Bhanwari persisted, with senior program and police officers following up and actively preventing a marriage. It was clear that all parties in the village had two positions on the issue of child marriage. While they campaigned for its abolition, they continued to perform marriages in their homes.[31] Bhanwari's attempt to reconcile rhetoric with practice threw the society into a crisis. Clearly, for Bhanwari, the problem of child marriage was not one of dichotomized conflict but a dilemma fraught with contradictions and multiple perspectives, something she recognized because of her own belated awareness of the "problem." The solution therefore lay in persuasion, which would no doubt create anger and tension, but could be resolved with further persuasion. Spread out as the problem was, not confined to a single caste, not a problem precipitated by men alone but one that adult women participated in as well, the solution, it would appear, lay in "'imaginative integrations and reconciliations," which require attention to a particular context (Barlett 1990, 851). The context is clearly understood as that of politics with all its complexity: "The *saathins* prefer to work through persuasion and are against any police action because it makes people hostile and impedes the *saathins'* work."[32] People's unwillingness, their anger, their dishonesty even, would, in the ultimate analysis, present solutions, because new situations are generative and enable practical perceptions.

On September 22 Bhanwari's husband, Mohan, was physically assaulted and Bhanwari sexually assaulted in the fields while at work. She identified the men responsible for assaulting her. When Bhanwari was assaulted, the drama was played out to its logical end. Nobody in the village was willing to support her. The police were not willing to register her complaint. Ironically, the same officer who had led the police action as a "follow-up" to Bhanwari's work even asked if she knew the meaning of "rape." Doctors were not available in the public health centers, although Bhanwari knew that she must not change her clothes and she must go through the steps necessary to see her case through to the court, regardless of the trauma of the assault—a fusion of reason and emotion, even at the most difficult times. With coworkers her only support in the campaign, scattered in different villages, and her husband himself a victim of assault for the first two days, Bhanwari was able to get a medical examination forty-seven hours after she was assaulted.

The immediate convergence of interests between community, police, judiciary, the state-run medical services, and the executive cannot be understated as "negligence."[33] It is necessary to unpack this convergence and the complicity in the sexual assault—both in its perpetration and in the guarantee of impunity that marked Bhanwari's journey from Bhateri to Jaipur over four days, ending in her having to deposit the skirt she was wearing at the Bassi police station as evidence, walking three kilometers to a saathin's village draped in her husband's chador.

One month after Bhanwari was raped, when no action had yet been initiated against those accused of the assault, the saathins got together at a public meeting to speak out not just in solidarity with Bhanwari but also about their own experiences of assault that they had until then not made public.[34] So not only was it possible in the villages that the saathins lived in to speak about issues like rape, as Bhanwari had done in 1987, and to work with families around issues of child marriage, as she had done in her daughter's case, but it was also possible to push the panchayat—a patriarchal body—to deliver speedy justice in a case of rape and to confront sexual harassment in a manner unimaginable in the more enlightened metropolises.

The point to note is not that violence against women is a common experience: violence *is* our context (Misra, Rajan, and Srivastava 1993). What was the source of hostility in the environment? Bhanwari challenged both community and state through her persistence and effectiveness. Furthermore, the anger of communities against the state was deflected onto Bhanwari, and the anger of the state at the effectiveness of a working-class dalit woman's activism that surpassed its own practice of linear politics was also trained on Bhanwari, leaving her completely vulnerable.

This returns us to our early question in this section about whether a campaign against child marriage can, in fact, be constructed in terms of employment and what the pitfalls of that construction might be in the larger context of a convergence of patriarchies between state and nonstate actors—in this case, state and nonstate legal systems. Take the trial court decision in this case:

> Indian culture has not fallen to such low depths that someone who is brought up in it, an innocent, rustic man, will turn into a man of evil conduct who disregards caste and age differences—and becomes animal enough to assault a woman. How can persons of 40 and 60 years of age commit rape while someone who is seventy years old watches by; particularly in the light of Bhanwari Devi's acceptance that one of the rapists is a respected man in the village. The court believes that the assertion of the prosecution that Gyarsa, 60 years, Badri, 40 years, committed rape in front of the 70 year old Shravan and 59 year old Ramkaran is not to be believed, especially given that neither the medical report nor the FSL report corroborates this rape. To the contrary, according to the medical report there were no injuries on Bhanwari Devi's private parts. According to the FSL report, the semen stains on the ghaghra and in the vaginal smear belonged to group "AS," although neither of the accused belongs to that group. In our view, the prosecution, keeping in mind the above circumstances, has not proved its case rationally and beyond doubt that Gyarsa, 60 and Badri, 40 raped Bhanwari Devi while Ramsukh and Shravan, Brahmin and therefore of a different caste from the other accused, looked on.
>
> The accused Gyarsa and Badri are acquitted of all charges under Section 376 IPC and the accused Ramkaran, Ramsukh and Shravan are acquitted of the charges under Section 376/34 IPC. Owing to inconclusive evidence, the accused are given benefit of doubt on the above counts.[35]

The existence of multiple systems for redress, while disabling of women's entitlements, for the most part proved in Bhanwari's case to be the space for restorative justice. In terms of the resolution, clearly the trajectory of practical reasoning opens out space for negotiation within particular contexts where women live and work. While antagonism can take the form of extreme violence against women activists, Bhanwari made the difficult choice to return to Bhateri and renegotiate her position there by calling a *jati panchayat* in 1993. There was hostility (Misra, Rajan, and Srivastava 1993), yet she called a panchayat, not to deliver justice because she was sexually assaulted but to restore her, in some way, to her context with dignity. Since that context is specific and one of which she alone was part, she was clear that she did not want any members of the support group that had backed her to be present at that meeting.

In February 1995 Bhanwari, along with twelve women from Prempura and Bhateri, decided to participate in the meeting of the newly elected Bhateri panchayat, which consists of five villages, including Bhateri. Among those elected were four women—one Scheduled Caste, one Scheduled Tribe, and two Brahmin. To her surprise, the newly elected sarpanch, an educated Scheduled Caste man, Ramji Lal Ballai, garlanded Bhanwari and said that she was the *mukhiya sadasya* (first citizen) of the village.[36] Bhanwari had succeeded in her mission. She reported feeling welcome at the meeting and was happy at the outcome. Although around the same time the neighboring Bassi panchayat honored the men accused of assaulting Bhanwari and launched a virulent attack on her and the groups that supported her, the fact that Bhanwari had been able to renegotiate space and dignity within Bhateri points to possibilities for restoration that are located outside patriarchal discourses of honor and chastity that constrain deliberations on justice for women survivors of sexual assault. The fact of sexual assault, however, circulates in courts with no possibility of redress except in the reduced and circuitous terms of "sexual harassment at the workplace" through the *Vishakha* judgment.

It is not my intention here either to present a eulogy of caste panchayats or to suggest that panchayats can completely replace courts in redressing violations. Rather, my attempt here is to show that restoration, remedy, and redress (or the lack thereof), especially against sexual violence, takes place simultaneously on different tracks. Women then negotiate their claims on several tracks as well. In Bhanwari's case a resolution (howsoever tenuous) was possible at the level of the village even when the doors of formal justice were shut to her.[37]

Conclusion

To conclude, Gina Vargas frames the possibilities of feminism cogently: "Feminism is not merely a struggle to obtain equal opportunities laws or recognition of citizenship; it is, above all, a counter-cultural proposal, because the materialisation of its vision requires a new democratic political culture that is permanently expanding its limits. . . . And another democracy will not be possible without both women and men engaging in a personal, subjective revolution, nor without the active recognition of our diversity, which in itself constitutes a profound counter-cultural change" (2006).

This is the point at which Indian feminism finds itself today. Unarguably, the road in the past thirty years has been long and difficult. There have been tensions with the radical Left (Kannabiran, Volga, and Kannabiran 2004), irreconcilable contradictions with the fundamentalist Right (Sarkar 1999), and sustained confrontations with a violent, repressive state, particularly in the North East and Kashmir (Banerjee 2008); there have been successes on paper that have simply not translated into practice and successful campaigns that have not resulted in Ambedkar's dream of notional change in the minds of people at large. There have been tensions within democratic spaces: between movements for civil liberties (which for a long time reproduced the private-public distinction, writing women's rights out of the terrain of civil liberties) and women's groups; between women from dominant communities within the women's movement and minority women, which has resulted in a cogent critique of "secular" feminism (Agnes 1994); between dominant women and dalit women within the women's movement and the charting of a distinct course of struggle by dalit women (Kannabiran 2006); between women's collectives like the Meira Paibis and the Naga Women's Union in Manipur, a society that "lacks the patriarchal instinct" (Banerjee 2008); and between feminists with disabilities and a women's movement that has only just begun to recognize disability as a measure of diversity (Ghai 2008). There is also the challenge that shrinking possibilities of livelihood and escalating conflict place before the women's movement. On another track, the articulation of political representation for women is underwritten by antidiscrimination politics that are part of anticaste movements, making a linear, universalizing resolution impossible. The urgent need to reassert the politics of presence is also foregrounded by the glaring absence of women in public institutions (*Second and Third Alternative Report* 2006), even thirty-five years after the publication of the *Towards Equality* report (Government of India 1974).

In this situation, torn apart by conflict, contradiction, competing interests, and exclusion, yet building bridges and crafting solidarities, women continue to lead the way to a different method of doing politics. The "Shed No More Blood" campaign by the Naga Mothers' Association and its effort to sustain a dialogue on peace—between warring factions, between tribes, and between women's groups—has, for instance, signaled "an alternative way of doing politics *and* peace, one that is non violent, democratic and consensual" (Menon 2007, 116).

Notes

1. An independent survey of the Government Mental Hospital in Srinagar found that post-traumatic stress cases increased from 1,700 in 1990 to 17,000 in 1993 and to 30,000 in 1998. (Khanday 2005).

2. Rai 2002 is an update of the case study that was originally published in International IDEA's handbook, *Women in Parliament: Beyond Numbers* (Stockholm: International IDEA, 1998).

3. While statistics show that there is an increase in women contesting elections at the national level from 51 seats in 1952 to 307 seats in 1991, the percentage of successful women candidates has gone down, from 45 percent in 1952 to 10.75 percent in 1991. The judiciary and the civil services likewise have fewer than 5 percent women at different levels, the Supreme Court currently having no sitting woman judges. This is a clear indication that the problem does not lie in women's unwillingness to participate in politics.

4. CEDAW 2007 draws heavily on the *Second and Third Alternative Report* (2006).

5. I do not attempt here to provide a historical account of the different women's groups in India and the campaigns they have organized. For such a detailed account, please see the essays reprinted in John 2008 and Kannabiran and Menon 2007.

6. I will move back and forth between "revolution" and "insurgency" in this section, taking in the view of movements that see themselves as carrying forward a revolution although they are often seen from the outside as small outbursts, that is, as insurgencies or revolts. This difference in perspective is central to the appreciation of the change that women's resistance has effected.

7. Kandukuri Rajyalakshmi (1851–1910) was the first woman in Andhra Pradesh to plunge into the work of social reform, women's education, and widow remarriage. Duvvuri Subbamma (1880–1964), was married at the age of ten and widowed soon after. "Desabandhavi" Duvvuri Subbamma, born in Daksharamam in Godavari District, was a woman who was able to transform her life. A widely respected freedom fighter, she spoke powerfully on total freedom as early as 1921, at the Political Conference in Kakinada. A leader of the Civil Disobedience Movement and the Quit India Movement, who propagated ideas of freedom and self-rule with intensity and commitment, she was arrested and jailed in Rajamundry for a year and later at Rayavellore Jail for a year for her part in the Salt Satyagraha. Chityala Ailamma (1919–1985) is engraved in history as the woman who started off the most critical event in the Telangana Peasant Struggle. Coming from the Chakali caste in Palakurti village, Ailamma's struggle for land provided an inspiring example to the Telangana peasants. Suffering great hardship and oppression in the course of this struggle, she was a beacon of the Communist Party. Sugra Humayun Mirza (1882–1958) devoted her whole life to the cause of the education of Muslim women and their cultural progress. She stood firm in her resolve to work for women's rights, dignity, and self-respect in spite of strong opposition. Sugra Humayun Mirza, or Begum Sugra as she was called, used her creative writing to propagate her views on social reform. Her experiences of her travels abroad are published in a series of six books. She wrote under the pen name "Haya." Writing about Hindu Muslim unity, using *swadeshi* goods, campaigning against purdah, setting up national universities, and demanding education in the mother tongue, Begum Sugra's achievements set her apart as a trendsetter in her time. See Volga, Kannabiran, and Kannabiran 2001.

8. M. Ratnamala, "Adimanavi," *Nutana,* 1979 (in Telugu, translated into English by Vasanth Kannabiran). Ratnamala is one of the founding members of Stree Shakti Sanghatana, one of the first feminist collectives in India, located in Hyderabad. A poet and writer, she has had a long association with the Marxist-Leninist movement in the state and played an important role in bringing feminist politics into leftist revolutionary discourse. She then went on to become the first woman president of the Andhra Pradesh Civil Liberties Committee, which addressed primarily the question of state repression.

9. There are, of course, differences in the sequence of issues taken up by the women's movement from one state to another, but this order is true of Andhra and some parts of northern and western India.

10. I have, in a recent essay, used a similar framework to understand violence against women in India (Kannabiran 2008b).

11. *Tukaram v. State of Maharashtra* (1979), 2 SCC 143; "An Open Letter to the Chief Justice of India" (1979), 4 SCC 17–22, a letter written by Professors Upendra Baxi, Vasudha Dhagamwar, Raghunath Kelkar, and Lotika Sarkar. Custodial violence designates violence against persons held in custody by the state, or persons in residential facilities like hostels, hospitals, asylums, and so on. Custodial rape is defined in Section 376 (2) and custodial violence not amounting to rape is defined in Sections 376 B, C, and D of the Indian Penal Code as "Rape/Intercourse by public servant with woman in his custody," "Rape/Intercourse by superintendent of jail, remand home, etc.," and "Rape/Intercourse by any member of the management or staff of a hospital with any woman in that hospital."

12. Rameeza Bee was eighteen years old in 1978, when she was gang-raped by four policemen and her husband, Ahmed Hussain, was beaten to death. The initial campaign in support of Rameeza was led by civil liberties activists and lawyers and consisted of an all-opposition coalition that included the Majlis Ittehadul Muslimeen. Later, women's groups in Hyderabad and Karnataka followed up on the case. There was a public protest, where the police treated the crowd as an unlawful assembly and opened fire indiscriminately, killing more people. After the firing, a one man Commission of Enquiry was constituted with the appointment of Justice Muktadar, a High Court judge.

13. Kiran Singh, a twenty-five-year-old student, petitioned the Supreme Court in November 1982 to seek protection from her father, who threatened to kill her if she married according to her own choice. She hid in a crouched position in a three-foot *almirah* (metal closet) for forty hours before escaping to Delhi. The prison was the family. See Kishwar 1984.

14. For an analysis of the subjugation of dalits, and dalit women by caste panchayats, see Dhagamwar 2005.

15. Especially evident in the recent case of the death of Rizwanur Rehman after his marriage to Priyanka Todi in Kolkata, a city with a very visible and vocal feminist presence for more than three decades. For a detailed analysis of the complexity of the love marriage versus arranged marriage dichotomy that reduces activism to a description after the tragedy, see Mody 2008.

16. Cases filed by feminist and human rights health collectives asking for the prohibition of sex-selective abortions: *Centre for Enquiry into Health and Allied Themes (CEHAT) and Ors. v. Union of India (UOI) and Ors*, AIR 2003 SC 3309; *Malpani Infertility Clinic Pvt. Ltd. and Ors. v. Appropriate Authority, PNDTAct, and Ors.*, AIR 2005 Bom 26.

17. Andalamma, testimony given at the public hearing on violence against women, Hyderabad, March 7, 2004, in front of a gathering of 5,000 women and the jury consisting of Mohini Giri, Nalini Nayak, Ruth Manorama, and Jeelani Bano.

18. For a more detailed analysis of sexual assault, see Kannabiran 2008a.

19. See, for instance, *Chairman, Railway Board, and Others v. Chandrima Das (Mrs.) and Others*, 2000 (2) Supreme Court Cases 465. Hanuffa Khatoon, a Bangladeshi national, and an elected representative of the Union Board, was gang-raped in February 1998 in the railway restroom of Howrah Station and again at a private residence outside the station by a group of men who included railway employees and touts. The High Court awarded Rs. 10 lakhs [1 million] compensation. The Supreme Court of India, upholding the decision of the High Court, observed that "International Covenants and Declarations as adopted by the United Nations have to be respected by all signatory States and the meaning given to the above words in those Declarations and Covenants have to be such as would help in effective implementation of those rights. The applicability of the Universal Declaration of Human Rights and the principles thereof may have to be read, if need be, into the domestic jurisprudence."

20. Sakshi petitioned the Supreme Court. As part of this process, three other organizations, namely, Interventions for Support, Healing, and Awareness; the All India Democratic Women's Association; and the National Commission for Women also presented their views on the proposed suggestions. See the *172nd Report of the Law Commission of India on Reform of Rape Laws* (2000).

21. *State of Punjab, Appellant v. Gurmit Singh and Others, Respondents* (1996), AIR (SC) 1393.

22. *Visakha and Others v. State of Rajasthan and Others* (1997), 6 SCC 241.

23. "The prostitutes take upon themselves to train up their children from their infancy and teach them nothing but how to lure the other sex. How, then, can we allow our children to read with these? . . . Is this the same thing as arguing that a Brahmin cannot sit with a Pariah? No, we are strenuous in upholding the cause of education. . . . Let the Government establish one school in each Division exclusively for the children of prostitutes" (*Report on Native Newspapers in the Madras Presidency*, Report on Tamil Newspapers for the Week ending 3rd August 1878, Tamil Nadu Archives, Chennai).

24. G.O. No. G Law 1539 (Councils, Leg. Councils, Prisoners), 15/4/32.

25. The International Committee for Prostitutes' Rights (ICPR), Amsterdam, 1985. See also VAMP and Sangram 2007.

26. Jean D'Cunha's long engagement with this issue is well known, as is also the work of groups like Sangram in Sangli, Sanlaap in Kolkata, and Prajwala in Hyderabad—each having a distinct position but contending with the criminal law on the ground. For an extensive review of the debates, see Rajan 2002; and Kotiswaran n.d.

27. *Dr. Upendra Baxi (1) v. State of Uttar Pradesh* (1983), 2 SCC 308; *Dr. Upendra Baxi and Ors.(II) vs. State of UP and Ors.* (1986), 4 SCC 106.

28. http://www.prajwalaindia.org/leagaladv.htm.

29. See, for instance, in the context of Andhra Pradesh, three essays on feminist engagements with peace processes by Volga, Kannabiran, and Kannabiran (2005a, 2005b) and Kannabiran, Volga, and Kannabiran (2004).

30. My argument here is that whether or not it is applied consistently, what is significant is the enunciation of a principle in the jurisprudence on sexual harassment at the workplace, which in itself demonstrates the inroads made by feminist politics.

31. Report of the meeting (*jajam*) in Bhateri on June 22, 1992. "Bhateri Gang Rape: Dateline," Archives of Jagori, Delhi, n.d.

32. Letter to the home minister signed by women's organizations from all over the country, dated November 4, 1992 (Archives of Jagori).

33. Ibid., for instance, says, "Government doctors, magistrate and other officials were all negligent" (Archives of Jagori, Delhi).

34. "Nyay Karo Ya Jail Bharo: Saathins Break the Silence" (Archives of Jagori, n.d.).

35. Excerpt from the Bhanwari Devi judgment.

36. Kavita Srivastava, report of meeting held on February 21, 1995, of the Bhateri panchayat, as told by Bhanwari (Archives of Jagori).

37. There is also the story of Basanti and Urmila from the village Karauli in Rajasthan. Basanti was raped by Urmila's husband, Mahesh. The all-male panchayat decided that the ends of justice would be served if Basanti's husband, Raja, raped Urmila. Basanti did not accept the verdict. Urmila walked in and declared that her husband should go to each woman in the village and beg her forgiveness. That being unacceptable to her husband, she declared she would not live with a rapist (*Second and Third Alternative Report* 2006).

5

The Chinese Women's Movement in the Context of Globalization

NAIHUA ZHANG AND PING-CHUN HSIUNG

In this chapter, we analyze the challenges and opportunities the Chinese women's movement has encountered in the global era. We take a historically grounded approach, examining the dialectic exchange and engagement between indigenous activism and global feminism. We argue that the politics and development of the contemporary Chinese women's movement are shaped by three distinct forces: the socialist legacy, economic development and political reforms since the 1980s, and influences of global feminisms resulting from China's hosting the Fourth World Conference on Women (FWCU) in 1995.

As an integral part of the Communist Revolution led by the Chinese Communist Party (CCP), the women's movement figures prominently on the national, state-building agenda. Guided by the doctrine of *nanu pingdeng* (equality between men and women) and *funu jiefang* (women's liberation), the All China Women's Federation (ACWF) represents and safeguards women's welfare. As the umbrella national women's organization sanctioned by the state and subordinate to the party, the ACWF is responsible for mobilizing women to achieve the tasks and goals of the party state. At the same time, it is the institutional base and battle front for women to stand fast on the principle of gender equality and make demands and propose policy on women's behalf.[1] With an organizational structure extending from the village to the national level and integrated into the state apparatus from the township level up, the ACWF remains a prominent player in the contemporary Chinese women's movement. It is therefore important to examine the ways

CHINA

Human Development Index ranking: .777
Gender-Related Development Index value: .776
Gender Empowerment Measure value: .534

General

Type of government: Communist Party–led state
Major ethnic groups: Han Chinese (91.5%); Zhuang, Uyghur, Hui, Yi, Tibetan, Miao, Manchu, Mongol, Buyi, Korean, and other nationalities (8.5%)
Languages: Mandarin; Cantonese; local dialects
Religions: Officially atheist; Buddhist; Daoist; Christians (3%–4%); Muslims (1%–2%)

Demographics

Population, total (millions), 2005: 1,313.0
Annual growth rate (%), 2005–2015: .6
Total fertility (average number of births per woman): 1.7
Contraceptive prevalence (% of married women aged 15–49): 87%
Maternal mortality ratio, adjusted (per 100,000 live births), 2000: 45

Women's Status

Date of women's suffrage: 1949
Life expectancy: M 71; F 74.3
Combined gross enrollment ratio for primary, secondary, and tertiary education (female %), 2005: 69
Gross primary enrollment ratio: 112[*]
Gross secondary enrollment ratio: 74
Gross tertiary enrollment ratio: 20
Literacy (% age 15 and older): M 95.1; F 86.5

Political Representation of Women

Seats in parliament (% held by women): 20.3
Legislators, senior officials, and managers (% female): 17
Professional and technical workers (% female): 52
Women in government at ministerial level (% total): 6.3

Economics

Estimated earned income (PPP US$), 2005: M 8,213; F 5,220
Ratio of estimated female to male earned income: .64
Economic activity rate (% female): 68.8
Women in adult labor force (% total): 44 (this figure obtained at the CEDAW Statistical Database)

[*]Gross enrollment ratios in excess of 100% indicate that there are pupils or students outside the theoretical age groups who are enrolled in that level of education.

in which ACWF juggles its dual functions amid marketization, political reforms, and international influences.

The backbone of the women's movement emerging in the mid-1980s was a cohort of urban-based professional women who were raised on the Maoist slogan "women holding half of the sky." Researchers and activists within and outside the ACWF began organizing themselves from the bottom up, searching for solutions. These new groups are locally positioned as the structural bases symbolically connecting the Chinese railroad to the international tracks. Contrary to the view that Chinese women are silent victims of the authoritarian CCP state, the movement seized the opportunities of international engagement when the Chinese government offered to host the Fourth World Conference on Women in 1995. A new chapter in the history of Chinese women's organizing has since unfolded.

An essential thread that runs through our analysis of Chinese women's movements in post-1995 China is the interplay between local and global forces. We identify the influence of global feminism coming to China through UN documents, international funding, training workshops, and frequent, intensive engagement between local and global groups. The fruition of such local-global engagement is evident in a wide range of indigenous initiatives in recent years. To illustrate the expansion and deepening of the Chinese women's movement, we examine the process, mechanisms, and effects of indigenization. Although an issue-based approach to gender inequalities has gradually eclipsed the state-mediated, Marxist-based women's liberation, the ACWF, NGOs, and academic groups continue to engage the state and hold it accountable.

This chapter contains three parts. First, we provide a historical overview of the connections between Chinese women and the outside world, particularly in the reform era. Second, we discuss the development of the Chinese women's movement as a result of the 1995 Beijing Women's Conference.[2] We are especially interested in gender mainstreaming and the development of NGOs, women's studies, anti-domestic violence work, political participation, and employment and economic well-being. We conclude with critical analysis of the interplay between local and global feminisms and the relationship between the Chinese women's movement and the state, and urge the adoption of new paradigms to better understand the women's movement in China.

History of International Connections

The Chinese women's movement has long faced the challenge of working with the state and international forces while maintaining autonomy from them.

When Western feminism first entered public discussion in China during the May Fourth era (1919–1925), some founding members of the CCP were inspired by its liberal ideas of sexual equality. But early feminism was characterized as "bourgeois," inspired by Western cultural ideals, and in direct conflict with the CCP's Marxist approach to the "woman question," which was influenced by the Soviet Comintern's subordination of gender to class inequality.

In 1949, the All-China Democratic Women's Federation (ACDWF) established, anticipating the founding of the People's Republic of China (PRC). It comprised women's federations from CCP-controlled areas and three non-partisan women's organizations from the Nationalist Party–governed urban areas. In 1957, against the backdrop of the CCP's announcing the arrival of socialism, the ACDWF was forced to declare that women's liberation and equality had been achieved and that its new goal was simply to provide social services to women. Two of the non-partisan women's organizations were disbanded amid the anti-rightist campaign. One lost its autonomy. The ACDWF changed its name to the All-China Women's Federation, and was subsequently incorporated into the administrative structure of the state to take charge of women's affairs with dual functions of (1) assisting the government with policy making and implementation and engaging in "woman work" and (2) representing the interests of all women and conveying their demands to the party/state. It was in this dual capacity that the ACWF became both the official and the popular representative of Chinese women to their counterparts outside China.

However, the ACWF's outside contact was mediated by the state, shaped by the CCP's official ideology on women's issues, and subject to the political and diplomatic needs of the country. This is evident in the ACWF's engagement with the Women's International Democratic Federation (WIDF), a key consortium among the communist countries in the 1950s and 1960s, and the World Conferences on Women organized by the United Nations from 1975 on. Although the ACDWF was actively involved in the WIDF's activities and took a leading role in expanding the WIDF's influence in Asia, its ties to the WIDF weakened as ideological and political conflicts between China and the Soviet Union spilled into women's activities and affairs. The Chinese delegation to the UN Women's Conference in Mexico City in 1975 expressed suspicion about autonomous women's movements and questioned the utility of achieving gender equality through laws and public policies. Echoing the CCP leaders' views, the delegation objected to the peace and disarmament goals of the women's movement. It supported the CCP state's foreign policy, which opposed imperialism and Western global hegemony.[3]

China's official position on international women's issues and activities began to change in 1979 when Chinese leader Deng Xiaoping initiated economic reforms opening China to the outside world. Over the next decade the ACWF's engagement with international women's affairs changed. In 1980 the honorary chairwoman of the ACWF expressed the Chinese government's support for the UN International Decade for Women and its themes of equality, development, and peace (*People's Daily*, May 15, 1980, 1). China sent delegates to the Second (1980) and Third (1985) World Conferences on Women and signed the Convention on the Elimination of All Forms of Discrimination against Women (see Wanru 1980, 12:20). It also worked with UN organizations and other international bodies addressing women and children. At the 1985 conference in Nairobi, inspired by the NGO Forum, the official Chinese delegation, primarily composed of ACWF members, organized its first ad hoc panel to discuss Chinese women's progress.

The ACWF's earlier encounter with global feminism was relatively superficial. It did not participate in heated debates about issues such as the meaning of feminism and the agenda of the international women's movement. As activists from the global North and South distinguished gender from class and national inequalities, the ACWF continued to voice its strong opposition against imperialist domination. However the ACWF's international involvement had virtually no effect on Chinese women, the society as a whole, or state policies.

Rise of the Chinese Women's Movement in the Reform Era

For the women's movement within China, the turmoil of the Cultural Revolution (1966–1976) aggravated many women's problems, frequently shredding families and delegitimizing women's issues. The Cultural Revolution slogan "What men can do, women can also do" confirmed the ideology of gender equality at the very time that the ACWF was disbanding, leaving no national organization to address women's issues in the years 1966–1978. Economic reforms after the Cultural Revolution resulted in certain gains for women, such as rising incomes and greater autonomy, but also brought a host of new problems and made some previously existing problems more visible. There were increasing incidents of trafficking in women, purchased and forced marriage, and intense pressures on women associated with the rigorous enforcement of birth control, leading to female infanticide and abuse of rural women who gave birth to daughters. Discrimination against women in state-sector employment increased as enterprises gained more control over personnel and hiring. Rural girls dropped out of school to help with family farming, as agriculture once again was organized by households rather than collectives. The number of women holding political positions declined as a result of direct election.

These problems shocked a generation of women who had grown up under the Maoist slogan of "Women holding up half of the sky." They prompted women intellectuals and professionals inside and outside of the former ACWF into action. The ACWF was revived and launched a nationwide campaign in the early 1980s for the protection of the rights and interests of women and children. By the mid-1980s, an urban-based women's movement had emerged in China, characterized by the heightening of women's consciousness, attempts to combat the old and new problems women faced, and, most important, the development of women's organizations and women's studies groups and programs at Chinese universities (Zhang and Xu 1995).

Beside the Women's Federation and other established women's organizations, new types of organizations also emerged. They are bottom up, independent from the state, and led by urban intellectual or professional women who have benefited from socialist gender policy, embraced women's right to work, and internalized a strong sense of equality. They engage in research on women, form discussion groups and women's studies centers to discuss women's issues, investigate and document inequalities, and search for solutions. Their organizing efforts led to two distinctive developments. One was to carve out spaces within the CCP state, for example, by creating the National Working Committee on Women and Children under the State Council in 1993. The committee has since exercised greater power and authority than the ACWF to advance women's welfare. The other was women's studies endeavors that created new discourses on women and brought ACWF activists and women scholars together to form research associations at the provincial and municipal levels, as well as creating women's studies centers in universities.[4]

The agenda of the Chinese women's movement in this period of the reform era was largely domestically driven. The theoretical perspectives used to frame its issues were locally derived, centering on critical analyses of Marxist theoretical frameworks on women.[5] This entailed analyzing the problems women faced in society, envisioning how women's studies as a discipline in China should be structured,[6] and critically examining the CCP's theoretical and practical approaches to women over the past forty years, resulting in recognition of the inadequacy of Marxist theory on the women question. "Women's perspective" became a new concept and approach that challenged the class-dominant CCP framework.

By the 1990s participants in the women's studies endeavor went outside of China for intellectual inspiration, exchange, and organizational connections.

The collaboration between Chinese women scholars on the mainland and the Chinese Society for Women's Studies (CSWS), a feminist organization formed in 1989 primarily by PRC women pursuing graduate study in the United States, has been particularly fruitful.[7] This and other international engagements sowed the seeds for exchange between intellectuals and activists both within and outside of China in the years leading up to the UN's FWCW in Beijing in 1995.

The Fourth World Conference on Women, Beijing, 1995

Reflecting on the impact of China's hosting of the FWCW and the concurrent NGO Forum, many Chinese women scholars and activists believe that the 1995 conference was a seminal event in the development of the Chinese women's movement. It marked China's integration into the international women's movement, contributed to changes in the domestic political and social contexts for the movement, and expanded the movement's agenda, activities, and organizational strength. Seen not as a single event but as a series of events between 1993, when the preparatory work began, and September 1995, the convening of the FWCW, the conference provided a textbook example of the interaction and interplay between local and global feminisms. Different from the earlier encounters, when state-centered women's liberation was upheld and virtually no women's organizing endeavor existed outside of the ACWF, the FWCW presented a platform for the CCP state, ACWF, and grassroots women's groups to renegotiate their relationship with each other and with feminist forces internationally. It was also the first time since the founding of the PRC that women's groups from the West were to engage Chinese women on issues related to women's liberation and gender inequality.

For the CCP state, the FWCW was the first and most important international event to be held in China since the Tiananmen Square event of 1989. The state treated the FWCW not just as an event for women but as a nationalist project showcasing China to the outside world. There was unprecedented publicity and organized activity leading up to the conference. For the first time, China fully participated in both the official conference and the NGO Forum, with more than 5,000 women attending the forum, sponsoring forty-seven panels and workshops. In its formal presentation at the official UN conference, the Chinese government focused on gender rather than on foreign policy issues and fully and unreservedly endorsed the Beijing Platform for Action, signaling the turning of a page for the women's movement in China and its relationship with its counterparts around the world.

For the ACWF, the Asia-Pacific Regional Preparatory NGO Forum in Manila in 1993 was a challenging and eye-opening experience. It found the vigorous, spontaneous interaction and exchanges among the participating NGOs at the meeting refreshing, but was also unprepared to answer challenges concerning its legitimacy as an NGO.[8] Controversies with regard to the conference permeated both the preparation and conference phases.

Without adequate knowledge of the historical development of the Chinese women's movement, its relationship with the CCP state, and the emergent organizing forces in the reform era, women's groups from the West considered Chinese women victims of an authoritarian state, and the conference an occasion where "36,000 feminists meet 1 billion communists."[9] Global media coverage of the conference, as well as comments made by some Western feminists, focused on the controversial role played by the Chinese government (Wang 1997). Immediate postconference evaluation of the effect of the conference on the Chinese women's movement was reserved, describing the conference as just "creating ripples" (Howell 1997). In contrast, experiences of the Chinese participants were overwhelmingly positive (Hsiung and Wong 1998). Historically speaking, the FWCW marked the beginning of a new era of Chinese women's movement and its engagement with global feminism.

The Women's Movement in Post-1995 China

China's hosting of the conference was no accident. After suffering a serious setback both domestically and internationally due to its suppression of the student protest movement of 1989, in 1992 the Chinese government decided to deepen the economic reform and integration with the global economy. "To connect the Chinese railroad to the international tracks" became the slogan and obsession of the government and the public. The women's movement thus benefited from the greatest openness and access to external contacts available to social groups in PRC history.

The 1995 conference helped women's issues receive a "status lift" on the national agenda through publicity and renewed commitment and resources from the government. In his welcoming speech at the official conference, Chinese president Jiang Zemin stated that equality between men and women was "a fundamental state policy for promoting social development." This wording linked gender equality for the first time to other "crucial state matters," including family planning, land, and environmental protection. Women's organizations, in particular the Women's Federation, wasted no time using the elevated status and symbolic value of the official commitment to challenge any measures that ran counter to the spirit of this "fundamental state policy" and used the Chinese Women's Development Program (1995–2000) as a mechanism to evaluate women's situation and to demand needed resources to fulfill specific goals.

The UN documents based on the discourse and agenda of the international women's movement helped shape the official gender rhetoric and policy agenda. For example, China's country report to the United Nations in 1994 and the Chinese Women's Development Program were based on the 1985 Nairobi Forward-Looking Strategies for the Advancement of Women, while the new National Program for Women's Development (2001–2010) was framed according to two international documents: the Beijing Platform for Action and the Millennium Development Goals. It covered the twelve critical areas of concern specified in the Beijing Platform for Action, with a focus on six areas in particular, elaborated into thirty-four goals and one hundred measures. This facilitated the work of the Women's Federation, as some commended the measurable indicators are easier for the women's organization to pursue (D. Liu 2006). As a result, new issues have now entered public discussion, often formulated with language and ideas from international documents. They include women's health, violence against women, domestic violence, the welfare of girls, a national mechanism for the advancement of women, and so forth. Thus, ideas from the international women's movement are becoming normalized in China, pressuring the government to support them. They hold the government directly responsible for protecting women's rights and interests, instead of blaming external factors such as residual feudalism and bourgeois influences for gender inequality.

China's hosting of the Beijing conference also opened the door to more foreign funding and international organizations. The Ford Foundation Beijing became a leading source of funding for projects concerning women.[10] Its funding is crucial for the development of reproductive health as a new area of research and action in China; its grants also have a major impact on women's studies, gender and development, and NGO capacity building. Additional major funding comes from organizations and agencies working in international development. The ethnically diverse Yunnan Province in the less developed southwestern part of China became a target for overseas assistance. In the words of a woman activist located in the principal capital, Kunming, "There is so much money that we cannot take all the projects there are."[11] All of these resources contributed to the birth of the gender and development field in China, with Oxfam Hong Kong as the foremost international NGO providing financial, theoretical, and organizational support to its practitioners. According to the *China Development Brief*, a private newspaper registered in the United States and focusing on Chinese NGOs, in Beijing alone there are two hundred international NGOs (http://www.chinadevelopmentbrief.org.cn/ml/index.jsp). Because of the acute shortage of domestic funding, China's independently organized women's groups are sustained mainly by funding from outside China. Even the ACWF now relies on foreign funding for most of its projects, since the government covers mainly its operating costs. Foreign funding thus inevitably draws researchers and activists to issues and concerns that were initially externally defined, and this further shapes the agendas and perspectives of the funded groups. The ideas and organizations coming to China are diverse. A case in point that reflects the complexity and variability of external influences are ultraconservative religious groups from the United States that collaborate with some Chinese women's groups and government agencies, advocating abstinence and opposing safe-sex education as the way to avoid HIV/AIDS (Milwertz 2002). China's eagerness to "connect the Chinese railroad to the international tracks" after decades of isolation made the nation less critical of and more vulnerable to global influences.

In addition, China's hosting of the 1995 NGO Forum allowed women activists to become the first citizen group (as compared to youth and workers, the other two of the three major "mass organizations" in China) to travel outside the country, conducting direct nonofficial exchanges with their follow NGO groups. Leaders of self-initiated women's groups participated in various conference-related activities and events, including the World Conference on Human Rights (Vienna, 1993) and the International Conference on Population and Development (Cairo, 1994). They were greatly inspired and empowered by their encounters, impressed by the enthusiasm, passion, and strong sense of participation displayed by their overseas NGO counterparts and by their varied and effective organizational formats and activities.[12] Some of them played a vital if constrained role in shaping the organization and the outcome of the 1995 conference. This was also the beginning of much broadened exchange and collaboration between Chinese women scholars and activists and their overseas counterparts.

New Concepts, New Organizational Practices

As one NGO leader said, "The 1995 World Conference on Women brought in many new terms and concepts to Chinese women. Among them, the most influential, the most widely spread, would be *gender* and *NGO*" (Gao 2000). There is no equivalent in the Chinese language for either of these two English terms.

To highlight that the feminist concept of *gender* is new in Chinese vocabulary and is different from the Chinese term *xingbie* (sex or sexual distinction), *gender* was translated by CSWS members as *shehui xingbie* (social sex)[13] when it was introduced to Chinese scholars in 1993 at a workshop jointly organized by CSWS and the Center for Women's Studies at Tianjin Normal University (Du 1993). The term *NGO* entered Chinese consciousness in conjunction with the NGO Forum. "Nongovernmental," translated as *fei zhengfu*, sounds alien to Chinese ears. The Chinese make a distinction between *guanfang* ("official" or "governmental") and *minjian* ("popular") organizations, but *fei* in *fei zhengfu* can also mean to "not conform to" government. Some university administrators at first did not want their faculty to attend the NGO Forum because of this negative connotation. Now both terms have entered formal Chinese political vocabulary. *Gender equality*, a central concept in UN documents and a goal of the international women's movement being popularized through China's hosting of the FWCW, now often appears in Chinese media and official documents, replacing *nannu pingdeng* (equality between men and women), the slogan that has inspired Chinese young people since the May Fourth movement. A politically savvy Chinese scholar commented in 2008 that "gender equality" is better because it can include equality for members of the LGBT community.

The introduction of *gender* and *NGO*, two concepts representing feminist ideas and practices from the international women's movement, poses a challenge to the CCP's theoretical framework and its organizational approach. Treating gender as a system of social stratification intersecting with class and other systems of inequality rather than being subsumed within class, as in Marxist analysis, is a theoretical breakthrough for Chinese scholars. The attention to the construction of gender at both macro and micro levels opens up investigation into the issues women face in the private sphere, such as reproduction, gender roles, sexuality, and domestic violence, and facilitates women's personal liberation and development. These issues were ignored or pushed aside by the CCP-led women's movement. The NGO concept legitimizes and gives impetus to the development of a large number of self-initiated women's organizations and expanded networks of horizontal connections, in contrast to the CCP model, where state-led "mass organizations" were vertically integrated into the state and society, mobilizing women from the top down.

The women's movement was transformed by the movement actors' engagement with the concepts of "gender" and "gender mainstreaming." Three groups are most active in using them to advance women's status in China. First is a group of women scholars and activists who are globally oriented and connected, and committed to using UN standards as leverage to push for women's causes in

China. They came together on occasions such as Beijing +5 and Beijing +10 to write NGO assessments of China's implementation of the Beijing Platform for Action and attended other related activities. They call attention to UN documents' declared commitment to gender equality and the measures and incremental goals proposed for all UN member states to take and reach.[14] "Gender mainstreaming" is thus used as a rallying point for promoting gender equality in China.[15] A leading activist and women's studies scholar calls for the reading and better implementation of three UN documents—the Convention of the Elimination of All Forms of Discrimination Against Women, the Beijing Platform for Action, and the Millennium Development Goals—because these documents are signed by the Chinese government, yet not many people know about them, including government officials and members of women's organizations. She examines how each document is implemented in China, outlines where China has gaps, and points out that these documents are framed as fundamental human rights as established in the Universal Declaration of Human Rights by the UN Assembly in 1946 (Liu 2006). The term *human rights* has already entered official and legal documents. "The State respects and protects human rights" was added to the constitution of the People's Republic of China (fourth revision, 2004) in April 2009, and the Chinese government issued the National Human Rights Action Plan of China (2009–2010), which outlines goals and measures for all of the government to follow in the next two years.

Another push comes from the field of women's studies, with a concerted effort to engender teaching and research in universities, one discipline at a time, as a cross-disciplinary/multidisciplinary field of studies in China, as will be discussed in a later part of the chapter.

The field of gender and development facilitates the dissemination of the gender concept to remote villages in the country. The theories and practices of women and development were introduced at the 1993 seminar, and long before that, development projects had been carried out in China. But it is the incoming international development organizations and projects that induced the formation of groups and organizations working on development projects and issues. As a new field in China, it leapfrogs to gender and development; quite a few of the new organizations name themselves Gender and Development Groups, such as the Yunnan GAD Group, the Guizhou GAD Group, the Beijing GAD Group, and so forth. The national network of development organizations is named the China GAD Network.

Xiehui xingbie peixun (gender training) is a core activity of these groups (as it is a requirement of almost all international development projects coming to China) and a major tool for incorporating gender perspectives into projects and consciousness raising. For example, it has been given to police officers and judges to raise their awareness about domestic violence. In this way, gender training brings the concept of gender to villagers, Women's Federation cadres, government officials, journalists, and others through a participatory approach typical of such training workshops. One major source of teaching material is *Handbook of Gender Training*, compiled by Gender and Development (GAD) activists together with an Oxfam Hong Kong officer. Many GAD members learned about gender training from this source and also use the text for the training they give to others. Many other concepts and approaches have become popularized this way, such as sustainable development, empowerment, participatory approaches such as Participatory Rural Appraisal, Training of Trainers, capacity-building training, and organizational capacity assessment. The rise of gender and development allows more attention to be paid to rural women and women of minority ethnic groups. Development NGOs play an active role in poverty alleviation, disaster relief, and, more recently, rural community development.

The contours of the current Chinese women's movement are quite different now from what they were before 1995. The women's movement is now composed of three larger areas of activities or networks: women's studies, gender and development, and issue-specific research and activism. The last category includes the networks against domestic violence, Media Monitor for Women, women's legal aid, networks of lesbians and LGBT, and a broad range of women's groups geared toward different segments of the female population, such as female migrant workers, girls, women with AIDS, women with disabilities, and others, to provide service and support. These groups, together with organizations from the gender and development field, are loosely connected as NGOs. They are more influenced by international NGO discourse and practices.

Women's NGOs have seen great development in post-1995 China. The pioneering women's organizations that began as research organizations remain strong and have grown. For example, the Shaanxi Research Association for Women and Family (SRAWF) was established in Xi'an, the capital city of the Shaanxi Province, in 1986 with the coordination of the Shaanxi Women's Federation. It is now the largest women's development NGO in China's northwestern region, engaging in advocacy, legal and counseling services, rural community development, and action research, with 130 members and 24 full- and part-time staff. Xie Lihua was a founding member of Women's Research Institute of China Academy of Management Science, the first women-initiated grassroots research organization, founded in 1988. She started *Rural Women Know All* (now *Rural Women*), the first magazine for rural women, in 1993. The institute has since grown into the Cultural Development Center for Rural

Women (CDCRW), providing support to migrant women working in Beijing, vocational training and literacy courses to rural women, and strong backing to women who are elected heads of village committees. It established the Women Village Heads Supporting Network in 2003 and launched *Women Village Heads* magazine in 2008, free for women leaders at the grassroots. The SRAWF and the CDCRW were selected to be among the seven winners of the "Model Public Welfare Programs" unveiled in November 2008 by the One Foundation of the Red Cross Society of China. Each winning organization received 1 million yuan (*renminbi*)[16] from the foundation.

Many new women's organizations have emerged. Among them, organizations of lesbians and gays have seen the fastest development. Spaces for them to get together began to appear in the summer of 1995 in Beijing. They refer to themselves as *tongzhi*, copying the term from their counterparts in Hong Kong, who first adopted the word to describe homosexuals. In Chinese, *tong* literally means "common," and *zhi* means "will"; the two were put together to translate the word *comrade* from Russian, used by CCP members, to express common interests and a common path. In 1997, six tongzhi living in Beijing (foreigners and Chinese, lesbians and gays) started the Tongzhi Pager Hotline. In 1998, the Queer Women Group was formed, followed by the convening of the First National Women Tongzhi Conference, extending connection and organization among activists (He 2001). In 2001, China's psychiatric association removed homosexuality from its list of mental illnesses. Now Chinese women tongzhi have established their own communities in some large cities, and many groups are very active, such as Beijing Tongyu (common language); the group publishes an online journal, *Les+*, and engages in advocacy, service, and other activities, such as community education and outreach, giving lectures, and organizing forums on university campuses. They work closely with other women NGOs and are part of the LGBT network in China with close connection to international organizations such as the Information Clearinghouse for Chinese Gays and Lesbians, registered in the United States. Besides organizing domestic activities, such as a queer art exhibition, annual queer movie festivals, and the like, Chinese LGBT activists have joined their overseas counterparts in celebrating Gay Pride Month and supporting the International Day against Homophobia on May 17.

Compared to their early days, women's NGOs are now more diverse, mature, and better connected. They are utilizing Web sites, e-mail, QQ groups, and other IT tools for their organizing efforts, and are receiving much better support—resources, training workshops, and published materials from NGOs, such the China NPO Network, a Beijing-based umbrella body providing information and consultation to NGOs; some women's organizations have joined the network. More established women's NGOs now have full-time staff. These women are harbingers of China's budding third sector.

Some visionary women NGO leaders are also leaders in NGO sustainability and development. Gao Xiaoxian, head of the SRAWF, was the first NGO leader to buy an apartment for her organization. Instead of using the grant money budgeted for paying rent, she used it to pay the mortgage to build the group's assets, saving money at the same time. The SRAWF was also the first to initiate an organizational building effort in 2000, through strategic planning, to find a way to build a "participatory, democratic, sustainable NGO." In 2002, the China NPO Network started a three-year training series on capacity building for NGOs, NGO governance, accountability, professionalism, leadership training, and organizational capacity assessment. Independently organized NGOs, especially the high-profile ones, were going through capacity building, where the biggest pressure is to build a culture of shared leadership, ending the "era of heroes," where the leader of the organization makes all the decisions, and beginning the "era of the system," where the leader acts as the chief executive and the board of directors makes the decisions. This is one example of the strong influence of foundations and international organizations.

Funding remains an important issue for Chinese NGOs. The Ford Foundation launched a program in 2003 to grant selected NGOs three-year "institutional development funds" (Ma 2006). All pioneering NGOs have received major funding for their operations, from Ford or other sources. Domestic funding sources are growing, as illustrated by the One Foundation's support, but are still limited.

Women on the Move: Agendas and Strategies

To illustrate how the Chinese women's movement tackles the issues women face in today's China, we provide a snapshot of women's organizing efforts in four areas. Two developed in the reform era: women's studies and combating domestic violence. The other two—women's employment and economic well-being and political participation—have been the central focus of the women's movement since the founding of the PRC. Women are fighting to curb regression in some aspects and gain new ground with new tactics.

Women's Studies: Gender Perspective and Institutionalization

By the time China embarked on preparation for the 1995 conference in the latter part of 1993, the landscape of women's studies had already taken shape, with four centers and one institute, namely, women's studies centers at Zhengzhou University, Hengzhou University, Beijing University, and Tainjin Normal University and the Women's Studies Institute of China, a research arm of the ACWF. The women's studies center at the CCP Central School later joined the ranks.

The effort to mobilize people to participate in the NGO Forum resulted in a surge of women's studies centers in universities. In less than two years, from September 1993 to May 1995, eighteen women's studies centers came into being, with another thirteen established by December 1999. Women's studies centers also found their way into the Chinese Academy of Social Sciences and other social research institutions, signaling a significant shift in the development of women's studies institutions in China, from concentration in the ACWF system in the 1980s to growth in academe in the 1990s (Du 2000; Yi 2000). This politically triggered expansion, however, produced great variations among the centers. While more established centers remain vibrant, some became inactive; some lacked critical feminist perspectives, teaching commercialized femininity in courses with "women" in their titles. Some scholars were also bothered by the fact that in order to sustain their organization, they had to focus on applied research—referred to as "doing projects"—to get funding. A scholar lamented that as projects became "hot," curriculum development and disciplinary construction in universities "cooled" (Du 2005, 35).

In the summer of 1999, the "Reading and Discussion Seminar on Disciplinary Construction of Women's History" was launched jointly by local and diasporic Chinese women's studies scholars, with private funding they had raised. It grew into "Developing Women and Gender Studies in China," a multiyear joint project headed by the Women's Studies Center at Tianjin Normal University, funded by the Ford Foundation (2000–2006). This project is unique in its guiding principles and approaches, emphasizing: (1) a commitment to make feminism and gender the theoretical bases and the principal analytical concepts of women's studies; (2) an engagement with scholarship from outside China through a series of reading and discussion seminars to "connect to, draw from, carry on [what has been established], and blaze new trails" (Cai, Wang, and Du 1999); (3) multidisciplinary and interdisciplinary approaches targeting three disciplines—history, sociology, and education—with each discipline holding separate seminars to produce its own textbooks and syllabi while all getting together to learn feminist theoretical frameworks and methodological approaches to forming a common ground for teaching all women's studies courses; and (4) faculty training and curriculum development through combining scholarship with teaching practice from inside and outside China for theory building, pedagogy exploration, and the establishment of a database with resources for teaching women's studies courses. The "Young Scholars Scholarship" set up within the project provided a small amount of money for new course development.

By mid-2004, the project had completed its first phase, producing twenty published books covering the three disciplines as well as gender and feminist scholarship in general. Three of these publications are translated works; the rest are works by Chinese local or diasporic scholars, including a CD on feminist pedagogy. The project supported thirty-four women and gender studies courses (nine of them at the graduate level) in fourteen Chinese universities. Of the dozen Chinese universities that have master's programs in women's studies or a specialty in women's studies in various disciplines, more than half of the directors or leading professors have participated in this project.

The project also established the Network of Developing Women/Gender Studies, with a Web site that contains materials and other resources for teaching women/gender studies courses in the three disciplines covered by the project, later adding materials on gendering the teaching of literature—a product of another project jointly run by local and diasporic Chinese scholars following the same model with a grant from the Ford Foundation.

The project signals two changes in women's studies in China. First, it reflects renewed efforts in discipline construction, emphasizing curriculum transformation and knowledge production in institutions of higher education. For this reason, some scholars further propose reserving the term *funuxue* (women's studies or women-ology) to highlight its academic nature exclusively for feminist teaching and research in universities in China and abroad, while using *funu yanjiu* (women's research or research on women)[17] for studies of "any issues related to women." This practice seems to be taking hold due to the effort of those in academe who consistently use *funuxue*.

Second, the project illustrates Chinese scholars' desire to bring gender into research and teaching, representing a shift of perspective in women's studies. But gender remains a highly contested concept. To clearly define the nature of their project and their position, Du Fangqin, the lead scholar of the project, made a point by naming the project and network *funu yu shehuixingbie xue* (women and gender studies) for two reasons. First, gender in the title is translated as *shehui xingbie* (social sex) to distinguish the orientation of their teaching and research from *xingbei yanjiu* (gender studies) at the Gender Studies Center of Dalian University, where they translate *gender* directly to the Chinese word *xingbie* (sex) to depoliticize the program and attract both male and female students.[18] Second, by keeping *women* in the title of the project, Du says they want to "emphasize [the project's] efforts of always locating women in the central position" when reconstructing knowledge in the "indigenous women/gender sphere, with the concept of gender (*shehui xingbie*)," to distinguish themselves from those who promulgate a "femininity" (*nürenwei*) discourse that "takes Chinese gender relations for granted as defined by the "harmony between yin and yang" (*yingyang hehe*) without analysis and criticism" (Du 2005, 7). She and her colleagues are also critical of the term *niuxing xue* (female studies or female-ology) that is used by some scholars in their writing or in the course catalogs of some universities. Contestation over the content and theoretical perspective of women's studies continues.

The ACWF is not a bystander to scholars' institutionalization effort in higher education. In the reform era, it has expanded its central school, originally set up as a women cadres' school in 1950, to offer degree-and-diploma-conferring programs to women students (Gu 2001). In 2001, the school moved to a new campus and changed its name to China Women's College. It has a women's studies department (the country's first), offering a four-year bachelor's degree. It also offered a pre–master's degree program in women's studies in conjunction with the Chinese University of Hong Kong and the University of Michigan from 2000 to 2004. Although women's studies course offerings are still limited across the country (less than 1 percent of all universities), progress has been made. By June 2006, university-level women's and gender studies institutions were offering 250 courses. About a dozen women's and gender studies programs have academic degrees at the master's level (Du and Wang 2008).

The large field of women's studies in China has also become stronger institutionally. By 2005, it was estimated that about thirty women's studies and research units were located within the ACWF system at the provincial level, nine in the Chinese Academies of Social Sciences, and fifty at major universities (Tan, Wu, and Li 2005). Another major achievement was the formation of the Chinese Women's Research Society (CWRS) in December 1999. It was initiated by the Women's Studies Institute of China (WSIC), registered as a nonprofit member-based organization for research, with 98 institutional members, 180 individual members, and a committee on women's education. *Collection of Women's Studies,* a bimonthly journal launched by the WSIC in 1992, became the official journal of the CWRS. It has some funding and organizes conferences on current issues concerning women. In recent years, activists within the CWRS have made creative use of the organization, extending their activities beyond promoting research. For example, in 2007, three Chinese laws—Chinese Property Law, Employment Promotion Law, and Labor Contract Law—were to be discussed when the People's Congress was in session, and the drafts of the laws were released to the public for feedback. The CWRS organized three small conferences, gathering specialists, scholars, and activists to suggest revisions to ensure gender equality in legislation. Their opinions were reflected in two of the three laws passed by the People's Congress (Liu 2009).

Combatting Domestic Violence

The Chinese language didn't include the term *domestic violence* until 1995. This new terminology is different from the well-known Chinese idiom of *dalaopo* (wife beating), which portrays the wife as the husband's property. Since the introduction of the new term, local initiatives against domestic violence have transformed the state-centered approach to "management of the public order" into an NGO-initiated "comprehensive community intervention." The former approach puts domestic violence in the same category as personal assault in the criminal code; it overlooks gender inequalities in domestic violence, and its remedial legal measures are superficial and short-term. The latter approach addresses both the outcome and the roots of domestic violence. Employing the legal framework of individual rights, the term and the concept of *anti–domestic violence* emphasize women's rights and call for their legal protection (Bu 2005).

The leading NGO, the Domestic Violence Network, founded in 2000, is affiliated with the China Law Society and aims to establish an anti–domestic violence network and information center, to propose legal codes rectifying domestic violence, to explore community-based intervention, and to develop anti–domestic violence materials and approaches relevant to Chinese society and culture (Bu 2005). Structurally, the Domestic Violence Network is positioned firmly at the junction between the local and the global. Within China, it engages in ongoing collaboration with government offices, the ACWF, the Chinese Academy of Social Sciences, and other academic institutes and NGOs. It has developed training materials and organized training workshops on domestic violence for officials in the judicial system, social workers, medical personnel, and others who work in relevant social and legal organizations. Its members have conducted research projects to analyze the patterns and scale of domestic violence in urban and rural settings. The findings have contributed to anti–domestic violence laws and regulations. The Network has received international funding and has organized international seminars to identify the best practices from around the world. Its Web site has links to other Web sites in Western industrialized countries on domestic violence (Bu 2005, Mulwertz 2003, and Web site).

The "Chinese character" of anti–domestic violence activism is evident in its use of traditional folk performances to oppose domestic violence. In 2001, the Henan Community Education Research Center began to explore community-based intervention into domestic violence in rural areas. In addition to intervention and victim support, it has successfully employed a popular form of folk performance as a means of public education to fight domestic violence in the countryside. Since 2002, several popular theater troupes have formed. They present plays such as *Why Doesn't She Divorce?* Writing new lyrics for well-known folk songs and new scripts for well-known scenes, these troupes have become a sensational hit in the countryside. For the women victims-turned-players, it is an outlet and form of empowerment. For male performers, it provides a deeper understanding of the nature of domestic violence. By appropriating folklore as an alternative medium, the popular theater troupes' performances bring *dalaopo* out of the closet of strictly familial, personal issues. They not only send a clear message that domestic violence is a community affair deserving public attention but also widely publicize its legal ramifications in the countryside. The troupe initiative therefore exemplifies feminist indigenization (Bu 2005).

Two other initiatives in Beijing suggest that international activism is taking root in Chinese soil. On November 25, 2002, the international date of increased attention to domestic violence, a group of Chinese men formed a group entitled "Group for the Growth of the Happy Family" (*Xingfu jiating chengzhang xiaozu*) to oppose domestic violence. As the Chinese version of the White Ribbon Campaign,[19] the group announced its commitment never to participate in or keep silent about violence against women. Since its establishment, similar units have been formed in Beijing's neighborhoods and in Changsha, in Hunan Province. The group has organized training workshops and offered counseling services to male abusers and to children of affected families (Li 2005).

In 2005, a lesbian and bisexual organization *Tongyu* (common language) formed in Beijing. This group refers to itself as *Lala*. This term comes from the English word lesbian, and also means "hand in hand" in Chinese. Over the past few years, similar groups in several major cities and urban centers throughout China have also arisen. The Lala Group receives funding from the Domestic Violence Network to eliminate domestic violence among lesbian and bisexual couples. Its objectives are to study the frequency and nature of domestic violence in China, to publish anti–domestic violence booklets, and to disseminate findings through mass media and training workshops (*Lala fanjiabao xiangmu*).

Incorporation of Gender Perspective into Policy and Policy Making

The more open political environment of recent years has enabled feminist groups to make their critical and diverse views heard. Concerted organizing effort has germinated around key policies, particularly women's rights and gender equality. In order to institutionalize gender equality, its principles must be written into policies and laws that were once assumed to be gender neutral. Such an endeavor is critical, as many new laws and policies have been drafted and existing laws revised in recent years as economic reform has altered the fabric of society. Furthermore, deliberate effort must be directed at establishing a much needed infrastructure to effectively enforce such laws and policies.[20] In the following section, we examine the actions and endeavors surrounding the Law to Protect Women's Rights in Beijing as well as three sets of laws, the Property Law, the Employment Promotion Law, and the Labor Contract Law. The first is a good example of the advocacy focus of the Women's Federation, as well as citywide collaboration among established NGOs. The latter demonstrates, at the national level, the cross-fertilization between research and activism, a development we will explore in later sections.

In December 2008, when the Beijing Municipality called for public input on its proposed Law to Protect Women's Rights in Beijing, the Women's Federation of the municipality seized this opportunity to propose some revisions. The amendments incorporated clauses to safeguard women's rights in family, education, employment, and political participation. The provisions not only addressed issues raised by feminist researchers and activists in recent years but also aimed to rectify discriminatory practices and gender inequalities that emerged as a result of economic reform.[21] To ensure enforcement, the proposed revisions not only specified the responsibilities of various government offices but also spelled out ramifications for specific discriminatory practices.[22] Most significantly, the Committee of Women and Children's Affairs and various levels of the Women's Federation would now monitor and hold accountable various government offices.[23]

One of the most controversial issues in the draft Law to Protect Women's Rights in Beijing was the proposed extension of the retirement age of women cadres and intellectuals to sixty, equivalent to that of their male counterparts.[24] The proposal aroused opposition, as expressed in media debates and Internet discussions. Meanwhile, four well-respected and well-positioned feminist groups published a position paper to voice their support for the law. Their widely publicized paper was addressed to the Beijing Municipality's official body in policy making and implementation. Although the so-called extended retirement age was, unfortunately, deleted from the final reading of the law, the *China Women's News Daily*, the official newspaper of the ACWF, announced its decision to extend the retirement age of its editors and executive staff to sixty years (Guo 2009). This announcement not only signaled a dissident voice but also reflects the lenient political climate in recent years.

The Property Law, the Employment Promotion Law, and the Labor Contract Law

In February 2007, the Chinese Women's Research Society (CWRS) called a meeting to share with women's NGOs in the Beijing area the review of the Chinese government's implementation of the Convention on the Elimination of All Forms of Discrimination Against Women. The gathering quickly turned into an organizing rally when its participants unanimously decided to take advantage of the upcoming meetings of the tenth National People's Congress and its Standing Committee, when three sets of laws (the Property Law, the Employment Promotion Law, and the Labor Contract Law) were to have their final readings before they were enacted. To ensure that the laws recognized local realities and specific practices that perpetuated gender inequalities, the participants promptly decided to act when the Standing Committee invited the public to air their positions. Their concerted organizing effort took three forms.

First, the CWRS and the Chinese Women's Research Institute of the ACWF invited input from the Bureaus of Labor and Social Security, the Labor Union, the Enterprise Association, and legal scholars and practitioners. The participants quickly reached a consensus on the prevalent forms of gender-based employment discrimination and the appropriate legal ramifications for this discrimination. In their proposed revisions, they adopted international protocols and legal positions alongside propositions grounded in China's local realities, after analysis of statistical data and case studies.

Second, the CWRS worked within the existing system. As Liu points out, representatives of the ACWF in the People's Congress and its Executive Committee were seasoned in law and policy making. Involving them in drafting the proposed revisions made it easy for them to proactively bring gender equality into policy making at the Congress. Furthermore, individual researchers contributed their research findings to substantiate arguments made in the amendments.[25] The CWRS also took full advantage of the expertise of legal professionals. By adopting the legal profession's terminology and technical expressions, the proposed revisions "creatively" employed discourse and language "understood or accepted by mainstream legal scholars, policy makers, members of the Congress" (Liu 2009, 13).

Third, the CWRS activated its mass base through its newsletter, the *Research News*, asking its members to respond to the Congress's calls for public input. It urged its members to use the CWRS's proposed amendments to submit their own individual input. It further extended its call for civil participation beyond its members, summoning all disadvantaged groups, such as rural workers, the disabled, minorities, HIV patients, and carriers of infectious diseases, to oppose employment discrimination.

Rural Women's Political Participation in Local Governance

Concerns over women's political participation caught national attention when the percentage of women cadres in national, provincial, and local party/government offices dropped to an all-time low in the 1980s. Efforts to ensure that women's representation and participation in local governance are not compromised have been the focal point of feminist activism in recent years as local governance becomes one of the key issues in the CCP's agenda for political democratization and rural revitalization in the new millennium. Since 2005, several provinces have adopted different strategies to improve rural women's political participation through elections at the village level.[26] The term *nucunguan* (woman village head) was coined to identify this particular group of rural women who enter the political arena through local elections. It is also a discursive idiom that encapsulates the debates about women's political participation in recent decades. The Cultural Development Center for Rural Women and the Shaanxi Research Association for Women and Family have been active in the nucunguan initiative. The CDCRW has been working on getting women elected to village committees since 2000. Besides conducting training workshops at the grassroots, it has established the national Nucunguan Support Network and website for all women village heads.

The CDCRW organized a Nucunguan Forum in November 2008. At the closing session, its director's words of encouragement revealed both conventional ideas about women's gender roles and new inspiration for women officers. Since loving and caring are women's strengths, the director stated, women officers' main focus of political participation should be in areas that will enhance the welfare of the elderly, weak, sick, and disabled. Women officers not only need to know how to listen and collaborate but also need to master the skills of effectively writing, speaking, and conducting official duties.

The SRAWF used the election of members and directors of the Villagers Committee as points of intervention. With international funding, their work began with improving the chances for rural women to be elected as members or directors of the Villagers Committees, and extended to addressing rural women's participation in local governance and implementation of gender equality (Gao 2009b). Reflecting on her group's intervention, the director of the association argued that it is important to turn abstract debates over women's equality and superficial descriptions of forbidding structural obstacles into specific, actionable questions, such as how to make women competitive candidates in elections, how to make women officers "reelectable," how to bring the principles of gender equality into everyday governance when in recent years it has been mainly driven by indicators of economic development, and how to handle hostile male-dominated environments in the political arena.

Clearly, increasing and sustaining rural women's political participation demand interventions that simultaneously enhance women's individual capacity and challenge structural obstacles. Methods of enhancing individual capacity range from organizing leadership workshops for nucunguan, making government grant information accessible to nucunguan, and holding specific forums so nucunguan can share their experiences in government to publishing their personal narratives and establishing networks among the nucunguan. These initiatives obviously go beyond conventional notions of striving for women's equality; their organizing objectives are to break through isolation, instill a collective identity, and claim the public persona of the nucunguan.

But before rural women in China can reach the international benchmark of 30 percent political representation, structural challenges must be overcome.[27] For example, in recent years, rural elections have become more competitive, as formal tangible benefits, such as a regular salary and retirement benefits, are now attached to various positions. As these positions become more attractive to men, it is increasingly difficult for rural women to be elected. Furthermore, with neither inherited nor currently available political capital, the learning curve for the first-term nucunguan is particularly steep. By the time they figure out various aspects of their job, the three-year term is over. Moreover, the male-dominated political arena proves formidable for many of them. Unless a nucunguan has a good relationship with the (male) party secretary, she cannot be reelected, no matter how outstanding her performance. Finally, village finances are managed by the superior administrative unit of the township, and many nucunguan end up investing their personal money to fill in the "black holes" created by their superiors.[28] And, of course, nucunguan continue to face the double burden of responsibilities in the public and private spheres

(Gao 2009b). To deal with the hostile environment and structural obstacles, training materials addressing locally relevant matters were used in province-wide workshops. About 2,400 women cadres and 1,000 administrative leaders attended the workshops (Gao 2009b).[29]

The intervention led to a marked improvement in elections. The percentage of women as members or directors of the Villagers Committees has increased at both the local and the national levels.[30] Most significantly, organizing experiences have led to discussions and initiatives that have expanded the notion of rural women's political participation from having women elected to the Villagers Committee to a general increase in women's participation in rural governance and civil affairs. Such expansion constitutes a groundbreaking trajectory of activism, advancing from a single quantity-based focus to an all-inclusive approach to women's political participation. Evidence of that expansion is found in a statement by the director of the SRAWF: "We argue that women can and should become active as citizens in local governance and that the principles of gender equality should be incorporated into all aspects of governance and public life" (Gao 2009b). Thus, the nucunguan initiative and its subsequent development call for innovative thinking and practices that promise to consolidate gains in newly entered male-dominated territory without losing ground in previously held areas.

At a conference where activists reflected on the progress made and challenges ahead in rural women's political participation, the Women's Federation was urged to encourage one-term nucunguan who had not been reelected to enter other public platforms and to support these women in their attempts to do so. It was argued that to remain active on the public stage, women should not shy away from high-profile competitions, such as for the annual Nunengren (Women of Outstanding Capacity) Award, even though it was a conventional category in the state feminist framework (Gao 2009b). The challenge, of course, is to overcome stigma and avoid the hazard of the preexisting gender-segregated model, where women are active only in officially designated fields. Organizing endeavors and critical reflection surrounding rural women's political participation further raise the question of how to adequately recognize women's active participation in public life outside the narrowly defined political arena. For example, women have assumed preeminent leadership roles in religious activities and groups. Their genuine interest and active participation are fertile grounds for deepening women's roles in good governance (Jiang 2007; Jiang and Tang 2007). The prospect of women's increasing participation in public affairs will improve when the nucunguan initiative is mainstreamed.

As discussed earlier, the nucunguan intervention in Shaanxi Province was led by the SRAWF. In collaboration with the Women's Federation in Shaanxi Province, the project grew from an experimental initiative in three local counties, with funding from international sources. After painstaking negotiations, the project eventually received backing from governmental offices such as the Policy Research Office of the Provincial Committee, the Provincial Civil Affairs Department, and the Organization Department of the Provincial Committee. Their open support and endorsement were extremely hard to secure but invaluable, for the legitimacy and tangible political capital they conferred.[31] By the end of the third project, the work was placed under the budgetary umbrella of the Women's Federation in Shaanxi Province and involved governmental offices. After April 2009, the ACWF, Bureau of Governance, and Ministry of Civil Affairs took over the undertaking. The ACWF embraced rural women's political participation in elections and governance as part of its main agenda. It is fair to state that rural women's political participation has now been mainstreamed (Gao 2009b, 2). Given China's political system and bureaucratic ethos, the mainstreaming is particularly meaningful and significant, as women and NGOs can now tap into formal political resources for their gender-specific causes.

Economic Issues

In China's planned economy, the state drove the advancement of women's participation in the labor force. However, the state has yet to establish a comparable mechanism and effective measures to counterbalance emergent forces instigated by privatization, marketization, and globalization, which have led to increasing gender inequalities over the past three decades (Jiang and Tang 2007). We now turn to key issues in this area: women's right to employment, land, and property and the issue of women in poverty.

Since the economic reforms of the 1980s, there have been recurrent arguments in favor of sending women home in tough economic times and at certain stages of their lives. State policy on employment and the labor market is essential to ensure women's economic rights and to mitigate unfavorable market forces. The ACWF and other NGOs have successfully rallied against measures to limit women's employment to certain stages of their lives into the "Tenth Five-Year Plan on Economic and Social Development."

Researchers have focused on other policy-related topics, such as employment for women university graduates, reemployment of laid-off women workers, and informalization of women's employment. Recommendations include involving women NGOs as the legitimate partners of the state, employer, and union in policies relating to women's employment; mainstreaming gender equality in employment-related policies; and proposing that the government should not only adopt nondiscriminatory practices in hiring and assessment but also establish effective mechanisms to monitor the labor market. Specific aspects of marketization have been identified as focal points of intervention.

Generally, women's rights in employment are most compromised in the nongovernmental and informal sectors. Under the pressure of finding paid employment, recent rural migrant and laid-off workers are most likely to enter the service and informal sectors, which are insecure, poorly paid, and provide limited opportunities for upward mobility (Jiang and Tang 2007, 56). Studies have found that not only are the conditions experienced by those women inferior to those of their female counterparts in the formal sector, but they are also worse off than their male counterparts in the informal sector (Jiang and Tang 2007). The policy vacuum in this area leads to inferior employment status, pay level, security, and unionization of women. Their precarious situations include no employment contracts, no social security, delayed pay, being overworked, and receiving no payment during pregnancy and maternity leaves (Jiang and Tang 2007, 58). In 2009, two NGO-based initiatives were launched in this area.

The newsletter, *Equality at Work in China*, first published in March 2009, aims to support, promote, and apply ILO Convention no. 111, the Discrimination (Employment and Occupation) Convention in China. In the same month, the Chinese base of the Global Call to Action Against Poverty put out a call for collaboration with community groups, NGOs, and researchers to study the employment and enterprise ventures of returned rural migrant workers during the global economic recession, to understand the views of local communities on the government's poverty-alleviation policy, and to propose alternative strategies for collaborating with various departments of the government.[32]

Although it is too early to assess the effects of such activist endeavors, two issues deserve comment. First, international financial support is being used to apply the global consensus sanctioned by the United Nations to China. It resembles the typical pattern of local-global engagement we discussed earlier in this chapter. The newsletter provides a venue for the dissemination of international norms on equality in employment, as well as a forum to discuss local practices and possible ramifications. To actually address abuses and violations requires joined forces and an adequate mechanism beyond publication of the newsletter. Second, as a consortium of local NGOs, the Global Call to Action Against Poverty is advantageously positioned to reach the local community. The call for proposals suggests deliberate effort to build networks and collaboration not only with NGOs but with government offices as well.

In 1978, the collective-commune system that had operated in China since 1958 was replaced by the household-responsibility system. Each household was given land-use rights according to its demographic composition (the number of people and laborers within the household). Even though Chinese women are legally entitled to contract land, laws and regulations remain ineffective because they are not backed by specific implementation guidelines. Patrilineal practices in the countryside mean that a woman's right to use contracted land is severed as soon as she marries, divorces, or is widowed. A report in 2001 on women's social status indicates that 70 percent of those without any property were women. Of propertyless women, 20 percent never received land, 44 percent lost their entitlement upon getting married, and 7 percent lost it upon divorce (Li and Wang 2007, 166).

Recent studies on poverty alleviation focus on the sources of poverty, the relationship between gender and poverty, and the gendered effects of poverty-alleviation projects. It has been found that poverty-alleviation projects often intensify gender inequalities. For example, most projects designate villages or households as aid recipients, without recognizing gender inequalities in the village or within the household. This leads to women's having unequal access to and control over resources provided through poverty-alleviation programs. Nor do women have equal opportunities for training and services in technology. Therefore, researchers find that poverty alleviation has not been an effective means to confront gender inequality and change traditional gender relationships (Jiang 2007, 6). Some development programs, in fact, increase women's labor and psychological burden because of women's continuing roles in reproductive labor.

Since 2001, the State Council has taken a participatory approach toward 592 poverty-alleviation projects (Li and Qi 2007, 63). It also emphasizes the importance of maintaining a gender perspective in poverty alleviation. One noteworthy change is the inclusion of the percentage of women experiencing chronic illness and the dropout rates of female elementary and middle school students as two of the eight indicators identifying poverty at the village level (Li and Qi 2007). Although it is too early to evaluate the result of such efforts, much of the work in poverty alleviation is carried out by government offices or relies on preexisting official setups. For example, various levels of the Women's Federation are involved in implementing and releasing funds for microcredit projects (Lin 2008, 33–34).[33] In addition, the China Population Welfare Foundation, an NGO under the supervision of the National Population and Family Planning Commission, initiated the "Happiness Project" in 1995 (ibid., 33). This project provides financial assistance to impoverished mothers of families that have complied with the government's family-planning program in poor regions (http://www.cpwf.org.cn/en/do1.asp). By using compliance to the family-planning program as a criterion, it inadvertently lends symbolic, if not substantive, support to the state and its population policy. Therefore, the underlying principle of the project stands in distinct contrast to other initiatives discussed in this chapter, which challenge and strive to transform the status quo.

The Chinese Women's Movement in Global Context: Assessment and Reflections

The preceding discussion provides an account of the development of the Chinese women's movement in the reform era. It emerged over the backdrop of China's economic reform, responded to the problems facing women, and was radically transformed by China's preparation and hosting of the 1995 FWCW and women's participation in this effort. Global influences and forces have become more important than ever in shaping domestic gender politics and the women's movement. The Chinese women's movement has expanded its agenda, taking on issues highlighted in the Beijing Platform for Action. Gender has become a new lens through which to view women's issues; gender equality is increasingly framed as a human rights issue. Women's organizations have continued to expand and have increased their organizing capacity. NGOs have been firmly established. Approaches, programs, and discourses from the international NGO community have influenced the way the movement is organized.

The women's movement faces many challenges. The strategy of gender mainstreaming has greatly extended the women's movement, bringing virtually everything into the purview of the movement and is effective in combating gender discrimination of various kinds within the legal framework. However, it also has drawbacks.[34] The strategy does not treat women as a special group in an unequal relationship with men, nor does it demand transformative changes to end such inequality, as opposed to *nanna pingdang*, or the official Marxist perspective on women. Although a "Marxist perspective on women" remains central to the official discourse and the ACWF's documents, there is a lack of scholarly work and public discussion among women's activists on the structural causes of gender inequality in China. Critiques of the government's macro economic-development policies are lacking at the very time when such an analysis is most useful and needed. Some activists do not see much difference between a "Marxist perspective on women" and gender mainstreaming, as both are committed to equality for women. But this is not true, especially when feminist gender theory is equated with a gender mainstreaming strategy alone. The women's movement, especially the ACWF, has yet to face this issue more seriously at both theoretical and practical levels.

The development of NGOs brought new energy, vision, and spirit to the women's movement and signaled the development of civil society in China. The challenge the women's movement now faces is that NGOs are generally confined to urban areas among educated women, and rare in remote areas. Many issue-based NGOs have become the movers of the women's movement, signaling the NGO-ization of the women's movement in China. As a result of international foundations and organizations' supporting NGO capacity-building training, Chinese NGOs are becoming more formalized and professionalized to live up to international standards. This makes it difficult for small new groups to receive recognition and funding. NGOs rely heavily on external funding, though the internal funding situation is improving.

China's hosting of the 1995 conference put the Chinese women's movement and its actors at the center of political debate. A few Chinese scholars believe that Western feminist ideas coming with the 1995 conference have hindered *bentu yanjiu* (indigenous research), which characterized women's studies before the conference (Li 2005). Some in the feminist community outside China view Chinese women's studies and the Chinese women's movement as being heavily influenced by international feminism, which is defined as "an ideological package—a well-financed, resurgent, neo-liberal, United States–focused effort to establish common ground for feminism," and refer to scholars who propose *bentuhua* (indigenization) as "agents of internationalization" (Spakowski 2000). Some Western feminist scholars challenge these Chinese scholars from yet another direction, suspecting that "indigenization" is actually a process whereby the Chinese reject foreign ideas: "What do you mean by indigenization? If a theory is useful, it should be universal, not to be confined by national boundaries" (Gao, Jiang, and Wang 2002, 15). These arguments, taken together, reflect the precarious position in which Chinese women scholars and activists find themselves when interacting with international feminism.

We believe it is important to keep a historical perspective when examining the consequences of the 1995 conference and to be sensitive to the complexity of local-global dynamics. Just as the Chinese women's movement emerged in the first quarter of the twentieth century amid a vigorous exchange of ideas between Chinese intellectuals and their counterparts outside China, the current Chinese women's movement, including those who call for "indigenous research," meaning "research without any outside influence" (Li 2000, 62f, cited in Spakowski 2000, 94), is benefiting from contact with global feminism. The FWCW helped push open the door for Chinese women's groups to reconnect with the international women's movement after decades of isolation. This explains the strong desire of Chinese women scholars and activists to learn from their counterparts outside of China. The interaction between the local and global is complex. Discourse is created in the process of interaction, negotiated from all sides—no one side can maintain unilateral control. The fact that the Chinese women's movement and NGOs emerged *before* the convening of the conference, rather than after, makes all the difference in the dynamics of the interaction and outcome.

The Chinese women's movement has the following characteristics: concerted efforts to effect legislative change, greater willingness to cooperate with the government on women's issues than its Western counterparts, cooperation between self-initiated women's organizations and the ACWF, thereby combining change from both bottom up and top down, and the institutional embeddedness of women's organizations in China's society.[35] This last aspect is best reflected in the ACWF, as described by a women's NGO leader: the ACWF "is currently the largest women's organization in China. It has a well-established organizational network from top to bottom, supported by huge groups of professional women cadres, the Party, and the government. It also has an existing channel for promoting polices or proposing legislative measures. All this is an important resource for Chinese women's activism." She goes on to outline the many changes that have taken place in the ACWF but comments that "the current structure of the Federation means that it cannot shed its features as a government organization" (Gao 2001a, 206). The ACWF had to take the party line in 1957 when women's gender interest was in conflict with that of the CCP, a primary example of its subordination to the party and the constraints it faces.

On the other hand, its established status as the representative of Chinese women also provides legitimacy for the ACWF to maintain and expand its space, and it has been the principal organization pushing for the advancement of women. It has bureaucrats but also very dedicated feminists (whether they identify themselves that way or not) who are among the core of the women's movement actors. Some of the high-profile NGO leaders are federation cadres, such as Gao Xiaoxian of the SRAWF and Xie Lihua of the Cultural Development Center for Rural Women. As deputy chief editor of *China Women News*, Xie has access to resources that helped her launch the magazines *Rural Women* and *Woman Village Head*. When the Tongzhi Pager Hotline opened in 1998, it was *China Women News* that advertised its number.

The Chinese women's movement does not fit prevailing models of women's movements as being autonomous from the state. Studies of state feminism since the 1980s examine the effects of the women's movement *entering* the state—that is, women's policy agencies set up by the governments of Western democratic countries in response to the demand of the Second Wave of the women's movement. But Chinese women were *inside* the state when the PRC was founded in 1949. At the time, some of the women's movement leaders, including nonpartisan women figures, held high party or government positions, a victory for the women's movement. This also makes the AC(D)WF an inside player in the ongoing process of state formation, interacting with the state.

We believe that to better understand the relationship between the Chinese women's movement and the state, new paradigms should be adopted. Insights from state theorists who bring culture into their study would be useful here (Steinmetz 1999). They see state formation as a process and analyzes the state as both a system and an idea—the "state effect." State and society are not viewed as two discreet entities with fixed, externally drawn boundaries; rather, boundaries are drawn internally by its players through structure-affecting policies, practices, and techniques that create both the institutional arrangement and the cultural effect of the state (Mitchell 1991). Seen from this perspective, the ACWF has been actively appropriating its dual status and role to interact with the state in drawing the boundaries between state and society. In the early years of the PRC, as there was no government agency for women's work, the ACWF took the opportunities of state administrative restructuring to have representation of the ACDWF in the newly established administrative organs. When its grassroots women's organization was threatened with elimination twice in the 1950s, the ACWF rose to stop it. Without this action, there would be no ACWF as a "mass organization" as it is known today. Although the ACWF is clearly defined in the official discourse as a "bridge connecting women to the Party and state," there are numerous examples of its creating the "state effect" by establishing itself as the authoritative women's organization for women: running women's media, institutionalizing practices such as having the ACWF be the first place women go for relief of grievances, receiving permission for women to be present in court hearings on women's divorce cases (during the

1950s when the new marriage law was released), and being specifically recognized in the PRC Law for the Protection of Women's Rights and Interests for its role in this regard. These measures resulted in the ACWF's dominance in representing women in formal official channels, but it had also gained space and representation for women. It is obvious that the ACWF is not a pawn to be manipulated by the state but an active agent drawing the boundaries.

It is also useful to examine the ACWF as an institutional actor in the framework of state feminism studies, by first asking, "What state? What feminism?" The first question draws attention to the legacy of Chinese socialism for the movement. Women's committees were established in both the former Soviet Union and China, following the instruction of the Comintern.[36] Women's delegate meetings as a form of organizing women at the grassroots level were copied from Soviet Russia in the early 1930s in the CCP-occupied area, but it was institutionalized in the PRC and not in Soviet Russia. Why? How does this affect the way the women's movements are carried out in both countries? In contrast to Russian women's rejection of the Communist Party's program to get women into the labor force, Chinese women rallied around the issues of women's employment and political participation, two central topics focused on by the state and women in the prereform era. Why is this the case?

The second question requires international feminist scholars to consider whether to associate the term *state feminism* with an authoritarian socialist state. We consider Chinese state feminism to fall within the framework of Marxist feminism; it was consciously followed in practice before the reform era by the ACWF whenever possible. The first generation of NGOs and the leaders of the women's movement are now the products of this tradition. What kind of feminism is developing in China? Where will the next generation of women go? These are the complicated questions the Chinese women's movement is facing today.

Notes

1. The demands are typically not made in a confrontational manner, though. The ACWF officials who are members of the CCP are subordinate to the party committee of the same administrative level, and have to go through the official channel for their demands. Party chairman Mao Zedong, aware of the indifference of some party bosses to women or woman-work, had taught the ACWF leaders the three steps in dealing with this problem: first submit proposals to the party committee; second, push for reply; third, just curse and swear if the first two methods did not work (Wang 2006, 914), an illustration that maneuvering within the system is the common strategy.

We appreciate Dr. Amrita Basu's patience, support, and intellectual input. Without her extraordinary commitment, this chapter would not have been completed. We would also like to thank Linn Clark for her editorial assistance and support, Liu Bohong for her support and provision of research materials and data, and Susan Joel's editorial assistance in the early stage of the project.

2. For a review of the Chinese women's movement prior to the 1995 conference, see Zhang and Xu 1995.

3. See the speech by Li Suwen, head of the Chinese women's delegation (Li 1975), and "Curtain Falls on World Conference on UN Year of Women," *People's Daily*, July 4, 1975, 6.

4. For scholars' personal accounts, see Liang 2001; Du 2000; and Gao 2000.

5. However, there were some Western feminist influences, such as Simone de Beauvoir's view expressed in *The Second Sex*.

6. For more detailed study of development of women's studies in China, see Chow, Zhang, and Wang 2004.

7. For more detailed discussion, see Wu and Xiaolan 2001.

8. From a personal conversation with a participant of the meeting in 1995. See also Wesoky 2002.

9. For discussion of the debate, see Hsiung and Wong 1998, 474–475.

10. For more on the role of the Ford Foundation Beijing and the influence of international feminism, see Spakowski 2000.

11. Conversation with a Yunnan activist, 2000.

12. For their personal stories and experiences with the 1995 conference, see Wong 1995.

13. This translation is now widely adopted by feminist scholars and in official documents, though the drawback of this translation has also become more visible, that is, those without a better understanding of the concept may treat gender and sex as two totally different entities, failing to see the connection between the two.

14. This is in contrast to the response of their Indian counterparts, who rejected the Beijing Platform for Action, faulting the document for endorsing a dominant development model and not challenging the existing macro systems oppressive to women (Liu 2006).

15. As shown in the following statement: "From Beijing Declaration, Platform for Action of 1995 at the Fourth World Conference on Women, to 'Political Declaration' 'Outcome Document' of Beijing +5 in 2000, to the Millennium Development Goals formulated by the United Nations, [these documents] all point out for us the direction of striving to building a society with gender equality. The reason we promote gender mainstreaming is to make the blueprint described by [these documents] a reality" (China Project Group 2004, 82).

16. About US$146,455; US$1=6.828 CNY.

17. When research on women's issues was taking off in the early 1980s, the term *women's studies* was introduced to China from the West in three different versions of Chinese translation: *funuxue* (women's studies or women-ology), *funu yanjiu* (women's research or research on women), and *nuxingxue* (female studies or female-ology).

18. Li Xiaojiang, the founder of the center and a pioneer in women's studies in China, said that "the advantage of the name *xingbie yanjiu* (gender studies) [is that it] not only easily attracts participation of male teachers but also benefits the discipline itself by going beyond 'women' and addressing 'gender.' It eliminates the excessive politicization of *funü xue* (women-ology) and breaks the parochialism of a single sex. Moreover, as a method of academic penetration, it has the advantage of integrating women's studies into other disciplines" (Du 2005, 7).

19. In 1991, a handful of men in Canada pledged to speak out about violence against women, wearing a white ribbon as a symbol. The White Ribbon Campaign quickly became a worldwide movement for men to combat all forms of violence against women and girls. For detailed information, see the Web site of the White Ribbon Campaign Against Domestic Violence, http://whiteribboncampaign-nh.org/.

20. In addition to examination of the content of various laws and policies, there has been much discussion of problems pertinent to enforcement. We consider this development a meaningful sign of the advancement of the women's movement in China.

21. For example, the revisions included a clause to ensure the educational rights of daughters of migrant workers. On individual rights, the amendments contained a provision that would prohibit unnecessary prenatal checkups that would reveal a fetus's sex, as well as various modifica-

tions that defined and criminalized sexual harassment. For additional details of the proposed changes, see http://www.bjfzb.gov.cn/advice/user/content.asp?UNID=291.

22. For example, the mass media would be accountable for "degrading and damaging women's reputation." For additional details, see ibid.

23. Both the Committee of Women and Children's Affairs and various levels of the Women's Federation have been criticized for having only symbolic, decorative status without real directive and administrative authority. It is therefore particularly significant that the committee and the offices of the Women's Federation proposed that they be authorized to demand written reports from various government offices within fifteen working days and to notify, and invite input from, the public through the mass media (ibid.).

24. The retirement age of male government employees in China is sixty; for female government employees it's fifty-five. This is based on the "Temporary Placement Regulation on Sick, Disabled, and Elderly Cadres," issued by the State Council in 1978.

25. Three specific research endeavors made significant contributions to the proposed revisions. The China Association for Employment Promotion and its researchers used their findings from a project devoted to incorporating gender equality into a "draft of employment advancement law." Researchers in the women's studies field participated in a project on "equity in employment" at the Ministry of Labor and Social Security's International Institute for Labor Studies. They brought insights from their research findings on antidiscrimination to the proposed revisions. The Center for Women's Law and Legal Services of Peking University, with women's employment rights as one of their objectives, used cases they had been involved in to enrich the revisions (Liu 2009, 14).

26. The Qianxi Model works through direct election of the chair of the Women's Committee, preparing potential women candidates to enter the Villagers Committee. The Hunan Model drafts the local "Guidelines on the Implementation of the Organic Law of the Villagers Committee." The guidelines require at least one female member on each Villagers Committee. The guidelines are posted in the names of the provincial Women's Federation and the Department of Civil Affairs. The so-called Tangu Model is directed by the Department of Civil Affairs. It includes a slot on the ballot specifically for a woman candidate. If there is no woman candidate listed, the ballot is considered invalid (Gao 2009b).

27. In 1990, following its review of progress made since the commencement of the Nairobi Forward Looking Strategy (1985), the Economic and Social Council of the United Nations aimed for 30 percent political representation by women by 1995 and 50 percent by 2000 (United Nations 1991).

28. What exactly the "black holes" are is not specified. These could be legitimate or not-so-legitimate administrative fees, overhead, or surcharges. This issue concerns both men and women village heads and members of the Villagers Committee (see Gao 2009b; and Wang, Gong, and Cheng 2007).

29. See http://www.westwomen.org/jigou/2009/0205/article_170.html.

30. The percentage of women as members or directors of the Villagers Committees in Heyang County, Shaanxi Province, increased from 0 percent in 2003 to 5.7 percent in 2006. For members of the Villagers Committees, the percentage rose from 14.7 percent in 2003 to 25.2 percent in 2006. For Shaanxi Province as a whole, the figures were 0.6 percent to 1.1 percent for directors and 9 percent to 12.2 percent for members (Gao 2009a). At the national level, the increases were 1 percent in 2003 to 2.3 percent in 2006 for directors and 15.7 percent in 2000 to 23.2 percent in 2006 for members (Gao 2009b).

31. These governmental offices are known to render "lip service," not "hard currency," when it comes to "women's work." Therefore, "gender equality" written into national policy has been repeatedly cited as a monumental success in the recent history of the Chinese women's movement. It is often referred to by feminist NGOs and the Women's Federation as "symbolic" hard currency, justifying their endeavor publicly and in negotiation with various governmental offices.

32. The Chinese base of the Global Call to Action Against Poverty was established in September 2005. It consists of six local NGOs in China (Gender and Development in China, China and Philanthropy Times, Magrove Support Group, Beijing Brooks Education Center, Fuping Development Institute, and Hui Tian Yu Center) and two international NGOs (Oxfam Hong Kong and Action Aid).

33. The United Nations first introduced microcredit programs in China in the 1980s. Other international agencies followed suit in their poverty-alleviation or agricultural development projects.

34. The United Nations Economic and Social Council (ECOSOC) definition cited by the International Labor Organization. http://www.ilo.org/public/english/bureau/gender/newsite2002/about/definition.

35. Even the self-initiated women's NGOs are not truly "independent," as they have to be affiliated with an official institution to legally register.

36. According to Elizabeth Waters, the Communist Parties were directed "to establish women's agitational commissions at every level, from the local to the national, with permanent representation on the relevant party committee, a full vote on matters relating to women, and a consultative vote on other issues" (1989, 37).

6

Polish Feminism Between the Local and the Global: A Task of Translation

ELZBIETA MATYNIA

The polis was distinguished from the household in that it knew only "equals," whereas the household was the center of the strictest inequality. To be free meant not to be subject to the command of another and not to be in command oneself.

—Hannah Arendt, *Human Condition*

Bitter Freedom

When I first returned to my native and already virtually "postcommunist" Poland in the summer of 1989 after eight years in New York—and just a few months after the Round Table negotiations—there was one thing that struck me most vividly. In the new and exuberant public life of the country there was an almost total absence of those capable women who had played such an active and essential role in the clandestine operations of the prodemocratic movements of the 1970s and '80s. I knew many of them well and had been active along with them, but I realized now that, like them, I had never defined the critical problems of the society I lived in, in terms of gender. The primary objective of every social protest and movement then was to fight for the political rights of *all* members of society. All other issues seemed to be of secondary importance, and could be dealt with after the battle for democracy had one day

POLAND

Human Development Index ranking: .870
Gender-Related Development Index value: .867
Gender Empowerment Measure value: .614

General

Type of government: Republic
Major ethnic groups: Polish (96.7%); German; Belarusian; Ukrainian
Language: Polish
Religions: Roman Catholic (94%); Eastern Orthodox, Uniate, Protestant, Jewish (6%)

Demographics

Population, total (millions), 2005: 38.2
Annual growth rate (%), 2005–2015: -.2
Total fertility (average number of births per woman): 1.3
Contraceptive prevalence (% of married women aged 15–49): 49
Maternal mortality ratio, adjusted (per 100,000 live births), 2000: 8

Women's Status

Date of women's suffrage: 1918
Life expectancy: M 71; F 79.4
Combined gross enrollment ratio for primary, secondary, and tertiary education
    (female %), 2005: 91
Gross primary enrollment ratio: 98
Gross secondary enrollment ratio: 99
Gross tertiary enrollment ratio: 74
Literacy (% age 15 and older): M 99.8; F 99.7

Political Representation of Women

Seats in parliament (% held by women): 19.1
Legislators, senior officials, and managers (% female): 33
Professional and technical workers (% female): 61
Women in government at ministerial level (% total): 5.9

Economics

Estimated earned income (PPP US$): M 17,493; F 10,414
Ratio of estimated female to male earned income: .60
Economic activity rate (% female): 47.7
Women in adult labor force (% total): 46 (this figure obtained at the CEDAW Statis-
    tical Database)

been won. But now, watching the freewheeling debates in the new parliament, and the quickly emerging institutions of public and political life all staffed by men, I found myself wondering where all the women were. Democratically, but quietly, women were being squeezed out of the new polis and sent back to the household.

During the first four years following the collapse of the Berlin Wall, while visiting various countries of the region, I could sense tensions building around "the problem of women." On the one hand, the issue of gender, never really discussed in those countries before, was quickly emerging as a response to the deteriorating legal and economic status of women. On the other hand, in those first years of transformation, there was enormous sociocultural and political pressure coming from both men and women to disregard the issue and even to ridicule those involved in discussions of it.

It was in the early 1990s, soon after the collapse of communism, that I observed a pair of striking paradoxes concerning the situation of women throughout the region. First of all, for many in public life the most politically rewarding behavior in the first years of postcommunism seemed to be that which focused on eradicating all remnants of the previous system, which included, ironically, the never-fulfilled commitments to human rights in general and to women's rights in particular. The second paradox was that the spheres of relative freedom available under communist rule—those provided by the church in Poland, by the so-called second economy in Hungary, and by the family in Czechoslovakia—had now, for women, become spheres of constraint (see Matynia 1995).

In the years that followed I witnessed a broadening expression of discontent. In March 2007 I participated in a Manifa (a term of endearment for "manifestation") that marked the start of International Women's Day. Many who joined that parade would not have cared to do so several years before. This time, dissatisfaction with the prevailing political discourse, dominated by the dogmatic and divisive voice of the ruling camp, turned the Manifa into a setting for challenging the growing discrimination not only against women but against various open-minded groups in the society who felt increasingly marginalized and whose voices were officially considered perilous to the health of the country.

A colorful group of a few thousand women and men gathered in front of the parliament and then advanced through the main street of Warsaw in a carnivalesque parade of popular dissent, under banners that sharply attacked government policies, spelling out "We are equal, we are different, and we are in solidarity." One could see among the posters and banners the declaration, "I've had enough," signed, "Mother Pole."[1]

FIGURE 6.1 The March 2007 "Manifa" in Warsaw (Courtesy Agnieszka Graff)

The First Gender Revolution

Growing up in Poland in the 1950s and '60s, my identity was shaped by a culture that—perhaps surprisingly for an outsider—offered women an expanded repertoire of choices, thanks not to any immediate communist policies but to the deep gender rearrangements that were a by-product of the war and the anti-Nazi resistance movement. I remember being impressed by various women, friends of my father's from the underground who visited our home, and by the conversations they had at the dinner table. I remember trying to bargain with my father, a former officer in the Polish underground in the 1940s, for some position in a clandestine resistance unit when the next invasion came. And in fact the air was full of war and the fear of war. Thanks to the state propaganda, there was no doubt that we were already surrounded, and the question was not *whether* "they"[2] would invade but *when*. I needed to be assured by my father that when war came I would not be a nurse, the traditional role for a woman in wartime, but somebody dealing with arms and logistics, maybe even a *laczniczka*, a courier running between units of the larger underground army operating in the deep forests near my hometown in central Poland.

It was on Polish territory that the biggest atrocities on a civilian population were committed, but it was also there that the largest anti-Nazi underground

FIGURE 6.2 "I died during an illegal abortion." Manifa 2008, Warsaw (Courtesy Agnieszka Graff)

FIGURE 6.3 Izabella Jaruga-Nowacka (on the left), first Governmental Plenipotentiary for the Equal Status of Women and Men. A prominent bishop called her "a feminist hardliner who will not change even under hydrochloric acid." Manifa 2008, Warsaw (Courtesy Agnieszka Graff)

emerged and functioned for five years. During World War II, Poland's wide-spread, youth-based resistance movement instigated what may well have been the most far-reaching cultural and gender revolution in Europe. Though it was rarely commented on at the time, the rules of conspiracy indeed broke and eventually eliminated prewar standards of propriety, including the roles tra-ditionally assigned to women. Young men and women disappeared together in the thick of the night with concrete covert assignments. Women were no longer just the moral guarantors of their sons' and husbands' courage to sac-rifice: they themselves fought alongside the men, and thus participated di-rectly in self-sacrifice.

The experience of war, occupation, and in particular the resistance chal-lenged, altered, and liberalized traditional perceptions of the gender dichotomy in Poland, bringing about a whole generation of independent and audacious women and opening up for them beyond family, motherhood, and church a space in the midst of public matters. The irony was that even before such a space for women fully opened up, it was shut down—as was any public space—by the autocratic communist regime, and the citizenry, both women and men, found themselves equally squeezed out of it. Equality in a time of anti-Nazi struggle had not entirely invalidated the cultural contract between ladies and knights, but the pronouncements of the postwar communist regime introduc-ing gender equality were taken for granted, because they did not sound as pro-gressive as had been expected.

Freedom, or the relative freedom during communist thaws, rarely created the conditions for equal participation by women in the institutions of political life. In Poland, paradoxically, it was in periods with drastically curtailed free-dom—in particular the Nazi occupation in the 1940s, and the period of mar-tial law in the 1980s, known in Poland as the "state of war"—that women came closest to earning equal status with men.

The Gendered Dialectics of Freedom and Equality

The communist system did not generate identical outcomes throughout the re-gion. Despite pressure from Moscow, each state within the bloc developed cer-tain peculiarities of its own. In the Polish case three well-known specifics stand out. The first was that most of its farmland did not undergo forced collec-tivization and that most individual peasants thus remained owners and man-agers of their own farms, guaranteeing them a measure of economic independence from the state, with a fairly equal division of labor between male and female members of the family. Even though limited, the farm was a site—

contrary to the situation in any other communist countries—where both men and women jointly decided about their daily lives and exercised a degree of autonomy unknown to those who lived in the cities under the close watch of the one-party state.

The second specific, not entirely unique to Poland but certainly far more pronounced there, had to do with the frequent changes in the political climate. When periods of extensive ideological frost were followed by thaws, there were variably extended periods of relaxed censorship, curbed secret police activity, freeing of political prisoners, openings to the West, a green light given to associational life, a more outspoken press, foreign movies, and translations of Fromm, Tocqueville, or Beckett. Thaws were a time for people to get a taste—however limited—of freedom and the possibilities for greater self-realization. The question is whether everybody participated in these moments equally.

The third peculiarity in Poland was that the church, too, had retained much of its autonomy, as the only national institution to survive the nineteenth and twentieth centuries intact. For the forty-five years under communism, Poles were as much affected by the Catholic Church—the only institutional survivor from the past—as by the institutional framework of "real socialism." The threatened position of the church vis-à-vis the communist regime afforded the church a particularly strong position vis-à-vis Polish society. Its already high moral authority was further strengthened in the early 1970s when the church became an ally of the democratic opposition and provided a base for many oppositional activities. Before 1980 (pre-Solidarity times) and after the imposition of martial law in December 1981, the church provided the only space where Poles could feel a real sense of freedom and dignity, protected from state control, and it was perceived by the majority of the society as the only possible guardian of spiritual values. Among the closely related elements of the dominant value system was the identification of Catholicism with Poland, or, to put it another way, the identification of Catholicism with the national tradition of struggle for the independence of the motherland.

A specifically Polish religiosity centers on the cult of the Madonna. The content of this folk-type religiosity committed to a Marian tradition—through its iconography, religious festivals, and pilgrimages—celebrates heroic, self-sacrificing women and motherhood in a national context provided by Polish history and romantic patriotic literature. In this literary tradition, the main duties of Polish women are to maintain the family and preserve Poland's national identity, while men (husbands and sons) fight for the *motherland*, conspire against foreign occupiers, and often spend their lives in prison. This form of "managerial matriarchy" (best captured by the ideal of the *Matka Polka*, the

"Polish Mother," the still widely revered role model for Polish women) historically provided women not only with dignity and prestige but also with psychological gratification. But these could be gained in virtually no other way than through this role of mother and family caretaker.

After 1945—just as in the other countries of the bloc—this traditional model was upset by a massive enlistment of women into the labor market as a result of ideological and economic pressures. Women were urged to assume new roles, becoming workers and building a new social order alongside men. But with the thawing of Stalinism, prompted by the events of October 1956, when the communist state suffered its first setback with a workers' protest in Poznan, this crudely promoted concept of a "new breed of socialist women" had to be discarded. At the same time, the collectivization of private farms was suspended, the primate of Poland, Stefan Cardinal Wyszynski, was released from internment, and religious instruction was reintroduced into the schools. Since then, the officially promoted model of Polish women has been largely a by-product of the intricate relationship between the Catholic Church in Poland and the communist state. The socialist model never recovered its original hard-line position, while the conservative model continued to gain visibility, especially during times of relative freedom (e. g., Solidarity, during 1980–1981), when the Catholic Church increased its influence and presence and thus had a greater impact on public affairs.

According to popular wisdom, as manifested in the parliaments throughout East and central Europe, the first step toward a successful transformation to democracy must be a radical departure from the communist past. The vacuum left after the collapse of communism in Poland—and after the official ideology had vanished—was quickly filled by the Catholic Church. The new political correctness that emerged is visible in parliamentary laws (religious instruction in school, antiabortion laws, restitution of church property), in the signed concordat with the Vatican, in the media (now obliged to observe "Christian values"), and in public life. The Polish debate on women's issues therefore examines the impact of the church on the past and current role of women.

The relatively long experience of the Solidarity movement of 1980–1981, in which an organization of citizens independently formed governmental structures, is an important source of the difference between the state of the women's movement in Poland and that in the other countries of East and central Europe. There is a growing body of literature analyzing the key role played by women in mending the banned trade union Solidarity after the devastation it suffered as a result of the military coup in December 1981, and in reconstructing its civic activities and structures underground (see Penn 2005; Kondratowicz 2001; Simpson 2001; and Graff 1999). As all this was highly illegal activity in defiance of harsh military law, it required the most rigorous conspiracy, and in part because the identities of female leaders (like those of the men) were kept secret, they rarely got any credit for their efforts afterward.[3]

Nevertheless, the experience was an extraordinary demonstration and test of their political wisdom, leadership, fiscal responsibility, and management skills, as well as their creativity in the realm of communications and logistics—not to mention ordinary courage. In effect, underground Solidarity brought to light and developed an impressive human capital in women that had not been recognized before.

This participation in the struggles for freedom was never really translated into participation in power when freedom finally came. In South Africa, women fighters from the African National Congress talk about a similar experience following the end of apartheid. This is also strikingly analogous to the history of African American men repeatedly demonstrating their patriotism and sacrifice in war after war yet returning home to second-class citizenship and racism.

In early 1989, when the communist government was ready to negotiate at the Round Table a compromise with the still-delegalized Solidarity movement, only one woman was actually seated at the Round Table (on the Solidarity side), and in the several separate subtables only five women took part (four of them on the Solidarity side). No woman was included in the informal negotiations in Magdalenka, where decisions were finalized.

Malgorzata Fuszara (2006), Poland's major academic and civic feminist, discovered a negative correlation between the times of political thaw and women's representation in parliament. In the two most memorable periods of political relaxation, after October 1956 and after the Round Table negotiations in 1989, the percentage of women parliamentarians dropped sharply from 17 percent to 4 percent in 1956, and in 1989 from 20 percent to 13 percent (and eventually, in 1991, in Poland's first fully democratic elections since the war, to 10 percent!).

When Fuszara says that the participation of women in parliament decreases abruptly when the parliament itself gains an unaccustomed degree of power, or when it in fact acquires true legislative power, her observation rings a familiar "bitter freedom" bell for the region (Matynia 1994). But what is interesting in Fuszara's analysis, examining as it does the communist and the postcommunist periods, is that it debunks a lingering belief—still prevalent especially outside the region—that the disappearance of the communist system is solely responsible for stripping women of their status and the opportunity to participate in political life. She herself tends to think that it was a mechanism

of a more universal character, revealed in all those new democracies, one that—
while placing legislative power in the hands of the parliaments and eliminating the compromised quotas established by the previous system—set off the
noticeable dwindling of the number of women representatives.

In the case of Poland, ironically (or perhaps not), it was precisely a women's
issue that became one of the key battlegrounds in the last communist and all
succeeding post-1989 parliaments. That battle, part of a more extensive cultural war, was over a woman's right to self-determination, and specifically
over her reproductive rights. The key soldiers of this legislative battle appeared in parliament armed with the paraphernalia of the Polish idiom:
"dressed" as knights and ladies, as peasants hiding behind the icon of the
Madonna, with male politicians cross-dressed as those patriotic "Mother
Poles," and finally bishops—not as shepherds but as the sheepdogs of a
Poland lured by the New Europe.

The year 1989 was critical for the Polish women's movement, less because
of the final break with the communist system than because of the abortion bill
prepared by a group of Catholic deputies for the last communist parliament.
The first draft of this bill specified a five-year prison term for a woman who
had an abortion. This provoked the rapid establishment of numerous new
women's organizations. Among the first registered were the Polish Feminists'
Association and Pro-Femina, both of which are relatively small, urban, young,
and intelligentsia based. The abortion issue and the general feeling of help-
lessness on the part of society vis-à-vis its elected representatives became major
catalysts for the most impressive liberal-oriented social movement in post-
communist Poland: the "proreferendum movement." Between November 1992
and March 1993 hundreds of committees established themselves throughout
the country to exert pressure on parliament to refrain, at the very least, from
criminalizing abortion. The committees collected 1.5 million signatures of adult
Poles requesting that a referendum be held to decide whether abortion should
be punishable.

In the favorable context of the fresh and authentic gratitude that society felt
toward the church for its long service on behalf of the survival of the Polish nation, harsh antiabortion measures were voted into law in 1993. Abortion was
virtually delegalized, sex education was removed from the schools, and state
subsidies for contraceptives were canceled. Now the Polish abortion law has
become a "cultural specificity," an exception protected in accordance with the
principle of a multicultural Europe. Yet the referendum committees have continued to have a life of their own, even after their movement was effectively
disarmed by parliament's decision in the final bill that only the physician per-

forming an abortion is to be punished and not the woman undergoing it. It was not long thereafter that women deputies established the Women's Parliamentary Group, an "across-the-aisle" initiative, and successfully competed with men in the autumn 1993 elections to parliament, increasing their participation from 9 to 13 percent.

In its often Sisyphean effort to build and strengthen women's organizations, to communicate its concerns effectively to broader groups of women, and to win sympathizers, readers, members, and activists, the emerging women's movement downplayed some issues that were regarded as too radical for the general public. Only rarely did one hear women's groups addressing in public the problem of sexual harassment or domestic rape and, almost never, sexual difference. Lesbian women involved in women's groups were choosing, usually for tactical reasons, not to confront the issue and further jeopardize the movement's chances of growing. It is hard enough in some women's groups just to call oneself a feminist; one must struggle to overcome a prejudice against the very word.

The whole situation was additionally complicated by a priori negative attitudes toward feminism in this part of Europe. Both the old and the new constitutions guaranteed fundamental rights and freedoms for all regardless of differences in sex, race, religion, ethnic background, and so on. Yet equality for women never did—and still does not—extend much beyond their participation in employment. The high participation of women in the labor market resulted from the needs of postwar industrialization, from the priority given to ideological principles, and from the pressure on individual families to supplement family income. However, the principle of equal pay, explicit in the legislation, was and remains a purely theoretical declaration, and in the context of the market economy gender discrimination, especially in hiring practices, is more pronounced than ever. Additionally, it was only in the late 1980s that it became obvious that there was no language that could be used to launch a debate on women's rights. The very word *gender* does not exist in any Slavic language, and initially the only option for those interested in the analysis of gender as a social construct was to use the term *sex*, and to qualify it at each and every application.

Feminism, the word, which exists in those languages, is so pejoratively loaded that for a long time it was considered political suicide for a woman active in public life to identify herself with feminism and feminist issues. When in April 1989 a team of sociologists asked a representative sampling of Poles to choose from a list the one category that best defined their identity, gender came in last place, after (in this order) human being, Pole, parent, and occupation. The survey was conducted at the time of the Round Table negotiations between the Solidarity-rooted opposition and the ruling Communist Party, during which the communist regime was being forced by society to share power. The feeling of solidarity against the system on the part of all citizens was very strong, and in this struggle gender was a negligible social variable (Matynia 1995, 395). Until the mid-1990s it was still the exception rather than the rule that the small number of women involved in politics paid any attention to the mounting problems facing women, or acted on behalf of their lost rights. On the contrary, there was an assumption at work among women policy makers that women's problems are inseparable from the problems facing society as a whole. It would be premature to say that the silence concerning women's problems was orchestrated or imposed, but it did not take long for women to speak up.

There was a quota system designed in Poland by the communists to ensure that women's participation in parliament would be numerically high but passive. Various analyses of the composition of the Polish parliament show that women had always been selected to demonstrate the thesis that even young, inexperienced nonprofessionals, with little education and without political backing, could become members of parliament. This is why women, to a greater extent than the male members of parliament, played the role of *fillers*. They were always a numerical minority, but their influence was even smaller than their numbers might have suggested.

Since the quota was dropped after 1989, the participation of women in parliament has been numerically much smaller still. But those women who otherwise entered the public life of the country became not only more visible but also much more active, which is attributed both to the emergence of an authentic public space and to their average level of education, which is statistically higher than that of men.

The issue of quotas, or—as it functions in a recent public discourse—of gender parity in electoral tickets, is important in Poland, as the chances of a candidate depend solely on the political parties. It is the parties that decide who will be put on their lists, and above all how high on the list a name will appear. It took another decade for the three leftist and center-leftist political parties to reserve on their lists of candidates for parliament 30 percent of the slots for women. In 2001, shortly before the elections in which seven political parties took part, three of them—two post-Solidarity parties (Union of Freedom and Union of Labor [UP]), and one postcommunist party (Alliance of the Democratic Left [SLD])—came up with internal policies that were to ensure a larger presence of women in both chambers of parliament. The effect was immediate: in the 2001 elections women constituted 20–21 percent in the lower chamber (a 54 percent increase) and 23 percent in the Senate (more than double the previous contingent of female senators!).[4] But when in the next two elections (2005, 2007) the issue of women quotas fell off the parties' agendas, the number of women parliamentarians went slightly down in both chambers of parliament (to 19.1 percent in 2007). The main obstacles are the smaller number of women designated as candidates by the parties and the low place given to women candidates at the bottom of the party lists. Though the 2001 party quotas have not been institutionalized, and in the more conservative climate of the next two elections no quotas were introduced to ensure a larger participation by women in public office, something has really changed, and not only symbolically. Starting approximately with the new millennium, all political parties became aware of the strategic usefulness of women running for elected office. They saw that a woman candidate perceived as efficient and trustworthy—if given an opportunity to run for a key position—performs better in the electoral campaign and usually has a much better chance of being elected than does her male counterpart. Perhaps it has something to do with the increasingly tarnished image of a political class associated with male politicians. For many it is clear that there was a good reason that in 2006 the Civic Platform Party proposed a woman for the powerful position of mayor of Warsaw, as only a woman could have won against the very popular former prime minister of Poland proposed by the rival Law and Justice Party. Indeed, Hanna Gronkiewicz-Walz won out over Kazimierz Marcinkiewicz and is considered one of the most effective mayors the capital city has ever had, and one of the most influential political figures in the country.

But it was already in the mid-1990s in Warsaw, Budapest, Prague, and Bratislava—places where the political scene was being looked upon more and more frequently with disappointment and disgust—that one could detect the emergence of a new *public-spirited ethos* exemplified more often than not by certain individual women and women's groups. Such an ethos combined the experience, commitment, and unselfishness of former dissidents with a readiness to address imaginatively the unfamiliar challenges of new political and economic circumstances. And it was speech in a variety of its forms, as I will try to show later, that brought women back into the political realm. Gradually, and not without resistance, they began to be accepted, and sometimes even respected, both by the broader public and by the political elites, either because of or in spite of their commitment to women's issues. The biggest qualitative leap took place in the realm of mentality, and today nobody would question— as was the case in the '90s—the fact that women are indeed discriminated against everywhere, from politics to private life. It was the Parliamentary

Women's Group that made sure that the new constitution of democratic Poland included a separate article decreeing equal rights for men and women.[5] Yet it is precisely in the realm of law, and in specific policies addressing the position of women in public life, but not mentioning reproductive rights, that their achievements are still very limited. This is why the presence of women in parliament (especially its lower chamber, the Sejm, which the constitution designates as the principal lawmaker) is of such importance.

The Politics of Locality and its Gender Implications

In the mid-1990s one could still observe a considerable discrepancy between the dynamic growth and vitality of women's civil society in the new democracies of central Europe and their virtual exclusion, for all practical purposes, from access to policy-making circles, and their consequently limited impact at the national level. In the early transitional period the nongovernmental organizations (NGOs) in general, and women's organizations in particular, tended to be given the "Hyde Park Corner" treatment, as an outlet for non-threatening, nongovernmental initiatives. Thus, women's organizations—though performing a crucial role as incubators of women with leadership skills—have generally been seen by their own members as fenced playgrounds within which women can do what they want but from which they cannot graduate (Matynia 1998).[6]

"Until recently," confessed Olga Krzyzanowska, a physician who was then deputy speaker of the Polish parliament, in the fall of 1992, "I never divided issues into male and female issues. Now I am noticing that actual women's rights in Poland are being threatened. So women's issues have faced me right here on our own front doorstep, and not just slipped in through the international back door" (Metelska and Nowakowska 1992, 145). Krzyzanowska's admission reflected a larger process, which slowly, in the face of much resistance, took place throughout central and Eastern Europe: the process of discovering and acknowledging that there is a problem of women in the first place.

But a few years later a first and very impressive cohort of women finally "graduated" in Poland and began to enter the politically relevant public sphere. There were several points of entry: at major universities women have managed to establish varied and impressive gender studies programs, popularly known as "gendery" (for lack of a Polish word, giving the English a Polish plural ending); they have developed shrewd media strategies; and there is the remarkable phenomenon of conceptual women's art, causing major controversies and debates.[7] Women have appeared in politics, in business, in the arts, in academe;

they have organized themselves in women's or feminist organizations; and they cannot be ignored anymore. The feminist debate has gone mainstream.

In June 1999 *Gazeta Wyborcza*, a major Polish daily, published an extensive and provocative essay by a young feminist and literary critic, analyzing the nature of patriarchal rule after communism (Graff 1999). In the course of the next two months, thirteen sizable articles followed: polemics and counterpolemics, not just letters—a phenomenon so striking that it was eventually noticed by the U.S. media (Penn 2001). Since then feminist writing has been flourishing in the press, everything from regular columns to very readable essays obviously addressed to a broad, intelligent audience.

There has also appeared a rising tide of sophisticated books produced by this first cohort of local feminists, often witty and always a "good read," widely discussed and reviewed, and often nominated for major awards. The books have generated new knowledge, and as they discuss the subordination of women, using categories and cultural references that are immediately recognizable by Poles, they have generated a new, informed, and critical public. The titles, which sound better in the original Polish than in these translations, convey a combination of freshness and savvy: *A World Without Women: Gender in Polish Public Life; Cinderella, Frankenstein, and Others; Sparrow with a Broken Wing, or, A Shot of Vodka: Constructions of Femininity in Polish Postwar Visual Culture; Ladies, Knights, and Feminists; Body, Desire, Attire; Lipstick on the Flag; and Silence of the Lambs: The Thing on Abortion.*[8]

Women's NGOs—three hundred of them—as strong as they are diverse, have become recognizable actors on the Polish political stage, even if their influence on the politics of the state is still relatively limited (Fuszara 2006, 4). An insistence on horizontal autonomous structures results not only from the negative reaction to the superhierarchical communist organizations but also from the experience of Solidarity, both during the period of the triumphantly self-governing society tolerated by the regime in 1980–1981 and, after the government crackdown, during the years of rebuilding the union's structures underground. The less centralized the activities, the more successful they were—and the more difficult for the police to disrupt. This is one of the reasons women in Poland prefer very loose networks or, as they put it, just "a directory of groups." The ethos of hard, foundational, organic work, aimed at specific issues needing attention (e.g., self-help groups, infrastructure, provision of legal advice, retraining for the unemployed, working with media on matters of domestic violence) is rarely visible and often taken for granted. (The Party of Women, registered in 2007, which appeared frivolous, perhaps because of what appeared to be a lightweight, sensationalist, and limelight-seeking launch, did not receive any serious support from established women's organizations and their leaders.) One of the questions raised I am sure—and not just by those active in Polish women's groups—is to what extent it is important that women who are to be supported in their run for parliament be concerned with women's issues in the first place. The strategy prior to what turned out to be the watershed elections of 2001 had been: it does not matter—the more women, the better. Women's organizations worked closely with the Parliamentary Women's Group to establish the Preelectoral Women's Coalition and launched and maintained public debate on the scandalously low number of women in the legislative and executive bodies. There is no doubt that their concerted action prompted the three parties to come up with the offer of quotas for their female members. Interestingly it was the coalition of the two left-of-center parties (SLD and UP), which brought to the parliament fifty-five women (25 percent of the coalition's parliamentarians), that decisively won the election then.

Though the 2005 and 2007 parliamentary elections did not spectacularly raise the number of women in either chamber of parliament as compared with memorable 2001 (in fact the numbers went down in the Senate but remained on the 20 percent level in the lower chamber), it became clear that women had made enormous strides in entering the world of both politics and the economy. Even though this did not initially translate itself into increased gender sensitivity, women now run the largest news organizations, constitute more than 30 percent of the country's managers, and represent an impressive—especially when compared with women in other EU countries—35 percent of all the self-employed (already in 1998 they owned 20 percent of small companies, those with eight to twenty workers).[9] All these advances in the presence of women and women's issues are accompanied by an increasingly sympathetic climate for an albeit moderate feminist agenda. There is a steady decrease in the number of people who support the traditional role of woman as homemaker, including those who still in the early '90s believed that women ought to sacrifice their professional careers for the sake of their husbands.[10] And according to a 2002 opinion poll, 92 percent of Poles wanted the government to put on its agenda the issue of equal status for women and men.[11] Most recently the "parity" discourse gained momentum after the impressive Women's Congress in Warsaw in July 2009 (3,000 women participated from all over the country), after which women conducted meetings with leaders of the key political parties to request 50 percent parity in the upcoming elections. The public debate and ensuing opinion polls revealed that "the Polish public wants more women in politics. In a recent poll for Gazeta, as many as 61 percent of respondents spoke in favor of gender parity in election tickets" ("Tusk" 2009).

These gains, which serve in the West as markers of women's relative success, are accomplished here in a sharply gender-contentious context, in which the state with its successive governments and parliaments, no matter whether right, center, or left oriented, have bred a political class and perfected a party system that is still virtually closed to women. Hence, civil society is the main terrain where strategies are articulated and where debates on equality as a principle of democratic politics are instigated. Just as in the dissident circles of the 1970s and '80s, where intellectuals and workers were joined with poets and artists, today women's NGOs, and a growing mass of feminists of both genders, are joined by a community of conceptual artists who struggle to sustain a barely reestablished but already taken-for-granted public sphere. And it is above all the women artists, through their dialogical and often unsettling artworks, and through the discursive web they have stimulated, who contribute to the public discourse on matters of gender and nation, gender and identity, and finally gender and democracy. Other elements of the traditionally gender-contentious context are harder to translate, as they cannot be readily understood in terms of categories designed to grasp Western patterns of subjection and oppression. Such a mechanical application causes real problems for the practical work of women in the region. One of its results is the EU's mishandling of the gender question in the process of European enlargement. Another is the tendency to look at the trafficking in women exclusively in terms of women's human rights.

This experience of women organizing themselves in the countries of postcommunist Europe, in spite of the feminism-hostile context, substantiates further the reasons given by Anne Phillips (2002) as to why feminism ought to be interested in a conception of civil society. Indeed, contemporary feminist thought does need to examine closely the concept itself, as well as the ways in which women in different local contexts have organized themselves to mediate with the state the key issues of rights and gender equality. And yes, the feminist conception of civil society has to be broad and generous in providing space for diverse responses to the challenges occurring locally. There is no one blueprint for civil society, and in many parts of the world there may be neither a need to copy Western civic know-how nor a need to forcibly adjust theory that does not either recognize or inform local realities. Also, in the so-called new democracies, once imaginative sites of civic movements and initiatives, the current much more rationalized and professionalized civil society organizations, identically designed and governed, are a source of disenchantment on the part of those who built the hard-to-imitate structures of civil society under the constraints of nondemocratic regimes.

Perhaps the usefulness of the broad civil society concept is best seen in instances of local feminisms, which, whether in democratic or nondemocratic states, found themselves marginalized by the gendering of politics anchored in local culture. The broad concept of civil society, not identical with what is commonly known as the NGO sector, neither prescribes one best way of action nor enforces any one agenda. Rather, it provides an inclusive space for diverse, indigenously inspired initiatives to conduct public dialogue with a concrete state, which in the case of women's organizations means negotiating matters of gender justice in specific social and cultural contexts.

This is why knowing that civil society in Poland was conceived in the 1970s and '80s in a search for consensus rather than confrontation with the regime may be of assistance to those of us who want to understand the strategies behind women's initiatives there and may protect us from the pitfalls of appearing patronizing. One of the responses to systemic transformation in the region was the mobilization of women's civil society, driven by a newly initiated discourse on the deteriorating status of women and grounded in locally cultivated civic experience. The agenda and praxis of this feminism were less concerned with issues of identity and more with equal participation in social and political life. As such they were close to what on an analytical level is proposed by Nancy Fraser (2003) when she suggests treating recognition as a question of social status.

Feminism and Democratic Performativity

Speech and action are not only attributes of freedom, as Arendt says, but a key source of individual dignity and of societal hope, as they contribute to the sense of a democratic polity in which people and their different voices matter in both making and maintaining it. Though the main roles in the theater of political life, whether democratic or not, are typically played by men, it has been striking how womanless the newly established democratic order in central Europe is.

The response of Polish women to their exclusion from the institutions of democratic governance and policy making was *performative*, as their actions resided in speech: the resolute media performance, books and journals that reached an ever-increasing audience, commentary on legal matters concerning domestic violence, carnivalesque street performances, seminars, letter campaigns, legal clinics, and hotlines.[12] The concept of performativity is usually associated with J. L. Austin's set of lectures on language, in which he discusses sentences that do not just describe reality or state facts but have the quality of enacting what they actually say. "There is something which is at the moment of uttering being done by the person uttering," and such a "speech act" has more than just a meaning, as it has, above all, an effect, explains Austin (1962, 60). Though not contractual or declaratory, not immediate, purely illocutionary acts, these action-oriented utterances have been implicit performatives, utilizing in a new political context the strategies of the civic movements of the 1970s and '80s that women had cocreated, to reenter the public space, to retrieve the weakened status of cocitizens with access to power. Just as before, in the time of self-limiting revolution conducted by civil society, their current speech actions were mostly of what Austin calls the *perlocutionary* kind. It was acting *by* saying something, acting to convince and to persuade, that produced follow-up consequences. One set of performative actions was generated by the articles, television interviews, panel discussions, "gendery" seminars, and above all books disclosing the cultural blueprints that had facilitated the removal of women from the newly created polis. The other was generated by massive letter campaigns, theatrical Manifas taking place on the streets of the cities, legal actions undertaken by women's groups and concluded by rulings on behalf of women (including the victims of trafficking), and finally voting for women in the parliament.

At the same time, a major change took place on the level of language, both its vocabulary and its grammar, where new gender-specific words, mostly nouns, gradually invented, translated, or adopted, entered linguistic usage. The most striking but also the most visible in the bylines of the press articles were the new words designating the professional or occupational status of women. In a conspicuous difference from their pre-1989 position, women acted to be recognized for who they are as women. Instead of a *sociolog* (sociologist), which used to indicate—as in English—both male and female, a grammatical female ending was added, and a woman sociologist, especially the independently minded and feminism-friendly one, now called herself *sociolo-zka* (*psycholozka*, or *antropolozka*), an initially awkward-sounding but now popular and progressive form of expressing both gender and occupational identity.

The growing and better-connected civil society organizations provided local feminism with the community and space where actors could be nurtured, issues identified, "subversive" strategies addressing the gender exclusive enumerated, male democracy worked out, and actions launched. The media, not particularly friendly but initially curious about a few women authors, were then compelled to open a space of appearance for savvy local feminist discourse. Only in such an accepted setting where conventional language is invoked (in this case the language of rights) could performative utterances take place. The public revelation of the once-unnoticed exclusion of women from institutional democracy, done in a powerful combination of conventional and fresh words, was a key to felicitous acts of performative feminism. Such local feminism-in-the-making, far from reaching its goals, nevertheless managed to transform the climate surrounding women's issues in post-1989 Poland (ibid.).[13] The more recent response to globalization has opened yet another opportunity for the mobilization and further articulation of local feminism in this part of Europe.

Economic Transformation Meets Globalization

Is globalization a threat or an opportunity for local feminism? In Poland the processes of globalization intersect with three relatively localized political and cultural processes: the post-1989 systemic transformation, the process of integration into the European Union, and a celebration of certain elements of the national past long censored and now retrieved. When one looks at these processes through the lens of gender, one ends up with if not necessarily an unclear, then certainly a perplexing, picture, the dynamics of which are driven by various paradoxes, by contradictions not easily reconcilable, and by the co-existence of different pasts and bizarre figures. The relationship between globalization and feminism in Poland makes me think of the murals of Marc Chagall: thoroughly modern but idiosyncratic, and, as such, not founded on the premises of modernity.

The process of accession to the European Union revealed some new aspects of the systemic transformation in the region, which in the first decade of the twenty-first century is by no means completed. One of the main foundations of the liberal-democratic order was an economic reform that led—through the structural privatization of enterprises and entire industries—to a market economy. Thus, both processes, the so-called transition to democracy and globalization in postcommunist Europe, were processes unfolding in the context of extensive privatization and the dismantling of centrally planned economies. What followed in the mid-1990s was the mismanaged and famously corrupt privatization of state utilities and enterprises (Transparency International 2001), commonly known as the "privatization," or "propertization," of the communist *nomenklatura*, accompanied by the collapse of whole industries, economic dislocations, unemployment, and the rapid impoverishment of entire regions. Though in the course of the next decade the economic situation of the country improved, unemployment went down, and the management of the human and economic capital became more transparent, the jury is still out on whether the steep costs of transformation were necessary and whether they brought real economic rewards and a degree of equity to the most affected part of the population.

At this point it is difficult not to observe that there is a very close connection between the devastation of the national economies and the emergence in the region over the first decade of transformation of a certain massive profit-making option: trafficking in women.[14] There is also a close link between the illegal trafficking in women and their powerlessness in the face of new and confusing, but still gendered, realignments in the marketplace. The UN Office for Drug Control and Drug Prevention has been warning—since the beginning of the century—that the traffic in women is now the fastest-growing business of organized crime, and its rate of growth is fastest in central and Eastern Europe and the former Soviet Union. According to estimates, the industry is now worth several billion dollars a year. Russian trafficking victims working in the sex industry in Germany reportedly earn on average $7,500 a month, of which the exploiter takes at least $7,000.[15]

This trafficking is obviously a global phenomenon. It moves across borders, continents, and oceans. And central Europe, at the interface between the wealthiest and the poorest countries of Europe and Asia, is the point of passage. As economic differences between the countries of the former communist bloc become sharper, the trafficking runs not only from east to west (Ukraine to Germany) but also from east to east (Bulgaria to Poland), because even within "The East" there is always some place west—or north—having relative economic success, proximity to the European Union, greater density of international transit on major highways, or greater strength of the local currency vis-à-vis the dollar and the euro. Hence, victims trafficked to (and through) Poland come mostly from rural and impoverished regions in which trading is the only occupation, and for a young, unemployed woman with little education, the only merchandise available for trading is her body.

They come from Russia, Belarus, Ukraine, Moldova, Romania, and Bulgaria, and—what is rarely mentioned—increasingly they turn themselves desperately into wares to improve their own and their families' impossible living conditions. The most common outcome of the growing trade in women is forced prostitution, which is often characterized as an organized crime, to be addressed in legal terms and to be prevented by a further tightening of the borders between the European Union and the rest of Europe. Such a response comes from people who would seem to prefer to be blind. The countries of the EU are not interested in seeing that the traffickers are not the sole culprits, that it was not they who coerced women into bonded labor abroad in the first place, even if it is indeed the work of criminal gangs and unscrupulous male traffickers who profit from all this enormously. Yet it is obvious for key international organizations that "the search for work abroad has been fueled by economic disparity, high unemployment, and the disruption of traditional livelihoods."[16]

The response of women activists in the region was to launch La Strada, a dynamic network of women's organizations in central and Eastern Europe established in 1995 to fight the trafficking in women. La Strada increasingly sees the trafficking in women and children not just as a result of powerful criminal networks operating in this part of the world or in terms of violations of human rights but above all as a violation of social and economic rights.[17] Saskia Sassen, a scholar with a critical activist edge, struggling to define the trafficking in women, said, "This is not crime, this is something else." And this "something else" will remain with us until some vast campaign is undertaken to improve the condition of women—and men—in the poorer countries ("Finding Women's Security" 2002).

The Politics of Europeanization

The goal of European Enlargement is to equalize the differences between the eastern and western parts of the continent.

—Sueddeutsche Zeitung, April 2001

The major enlargement of the European Union in May 2004, which included eight postcommunist countries, evaluated as the most advanced in democratic and economic reforms, created a new divide, this time between countries of the former communist bloc, between the lucky ones who made it to the club, and the poor, unlucky ones who did not.

The eastward enlargement of the European Union, the most significant growth it has experienced so far in terms of both scope and diversity—from fifteen to twenty-five member states—has obviously had enormous implications for the applicant countries. Of the ten countries invited to take part in the lengthy process of preparations and negotiations for EU entry, completed on May 1, 2004, all but Cyprus and Malta were former members of the communist bloc.[18]

Poland completed its negotiations with the European Union on December 13, 2002 (for Poles an interesting, though pure, coincidence, that being the anniversary of the 1981 imposition of martial law that temporarily crushed Solidarity). Although the talks had been stormy, as the Polish negotiators frequently rose from the table, ready to break off the talks, it was finally agreed that Poland had met the EU criteria for membership, which were organized into three clusters of requirements and thirty chapters of negotiations focusing on various areas of EU law and policy. The first cluster called for stable democratic institutions, founded on the rule of law, human rights, and respect for and protection of minorities. The second group required the existence of a functioning market economy capable of coping with the competitive pressures and market forces within the EU. The third cluster included the ability to take on the responsibilities of membership, which include adherence to the aims of political, economic, and monetary union.[19] The return of the Polish negotiating team from Copenhagen, with Prime Minister Miller at the helm, was greeted with considerable euphoria, especially by the liberal media. On April 16, 2003, the ten applicant countries signed the Treaty of Accession in Athens.

It is widely believed—at least among the original EU members—that the carrot of membership contributes to a strengthening of the causes of democracy and tolerance within the applicant countries. Women's groups in Poland—a country known for its regressive policies concerning reproductive rights—had been following the process of negotiation closely, in the expectation that the process itself and the very act of joining the European Union would force the Polish state to adjust its laws to the standards and norms of the EU, including equal treatment legislation, and the European Commission's provision for comprehensive gender equality, known as *gender mainstreaming*. In short, women were actively anticipating that this European approach would become a commanding guarantor of gender justice in the region and that the principle of gender mainstreaming would gradually produce a major change in mentality, especially within the Polish political class.

Gender mainstreaming[20]—actively promoted in the 1990s by various intergovernmental organizations in Europe, especially by the Council of Europe—is a strategy aimed at integrating the gender perspective into every fiber of society. More specifically, it means incorporating a gender-equality perspective into all policies at all policy-making levels, primarily by those who deal with the given policies (i.e., in education, health care, transportation, and so on). Gender mainstreaming, as defined by the Council of Europe, is the "re-organization, improvement, development, and evaluation of policy processes, so that the gender-equality perspective is incorporated in all policies at all levels and at all stages, by the actors normally involved in policy-making."[21]

One would think that the painstaking process of negotiation would have provided the EU with an excellent opportunity for the coherent introduction of the principle and culture of gender mainstreaming to each country through its extensive teams of experts negotiating separately in thirty different policy areas. One would have thought that this was a major opportunity, since the applicant countries were adjusting and reorganizing their structures, learning to take on new responsibilities, and at that very sensitive moment having to exhibit their political goodwill. But a closer examination of the thirty chapters of negotiations on the conditions under which applicant countries can join the EU reveals a priority given to economic issues over social or political concerns.

And under the pressure exerted by the EU to synchronize the legal, social, and economic spheres, gender was not the primary or even a secondary lens through which these concerns were examined. In fact, women's issues appeared in only one of the thirty areas of negotiation, specifically in the thirteenth, concerning the problems of social policy and employment. And there were no negotiations concerning the question of gender equality as such. This prioritizing makes one think about the double standards already applied now vis-à-vis candidate countries. After all, the EU has been for many years openly promoting gender mainstreaming among its original members, setting aside human and financial resources to ensure the implementation of policies that support further equality for women. The applicant countries, however (or, rather, their women's rights groups), it was tacitly decided, ought to be satisfied that the employment status of women has been considered.[22]

Ironically, for the EU to highlight this partial standard not only is misleading but can also undermine the efforts of the local women's movements in the new member countries. A high level of women's employment (70–80 percent) and education was experienced by two generations of women and is generally taken for granted in the region. While the current inequalities between men and women in the labor market are widely recognized by Polish society, it is also clear to women that equality in the labor market, still very high in Poland, does not automatically advance their equality in other spheres of life (Fuszara 2000).

The main preoccupation of the EU negotiations—the policy of equal opportunity for men and women in the realm of employment (on the premise that women can handle simultaneously both household responsibilities and full-time employment)—does not actually address the real problems faced by women in Poland, argued Polish scholars and activists. Such problems are issues of importance to current members of the European Union, where even a few years ago the participation of women in the labor market was much lower than in central Europe. In Poland women had been managing double duty for years, and now many of them would prefer to have some flexibility in making their choices, especially at a time when the state is pulling back from its provision of support systems for working mothers.[23]

The absence of such flexibility on the part of Brussels, and the insistence on selected, mostly economic, standards that were devised in one context and cloned for another, may help in forcing women in central Europe to retreat into the roles envisioned for them by the church, as mothers and homemakers. As one of the most perceptive feminist writers in Warsaw has bitterly observed, the EU may simply be willing to accept gender discrimination in Poland as a matter of local color: "The French have their cheeses, the Brits their Queen, and the Poles have their discrimination against women" (Graff 1999, 22–23). She said this in 1999, and it seems that what sounded then like a sardonic observation about a misapplied idea of the cultural rights of the community has turned into an accurate prediction.

One may argue that the principle of gender mainstreaming has been unevenly realized among the member countries of the EU itself. While it seems to be fairly well entrenched in Germany and in the Nordic countries, its realization in France, for example, seems to be taking place mostly at the local level. But the lamentable absence of any general discussion with the applicant states on the strategy concerning gender issues—a comprehensive strategy that for the member states is already a guiding strategy—has already had detrimental effects. Perhaps such a discussion could have helped to create a larger consensus around the need to introduce gender-equality policies, or at least discourage manifestations of openly antiwomen attitudes that originate in official circles and constitute a further assault on the women's rights community.

As one might expect, the reasons Polish feminists looked with hope toward Poland's entry into the European Union were the very reasons cited by the local conservative groups in warning against accession. The growing split between the progressive and reactionary publics, the latter spreading fear about accession and further aggravated by the patronizing stance of some Western politicians vis-à-vis the "New Europe," has put the government negotiating the accession treaty into a state of anxiety, especially in view of the June 2003 national referendum in which Poles were to cast their votes for or against accession to the EU. And, paradoxically, Polish feminists were nervous that even if accession were accomplished, they might discover that the EU had been stinting all along on the question of women's rights when it came to the "New Europe."

The feminists' disappointment with the EU approach toward the candidate countries, which applied scrutiny to everything except women's rights, broadly understood, was based on a decade of either unworkable or straightforwardly hostile relationships between women's civil society and the state. Following the

1997 elections the Polish government replaced its office dealing with gender equality with one called the Governmental Plenipotentiary for Family Affairs, whose representative, sent in June 2000 to the UN conference "Women 2000," spoke out against women's rights without hiding her disdain. But the hard work of women's organizations paid off in 2001, when women candidates won 22 percent of the seats in the parliamentary elections and a new Office of the Governmental Plenipotentiary for the Equal Status of Women and Men was established. Its appointed head, Izabela Jaruga-Nowacka, a longtime leader of a women's organization affiliated with a left-wing party, announced that her office, which would also defend men's rights (including those related to reproductive health), had taken upon itself, as one of its goals, a campaign to liberalize the antiabortion law. She pointed out that this very strict law had resulted in the massive emergence of underground abortion clinics and dramatically affected the lives of thousands of women, particularly those who are less affluent. Making her first major presentation of the program in January 2002, she set the stage for acts of constructive performativity, making it clear that she intended to work toward liberalization of the law criminalizing abortion, through dialogue and the building of societal and political consensus around the issue, rather than through a declaration of ideological war against the conservative, populist faction in parliament (for more on women and performativity, see Matynia 2009).

Yet Jaruga-Nowacka's refreshingly independent position and visible presence in public debates soon began to be perceived not only as a threat to those at the right end of the political spectrum but also as an *obstruction* to the work of the new government, which—despite its communist pedigree—liked to present itself as an enlightened European-style social democracy. Nevertheless, a governmental spokesman, during the plenipotentiary's January presentation, immediately stated that the Council of Ministers had no plans to revisit the antiabortion law in 2002 ("Minister Jaruga-Nowacka" 2002).

Soon afterward, in an interview given to a Warsaw daily, a Polish bishop who had been generally considered one of the most reasonable and moderate[24] came out with a surprising statement, calling the new Governmental Plenipotentiary for the Equal Status of Women and Men "a feminist hard-liner who will not change even under hydrochloric acid." This tipped the scale, and the bishop's vitriolic remarks were immediately greeted with a barrage of criticism in the media, including the voices of well-known professional women who had never associated themselves with the feminist movement.

In early February 2002, more than one hundred well-known women—intellectuals, scholars, and artists, including a Nobel Prize Laureate—signed a letter of protest written by a widely respected senior professor and literary critic, Maria Janion, and addressed to the European Parliament and to Anna Diamantopulou, the EU's commissioner for labor and social policy (the very area, chapter 13, that considers women in the enlargement negotiations). The letter, widely circulated throughout the country and abroad, expressed distress over the direction of the debate on the situation of women in Poland and suggested that behind the scenes in Poland's negotiations with the EU some very specific trading in women's rights had taken place.[25] And looking at the entire political stage from overseas, one could not help thinking that the government's caution about not antagonizing the church hierarchy was closely related to its anxiety concerning the issue of European enlargement. Popular support for joining the EU had been steadily dropping in Poland (from 80 percent in 1996 to 55 percent in 2001),[26] and it became clear that the post-communist government had been courting the church to gain an advocate vis-à-vis its large rural constituency, which was most resistant to the idea of enlargement. At some point it seemed as though this disturbing antifeminist alliance might only have been a temporary strategic constellation: this alliance of globalizing Eurocrats, cloning their mostly economic laws and regulations for others but unwilling to see the candidate countries as they really were and to set in motion the general idea of gender mainstreaming; individual governments that were itching to join the European club and that to get there were willing, despite earlier promises, to close their eyes and sacrifice women's rights; and the "universal" Catholic Church, which—at this historic juncture—was happy to play its illiberal card openly, hoping to hinder at least for a while the unavoidable.

Even though the process of European enlargement has not provided the expected program of prerequisites, instruments, and climate that would empower women's rights groups in the region (certainly nothing comparable to the Convention on the Elimination of All Forms of Discrimination Against Women), membership in the EU inevitably has to open up access to the broader family of standards implied by the notion of gender mainstreaming and to provide mechanisms through which their implementation could be monitored and accounted for. But the mechanics of enlargement, as seen through the lens of gender, reveal major flaws and deficiencies in the European institutions themselves. When in July 2002 the European Parliament accepted a resolution recommending that abortion be legal in the candidate countries, the Polish Episcopate retorted, "We do not need any instruction from Brussels in order to learn when one can kill a baby. We know that one cannot do it ever, and that's it. It is a scandal that the European Parliament is trying to intervene in countries that are not even members of the E.U." (Brzeziecki and Fik 2003). And yet as soon as the government delegation, with Prime Minister Miller, returned from the final accession negotiations in Copenhagen in December 2002, church representatives expressed their satisfaction and support for the successful conclusion of the process.

Later the government, pressed by the episcopate of the Catholic Church, was trying to hammer down a separate protocol (like the one forced by Ireland in Maastrich) to be added to the Polish treaty, stating the inviolability of Polish antiabortion law. And Prime Minister Miller—even though he knew from the opinion polls that the overwhelming majority of Poles support a liberalization of the antiabortion law—announced that in today's Poland the conditions were not right for a modification of the abortion law.

One ought to admit that even though a rare opportunity to change or to modify the Polish antiabortion law was lost, the very fact that the European Union has invested itself in employment issues brought about a new law concerning sexual harassment in the workplace. Some feminists in Poland observed with some satisfaction that in this respect the implementation of the European Union legislation paved the way for a transformation in the attitudes of the general public. There are also some other related legislative changes: family-leave policies are already extended to eighteen weeks, and they are to be further lengthened to match EU recommendations, and a one-week paternity-leave policy was introduced in 2008.

Paradoxically, it was the country's democratic transformation that for some political forces opened up an opportunity to rebuild the wall between the polis and the household that had been perforated during the time of the self-limiting revolution. It was Poland's accession to the European Union—in particular the favor expected of the church to support the accession and to convince the people to vote yes in the upcoming referendum—that postponed any revisiting of women's reproductive rights. And it was the process of European enlargement that made it tricky for local feminism, with its impressive analysis of Poland's indigenously gendered culture, to "undress" the pageant (so effective in its restriction of women's right to self-determination) and thus to disarm it.

One could, of course, toy with the idea of a radical unilateral rejection by Polish feminism of the entire cultural idiom, but that would include its other modern and often whimsical elements, which, like the experience of World War II, the imaginative forms of Solidarity's resistance, and the street-theater experience of the late 1980s, remain for many women in Poland a source of autonomy, agency, creativity, and strength. It is particularly important under the present circumstances to consider that the response to such a unilateral rejection may come from relatively recent ideologies based on ultraconservative values (mostly religious and national), from populism, or from fundamentalism. Thriving in times of rapid social change, such ideologies provide emotional, cognitive, and political answers for those whose own modernizing efforts have been challenged and systematically frustrated. In the case of Poland the crowning moment of civil society—often referred to as the first Solidarity period (1980–1981), which had put the first serious crack in the system—was itself an alliance of various forces united only by their broadly anticommunist attitudes. Its three main original constituencies were the workers at large enterprises, bringing a populist hue to the language of material claims and entitlements; the secular intelligentsia, including many lay Catholics, speaking the language of human rights, cultural liberties, and strong democratic commitments; and many in the broader Catholic milieu who were unambiguous about their national colors, speaking the language of national values and claims. In the political scene of the late 1990s and early 2000s, that second current, representing a civil society–based agenda of human rights, democratic practice, and civic responsibility, seems to have been gradually marginalized, especially in the parliament. It was overpowered by the two pillars of the various ruling coalitions, namely, the so-called postcommunist Left, "reformed" in its dissociation from any communist principles and in its support of a free market and accession to the European Union, and the radical Right, which had emerged, in turn, through a kind of symbiosis between the first and third constituencies of Solidarity, that is, the proletarian-populist and the Catholic-nationalist groupings.

The resulting civic vacuum is only partially filled by the existing NGOs, with their separate niches of expertise, often performing auxiliary functions for the various governmental agencies. Even though they greatly enhance the institutional landscape of democracy, the public debate that they generate is fragmented and limited to their specific concerns. Understandably, their commitments may be linked not to the human rights agenda of the original Solidarity but to the civil society activities mobilized by the populist Radio Maryja, the principal defender of the Polish cultural idiom.

Still, Poland's own systemic transformation, its opening to markets, ideas, and people, as well as its joining the European Union, provoked a manageable measure of moral-majority and populist-fundamentalist response.[27] The real danger may lie, rather, in impoverished, isolated, and autocratic places like Belarus or the countries of central Asia.

Censoring Feminism in Central Europe:
Paradoxes of the Western Feminist Critique of Liberalism

There is now a considerable literature by American authors focusing on the systematic tensions between Western and Eastern women (Funk 1994), the jamming of communication while trying to translate Western feminism into postcommunist realities (Holmgren 1995), the difficulties in discussing gender issues in the region (Snitow 1993), the prospects for feminism after communism (Goldfarb 1997), or the straightforward rejection of feminism in Eastern Europe (Watson 1997). Similar literature has also been produced by women from the region, who address questions frequently asked by Western women: "Why am I not a feminist?" (Marody 1993), how to smuggle feminism across the post–Iron Curtain (Šmejkalová 1996), why feminism is not successful in the Czech Republic (Siklova 1996), and the frequently raised issue of intellectual patronization by Western authors (Nemenyi 2001).

Paradoxically, the relative success of Polish feminism in its efforts to find a voice, which allowed for such a compelling Polish debate, is also one of the reasons Polish feminism is the most open to the West. Yet there are some latent issues that are continuously causing tension and misunderstanding in East-West debates and are rooted in the different evaluation of liberalism offered by feminists from the East. To list some of the contentious issues may open up possibilities for future discussion. And liberalism is important here not because—as the exact opposite of communism—it has to have some bearing in the region on new directions in thinking but because liberalism is also, of course, a convenient vehicle for globalization, or "universal" civilization, with its emphasis on universal standards, free markets, individual freedom, individual rights, and the rule of law. This underscores one of the seeming paradoxes, mentioned earlier, that characterize feminism in Poland: the attention given simultaneously to the specificity of the Polish idiom formed by the politics of locality and to the language of universal human rights and consensus-based civil society. Here are some issues that further explain why Polish feminism reacts so differently to liberalism.

Issue 1: Liberalism never really made it to Poland, but nationalism did. The cultural idiom that has framed gender relations in Poland is not only the outcome of a particular historical and cultural experience but also heavily oriented toward collective rights and community needs, above all the needs of the national community. For local feminists trying to free themselves from such constraints, which are experienced in Poland as the constraints of nationalism and a recently vibrant populism, it is difficult to enter a Western feminist discourse that talks predominantly in terms of collective rights. It would also bring them dangerously close to those populist sentiments.

Issue 2: While the biggest foe of globalization may be religious nationalism, one of the main foes of liberalism, and the biggest factor impeding the reception of liberalism in Poland, has been, and remains, the Catholic Church (Szacki 1995). Whereas in the most difficult times the church provided Poles with a space in which they could experience personal freedom and dignity, since the collapse of communism it has become the major antiliberal force redefining the role of women in terms of motherhood and family responsibilities. Thus, in Poland the liberal principle of keeping the church away from the public is considered both attractive and progressive, and so is the liberalism-rooted critique of the church, which rejects all forms of dogmatism and any limitations on discussion and criticism. This is at a time when Marxism-derived theories are simply not an option in this part of the world, particularly as they are now often embraced, under various guises, by the populist Right.

Issue 3: The absence of a liberal tradition, along with the specific political circumstances prevailing in Poland for fifty years (1939–1989), have made the private-public divide postulated by the liberal tradition a useless tool as far as feminist theory in Poland (and most of its discourse) is concerned. Poland's politics of locality required a peculiar merger of the private and the public. The boundaries had already become blurred in the nineteenth century. Education, art, and self-help organizations—all activities that in a normal society constitute the public sphere but that in Poland were illegal throughout the nineteenth century and both world wars—had already moved into the domestic, private sphere long before communism was installed there. It was the extended family with its close circle of friends that hosted and cultivated a public sphere within the private. The public became private, whereas the so-called publicness of the sphere sponsored by the state was staged, as Habermas might put it, "for manipulative purposes" (1996, 235).

From the 1970s on, for a growing number of Poles the private sphere developed into a civic realm inhabited by private agents acting on behalf of the public good. Were the seminars of the *flying university* that were regularly organized in private apartments and announced through the underground press public or private? Were the studies and research on Polish society, conducted by private groups of university professors, a civic initiative known as Experience and the Future, and published by the underground publishing house NOWA, public or private? What about the private performances of the 8th Day Theater or poetry readings at home or in churches? Yes, it was all unofficial, very often illegal, but it did not easily fit the Western notion of a private sphere.

The private spaces became public as they blurred the lines between exclusively personal or domestic matters and public matters and agendas.

What looks like a paradoxical privatization of the public (closely related to "depublicization" of the official sphere or a going underground by the public) does not make it a lesser public. The names of the editorial board of the biggest underground periodical, called *Censored*, were openly printed along with their home addresses and phone numbers. The general rule was that "Things may not be normal here but we have to act as though they are normal." To expand in this way the realm of the private in order to accommodate the public was, in effect, to dissolve the boundaries between the two spheres, or at least to install multiple openings between already porous walls (Matynia 1998, 16–17).

Issue 4: Acknowledging this peculiarly Polish experience of a private but public sphere helps us to understand the emergence here of civil society, which is the domain of an expanded private sphere. As Western social science theorists have suggested, Poland was the place where civil society was reinvented. The lack of a liberal tradition and liberal discourse in Poland did not become an obstacle to devising a set of practices in the 1970s that later came to be labeled by Westerners "civil society." Obviously, civil society in the late '70s was an emancipation project, empowered by the notion of human rights as adopted in the Helsinki Accords signed by the Polish government in 1975. Yet this paradigm of civil society did not prescribe as best any one way of acting but recognized the value of locally cultivated civic imagination and homegrown initiatives. It was, and is, a specifically Polish experience of applied liberalism, closer to the democratic potential of Habermas's theory of deliberative action than to conventional rights-based liberal theory (Matynia 2001). This also sets it apart from the populist environment dominated by a monological black-and-white vision of the world, an environment in which fear reigns supreme.

In a society where democracy is a reasonably well-functioning mechanism, civil society functions as a partner of the state. Women's organizations in Poland, although amazingly numerous, as they are still building their home base, are still not strong enough to be recognized as a full partner of the state, but, with or without the help of the European Union, they are getting there. The problems begin when gender—by becoming an issue-driven grant vehicle—often creates conditions in which a comprehensive, locally derived agenda for women's groups does not overlap with the programmatic guidelines of some Western donors or, as in the recent case of accession to the EU, chapters of negotiation. This asymmetrical relationship causing multilateral dependencies is very much a feature of globalization.

The Challenge of Translation

While pointing out both the understandable liberal leanings of Polish feminism and its seemingly antiliberal imperative in exploring local idiom, I tend to agree with Anne Phillips when she observes that "the universal discourses of rights are often formed in context, and they often fail to engage adequately with difference" (1991, 149). At the same time I would like to emphasize that the work Polish women do on disarming the cultural idiom is strategic, as it directly addresses the sources of violations of rights and gender equality. Hence, it is important to caution against the natural temptation to translate regional or national differences into terms that are our own: to understand the nature of their distinctiveness, yes; to extend what Ann Snitow (1997) calls "hermeneutical generosity," yes; and to build transnational initiatives based on real partnerships where local women, who know intricacies of their own situation best and can address it with strategic savvy, indeed have a voice, yes.[28]

Feminism is a political and cultural project of global dimensions, but with its own local expressions and accomplishments that do not always lend themselves easily to exact translation. And perhaps feminism's biggest strength is its polyphony of voices and strategies. Even within the *local* there are a variety of feminisms. Just as there are Muslim women's organizations in many countries, there are also some women's organizations associated with the Catholic Church. Perhaps the most intellectually impressive, observed with some sympathy by the country's mainstream feminists, is a modest movement known as the *New* Feminism, concerned with recognizing men and women as equals in both Catholic theology and everyday life, and thus trying to build bridges between feminism and educated Catholic women. It is a relatively modest project, but its role in a country that is almost 90 percent Catholic, and a nation whose imagination has been shaped by the Marian cult, should not be underestimated.[29]

While the notion of local multiple feminisms does not necessarily deglobalize feminism as such, it does *decenter*, or *provincialize*, the center (see the interesting Chakrabarty 2000), which is where Western and Northern feminism tends to locate both itself and most of its discourse. On the other hand, these local feminisms operate within the same set of concerns but address them through indigenously developed strategies. Such strategies may be, as in the Polish case, a mixed bag of blueprints developed under communist rule by the democratic opposition in the 1970s and '80s (if you cannot talk to your government, talk to foreign media or international institutions, such as the Helsinki Human Rights Committee) and by local gender studies programs (if you cannot reach a wider public using the detached language of rights, gradually create a thicker feminist culture by launching a critical debate on the gendering outcomes of the core cultural tradition). Saskia Sassen talks about the importance of multiple microinterventions, which have in fact a global character even if they are not thoroughly cosmopolitan (2002). I think we should take her advice.

The Polish feminists discovered how badly they needed a language and some key concepts to make their efforts both understandable at home and connected to other feminisms. *Gender* is one of them; *civil society* and *women's rights* may be others. And perhaps such feminisms—provincialized, decentered, but linked to each other and seeking indigenously based solutions to global problems—could serve as an attractive, inclusive, and less arrogant model for globalization itself.

Notes

1. Manifa, which is a carnivalesque event that attracts the media and demands equal rights for women, is organized annually by the younger generation of Polish feminists, among them accomplished author Agnieszka Graff.

2. Interestingly, "they"—perhaps because of successful efforts of the state propaganda—were always envisioned as Germans.

3. Shana Penn describes the most drastic case in "The National Secret," *Journal of Women's History* (Winter 1994): 55–69, also in Penn 2005.

4. "The Politics of Gender Equality: Poland 2007" (Polityka równosci plci: Polska 2007), prepared as a part of the project "Gender Mainstreaming Initiative," UNDP and Gender Thematic Trust Fund. Available at http://www.gm.undp.org.pl/files/63/Polityka_rownosci_plci.pdf? PHPSESSID=79b304e3a8bfbdace428f87c9c53a086.

5. Article 33 of the constitution states: "(1) Men and women shall have equal rights in family, political, social and economic life in the Republic of Poland. (2) Men and women shall have equal rights, in particular, regarding education, employment and promotion, and shall have the right to equal compensation for work of similar value, to social security, to hold offices, and to receive public honors and decorations." Available at http://www.servat.unibe.ch/icl/pl00000_.html.

6. The reasons for that situation were many: a still not yet fully developed appreciation of the representative role of elected officials, a tendency toward a certain disdain for the general public, and a rather widely ingrained indifference to "women's issues" on the part of traditionally male-dominated governments.

7. For full analysis of this phenomenon, see Matynia 2009.

8. A. Graff, *Swiat bez kobiet* (Warsaw: WAB, 2001); K. Szczuka, *Cinderella, Frankenstein, i inne* (Kraków: eFKA, 2001); E. H. Oleksy, "Wrobelek ze zlamanym skrzydlem[. . .]i kieliszek czystej: Konstrukcje kobiecosci w polskiej powojennej kulturze wizualnej" (in *Gender, Film, Media,* ed. Elzbieta H. Oleksy and Elzbieta Ostrowska [Kraków, 2001]), English translation: *Sparrow with a Broken Wing [. . .] or, A Shot of Vodka: Constructions of Femininity in Polish Postwar Visual Culture*; S. Walczewska, *Damy, rycerze, i feministki* (Kraków: eFKA, 1999); K. Klosinska, *Cialo, pozadanie, ubranie* (Kraków: eFKA, 1999); E. Kondratowicz, *Szminka na sztandarze* (Warsaw: Sic! 2001); K. Szczuka, *Milczenie owieczek: Rzecz o aborcji* (Warsaw: WAB, 2004).

9. There have been many articles in the West featuring Wanda Rapaczynska and Helena Luczywo, the two women behind the media giant Agora (Ash 1999; Simpson 2001). See also "Women Entrepreneurs in Poland," http://www.polskainstitutet.se/doc/uppsala-10april.ppt.

10. The decrease in those who support the role of woman as homemaker: from 86 percent in 1992 to 76 percent in 1998. The decrease in those of the opinion that women ought to sacrifice

their professional careers for the sake of their husbands: from 46 percent in 1992 to 32.9 percent in 1992. See Domanski 2002.

11. Report of the Public Opinion Research Center (CBOS), February 2002, no. BS/39/2002, available at http://www.cbos.pl.

12. There is an impressive set of handbooks by dedicated women lawyers that expand knowledge on new legislation directly affecting women, such as domestic violence (Sylwia Spurek, *Ustawa o Przeciwdzialaniu Przemocy w Rodzinie. Komentarz* [Warsaw: Wolters Kluwer, 2008]), gender equality (M. Mazewska and M. Zakrzewska, *ABC Rownosci, NEWW* [Gdansk: Polska, 2007]), and electoral processes (S. Spurek, *Kobiety, partie, wybory* [Lodz: Centrum Praw Kobiet, 2002]).

13. Felicitous, or happy, performatives do not just act as though they are doing what they are saying but actually have a real immediate (illocutionary acts) or delayed (perlocutionary acts) effect.

14. Saskia Sassen links the trafficking in women more specifically to the hyperindebtedness of many countries. See her work "Strategic Instantiations of Gendering: Global Cities and Survival Circuits," available at http://portal.unesco.org/shs/en/ev.php-URL_ID=7374&URL_DO=DO_TOPIC&URL_SECTION=201.html.

15. ODCCP—Internet/United Nations Office for Drug Control and Crime Prevention (ODCCP), http://www.odccp.org.

16. See the Web site of the UN Office for Drug Control and Crime Prevention.

17. J. Regulska, quoting Barbel Butteweck from La Strada's Prague office: "W poszukiwaniu przestrzeni dla kobiet. Integracja Europy a Rownosc Plci," *Biuletyn OSKa,* no. 12, available at http://www.oska.org.pl/biuletin.

18. The others are the Czech Republic, Estonia, Hungary, Latvia, Lithuania, Poland, Slovakia, and Slovenia. In 2007 two other countries of the former Eastern bloc, Bulgaria and Romania, were admitted to the European Union.

19. For more details, see the very informative Web site http://www.unc.edu/depts/europe/conferences/eu/cfsp/enlarge.

20. The concept, brought up for the first time at the UN Third World Conference on Women in Nairobi in 1985, launched a vigorous debate, especially in Western Europe, was adopted as part of the Platform for Action, and was eventually further highlighted as a key strategy at the 1995 Beijing conference. See also "Gender Mainstreaming: Conceptual Framework, Methodology, and Presentation if Good Practices," issued by the Council of Europe, available at http://www.coe.int/T/E/Human_Rights/Equality/PDF_EG-S-MS_98_2rev_E.pdf.

21. Ibid., 15.

22. J. Regulska, "W poszukiwaniu przestrzeni dla kobiet"; Stephane Portet, "Integracja Polski z Unia Europejska a Relacje Plci," *Biuletyn OSKa,* no. 12.

23. Joanna Regulska was one of the first to point out major difference of employment status between women from Western and Eastern Europe ("W poszukiwaniu przestrzeni dla kobiet"; see also M. Fuszara 2000, 2006). The emphasis on gender mainstreaming in the realm of employment was still visible in the conferences organized in Poland in 2007 and 2008 co-sponsored by the Ministry of Labor and Social Policy. Nevertheless, once Poland joined the EU, both the concept and the practices of gender mainstreaming entered the language of both nongovernmental organizations and governmental agencies, indicating a measure of unquestionable progress.

24. The bishop was Tadeusz Pieronek.

25. The "Letter of One Hundred" was published in *Gazeta Wyborcza,* March 7, 2002, one day before International Women's Day, and opened a flood of polemics in the Polish media.

26. CBOS, October 2001, http://www.cbos.pl.

27. Examples of populist manifestations are Radio Maryja and Samoobrona (a political party led by Andrzej Lepper, stripped of his position as a deputy speaker of parliament and his immunity as an member of parliament). The ultra-right-wing political party Liga Rodzin Polskich exhibits a fundamentalist mentality.

28. A good example of a transnational network where the initiative is placed in the hands of the local organizations and local voices is the Network of East-West Women, an organization

supporting women's rights in East-central Europe, in the Balkans, and in the countries of the former Soviet Union. Launched in 1990 as an initiative of U.S. feminists, its international secretariat has been moved from Washington, D.C., to the region and is run now by the NEWW-Poland branch (http://www.neww.org.pl).

29. The key representative of this intellectual project in Poland is Elzbieta Adamiak, author of a widely discussed book *Milczaca obecnosc: O roli kobiety w kosciele* [Silent presence: On the role of a woman in the church] (Warsaw: Wiez, 2005).

7

Russian Women's Activism:
Two Steps Forward,
One Step Back

LISA McINTOSH SUNDSTROM

W omen's activism in Russia has undergone dramatic transformation since the collapse of the Soviet regime in 1991, and indeed since Elizabeth Waters and Anastasia Posadskaya penned their 1995 chapter, "Democracy Without Women Is No Democracy: Women's Struggles in Postcommunist Russia," in *The Challenge of Local Feminisms*. On one hand, formally organized women's groups have grown exponentially since the early 1990s, and women activists have become savvy managers, fund-raisers, and organizers. Many have established strong ties with global feminist networks to strengthen their effectiveness. But, on the other hand, enormous weaknesses remain, to the point that it is difficult to truly say there is a "women's movement" of any significance in the country. Feminists have had only very minor and sporadic influence on some small portions of Russian society, and it is safe to say that most Russians have a decidedly negative orientation toward the term *feminism*, although their actual beliefs about gender equality vary greatly. While a dramatic growth in women's organizing occurred in the 1990s immediately after the collapse of the Soviet regime, there has been a subsequent contraction in the visibility of women activists and their ability to work for change over the past decade. This is in many respects due to a decline in foreign donors' funding for civil society organizations in Russia in recent years, which has seriously depleted the resources of women's organizations and endangered their ability to continue working. Foreign funding has been a double-edged sword, encouraging women's organizations to become focused on professional project execution

RUSSIA

Human Development Index Ranking: .802
Gender-Related Development Index value: .801
Gender Empowerment Measure Value: .489

General

Type of Government: Federation
Major Ethnic Groups: Russian (79.8%); Tatar (3.8%); Ukrainian (2%); other (14.4%)
Languages: Russian (official); more than 140 other languages and dialects
Religions: Russian Orthodox; Muslim; Jewish; Roman Catholic; Protestant; Buddhist;
    other

Demographics

Population, total (millions), 2005: 144.0
Annual growth rate (%), 2005–2015: -.5
Total fertility (average number of births per woman): 1.3
Contraceptive prevalence (% of married women aged 15–49): not available
Maternal mortality ratio, adjusted (per 100,000 live births), 2000: 28

Women's Status

Date of women's suffrage: 1918
Life Expectancy: M 58.6; F 72.1
Combined gross enrollment ratio for primary, secondary, and tertiary education
    (female %), 2005: 93
Gross primary enrollment ratio: 128
Gross secondary enrollment ratio: 91
Gross tertiary enrollment ratio: 82
Literacy (% age 15 and older): M 99.7; F 99.2

Political Representation of Women

Seats in parliament (% held by women): 8.0
Legislators, senior officials, and managers (% female): 39
Professional and technical workers (% female): 65
Women in government at ministerial level (% total): 0

Economics

Estimated Earned Income (PPP US$): M 13,581; F 8,476
Ratio of estimated female to male earned income: .62
Economic activity rate (% female): 54.3
Women in adult labor force (% total): not available

and grant management, to follow trends in donor-funding priorities, and to spend little time reaching out to Russian women at large for agenda development and support.

Overall, as I discuss at length below, women's post-Communist activism on the issue of gender-based violence has been rewarded with a number of mobilizational and public policy victories (albeit limited and unstable), while activism on women's economic inequality and political representation has been more muted and produced far less tangible improvement. This is partly because preventing violence against women seems to be a universally appealing goal for feminists worldwide and therefore an issue for which transnational material resources and advocacy support have been relatively abundant. But in addition, because of its universal nature, the norm against physical violence resonates with Russian citizens, while the goals of economic and political equality are more controversial because of Russia's legacy of gender norms under Communism.

Self-identifying feminists are few in Russia, and they struggle to persuade public officials and citizens at large to consider their ideas seriously. The resistance that feminists face has sources that are more intractable than in many Western countries where liberal values have played a strong role in politics and society. The Soviet state labeled feminism a bourgeois, Western ideology, and claimed that it was unnecessary in the Soviet Union since socialism had brought about equality between the sexes. Women thus tended to react by looking at their "equality" (which really was a heavy double dose of paid public and unpaid household labor) and deducing that equality brought nothing positive for women's lives. Russian feminist Olga Voronina captured the reaction well: "For the average Soviet woman, emancipation is what she already has, that is, a lot of work, under the guise of equality with men" (1993). The legacy of Communist rhetoric as well as policy efforts to promote women's inequality in some areas but undermine it in others has meant that women are equal in law but not in practice. Though treated unequally in everyday life, their equal status in many official respects makes it difficult for women to argue that they face significant discrimination. Once post-Soviet politicians launched marketization processes and a laissez-faire model of the state became popular among various political and economic elites, gender segregation in the labor sphere increased, and women's representation in politics declined, while the myth that the Soviet regime rendered women equal to men persisted. The myth of equality and the accompanying sense that Soviet equality ruined women's femininity has led to an open resurgence (kept largely out of Soviet-era public discourse) of some traditional gender ideals of women as nurturing mothers and keepers of the hearth (not to mention sex goddesses) and men as strong providers (ibid., 223; Jurna 1995, 477). Moreover, this history has made it difficult for post-Soviet Russian feminists to mobilize successfully by framing political claims as demands for gender equality. Renewed popularity of the Russian Orthodox Church after the Soviet period of religious suppression has also contributed to the growth of traditional gender ideals.[1] Yet the situation is complicated and in flux: as I discuss below, these reactions *against* Soviet gender ideals are matched by enduring *positive* orientations toward women's labor-force participation, which themselves stem from Soviet labor patterns.

Some Historical Context: Gender Politics in the Soviet Period

Russia is an extremely interesting case to consider and compare with other countries in terms of women's activism and feminism. Its twentieth-century history (like the history of other post-Communist states) would seem at first glance to be conducive to the development of strong feminist activism and gender equality in society. Soviet women were extremely well educated, and high female labor-force participation developed relatively early compared to most other countries. Moreover, the early revolutionary Bolshevik regime, and especially feminists within the Bolshevik movement, emphasized gender equality.

Some Russian women attained full suffrage and the right to hold elected office under the Provisional Government between the February and October 1917 revolutions, and this was extended to all Soviet women in the 1918 Soviet Constitution. The Bolshevik regime instituted (although not always implemented) various labor and welfare rights that women still struggle for in many countries: for example, the principle of equal pay for equal work, rights to maternity leave with full pay for eight weeks before and after birth, and equal entitlement to employment benefits (Buckley 1989, 34–35). The regime lifted divorce restrictions, recast marriage as a decision of mutual consent between partners, and legalized abortion (ibid., 35–37).

Bolshevik feminists Aleksandra Kollontai and Inessa Armand advocated radical reorganization of family structures to emancipate women from the oppression of bourgeois marriage. Armand and Kollontai were radical enough to argue that family as a social institution enslaved women. Armand stated that "it is necessary to demolish this fortress" of the family (ibid., 44). Kollontai in a similar vein argued that "the individual household is dying" and that under socialism, brigades of domestic workers (both men and women) would do the housework of society (ibid., 45).

Lenin, following Engels, was sympathetic to these ideas, but viewed gender inequality as a problem that would disappear once Communism established itself (Zetkin 1934). During the Soviet period, the party's ideology both reified and tried to break existing gender stereotypes, depending on the era and realm of society. Beginning in the 1920s the regime's commitment to gender equality began to fade in the face of insufficient resources to truly collectivize domestic tasks and a great deal of hostility among both men and women toward these goals (Buckley 1989, chap. 1; Lapidus 1978, chap. 2; Aivazova 1998). In 1930 the state's abandonment of gender equality became official when Stalin closed the Women's Department (Zhenotdel) that Armand and Kollontai had founded, declaring the "woman question" officially "solved" (Buckley 1989, 108). Ultimately, as Waters and Posadskaya (1995) depict so well, the Soviet state warped the ideas of the Bolshevik feminists in ways that ended up increasing the burdens of Soviet women by requiring that they fulfill both traditional domestic roles and full-time participation in public life (work and public organizations). Because the development of communal services to reduce women's domestic labor time lagged behind the pace at which women were entering the paid employment sector, Soviet women endured the "double burden" of domestic and paid labor. It is estimated that nearly 75 percent of all domestic tasks fell exclusively to women in Soviet households in the 1970s (including many much more time-consuming ones than women in the industrialized West endured, due to the lack of consumer goods and labor-saving household devices), in addition to full-time work outside the home, in which nearly all of them participated (Lapidus 1978, 272). More recent studies indicate little change in this pattern of housework responsibilities (Vannoy et al. 1999; Ashwin 2006b).

During the Soviet period, the only women's organizations the government permitted were the official Soviet Women's Committee and the vast official network of small women's councils (*zhensovety*) in cities, towns, and workplaces across Russia. The government originally created the SWC in 1941 as a mechanism for mobilizing women in the war effort during World War II. Khrushchev revived the zhensovety (which Stalin had closed down along with the Zhenotdel) beginning in 1959 in his general effort to activate the Soviet mass population. Eventually in the 1980s, Gorbachev appointed the SWC in charge of leading the network of zhensovety, creating a single hierarchical umbrella network to represent women's interests. Yet these organizations had a primary mission of transmitting government and Communist Party messages to women to encourage them to fulfill regime goals in their daily lives, rather than acting as advocacy organizations to communicate women's demands or lobby for their interests at the national level (Buckley 1989). The SWC also had a secondary mission of promoting a rosy image of Soviet women's status to the outside world: as Zoya Khotkina has stated, the SWC "had, like Janus, two faces: one for Soviet women and another for Western women" (1999).

The Beginnings of Independent Women's Activism

In the 1970s and 1980s, prior to the collapse of the Soviet Union, there were some small groups of underground women feminists working in Russia, including publishers of the underground *samizdat* (self-published) journals *Women and Russia* and *Maria*. The Soviet government punished these activists quite severely, exiling some and sentencing others to hard-labor camps for advocating "bourgeois feminism" (Waters 1993; Dyukova 1998). In the late perestroika period, when independent social organizations were first permitted to associate more openly, many women's organizations were established informally, though they were not allowed to register.

A crucial organizational moment of these nascent groups came when several of them arranged two forums for independent women's organizations, called the First and Second Independent Women's Forums. The first took place in March 1991 and the second in late 1992, both in the small city of Dubna, outside Moscow. These forums proved to be crucial to the early mobilization and networking of the post-Soviet women's movement. Forum participants created a loose network of women's organizations, scholars, and activists called the Independent Women's Forum (V. Sperling 1999, 20). The IWF never really mobilized formally except when some of its members created an organization later, called the Information Center of the Independent Women's Forum, which exists at least as an information network to this day. Women developed other networks through different routes and other conferences over the same time period, with somewhat overlapping memberships across the multiple networks. One was the Women's League, which emerged out of a conference in Moscow in 1992 called "Women and the Market Economy." While independent of the state, the Women's League was somewhat less radical in outlook than the IWF (ibid., 21). Another network was the Union of Russian Women, which emerged in 1991 as a renamed version of the former Soviet Women's Committee, albeit no longer state sponsored. The URW also adopted a number of other fairly mainstream women's organizations under its umbrella. The final network was the US-NIS Consortium, later renamed the Russian Consortium of Women's Nongovernmental Organizations, which was cofounded by Russian and U.S. women activists in 1994 and brought together an "uneasy coalition" of members from the IWF and the Women's League (ibid.). Eventually, the consortium outlived the IWF and the Women's League in terms of ongoing activism and was one of the most prominent women's NGOs in Russia during the 1990s, while the other two became relatively dormant.

It is interesting to note that, in comparison with the material resources needed to organize large women's conferences in Russia today, the women who organized the Dubna forums did so with very little money. Workplace contacts of the organizers donated most of the supplies and venue costs in kind. Today, organizing conferences in Russia's market economy requires substantial funding, if only to rent a venue, duplicate materials, and provide food and beverages. Feminist Zoya Khotkina of the Moscow Center for Gender Studies has stated that "it was all done of the solidarity of women alone. Now, it's impossible to work like that" (1999).

Waters and Posadskaya noted in "Democracy Without Women Is No Democracy" (1995) that some women's groups were involved in the broader democratization movement as Russia transitioned from Soviet rule to multiparty democracy in the early 1990s. There were women in the prodemocracy movement who were fairly sympathetic to feminist ideas but did not identify openly with feminism or women's rights. Examples include Galina Starovoitova (a politician who was tragically murdered in 1998 in a targeted assassination), Irina Khakamada (who rose to the senior leadership of the Union of Right Forces Party), and, at more grassroots levels, many of the women involved in human rights organizations, who were not necessarily self-identifying feminists. Some feminists were actively involved, such as Olga Lipovskaya, a feminist poet widely recognized as a leader in the development of the Russian women's movement, who edited the samizdat journal *Zhenskoe chtenie* (Women's Reading) in the Soviet period. Lipovskaya was active in the St. Petersburg division of the Democratic Union in the late Soviet and early post-Soviet period, and then became head of the St. Petersburg Center for Gender Issues when it was founded in 1992.

However, the extent to which feminists or women's groups were active participants in the democracy movement was significantly less than in some other cases, particularly in Latin America (Jaquette and Wolchik 1998, 250; E. Friedman 1998; Franceschet 2003; Waylen 1994, 347). In many other countries' prodemocracy movements women were angered and disappointed by male activists' failure to include women's issues in the democracy agenda, and this spurred the growth of a separate feminist movement (Waylen 1994, 342–343; E. Friedman 1998, 107–109). While some Russian prodemocracy activists who were already feminists experienced similar frustration, as Posadskaya notes (Waters and Posadskaya 1995, 364), such feelings of alienation did not promote the development of an autonomous feminist movement. This difference in the genesis of women's activism in Russia compared to Latin America is undoubtedly related to the earlier-discussed normative resistance to feminism and gender equality as mobilizing concepts among Russian women, stemming from the Communist legacy.

The Shape of Post-Soviet Women's Activism

What exactly is a women's movement? Mario Diani sets out a definition of a social movement that synthesizes aspects of different schools of social movement theory: "A social movement is a network of informal interactions between a plurality of individuals, groups and/or organizations, engaged in political or cultural conflict, on the basis of a shared collective identity" (2000, 162). Crucial aspects of this definition include sustained networks of formal or informal interaction, or both, among individuals, groups, or organizations; a sense of a broad shared agenda of creating (or preventing!) change in society; as well as a shared set of beliefs and self-identification as members of a movement. I define a women's movement as a social movement in which members are participating on the basis of a shared agenda of improving women's status in society. Of all the characteristics of a social movement, perhaps the only one that could be said to be present among women's organizations in Russia is interaction of informal networks in a sustained, but infrequent, manner. Self-identification as being a member of a general women's movement is rare. In my interviews with Russian women activists over the years, those who use the term *movement* tend to employ it in reference to issue-specific mobilization (such as the movement against violence against women) or in reference to formal networks of women's organizations. For example, leaders in the large network of women's councils under the umbrella of the URW will sometimes refer to their network as "our women's movement." Women in the political party Women of Russia also frequently referred to their network of local branches as a "movement," but in legal terms, their political party was called a "political movement," so they likely used the term in an official sense.

The scale of women's activism in Russia, especially the small subset occurring on the basis of feminist ideas, is relatively small and lacks the kinds of sustained, mobilized networks of contention that exist in social movements. Some Russian feminists have actively rejected the idea that a "women's movement" exists in Russia (Marianna Muravyeva in Sopronenko 2008), and there is considerable justification for this assessment. Some non-Russian scholars have deemed the configuration of women's activism to constitute a "women's movement," although they admit that the movement is fairly weak (Waters 1993; V. Sperling 1999; Henderson 1998).

Most women activists in Russia decline to call themselves feminists. For instance, in a directory of women's organizations produced by Natalia Abubikirova and collaborators in 1998, only 3 percent of surveyed organizations across Russia and the Newly Independent States listed themselves as engaging in feminism (Abubikirova et al. 1998, 15). This is despite widespread attitudes among activists and even mainstream Russian women and men that are recognizably feminist (i.e., advocating gender equality or women's full-fledged status as human beings) to Westerners.

An excellent example is Russian citizens' attitudes toward women's employment in the public sphere, which can be traced back to Soviet-era patterns of the vast majority of women working outside the home. By the late 1990s women's labor-force participation had declined slightly, but so had men's, and the rate for women was still high by world standards at 75.1 percent (Ashwin 2006a, 2). In the multicity collaborative study that Sarah Ashwin and Russian colleagues conducted in the late 1990s, interviews revealed strong beliefs among both women and men that women should be able to work outside the home, and the researchers found that "working mothers are not subject to social sanction" (Ashwin 2006b, 37). Similar findings came from a fascinating study by Tania Rands Lyon, based on in-depth interviews with Russian families who raised children in the 1990s. While the vast majority of both men and women in her study professed that traditional spousal roles (man as breadwinner, woman as keeper of the hearth) were preferable for society, very few attained these roles in their actual lives, and some of the women advocating traditional gender roles as ideals also stated that they personally would be unhappy as full-time housewives. Thus, "there seems to be a difference in many minds between what is better for 'everyone' and what is better for individual women" (Lyon 2007, 31). So although large-N surveys have found that traditional attitudes about gender roles are extremely widespread in post-Soviet Russia among both men and women, such abstract views may not accurately affect women's actual roles and individual perceptions of self-identity in their concrete lives (Vannoy et al. 1999, 52–53; Inglehart, Basáñez, and Moreno 1998, 128).

Sometimes women activists will cope with these contradictory societal norms by voicing feminist views to certain audiences (such as within the walls of their organization or to Western interlocutors) but articulating nonfeminist

rationales for improving the status of women to other mainstream domestic audiences. For example, leaders and members of parliament from the political
party Women of Russia, much hailed in the West as a sign of an emergence of
women's political power in Russia in the early 1990s, had ambivalent reactions
to being labeled as feminists. The party's leader, Ekaterina Lakhova, stated at
one point, "Men are calling us feminists. That word doesn't frighten me; we're
just fighting for our rights." Yet the party's campaign brochure distanced itself
from "radical feminists," and another parliamentarian from the party, Galina
Klimantova, only reluctantly admitted that she was "probably" a feminist (V.
Sperling 1999, 122–123). Similarly, in one detailed case study of individual crisis centers in the city of Izhevsk, Maija Jäppinen uncovered a complicated and
contested relationship to feminist ways of framing the problem of violence as
a structured societal phenomenon based on gender roles and power dynamics.
An NGO-based crisis center's staff used recognizably feminist concepts in their
everyday work with victims of violence but presented a much more family-
based, gender-neutral perspective on violence in public documents (Jäppinen
2008, 8–9). In addition to asserting varying relationships to feminism in different circumstances, the most successful women's organizations have adapted
to society's hostility to feminism by making claims that relate to general human
rights rather than women's equality (Sundstrom 2005; Schatral 2007, 49).

There was a surge in the development of women's organizations and networks among them in the late Soviet and early transition period. Abubikirova
et al. found from their survey of women's organizations that in the 1980s, there
was a "preparatory period, in which (especially against the background of reforms of the late 1980s) a hidden accumulation of strength occurred" (Abubikirova et al. 1998, 12 [author's translation]). Then the first real spike in creation
of women's organizations began in 1990 when independent organization outside the state became permitted, and a major peak of organizing occurred in
1994 (ibid.). This was encouraged to a great degree by funding from foreign-
aid agencies and private foundations for the development of civil society and
gender equality in Russia, as I discuss further below. However, particularly since
2001, as foreign donors' resources have shifted elsewhere (namely, Afghanistan
and Iraq), groups in Russian civil society, including women's organizations, have
experienced a huge vacuum in availability of funding for their initiatives.

Some observers have noted that in the context of the transformation away
from Communism, as private business has grown more profitable, the nonprofit sector of civil society has become extremely feminized in nature—not
only in Russia but also in many other post-Soviet states (Kuehnast and Nechemias 2004, 1–10; Kedzie 1999). Civic activism became the "housework"

sphere of politics, in which highly important community organizing and support roles are relegated to women, with men fulfilling the high-profile decision-making roles (Sperling, Ferree, and Risman 2001, 1171).

Overall, women's activism in Russia has adopted a fairly moderate, conciliatory outlook in terms of both feminist philosophical approaches and stances toward cooperation and dialogue with the Russian state. The varieties of feminism that Russian women activists express—for the minority who admit to being feminists at all—tend to be social democratic, liberal, or "gynocentric" (asserting that women have a special relationship to the environment or peace) (V. Sperling 1999, 63). Radical feminism, in the sense of a feminist approach disavowing dialogue with a fundamentally patriarchal state, or consciously rejecting partnership with men, has been largely absent from the Russian women's movement. There are some exceptions, and a few lesbian organizations have existed, such as MOLLI (Moscow Organization of Lesbian Literature and Art), but organizing publicly based on homosexual identity requires extreme courage in Russia as homophobic attitudes are highly prevalent in society (Essig 1999).

Women activists have also generally been willing to work with the state when the state expresses interest in dialogue, but most have shied away from attempting to influence state policies, and those who have made such attempts have rarely been successful. This lack of emphasis on lobbying is largely due to the widespread ineffectiveness of much of the post-Communist Russian state until recently, as well as an accurate perception that much political influence derives from insider patron-client networks rather than open, transparent communication channels.

I turn now to discussion of some specific areas in which avowed feminists and nonfeminists alike have mobilized in order to improve the status of women in Russia. Three particular areas of concern, with varying levels of success in outcomes of mobilization (in terms of both attracting supporters and improving actual equality for women), are violence against women, women's economic inequality, and women's political representation.

Violence Against Women

According to Zabelina, in the 1980 edition of the ubiquitous Soviet encyclopedic dictionary, the entry on "violence" did not mention violence against individuals in any way. Instead, it only referred to violence as existing between classes or nations. Thus, "several generations of Soviet people . . . did not think of violence as a violation of human rights" (2002, 6). The Soviet state concealed crime statistics, including on domestic violence (Stickley, Timofeeva, and Spären 2008, 483). Crimes occurring within families were not addressed by the Soviet state until the perestroika era, and no analysis tried to quantify family violence until the early 1980s (Gondolf 1997, 65).

Statistics regarding the frequency of occurrence of intimate partner violence are still unclear. Yet a survey of 1,000 women in Moscow in the 1990s showed a quarter of respondents indicating that they had experienced physical abuse in their relationships, while another survey of 3,900 women in smaller regional cities of Novgorod, Perm, and Berezniki in 2000 indicated 15 percent of women suffer from intimate partner violence (Stickley, Timofeeva, and Spären 2008, 484). One cross-national study over a decade ago indicated that Russian women may be two and a half times more likely to be killed by their partners than American women (Gondolf 1997, 70). These data are no doubt inaccurate, given the low reporting levels of sexual violence in general and the fact that Russian women's inclination to report such violence is even lower than in the United States due to traditional societal rejection of the idea of spousal violence as a crime. Estimates of rape reporting rates range from only 3 percent up to 20 percent (Zabelina 2002, 10).

Women suffering from domestic violence and activists trying to combat the phenomenon face some hostile societal norms. There is a widespread belief among law enforcement officials and the general public that victims are responsible for provoking the violence against them (Johnson 2009, 28; Sinelnikov 1998; Attwood 1997, 99; Human Rights Watch 1997). Indeed, in my research on Russian women's organizations, I found that even some women's organizations accepted this stereotype. In 1999 one leader of a women's organization in St. Petersburg who was attempting to secure funding for a violence prevention program told me that "women sometimes provoke these incidents," and wished to concentrate on training women to speak to their husbands less aggressively as a way to prevent beatings.[2] In a case study of organizations in the Siberian city of Barnaul, Johnson cites the head of the regional government's education committee stating, "Russian women love to be martyrs, they love to be beaten" (2007, 40–59; Attwood 1997, 99).

Yet as a small movement against gender-based violence began to grow in Russia, the problem began to emerge from the shadows of discussion, and public awareness rose. The transnational links of the developing antiviolence movement were crucial, particularly in the early years. In the early 1990s several American feminists, most notably Martina Vandenberg and Lisa Hoffman, were involved in the founding of Syostri (Sisters), while a Swedish crisis center and the U.S.-based Family Violence Prevention Fund mentored Marina Pisklakova, the founder of ANNA (the acronym for the "No to Violence" Association) (Chernenkaia 1999; Potapova 1999). Other Western feminists, such as the lawyer Dianne Post working from the American Bar Association's Central and East European Legal Initiative, continued to provide advice to antiviolence activists almost a decade later. Many of the slogans and methods used by women's crisis center NGOs are adopted from Western feminist crisis centers (Sundstrom 2006). Several of the women who went on to form the Russian Association of Crisis Centers for Women (RACCW) met one another for the first time while on an internship in the United States in 1994 to learn about American crisis centers for women (ibid.).

The first crisis centers in Russia were founded in Moscow and St. Petersburg between 1993 and 1995. The first three centers were ANNA and Syostri in Moscow (the former focusing mostly on domestic violence and the latter on sexual assault), and the St. Petersburg Crisis Center, which began unofficially in 1991 and was formally registered in 1994 (Johnson 2009, 49). All three primarily offered a telephone hotline and in-person counseling and, usually with financial support from Western donors, began to spread this model across Russia. Most of the crisis centers that resulted provided a telephone hotline for victims of sexual and domestic violence as the mainstay of their activity. Many also conducted group or individual counseling sessions in person. This particular model of crisis counseling was inexpensive and therefore well suited to Russia's meager resource circumstances of the 1990s, compared to the investment required to open overnight shelters for women experiencing violence (ibid., 52).

Many of these organizations are also active in public education campaigns and political advocacy work and seek to reform the practices and views of social workers, doctors, police, lawyers, and judges who deal with victims of violence. They have battled stereotypes, often with posters that mimic the startling images and slogans of anti–domestic violence organizations in the United States: "There is no excuse against domestic violence" with statistics that one in four Russian women suffers from domestic violence, and that every hour a Russian woman dies as a result of it, and "He said that he won't hit you anymore . . . but that's what he said the last time" (posters by ANNA gathered during research in Moscow, 2005).

A few of the key organizations, such as ANNA and Syostri, have been involved in public policy lobbying and have contributed their expertise for the development of legislation. Some have participated in a working group within the State Duma Legislation Committee to draft legislation to prevent trafficking of women (Schatral 2007, 50). They also lobbied successfully to have several bills on domestic violence introduced in the State Duma, beginning in 1995, and provided input on the draft legislation to the legislative working group (Gondolf 1997, 66). Notably, none of the bills successfully passed into law.

A national organization linking crisis centers for women, called the Russian Association of Crisis Centers for Women, was formed in the 1990s, supported heavily by Western donors and launched through a project funded by the U.S. Agency for International Development and implemented by IREX (the International Research and Exchanges Board, a U.S.-based nongovernmental organization).[3] The RACCW was officially registered in 1999 and by 2004 had formed a network of fifty organizations in forty Russian cities.[4] According to the RACCW, in the year 2001 more than 65,000 women turned to their member centers for help in instances of domestic violence and sexual violence (Zabelina 2002, 8). The total number of crisis centers operating across Russia in 2004 is estimated by Johnson to have been approximately two hundred (Johnson 2009, 43). This is an astounding accomplishment over a period of scarcely more than a decade of activism on the issue of violence against women.

The movement against violence against women has experienced some important successes in changing the normative views of individual government officials and professionals, such as law enforcement officials, judges, and medical professionals, who interact with victims of violence. A major development, indicating the movement's persuasiveness, has been the increasing involvement of regional and municipal governments in either founding their own crisis centers or materially supporting or even co-opting formerly nongovernmental crisis centers. This development carries both advantages and dangers. A positive element of state funding is that it is usually more reliable than short-term funding from Western donors, although state funding too is subject to the whims of individual local politicians and bureaucrats. Only state crisis centers have had sufficient resources to maintain overnight shelters in which victims of domestic violence can safely stay while they rebuild their lives. Yet state crisis centers typically have a much more family-centered, less feminist outlook on the problem of violence (Jäppinen 2008; Johnson 2009, 57). A small pilot survey of Russian crisis centers for women found that only a minority of centers considered feminism important to their work but that far more NGO-based crisis centers than state-run crisis centers embraced feminism. A few NGO-based centers even considered themselves "feminist organizations" (Johnson 2008, 10). Thus, operation as a state institution does seem to deradicalize crisis centers and limit their ability to alter gendered power relations in society.

Despite the mobilizational victories of the movement, in the past five years, as foreign donors have increasingly shifted resources to other causes and other regions of the world, many of the NGO-based crisis centers in Russia have faced significant resource obstacles. Reports cited by Johnson found only nineteen nongovernmental women's crisis centers remaining in 2007, while 40 percent of crisis centers could not afford to pay any staff and 50 percent could not pay a decent living wage and therefore experienced high turnover of qualified staff (Johnson 2009, 67).

Until 2001 ANNA, which had been the lead managing organization of the RACCW, had worked with an organizational structure in which leadership and resources overlapped between the crisis center ANNA and the national association. After criticism of this intermingled organizational structure from one of its major funding donors, USAID, ANNA severed RACCW's resource stream and governance structure, which meant that the RACCW would need to seek its own independent sources of funding, losing the benefit of ANNA's highly successful funding record and the skillful leadership of ANNA's founder, Marina Pisklakova (ibid., 64).

Unfortunately, by 2008, with no substantial funding, the association had lost its office space and no longer had any grants from donors to support their work building a crisis center network and conducting trainings for crisis center professionals. As a result, the association had fallen into a period of relative hibernation at the time this chapter was written. Thus, this relatively "good news" story of Russian women's mobilization to stop violence against women has a rather tenuous future. Crisis centers seem to be caught between the restrictions on gender-based approaches to violence that state affiliation requires and the perpetual instability of funding that reliance on foreign donors entails. There is no foreseeable exit from this precarious position unless feminist perspectives on violence and a culture of charitable donations develop eventually in Russian society to provide a more stable resource base.

Women's Economic Inequality

Women's economic inequality in Russia occurs in multiple arenas. Major sources of inequality have been hiring discrimination, occupational segregation, and a significant gender wage gap—all of which have their roots in entrenched societal views about distinct "men's jobs" and "women's jobs." However, despite fears among feminists in the early 1990s, women have not been the primary victims of unemployment in post-Soviet Russia, nor have they exited the workforce in significant numbers (Ashwin 2006a, 2).

Part of the reason for high levels of gender segregation is that Russian workers tend to self-select into "gender appropriate" professions (Kozina and Zhidkova 2006, 57). Yet interview and survey studies indicate that both men and women agree that women face discrimination in hiring and firing decisions and that there are widespread norms among employers and employees about the disadvantages of women as employees compared to men (ibid., 70). Inequalities between sexes have increased (quite predictably) with the introduction of a market economy (Johnson and Robinson 2007, 6). According to Marina Baskakova, while women's wages in the 1980s and early 1990s were 60–70 percent of men's (largely due to occupational segregation), by 1999 they were only 56 percent of men's (Baskakova 2000, 63). Men are hired for any higher-paying jobs, while women are hired in lower-paying jobs (Kozina and Zhidkova 2006; Mezentseva 2004). Svetlana Aivazova wrote in 2000 that in "female" occupational sectors (dominated by women), the average salary is 40 percent of the average salary for all occupations throughout the country, while in some "male" occupational sectors, like the oil industry, the average salary is 360 times the average national salary. Jobs that were once women's have become men's over time as those employment sectors have become more lucrative; the banking sector in post-Soviet Russia is a highly illustrative example (Mezentseva 2004, 317).

One advantage Russian women have in the labor market, despite widespread gender stereotypes, is that Russian society generally views women's labor participation as a desirable and normal phenomenon. This is due to the long Soviet legacy of encouraging women's full-time participation in the labor force outside the home. Rapid Soviet economic development made women's mass participation in the workforce a necessity (Lapidus 1978, 98). By 1960 women's labor-force participation is estimated to have reached 77.4 percent, and by 1980 88.2 percent (versus 56.2 percent in Germany and 51.3 percent in the United States) (Newell and Reilly 1996, 341). Russian surveys of women's attitudes toward work indicate that "work is crucial to Russian women's sense of identity; provides them with a sense of meaning . . . even when the work itself is unpleasant and provides little intrinsic satisfaction" (Ashwin 2006b, 35).

However, norms that question women's role in the paid labor force began to rear their heads in the early post-Soviet period. A number of politicians have stated that women should be the first workers released when layoffs are necessary—expressing a strong preference for men as primary breadwinners for families (e.g., *Moscow Times*, May 20, 1993). Public opinion surveys also indicate the acceptability of such ideas among many Russians. For example, the massive World Values Survey indicated in 1999 that 34.9 percent of Russian citizens agree with this statement: "When jobs are scarce, men should have more right to a job than women." In contrast, only 2.3 percent of Swedish respondents, 9.8 percent of U.S. respondents, and 29.3 percent of Portuguese respondents agreed (http://www.worldvaluessurvey.org/).

Strikingly, even though there is widespread understanding among women that they face discrimination in competition with men on the labor market, women in general and feminists in particular have not mobilized extensively on issues of employment discrimination. The activism that has taken place to a small extent has been through women's organizations lobbying at very formal levels for changes in legislation concerning employment equality—rather than at the level of addressing individual women employees' grievances or consciousness-raising campaigns about the injustice of employment discrimination. Those organizations that have worked with individual women to tackle unemployment (particularly in the early to mid-1990s) have focused mainly on retraining women for new jobs rather than contesting gender discrimination. In this sense, they have avoided addressing discrimination and worked around it in pragmatic ways. Moreover, many of the women's organizations engaged in retraining have focused on alternative career paths that are heavily gender stereotypical and even hold the potential for labor exploitation, such as hairdressing, cosmetology, or home-based piecework (Sundstrom 2006, 88; Bridger, Kay, and Pinnick 1996; V. Sperling 1999, 163).

Lobbying efforts have produced some legislative victories in improving the legal conditions necessary to elevate women's economic status. The Consortium of Women's Nongovernmental Organizations claimed that Russian pension legislation was amended as a direct result of a meeting between the head of the Russian Pension Fund and several consortium member NGOs. The amendment allowed women's years of maternity leave to be included in their accumulation of employment years contributing to their state pension levels (Ershova 1998). The consortium also argued that it was influential in amending two clauses of the draft Russian Labor Code concerning banning women's labor in heavy or dangerous forms of work (women's organizations argued that a narrow, specific list of jobs should be named rather than a general clause banning women from dangerous labor), and provision of employment protection for pregnant women and mothers with children under one and a half years of age (Sundstrom 2006, 87; Levina 2001). Indeed, one small victory is that these amendments remained throughout an extremely contentious and drawn-out debate period over the content of the new Russian Labor Code, which was adopted only in December 2001 and included vigorous battles between Russian trade unions and employer groups in which many aspects of the code were modified (Levina 2001). In general, though, these declaratory legislative changes have not affected levels of employment discrimination against women on the ground. As I have argued elsewhere (Sundstrom 2006, 88; 2005, 436–437), feminist scholars in Russia have been the major supporters of activism on employment discrimination. Their activism has generally been confined to seminars with politicians and bureaucrats as well as writing "gender expertise" reports on the implications of government legislation and welfare policies. They have not engaged in mobilization to rectify individual women's grievances through legal clinics or mass media campaigns, nor have they mounted demonstrations to protest the problem.

There are a couple of reasons for the differences between activists' approaches to employment inequality and to violence against women. One is that domestic violence against women is an issue in which victims and perpetrators are more clearly identifiable than in cases of employment discrimination, which is a product of macrolevel structural causes. Thus, violence against women is more conducive to action by feminists on a concrete, individual basis. There are clear victims who need immediate physical assistance. But second, and I believe more crucially, there are distinct societal norms surrounding the two issues, which facilitate activism in the case of violence against women but create obstacles in the case of employment discrimination. As I argued earlier, there is a particular resistance to claims for equality in Russia as a result of the Soviet framing of gender equality. Since it is difficult to frame employment-discrimination grievances in terms other than equality, it is very difficult for feminist activists to raise public concern about the problem. In contrast, on the issue of violence, the problem can be framed as the right of every human being to be free from physical violence, which, as I and others have argued elsewhere, is a widely accepted norm that has been a successful basis for women's mobilization around the world in recent decades (Sundstrom 2005, 430; Bunch 1990; Keck and Sikkink 1998).

Women's Political Representation

Women in post-Communist Russia have generally been underrepresented in political institutions compared to in the Soviet period when quotas for women existed at various legislative levels. In the Soviet system, generally one-third of the USSR Supreme Soviet and Congress of People's Deputy seats were delegated to women. In the more powerful party body, the Central Committee of the Communist Party, fewer than 5 percent of deputies were women (V. Sperling 1999, 116). Only a handful of women were ever appointed to the Politburo, the most powerful decision-making body of the CPSU (Noonan and Ne-chemias 2001, 184). This low level of female representation at the executive level continues today. At the time of writing, there is only one female regional governor in Russia: Valentina Matvienko, the governor of St. Petersburg, who has been a prominent, nationally known politician (and former cabinet minis-ter) since the Yeltsin era. Only three of seventeen federal cabinet ministers at the time of writing were female: the minister for health and social develop-ment (a traditionally female cabinet post in Russia), the minister of agriculture, and the minister of economic development (an unusually powerful post for a female minister).

An early high point of women's parliamentary representation in the post-Communist period was in the 1993 elections to the lower house of the national parliament, the State Duma. Three major women's organizations (the Union of Russian Women, the Association of Russian Businesswomen, and the Union of Women of the Naval Fleet) collaborated in 1993 to form a women's party called Women of Russia (WOR). The leaders of the organization were Alevtina Fed-ulova of the Union of Russian Women and Ekaterina Lakhova, adviser to the Russian president on family, mothers, and children. While the party has advo-cated many social policies that would benefit women and children, promoted efforts to combat severe human rights violations against women such as the sex trade and sexual harassment, and campaigned for women's and children's rights, its candidates' relationship with feminism has been an uneasy one.

In their inaugural electoral participation during the Russian Duma elections of 1993, WOR attained a surprising high-water mark of 8 percent of the pop-ular vote, which resulted in twenty-three seats in the Duma. Then, in the 1995 parliamentary elections, WOR garnered only 4.7 percent of the vote, falling just short of the 5 percent vote threshold necessary to win seats in the Duma (Schevchenko 2002, 1201). However, since Russia had a mixed electoral sys-tem of plurality and proportional representation (each electing half of the seats in the Duma) until 2007, three WOR members were elected in the single-member districts.

In 1997 one of the leaders of WOR, Ekaterina Lakhova, left the party and founded her own similarly named "Sociopolitical Movement of Women of Rus-sia." Yet by December 1998 both fragments of the original party opted to join the Otechestvo (Fatherland) Party, headed by Yuri Luzhkov, mayor of Moscow, since their prospects of exceeding the minimum-vote threshold as a separate party were extremely low. In 1999, Otechestvo joined forces with another po-litical bloc to form the Otechestvo-Vsia Rossiia (OVR) bloc. Soon afterward, before the next election occurred, Fedulova's WOR left OVR because the party's members were granted very low priority in the OVR party electoral list, while Lakhova remained with the bloc since she was assigned a relatively high position on the list. An official letter issued by WOR stated that OVR had "demonstrated a traditional, conservative approach to the role of women in society . . . confirming that they do not view women as partners or believe in their strength and potential" (Cherkassov 2000). Standing for election on its own, WOR attained its lowest-ever percentage of the national vote—only 2.04 percent. Undoubtedly, this poor performance was due to its belated campaign start because of the defection from OVR, ongoing rivalries and voter confusion between the two similarly named women's blocs, and WOR's tiny funding base compared to the large so-called parties of power that come and go in Russia and are granted significant government and business-sector resources.

The overall number of women in the Duma paralleled the trend in votes for WOR until recently, since WOR had provided a strong boost in women's representation. Most other political parties have included very small minorities of women among their candidates and have tended to place women near the bottom of party lists. For example, in the 2003 elections, Ekaterina Lakhova, who had by that point migrated to the dominant United Russia Party, was the top-ranked woman on the party's candidate list at position number 20.[5] Lakhova retained her seat due to her party's strong share of votes (38%), but more widely, women have tended to lose out when votes translate into seats. The total number of women elected to the Duma was sixty (13 percent) in 1993, forty-six (10 percent) in 1995, thirty-four (8 percent) in 1999, and forty-four (10 percent) in 2003.

Surprisingly, in the December 2007 elections, a record sixty-four (14 percent) elected Duma deputies were women (Inter-Parliamentary Union 2008a). This is an extremely interesting and thus far underexplained development. Since women are located near the bottom of the various party lists, one would expect that the number would decrease with the change of Russia's electoral system to purely party-list proportional representation (eliminating the 50 percent of seats that were previously single mandate). Approximately half of all women candidates elected in 2003 came from the single-mandate constituencies (Russia Profile n.d.), and in previous years, in fact, the single-mandate districts produced more female deputies than the PR seats (R. Moser 2001; V. Sperling 2005, 194). One factor explaining the 2007 boost in women attaining Duma seats is that a slightly higher proportion of electoral candidates on the party lists in 2007 were women. The percentage of women among party-list candidates has generally increased gradually since 1993, without any formal quotas in place, but the proportion of women candidates is still dishearteningly low. In 1993 only 7 percent of Duma party-list candidates were female, while by 2007 the proportion had increased to 17 percent (Aivazova 2000; Russia Profile n.d.; "Predvybornye spiski partii" n.d.). The new Kremlin-allied party (often called a "puppet party") competing in the 2007 election, "Just Russia" (*Spravedlivaia Rossiia*) included an especially high number of women candidates (29 percent), and on the federal and many regional candidate lists, women appeared within the top three candidate positions. The party won just under 8 percent of the popular vote, meaning that it passed the threshold to win Duma seats. The curious fact that Just Russia's candidate list included more women than the much more powerful United Russia Party fits with the usual feminist observation that the more women present in a given political or economic sphere, the less power resides in it.[6] Yet there is another institutional change that helps to explain the 2007 increase of women in the Duma: the increase of the minimum-vote threshold for parties to win Duma seats from 5 percent to 7 percent. This meant fewer parties than ever before were elected to the Duma, and thus each of the parties crossing the threshold was able to elect candidates farther down its list; hence, more women were elected. This is a surprising side effect of the increased minimum-vote threshold, which is otherwise seen as harming democratic representation in Russian politics.

Some women's organizations with a keen interest in formal politics have allied with political parties during election campaigns, but this has been rare. As Suvi Salmenniemi has argued, "Elections do not seem to attract much attention in the Russian women's movement" (2003, n.p.). When WOR held Duma seats, women's NGOs had fairly friendly and mutually responsive relationships with WOR Duma deputies, with women activists obtaining greater access to Duma committee discussions and drafts of legislation as a result. Yet the alliance was never formal, and feminist women's NGOs were not actively involved in campaigning for WOR, most likely because many feminist activists viewed WOR as too much a part of the political establishment and not sufficiently feminist in orientation (V. Sperling 1999, 127–128).

Women's NGOs have been somewhat active in increasing women's representation in politics, though their efforts have been largely unfruitful. Some women's organizations, including the Consortium of Women's NGOs, advocated quotas for female candidates in the mid-1990s. In 1997 a bill was introduced in parliament proposing a quota of 30 percent women in parliamentary seats, but it was defeated in a second reading in the Duma (*Moscow Times*, September 17, 2003). In 2004 the question was again raised at the level of the Central Electoral Commission, with a female member of the commission from the Yabloko Party, Yelena Dubrovina, proposing a change to electoral legislation that would mandate a 30 percent quota of female electoral candidates included in political parties' lists. The head of the CEC, Alexander Veshni-akov, supported the proposal, although most other members of the commission opposed it. The proposal, sponsored by Deputy Ekaterina Lakhova, went on for consideration within the draft 2005 electoral legislation that introduced the 100 percent PR system for the Duma. Once again, the Duma rejected the quota proposal, and the debate was accompanied by some politicians' statements to the effect that women were not serious political figures (*St. Petersburg Times*, April 19, 2005).

Transnational Linkages of Russian Women Activists

Russian activists' connections with transnational actors have been extremely important and influential for self-proclaimed feminists. Russian activists have developed links with global feminist networks for the purposes of solidarity, support, and strategic development. In the area of violence against women, for example, many of the terms used in Russia have been translated directly into Russian from English (for example, "violence against women," "domestic violence," "violence in the family") (Johnson 2007, 44). More broadly, the term "gender" itself is translated letter for letter into Russian, with a hard "g" sound. But probably the most influential transnational connection that Russian women activists have established is with Western funding organizations. These linkages have been sources of strength in some respects and of weakness in others.

Activists' linkages with Western donor organizations in the area of violence against women are indicative of some general patterns in the transnational funding of Russian women's activism. In the mid- to late 1990s, funding from Western (especially American) donors was especially extensive in the area of domestic violence. For example, the development of the RACCW was funded by a number of grants from IREX and USAID. These grant funds have been crucial to the development of the crisis center movement and the progress that activists have made in combating violence against women.

However, these relationships with Western donors have also been fickle. The fate of the RACCW described earlier is an excellent example. While donors were extremely active in funding women's activism against violence, and in particular in fighting domestic violence in the mid- to late 1990s, by the early 2000s this enthusiasm of donors (at least the largest American donors) had begun to wane and shift into initiatives to combat trafficking of women. This led some crisis centers to reorient some of their programmatic focus into antitrafficking, largely in order to sustain themselves financially rather than due to any inherent interest in the issue. Indeed, many activists have complained about this agenda drift as well as the security risks involved for their organizations, since trafficking of people is closely bound up with powerful organized criminal networks.

Transnational linkages—both as funding and as networking—have been widely criticized for their tendency to strengthen elite figures and the elitist nature of the Russian feminist movement. Several analysts have noted that leaders of women's NGOs who speak English fluently have been particularly privileged in their relationships with Western donors and the global feminist movement (Sundstrom 2003, 150; Richter 2002, 37). Again, in the example of the crisis centers movement, it is notable that the founding leader of the RACCW, Marina Pisklakova, spoke excellent English and was thus able to build a strong reputation among Western donors, while the leader who followed Pisklakova, Natalia Abubikirova, was not as adept in English and was thus less successful in winning Western grants. Indeed, Richter cites an unpublished article Abubikirova wrote with Marina Regentova in the 1990s, in which they argued that the English language is used as a "means of power and control" and "a convertible currency" in the Russian women's movement (Richter 2002, 37). This privileging of English-language abilities has helped to create new hierarchies and reinforce some already existing in Russian society. Highly educated members of the intelligentsia (who are more likely to take a feminist stance toward issues affecting women) are more likely to speak English than women with less education and income, while women in major cities are also more likely to possess a good command of English than women in rural areas.

Inequalities in access to information technology have exacerbated these hierarchies as well. Women in smaller communities were often ten years or more behind their counterparts in major urban centers in acquiring access to the Internet, which is vital for learning about transnational funding and partnership opportunities. In a country like Russia, which is so large it spans eleven time zones, physical travel, snail mail, and even telephone communication are unaffordable or impractical in many cases. So a vast disadvantage in Internet access made it much more difficult for women's organizations in smaller, more remote locations to compete in the funding and transnational mobilization game. Moreover, the fact that when Western donors had offices within Russia those offices would be located first and most prominently in Moscow gave Muscovite activists a distinct advantage in becoming friendly with Western donors.

Probably the greatest overall negative side effect of Western funding is that it appears to have inhibited the long-term institutionalization of Russian women's organizing. Some scholars of feminist movements define institutionalization as "the development of regular and routinized relationships with other organizations" (Ferree and Yancey 1995, 6). There is significant debate in feminist literature concerning how positive or negative this kind of institutionalization is—positive in the sense that the longest-lasting organizations and movements tend to be highly institutionalized but negative in that they tend to lose a degree of radicalism in their demands and are forced to create hierarchical decision-making structures (ibid., 474). Indeed, some Russian feminist activists have lamented that Western donors have forced them to formalize their organizations and create strict hierarchies in their governance procedures in order to be eligible for grant funding. This erodes feminist models of decision making, which aim for egalitarianism and consensus building. One could argue that *perhaps* the Russian women's movement would have been more vocal or radical in its public claims in the absence of Western funding. Yet in my interview research on women's organizations across seven Russian cities in the late 1990s, I found that the few organizations that engaged in public demonstrations were nearly all funded by Western donors (and most were women's crisis center activists) (Sundstrom 2001, 188–193). Western funding may well have granted these specific organizations sufficient financial autonomy from the Russian state to feel free enough to engage in public demonstrations. In short, in the Russian case, this debate on the effect of institutionalization on radicalism is largely moot because radical groups—whether in terms of their feminist viewpoints or repertoires of protest—are rare.

Another way of defining movement institutionalization comes from the literature on civil society in democratization processes. Valerie Sperling asks whether women's organizations in Russia have become institutionalized in the sense of "acting as established channels between state and society," which entails resources to act, the ability to promote concerns to the state, and organizations' connection with and responsiveness to constituencies in society (2006, 161). It is important to be clear that "institutionalization" in this form refers to acting as an intermediary to interpret and make claims on the state rather than women's organizations becoming actual arms of the state. This distinction has blurred under recent institutional innovations introduced by former president Putin, such as the Public Chamber, a state-formed body designed to create dialogue between the president and various organizations in Russian civil society, to which only a few leaders of women's organizations have been appointed since its initiation in 2006.[7] As mentioned earlier, the SWC played such a transmission role in the Soviet period, and it was clear that it acted more according to the state's wishes than to communicate women's claims on the state. Organizations with more "radical" (or at least feminist) demands in Russia tend not to have any impact on Russian politics or societal norms because they do not regularly engage in public protest or dialogue with either government or the mass public. Perhaps if there is not a significant portion of society that sympathizes with feminist norms, a noninstitutionalized movement with radical demands cannot play an influential role anyway—so that institutionalization on balance has a positive role to play.

Foreign funding of Russian women's NGOs has institutionalized recipient organizations in some ways but only temporarily. It gave them initial funding through which they could begin to function on a full-time, professional basis, and by which they could begin to build networks with other women's organizations. Yet in other ways foreign funding has profoundly harmed institutionalization. It has dissuaded NGOs from locating other domestic mechanisms for resource mobilization (such as domestic philanthropists, individual volunteers, or donations), so that when foreign donors began to withdraw their enthusiasm for feminist organizations in Russia, the organizations found themselves at a loss to locate other resource bases. Most damaging for long-term institutionalization, foreign funding has failed to encourage women's groups to reach out to the wider public and build domestic constituencies of support for their goals, instead incentivizing women activists to base their activities on donors' programmatic agendas (Sundstrom 2006; Richter 2002, 30; V. Sperling 2006, 163; Henderson 2003).

Conclusion

Women's organizing in Russia—particularly on a feminist basis—faces serious obstacles in the foreseeable future. While some of the obstacles are particular to women's organizations, such as a hostile societal reaction to feminist ideals, many are common to other social movements in Russian civil society today. Regardless of the kind of movement, independent activists in Russia face serious resource-mobilization challenges, including having to choose between a meager and unreliable existence as an NGO with sporadic foreign funding or a more stable existence as a state-supported organization dependent on government approval. Foreign funding encourages many pathologies, including unstable organizational agendas and diversion from developing domestic constituencies.

The trajectory of the women's crisis center movement outlined above illustrates many aspects of the challenges facing Russian women's mobilization in general. An initial blossoming of organizations in the 1990s, many supported by Western donors, ended when foreign donors moved programs elsewhere in the world or on to different issues in Russian society. What seemed at one point to be a growing women's movement has stalled in recent years, leading many feminists to look for sustainable careers outside the activist realm. In a country where individual charitable donations are extremely rare and political participation by citizens is extraordinarily low—never mind the general hostility to feminism—the prospects for the growth of a mass-supported women's movement are exceedingly slim.

Yet some activists persist heroically in their missions and do manage to attain small victories through sheer persistence. Gender studies programs, which did not exist until the 1990s, are now alive and well in many universities around Russia, inspiring a new generation of feminists. Perhaps this is where hope lies: in the gradual development of activists and changing of societal norms on an incremental, individual basis.

Notes

1. In fact, recently the Orthodox Church has actively begun to foment opposition to abortion in Russia, in convenient tandem with state concerns about Russia's rapidly declining population (*Moscow News*, February 1 and July 24, 2008). Abortion had been legal and largely depoliticized since the 1920s (with the exception of the Stalin period), and the major problem related to abortion has been its status as virtually the only form of available, affordable birth control during much of the Soviet and post-Soviet periods.

2. Interview with director of a St. Petersburg women's NGO, St. Petersburg, October 5, 1999.

3. The association is now officially called the "Let's End Violence" Association of Crisis Centers for Assistance to Women Victims of Violence (Assotsiatsiia krizisnykh tsentrov pomoshchi zhenshchinam, perezhivshim nasilie "ostanovim nasilie").

4. Information submitted by the association at http://www.db-is.net/index.php?id=pnbpt 0p0000fa.

5. Data gathered from Arkhiv politicheskoi reklamy (http://www.33333.ru/elections.php), November 19, 2008.

6. I am grateful to Valerie Sperling for this observation concerning Just Russia.

7. It remains unclear to what extent the Public Chamber was having any influence on government policy rather than simply creating the appearance of regularized government consultation with civil society through dialogue with organizational leaders handpicked by the president (Evans 2008, 2005, 151; Henderson 2008, 25). The most prominent leader of a women's organization to be appointed to the Public Chamber thus far is Elena Ershova, who was appointed in 2006 but did not remain in the term that began in 2008.

The author wishes to thank Anna Shapovalova for superb research assistance; Janet Johnson, Valerie Sperling, and James Richter for input and reactions; and the volume editors for excellent guidance. Any weaknesses that remain are the fault of the author.

8

Contemporary Feminisms in Brazil: Achievements, Shortcomings, and Challenges

CECILIA M. B. SARDENBERG AND ANA ALICE ALCANTARA COSTA

B razil has been known for the strength and diversity of its social movements and particularly for women's activism in these movements. Over the past three decades, women in Brazil have forged and carried their own struggles, with feminists representing a small, but very active, segment of women's movements at large in the country (Soares et al. 1995; Costa 2005). Contemporary feminist activism in Brazil emerged in a moment of political upheaval, playing an important role in the process of redemocratization of the country and stretching the very concept of democracy in the process (S. Alvarez 1990; Pitanguy 2002). Moreover, it has expanded and diversified considerably since then, to the point that it is always best to refer to feminisms in Brazil in the plural. Indeed, within Latin America—and even beyond—Brazilian feminisms have been regarded as "perhaps the largest, most radical, most diverse, and most politically influential of Latin America's feminist movements" (Sternbach et al. 1992, 414).

This recognition is certainly not unfounded. Brazilian feminisms have made important contributions, not only in terms of a change of values regarding women's place in society but also toward building a more gender-equitable society (Costa and Sardenberg 1994; Soares et al. 1995). Feminisms in Brazil have been instrumental in the passage of new legislation promoting gender equity and in the formulation of public policies for women, carving new spaces in state machineries and apparatuses to implement and monitor them (Costa

BRAZIL

Human Development Index ranking: .800
Gender-Related Development Index value: .798
Gender Empowerment Measure value: .490

General

Type of government: Federal Republic
Major ethnic groups: Portugese, Italian, German, Spanish, Japanese, Arab, African, indigenous people
Language: Portuguese
Religions: Roman Catholic (74%)
Date of independence: 1822
Former colonial power: Portugal

Demographics

Population, total (millions), 2005: 108.1
Annual growth rate (%), 2005–2015: 1.2
Total fertility (average number of births per woman): 2.3
Contraceptive prevalence (% of married women aged 15–49): 77
Maternal mortality ratio, adjusted (per 100,000 live births), 2000: 110

Women's Status

Date of women's suffrage: 1932
Life expectancy: M 68.1; F 75.5
Combined gross enrollment ratio for primary, secondary, and tertiary education (female %), 2005: 89
Gross primary enrollment ratio: 135*
Gross secondary enrollment ratio: 111*
Gross tertiary enrollment ratio: 27
Literacy (% age 15 and older): M 88.4; F 88.8

Political Representation of Women

Seats in parliament (% held by women): 9.3
Legislators, senior officials, and managers (% female): 34
Professional and technical workers (% female): 52
Women in government at ministerial level (% total): 11.4

Economics

Estimated earned income (PPP US$): M 10,664; F 6,204
Ratio of estimated female to male earned income: .58
Economic activity rate (% female): 56.7
Women in adult labor force (% total): 43 (this figure obtained at the CEDAW Statistical Database)

*Gross enrollment ratios in excess of 100% indicate that there are pupils or students outside the theoretical age groups who are enrolled in that level of education.

2005; Sardenberg 2004). As a consequence, "state feminism" has expanded significantly in Brazil. This expansion has been especially pronounced over the past fifteen years, contrary to the belief that women's movements tend to fade in the context of postauthoritarian regimes (Razavi 2000; Craske 2000). But in contemporary Brazil, a "participatory" form of state feminism is at work: not only has it strengthened the demands of feminist and women's movements, but it also formulates its policies for women—at least at the federal level—on a more participative basis. This has been especially evident in the two national conferences on public policies for women (2004 and 2007), promoted by the Lula administration. Each of these processes involved more than 300,000 women all over the country in preparatory conferences to discuss and present policies.

However, despite these significant gains for women in Brazil, and in spite of a pledge by those in power to implement "gender mainstreaming" in all spheres and at all levels, major changes in that direction have yet to be enacted in the legislative, judicial, and executive branches (Costa 2008; Araújo 2003; Nogueira 2005). These branches have remained notoriously resistant to the inclusion of women, such that, to quote Razavi in reference to similar circumstances elsewhere, "the new wave of democratization has not, by any means, had a feminizing effect on the parliaments, cabinets and public administrations of the new democracies" (2000, 2). This has resulted in a major paradox for Brazilian feminists: on the one hand, there is the presence of a wide and well-articulated women's movement and, on the other, a notorious absence of women in decision-making positions (Costa 2008). One of the consequences of this state of affairs is that we still lack a "critical mass" of women to push forth the implementation of new state institutions and policies, such as those designed to confront violence against women (Sardenberg 2007a). There is also little legislative or judicial support for greater advancements concerning women's sexual and reproductive rights. As such, legal and safe abortions in Brazil have remained strictly limited, resulting in high rates of maternal mortality, particularly among young black women living in poor neighborhoods throughout the major cities (Sardenberg 2007b; Soares and Sardenberg 2008).

In this chapter we highlight the major achievements, as well as the shortcomings and challenges of feminist struggles in contemporary Brazil, focusing in particular on the expansion of "participatory" state feminism despite the still-low representation of women at the upper decision-making levels. In so doing, we will argue that this form of state feminism has emerged in Brazil on the one hand, as a result of growing activism and articulation of feminist and women's groups and, on the other, as a response to the persistence of a patriarchal political system sustained by a political culture that remains resistant to the empowerment of women. "Participatory" state feminism has also been fostered by the rise to power of more progressive parties, such as Partido dos Trabalhadores (PT, or Workers' Party), and their commitment to participatory forms of governance (Cornwall and Coelho 2006). Of course, this does not mean that "participatory" state feminism has obviated the tensions between feminist and women's movements and the state, or that feminisms are free from state "co-option." Despite low representation in the upper echelons of the legislative, judiciary, and executive branches, "participatory" state feminism has made it possible for feminists to take a greater part in the formulation and monitoring of public policies that respond to women's demands in building a more equitable society.

As we hope to show, however, meeting these challenges will not be an exercise free of tensions; tensions have been an integral part of the outstanding capacity of feminism in Brazil to "diversify" and become more plural. Note that plurality, in this case, does not pertain only to the incorporation of different segments of women's movements into the ranks of feminism. Carving new spaces of action, be they in the state apparatuses or in institutions of civil society (the nongovernmental organizations, universities, unions, and political parties, for instance), or in local, national, or global arenas, is equally important and mutually reinforcing (S. Alvarez 2000; Costa 2005). This process demands and promotes the "professionalization" of feminist activists (S. Alvarez 1998b) and the development of what we may regard as new "feminist careers," including academic ones. We believe that both of these processes, that is, diversification and professionalization, have been positive developments for feminisms in Brazil, in spite of the tensions that they might have incurred. Diversification responds to the diverse character of Brazilian society and professionalization to the need to have trained feminists to meet the challenges of incorporating a feminist gender perspective—that is, one geared to women's empowerment—in the state apparatus and in the different institutions of civil society.

As feminists who are engaged in activism within and outside academe, we have tracked these different paths of feminist activism in Brazil and engaged in many of the struggles discussed in this paper. We are conscious that our expectations and frustrations regarding feminisms and women's movements in Brazil will emerge in our analysis, revealing the intricate symbiosis established here between subject and object. We assume the duality of those who attempt to exercise and analyze transformative actions in society (Durham 1986, 26), and we are well aware of the epistemological and political underpinnings of such an attempt (Sardenberg and Costa 1994).

Achievements: "We Made History"

Feminism may be understood as critical thinking as well as political action that challenges the existing gender order, seeking to improve women's position in society. By this definition, feminism has a long history in Brazil (Sardenberg and Costa 1994; Soares et al. 1995). From the last quarter of the nineteenth century into the first three decades of the twentieth, the so-called First Wave of feminists in Brazil defended women's education rights and struggled in parliament for the extension of suffrage to women, which was granted in 1932.[1] "Second Wave" feminisms emerged in the mid-1970s, bringing into the public arena women's demands for the criminalization of domestic violence, equal pay for equal work, equity in decision-making spheres, and sexual and reproductive rights—demands that still remain unanswered in many respects. As such, Second Wave feminism in Brazil has not come to an end—it has been thriving for more than thirty years, although incorporating new discourses, diverse strategies, and different forms of organization.

The UN designation of 1975 as "International Women's Year" played a decisive role in the launching of the contemporary Brazilian feminist movement. Until then, the military-dictatorial regime that had been established with the 1964 coup had succeeded in keeping women's struggles off the streets by violently repressing public demonstrations (Sardenberg and Costa 1994). The UN initiative not only granted a new status to the cause of women in Brazil (Pinto 2003) but also opened the way for local expressions in that direction—such as the UN-sponsored conference held in 1975 in Rio de Janeiro that resulted in the creation of the Centro de Desenvolvimento da Mulher Brasileira (Centre for the Development of the Brazilian Woman). The Brazilian Society for the Advancement of Science began holding feminist meetings during its annual conferences in 1975 and continued to do so over the next decade (Costa and Sardenberg 1994; Sardenberg and Costa 1994; Pinto 2003; Sardenberg 2004).[2]

In 2005 a number of events, academic and otherwise, were held to commemorate "30 years of *uninterrupted* feminism in Brazil."[3] One such event occurred in the Rio de Janeiro State Congress in December of that year, when Congresswoman Inês Pandeló of the PT offered perhaps one of the best assessments of the history of feminism in Brazil: "In the last thirty years, we made history. But we cannot stop here. Every day, every hour, we must take significant strides in the struggle for women's rights in society. May we renew today, right here, our energies to continue fighting for our full citizenship."[4]

Feminist struggles in Brazil have changed with the political context in which they have unfolded. Jacqueline Pitanguy distinguishes three major periods: "the first, running from the mid-seventies to the mid-eighties, marks the appearance of feminism as a political actor and its struggle for legitimacy and visibility. The second period, which occurred in the eighties, is dominated by the inclusion of a feminist agenda in public policies and normative frames. The third, in the nineties, sees the internationalization of this agenda through transnational coalitions that will play a major role in the re-conceptualization of human rights language" (Pitanguy 2002, 1–2). We would add a fourth period to this chronology, from 2000 on, characterized by the strengthening of state machineries for the promotion of gender equity and, thus, of "participatory state feminism." This came in response to demands forged by women's movements, feminists in particular, aided by international agendas on human and women's rights. Furthermore, the expansion of "identity feminisms" (Costa 2005) as well as the widening of the spheres of feminist activism, particularly evident since the mid-1990s, have also contributed to this process.

The Dual Struggles of the 1970s

While women's activism in Brazil has been expressed in different social movements, we define *women's movements* as only those centered on gender-based interests, that is, "those arising from the social relations and positioning of the sexes and therefore pertained, but in specific ways, to both men and women," as Maxine Molyneux suggests (1998a, 231–232). Molyneux has further distinguished women's interests as "practical" and "strategic," the former "based on the satisfaction of needs arising from women's placement within the sexual division of labour" and the latter "involving claims to transform social relations in order to enhance women's position and to secure a more lasting re-positioning of women within the gender order and within society at large" (ibid., 232). We consider *feminist movements* those that are centered on women's strategic gender interests, recognizing, however, that these interests are contextually defined.

As in other countries of the so-called Southern Cone, contemporary feminisms emerged in Brazil in the context of the democratic struggles and resistance against the military regime, which came into power with the coup of 1964. In this first period feminisms had a dual role, fighting both for the reestablishment of democracy as well as for the inclusion of gender equality as a "central democratic theme," thus widening the issues in the democratic agenda (Pitanguy 2002). This also involved the redefinition of the concept of politics in order to include the "personal," for the practices of everyday life should also be considered in the realm of the exercise of citizenship. This perspective was not easily accepted by progressive forces at that time (S. Alvarez 1990).

Feminists in Brazil participated in a much wider women's movement that included in its ranks groups with different interests and forms of organization. Following similar tendencies within Latin America at the time, these groups comprised three major "streams" or segments: human rights groups, popular women's movements, and feminist groups (Vargas 1992). In Brazil, however, human rights groups, such as the Movimento Feminino pela Anistia (Feminine Movement for Amnesty), were never as strong as the Madres in Argentina and the Agrupación in Chile, nor did they take a major leadership role in the wider women's movement. Besides, they tended to fade away after 1980, when amnesty was conceded to those in exile, in prison, or otherwise condemned for political reasons. In contrast, popular women's movements, as well as feminist groups, not only became more visible but also have remained much more active than their "human rights" counterparts since the 1980s. During the 1970s popular women's movements grew around the *clubes de mães* (mothers' clubs) organized by the more progressive sectors of the Catholic Church in the periphery of the larger cities. These "clubs" grew in number and visibility as they came to lead the Movimento Contra a Carestia (Movement Against the High Cost of Living), which gained nationwide attention.

We could characterize the feminist movement in Brazil in the 1970s as being part of a wide and heterogeneous movement that articulated the struggles against the oppression of women in society with the fight for the redemocratization of the country. Other social movements against the military-dictatorial regime downplayed women's strategic interests (Lobo 1987). Nevertheless, feminist organizations strove to enlarge the debate on gender inequality by bringing forth new issues into public debate, such as domestic violence, the discrimination against women in the labor force, and women's exclusion from decision-making spheres. Although feminists raised issues such as sexuality, contraception, and abortion, they did so "gradually and awkwardly, since these issues were considered taboo by the Catholic Church and rejected by democratic forces allied with the church against the military" (Pitanguy 2002, 2).

In the 1980s women became active in neighborhood movements, leading the struggle for the creation of community day-care centers (see Sardenberg 2007). They gained support from feminists and formed partnerships and coalitions within the wider women's movements. Most feminist activists in this period came from middle-class families, had access to college educations, and were characterized as "professional" women. But many came from organizations recognized as part of the "Revolutionary Left," espousing a Marxist perspective on national liberation. These and other activists suffered through the experience

FIGURE 8.1 Members of the Domestic Workers' Union participate in the International Women's Day March in Salvador, Bahia, March 2007. (Photo by Cecilia Sardenberg)

of armed struggle, underground clandestine lives, imprisonment, torture, exile, and, in particular, authoritarianism and sexism both from the left-wing organizations in which they were active and from repressive state mechanisms (Costa 2005). Nevertheless, in spite of their critical stance toward these left-wing organizations, Brazilian feminists promoted a wider project of social reform that involved women from the popular sectors (Molyneux 2003, 269).

The 1980s: Dialogues with the State

The 1980s ushered in the process of redemocratization, in which social movements played an important role and forged demands on the state. Two relevant developments marked this process: the granting of amnesty to political prisoners and those in exile and reform of political parties (Pinto 2003). Amnesty brought leftist activists back to Brazil, among them many women who had participated in feminist groups in Europe and the United States. Their return strengthened feminisms in Brazil, particularly by creating more demands for the legalization of abortion and the criminalization of violence against women. At the same time, party reform opened the way for negotiations and alliances with newly created progressive parties and, consequently, created space for the demands of the women's movements.

Feminists also developed an agenda for women in public policy and normative frames (Pitanguy 2002). One of the major policies in question responded to issues regarding women's health; the 1983 launch of the Programa de Assistência Integral à Saúde da Mulher (PAISM, or Program of Integral Assistance to Women's Health) helped open an important and much needed dialogue between officials in the Ministry of Health and feminist activists (Villela 2001).[5] It was also in this period that, as a result of campaign negotiations with opposition candidates in the state of São Paulo, "state-sponsored feminism" first appeared, with the creation and expansion of state apparatuses—or specific "state machinery"—to implement and monitor public policies for women. In 1983, for example, the Conselho da Condição Feminina (Council for the Condition of Women) was created, followed in 1985 by the implementation of the first major public policy related to combating violence against women with the creation of DEAMs (Delegacias Especializadas de Atendimento à Mulher, or Police Stations for Battered Women). By 1992 there were 141 DEAMs across the country; at present, there are more than 300 (Pinto 2003). The creation of local and state councils for women's rights did not follow at the same pace, but it is important to highlight the creation, in 1985, of the Conselho Nacional dos Direitos da Mulher (CNDM, or National Council for Women's Rights).

Prior to this period, government-appointed organizations had limited autonomy in making critical decisions. In response to feminist demands, feminist organizations appointed at least half of the members to the new councils, granting the councils room for independent decisions and greater efficacy in meeting women's interests and demands.[6] However, many of these councils were still made up of party recruits, and this led to a loss of autonomy (Pinto 2003, 71). As a result, some segments of the feminist movement refused to participate in the councils, and this became a controversial issue in the National Feminist Encounter, held in 1986 in Belo Horizonte (Sardenberg and Costa 1994).

Indeed, participation in the new organizations and state support for these new policies created dilemmas for feminists concerning the movement's relationship with the state. Because the state was no longer considered the "common enemy" (Costa 2005), feminists had to recognize the capacity of the "modern state" to influence society as a whole—and not only through coercive means. It became evident that it was just as important to recognize the relevance of legislation and social and economic policies as it was to recognize cultural regulation mechanisms in the education and public communication processes and to look at the state as a potential ally in the transformation of the condition of women (Molyneux 2003, 68). Feminists also began to understand the role of the state in guaranteeing the viability of a set of social, economic, and political rights for the entire population and in amplifying citizenship rights (Costa 2005).

The emergence of state feminism led the movement to become involved in the formulation of the 1988 constitution.[7] A direct action campaign led by the CNDM—identified by the media as the "lipstick lobby"—and supported by social mobilization and political pressure convinced parliament to include 80 percent of women's demands in the new constitution.[8]

The *Bancada* (Women's Caucus) in the National Congress also played a fundamental role in the defense of women's rights in the new constitution. The Bancada, which consisted of twenty-six women elected for the 1986–1990 legislative mandate and representing several different political parties, included only one self-identified feminist (Dep. Moema San Tiago). Nevertheless, the women in the Bancada were able to "rise to the occasion," assuming a suprapartisan identity and presenting thirty amendments defending women's rights in the new constitution (Pinto 2003, 74–75). They were backed by women's groups all over the country who, under the general coordination of the CNDM, were active in collecting signatures in support of these amendments.[9]

Under Jacqueline Pitanguy's presidency, the CNDM achieved widespread support throughout the country. As its power increased, it directly challenged institutional sexism and racism in Brazil. Not surprisingly, under new leadership, the Ministry of Justice eventually attempted to curtail the autonomy and leadership enjoyed by the CNDM. The new minister of justice not only cut the annual budget allowed to the CNDM but also restricted its autonomy. This led to the resignation of Pitanguy and all other members and staff of the CNDM, an act that had the support of feminist and women's organizations throughout the country. Unfortunately, it took nearly a decade before a National Council, equally representative of feminist and women's movements in Brazil, could be formed again (Sardenberg and Costa 1994).

The 1980s saw the emergence of new segments within the wider women's movements, many of them opened to in-depth dialogues with feminism. In the 1987 National Feminist Encounter, for example, nearly 79 percent of the participants were active in "labor unions, in the black movement, in neighborhood associations, in mothers' clubs, in the church, and in political parties" (Soares et al. 1995, 309). In this National Feminist Encounter—held in the city of Garanhuns, Pernambuco—a black women's movement emerged. Although black feminists had been a part of the so-called Second Wave of feminism in Brazil, right from its emergence in the mid-1970s, it was only in that encounter that they came together to mark a black women's movement within

Brazilian feminisms. Since then, several national and regional encounters of black women have taken place, and a number of black feminist NGOs have been created in Brazil, leading to the articulation of the Forum of Black Women's Organizations.

The 1980s also saw the emergence of academic feminism. Indeed, in national scientific and academic organizations, as well as within universities throughout the country, research and study groups on women's and gender issues were formed (Costa and Sardenberg 1994), leading to demands for new "professionals" and thus the creation of new "feminist careers." Academic feminism has been expanding ever since, as is evident not only in the proliferation of women's and gender studies groups, primarily in public universities throughout the country, but also in the special events, publications, theses, and dissertations in this field of study in the past two and a half decades (Sardenberg 2003).

The 1990s: The Professionalization and Transnationalization of Feminisms

Jacqueline Pitanguy has observed that with the dismantlement of the CNDM "the feminist agenda in Brazil was carried forward during the 1990s mainly by nongovernmental organizations." She adds that "the significant role played by women's NGOs in the national arena and the efficacy of the advocacy strategies developed by regional and international networks and coalitions of NGOs characterize this third moment of feminism in Latin America. The internationalization of the feminist agenda and the impact of globalization mark the political actions of women's movements in the nineties and in this new century" (2002, 5).

Indeed, the increase in the number of government agencies promoting women's public policy, such as DEAMs, spurred the growth of the demand for professionals specializing in gender and women's issues.[10] This led to the development of a process of professionalization among feminists, who began to assume the task of expert lobbying for policies for women, in many cases becoming planners and practitioners. This, in time, has engendered the emergence of feminist NGOs, many of them springing from the formalization of feminist women's groups (Thayer 2001). They have assumed the leadership in lobbying the state, creating new challenges and dilemmas for feminist movements (S. Alvarez 1998b).

In the early 1990s Brazilian women were active in a number of different organizations emerging from various segments of Brazilian society, giving rise to

distinct "feminist identities" (Lebon 1997). Women of the working classes—
also known as *classes populares* (popular classes) in the country—were organized
in neighborhood associations, factory workers in women's departments of their
unions and national union coalitions, and rural workers in their rural organizations. These groups also constitute different segments of the wider women's
movement that began to self-identify with feminism, thus joining the ranks of
what has since become identified as "popular feminism," that is, as a feminism
that involves women from the working classes, as well as a nonwhite feminism.
Black feminist associations continued to grow and amplify the feminist political agenda and the parameters of feminist struggles themselves, such that, in
Brazil, in accordance with Sonia Alvarez's observations regarding Latin America as a whole, "the existence of various feminisms, with diverse points of view,
major issues, means of organization and strategic feminist priorities were widely
recognized in the 1990s" (1994, 278).[11]

The growth of popular feminism had a major impact on the wider women's
movements by diluting the ideological barriers and resistances to feminism.
The diversity of "feminisms" in the Brazilian women's movement was already
evident in the movement's preparation for the Fourth World Conference on
Women, which took place in Beijing in September 1995, in that women from
the different segments actively participated in this process (Costa 2005). Indeed, the Beijing preparatory process brought new energy into the Brazilian
feminist movement, stimulating the creation of local Women's Forums[12] in
cities in which they did not exist or had been inactive, the formation of new
coalitions, and the establishment of new women and gender departments in
unions and in other institutions of civil society. As a result, pre-Beijing preparatory meetings were held in twenty-five of Brazil's twenty-seven states, involving more than eight hundred women's organizations. The Articulation of
Brazilian Women (AMB) was created in 1995 precisely to organize Brazilian
women's participation for the Beijing conference.[13]

The AMB was able to bring forth important advancements. In spite of the
lack of support from the CNDM, then in the hands of conservative leadership, feminists were able to establish, for the first time in Brazilian history, a
participatory dynamic for the elaboration of the official report of the Brazilian government to the Fourth Conference. This was also made possible by the
Ministry for External Relations, the Brazilian governmental organization responsible for the report. For this specific purpose, the MRE created a special
working group that included notable feminists responsible for the organizing
and integrating of dozens of activists by means of special seminars.[14] Many of
the recommendations presented by activists in these seminars were included

in the final report. This articulation of feminist and women's groups guaranteed not only the presentation on the part of the Brazilian government of a representative product but also the approval of the Beijing Platform in its entirety by the Brazilian government. More important, it ensured a better assimilation, on the part of the federal government, of the demands put forth by women's movements.

Indeed, the experiences of Brazilian feminists in these regional meetings, as well as in the transnational spaces of the UN conferences, introduced new strategies and discourses in national activism (S. Alvarez 2000, 1998a; Pitanguy 2002). In particular, the affirmation of women's rights as human rights lent greater legitimacy to feminist struggles in Brazil, opening the way for the expansion and strengthening of state feminism throughout the decade.

The 2000s: Strengthening State Feminism

The new millennium inaugurated space for transnational feminisms in the World Social Forum Conferences. The first three of them, held in 2001, 2002, and 2003, took place in Porto Alegre, Brazil. Brazilian feminists were present not only in these regional transnational spaces, but also in the WSF Conferences held elsewhere (such as in Mumbai), organizing panels, events, and public manifestations, be it as part of their organizations and groups or as members of regional or global networks (Conway 2007; Vargas 2003).

One of the more important positive consequences of Brazilian feminists' presence in these international and transnational spaces is the boosting of their position locally and nationally to fight for public policy for women (S. Alvarez 2000). This is what Margaret Keck and Kathryn Sikkink (1998) call the "boomerang effect" of influence, the cycle of transnational coalitions pressuring more powerful states and international agencies (such as the UN ones) so that they, in turn, will attempt to "convince" a particular government to implement a policy change in the desired direction.

Indeed, the national and transnational articulation of feminists in the Beijing conference process eventually paid off with the creation of the position of the national secretary of women's rights in 2002, to which was nominated Dr. Solange Bentes, a lawyer from the state of Alagoas and also then president of the CNDM. One of her first tasks as the new secretary was to draft Brazil's first report to the Convention for the Elimination of All Forms of Discrimination Against Women, a task that should have been done more than ten years earlier. For that purpose, the secretary commissioned a number of feminist NGOs.[15]

In a parallel process, following the practice established by the CEDAW committee, Ações em Gênero e Desenvolvimento (AGENDE, or Actions in Gender and Development) and Comitê Latino-Americano e do Caribe para a Defesa dos Direitos da Mulher (CLADEM/Brazil, or Latin American and Caribbean Committee for the Defense of Women's Rights)—two feminist NGOs that were focal points for the "Women's Rights Are Not Facultative" campaign in Brazil—created a network of thirteen organizations and other larger networks[16] involving more than four hundred entities to elaborate the Alternative Report, also known as the "Shadow Report." Representatives of the organizations and networks that participated in the writing of the document presented it at the same time that the government submitted the Official Country Report to the twenty-ninth session of the CEDAW committee in New York.[17]

As a result of an initiative of the AMB, the feminist movement was also mobilized in 2002 to draw up the Plataforma Política Feminista (Feminist Political Platform), to be presented to all candidates in the forthcoming presidential elections. This platform represented an important shift in feminist discourse: instead of focusing strictly on women's issues, feminists voiced their perspectives on issues of general interest, formulating a proposition to the construction of a more equitable society on the basis of the principles of a nonracist, nonhomophobic, and anticapitalist feminism. The formulation of this platform involved the participation of women active in local "women's forums" throughout Brazil's major cities in state conferences, culminating with a Brazilian women's conference held in Brasília, the national capital, at which more than 1,000 women represented various "feminist identities," followed by the presentation of the Feminist Platform to the candidates.[18]

Modeled after this conference, and as a result of a proposition formulated by feminists involved in the PT presidential campaign, a similar process was put into effect for the First and Second National Conferences for Public Policies for Women. This process was launched by President Luis Inácio Lula da Silva's government, which established 2004 as Ano da Mulher (Women's Year) through federal law. As part of the events for that year, the SPMulheres (Secretaria Especial de Políticas para Mulheres, or Special Secretariat for Women's Policies), a cabinet-level position created by the Lula government in 2003, organized the I CNPM (I Conferência Nacional de Políticas para Mulheres, or First National Conference on Policies for Women), which took place in Brasília in July 2004. Elected by their peers in the state conferences held all over the country, nearly 2,000 women delegates assembled in Brasília.[19] The stated purpose of this nationwide process was to establish a dialogue between civil society and government—from the municipal through the federal levels—for the formulation of the I PNPM (I Plano Nacional de Políticas para Mulheres, or First National Plan of Public Policies for Women), toward the eradication of gender inequalities in Brazil.

Feminist activists of all walks and faiths participated in this process, conscious that it could revitalize the feminist movement as an "actor in the national political scene." However, feminists were aware of the risk of being used "for a merely illustrative participation, with few concrete results as to definitions of the future plans" (AMB 2004, n.p.). In order to avoid falling into this trap, the AMB intervened in the municipal and state preparatory conferences, thus guaranteeing the largest possible number of delegates who identified as feminists and thus ensuring the incorporation of the demands formulated in the Feminist Political Platform into the I PNPM. This strategy paid off: in all but one of the state conferences (the state of Minas Gerais), the legalization of abortion on demand was approved by a wide margin (Sardenberg 2004). In addition, as observed by the AMB, as a recommendation to this plan, it was approved in the I CNPM the "feminist position that affirms the responsibility of the State over the financing, formulation, and implementation of public policies for women, and the articulation between social and economic policies, both with a distributive character, in addition to the maintenance of budget links to health and education, the relevance of affirmative action, and the principles of equality and equity, the lay nature of the State, and the intersectorial character of the actions needed for the implementation of these policies, and thus the need for the participation of all governmental areas" (AMB 2004; our translation).[20]

A second conference, the II CNPM, was held in Brasília in August 2007, once again bringing together more than 2,000 delegates from all over the country, this time to evaluate the I PNPM and suggest needed adjustments.[21] The resulting final document recognized and reaffirmed some important achievements, such as the launching of the Pact Against Violence and the passage of comprehensive legislation to combat domestic violence, known as "Lei Maria da Penha" (discussed below). Likewise, the demand for the legalization of abortion was also reaffirmed by a wide margin (Sardenberg 2007).

The II CNPM also included the issue of "gender and power" in the discussions that were to serve as basis for the elaboration of the II PNPM. Feminists were successful in guaranteeing the inclusion of the principle that "to widen women's participation in power and decision-making spheres is to work for the consolidation and perfection of Brazilian democracy" (SPM 2008, 118; our translation). This principle has fostered the creation of government machinery at the municipal and state levels to oversee the implementation of the policies in question, including the implementation of councils for the defense of women's rights, formed by representatives of civil society.

Shortcomings and Challenges

In the past three decades, Brazilian society has experienced two distinct, even contradictory, processes that have profound implications for the formulation of policies regarding women's issues. As noted in the previous sections of this chapter, the gradual redemocratization of political institutions, a process marked by the emergence of new actors in the national arena, opens the way for events, such as the National Conferences for Public Policies for Women, to take place. Yet at the same time, we suffer the effects of a perverse combination of the processes of globalization, production restructuring, and the large-scale advancement of neoliberalism, which make labor relations even more fragile and result in the widespread impoverishment of the population. In particular, the implementation of fiscal adjustment policies demanded by the International Monetary Fund, with the consequent cuts in social programs, has rendered the life of the Brazilian laboring classes even more difficult, if not downright painful.[22] As such, despite the important advancements made toward the reestablishment of political and citizenship rights that have culminated with Lula's swearing-in as president, and despite his commitment to offset the impact of the neoliberal politics of previous governments, Brazilian society is still profoundly marked by social inequalities, particularly those resulting from the intersection of gender, class, race, age, and other equally widespread social determinants.

This means that feminist thought and action in Brazil must proceed from a consideration of these intersectionalities, giving rise, as they must, to distinct gender experiences—and thus to distinct gender needs and interests for women placed at different intersection nodes. Therefore, it is not surprising that the wider women's movement in Brazil is made up of distinct segments, and that, as observed by Soares et al., "each part of the women's movement could be analyzed as a social movement in itself, with its own dynamics and modes of expression. These parts intersect, interrelate, and, at times, conflict" (1995, 310). This situation responds to the building of tensions within the women's movement that must be faced in the formulation and implementation of public policies tending to different demands.

Other challenges come as a result of the continuing strength of patriarchal values in Brazilian culture, which have prevented advancements in the legis-

FIGURE 8.2 Feminist group Loucas de Pedra Lilás's stage performance advocating legalization of abortion during II National Conference for Public Policies for Women, August 2007. (Photo by Cecilia Sardenberg)

lation regarding sexual and reproductive rights, particularly the decriminalization of abortion, and have created a number of obstacles in the implementation of new legislation to combat domestic violence. Likewise, deep-seated patriarchal values are in the way of women's rise to decision-making positions in formal power structures, despite the establishment of quota systems to offset the imbalance of power on gender lines. In this section, we shall look at some of these pressing issues for feminisms in contemporary Brazil.

Gender and Race Inequalities

To this day, Brazil is characterized by deep-seated social inequality; the opulence of a few stands against the misery of millions.[23] The rise to power of the PT, with the election of President Lula in 2002 and again in 2006, has yet to alter the structure of inequalities, although some important strides have been made in that direction. Women are among the most disenfranchised, representing the absolute majority of the unemployed. Those who are in the labor market face low wages, often in the lowest-paying and least-prestigious occupations.

While, in the past two decades, inequalities between men and women have tended to narrow *within* certain social groups, inequalities *among* women, specifically between black and white women, have widened considerably.

Insofar as educational levels are considered, for example, data from the 2000 census indicate that women have surpassed men in all levels of schooling, particularly the university level. However, this does not apply to all women in the same way. Indeed, while the proportion of white women who have completed secondary schooling has grown to 17.2 percent, only 10.2 percent of all black women have reached the same status. Similar differentials exist in terms of college education: 7.7 percent among white women, and a mere 1.9 percent for nonwhite females (IBGE 2003). Of course, women on average still earn lower incomes than men, regardless of their color or ethnic group and independent of their levels of schooling. Black women tend to face the most precarious conditions in the labor market, with a large proportion still working as domestic workers.

Another issue that deserves special attention from feminists is the noticeable increase, in recent decades, of the proportion of women-headed households. For example, in the state of Bahia, this proportion rose from 20 percent of homes in 1991 to 27.1 percent in 2000, corresponding to growth of 35.3 percent (ibid.). This rise was more pronounced in urban areas than in rural ones. In the city of Salvador, for instance, female-headed households, composed of "women and their children," correspond to 37.5 percent of all the homes (ibid.; Berquó 2002).

These statistics are particularly important within the context of the current debate regarding the "feminization of poverty." Studies have revealed that households headed by women face greater vulnerability to poverty than other households, because female heads are more likely to be among the unemployed or working part-time and to earn, on average, lower wages (Lavinas 1996). Indeed, according to the 2000 census, nuclear family households headed by men earned, on average, $295,80 *reais* (about US$140) per year, while this average was reduced to $263,90 *reais* (about US$120) in the case of households headed by a woman living alone with her children. And the situation is considerably worse in households headed by black women: these households earn, on average, 74 percent less than households headed by white men (ibid.).

Because income disparity is more critical in the case of families headed by black women, poverty-reduction policies in Brazil must take both gender and race into account. By the same token, poverty reduction and the fight against racism are among the most important challenges posed to feminist activists in the decades to come. Feminists need to take a strong stand in favor of affirmative-action policies along gender and racial lines, as well as pressing for stronger and more inclusive social programs geared to poor families, particularly those headed by women.

Women's Representation in Power Structures[24]

Despite actively participating in the so-called informal political spheres, women in Brazil have not been able to break into the traditional political structures. In Del Campo's words, "After the transitions to democracy, a participatory modality was established in Latin-America that we could say combined, on one side, the predominant classical participation structures—in which women were still excluded in good proportion—and on the other, new channels of expression where feminine incorporation had a space in an increasing way" (2005, 1701).

Although women gained the right to vote in 1932 and today represent 51 percent of the electorate, women do not fill more than 10 percent of elective positions in the country. According to the data computed by the Inter-parliamentary Union, Brazil occupies the 100th position in a total of 135 countries according to their rates of women's political representation. Of course, this low rate of representation stands in contrast to the strength, reach, and political influence of Brazil's feminist movement. Despite three decades of vibrant activism and evolving engagement with the state, increasing women's political participation has been an all but insurmountable challenge. This remains a key paradox in Brazilian feminism: it has succeeded, through its political strength, in putting women's demands on the table, but it has failed to open formal political spaces to the women themselves.

A number of factors have contributed to the historical exclusion of women from these spaces: first, women's social trajectories and their gender markers, geared as they are to the domestic sphere, and, second, elements more directly related to the political system, such as political party structures, the electoral system, and the overall political culture, which has been traditionally based on patronage and patriarchal values (Araújo 2003). Despite women's participation in informal political arenas such as social movements, it was only in the 1980s that significant numbers of women became active in formal politics and institutions. The process of redemocratization of the country also opened the way for the greater presence of women in those arenas. After 1986 this process slowed, only to emerge from a hiatus with the 2002 elections, and mainly within the more progressive-leftist parties. Nevertheless, because the electoral system requires party affiliation, and because feminists have been weary of party control of social movements and, in claiming "autonomy," have tended to stay away from party involvement, it has been difficult for feminist candidates to be successful.

Feminists first organized to address women's political representation in 1995. Working closely with federal congresswomen and men, they pushed for the passage of Law no. 9.100 of 1995, known as the "Quotas Law," which guaranteed that 20 percent of all candidates in proportional elections (town councilors and state and federal deputies) would be women. Though it was applied in the municipal elections of 1996, the new legislation was not enough to change the situation of women's exclusion. In 1997 Law 9.504 was approved, raising the mandatory female-candidate percentage to 25 percent for the 1998 elections and to 30 percent for subsequent elections. However, despite this legislative success, the quota has not translated well into practice. One major problem is that the law does not include a penalty for parties who fail to meet the quota, so many simply ignore it. In addition, it provides no concrete support for female candidates, such as public campaigning funds or free television and radio advertising. Finally, it neither establishes nor offers incentives for the creation of any mechanisms within political parties to encourage women's political development and education.

Increasing the proportion of women who hold public office in Brazil has remained an elusive goal. Aware of this fact, in June 2007 the CNDM and the Women's Caucus in the National Congress, with the support of the SPMulheres, organized a public demonstration on the front yard of the National Congress with the objective of calling attention to the persistent exclusion of women from decision-making spheres and for Congress to pay attention to gender issues in proceeding with the political reform. With the theme *"Nem menos nem mais: apenas iguais"* (Not more or less: just equal), women demonstrated their commitment to the needed political reform, demanding greater space for women in the Brazilian parliament (SPM 2008, 117). A few weeks later, in the midst of the heated discussions going on in Congress, our own Research Center—the Nucleus of Interdisciplinary Women's Studies (NEIM) of the Federal University of Bahia (UFBA), along with two feminist NGOs (AGENDE and Project Women and Democracy of the Casa da Mulher do Nordeste) and the Women's Caucus at the National Congress, promoted an international seminar called "Pathways of Women's Empowerment: International Experiences on Affirmative Action" in the Congress Hall, to bring forth examples of successful experiences in that direction.[25] Among the participants were representatives from Argentina and Costa Rica, countries that hold the highest percentages of women in parliament in Latin America (30 and 40 percent, respectively), as well as Rwanda, where women occupy 49 percent of seats in congress. Although these countries employ distinct quota systems, their presentations made it clear that, to be effective, quota systems need to include sanctions for parties that do not comply with the stipulations. Unfortunately, this lesson has yet to be incorporated in Brazil.

Indeed, Clara Araújo (see also Araújo 2003) from the State University of Rio de Janeiro, also present at the seminar, provided a real insight into the Brazilian experience, identifying a number of weaknesses in Brazil's political system—in particular, the government's inability to redistribute power over the past thirteen years, which has consistently kept women (among others) outside the decision-making sphere. This analysis was confirmed by the reform process that ensued that very same week. Despite a unified set of proposals backed up by international experience and strong partnerships between the government and civil society, feminists and their allies in the Brazilian legislature were able to secure only a few measures aimed at ensuring gender parity in political representation.

Very few of women's demands were incorporated into the Political Reform Project's official report (PL 1210/07), and still fewer made it onto the list of final reforms. The Brazilian women's movement is accustomed to transforming experiences of struggle into opportunities for learning. It managed to guarantee that free television and radio advertising for political parties would address the political participation of women, and it succeeded in ensuring that 20 percent of public campaigning funds would be set aside for female candidates (less than the desired 30 percent, which would correspond to the current quota). Despite the overall defeat, women used the political reform process to organize, raise awareness, build new alliances, and strengthen existing collaborations with members of the executive branch and female deputies and senators from the legislative branch.

Another means of pushing for reform to the quota system was to include quotas as part of the PNPM. Part of the democratization process in Brazil is a participatory governance structure that operates in parallel to the representative democratic system. At each of the three tiers of government, sectoral secretariats—for areas such as health, education, women, environment, and so on—are obliged to hold regular conferences to engage with organized civil society in shaping and monitoring public policies. These conferences, such as the National Conferences for Women previously discussed, offer a significant opportunity for social movements to engage with the state, because the conferences are composed of 50 percent civil society members and 50 percent representatives of the state. Thus, two months after the debate on political reform in Congress, the women's movement entered the Second National Conference on Women's Policies armed with new allies and broader public and political support for its original proposal. At that conference the proposal was strongly reaffirmed, and the women's movement was able to secure a commitment from the federal government to make building representative parity among men and women a national priority.

It is important to emphasize that not only in the legislating bodies but also in the other two branches of government—executive and judicial—women's exclusion from the higher posts continues to be notorious. In fact, women's participation in top positions in the executive branch, despite showing an increase from 13 percent during President Cardoso's terms to 19 percent with President Lula, still falls far behind that of men. For instance, at present, among the thirty-seven cabinet members, only four are women, and only eleven of the thirty-seven ministries have women occupying positions in the higher echelons of decision making. As Montecinos observes, "It cannot be expected that women in positions of power will represent the interests of women above other considerations, as it cannot be argued that the interests of all women could be unambiguously reflected in a demarcated set of preferences" (2001, 191). However, the success of the "lipstick lobby" in passing legislation favoring women in the 1988 National Constitution suggests that a "critical mass" of women in the power positions can make a positive difference.

Criminalizing Domestic Violence Against Women: The Maria da Penha Law

One area in which this "positive difference" is certainly needed is in the judiciary, particularly concerning the implementation of Lei Maria da Penha, the new legislation regarding the criminalization and prevention of domestic violence.[26] This new legislation comes after more than thirty years of feminist organizing and campaigning for the criminalization of violence against women, but, as we shall see below, its implementation has encountered a number of obstacles from judicial authorities.

As explained by Dollarhide and Bouabid's report in 2004, "Domestic violence is the main cause of injuries suffered by women between the ages of 15 and 44 in the region. Between 30 and 40 percent of women have suffered some type of family violence. One out of every 5 women misses work due to domestic violence and more than half of men who beat their wives also beat their children." Throughout Latin America, therefore, the eradication of domestic violence has been a major focus of feminist struggles. Latin American feminists have worked steadily and consistently not only for official recognition of the legitimacy of the demands for legislation and public policy in that direction but also to eradicate patriarchal values regarding gender relations, so as to put "private violence in the public eye." The first major break toward that end came in 1994, with the adoption by the Organization of American States of the Interamerican Convention to Prevent, Sanction, and Eradicate Violence Against

Women, better know as the "Belém do Pará Convention," after the name of the city in Brazil where it was passed.

As previously noted, Brazil's first step in this process was creating DEAMs (Police Stations for Battered Women), ideally staffed by policewomen. The first such station was created in São Paulo in 1985. Today, there are more than three hundred DEAMs in the country. Many states also created reference centers and shelters for battered women, as well as a network of services, including coroners' offices, hospitals, and so forth, to assist women victims of violence. A new law increases the period of imprisonment for such violent acts and also allows preventive arrests and a number of measures to protect women.[27] This law was formulated on the basis of a legal document elaborated by a consortium of feminist networks and organizations, passing through a long process of discussions and reformulations by a working group formed by representatives of several government ministries coordinated by the SPMulheres.

Legislation that criminalizes domestic violence has not been easily accepted. Several judges have claimed that the Maria da Penha Law is "unconstitutional" because it "discriminates" against men. Aware of these possible drawbacks to the Maria da Penha Law, the SPMulheres wrote and has been strengthening the Pacto Nacional pelo Enfrentamento à Violência Contra a Mulher (National Pact for Combating Violence Against Women) with the twenty-seven state governments in the country, with the objective of consolidating the National Policy for Combating Violence Against Women.[28] SPMulheres has also promoted the articulation of consortia to monitor the implementation of Maria da Penha Law throughout the twenty-seven states, by means of a competitive bidding process.[29] Observe (the Observatory for Monitoring the Implementation of the Maria da Penha Law), created by the winning consortium, has conducted research in six state capital cities, revealing that in nearly two years since the passage of the new legislation, few strides have been made toward its implementation according to what the bill states, with the greatest obstacles to be found in the creation of the needed courts. The study also reveals that feminist and women's movements have been active in pushing for the implementation of the law, as it is clear that it will not be enacted without pressure from interested groups, which, in this case, are women of all walks of life.

The Fight for the Legalization of Abortion

Because domestic violence has no "boundaries"—it affects women of all classes, races, ethnicities, and ages—it is an issue that has brought together different segments of the women's and feminist movements in a common struggle.[30]

Sadly, the same cannot be said of the fight for the legalization of abortion. Given its controversial character and the strong opposition to it from religious groups, it is a struggle carried out mostly by self-declared feminist activists. Although this struggle in Brazil spans the past thirty years, it has grown in prominence within the past decade.

Since the 1940s abortions in Brazil have been legal under two conditions: when pregnancy occurs as a result of rape and when pregnancy endangers the life of the mother. In spite of its being prohibited in all other instances, however, it is believed that between 750,000 and 1 million clandestine abortions are performed in Brazil every year, resulting in the admission of nearly 250,000 women into public hospitals due to abortion-related complications. Studies show that nearly 10 percent of the admitted women die, and close to 20 percent suffer severe damage to their reproductive organs (Sugimoto 2005; Martins and Mendonça 2005). For the most part, these women are black and poor, since middle- and upper-class women are able to find safe abortion services in clandestine clinics.

Even in the cases permitted by the legislation, "women could not count on the support of the State to have their rights recognized. They not only had to deal with the many bureaucratic obstacles to have access to the procedure, but also faced the refusal of medical personnel in the public hospitals, as no legal and infrastructural provisions existed to guarantee what the law prescribed" (Soares and Sardenberg 2008). It was only in the late 1980s, with the launching of PAISM and the closer association it created between feminists and the Ministry and Secretariats of Health, that the first public health service providing legal abortions was created in the state of São Paulo. It was not until the 1990s that similar services emerged across the country.

The 1990s would be characterized by a "change of mood" regarding abortion, sparking public debate around the issue. This change began in 1990 with the launching of the September 28 Campaign for the Decriminalization of Abortion in Latin America during the Fifth Latin American and Caribbean Feminist Meeting. The initiative garnered the support of women from twenty-one countries and seven regional networks. This was followed by a series of international conferences—Rio in 1992, the 1994 International Conference on Population and Development in Cairo, the Copenhagen Conference in that same year, and the 1995 International Conference in Beijing—that increasingly supported women's struggles for reproductive rights.

Since 1991, when the September 28 Campaign was first launched, it has gained supporters across the country. Indeed, the Rede Feminista Saúde (Feminist Network for Health, Reproductive Rights, and Sexual Rights, or simply the Feminist Health Network) has been a major actor in that regard, leading the September 28 Campaign along with CLADEM, a Latin American network with similar goals. They have focused on three major paths of action: working with the Ministry of Health and local health officials and professionals to guarantee the availability of services for legal abortions; building and monitoring changes in public opinion in favor of the legalization of abortion, which has included monitoring the media; and dealing with the law, particularly with the situation in the legislature (Villela 2001; Soares and Sardenberg 2008).

The campaign for the legalization of abortion in Brazil has also benefited from the rise to power of more progressive political parties, such as the PT, which brought Lula to the presidency in 2002. Lula's Ministry of Health has been especially supportive of the legalization of abortion in Brazil, building a strong argument around the issue of public health (Sardenberg 2007a). Likewise, the Special Secretariat for Women's Public Policy has also been instrumental in that direction, pressuring the government from within for legislative change. Nevertheless, it also faces growing opposition from conservative religious groups, particularly elements of the Catholic Church that were notably strengthened by the visit of Pope Benedict XVI to Brazil in 2007 (Sardenberg 2007a). In May 2007, for instance, more than 5,000 people connected to various religious groups staged a protest in São Paulo, denouncing abortion as "murder." They highlighted the case of a baby called Marcela, who, although born without a functioning brain, lived for four months, thus challenging medical claims that life outside the uterus is impossible for anacephalus infants. Such a case, they argue, invalidates arguments in favor of the legalization of abortion (Soares and Sardenberg 2008).

The response of Brazilian feminists to this countereffort has been to avoid a head-on collision, with campaigns and other efforts directed toward creating the conditions for a more favorable public opinion. This is a strategic choice: recent polls indicate that public opinion in Brazil has taken a strongly conservative turn in relation to abortion. In 1993 54 percent of those polled defended the maintenance of abortion laws as they stood, while 23 percent supported full legalization; a poll in Folha de São Paulo in October 2007 suggests that the percentage favoring legalization has fallen to 16 percent (ibid.).

In any event, it is clear that the Catholic Church has emerged as a major enemy of women's rights and women's lives. The church has the financial backing needed, as well as the scope, through its parish system, to carry a strong campaign, and it is not scrupulous about the means that are used. An example of how low the church can stoop to achieve its goals is found in the distribution of plastic aborted fetuses to people who attended Sunday mass in the city of Rio de Janeiro's parishes this past December, with the full support of the local bishop. The church has also been behind the approval of local legislation prohibiting the distribution of the "morning-after pill" through the public health system in cities such as Recife, in Pernambuco, and Jundiaí, in São Paulo. Even if these approvals have been overthrown on the basis that they are unconstitutional, they have an impact on public opinion. And recently the church scored two major points: it was instrumental in having a project elaborated by the Triparty Committee formed by SPMulheres defeated in the Congressional Committee for Social Security and the Family, and it is backing the Parliamentary Investigating Committee to investigate abortion practices in Brazil.[31]

The backlash against the gains obtained for women by the feminist movement is also thriving in the judicial system. Nearly 10,000 women in the city of Campo Grande, in the state of Mato Grosso do Sul, are being tried for having had abortions, with some of them already convicted. Of course, this backlash will not stop the campaign for the legalization of abortion in Brazil. As we move forward, resistance to securing women's reproductive rights, fostered by the conservative forces in our society, will continue to try to impose patriarchal restrictions on our way toward achieving full autonomy (Soares and Sardenberg 2008). Combating these forces will constitute a major challenge to feminists in the years to come.

Final Considerations

In reflecting upon the achievements as well as the challenges facing feminisms in contemporary Brazil, it pays to consider Razavi's observation that the expansion of "state feminism" may be seen as resulting from blockages to women's participation through more traditional processes (party politics, for instance). In these circumstances, one strategy "is to enter and work directly through the state bureaucracy." For Razavi, therefore, "State feminism, as it is more widely known, is essentially a post-liberal democratic solution and one possible institutional channel for giving voice to women" (2000, 210). She further observes, however, that state machineries alone cannot be expected to bring significant policy changes without the building of feminist constituencies to support them. At the same time, she argues, "state feminism" tends to depoliticize women's movements, thus cutting short its very basis of support. Should we therefore expect that the strengthening of state feminism in Brazil will be the downfall of feminist activism in social movements? Will only time tell, or can we imagine a different future for feminisms in Brazil?

An important point to consider in this regard is that state feminism in Brazil is not imposed from the top. On the contrary, it is a response to pressures from the feminist and wider women's movement. Furthermore, it has become more "participatory" within the past decade, in that more participatory mechanisms, such as councils and conferences, from the local to the national levels, have played an important part in the formulation and monitoring of public policies for women. Finally, the new decision-making positions in the state machineries that are being created, particularly at the federal level, are being occupied by feminists: they are the ones pushing forth, advancing the National Plan of Public Policies for Women. Of course, there are spaces in these machineries that women who are not in the movement have occupied as a result of party pressure. In the absence of pressures from the movement, these state machineries become mere bureaucratic bodies; they do not present the same success and advancements as those in the hands of feminists.

Indeed, the success of the present Special Secretariat for Women's Policies lies in its recognition of the importance of the feminist movement for the formulation and implementation of public policies that will make a difference in women's lives. As such, thus far, "participatory state feminism" has brought new energy to feminisms in Brazil, providing the means for more participatory channels for the formulation, implementation, and monitoring of public policies for women.

For feminism, it is not enough to have a state mechanism; it is necessary to have people committed to feminist causes advancing the issues at hand, as well as a more participatory form of governance. Thus, feminist organizations and women's forums monitor the actions of those in power and give or withhold their support. This means that if feminisms in Brazil are to continue expanding into the state apparatus, rather than allowing the state to control the movement, building feminist constituencies will continue to be a fundamental challenge for feminisms in the decades to come.

Notes

1. The notion of "waves" of feminism in Latin America has been proposed by Chinchilla (1993).
2. Since 1985 feminist meetings have been held independently of the SBPC Annual Meetings (Sardenberg and Costa 1994).
3. This was the title of a seminar organized by CLAM in Rio de Janeiro, available at http://www.clam.org.br/publique/cgi/cgilua.exe/sys/start.htm?infoid=217&sid=41.
4. Available at http://jbonline.terra.com.br/extra/2005/12/05/e0512343a.html.
5. Indeed, as a result of this "dialogue," abortion services in the cases prescribed by law began to be performed in public hospitals for the first time, the city of São Paulo being the first to provide these services (Pinto 2003). Since the 1980s feminists have worked closely with health secretariats and numerous integrating health councils throughout the country to promote campaigns on issues regarding women's reproductive health (Villela 2001).

6. The process differs by state, but, in general, feminist and women's organizations nominate women to the councils, half of the members being chosen from this pool of women and the other half appointed by different state bureaus and agencies. The governor or other authority in charge then formally approves the nominees.

7. During the military regime a severe constitution, taking away all citizenship rights, was put into effect. With the process of redemocratization, a new constitution had to be elaborated.

8. In accordance with the procedures established by the National Congress, these demands had to be presented in the form of amendments, each being supported by at least 30,000 signatures. Four such amendments were presented by feminist and women's groups, one of them containing a "package" of demands, approved in its entirety, including, among others, changes in the wording of the law to include women, issues regarding women's health, equality for partners in marriage, medical and psychological support to women victims of sexual violence, freedom in family planning, and women's rights to ownership of land. For a more detailed discussion of these demands and of women's participation in the writing of the new constitution, see Pinto 2003, 72–79.

9. The CNDM also promoted a number of national campaigns, including the writing of the Carta das Mulheres (Women's Letter), presented to the Assembléia Constituinte (Constitutional Assembly). This consisted of a two-part document, the first one defending "social justice, the creation of a Unified Health System, free public education in all levels, autonomy to the labor unions, agrarian reform, tributary reform, negotiation of the foreign debt, among other propositions." The second part was completely geared to the defense of women's rights in different areas, including employment and work, health, property rights, and marriage relations. In particular, the Carta das Mulheres tended to the problem of violence against women, defending women's rights to physical and psychological integrity, and demanding the creation of special police stations for battered women. Although it did not explicitly defend the legalization of abortion, it also included a polemical point in discussing a woman's right "to know and decide about her own body" (ibid., 75).

10. On Police Stations for Battered Women in Brazil, see Hautzinger 2007.

11. On black feminisms in Brazil, see Carneiro 1999; Ribeiro 1995; and McCallum 2007.

12. The Fóruns de Mulheres (Women's Forums) are noninstitutionalized entities, constituted by feminist groups or organizations, women's groups in unions and other organizations, and independent feminists (feministas autônomas) operating in Brazil's major cities. They are responsible for organizing, articulating, and implementing campaigns, events, and other mobilizations of the feminist and women's movements throughout the country. The fóruns maintain thematic coordinations without a deliberating or representative power, except when such power is explicitly authorized by the participating women and organizations. At present these fóruns constitute the most organized manifestation of so-called autonomous or independent feminism in Brazil. Cecilia Sardenberg and Ana Alice Costa, authors of this paper, participated in the creation of the Women's Forum of Salvador, Bahia, and we have been active members for close to two decades.

13. Indeed, speaking of the impact of these conferences on women's movements in Brazil, Maria Aparecida "Shuma" Shumaher, one of the coordinators of the AMB, has observed, "This mobilization provoked and constituted [women's] Forums/Articulations in twenty-five Brazilian states, and the promotion of nearly 100 events (state meetings, seminars, research projects, etc.), involving more than 800 organizations. In the history of Brazilian women's movements, I do not know of any other international event that has counted on such an intense mobilization in the country. In some Brazilian counties, the Beijing event stimulated the creation of new spaces for debate. For the first time, women's movements elaborated twenty-two documents/diagnostics that showed the complex nature of inequality among women in the country, giving us the opportunity to evaluate the degree of organization of the movement in each one of these states, assess regional priorities, and propose the design of policies to be implemented" (Pinto 2003, 114–115; our translation).

14. Ana Alice Alcantara Costa integrated this work group, being responsible for the coordination of the Conference on Gender and Power, held in Salvador, Bahia, organized by NEIM/UFBA. Cecilia Sardenberg participated in this conference as cocoordinator.

15. The report was elaborated in 2002, during the presidency of Fernando Henrique Cardoso, but it was discussed by CEDAW only in the following year, with the presence of Minister Emilia Fernandes, nominated by the Lula government, who assumed the task of implementing the CEDAW committee recommendations.

16. The following networks and national coalitions participated in this process: AMB; Articulação de ONGs de Mulheres Negras Brasileiras; Articulação Nacional de Mulheres Trabalhadoras Rurais; Comissão da Mulher da CGT—Central Geral de Trabalhadores; CNMT/CUT—Comissão Nacional Sobre a Mulher Trabalhadora da CUT; MAMA-Movimento Articulado de Mulheres da Amazônia; REDEFEM—Rede Brasileira de Estudos e Pesquisas Feministas; REDOR—Rede Feminista N/NE de Estudos e Pesquisas sobre a Mulher e Relações de Gênero; Rede Nacional de Parteiras Tradicionais; Rede Feminista de Saúde—Rede Nacional Feminista de Saúde, Direitos Sexuais e Direitos Reprodutivos; Rede de Mulheres no Rádio; Secretaria Nacional da Mulher da Força Sindical; and União Brasileira de Mulheres.

17. Ana Alice Alcantara Costa, one of the authors of this paper, was one of the activists present at the CEDAW committee meetings, representing REDOR (an academic feminist network), and speaking at the United Nations in July 2003, for the coalition that elaborated the "Shadow Report" from Brazil.

18. Ana Alice Alcantara Costa participated in this conference as part of the delegation from Bahia.

19. Cecilia Sardenberg, the first author of this paper, participated in the I CNPM as a delegate from the state of Bahia and in the II CNPM as a delegate from the Ministry of Education, representing the Nucleus of Interdisciplinary Women's Studies of the Federal University of Bahia. Ana Alice Alcantara Costa participated in the II CNPM as group coordinator.

20. It is estimated that approximately 300,000 women were involved, directly or indirectly, in the entire preparatory process for the I CNPM, from the city to the federal levels. It is known that 14,050 women participated as delegates in the twenty-seven state conferences held during May and June 2004; 2,000 of these participants were nominated for participation in the I CNPM. Among these participating women, 47 percent were identified as members of organizations of the black women movement and about 3 percent from native indigenous groups, whose voices ensured the inclusion of race and ethnicity issues in all the points included in the I PNPM.

21. This time, a total of 2,559 were elected in the 600 municipal, regional, and state conferences that were part of this process, implying, once again, the direct or indirect involvement of more than 300,000 women across the country.

22. As explained by Montecinos, "In the past two decades, policy elites faced the challenges of political liberalization while attempting to implement comprehensive and painful economic reforms prompted, in part, by stringent demands from international creditors and investors. Social mobilizations to oppose market-oriented policies and protest unemployment and deteriorating wages were contained to avoid possible reversals to military control, perceived as an imminent threat in some countries. Elected governments placed unpopular policy choices in the hands of competent experts, shielded from the unpredictability of party coalitions, interest group politics, and public debate. Instead of looking for new avenues to expand citizens' rights and participation, the fragile new democracies pursued a policy-making strategy that insulated and empowered economic reformers" (2001, 176).

23. Portions of this section were published in Sardenberg 2004.

24. Portions of this section were published in Costa 2008.

25. This seminar was part of the Pathways of Women's Empowerment Research Program Consortium in which NEIM participates as a partner institution. See, for example, http://www.pathways ofempowerment.org. DFID, the Brazilian Congress, and the Pathways of Women's Empowerment RPC were the major funders of the event.

26. Portions of this section were extracted from Sardenberg 2007.

27. Law No. 11.340, sanctioned on August 7, 2006, and named the Lei Maria da Penha (in honor of a woman shot and crippled for life by her ex-companion twenty years ago), not only

triples the period of imprisonment for such violent acts (from one to three years now) but also allows preventive arrests. It also includes a number of other measures to protect the woman.

28. This policy package includes not only the implementation of the Maria da Penha Law, but also the promotion of women's sexual and reproductive rights, the combat against the feminization of AIDS and other sexually transmitted diseases, the combat against sexual exploitation and the traffic of women, and the promotion of human rights of incarcerated women.

29. The chosen consortium, composed of nine entities, including four academic research centers, four feminist NGOs, and three national feminist networks as partners, is coordinated by NEIM, with Cecilia Sardenberg as national coordinator. It is at present devising a methodology to carry out the monitoring process. They have created the Observatory Lei Maria da Penha (known as Observe), which can be reached at http://www.observe.ufba.br.

30. Portions of this section were extracted from Soares and Sardenberg 2008.

31. To carry out the policies included in the I PNPM, the Lula government created in 2004 the Comissão Tripartite (Triparty Committee), comprising representatives from civil society and from the executive and legislative branches. Their major objective was to formulate a legal framework for feminist demands to be presented to Congress.

9

Seeking Rights from the Left: Gender and Sexuality in Latin America

ELISABETH JAY FRIEDMAN

The majority of Latin Americans currently live under left or center-left governments. Given the shared commitments of governments and progressive movements to issues of social justice, state support for feminist and women's movements and a propitious environment for their cooperation seems a reasonable presumption. Historically, however, the political Left has an uneven record on women's rights and the fostering of gender-based solidarity. How do contemporary left governments compare? The preliminary answer, based on a comparative study of Chile, Bolivia, Brazil, and Venezuela, is one that echoes the historical record. These governments have improved the well-being of many women by promoting social welfare. Their support for women's access to the state, including decision-making positions, and sexual autonomy is less consistent. Even the most left-wing presidents seem unwilling to frontally challenge gender and sexual hierarchies, in great part because the Catholic Church defends—and depends on—these constructs.

In Venezuela and Bolivia powerful leaders pay at least lip service to women's demands as they mobilize them on behalf of political transformation, but their political projects only sporadically offer women opportunities to advance their rights. In the more stable political systems of Chile and Brazil, entrenched interests, partisan differences, and relations between state institutions prevent profound changes in gender and sexual power relations despite the efforts of progressive executives. In each country the preexisting relationships between feminists and women in other social movements have

VENEZUELA

Human Development Index ranking: .792
Gender-Related Development Index value: .67
Gender Empowerment Measure value: .542

General

Type of government: Federal Republic
Major ethnic groups: Spanish; Italian; Portuguese; Arab; others
Languages: Spanish; indigenous dialects
Religions: Roman Catholic (96%); Protestant (2%); other (2%)

Demographics

Population, total (millions), 2005: 26.7
Annual growth rate (%), 2005–2015: 1.6
Total fertility (average number of births per woman): 2.7
Contraceptive prevalence (% of married women aged 15–49): 77
Maternal mortality ratio, adjusted (per 100,000 live births), 2000: 57

Women's Status

Date of women's suffrage: 1945/1946
Life expectancy: M 70.4; F 76.3
Combined gross enrollment ratio for primary, secondary, and tertiary education
   (female %), 2005: 76
Gross primary enrollment ratio: 104*
Gross secondary enrollment ratio: 79
Gross tertiary enrollment ratio: 41
Literacy (% age 15 and older): M 93.3; F 92.7

Political Representation of Women

Seats in parliament (% held by women): 18.6
Legislators, senior officials, and managers (% female): 27
Professional and technical workers (% female): 61
Women in government at ministerial level (% total): 13.6

Economics

Estimated earned income (PPP US$), 2005: M 8,683; F 4,560
Ratio of estimated female to male earned income: .53
Economic activity rate (% female): 57.4
Women in adult labor force (% total): 35 (this figure obtained at the CEDAW Statis-
   tical Database)

*Gross enrollment ratios in excess of 100% indicate that there are pupils or students outside
the theoretical age groups who are enrolled in that level of education.

CHILE

Human Development Index ranking: .867
Gender-Related Development Index value: .859
Gender Empowerment Measure value: .519

General

Type of government: Republic
Major ethnic groups: Spanish-Native-American (Mestizo); European; Native-American
Language: Spanish
Religions: Roman Catholic (89%); Protestant (11%)
Date of independence: 1818
Former colonial power: Spain

Demographics

Population, total (millions), 2005: 16.3
Annual growth rate (%), 2005–2015: 1.0
Total fertility (average number of births per woman): 2.0
Contraceptive prevalence (% of married women aged 15–49): 56
Maternal mortality ratio, adjusted (per 100,000 live births), 2000: 16

Women's Status

Date of women's suffrage: 1949
Life expectancy: M 75.3; F 81.3
Combined gross enrollment ratio for primary, secondary, and tertiary education
    (female %), 2005: 82
Gross primary enrollment ratio: 101*
Gross secondary enrollment ratio: 91
Gross tertiary enrollment ratio: 41
Literacy (% age 15 and older): M 95.8; F 95.6

Political Representation of Women

Seats in parliament (% held by women): 12.7
Legislators, senior officials, and managers (% female): 25
Professional and technical workers (% female): 52
Women in government at ministerial level (% total): 16.7

Economics

Estimated earned income (PPP US$), 2005: M 17,293; F 6,871
Ratio of estimated female to male earned income: .40
Economic activity rate (% female): 36.6
Women in adult labor force (% total): 36 (this figure obtained at the CEDAW Statistical Database)

*Gross enrollment ratios in excess of 100% indicate that there are pupils or students outside the theoretical age groups who are enrolled in that level of education.

BOLIVIA

Human Development Index ranking: .695
Gender-Related Development Index value: .694
Gender Empowerment Measure value: .500

General

Type of government: Republic
Major ethnic groups: Indigenous (55%); Mestizo (30%); European (15%)
Languages: Spanish; Quechua; Aymara; Guarani
Religions: Roman Catholic
Date of independence: 1825
Former colonial power: Spain

Demographics

Population, total (thousands), 2004: 9,182
Annual growth rate (%), 2005–2015: 1.7
Total fertility (average number of births per woman): 4.0
Contraceptive prevalence (% of married women aged 15–49): 58
Maternal mortality ratio, adjusted (per 100,000 live births), 2000: 290

Women's Status

Date of women's suffrage: 1938 and 1952
Life expectancy: M 66.9; F 62.6
Combined gross enrollment ratio for primary, secondary, and tertiary education
   (female %), 2005: 82
Gross primary enrollment ratio: 113*
Gross secondary enrollment ratio: 87
Gross tertiary enrollment ratio: not available
Literacy (% age 15 and older): M 93.1; F 80.7

Political Representation of Women

Seats in parliament (% held by women): 14.6
Legislators, senior officials, and managers (% female): 36
Professional and technical workers (% female): 40
Women in government at ministerial level (% total): 6.7

Economics

Estimated earned income (PPP US$), 2005: M 3,584; F 2,059
Ratio of estimated female to male earned income: .57
Economic activity rate (% female): 62.6
Women in adult labor force (% total): not available

*Gross enrollment ratios in excess of 100% indicate that there are pupils or students outside the theoretical age groups who are enrolled in that level of education.

BRAZIL

Human Development Index ranking: .800
Gender-Related Development Index value: .798
Gender Empowerment Measure value: .490

General

Type of government: Federal Republic
Major ethnic groups: Portugese, Italian, German, Spanish, Japanese, Arab, African, indigenous people
Language: Portuguese
Religions: Roman Catholic (74%)
Date of independence: 1822
Former colonial power: Portugal

Demographics

Population, total (millions), 2005: 108.1
Annual growth rate (%), 2005–2015: 1.2
Total fertility (average number of births per woman): 2.3
Contraceptive prevalence (% of married women aged 15–49): 77
Maternal mortality ratio, adjusted (per 100,000 live births), 2000: 110

Women's Status

Date of women's suffrage: 1932
Life expectancy: M 68.1; F 75.5
Combined gross enrollment ratio for primary, secondary, and tertiary education (female %), 2005: 89
Gross primary enrollment ratio: 135*
Gross secondary enrollment ratio: 111*
Gross tertiary enrollment ratio: 27
Literacy (% age 15 and older): M 88.4; F 88.8

Political Representation of Women

Seats in parliament (% held by women): 9.3
Legislators, senior officials, and managers (% female): 34
Professional and technical workers (% female): 52
Women in government at ministerial level (% total): 11.4

Economics

Estimated earned income (PPP US$): M 10,664; F 6,204
Ratio of estimated female to male earned income: .58
Economic activity rate (% female): 56.7
Women in adult labor force (% total): 43 (this figure obtained at the CEDAW Statistical Database)

*Gross enrollment ratios in excess of 100% indicate that there are pupils or students outside the theoretical age groups who are enrolled in that level of education.

not been fundamentally transformed, but there are more opportunities for making common cause.

This tension is not new. Feminists and women from other social movements have championed women's human rights in the face of political repression, economic austerity, and everyday violence. But their periodic collaboration has alternated with disagreement and distance over priorities, strategies, and allies. This chapter focuses on women's activism and its outcome with respect to women's rights and gender equality within the larger political context of the region. It also takes into account parallel organizing among lesbian, gay, bisexual, and transgender (LGBT) people,[1] given their common challenge to the conservative Catholic inheritance of patriarchy and heteronormativity by championing bodily integrity and autonomy.[2]

To trace the connections between past and present, this chapter begins with a definition of the terms *feminism* and *women's movements* in the Latin American context. It then moves to a historical overview of the relations between feminist and other women's movements, focusing on external influences including regime change, left parties and movements, the Catholic Church, and transnational organizing opportunities. The section traces feminist and women's activism through the 1990s. The second half of the chapter offers a four-case study comparison of more recent developments under left-leaning governments, ranging from feminist state-society relations to sexual rights.

Women's Movements in Latin America: Negotiating Boundaries

Movements of women have assumed three forms: feminist movements, women's movements, and movements in which women play significant roles. The first seek to end women's subordination, or the existence of hierarchies based on gendered relations of power, by challenging the traditional roles of women and men; following an early scholarly characterization, in Latin America these movements have been called movements for women's "strategic gender interests" (Molyneux 1985a). The second focus on a range of issues, including basic material survival, defense of human rights, or even conservative demands such as the continuance of an authoritarian regime. Movements composed and led by poor and working-class women who do not explicitly challenge gender roles, but often organize in order to be able to fulfill those roles, have been called movements for "practical gender interests" (ibid.). The third are movements in which women are primary actors but include men and are often led by them.

These movements have not developed independently of one another, and the considerable cross-fertilization of activists, issues, and ideas has meant that it is difficult, if not counterproductive, for both analysts and activists to try to make bright-line distinctions. Unlike in the United States and Western Europe, for example, the "Second Wave" middle-class feminists of the 1970s, emerging from left movements, recognized class as well as gender oppression, and initially prioritized poor and working-class women's issues (Sternbach et al. 1992, 402). Moreover, observers note the extent to which all women's movements, regardless of their explicit goals, implicitly challenge traditional gender roles, since they are vehicles for women to actively engage with public affairs. Decades of feminist work inside other movements have resulted in more "general" movements—environmental, antipoverty, anti-imperial, peace—accepting women's participation and equality as central to their goals. Indeed, different movements of women have sought areas of confluence on which to work together, whether on gender-specific issues such as violence against women, or more general challenges, such as the detrimental impact of neoliberal economic reform on their families and communities.

Periodic attempts to draw boundaries around feminism have taken place in the region. From the emergence of "First Wave" feminism at the end of the nineteenth century, feminists have debated the relevance of theories and approaches, issues and allies. As women's movements sought to engage the places and spaces of "Second Wave" feminism in the 1970s, "historical" activists grew frustrated by the impact of new participants who often brought new issues to the table at national and regional feminist meetings. Analysts have called these moments "crises of expansion and inclusion," and their resolution has been far from easy (S. Alvarez et al. 2003, 541). At one regional meeting, critics of "hard-line" feminism pointed out the difficulty of measuring feminism in their rejection of a feminist yardstick (*feministómetro*), and a proposal to hold separate meetings for experienced and inexperienced feminists in the future was met by hundreds of women chanting "We are all feminists!" (*"Todos somos feministas!"*) (Sternbach et al. 1992, 421). One outcome of these controversies has been the differentiation of a range of feminist positions, such as autonomous feminist, lesbian feminist, and "popular" feminist, a term from Chile used by those focused on the needs of working-class women (Schild 1998, 108).

From opposite ends of the political spectrum, some female advocates for women have rejected the label *feminist* as associated with middle-class women whose primary intent is to critique men. They picked up on the term *gender*, which diffused from academic into policy circles in the 1990s. Although many feminists found that state actors' adoption of *gender, gender theory*, and *gender perspective* co-opted the original intent of gender analysis, which was not only to identify gender inequality but also to seek to change it, other advocates embraced the new terminology. In an ironic move, gender theory "was defended both by working-class women who thought that the feminists were not sufficiently concerned about ending class inequality and by right-wing women who thought that the feminists were too concerned about ending class inequality" (Kampwirth and Gonzalez 2001, 16).

Latin American feminism is multifaceted. Understanding its richness means foregrounding women's agency on the issues that women identify as central for survival. Privileging safe abortion over prenatal care or equal pay over microcredit, or excluding issues of race or ethnicity from a liberal or even radical interpretation of feminism, risks neglecting the situated meaning of women's interests in societies crosscut by multiple sources of oppression.

"[Wo]men Make Their Own History, But They Do Not Make It As They Please": Organizing in Context

In the late nineteenth and early twentieth centuries, "First Wave" feminists in Latin America sought social reform under the banner of women's "different mission" from men, similar to the Catholic precept of gender "complementarity." Believing that women's proper focus was on issues of home and children, many early activists did not prioritize their own rights (Miller 1991). However, others realized that without the vote, their efforts would be stymied. Leaders such as Bertha Lutz, founder of the Brazilian Federation for Feminine Progress, sought transnational alliances, collaborating with the International Women's Suffrage Alliance in advancing Brazilian women's suffrage in the 1920s (Hahner 1990, 138–161).

Avid feminist participation in left parties did not always result in support for suffrage. Male leaders assumed that the enfranchisement of women would give the Catholic Church increased political influence, considering women's perceived attachment to the institution. Suffrage was championed by confessional parties pleased with such potential results, and by small communist and socialist parties. Following World War II, however, left-leaning nationalist and populist parties mobilized women. They decreed female enfranchisement and incorporated women through women's branches or affiliated parties such as the Peronist Women's Party (Miller 1991, chap. 5). Though women gained political access, they were seen as the "housekeepers" of the public sphere, responsible for the daily life of the party organization rather than the promotion of their own interests (E. Friedman 2000, 38–39).

The "Second Wave" feminists of the 1970s also had mixed experiences with the Left. Although they often cut their political teeth in the revolutionary Left or left-leaning parties, they became frustrated with the subordination of gender-based to class-related goals in both theory and practice: women found themselves, and their issues, subordinated to male leadership (Luciak 2001). While some chose to create feminist organizations, others opted to engage in "double militancy," fighting from within their movements and parties to put gender on the agenda. This division between feminists (*feministas*) and party cadre (*militantes*) led to intense debates over whether the former were enjoying the latest imperial bourgeois import from the United States or Europe or the latter sacrificing their feminist ideals to mobilize masses for the socialist patriarchy. Despite their differences, both "sides" agreed that their natural constituency was the poor and working-class, and often indigenous or Afro-descendant, women who made up the majority of female Latin Americans. But because militantes often sought to recruit activists from women's movements to serve only party interests and feministas insisted that gender oppression was as important as class oppression, both found it difficult to create lasting multi-class alliances. Mobilized by the economic decline and political repression that characterized the region from the late 1960s through the 1980s, women's movements grew in strength and numbers, informed by—but always in uneasy tension with—the feminist ideals and organizing principles of largely middle- and upper-class white and mestiza women.

Women mobilized through several arenas. Some organized on behalf of authoritarian governments, in agreement with a conservative ideology that claimed an "ordered" traditional family as the cornerstone to restoring order to society, polity, and economy (Power 2001). Against authoritarianism, the now-famous "mothers' movements," which sought information about their missing children and partners, often formed the backbone of a growing opposition movement (Jaquette 1991; S. Alvarez 1990, chap. 3). In Chile, Brazil, and elsewhere, poor and working-class women organized for family survival, creating communal soup kitchens, and Chilean women created tapestries portraying the violation of their and their communities' human rights. Often these efforts took place under the protection of the Catholic Church, particularly where repression of left parties and unions was the most draconian. The Church was an inconsistent ally for women: while it protected grassroots organizations, and recognized the difficulties poor women faced in supporting their families and communities, it held the line on issues challenging women's bodily autonomy. Where parties organized clandestinely, such as in Venezuela, women proved to be ideal underground cadres, as their gender made them less suspect in the eyes of the authorities (E. Friedman 2000, chap. 3). Finally, feminists, often inspired by ideas acquired during exile in Western Europe, made connections between authoritarianism in the polity and the family, fighting for "democracy in the country and the home" (Baldez 2002, 161).

The growth of opposition movements provided an opportunity for women to form cross-class and nonpartisan coalitions to demand an end to authoritarianism. Women's gender solidarity, based on their common identification as "political outsiders," often allowed them to unite where men were unable to cooperate. For example, in Chile, the mass organizations Women for Life (1983) and Coalition of Women for Democracy (1988) brought women together across class and party lines to unify the opposition against Pinochet, and then to make gender-based demands on the new democracy (ibid., chaps. 7–8; S. Alvarez 1990, chap. 5; E. Friedman 2000, 117–121). Although this coalition building did not survive the transition to democracy intact, it fostered relationships and shared understandings, particularly the saliency of the human rights framework for women's struggles, that would continue to inform organizing.

In the Cuban and Nicaraguan revolutionary regimes, women played key roles in achieving state power. Mass women's organizations, the Cuban Women's Federation (FMC) and the Luisa Amanda Espinoza Association of Nicaraguan Women (AMNLAE), were created as the official channel for women's integration. While important gains—workplace-equality measures, antisexist education, day-care provision, and, in the case of Cuba, access to legal abortion—were made, women's rights were often subordinated to national needs. Both the FMC and the AMNLAE mobilized women on behalf of the revolutionary states, whether that meant taking on significant community work or postponing their demands in order to fight against the Contra War in Nicaragua (L. Smith and Padula 1996).

Early LGBT activists had similar experiences to feminists vis-à-vis the Left in the 1970s.[3] Although stalwart members of left parties, their sexuality was seen as a taboo subject, contrary to "revolutionary morality." This attitude was reflected in the homophobic policies and practices of the revolutionary regimes in Cuba and Nicaragua. Thus, some activists split off into separate gay liberation groups that included men and women.

For lesbians, the move from partisan to identity-based organizing was often unfulfilling. Although they participated in the formation of an identity distinct from partisan ideology, they often found themselves and their issues sidelined or subordinated to gay men. They thus turned to burgeoning feminist and women's movements, directing their energies to "larger" women's issues such as reproductive rights and ending violence against women. But here again they found themselves sidelined, if not silenced. Many feminists feared their movements would be "tainted" by association with lesbianism, given the widespread societal assumption that feminists were driven by hatred for men rather than for patriarchal structures of power, and refused to directly engage with issues of nonnormative sexuality or family structure.

As a result of their double marginalization, some lesbians began organizing autonomously in the 1980s, often forming the most radical feminist groups, such as the Bolivian group "Women Creating." The AIDS crisis led to rapprochement between mixed-gender groups and feminists. Although the disease tragically deprived movements of some of their most committed supporters, it created new sources of national and international financial and institutional support for LGBT groups, as well as opening up public dialogue on sexuality (Pecheny 2003). Following on these developments, coalitions between LGBT and feminist movements emerged around issues of bodily integrity and autonomy in the 1990s.

With the regionwide transitions to liberal democracy beginning in the 1980s, many feminists began to engage directly with the state. Some continued in or rejoined party politics. In Brazil and Chile women demanded, and received, a full-fledged ministry of women's affairs. Opportunities for policy development and implementation also stimulated a process of "professionalization" of feminist movements, as many middle-class and elite women formed nongovernmental organizations (NGOs) to work on issues such as microcredit, domestic violence, and women's leadership (S. Alvarez et al. 2003, 548). This dramatically changed the nature of feminist efforts, given that NGOs were subject to the demands of granting agencies, whether international foundations, organizations, or governmental ministries. Organizations often adapted their structure, projects, or even missions to coincide with the priorities of funders. While it nurtured the feminist policy sector, democratization paradoxically debilitated movements by opening new avenues of action within the formal political arena.

Moreover, engaging with the state provoked tensions with allies and the very women organized feminists sought to help. Feminists entered the state precisely as such states were beginning to shed their responsibilities for social welfare and economic growth under the dictates of neoliberal economic models. Those who remained outside the state criticized the resulting "gender technocracy" that supported the "global neoliberal patriarchy" by teaching poor and working-class women how to cope with neoliberal citizenship (Monasterios 2007, 33–34; S. Alvarez et al. 2003, 547; Schild 1998). The division between the self-proclaimed *autonomas*, who continued to work in movement arenas, including those of the political Left, and those they identified as *institucional-izadas*, who sought change through more formal institutions, marked another painful rending of feminist energies. The four case studies below help to shed light on the question of the extent to which "institutional" feminism helps to realize its goals or weaken its bases.

In addition to national politics, transnational networking remained critical to Latin American women. This networking, which included the circulation of ideas, strategies, resources, and people themselves, was facilitated by both formal state-oriented UN world conference processes and movement-based transnational meetings. The Latin American and Caribbean feminist *encuentros* (encounters) began in 1981. Intended to bring together movement activists from throughout the region, encuentros have taken place in Argentina, Brazil, Chile, Colombia, Costa Rica, the Dominican Republic, El Salvador, Mexico, and Peru. While changing in format and theme, these multiday experiences provide a host of different ways for activists to interact, becoming "key transnational arenas where Latin America–specific feminist identities and strategies have been constituted and contested" (S. Alvarez et al. 2003, 539).

The encuentros inspired the creation of regional networks, including the 28 September Campaign for the Decriminalization of Abortion in Latin America and the Caribbean; the Network of Latin American and Caribbean Women's Health; the Network of Afrolatinamerican and Afrocaribbean Women; and the Latin American and Caribbean Feminist Network Against Domestic and Sexual Violence. These networks coordinated their own face-to-face meetings as well as making use of new technologies to circulate information and strengthen regional campaigns.

These regional networks helped feminists prepare for a series of UN world conferences: on the environment (Rio de Janeiro, 1992), human rights (Vienna, 1993), population and development (Cairo, 1994), women's rights (Beijing, 1995), and habitat (Istanbul, 1996). Preparations for the conferences mobilized women's rights activists. The conferences themselves produced documents, such as the Vienna Declaration and Programme of Action and the Beijing Declaration and Platform for Action, that women used to legitimate demands at home. But it was not a one-way process: Latin Americans were at the forefront of the Vienna-oriented transnational movement that famously established "women's rights are human rights"; their experiences fighting authoritarian rule left them with a keen awareness of the power of the human rights discourse (E. Friedman 1995).

However, feminists became frustrated at the degree of backlash they experienced at the "+5" meetings following up on the conferences in the 2000s, as more conservative governments and NGOs, led by the Vatican, attempted to roll back gains. Moreover, many found that the conferences provided paltry results in comparison with the enormous effort invested in organizing around them, given the roadblock that global neoliberal economic policies threw in the way of improving most women's lives. Upon the initiation of the World Social Forum in Brazil in 2001, activists turned to this social movement–oriented "counter-hegemonic transnational space." Brazilian feminists became aware of the lack of attention to gender in the initial programming and quickly organized transnationally to convince the organizers to include it (César de Oliveira 2002). Since that time, Latin American feminists have sought to have an impact on the forum as a whole, continuing to debate whether carving out their own spaces or bringing feminist perspectives into other arenas is more effective (S. Alvarez, Faria, and Nobre 2004).

Transnational actions had a mixed outcome. Formal international opportunities helped Latin American feminists legitimate their demands at the national and local levels. In many countries these opportunities energized organizing and nurtured transnational connections.[4] But they exacerbated the divisions among feminist groups and between feminist groups and women's movements. International resources, often targeted at the most professionalized groups, and discourses, such as the importance of "mainstreaming a gender perspective," reinforced the split between those focused on policy making and those focused on movement building. Engaging with formal international processes drew resources and attention away from national contexts, sometimes "unsettling intra movement solidarities while accentuating class, racial-ethnic, and other inequalities among activists" (S. Alvarez et al. 2003, 554).

Less-official forums, oriented to the agendas of activists, strengthened solidaristic contacts, particularly through regional networks, and circulated new conceptualizations of issues. Despite their often idyllic settings in places such as the Brazilian and Dominican coasts, they were not free from conflict over funding and inclusion. At times they magnified national controversies that might not have otherwise diffused as rapidly and destructively, such as when a group of Chilean feminists oriented the seventh *encuentro* around their bifurcation of the feminist world into autonomous and co-opted camps (S. Alvarez et al. 2003, esp. 554–557).

As important as transnational opportunities were, the national contexts of the 1990s remained key to the mediation of women's demands. Although feminists could now lobby democratic governments, they operated in a center-right context with inconsistent left support, and in many countries the Catholic Church had renewed legitimacy as a political actor following its staunch opposition to authoritarian rule. Key successes included the nearly regionwide adoption of statutory candidate gender quotas and legislation prohibiting domestic violence. At almost 40 percent, Argentina and Costa Rica pulled ahead of other countries in female representation in their lower houses, although a regional advance was evident: in 2008 the percentage of women in countries with quota provisions reached 20.5 percent, an increase of nearly 60 percent from a decade earlier (Llanos and Sample 2008; Inter-Parliamentary Union 2008b).

The negotiations for these laws and other proposals did not show a clear correspondence between feminist demands and left party support. Right-wing parties, influenced by the Catholic Church, ensured that family values underpinned much of the antiviolence legislation, and some recognized that including women on party lists might benefit them at the polls (Macaulay 2006; Baldez 2004). Meanwhile, the Left refused to spend political capital supporting the feminist demand for reproductive rights, given the unpopularity of abortion in opinion polls across the region and active lobbying by the church. In 2006, in the most notable contradiction between left governance and reproductive rights, Nicaragua criminalized therapeutic abortion under the leadership of former revolutionary Daniel Ortega. Ortega's compromises with the Right and the Catholic Church, his political manipulation to defeat former allies, and the still-unresolved accusations by his stepdaughter of sexual slavery alienated feminists (Kampwirth 2008).

Left parties and revolutionary governments thus incorporated some feminist demands but subordinated women and their issues to "larger" goals—and for political expedience. The agenda for social change around gender and sexuality proceeded without consistent support from the Left.

Today's Left on Gender and Sexuality: Making a Difference?

The historical context outlined above took place with the Left out of power— or fighting for the survival of a revolution. Does the Left's entry into democratic governance make a difference? To answer this question, this section provides a comparison of four countries: Chile, Brazil, Venezuela, and Bolivia. These countries offer a seemingly wide spectrum of political transformation. Chile and Brazil are representative democracies based on principles of political competition and separation of powers and underpinned by neoliberal economics. Although Venezuela and Bolivia run elections, they have consolidated executive power and promote more direct participation through national popular movements, undergirded by heterodox economic policies. Some analysts have offered normative distinctions between their political and economic projects, characterizing the first two as a more reformist "right Left," seeking to promote liberal democracy and equitable social policies, and the second two as a more radical "wrong Left," mired in an outdated and power-hungry populism (Castañeda 2006). Similarities across the "good-bad" divide, differences within each "side," or each country's complex contextual realities complicate such dichotomous assessments.

To assess change within each country and across them, the rest of this chapter focuses on six areas pertaining to women's status and rights, as well as addressing sexual rights. It first presents the record of three of the four governments with respect to improvements in women's socioeconomic status. To demonstrate the impact of left governance on feminist state-society relations, the next section examines contemporary feminist and women's movements and their relationship with state feminism in the form of national women's machinery. The following section evaluates women's representation in national decision making. The final three sections look at three key policy issues: violence against women, reproductive rights, and sexual rights.

To briefly summarize the findings of this analysis, Venezuela's "twenty-first century socialism" depends on the mobilization of women, but, as with its twentieth-century predecessors, mainly to support the political project of its current president, Húgo Chávez. Although they have made some important rhetorical gains, feminists struggle to convince state actors to implement gender-equitable policies. There are clear parallels in Bolivia: reflecting the impact of a women's coalition, the new constitution in Bolivia offers progressive language on gender-related rights. President Evo Morales has acknowledged the important political role of indigenous women, but it is unclear whether they are able to advance their own demands. In Chile President Michele Bachelet is seeking to advance women's rights but faces overwhelming opposition on more controversial issues. Working through her women's ministry, she has reformed a weak law against domestic violence, but the partisan divisions within the ruling coalition, exacerbated by the political power of the Catholic Church, make it impossible to pass legislation on reproductive and sexual rights. President Luis Inácio Lula da Silva (known by the nickname "Lula") of Brazil has opened important avenues to feminist advocates through his women's machinery and come out strongly on behalf of sexual rights. But he faces institutional challenges, including a legislature unwilling to change its male profile and increasingly open to religious influences.

Women's Socioeconomic Status

Venezuela, Brazil, and Chile[5] seem to be making good on the leftist promise to ameliorate material inequalities among their male and female citizens; all have addressed the welfare of poor women and their families. Chávez's administration introduced a parallel social service infrastructure of *misiones* in 2003 that have incorporated large numbers of poor and working-class women as recipients, volunteers, or employees; since 2001 the Women's Bank has offered microloans for poor entrepreneurs. The conditional cash-transfer *Bolsa Família* program, expanded under Lula, now covers a quarter of the Brazilian population (Hunter and Power 2007, 18) and thus supports almost all eligible poor women and their families. But the attempt to hold down social spending has taken its toll. In one review of a collection of fifty-seven federal programs that have a direct impact on Brazilian women, only those funds associated with basic health care and the *Bolsa Família* (39 percent of the total) were fully paid out ("Em 2007" 2008). Although Bachelet has not implemented national programs similar to those of Venezuela and Brazil, she has taken action on senior health care, education, and employment for the poorest sectors (Savelis 2007, 73). More than eight hundred new day-care centers have opened since she took office; free preschool is also on the agenda.

While it is hard to determine cause and effect when dealing with secular trends such as life expectancy and the impact of previous policies, over the past decade these kinds of programs seem to be having an effect. As the snapshots of tables 9.1 and 9.2 show, although women are still earning far less than men, they have largely higher rates of educational enrollment. Table 9.3 shows some improvement in life expectancy. This evidence suggests that left governments do make a difference on material elements of women's status.

Feminist State-Society Relations

In moving from women's socioeconomic status to questions of whether feminist voices are heard by and can have an impact on state institutions, the picture of Left support becomes more complex. Left governments often incorporate feminist activists and, in some cases, expand the abilities of their national women's machinery. But to what ends? Sometimes it is to further national projects, rather than advance women's rights per se. This goal can exacerbate preexisting tensions between feminist and women's movements, as state actors seek to mobilize the latter. However, feminists within the state can make a difference on the direction of policy.

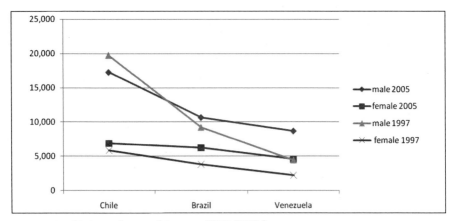

TABLE 9.1 Estimated earned income (PPP US$) by sex.
Data are drawn from UNDP, *Human Development Report 2007* and UNDP, *Human Development Report 1999*.

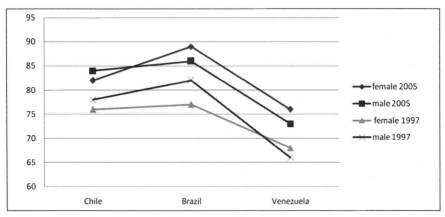

TABLE 9.2 Combined gross enrollment ratio for primary to tertiary education by sex.

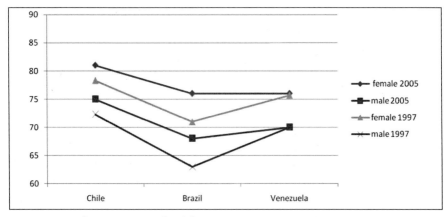

TABLE 9.3 Life expectancy at birth by sex.

Although affected by the political polarization that has characterized Chávez's rule, feminist activists have advanced issues from their "minimum agenda": the application of antiviolence statutes, the decriminalization of abortion, gender parity for electoral lists, prohibiting gender stereotyping in advertising, and achieving a minimum wage for homemakers. The incorporation of feminists from left parties into Chávez's government facilitated the institutionalization of parts of the "agenda." For example, feminist intervention in the 1999 constitutional convention resulted in the prohibition of gender discrimination and the promotion of gender equality, illustrated by the use of gender-inclusive language throughout the constitutions (for example, *cuidadanos y cuidadanas* [male and female citizens]). It also protects maternity, allows women to transfer their citizenship to foreign spouses, and recognizes housework as an economic activity. However, activists have not been successful at getting the majority of women on board with the "agenda" (Espina 2007, 2000).

In contrast, the Chávez government has made an effort to incorporate women into the "Bolivarian Revolution."[6] Although Chávez has not established the highly institutionalized mass women's organizations that characterized the Cuban and Nicaraguan revolutions, his National Women's Institute (INAMUJER) has attempted to bring together a "Bolivarian Women's Force" made up of members of the 22,000 *puntos de encuentro*, or "encounter points," which are small state-supported women's groups. These groups have been able to access microcredit and participate in health and women's rights campaigns, as well as national women's meetings (INAMUJER 2008). Even though men hold leadership roles in the misiones, women's participation in such opportunities can lead to their empowerment (Fernandes 2007b).

In general, INAMUJER has followed in the footsteps of other revolutionary women's organizations: its primary goal is to mobilize women for the revolution. As a prominent example, the International Women's Day marches it has sponsored have focused on protesting the U.S. invasion of Iraq, Colombia's violation of Ecuador's sovereignty, and Exxon's actions against the Venezuelan state oil company. These marches, attended by thousands of women, do not focus on their condition or rights.

Despite its political fealty, INAMUJER has an uncertain future. In March 2008 its head was named as the state minister for women's affairs, an advisory position to the president rather than a ministry with its own budget. INAMUJER, which remains part of the Ministry of Health and Social Development, has an unclear fate, becoming an example of how state feminism is subject to the whims of executives (Espina 2008).

In Bolivia the movement sector has not been able to overcome the preexisting polarization between feminists who worked with pre-Morales governments and those who rejected engagement with the state (Monasterios 2007). The latter, while small in terms of numbers, have been symbolically important both in Bolivia and in the region, seeking to support grassroots women while espousing radical, antipatriarchal politics.

As in Venezuela, some feminists have used the opportunity of a constitutional convention to create and lobby for a common agenda. Over two years the Women and Constituent Assembly movement brought together 25,000 women to formulate a consensus position (Mujeres y Asamblea Constituyente 2007). Its influence on the draft constitution is evident in many articles, some of which are discussed below.

Reflecting Chávez's efforts, Morales has begun direct dialogue with low-income indigenous women organized through neighborhood councils and the Bartolina Sisa National Federation of Peasant Women. Although they are present at some intermediate levels of leadership (Farthing 2007, 8), it is an open question whether such movements will go beyond mobilization to participation in national leadership and decision making (Monasterios 2007).

Morales has not used his women's machinery as a tool for mobilization; instead he has chosen to diminish it. He threatened to get rid of the Vice Ministry of Women, under the Sustainable Development Ministry, as a "form of discrimination": since "women will be ministers" there would be no reason to have a special office for the sector. In sharp contrast, women within Morales's MAS party and the leader of the Bartolina Sisa Federation insisted they would fight to keep it, and even transform it into a full-fledged "Gender Ministry." Nevertheless, by the end of the year the office was "demoted" to Vice Ministry of Gender, Generational, and Family Issues in the Justice Ministry (Bolpress 2006; NotiEMAIL 2006).

Under the four Concertación governments Chile has had since redemocratization, prominent feminists in this dominant political coalition established close relationships with state actors or entered the state. As in Bolivia, radical autonomous feminists critiqued those who engaged with the state, seeing them as co-opted by a liberal, capitalist, patriarchal system. Moreover, as in Venezuela, there was a disconnect between those feminists professionally active in the state and nongovernmental organizations and grassroots organizations of women (Ríos Tobar 2007).

Some of this disconnect, paradoxically, came through the relative success of Chile's national women's ministry. Compared to Venezuela and Bolivia, Chile's National Women's Service both is well established (begun during the Chilean transition to democracy) and has considerable political clout. Bachelet increased its budget by 13 percent in 2007, making it "one of the biggest, best-funded and highest-ranked national women's agencies in Latin America." Like the rest of the Chilean government, it has relied more on the technical expertise of professionals than on the incorporation of grassroots organizations, marginalizing nonelite actors (ibid., 28). However, Bachelet's appointment of a feminist to lead it had an immediate impact, including increased attention to domestic violence.

As in Chile, preexisting ties between organized feminists and Lula's Workers' Party have translated into feminist access to the Brazilian state. This access also reflects the strength of the multifaceted feminist movement. Its more prominent organizations span the spectrum from legislative watchdog to Afro-Brazilian empowerment, and the "feminist, antiracist" Articulation of Brazilian Women has served as a national network for fifteen years. But the government has received its share of criticism; for example, Afro-Brazilian women have shown how the neoliberal development model neglects their and their families' needs (Reis 2007).[7]

Lula has re-created his national women's machinery (also created during the transition to democracy) as the Special Secretariat for Women's Policies (SPM), an advisory body with ministerial rank charged with mainstreaming women's issues in public policies. It has coordinated two national conferences involving hundreds of thousands of women across the country; in 2007 the second conference approved a series of policies to challenge gender, race, and class inequalities. SPM's current national plan attests to the influence of its feminist leadership and civil society council: the plan is informed by an intersectional perspective that highlights issues such as the intertwined fight against racism, sexism, and "lesbophobia" and the need to provide health care for all women, including Afro-Brazilian women, indigenous women, lesbians, and transsexuals. But SPM's reach is wider than its impact, given the frequent lack of follow-through on gender-related policies by other ministries and the limitations in social spending from the government's attempt to stay on a neoliberal economic course (ibid.; SPM 2008; Osava 2007).[8]

This overview of feminist state-society relations under left governments reflects historical patterns but shows new trends as well. In line with his revolutionary predecessors, Chávez has attempted to mobilize women within his "Bolivarian Revolution." His national women's machinery has been crucial in this endeavor, prioritizing national goals over the fulfillment of women's rights. Morales also has sought to incorporate grassroots women into his national project, but instead of relying on Bolivia's women's machinery, he has diminished its role. Although his "mainstreaming" view ("women will be ministers") may garner political legitimacy in a society where ethnicity and class are more politically articulated than is gender, the defense of women's machinery by his supporters shows its continued relevance. In these "more left" cases, other political opportunities have been more fruitful for the articulation of feminist concerns. The constitutional reform processes overseen by Chávez and Morales have stimulated women's mobilization; in both countries they have had an impact on fundamental legal structures.

In Chile and Brazil feminist alliances with left parties have given them access to the state, and executives have championed long-standing and high-profile women's machinery. But the coexistence of state support for feminist issues and co-optation of movement energies continues, given the governments' commitments to technocracy and neoliberalism. Each country attests to the historical dependence of state feminism on the political will of the executive, as well as inequality of access between women with and without class and race privilege.

Women's Representation in Decision-Making Positions

The percentage of women in national parliaments is often taken as a proxy for gender equality—for example, as part of the United Nations Development Program's "Gender Empowerment Measure." Certainly, the number of women in decision-making positions indicates the extent of gender equality in descriptive representation. However, descriptive representation is not equivalent to substantive representation; female leadership does not automatically translate into the promotion of a feminist agenda. This is especially true when women's crosscutting identities have saliency. For example, in Bolivia, "elite urban women linked to the leadership of right-wing parties mainly benefited" from gender candidate quotas under former president Sánchez de Lozada, bringing their own political, class, and geographic perspectives to their governance objectives (Monasterios 2007, 34). They took advantage of an opportunity for women to promote conservative policy, much like their historical predecessors in the region. In addition, party systems and structures have an impact on what women are able to accomplish for women: strong parties in stable systems will be more able to exert discipline over all their members, whereas weak parties and fragmented systems will lead to more independence in their members' actions. Party platforms can have more impact on substantive representation than legislators' gender.

With the difference between counting and consciousness in mind, this section examines the extent to which women participate in national representation and decision making in the governments of Chávez, Morales, Bachelet, and Lula. The following discussion is based on the percentage of women in the lower or single house of parliament (the global comparative measure of women's representation) including the election before the executive (or her or his party) came to power, as well as the election(s) in which she or he came to power. The section also examines policies to address the underrepresentation of women and women's cabinet positions. This survey reveals that left governments are inconsistent in their support for women's descriptive representation.

A decade after his first election, Chávez is attempting to address women's representation. After increasing sharply with his first election (from 5.9 to 12.1 percent), it declined with his second (to 9.7 percent), in which Chavistas (Chávez supporters) won a large majority.[9] In his third election, when Chavistas again dominated the legislature, women increased their numbers nearly 100 percent, from 9.7 to 18.6 percent, just above the regional average of 18.5 percent. Despite feminist pressure, the Venezuelan government has not restored the statutory quota of 30 percent it suspended in 2000 (Espina 2007, 21). But Chávez's government has proposed other measures: gender parity for candidates for political office was part of the (defeated) 2007 constitutional reform plans, and the National Electoral Council decided in July 2008 that the candidates for regional legislative councils had to conform to gender parity.

When Morales was elected, the percentage of women in parliament declined slightly from 18.5 to 16.9, but 74 percent, including the president of the assembly, were from his MAS party (Draper 2006). In addition, 86 of the 255 members of the 2007 Constituent Assembly were women, achieving a quota of one-third of the representatives. The Women and Constituent Assembly movement lobbied for this quota and its fulfillment, as well as encouraging turnout among women (Coordinadora de la Mujer et al. 2007).

Bachelet has sought to improve the percentage of women in the Chilean lower house. It has risen slowly in the last three elections, from 10.8 percent to 15 percent. Recognizing her country's below-average status in regional terms, Bachelet introduced a bill in October 2007 to achieve equal political participation between men and women, specifying that party lists and party leadership positions can be no more than 70 percent of either gender. Parties opting to include more women than the minimum are eligible for extra state funds (Bunting 2007). However, the legislature has been opposed to such measures.

Although the percentage of female representatives has risen since Lula was first elected in 2002, from 6.2 percent to 9 percent, Brazil lags behind these countries with the second-lowest percentage in the region. This is particularly notable given the statutory 30 percent quotas for female candidates. Rather than placing the blame on the president's shoulders, the failure of quota measures has been attributed to its original design problems, including the ability for parties to manipulate the lists to ensure that men get the viable positions (Miguel 2008). The revision of the quota legislation is a priority for the Special Secretariat for Women's Policies, according to its 2008 Second National Plan, and feminist advocates are also seeking to improve representation.[10]

Cabinet positions, appointed by executives and changed at their discretion (with congressional oversight), are a sensitive measure of the commitment of executives to gender equality in decision-making posts. The finding that left presidents are likely to appoint women to their cabinets is partially confirmed here (Escobar-Lemmon and Taylor-Robinson 2005; executive branch Web sites for each government). Bachelet famously implemented gender parity in her appointments; Chávez has a 30 percent female cabinet; and Morales's cabinet is 25 percent female, including, at first, Justice Minister Casimira Rodríquez, a Quechua Indian and head of the union of domestic employees. Although she has since left the cabinet, her position continues to be held by a woman.

Cabinet positions can be as easily shuffled as a deck of cards, often in response to political crisis; one such shuffle, in March 2007, shifted Bachelet's cabinet away from parity (to thirteen men and nine women), as she brought in experienced politicians. This change resulted in her female cabinet members clustering in traditional positions, such as education and health, although they also hold positions in planning and agriculture. Chávez's cabinet assigns women to similar positions, with no women in prominent posts. Finally, in a development for which he can take full credit, Lula has not appointed a single woman to Brazil's twenty-three ministries. Adding in the additional authorities with ministerial rank brings the total to four women out of thirty-seven, including the head of the Special Secretariat for Women's Policies.

This section shows that although women have mobilized to demand equitable roles in decision making, left executives do not ensure it. Legislative representation is not necessarily in their hands; Chávez has more sway over his legislature than Bachelet, whose efforts to establish quotas are not being heeded by the coalition government she heads, or Lula, who operates within the constraints of Brazilian institutional design. This may help to explain the counterintuitive finding that the highest percentage of women in legislatures is in the populist democracies of Venezuela and Bolivia. Cabinet making, controlled by the executive, provides a more sensitive measure of executive commitment to gender equality. Here Bachelet made a significant, if ultimately curtailed, effort; Chávez and Morales are right behind her; and Lula trails far behind. No executive consistently puts women in important cabinet positions.

Violence Against Women

Moving from counting to consciousness, this section examines the first of three policy areas that, given the depth of their challenge to gender and sexual power relations, are serious "litmus tests" for the influence of advocates on left governments. New legislation against violence against women is reflective of feminist positions, although governments have been uneven in promoting it.

Bolivia's 1995 Law Against Domestic and Family Violence reflected the regional trend of protecting the family rather than addressing the gender-related nature of much violence in the home. The Women and Constituent Assembly movement offered new language for the constitution that embodies a more feminist perspective on violence against women: "All people, women in particular, have the right to not suffer physical, sexual or psychological violence, as much in the family as in society." Moreover, the state is obliged to take the remedies necessary to "prevent, eliminate, and sanction gender violence" (Article 15, paragraphs 2–3).

Extensive pressure has led to Chávez's and Lula's signing new statutes against violence against women. In 2006 Brazil became one of the last countries in the region to pass such legislation. The "Maria da Penha Law" commemorates the woman who lodged a complaint against Brazil at the Inter-American Commission on Human Rights (IACHR) to protest the government's repeated failure to protect her against her aggressive ex-husband. Although his maltreatment—including a murder attempt—left her a paraplegic, two different trials concluded without indicting him. Only after the IACHR found in her favor in 2001, followed by five years of continuous lobbying from civil society groups and the Special Secretariat for Women's Policies, did the law pass (Santos 2007). Again responding to executive pressure to cut spending, the federal program Oppose Violence Against Women only used half of its allotted resources in 2007 ("Em 2007" 2008).

Venezuelan women's organizations, outraged by the attorney general's 2003 decision to suspend restraining orders against batterers, successfully lobbied for the replacement of the Law on Violence Against Women and the Family with the 2006 Law on the Right of Women to a Life Free from Violence (Espina 2007, 21). But the government delayed its implementation: the first antiviolence courts were slow to open their doors, and INAMUJER's promised nationwide provision of women's shelters was marred by delayed openings.

In 1994, during the Christian Democrat–dominated era of the Concertación coalition, Chile adopted the law Establishing Standard Procedures and Penalties for Acts of Violence Within the Family. Advocates considered this legislation unsatisfactory, given the leeway that judges had over the fate of abusers and its lack of criminal sanction. Under Bachelet, the executive took the side of feminist legislators, backing a significant revision to the legislation that provided for criminal sanction; it also established family courts to deal with domestic conflicts and new shelters, walk-in assistance, and counseling centers for battered women (Estrada 2007; Haas 2007).

On the issue of violence against women, legislative efforts have improved older statutes by incorporating a more feminist perspective. But in this area the state is far from taking the lead, as illustrated by Lula's dilatory action and Chávez's backsliding on fulfillment. Implementation depends on more hard work from advocates.

Reproductive Rights

In the area of reproductive rights, especially the lightning-rod issue of abortion, left governments seem unable to resist the strong opposition from the political Right and religious leaders. This is true in all four countries, despite a vocal regional reproductive-rights movement.

Although feminist and LGBT activists lobbied hard to use the 2007 constitutional convention in Venezuela to advance reproductive rights, women's ability to interrupt pregnancies in the first trimester was not included. Religious leaders joined with secular politicians in defeating this effort. In Bolivia some headway was made during the constitutional convention. The new constitution states that: "men and women are guaranteed the exercise of their sexual and reproductive rights" (Article 66), and an attempt to protect life from the moment of conception was unsuccessful (Friedman-Rudovsky 2007). Meanwhile, work on the Bolivian law on sexual and reproductive rights, passed by the previous legislature but not promulgated by the then president under pressure from the church, has been "frozen" in the legislature due to the shift in priorities to the contentious constitutional reform process (Coordinadora de la Mujer et al. 2007).

In Chile, Bachelet—who as health minister allowed the legalization of the so-called morning-after pill—decreed that all contraception, including this method, be provided free of charge in public clinics to all girls and women over the age of fourteen. This move was denounced by the Catholic Church and the Right. Right-wing politicians took the policy to the Constitutional Tribunal, claiming that the distribution order for the morning-after pill violated the constitution's protection of the right to life since the moment of conception. The tribunal ruled in their favor in April 2008, in a decision that cannot be appealed. Meanwhile, although Bachelet's party has stated its support for the decriminalization of therapeutic abortion, the political opposition to this measure has meant a stalemate (Rompiendo el Silencio 2008).

In Brazil the first National Conference on Policies for Women (2004) declared unsafe abortion to be a violation of women's human rights and called for decriminalization. Lula backed a law to that end, but during his second presidential campaign he told the Brazilian Conference of Bishops that he was personally against abortion. In the 2006 elections the Parliamentary Front to Defend Life campaigned for "God's List," a slate of candidates who answered a questionnaire on abortion, contraception, and LGBT rights in accordance with Vatican positions. They have also proposed the so-called rape benefit to provide child support to any woman who agrees to continue a pregnancy occurring after a rape and raise the child (Rede Feminista de Saúde 2008).[11]

The impact of more than a decade of Vatican-inspired social mobilization against abortion and many forms of contraception is evident. Often trying to balance demands of political allies on a topic that has been characterized as a matter of moral absolutes, left executives seem either unable or unwilling to back a policy that deeply challenges gender roles—and religious belief (Htun 2003, chap. 6, 168).

Sexual Rights

Although national legislation on sexual rights remains elusive in these countries, there is no denying that, in contrast with reproductive rights, significant national efforts are under way in this area. Like feminists, LGBT activists have made use of constitutional reform "openings," and certain executives have responded positively to their demands for human rights.

In Venezuela's first constitutional reform in 1999, the Catholic Church blocked the addition of a clause stipulating nondiscrimination on the basis of sexual orientation. Eight years later, the clause was included in the unsuccessful 2007 constitutional reform. In Bolivia the new constitution promises a radical shift in antidiscrimination policy: Article 14 states, "The State prohibits and punishes all forms of discrimination based on sexual orientation [and] gender identity." This radical development places Bolivia in the vanguard of constitutional protection of gender identity. However, the constitution's definition of marriage as between a man and a woman reflects the continued power of the Catholic Church.

During the second Concertación government, in 1998, the Chilean parliament repealed the section of the penal code that criminalized same-sex relations between consenting adults. Although there is parliamentary support for a civil unions bill, including the reiterated backing of Bachelet and her Socialist Party, the government has not made a concerted effort to promote it (Rompiendo el Silencio 2008). A Law to Establish Measures Against Discrimination remains frozen in the congress (Movimiento de Integración y Liberación Homosexual 2008). However, the Civil Registry now allows for name and sex changes without undergoing sexual reassignment surgery, and the Labor Bureau will investigate claims against unjust firing on the basis of homophobia or transphobia.

Lula's government has taken the most wide-ranging steps to fight homophobia and support LGBT rights, although legislative change remains elusive. His party has been instrumental in advancing civil union legislation at the federal level,[12] and in October 2003 pro-LGBT congressional deputies formed the Parliamentary Front for the Freedom of Sexual Expression. The Special Secretariat on Human Rights coordinates the federal Program to Combat Violence and Discrimination Against GLTB and Promotion of Homosexual Citizenship, known as "Brazil Without Homophobia"; its mandate covers health, public security, work, education, and citizenship. The federal government also sponsors the world's largest gay-pride march, held in São Paulo: more than 2 million people attended in 2007. In June 2008 the government put on the First National Conference of Gays, Lesbians, Bisexuals, Transvestites, and Transsexuals. In Lula's opening speech, which six of his ministers attended, he advocated national civil unions and described discrimination on the basis of sexuality as "perhaps the most perverse disease impregnated in the human head" in his call to criminalize homophobia (Picheta 2008, n.p.).

Brazil has also been at the forefront of international and regional action on sexual rights. The Brazilian delegation to the UN's Commission on Human Rights proposed the 2003 resolution on Human Rights and Sexual Orientation (E/CN.4/2003/L.92 2003), which called on member states and the UN itself to "promote and protect the human rights of all persons regardless of their sexual orientation."[13] The Special Secretariat for Human Rights has advocated strongly within MERCOSUR, the Southern Common Market, for state and regional action against discrimination, including the adoption of the international "Yogyakarta Principles" on the equal rights of sexual minorities (Movimiento de Integración y Liberación Homosexual 2008). In June 2008 Brazil presented

Resolution 2435, "Human Rights, Sexual Orientation, and Gender Identity," to the General Assembly of the Organization of American States. This resolution is the first inter-American document to "express concern" about human rights violations based on sexual orientation and gender identity and request further OAS discussion.

Both Lula and Bachelet have taken steps to recognize sexual rights, even as legislative action has proved impossible. Brazil is at the forefront, with Lula calling for the criminalization of homophobia and his government taking action both domestically and internationally. Venezuelan and Bolivian constitutional reforms promised antidiscrimination clauses, although with one reform stymied and the other just passed, it is unclear what impact they will have.

Seeking Rights from the Left: Advances and Challenges

The findings of this chapter reflect the historical record: having the Left in power makes a difference in some areas and not others. The Left has included grassroots women through attention to their "practical" interests and put more women into decision-making positions. But it has offered inconsistent support for policies challenging gender and sexual hierarchies.

In terms of gains, the attention paid to socioeconomic inequality, a hallmark of these governments, has had a positive effect on women and their families. "Participatory" democracies such as Venezuela and Bolivia, as they seek to include women in "twenty-first-century" socialist or indigenous nationalist projects, echo revolutionary experiences in Nicaragua and Cuba, and although not at the scale of their predecessors, they do rely on women's mobilization (Fernandes 2007a). They have also opened periodic opportunities for cross-class and cross-ethnic collaboration.

Meanwhile, the representative democracies of Chile and Brazil have used executive branch resources, such as their (relatively) powerful women's machinery, to advance rights when legislative avenues are closed. Here state feminism has been more effective at promoting feminist goals, pointing to the importance of three elements: feminist leadership inside the state, good relations between state and civil society actors, and finding common ground to build upon.

Left governments are less willing to undertake direct challenges to gender and sexual power relations in the face of religiously inspired opposition. The church-state politics of the twenty-first century do not follow predictable lines, as the actions of Daniel Ortega or even Lula da Silva indicate, and right-leaning politicians and civil society groups have been energized by their own transnational networks, whether Catholic or, increasingly, evangelical. The implementation of antiviolence statutes, with all they imply for disrupting familial hierarchies, is weak. The decriminalization (let alone legalization) of abortion faces implacable opposition and little executive support. Where executive support exists for sexual rights, legislatures are slow to move.

But the alliances that feminist, female, and LGBT activists have struck up over the past decades, as well as their transnational influences, continue to inform those seeking deeper transformation of left governance today. The human rights framework, which gained powerful meaning in the fight against authoritarianism, continues to provide a legitimating discourse and a basis for cooperation across movement arenas. LGBT activists' demands for nondiscrimination clauses in constitutions, or "the same rights with the same names" in their struggles for marriage equality, show their strategic use of the human rights framework. The transnational frame of women's rights as human rights was key to regionwide diffusion of antiviolence statutes. And even reproductive rights advocates have tried to use it, whether in the more neutral framing of reproductive rights as a "right to health," drawing directly from language formulated at the 1990s UN conferences, or the "right to abortion" demanded by some advocates.

Cooperation among feminist, women's, and LGBT organizations is a vital resource for advancing unmet demands, and mobilization around the Venezuelan and Bolivian constitutional reforms and antiviolence legislation has demonstrated this potential. A burgeoning network of reproductive and sexual rights activists continues to advocate for an inter-American convention on sexual rights and reproductive rights. Beyond these conjunctural opportunities, more sustained connection faces the twin challenges of larger state agendas and enduring crosscutting interests such as class, race, religion, and political orientation.

Notes

1. Although this chapter uses the acronym LGBT, it varies across countries and specific movements, reflecting the dynamics and demographics of local activist communities.

2. See, for example, the campaign for an Interamerican Convention on Sexual Rights and Reproductive Rights, http://www.convencion.org.uy/.

3. Information on LGBT movements is drawn from Mongrovejo 2000 and Babb 2003.

4. Chapter 8 offers an illustration.

5. Bolivia is excluded here since the data for the tables below were not available for any time after Morales's election; the Chilean data cover a time in which Bachelet's party, but not Bachelet herself, was in power.

The second half of this chapter draws extensively on my article "Gender, Sexuality, and the Latin American Left: Testing the Transformation" (*Third World Quarterly* 30 [2]). I would like to thank Amrita Basu for her helpful suggestions and Kathryn Jay for her editing assistance.

6. Chávez has named his political project after Simón Bolívar (1783–1830), the "liberator of South America," in part because of Bolívar's (ultimately unsuccessful) plan to unite the Andean region following the defeat of the Spanish.

7. See Chapter 8 for a more expansive discussion of the feminist movement.

8. See Chapter 8 for more detail on this agency and its interaction with feminist activists.

9. All the data on female representation are from Inter-Parliamentary Union 2008a.

10. See Chapter 8.

11. In Brazil, abortion is legal for victims of rape who become pregnant.

12. Although much recent policy on LGBT rights has been implemented at the subnational level in Brazil's federal system, this chapter is focused on change at the national level. For more detail, see Marsiaj 2006.

13. The lack of consensus on the resolution to promote LGBT human rights led the Brazilian government to withdraw its support two years later.

10

Toward a Culturally Situated Women's Rights Agenda: Reflections from Mexico

ROSALVA AÍDA HERNÁNDEZ CASTILLO

In this chapter, I share a series of reflections based on the Mexican experience on how to rethink women's rights by taking into account the cultural context of our feminist struggles, and thereby developing a gendered perspective that promotes cultural rights. These reflections emerge from several years of research on the organizing processes of indigenous women, as well as from my own experiences as a feminist activist seeking to build political alliances with the indigenous movements in Latin America.

During the past decades, the intensification of migratory flows from the South to the North and the emergence of important indigenous movements throughout the Americas have placed group rights at the center of debate and called into question universalist and liberal visions of citizenship. Demands for state recognition of cultural and collective rights, which recognize the multicultural character of nations, have reopened old anthropological debates on cultural relativism and universalism. At one end of these debates are actors who conceptualize culture as a homogenous entity of shared values and customs, without considering relations of power. At a political level, they often idealize the practices and institutions of non-Western cultures (echoing the Rousseauian ideal of the Noble Savage that the West continues to seek in its former colonies). At the other extreme are liberals who negate the rights of particular cultures and, in the case of Latin America, reject the right to autonomy for indigenous people. They reclaim values that appeal to universal citizenship rights in order to justify assimilationist and integrationist policies. Both of these visions, the essentialist and the

MEXICO

Human Development Index ranking: .829
Gender-Related Development Index value: .820
Gender Empowerment Measure value: .589

General

Type of government: Federal Republic
Major ethnic groups: Mestizo (60%); Indian (30%); White (9%); other (1%)
Language: Spanish
Religions: Roman Catholic (76.5%), Protestant (6.3%); other, unspecified, or none
(17.2%)
Date of independence: 1810
Former colonial power: Spain

Demographics

Population, total (millions), 2005: 104.3
Annual growth rate (%), 2005–2015: 1.0
Total fertility (average number of births per woman): 2.4
Contraceptive prevalence (% of married women aged 15–49): 74
Maternal mortality ratio, adjusted (per 100,000 live births), 2000: 60

Women's Status

Date of women's suffrage: 1947
Life expectancy: M 73.1; F 78
Combined gross enrollment ratio for primary, secondary, and tertiary education
(female %), 2005: 96.9
Gross primary enrollment ratio: 108[*]
Gross secondary enrollment ratio: 83
Gross tertiary enrollment ratio: 24
Literacy (% age 15 and older): M 93.2; F 90.2

Political Representation of Women

Seats in parliament (% held by women): 21.5
Legislators, senior officials, and managers (% female): 29
Professional and technical workers (% female): 42
Women in government at ministerial level (% total): 9.4

Economics

Estimated earned income (PPP US$), 2005: M 15,680; F 6,039
Ratio of estimated female to male earned income: .39
Economic activity rate (% female): 40.2
Women in adult labor force (% total): 35 (this figure obtained at the CEDAW Statis-
tical Database)

*Gross enrollment ratios in excess of 100% indicate that there are pupils or students outside
the theoretical age groups who are enrolled in that level of education.

ethnocentric, generate polarizations and leave indigenous peoples, who are the focus of this essay, unable to construct their own futures or to rethink their relationships to nation-states. However, other visions emerge from indigenous movements' political practices and daily acts of resistance that attempt to transcend the dichotomy between essentialism and ethnocentrism. These practices identify creative ways to rethink ethnic and gender identities and to construct a politics of cultural recognition that considers diversity within diversity, while at the same time promoting a culturally situated women's rights agenda.

In this chapter I first present a brief summary of the processes that gave rise to the indigenous women's movement in Mexico, and I describe the diverse political genealogies that influence a culturally situated feminist agenda. I then analyze the genesis of universal discourses on women's rights and examine how these have been globalized and institutionalized, specifically from my personal experiences with international foundations that grant fellowships to indigenous women. The chapter concludes with reflections of the processes of globalization from below that are emerging from organized indigenous women throughout the continent. These processes demonstrate that despite the economic and political power that lies beneath liberal and universalizing definitions of women's rights, indigenous women are contesting and resignifying these discourses and practices.

My focus is on indigenous women's struggles for more just relations between men and women based on definitions of personhood that transcend Western individualism. Their notion of equality identifies complementarity between genders as well as between humans and nature. It considers what constitutes a dignified life through a different understanding of people's relationship to property and to nature than liberal individualism's. This alternative perspective on women's rights, which reclaims indigenous *cosmovisiones*, or indigenous epistemologies, as spaces of resistance[1] and as tools to build gender justice, is being transnationalized by a continental movement of indigenous women, most notably as part of an international network called the Enlace Continental de Mujeres Indígenas (Indigenous Women's Continental Alliance). In this sense, we can point to an emerging form of cosmopolitanism (de Sousa Santos 1997) or transnationalism from below, which is confronting not only ethnocentric universalism but also globalization from above.

If we consider feminism as a body of social theories and political practices that analyze and seek to change the inequality between men and women, then this budding indigenous women's movement can be seen as a new indigenous feminism. Even though indigenous women have allied with wider women's movements, they do not—in most of the cases—define themselves as feminists. Most indigenous women associate feminism with urban middle-class women and consider feminism detrimental to their shared struggles with indigenous men. Although these preconceptions are starting to change and some indigenous women's groups in Mexico and some Mayan feminists from Guatemala (Hernández Castillo 2008) are beginning to identify with feminism, there is still a long way to go in building bridges between urban and indigenous feminists and indigenous women's organizations in Latin America.

This chapter is a call to heed the indigenous women's criticism and to contribute to the construction of political alliances. From local, national, and international standpoints, organized indigenous women's discourses and practices have come to challenge noninclusive perspectives of Latin American feminisms and to reveal the limitations of a political program based on liberal perspectives of equality and universalist notions of citizenship. Whether they adopt or reject the concept of feminisms, organized indigenous women have questioned our urban middle-class feminisms, leading us to reflect on the need to build a *politics of solidarity* based on establishing alliances that recognize and respect women's diverse interests.

Snakes and Ladders in the Road Toward a Feminist and Indigenous Women's Understanding

The 1970s represented a groundbreaking decade for Latin American feminist histories. The UN legitimized feminists worldwide demands by designating 1975 as International Women's Year and holding the first World Conference on Women in Mexico City. During this decade many countries had growing feminist movements that promoted the creation of a "cultural climate" that denaturalized oppression and violence against women. Mexico, however, was one of the few Latin American countries that fostered the development of *feminismo rural*, or civil feminism centered in rural work. This was a nonindigenous women's movement, composed of women from an urban background who chose to organize in rural areas as their life project and favored a dialogue with peasant and indigenous organizations, contributing to the future development of indigenous women's organizing.

It was during the 1970s peasant movements that feminist activists started to engage in grassroots work in rural areas of Mexico, both implementing projects for women and encouraging a gender consciousness among indigenous women. I and other members of my organization, COLEM,[2] were part of the generation whose feminism developed in dialogue with indigenous and peasant women throughout the country. Many of us were former leftist activists who were engaged in solidarity efforts supporting national liberation struggles in Central America and worked with popular and peasant groups in Mexico.

Based on our experience working with rural women, we believe that the feminist agendas should address the social and economic inequality that taints the lives of poor women. The history of Mexican feminism has been characterized by friction between those whose main struggle to confront gender inequality has been centered in the prochoice agenda and those who seek to build their feminist agenda upon a strategy aimed at challenging gender and class differences. This is one of the multiple obstacles that need to be overcome in order to build a truly representative national feminist movement.

Since the foundation of the Feminist Women's Coalition in 1976 and the creation of the Liberation and Rights for Women National Front in 1979, legalizing abortion and fighting against domestic violence have been the main demands of hegemonic feminism in Mexico. This feminism, essentially urban and academic—theorized from a scholarly perspective and built from the center of the country—has been hegemonic, not by virtue of commanding widespread legitimacy but by virtue of the support it has garnered in international circles, where popular and rural feminisms have been marginalized.[3] The history of these feminisms is yet to be written.

Even today, Mexican scholarly histories on feminism (Bartra 2002; Lamas 1992; Lamas et al. 1995; Lau 2002) talk about "popular feminisms" when describing urban nongovernmental organizations (NGOs) that supported poor urban or rural women's organizing during the 1980s, but disregard poor women who independently developed a critique of gender inequality. These women of popular sectors (urban or rural) are seen as passive, in need of feminist deliverance, and mobilized for exclusively short-range purposes.[4] Gisela Espinoza Damián, a major activist in grassroots feminism, states that "popular feminism should not be applied to non-governmental organizations, since it was poor urban women who forged that name and adopted that identity" (2009, 87). She recommends distinguishing *civil feminism* composed of civil organizations organized mostly by middle-class professionals who work with working-class sectors from *popular feminism* in which poor working-class women or peasant women engaged in their own gender struggles and collaborated with men both to challenge gender inequality and to reposition themselves to have a greater voice in broader social movements. Espinoza Damián does not include indigenous women as part of the *popular feminism* of the 1980s, because although they were organized around economic demands, it not was until the 1990s that they started to develop their own gender demands.

During the political fervor that characterized the women's movement in the 1980s there were several joint gatherings of indigenous, peasant, and working-class women; one was the First National Women's Meeting held in 1980 in

Mexico City. This was a groundbreaking event in the history of popular feminism, because it was the first time that women of popular sectors gathered to discuss gender and class inequality in their own terms. It was organized by Liberation Theology and feminist civic associations such as CIDHAL (Communication, Exchange, and Human Development in Latin America).[5] More than five hundred women from both rural and urban backgrounds attended the meeting. They discussed women's roles in and problems with popular movements. Indigenous peasant women from the states of Veracruz, Chiapas, Michoacán, and Morelos and from organizations such as the Emiliano Zapata Peasant Organization and Emiliano Zapata Peasant Union all participated in the meeting (Espinoza Damián 2009). In Chiapas, as part of the 1980s peasant movement, leftist activists and indigenous women from different parts of the state had a chance to interact at meetings, workshops, and conferences. Although formal deliberations centered on agrarian problems, women started to informally share ideas and experiences. Gender inequalities within families, communities, and organizations became conversation topics during meetings. During such dialogues, organization advisers, nuns linked to Liberation Theology, and activist scholars not only were witnesses and supporters but also actively developed their own feminist agenda, expanding the criticism against capitalist inequality and reflecting on gender and racial exclusion.

Each of the participants in these workshops and meetings brought her own specific vision of the struggle, produced from her own experience of what it means to be a *campesina*, or indigenous woman. The campesinas of the Emiliano Zapata Campesino Organization, the Independent Central for Agricultural Workers and Peasants, the Proletarian Organization Emiliano Zapata, and the Plan de Ayala National Coordination were principally interested in the fight for land, not just for the men but also for themselves and their daughters. The indigenous women of the Sierra, linked to organic co-ops, brought to the debate the importance of women's work in the promotion of sustainable development and shared their experiences with organic agriculture. The testimonies of many of the participants included the theme of domestic violence and their concern to develop strategies against it. In one of the *Memoirs* of these workshops, there is also concern about creating laws that recognize women rights, including the right to political participation:

> We want to participate in the making of laws which relate to us and our people. We want to participate in the meetings in order to be able to be elected and respected as having authority so that men listen to us because as women we can think and make decisions and we are equal in body and blood. We

want to discuss and analyze among ourselves the importance of being a woman and, together with other women, search for a revaluation of our condition as women and as indigenous peoples. We demand recognition and respect to our campesino and indigenous women organizations in all governmental bodies and programs.[6]

A landmark event that signified coalescence of a growing civic feminism and an indigenous women's movement was the First Indigenous and Peasant Chiapas Women's Meeting held in the city of San Cristobal de las Casas in 1986, summoned by scholars and activists from the Chiapas Autonomous University and the Chiapas Indigenous Healers Organization. Sonia Toledo and Anna María Garza, promoters and chroniclers of the event, tell us how popular education methodology was used to explore with indigenous women their own conceptions of body, sexuality, and suffering. This line of work, they say, "sought to build alternative relations to those prevalent in traditionally male-dominated organizations. In spite of our own inherited divisions between the advice-giver from the advised, these kinds of meetings helped create new dynamics of reflection and understanding. Women's political work and participation were assessed; expressing feelings and self-esteem were underlined" (Garza Caligaris and Toledo 2004, 213). In spite of the structural gap between professional and indigenous women, these dialogues marked both parties' organizational processes and political agendas.

As a result of such dialogues, a number of feminist civic organizations arose that gave priority to organizing and assisting indigenous and peasant women. My experience as a feminist started in one of these organizations, COLEM. This organization grew after a series of sexual crimes against women working in NGOs in 1988 and 1989 came to light. We were originally organized as a wide front against sexual and domestic violence but soon consolidated into a civic association with legal, schooling, and health activities, including workshops on gender consciousness.[7] Similar organizations emerged in other indigenous regions throughout the country. These included Comaletzin A.C., created in 1987, whose members fostered development with gender perspective among indigenous and peasant women in the states of Morelos, Puebla, Sonora, and Chiapas;[8] the Center for Research and Action for Women, created in 1989 to promote indigenous women's organizing in the Chiapas Highlands and among Guatemalan refugees;[9] Women for Dialogue, an association working in Veracruz and Oaxaca; and Women in Solidarity Action Team, working in Michoacán.[10] These pioneering organizations have been followed by several others that have joined a positive dialogue with indigenous women. For instance, K'inal Antzetik, the Indigenous Women National Coordination, and many other feminist organizations gathered in the National Rural Adviser's and Promoter's Network (Berrio Palomo 2008; Mejía Flores 2008).

The National Indigenous Women's Movement in Mexico: Reinventing Culture and Redefining the Nation

The emergence of an indigenous women's movement with gender demands is also the result of the Zapatista movement, which I will describe after providing some background on indigenous organizing. It is impossible to understand the present force of the indigenous women's movements without taking into account their experiences in the indigenous and peasant struggles of the past three decades.

From the 1970s onward, an important indigenous movement emerged in Mexico and started to challenge the official discourse on the existence of a homogeneous and mestizo nation. Alongside demands for land, cultural and political demands made an appearance that foreshadowed what would become the struggle for autonomy of the indigenous peoples. At the same time, important changes were taking place in the household economy, and new spaces for collective reflection emerged into which indigenous women were incorporated.

In the case of Chiapas, the Indigenous Congress of 1974 is considered a turning point in the history of the indigenous peoples. Beginning with that meeting, in which Tzotziles, Tseltales, Choles, and Tojolabales[11] participated, cultural demands were added to the peasant demands for a just distribution of land. Although academic work on the indigenous movement of that time does not mention the participation of women, from testimonies of participants we know that they took charge of the "logistics" for many of the marches, demonstrations, and encounters described in these works. The role of logistic supporters for the land struggle continued to exclude women from decision making and active participation in the organizations, although it did allow them to meet and share their experience with indigenous women from other parts of the state.

While women actively participated in peasant mobilizations, some changes in household economy took place in the 1970s that resulted in an increased participation of women in the informal trade in agrarian and craft products in local markets. It would be impossible to understand the broader political movements without taking into account the local developments that affected the indigenous households. In a context of land scarcity, the "petrol boom" of the 1970s prompted the migration of many indigenous men from Chiapas, Oaxaca, Tabasco, and Veracruz to the oil fields, leaving their women in charge of the household. The process of monetarization of the indigenous economy may have had a disempowering effect on women in the household, arguably decreasing the significance of their domestic labor for the reproduction of the labor force (Collier 1994; Flood 1994). For many women, however, changes in the household economy were fraught with contradictions, because while their position within the household changed, their incorporation in informal trade activities brought them into contact with other indigenous and mestiza women through the creation of cooperatives that in the course of time became spaces for collective reflection (Nash 1993).

The Catholic Church, through its priests inspired by Liberation Theology, also played a major role in the creation of spaces for reflection, above all in the areas of influence of the San Cristobal Diocese (in Chiapas), Oaxaca and Tehuantepec (Oaxaca), and Tlalpa (Guerrero). Although Liberation Theology did not promote reflection on gender relations, the courses and workshops on social inequality and racism in mestizo society led indigenous women to question the gender inequalities they suffered in their communities.

In Chiapas in the beginning of the 1980s, a group of nuns began to support this type of reflection and supported the creation of the Women's Area in the San Cristobal Diocese. This encounter between nuns and indigenous women gave rise to the Coordinadora Diocesana de Mujeres (Diocese Coordination of Women), one of the most important spaces for the organization of indigenous women in Chiapas (Hernández Castillo 2008). With their organizational experience and their reflections on gender relations, these women have played a key role in the broader women's movement. Migration, organizational experience, religious groups, feminist nongovernmental organizations, and even official development programs have influenced the ways in which indigenous men and women have restructured their relations within the household and have reframed their strategies of struggle.

After the appearance of the Zapatista National Liberation Army on January 1, 1994, a set of laws were made public, including the Revolutionary Woman's Law published in *El Despertador Mexicano*, the informational bulletin of the Zapatistas.[12] Various testimonies indicate that the law was the product of a long process of consultation among Zapatista communities. Subcommander Marcos referred to this law as the "first Zapatista uprising," when chronicling the passing of the law in March 1993, and pointed out how the law challenged the traditional norms governing indigenous relationships:

> In March 1993 we were discussing what would later become the revolutionary laws. . . . Susana [a Zapatista commander] had the job of visiting dozens of communities to talk to women's groups and gather the content for the women's law. When the CCRI [the main Zapatista headquarters] met to vote on the

passing of the laws, the commissions passed to the front one by one— the justice commission, the agrarian law commission, war taxes commission, rights
and responsibilities commission, and the women's commission. Susana had to
read out the proposals she had written from the thoughts of thousands of indigenous women. . . . She began to read, and as she read, the CCRI assembly
grew restless. Voices whispered in Chol, Tzeltal, Tzotzil, Tojolabal, Mam, Zoque
and *Castilla*. Comments flew from one end to the other. Susana did not falter;
she went on, tearing down everything and everybody: "We don't want to be
made to marry someone we don't want. We want to have the number of children we decide we can raise. We want the right to hold posts in the community. We want the right to speak and have our words respected. We want the
right to go to school and even to be chauffeurs, if we choose." She continued
until she was finished. There was a heavy silence. The Women's Revolutionary Law that Susana had just read meant a real revolution for indigenous communities. . . . That is the truth: the first Zapatista uprising was in March 1993,
and was led by Zapatista women. There were no losses, and they won. Such
things happen in this land. (*La Jornada*, January 30, 1994)

The Revolutionary Woman's Law has had a very important political effect
in making public the gender demands shared by many indigenous women in
Mexico. Although not all indigenous women know this law in detail, its existence has become a symbol of the possibility of a better life for women.

Since the Zapatista uprising, indigenous women in various regions of Mexico have started to raise their voices, not only to support the demands of their
companions or to represent the interests of their communities but also to demand respect for their specific rights as women. Alongside their participation
in the struggle for land and democracy, a great number of indigenous women
have begun to demand that the construction of more democratic relations be
extended to relations inside the household, the community, and the organization. The emergence of this new indigenous women's movement is the expression of a long process of organization and reflection in which both Zapatista
and non-Zapatista women took part. Under the influence of Zapatismo, a nationwide movement—still incipient and not without contradictions—emerged
for the first time articulating local initiatives to incorporate gender demands in
the political agenda of the indigenous movement. In 1997, during the National
Encounter of Indigenous Women, "Constructing Our History," seven hundred
women from different parts of the country created the Coordinadora Nacional
de Mujeres Indígenas (National Coordination of Indigenous Women). It provides a national-level network that brings together some twenty indigenous

peoples in the states of Chiapas, Michoacán, Morelos, the Federal District, Guerrero, Hidalgo, Jalisco, Estado de México, Puebla, Querétaro, San Luis Potosí, Sonora, Veracruz, and Oaxaca.[13]

Indigenous women who took part in these organizing efforts have adopted the Zapatista Revolutionary Woman's Law for their own political efforts. This law recognizes women's rights to hold public office, inherit land, and make decisions about their bodies, rights that usually defy local tradition. As Margara Millan (2008) has stated, this law challenges the core of patriarchal domination because it removes family heads' control over their daughters' spouse selection and material resources, especially the land, and thereby create local spaces of power for women. This law has gained a symbolic significance not only for Zapatista women, but for many other indigenous women as well, who feel that demands they had been stressing for some time are now legitimized.

While these women have organized within their own communities to change traditions and community structures that exclude them, they also claim the right to their own culture and traditions. Within the new spaces formed under the influence of the Zapatistas, indigenous women have adopted their people's self-determination demand, while simultaneously critically challenging their communities and organizations from inside.

The National Coordination of Indigenous Women has been fundamental in the promotion of a gender perspective within the indigenous movement. The voices of many of their members are heard in the National Indigenous Congress (CNI). In the national debate over the proposal for reform of the constitution, they were prominent in challenging the static representations of tradition and vindicated the right to *cambiar permaneciendo y permanecer cambiando* (the expression, "to change while remaining and to remain while changing," refers to their will to maintain their indigenous identity and at the same time to maintain their work for changing gender roles).

In contrast to women in the national feminist movement, indigenous women have maintained a double struggle, knitting together their campaign for specific gender demands and the autonomy struggles of their peoples, and have continued to militate in the National Indigenous Congress. This double militancy, however, has met with multiple resistances, both from the feminist movement and from the indigenous movement. For many feminists, the indigenous woman's demands for indigenous autonomy and for the recognition of collective rights are considered a danger for the advancement of women's rights, and to the indigenous movement, their criticism of gender exclusion and patriarchal domination are seen as divisive. I think, however, that both movements actually benefited from this double militancy: the feminists were forced to incorporate cultural diversity in their analysis of gender relations, and the indigenous movement had to incorporate gender in its analysis of the ethnic and class inequalities suffered by indigenous peoples.

Mexican academic feminism, influenced by anthropologists in the 1980s, incorporated contextual diversity in its perspectives on gender relations and recognized that "the asymmetry between men and women means different things in different places. Therefore, the position of women, their activities, their possibilities and the limitations they encounter vary from culture to culture" (Lamas 1986, 184). However, this recognition did not result in an inclusionary feminist agenda that took into account the specific needs of indigenous women. As I have pointed out, the agenda of the national feminist movement has centered on demands regarding voluntary motherhood and recognition of reproductive rights, and the struggle against sexual violence and for the rights of lesbians and homosexuals, and it has not included the criticism of class inequality and racism (Tuñon 1997). Although some of these demands are shared by the indigenous women's movement (above all those regarding reproductive rights and the struggle against violence), this movement adds economic and cultural demands that are the product of the experiences of racism and exploitation that shaped their gender identities. We therefore can criticize hegemonic Mexican feminism in ways similar to Judith Butler's critique of homophobia in North American academic feminism when she argues, "Any feminist theory that restricts the meaning of gender to the suppositions of its own practice establishes exclusionary gender norms inside feminism, often with homophobic [in our case ethnocentric] consequences" (2001, 9).

Even my own organization, which, like other rural feminist organizations that from the 1980s onward have been working with indigenous women, has done so on the basis of our own feminist agenda and our own definitions of gender and self-esteem that derived from our own experience. In the 1990s processes of self-critique and reframing of working methods began, and the constructive dialogue with organized indigenous women became fundamental to such processes.[14] As a result of these dialogues with organized indigenous women, some of the members of feminist organizations working in rural areas have started to discuss an antiracist agenda in different feminists arenas, although in spaces that are still very marginal and have not yet impacted the main political agenda of the national feminist movement.[15] The feminist methodology that we have been working with, alongside other women who are academic colleagues and activists who identify as rural feminists, is based on questioning the homogenizing, generalizing perspectives of patriarchy and what "women's interests" are considered to be. By rejecting the idea of a preexisting homogeneous collective subject ("women") and by considering any collectivity to be the product of alliances between those who are different, we are presented with the challenge of building a political agenda on the basis of dialogue and negotiation. Within this task, research has a great deal to contribute in terms of knowledge and recognition of the cultural and historic specificities of social subjects. In contrast with the action research of the 1970s, this feminist proposal is not based on the premise that we have some historic truth to share but rather has the purpose of creating a space for dialogue with other women—through research and organizational work—to discuss and analyze the different conceptions and experiences of subordination and resistance. Here, I would venture to borrow the concept of *dialogical anthropology* developed by Dennis Tedlock (1990), referring to a new form of conducting ethnography in which dialogue is fundamental for text development and which proposes that the researcher is included and recognized as part of the dialogue established with those being studied. Taking this proposal beyond textual strategies, I would suggest that it can be applied to a new way of interacting in the field with social actors.

The feminist dialogical anthropology we are proposing, unlike coparticipatory research, does not intend to transform reality on the basis of a method or theory considered to be infallible. Rather, together with the social actors we work with, we seek to reflect upon and deconstruct the issues in a shared social reality—and to jointly develop a research agenda based on these dialogues that makes our knowledge relevant for those social actors.

New representations of indigenous women as active political agents who construct their own history emerged in the Mexican social sciences since the 1990s, and particularly after 1994 (see Garza Caligaris 2002; Hernández Castillo 1994, 1996; Marcos 1997; Millán 1996; Sierra 2004; and Speed, Hernández Castillo, and Stephen 2006), rejecting the tendency to construct indigenous women as passive subjects and victims of patriarchy or capitalism. It is in this theoretical reframing of the gender concept as a multidimensional category and the recognition that ethnicity and class matter that the input by indigenous women has been of fundamental importance. Their voices resonate in the documents that come out of encounters, workshops, and congresses and in articles written by and interviews with indigenous women that are published in feminist magazines and the national press.[16]

Parallel to this dialogue with feminism, indigenous women have maintained their exchanges with the national indigenous movement, in which they actively participate through the CNI. There they have confronted the idyllic imagery of indigenous culture that saturates the political discourse of many CNI members, indigenous leaders, and their advisers.

Although we can understand that during certain phases in the development of social movements an essentialist discourse that idealizes *"lo propio"* (what is ours) and excludes the "alien," as in the initial radical segregation of the feminist movement, may emerge, experience has taught us that such strategies only bring isolation and cancel the possibilities for forging political alliances. On many occasions indigenous women have indicated these dangers and have opted to vindicate the historic and malleable character of their cultures and to condemn those "uses and customs" that offend their dignity. Their struggle is not one for the recognition of an essentialized culture but for the right to reconstruct, confront, and reproduce that culture, not on the terms established by the state but on the terms established by the indigenous peoples themselves in the context of their own internal plurality.

In relation to the state, indigenous women are questioning those hegemonic discourses that continue to call for the permanence of a monocultural national identity. At the same time, in relation to their own communities and organizations, they are expanding the concept of culture by questioning static visions of tradition and striving for its reinvention.

The proposals and experiences of organized indigenous women point to new possibilities for rethinking the politics of cultural recognition from a gendered perspective. Their proposals go beyond liberal universalism, which in the name of equality negates the right to cultural differences, and beyond cultural relativism, which in their defense of the right to difference justifies the exclusions and marginalization of women.

Is the Recognition of Cultural Rights
Bad for Indigenous Women?

Indigenous organized women in Mexico, who have decided to participate in the political struggles for indigenous autonomy and for the recognition of collective rights, face this central question of cultural rights and women. This idea has generated quite some debate in the United States and in Europe, and it is a matter of concern in the United Nations when attempts are made to reconcile international legislation on indigenous rights with international legislation on women's rights. Political scientist Susan Moller Okin brought together a group of social scientists with different views on multiculturalism to debate the potential implications of the recognition of the collective rights of "minorities" for women. She argues that there is a strong tension between multiculturalism and feminism because the former is based on the vindication of ethnic minority cultures, whereas the latter is based on a critique of patriarchy regardless of culture. She argues that the women of such ethnic minorities, which in many cases in fact are majorities in their countries, "may be better off if the culture into which they were born is extinguished (through the integration of its members into a less sexist national culture)" (1999, 23).

Such ethnocentric feminism fails to scrutinize the problematic relation between liberalism and feminism because it starts from the simple assumption that liberalism has brought greater equity to women than these "minority" cultures in which women continue to be subjected to forced marriages, polygamy, genital mutilation, segregation, the veil, and political exclusion, to mention a few of the "backward" practices the author lists as mechanisms of control over and oppression of women. Feminists from India, like Chandra Mohanty (1991) and Lata Mani (1998), have respond to representations like those by Okin and the Mexican critics of indigenous rights by pointing out that portraying "third world" women (in our case indigenous women) as simple victims of patriarchy is a form of discursive colonialism that fails to appreciate how these women have created spaces of their own according to their own cultural dynamics.[17] The liberal feminist critique of multiculturalism assumes ingenuously that a "minority" culture is the culture vindicated by the hegemonic sectors within that culture and fails to see that the practices and discourses of contestation developed by women are also part of the cultures for which respect is demanded. They also assume that they know how gender inequality functions in any society, without bothering themselves with specific contexts or histories, and then they think that on the basis of such knowledge they possess the key to the liberation of their "sisters" from the so-called third world.

In Mexico the new indigenous women's movement that arose under the influence of Zapatism has set itself the task of reframing the demands for recognition of the multicultural character of the nation; it did so in the context of a broadened definition of culture that does not stop at its hegemonic representations and voices but instead reveals the diversity within and the contradictory processes that give meaning to the life of a human collectivity. Instead of rejecting cultural diversity because it might give rise to practices that oppress and exclude them, indigenous women decided to engage in a struggle over the very meaning of difference. Their aim is to give "cultural identity" an emancipatory and nonexclusionary charge.

In their demands for indigenous collective rights, indigenous women have supported the recognition of collective rights over land and the right to their own customary law, considered as Indigenous Law (Derecho Indígena). Confronting the liberal critiques of Indigenous Law, which accuse it of being backward and antidemocratic, indigenous women have pointed out the dynamic character of their normative systems, which are continuously being reconfigured and which, in recent years, reflect the transformations and struggles these women have promoted. Two indigenous women, Comandante Esther, the Zapatista leader, and María de Jesús Patricio, a National Indigenous Congress representative, defended the constitutional reform that recognizes indigenous autonomy and Indigenous Law in their speeches before the Mexican Congress. They challenged the static representations of tradition that have been used to dismiss indigenous practices and customs, saying instead that the indigenous communities' normative systems are being reworked and that indigenous women are playing a fundamental role in that process. In this regard, María de Jesús Patricio pointed out, "We, the indigenous peoples, now recognize that there are practices that we should combat and others we should encourage and this is seen in the more active participation of women in the decisions of our community. Today, we women participate more in the decisions of the assemblies; today we are chosen to hold positions; and in general, we participate more in community life." Comandante Esther focused on enumerating the inequalities and exclusions that the current legislation permits. She argued that the constitutional reform that Zapatista women were demanding would serve to "allow us to be recognized and respected, as women and as indigenous persons—our rights as women are included in that law, since now no one can impede our participation or our dignity and integrity in any endeavor, the same as men" (*La Jornada*, April 3, 2001, 9).

Their demands for recognition of a culture that itself is in a process of change thus converge with the ideas put forward by some critical feminists regarding a politics of difference that does not mean exclusionary alterity or opposition but rather specificity and heterogeneity and where differences between groups are conceived in relational terms instead of defined by essential categories or attributes (Minow 1990; Young 1989). At the same time that we are witnessing the emergence of an indigenous feminist agenda, we are also seeing the imposition of a women's rights agenda that does not consider the specific cultural context in which indigenous women are developing their own political strategies.

Women's Rights as Globalized Localism

On June 25, 1993, United Nations member-state representatives gathered in Vienna during the World Human Rights Conference. There they agreed to include as a human rights violation any violation of women's specific rights. Women's participation and initiative during this conference pushed forward a transcendental change in human rights theory, since it was established that human rights should be enjoyed in the private sphere as well as in the public, and, thus, there could be human rights violations in both as well. Before this point, the system recognized only those violations committed by the state within the social and political realms. Since this historical decision was made, acts done by citizens within the private sphere can generate state responsibility.

This decision was celebrated by feminist organizations throughout the world as a necessary step in the universalization of women's rights. In the Mexican city of San Cristobal de las Casas, in the heart of the Tzotzil region in the Chiapas Highlands, a small support group for women and children run by the feminist organization I worked with at the time celebrated the good news. That same year we came across a copy of a video called *The Vienna Tribunals*, in which women from all parts of the world gave testimony to shocking rights violations. Their different stories told us about rape within the domestic sphere, genital mutilations, forced marriage, domestic violence—the experience of patriarchal domination and violence brought together women from all over the world who claimed that their specific rights be recognized as human rights. This film became a keystone of our workshops on women's rights. Although *The Vienna Tribunals* moved me to tears, there was some uniformity in the voiced-over narration about patriarchy as a universal oppression and exclusion system that made me feel a little uncomfortable. My training as an anthropologist told me that comparing the raping of a woman in the United States with the forced marriage of a peasant in Africa was a parallelism that left too much context and history out.

The Vienna Tribunals could have easily influenced Mary Daly's classic work *Gyn/Ecology: The Metaethics of Radical Feminism* (1978). In this book Daly guides us through different parts of the world, describing assorted practices like incest and suttee, female genital mutilation, and rape, all of which, according to her, have the same origin: male patriarchal domination over women. Audre Lorde's criticism in "An Open Letter to Mary Daly" already showed in 1984 the lack of a context necessary to analyze African cultural practices, the reductionism of culture to patriarchal practices, and the silencing of other elements such as racism and colonialism.

My intuition and discomfort toward generalizing discourses on the effects of patriarchal domination over women's lives became clearer after listening to our Tzotzil friends' responses when confronted by my feminist coworkers about "the selling of brides" in indigenous communities. The term *selling of brides* was used by our feminist organization to denounce forced marriages that included the ritual exchange of gifts between families as part of traditional wedding arrangements. Even though several of these women were struggling within their families and communities in order to win the right to choose whom to marry for the younger generations, the idea of "selling women" seemed offensive and disrespectful to them and their families. In spite of the good intentions of our feminist practice, our universalistic discourses did not always resonate among those indigenous women we meant to rescue from patriarchal cultures.

Considering Boaventura de Sousa Santos's theoretical proposals (1997, 1998), I would like to examine the different ways in which women's rights discourses and practices have played a role as globalized localisms (that is, local knowledge that has been globalized), inasmuch as they strive to impose visions of a free and rational individual, the legal person, as well as conceptions of freedom and liberty whose roots lie in a particular time and space: the European Enlightenment. In this sense they can be considered as local knowledge that has been successfully globalized.

At the end of World War II the cause of human rights gained worldwide attention due to the Nazi genocide and to the large number of political prisoners and exiles. This was the context in which the Universal Declaration of Human Rights was approved in 1948. Since then, it has become a sword with many edges against the disposed that it was meant to protect. Because it was built without the contribution of most countries and failed to recognize group rights, its emancipatory character was uncertain from the start. The concept of human rights became globalized after this declaration, and it substituted the original concept in the original draft of the *Universal Rights of Man*.

A little-known fact is that four women signed the Universal Declaration of Human Rights: Minerva Bernardino from the Dominican Republic, Bertha Lutz from Brazil, Virginia Gildersleeves from the United States, and Wu Yi-Tang from China. This illustrious quartet struggled so that women would be considered in the declaration and also for women's incorporation as political officers of the UN. To some extent, they were also responsible for the fact that the concept of "Rights of Man" was at the end substituted by that of "Human Rights," making the declaration more inclusive.

In spite of the good intentions that might have moved the sponsors of the UN Charter, the political context in which it was written determined its double standard use according to hegemonic states' interests. During the cold war, the human rights declaration became a tool to justify U.S. intervention in domestic affairs of countries that did not comply with its interests. Such was the case with the direct intervention of the U.S. government in the overthrowing of Jacobo Arbenz's progressive government in Guatemala in 1954.

Recognizing the probable political misuse of human rights, the Executive Committee of the American Anthropological Association (AAA) prepared a document questioning the colonialist character of the declaration a year before it was approved. The document, submitted to the UN Human Rights Commission, argued that the assumed superiority of Western values had already been used as an excuse to justify control and domination over millions of people throughout the world. Accordingly, it stated, "How can the proposed Declaration be applicable to all human beings, and not be a statement of rights conceived only in terms of the values prevalent in the countries of Western Europe and America?" (1947, 539).

There are some human rights advocates like Karen Engle who refer to the AAA statement as an example of the "expression of unlimited tolerance" that characterizes cultural relativists and as one of the "historical discredits" of contemporary anthropology (2001, 542). Nevertheless, recent fieldwork carried out by scholars like Shannon Speed and Jane Collier (2000) in the Chiapas Highlands illustrates how the Mexican government has used human rights as a tool to limit the autonomy of indigenous people. Likewise, Sally Engle Merry (2003), through her ethnographic analysis of international organizations trying to understand cultural conceptions, has revealed to us how a limited and essentialist conception of culture, thought of as customs and traditions, has been used to *culturalize* conflicts and inequalities in so-called third world countries.[18] If cultural practices that generate gender exclusion, for example, are not understood in historical context, then the wider economic and political structure that feeds and gives meaning to them becomes obscured. At the same time that she explains how gender inequalities are *culturalized*, Engle Merry demonstrates how practices and conceptions of international organizations are being universalized after being deculturalized.

The same culturalizing and deculturalizing mechanisms have been present in feminist groups and international organizations in regards to women's human rights. Ever since 1979, when the UN assembly approved the Convention for the Elimination of All Forms of Discrimination Against Women, there has been a tendency to see women's rights as opposing cultural practices, deculturalizing the former and simplifying the latter.

Latin American states have played an important role in this gender-inequality-culturalizing process and the deculturalization of women's rights discourses with the contribution of feminist NGOs. The modernizing development discourse has blamed indigenous cultures for women's exclusion, while presenting development and women's rights as a *deculturalized* alternative.

Women's rights as "globalized localisms" have been promoted by nation-states as part of their programs to incorporate women in development while at the same time complying with international commitments to implement public policies that promote gender equality. The underlying logic of most state programs aimed at rural and indigenous women is that development—as a universal, not culturally situated, process—would move forward more hastily if women were a part of it instead of wasting their time unproductively. In the Mexican case the politics has focused on individuals, promoting access to credit and employment as means that would allow women to merge into the development process.

The United States Agency for International Development has been an important vehicle to globalize the women's rights agenda linked to the Women in Development perspective. The underlying logic of this perspective is that women are a barren resource that could contribute profitably to development (see Kabeer 1998). Under the influence of this sort of global discourses, to grant rights to women is part of assimilating them to the development process as a civilizing horizon of all humanity, while, on the other hand, local cultures "hinder development and exclude women."

Gender Hierarchy in Women's Rights: Complicities and Disappointments

In May 2004 I made the mistake of being part of a panel of reviewers, set up by international organizations and feminist NGOs, to allocate grant funds. Unfortunately, if you look closely, these committees turn out to be tribunals that judge poor women in third world countries. They investigate whether these women have and are working in accord with a "real" gender agenda, at least enough to receive such funding. But unlike the "Vienna Tribunals" these public judgments are not recognized as trials run by specialists that evaluate the projects offered to them, nor do we see that the power roles we play and our imposition of principles parallel the court system. At the time, the international financing was funneled through a Mexican feminist nongovernmental organization with a very high reputation, offering scholarships to indigenous women involved in sexual and reproductive rights issues in their home regions.

Perhaps naively, I thought that by partaking in these activities, I could bend the trend in the construction of wider, less ethnocentric definitions of women's rights. So I accepted the NGO's invitation to be a part of the board of specialists that would evaluate applications. The interviews and project presentations took place in a luxury hotel on the outskirts of Mexico City. Indigenous women from all over the country traveled there to make a public defense of their projects. The six reviewers were feminists: some academics, some activists. None of us were indigenous, and most were from Mexico City. Sitting in a semicircle beside the NGO's board of directors and the international funding agency's regional head, we began interviewing applicants.

One by one the indigenous women stood in front of the jury. Some spoke perfect Spanish, some a kind of pidgin, mixing Spanish with their own languages.

Some explained their projects using paperboards prepared in advance, and others preferred laptops and PowerPoint presentations while answering our questions. Then it was Amanda's turn, a Nahua woman from southern Veracruz with fifteen years of experience working as a health promoter. She chose the paperboard to explain the importance of traditional medicine for indigenous women's self-care, holistic concepts of traditional medicine on health, and the importance of rescuing them for the sake of women's health. The head executive of the financing agency, somewhat weary about the absence of women's reproductive rights references, interrupted and asked straightforwardly, "How do you define reproductive health? What has your project to do with women's reproductive rights?" Puzzled by the interruption, Amanda answered with a standard definition that she might have read in the scholarship-promotion brochures. The executive dashed back with another question: "What do you think of abortion?" Amanda was now bewildered and kept silent. So another question came through: "Do you think indigenous women have a right to decide about their bodies?" Amanda tossed back a different question: "Decide over what?" The executive seemed annoyed by the lack of sound answers. The rest of us sat silently, witnesses to evident bullying. "What do you know about feminism?" "Well," answered Amanda slowly, "I believe that it is good that we women have rights, but I don't agree with feminists that fight against men and want to separate both worlds." "Which feminists are those?" retorted the executive. "Can you name one?" Amanda was about to break into tears when I decided to question the "power performance" that we were watching, so I interrupted, saying I thought that she was mistaken about the place and the person to ask such questions, and added that "I could provide a long list of intolerant and secluding feminists." Amanda received the scholarship, and fortunately I was never again called for jury duty. Amanda's experience with reproductive rights scholarships is living proof of the ways that international organizations are influencing indigenous women's gender agendas, validating some struggles and invalidating others. National feminist organizations have been accessories to these impositions, giving way to a gender agenda that has reproductive rights, and particularly the right to abortion and birth control, as its core.

I do not mean to deny the importance of reproductive rights, but we must agree that after the International Reunion on Women and Health held in Amsterdam in 1984, the wider definitions of reproductive rights that included the right to economic and social conditions that favored women's health were replaced by a regulatory definition that narrowed the concept to birth control and abortion rights. In fact, third world feminists such as Shu-Mei Shi and Sylvia Marcos have drawn attention to the power networks underlying reproductive health discourse, its silences, and its limitations, stating that "the global women's health movement has focused its agenda to reproductive rights, as if other women's health issues lacked importance. Poor women are dying of malnutrition and diseases that are curable if proper medical care is provided. They lack many other things that are required for wellbeing and survival" (2005, 147). Also, "the most extreme negative implication of demographic control through the reproductive rights rhetoric is that it is tantamount to the old imperialist eugenics paradigm. While developed countries are promoting higher birth rates due to the aging of their population, in underdeveloped or developing countries reproduction is controlled in the name of women's 'right to chose' over their bodies" (ibid., 148).

At the same time that liberal definitions of women's rights are globalized and presented as universal, the U.S. government uses the same discourses to justify military intervention in countries whose "patriarchal and antidemocratic cultures" infringe women's rights. Charles Hirschkind and Saba Mahmood (2002) have analyzed the responsibility of the U.S. government in strengthening and consolidating the mujahideen in Afghanistan, and the Bush administration's subsequent justification of military intervention in Afghanistan in the name of supporting women's rights. Similar arguments have been used by the Mexican government and by national power groups to deny political rights to indigenous peoples. Faced with a growing indigenous movement that demands a constitutional reform that truly recognizes autonomy rights for Indian peoples, politicians and academics, who had never before written a line or spoken about indigenous women's gender inequality, suddenly showed great concern that indigenous legal systems might contravene women's rights. Fortunately, indigenous women's organizations have confronted such fixed representations of tradition and their use to disqualify their customs. They have argued that indigenous normative systems are currently being reviewed and that women are playing an important part in this process (see Sierra 2004; and Sierra and Hernández 2005).

Indigenous women's movements fight two fronts: on the one hand, they demand the recognition of their self-determination rights as indigenous people by the state, and on the other, they struggle in their own communities and organizations to transform their own legal systems. Nevertheless, in April 2001 Mexican deputies and senators decided to combat "the threats of traditions and customs" in order to "defend women's rights" by limiting autonomy and local conflict-resolution mechanisms through a limited legal reform on cultural recognition. The so-called Indigenous Rights and Culture Law left out the right of indigenous people to control their own territory and established a bondage mechanism that forces native authorities to have their decisions validated by state judges and tribunals.[19] Indigenous women never asked for any such protection that restricted indigenous autonomy. On the contrary, they demanded the right to self-determination and the protection of their culture. But at the same time they have challenged their own people to redefine the meaning of tradition and custom and their right to take part in the formation of alternative autonomic projects.

Reproposing Women's Human Rights: Globalization from Below

The lived experiences of indigenous women in Mexico are not isolated experiences. Throughout the past decade on the American continents, organized indigenous women have attempted to combine the political and cultural demands of their peoples with their own gender demands. It is in these spaces that they are proposing new conceptualizations of women's rights based on greater holistic perspectives, which encompass relationships between men and women and between humankind and nature.[20]

In 1992 the five hundredth year anniversary of the invasion of America presented an opportunity for women throughout the continent to meet and share their experiences of exclusion and of struggle as part of the indigenous movements of their countries. After the first Continental Gathering of Indigenous Women (the first held in Quito, Ecuador; the second in Mexico in 1997; and the third in Panama in 2000) as well as the Summit of Indigenous Women in the Americas (held in 2002 in Oaxaca, Mexico, and in Peru in 2005), many of these women opted for constructing their own spaces, independent of the national indigenous movements and all of the feminist movements of their countries, and later invited indigenous women's groups from other continents to participate. In this context the Continental Alliance of Indigenous Women emerged, where the indigenous peoples of Latin America converge with those of the United States and Canada. Within this continental movement, indigenous women have shared and complemented two different worlds of meaning: demands posed in terms of women's rights and demands posed in terms of indigenous worldviews (*cosmovisiones*) that generate a more integrated perspective of social subjects' relationship to their surroundings.

In the same vein as the concept of *dharma* of the Hindu culture and the *humma* of the Islamic culture, as analyzed by Boaventura de Sousa Santos (1997, 49–50), which establish relationships between the part (the individual) and the totality (the cosmos), the perspectives of equity and equilibrium linked to social justice for women, as claimed by a sector of the indigenous women's continental movement, speak to a local construction that confronts, and at other times complements, the global discourse on women's rights.

On many occasions indigenous women's discourses that claim the existence of an indigenous epistemology have been classified as essentialist and been delegitimized by nonindigenous academics and activists, who have failed in large part to explore the possibilities that these discourses can hold for people whose cultures and identities have been negated by processes of colonization. Some feminist academics have been particularly critical of these discourses for the ways in which certain men of indigenous movements in Latin America appropriate the concept of *complementarity* to represent an idealized version of their cultures and societies, hence ignoring the existence of power relationships between genders. However, from another perspective, indigenous women are reclaiming the concept of *complementarity* in order to critique and question the ways in which indigenous men are reproducing colonizing relationships of power that contrast to the Mesoamerican cultural principles of duality.

The ethnocentrism of academe and of feminist activism has prevented productive dialogues from surfacing with those indigenous women who reclaim the concept of *cosmovision*. The emancipatory potential that indigenous spirituality has for these women, as well as the ways in which the concepts point to different understandings of women's rights as part of the rights of their people, has been little explored.

Despite hegemonic feminism's resistances and rejections of culturally situated perspectives, indigenous women's proposals are beginning to find important spaces within the indigenous women's continent-wide movement. For example, these new voices played a central role in the first Summit of Indigenous Women in the Americas, held in the city of Oaxaca in 2002. The prepared documents rejected the concept of feminism and reclaimed the concepts of complementarity and duality as fundamental to understanding gendered relations: "This document does not share a feminist perspective, given that for indigenous peoples, our *cosmovision* values each being, and the concept of duality maintains great importance. We have to recognize that the influence of the cultures of the invaders have partially deteriorated this vision, in the role that women play in society, and it is for this reason that this principle is no longer reflected today and we suffer great social unbalances and inequalities. In an ever-changing world based on Western cultural models it has been difficult to maintain intact indigenous cultures" (Cumbre de Mujeres Indígenas de las Américas 2003, 126).

This explicit dissociation with feminism is based on a stereotype of feminists as separatists who are not concerned with political alliances, which informs many of the perspectives shared by popular women's movements and unfortunately continues to be reproduced by many feminists. The reluctance to understand the genesis of these political proposals and non-Western epistemologies, as well as the imposition of a feminist agenda that is insensitive to cultural diversity in Latin America, influences many indigenous women's rejection of the concept of feminism. Some Mayan women take this concept of cosmovision and spirituality in order to propose a concept of gender that implies the following:

> a respectful, sincere, equal, and balanced relationship—what in the West would be considered equity—of respect and harmony, in which both the man and woman have opportunities, without it presupposing additional responsibilities for the woman, but rather a facilitating element. Only then can one be well spiritually, with humankind, with the earth, the sky and those elements of nature that provide us with oxygen. . . . For that reason, when we talk of a gendered perspective, we are talking about the concept of duality based on an indigenous *cosmovision* in which all of the universe is ruled in terms of duality, this sky and the earth, happiness and sadness, night and day, and they complement each other—one cannot exist without the other. If we had ten days with only sun, we would die, we wouldn't be able to stand it. Everything is ruled in terms of duality, undoubtedly, men and women. (Estela, an indigenous woman from the Asociación Política de Mujeres Mayas, Moloj, Mayib' Ixoquib' [Political Association of Mayan women Moloj, Mayib' Ixoquib', Guatemala], cited in Gabriel Xiquín 2004)

It is evident that from these perspectives, the concept of complementarity does not serve as an excuse to avoid speaking about power and violence as part of gendered relations, but rather, on the contrary, becomes a tool to critique the colonizing attitudes of indigenous men and proposes the need to rethink culture from the perspective of gender equality. Each one of the principles and values is reclaimed by indigenous women as part of their cosmovision, and they are deemed fundamental to the construction of a just life for women.

In the memoirs of the First Summit of Indigenous Women in the Americas (Primera Cumbre de Mujeres Indígenas de las Américas) (Cumbre 2003), some of the main elements of this alternative epistemology are expressed in the following terms: In contrast to the stark individualism promoted by globalized capitalism, indigenous women reclaim the value of *"community:* by understanding this term as a life where people are intimately linked with their surroundings, under conditions of respect and equality, where nobody is superior to anybody." In contrast to predatory neoliberal development, they reclaim *"equilibrium:* which means to watch over the life and permanence of all beings in space and in nature. The destruction of some species affects the rest of beings. The rational use of material resources leads us toward balance and rectitude in our lives." In contrast to violence and domination of the strong over the weak, upon which is premised the liberal conception of survival of the fittest, they propose *"respect*: which is based on the indigenous concept of the elders being those who are most respected, an attitude that extends to all other beings in nature. The Earth is seen as a woman Mother and Teacher that conceives the sustenance of all beings. It is the equal treatment with other beings, under the same conditions." In contrast to the superiority of the masculine over the feminine, which is claimed by patriarchal ideologies, they propose *"duality or dualism*: in which the feminine and the masculine in a same deity are two energy forces found in one, which permit the balance of vision and action. They represent the integrity of everything which guides us toward complementarity. By considering the Supreme as dual, father and mother, one can act with gender equity. This attitude is basic for the eradication of machismo." In contrast to the fragmentation of the productive process promoted by *maquiladora [offshore contract manufacturers]* development, in contrast to the segregation of the labor force, in contrast to the fragmentation of collective imaginaries and the rejection of a systemic analysis that allow us to locate the links between different forms of struggle, they propose *"la cuatriedad*: which signifies the totality, a cosmic balance, that which is complete as represented by the four cardinal points, unity and the totality of the universe. By seeing both ahead and behind, by seeing to the sides, it is possible to struggle for unity. It is a force capable of transforming the inequalities that our people suffer due to neoliberal and globalized politics" (Cumbre de Mujeres Indígenas de las Américas 2003, 132).

Recuperating indigenous women's theorizations and recognizing their emancipatory potential does not imply an idealization of contemporary indigenous cultures. The proposals of these indigenous women speak to us of an indigenous epistemology based on important values that they want to recuperate as well as activate, which in no way suggests that they represent the cultural expression already shaping their daily lives.

To disqualify these proposals because they do not share our urban feminist perspective of equality or because they are not based on our concerns for sexual and reproductive rights, or at least not in the same way in which we understand these rights in urban and mestizo regions, means reproducing the mechanisms that silence and exclude those political movements marked by patriarchal perspectives. A questioning of our own ethnocentrisms and racisms is a necessary first step in establishing intercultural dialogues on the conceptualizations of women's rights and for constructing political alliances based on what we have in common, while at the same time recognizing our different visions of the world.

Notes

1. The concept of *cosmovision* is very important in the political discourse of the indigenous movements in Latin America and refers to the specific worldview that indigenous people claim to have that includes a more holistic perspective of social and natural processes. It is considered a specific epistemology to conceive and refer to the world.

2. The acronym stands for Colectivo de Encuentro entre Mujeres. COLEM also means "free" in the Tzotzil language, spoken in the Chiapas Highlands. This organization was founded in 1989 in the southern Mexican state of Chiapas to fight sexual and domestic violence, under the name of the San Cristobal de las Casas Woman's Group and changed its name to COLEM in 1994.

3. The feminist NGOs that have centered their work in rural and indigenous areas are usually integrated by urban mestiza women. There are some experiences of indigenous and mestiza women working together in feminist NGOs, as it was the case of my own organization, COLEM A.C., in the 1990s. These rural feminist organizations, as well as the indigenous women organizations, have been excluded from the political spaces and agendas of the hegemonic feminism.

4. Mexican feminism has represented women coming from popular backgrounds following a hegemonic trend in social movement literature of establishing typologies that create an implicit hierarchy of such movements. For example, differences between "practical interest" and "strategic interests" (Molyneux 1986) or between a women's movement and "women in motion" (Rowbotham 1992) tend to reproduce a political evolutionist perspective where scholars' values and utopian horizons are used as universal parameters to measure women's transformative capacities.

5. CIDHAL is one of the earliest Mexican feminist organizations with grassroots work in working-class areas, created in 1969 in the state of Morelos as an information and feminist document-distribution center. Later on it turned to popular-sector work, especially in urban areas and church-based communities. A deeper history of CIDHAL can be found in Espinosa 1988.

6. Memoirs of the workshop "The Rights of Women in Our Customs and Traditions" (1994).

7. For a complete account of this organization, see Freyermuth and Fernández 1995.

8. Comaletzin was formed as a civic association in 1987 and stated as its main line of action "training, organizing, educating and researching considering gender as the core line of analysis" (Comaletzin 1999, 6). This association played an important role in the establishment of the National Rural Adviser's and Promoter's Network in 1987, which gathered together organizations interested in gender and development in several regions in Mexico.

9. The Center for Research and Action for Women was created by Gloria Sierra, Begoña de Agustin, Pilar Jaime, and Mercedes Olivera and registered in Nicaragua, Guatemala, and Mexico. Their main goal was working with women uprooted due to armed conflicts (refugees, displaced, and returned) in Central America and Mexico, in order to promote the development of gender consciousness and identity, encourage them to adopt their rights as refugees, and demand their respect from UNHCR, their own refugee or displaced organizations, and the countries of asylum. They worked mainly with women organized in popular movements, refugees in Mexico, Nicaragua, Costa Rica, Belize, and Panama, and with displaced women in El Salvador, Nicaragua, and Guatemala (I would like to thank Mercedes Olivera for this information). These experiences themselves were headed by a number of efforts to uphold reflections on women's rights within peasant organizations like the Agricultural Workers Independent Center or the Emiliano Zapata Peasant Organization.

10. The Women in Solidarity Action Team was founded in February 1985, based on working in health and popular education with working-class groups in Mexico City and indigenous women from different parts of the country.

11. There are sixty-two formally recognized ethnic groups in Mexico whose demography sums up twelve million people, that is, about 11 percent of the national population. Among them, Tzotziles, Tseltales, Tojolabales, and Choles are the four largest groups found in Chiapas, all from the Mayan family.

12. This law has been reproduced by the national and international press. The content of the law can be read at Speed, Hernández Castillo, and Stephen 2006.

13. An account of the National Congress of Indigenous Women and its organizational work can be found in Artía Rodríguez 2001 and Hernández Castillo 2006b.

14. In the past eight years I have been working with organized indigenous women through co-participative research. A critical reflection on the relations between mestizo advisers and indigenous peasant women during the 1980s can be found in Garza and Toledo 2004. I participated in the process of self-critical evaluation of feminist methodologies in the Comaletzin and COLEM groups.

15. Such reflections have also developed in the spaces of encounter of Latin American feminists, as can be seen in the contents of the Workshop on Feminism and Cultural Diversity organized by Sylvia Marcos at the Eighth Latin American and Caribbean Congress. See Marcos 1999. In the Latin American Feminist Encounter, which took place in Mexico City in May 2009, there was a special panel, "Feminisms and Indigenous Women: Racism, Exclusions, and Disencounters," in which indigenous and nonindigenous women participated. But in a four-day congress, we were able to negotiate only a two-hour space for these issues.

16. A compilation of such documents can be found in Lovera and Palomo [1997] 1999. See also Sánchez 2005.

17. For other critiques of the ethnocentrism of liberal feminism, see Alarcón 1990 and Trinh 1988.

18. Sally Engle Merry (2003) uses the term *culturalize* to refer to the analytical move that explains any social or political process in cultural terms.

19. These changes are in Article 2d, Section II, of the new Law on Indigenous Rights. See *Perfil La Jornada,* April 28, 2001.

20. These new social actors are beginning to theorize their own understandings of women's rights, gender, and feminism as well as share their perspectives as part of the construction of intercultural dialogues. See C. Alvarez 2000; Grupo de Mujeres Mayas Kaqla 2000; and Sánchez 2005.

11

The Demobilization of a Palestinian Women's Movement: From Empowered Active Militants to Powerless and Stateless "Citizens"

ISLAH JAD

Palestinian women's movements in the Palestinian Occupied Territories are currently faced with two major tasks: continuing the national struggle and participating in state building while at the same time pressing for women's rights. Like women's movements worldwide, Palestinian women's movements are faced with both "old" agendas of mobilization and liberation (in this case, from the Israeli Occupation) and "new" ones concerning women's equality and empowerment (here, under the "rule" of the Palestinian Authority [PA]). Under normal circumstances, it is difficult to straddle these two agendas; it becomes much more difficult, if not impossible, in the extraordinary situation in which the very existence of the Palestinian state and society are threatened by the Israeli Occupation.

The past decade and a half since the conclusion of the Oslo Accords in 1993 have seen changes in local and national political and societal structures that have had profound impacts on the Palestinian women's movements, both locally in Palestine and in the wider exile. In particular, the establishment of the Palestinian Authority in 1994 and of all the quasi "state" apparatuses that followed have had a formative impact on all aspects of the women's movement.

The importance of state-building dynamics cannot be underestimated. In fact, the dual dynamics of state building and an accompanying phenomenon of

PALESTINE

Human Development Index ranking: .731
Gender-Related Development Index value: not available
Gender Empowerment Measure value: not available

General

Type of government: Transition; limited self-rule
Major ethnic groups: Palestinian Arab; Jewish
Languages: Arabic; Hebrew
Religions: Muslim; Jewish

Demographics

Population, total (millions), 2005: 3.8
Annual growth rate (%), 2005–2015: 3.0
Total fertility (average number of births per woman): 5.6
Contraceptive prevalence (% of married women aged 15–49): 51
Maternal mortality ratio, adjusted (per 100,000 live births), 2000: not available

Women's Status

Date of women's suffrage: Not applicable
Life expectancy: M 96.7; F 88
Combined gross enrollment ratio for primary, secondary, and tertiary education
   (female %), 2005: 84
Gross primary enrollment ratio: 88
Gross secondary enrollment ratio: 102*
Gross tertiary enrollment ratio: 39
Literacy (% age 15 and older): M 98.8; F 88

Political Representation of Women

Legislators, senior officials, and managers (% female): 11
Professional and technical workers (% female): 35
Women in government at ministerial level (% total): not available

Economics

Estimated earned income (PPP US$): not available
Ratio of estimated female to male earned income: not available
Economic activity rate (% female): 10.3
Women in adult labor force (% total): 13 (this figure obtained at the CEDAW Statistical Database)

*Gross enrollment ratios in excess of 100% indicate that there are pupils or students outside the theoretical age groups who are enrolled in that level of education.

"NGO-ization," have led to increasing fragmentation and demobilization of all Palestinian social movements. There are several reasons for this. First, both the nature and the limited life cycle of projects funded by donors induce fragmentation, rather than bringing about what Tarrow has called "sustainable networking" (1994), whereby ties are made, nurtured, and maintained with members and organizations. Nongovernmental organizations (NGOs) typically aim to advocate for or to educate a "target audience," which is usually defined for and limited to the period needed to implement a project. Here, the constituency is not a natural social grouping but is artificially constructed. Equally important, the targeted group is typically a temporary passive recipient rather than an ongoing active partner in the initiative. This relationship carries a cultural dimension, promoting values that favor dependency, lack of self-reliance, and new modes of consumption.[1] NGO-ization as a process also introduces changes in the composition of much of the women's movement, bringing to the fore a middle-class, professional women's elite at the expense of rural and refugee women activists from grassroots organizations. Such a transformation (Goetz 1997) results in a shift in power relations.

Each of the factors just mentioned contributes to a significant difference between NGOs and social movements—two phenomena that are often conflated. According to Molyneux, the term *women's movement* implies a social or political phenomenon of some significance, due to both its numerical strength and its capacity to effect change, whether in legal, cultural, social, or political terms. A women's movement does not have to have a single organizational expression and may be characterized by diversity of interests, forms of expression, and spatial location. It will comprise a substantial majority of women, although it may not be exclusively made up of women (Molyneux 1998b, 226). According to Tarrow, what specifically characterizes social movements is that "at their base are the social networks and cultural symbols through which social relations are organized. The denser the former and the more familiar the latter, the more likely movements are to spread and be sustained" (1994, 2). The same can be said of women's movements, as distinguished from "women in movement" (Rowbotham 1992, as cited Jackson and Pearson 1998). Tarrow adds, "Contentious collective action is the basis of social movements, not because movements are always violent or extreme, but because it is the main, and often the only, recourse that most people possess against better-equipped opponents. Collective action is not an abstract category that can stand outside of history and apart from politics for every kind of collective endeavor— from market relations, to interest associations, to protest movements, to peasant rebellions and revolutions" (1994, 3).

The transformation in the nature and role of Palestinian leadership in the PA era has left deep marks on the forms of women's activism. The creation of the PA, with its admittedly limited state-building mandate, pressured women's movements to shift their agenda from a combination of national struggle and women's emancipation to an agenda of targeting the state to promote women's rights. Many successful women's grassroots organizations were transformed into NGOs or came under the growing influence of NGO practices. A new Palestinian civil society emerged as a depoliticized arena that, while providing a forum to discuss democratization, human rights, and women's rights, effectively lost its previous capacity to organize and mobilize different groups, in particular women's groups aiming to combat the Occupation.

In addition to the changes in the nature of NGOs and their efforts at state building, various traumatic developments have contributed in some measure to the evolution of the women's movement. These include the second intifada, the separation of Gaza and the West Bank, the construction of hundreds of roadblocks throughout the territories, the complete closure of Gaza, the construction of the Separation Wall, and the election of Hamas in 2006. This chapter takes a broad look at Palestinian women's movements today to shed light on sweeping changes that have resulted in several important areas: the legal contours of Palestinian citizenship and gender, the idealized image of women in official Palestinian discourse, forms of women's activism and participation in civil society, the ability of grassroots movements to mobilize, and the balance between secular and Islamist forces.

In this chapter I argue that the establishment of the Palestinian Authority has had a demobilizing effect on all social movements, including the women's movement. I argue that the development of the NGO movement has further demobilized Palestinian civil society in a phase of national struggle. I show how the weakening of the secular Palestinian national movement under Israeli Occupation, including attempts at donor-funded promotion of civil society, has provoked a progressive depoliticization of the women's movement. I also suggest that the vacuum created by this retreat has been increasingly filled by the militancy of the Palestinian Islamic Resistance Movement known as Hamas.

NGOs Before and After the Arrival of the Palestinian Authority

At the turn of the twentieth century, women in Palestine, as in neighboring countries in the rest of the Arab world, established their own charitable organizations in urban centers. The pioneering women in that domain were mainly Christians who had benefited from and been empowered by the emergence of missionary education. Muslim women were encouraged to join the national struggle, establish their own organizations, and transcend religious boundaries. They were urban middle-class and driven by the desire to "modernize" the "traditional" social order through the "uplifting" of rural women by means of education (Mogannam 1937; Fleischmann 2003).

Charitable work and urban elites dominated women's activism until the formation of the General Union of Palestinian Women (*al-itihad al-'am lil-maraa al-falastineyya*) in 1965 as one of the popular organs of the Palestinian Liberation Organization. GUPW activism varied by the locality of the Palestinian communities. At the peak of the "revolutionary" era when the PLO was settled in Lebanon, the GUPW was controlled by activist women divided along factional lines. The GUPW played an important role in organizing and mobilizing Palestinian women in their different localities throughout the diaspora. In the West Bank and Gaza, charitable activities and elite women continued to dominate the work and activism of the GUPW until the formation of women's grassroots organizations beginning in 1978.

Israel's conquest and occupation of the West Bank and Gaza in the war of June 1967 expanded Israeli rule to all of historic Palestine. This opened a new chapter in Palestinian resistance and ushered in new political, social, and economic realities that profoundly affected women. The Palestinian women's movement that consequently developed was initially shaped by these forces. The women's movement contributed to both Palestinian national resistance and the creation of a new consciousness on the part of Palestinian women. During this period the Palestinian women's movement was linked inextricably to the nationalist movement and shared its fortunes, its burdens, and its vision of Palestinian independence. For both, ideology was shaped by the imperative to end the harsh rule of the Israeli military Occupation and attain national self-determination.

Both the nationalist and the women's movements developed in the particular and unique situation of a prolonged Occupation and the absence of a state. This absence, however deleterious to social and economic development, afforded space for mobilization and public activity that gave a special empowering character to Palestinian grassroots movements, including the formation of the women's movement in the late 1970s. This new formation, embodied in the women's committees, decisively widened the circle of activist women and played an important role in mobilizing women for the first intifada, the nationalist Palestinian uprising launched in December 1987.

During the Palestinian resistance, including the years of the first intifada, women formed organizations with the aim of enhancing women's participation in the battle for independence and defending the Palestinian people and cause, while simultaneously providing vital services for women in the realms of education, political participation, and cultural life. These women viewed realization of their social rights as a vital link toward the independence of Palestine. Their goals paralleled those of the nationalist movement, whose members also viewed these women as an integral component in the creation of the new nation-state. For its part, the women's movement unequivocally supported the nationalist movement in its future nationalistic vision of Palestinian independence.

Prior to the formation of the PA, Palestinian society was organized into political parties, grassroots mass organizations, and NGOs related to political parties, all under the umbrella of the Palestine Liberation Organization, which nurtured and financially supported these parties and their satellite organizations.[2] This was necessary since the PLO and its affiliated political parties were banned by Israel, while their satellite organizations, primarily seen as service providers, were allowed some freedom to work in the Occupied Territories.

The Oslo Agreement ended the PLO's armed resistance and allowed the organization, through negotiations, to constitute itself as a quasi state with control over all the symbolic trappings of statehood such as a flag, an anthem, an airport, and passports, but without sovereignty over its people, territory, or resources. The PA's failure to deliver national rights came as the Islamic Resistance Movement, or Hamas, emerged to continue the struggle and to contest the defeatist stand of the PLO over Palestinian communities. Hamas constituted itself as an Islamic national movement representing the historical national Palestinian right to self-determination and the return of Palestinian refugees to their homeland. Hamas sought to do this through the mobilization and organization of Palestinians in the West Bank and Gaza to resist the Occupation. Hamas borrowed the old ethos developed through the Palestinian national struggle led by the PLO around the core idioms of "struggle," "sacrifice," and "suffering" that constituted Palestinian national identity in the diaspora before the advent of the PA. As Islamist groups gained hegemony in civil society, other advocates lost out.

I shall describe, in what follows, the paradoxical process of depoliticization and demobilization of the previously powerful and locally grounded women's grassroots committees after the initiative passed to the PA, which became the main political actor and job provider and defined the role for NGOs as complementary to that of the new "state." I will trace the trajectory of one of the "new" NGOs, as an example of many others; describe the rise of "femocrats";[3] and then contrast these developments with the gradual demobilization of an earlier grassroots women's organization in order to examine whether this transition realized feminism and empowered women. I also briefly trace the parallel process of the growing power of the Islamists, who are now taking up the lead in the national struggle.

The Legal Contours of Palestinian Citizenship and Gender

With the establishment of the PA, Palestinian citizenship became a dilemma. The Oslo Agreements granted the PA the right to issue only a Basic Law. The first drafts of the Basic Law reflected the fact the Authority could not, within the existing political framework, define Palestinian identity according to the tenets of Palestinian nationalism. Rather than formalizing a separation between Palestinian nationality and nationality, or identity, and Palestinian citizenship, the first drafts of the Basic Law[4] postponed the definition of citizenship to some future period of legislation (Hammami and Johnson 1999).

In the latest version of the Palestinian Basic Law (March 2003), Article 12 specifies the ways in which Palestinian nationality might be transmitted. Under pressure from the women's movement, the criterion for nationality was changed from blood ties through the father, used before 1984, to blood ties through both parents. For the first time in an Arab state, women were given the right to confer citizenship to their children (Jad et al. 2003, 9). Earlier drafts of the Basic Law had already affirmed that Palestine respected and recognized a whole set of universal agreements and declarations, including the United Nations Convention for the Elimination of All Forms of Discrimination Against Women, which provide a basis for the adoption of universal conventions as sources for legislation. In the first four drafts of the Basic Law, which were subject to popular discussion, sharia was not mentioned as a source of legislation, nor Islam as the state religion. Under pressure from Islamists, as will be described later in this chapter, both were later added by the Legislative Council, which was composed mostly of secular members at the time.

Despite the positive provisions, there were some revealing passages in the Basic Law dealing with work and motherhood that suggest a less than full commitment to changing gender relations. Article 23, for example, declares that a "woman has the right to participate actively in social, political, cultural and economic life, and the Law will work to eliminate constraints that forbid women from fully participating in the construction of their families and society" (ibid.). However, the major dilemma of women's unemployment was not clearly addressed—not in terms of job availability, employers' reluctance to hire women, the need for child care and a change in family protective mores, or guarantee of equal pay for equal work. Nor did the article define clearly the obstacles and constraints that the law would work to eliminate; it only said that they related to the construction of the family and society. The same article also stated that "women's constitutional and shari'a rights (*hoqoq shar'eyya*) are protected, and that the law would stipulate punishment for any violations" (ibid.). Thus, the proposed law uses an obscure language that suits all ideological inclinations, whether secularist or religious, and leaves unclear which code, constitutional or sharia, would be used if the two were in conflict. Issues relating to motherhood, child care, and the family, all concepts central to Palestinian nationalism, were dealt with in most PA legal documents as the duty of society but without any official commitment on the part of the PA to help women carry out that duty (Jad, Johnson, and Giacaman 2000). Child care and maternity services, traditionally the task of women's organizations, did not receive enough support under the PA to keep them functioning. In many laws, such as the Civil Law and Civil Service Law, women were depicted as being dependent on men. More important, changes in the laws were not translated into policies; where financial support would have been required to develop policies and programs based on the new laws, it did not materialize.

Along with the unclear definition of citizenship, the PA lacks a coherent set of policies intended to enforce the rule of law as an important guarantor of citizens' rights. The most visible policy is related to the security responsibilities assigned to the Authority by the Oslo Accords. Accordingly, certain aspects of citizenship are severely undermined, especially in the PA's relationship with opposition parties in general and with the Islamic political movement in particular. Detention without charge, torture, maltreatment, and harassment are methods frequently used against the Islamic political opposition (Islamic Resistance Movement 1996). A higher security court was established by presidential decree as a parallel body to civil courts. Different security apparatuses are creating their own courts free of civil control (JMCC 2000a, 2000b, 2000c).

These repressive measures placed, and continue to place, women activists in a difficult dilemma. Various social organizations that demanded civil and social rights were already encountering antagonism from the PA; for women activists to criticize the PA's practices would invite similar repercussions. In order to strengthen their position, the women found it necessary to ally with other social organizations, such as Islamist groups, whose stances did not necessarily run parallel to their own. Failure to take a stand at all would have discredited the women activists, reducing their legitimacy in civil society.

To ally with the PA to the point of turning a blind eye to its unethical practices, however, was to risk being discredited by the larger women's movements. In fact, certain grassroots women's organizations linked to Fateh, the ruling party, were discredited for precisely this reason. Most notable among these was the General Union of Palestinian Women. When the PA was established, the leadership of the GUPW, an organization that Israel had previously banned in the Occupied Territories for its association with the PLO, returned from exile and set up an official organizational infrastructure to supersede the local unofficial committees that had constituted the women's movement when the entire West Bank and Gaza were solely under Israeli Occupation.

Conflict quickly arose between the "returnee" diasporic leadership and local leadership over a variety of issues. Additionally, while the GUPW tried to present itself as a nongovernmental body, its actions and funding indicated otherwise. The organization was financially dependent on the PA, and the PA showered it with sometimes flagrant manifestations of favoritism. The GUPW leadership and its administrative staff, for example, received monthly salaries from the PA, while the rent for their luxurious offices was also paid by the PA, a fact that eventually led the local leadership to challenge the Union's claim that it was an independent NGO. "We follow here (in the West Bank) our internal administrative culture as spelled out in our constitution of charitable societies, according to which an elected member should not get a salary or any financial grant. We consider this a conflict of interest. Besides, how can they claim independence from the PA as the representative of a group of society while they all get salaries from the PA?"[5]

Clearly, in the eyes of some, the GUPW had become mere pawns for the PA. Another woman from the local group put it this way in an interview:

Every time we want to publish a leaflet or any political document, they [the GUPW returned-from-exile leaders] always insist that we have to add some glorifying sentences about the president; they ask us to display his photos. We are rebellious here; we are not used to that. Also, they objected to one of our leader's attending a conference in Amman because she was one of the signatories of a leaflet published by an opposition group criticizing the corruption in the PA. Of course we have to criticize the government. This is our right: we are not representing the government; we represent our people, our women.[6]

The GUPW returnees recognized the gender inequality being practiced by the national leadership; however, they chose not to protest it overtly. As Agarwal put it, these women were compliant but not complicit with political hierarchy (1997, 25).

Changes in law, then, reflected an ambivalent commitment to women's rights and equality, and even those laws that represented an improvement were not supported at the policy level. This situation placed women's organizations in a difficult position vis-à-vis the political hierarchy.

The Idealized Image of Women in Official Palestinian Discourse

In addition to changes in legal status, changes in women's image and expected role also followed the establishment of the PA. In the historic discourse of the Palestinian national movement, women were typically portrayed either as militants or as self-sacrificing mothers (Peteet 1991; Jad 1990). In the face of death, dislocation, rejection, and annihilation, Palestinian poets glorified the woman who had a large number of children, especially male children.[7] The woman "freedom fighter" with a gun in her hand was an image glorified by different Palestinian factions, especially on the Left. However, national slogans like "the right of return" and "nation building" required a different model for women. What has happened to these images of women under the PA? And what has happened to the platforms of "struggle," "sacrifice," and "suffering" that constituted Palestinian national identity in the diaspora before the advent of the PA?

In her study of Palestinian nationalism, Helena Schulz underlines the "ambiguity of Palestinian nationalism and national identity" (1999, 156). In the new era of unachieved liberation the terms *belonging, loyalty,* and *commitment* have become the *mots d'ordre* for the new political regime around which the reconstruction of Palestinian nationalism is taking place. Belonging to Palestine is the main slogan, without specifying which Palestine or whose Palestine. Belonging to Palestine is also extended to mean belonging to Fateh, the main political party. This is manifested in the Fateh ideology that encompasses four core values, with belief in the Palestinian cause being the first, and the other three involving willingness to engage as a member of the Tanzim (i.e., Fateh) to carry out the work and responsibilities associated with the required commitment and to abide by the stands, programs, and decisions adopted by the Tanzim with respect to political framework. This ideology was not limited to Fateh members per se but extended to a broader national level and resulted in a proliferation of social organizations willing to follow the lead of the Palestinian Authority. These *mots d'ordre* were enforced among Fateh members after Hamas won the legislative election of January 2006.

As part of this process, media and propaganda signal the PA's "sovereignty" through two key symbols: the flag and the president.[8] Pictures of President Arafat in his military uniform as a symbol of the continuation of the struggle were hung in the streets, in stores, and in all PA offices. "Struggle" has been replaced with the "symbolic militarism"[9] reflected in many youth military marches and the use of military uniforms by young kids and young men. This symbolic militaristic orientation is reinforced through the mushrooming of the PA's security apparatuses, each one in a different military uniform. The new culture of symbolic militarism has come again to glorify the male fighter and to overshadow the earlier image of the woman militant that was prominent during the years the PLO was headquartered in Lebanon.

In those days, the most successful and respected women activists were not those who simply organized other women but rather those who got directly involved in the underground and militant activities of the political organization. In Fateh, there was always a clear distinction between the military wing and other mass-based organizations, including women's organizations, and being a member of the women's organization was not a sufficient criterion for inclusion in the higher ranks of Fateh. Those who joined the women's organization were nominally considered Fateh members to widen the popular basis of the organization—as one of the women's organization's members said, "to show our popularity" (Rafidi 2001)—but very few women were actually members of the Fateh political organization. In order to be a member, women had to prove themselves as *"bint* Fateh" (a daughter of Fateh) (ibid.). A real "daughter of Fateh" was constructed as masculine and tough, with short hair, simple trousers, a long shirt with long sleeves, and, as Islamism became popular, a head scarf. She had to be discreet, speak little, and remain steadfast under interrogation. The few but well-known women who headed militant cells were given male pseudonyms. As "Aisha," a former militant, remembers:

> I was known by the name of Abu Muhammad [Muhammad's father].[10] I talked, walked, and behaved exactly like men. If I showed my femininity, they [men] would take me as a weak, easy-to-crack person. I was tough, very tough. I had to show them that I was not less than they were, that I was a tough strong man. I only realized that I was a woman and that I should be proud of it after the establishment of the PA, when I joined a conference on what our gender agenda under the PA should be. (Maghassib 2001)

More recently, during the second intifada beginning in September 2000, women again projected an image of themselves as militants and fighters when a number of women persuaded some militant groups to recruit them for military actions. Lately, Islamist women, like women in the PLO before them, have persuaded male leaders in the militant al-Qassam Brigades to recruit them (Palestine Media Centre 2005).

The PA, however, has attempted to replace the image of the woman militant with the image of the ideal woman as fertile, self-sacrificing, and steadfast. In the national struggle the fertile woman was deemed necessary because the outcome of the conflict was perceived to depend partly on the demographic balance between Jews and Arabs. An extension of the ideal of the self-sacrificing mother is the official glorification of mothers of martyrs, an image extolled in the poetry of the Palestinian icon Mahmoud Darwish. With the essentalist depiction of women as passive, grieving, selfless mothers, it is easy to overlook the victimization of Palestinian men by Israeli violence.

Palestinian mothers, sisters, and daughters of martyrs are also subject to contradictory messages from multiple discourses. While nationalist discourse glorifies women as mothers, uplifting their maternal suffering into national defiance and resistance, another feminist discourse urges women to be themselves, to express their true feelings and grief.[11] Feminist women's activism presents a new image for the woman as urban, professional, elegant, and claiming her individual rights from the PA, society, and family; it portrays the woman as a "taker." At the same time, Islamist groups depict the model woman today, as in the past, as modestly veiled, patient, a pious caretaker for her husband and children. She is, most important, the bearer of male children sacrificed in order to continue the resistance; to them, woman is the selfless "giver."[12] For its part, most Palestinian official discourse, prompted by the demands of foreign donors and UN agencies to "mainstream gender" and to take it into account in all projects, employs up-to-date, gender-friendly language. These myriad and contradictory discourses, each projecting its own image of the ideal Palestinian woman, all coexist in today's Palestine.

In sum, with the establishment of the Palestinian Authority, militarism has taken on an increasingly male complexion, and women have had to retreat from this domain but have received confusing messages about what their ideal role in society should be. As most doors closed on women's chances for militant action, women's activism in Palestinian society has taken new forms, as the following section explains.

From "Self-Help" to "Self-Government": The Rise and Fall of Different Forms of Women's Activism

The changes in the NGO sector represent the most remarkable change of all affecting women's movements in Palestine. Before the formation of the PA, women activists belonged to what were known as "grassroots organizations"— women's committees that were branches of political formations and sustained the first Palestinian intifada. The success of the women activists lay in organizing and mobilizing the masses and was based on their skills in building relationships with other people. The women succeeded because they had a cause to defend and a mission to implement and because they believed strongly in the political formations to which they belonged. It was important for a woman activist to be known and trusted by people in the community, to have easy access to them, to care about them, and to help them when needed. The task required daily tiring, time-consuming networking and organizing. These women activists knew their constituencies personally and depended on face-to-face human contact for communicating with them.

But during the first Palestinian intifada and following the signing of the Oslo Agreement in 1993, a significant change occurred. The NGO sector began to be used as a channel for foreign aid, resulting in service delivery at the local level in the form of clinics, schools, kindergartens, and income-generation projects. Indeed, at this time, the NGO sector in the West Bank and Gaza operated as the main channel for the foreign aid that enabled service delivery at the grassroots level. In 1991, when the Madrid Conference initiated the state-building process, women's movements were pressured to shift their agendas from one that combined the national struggle with women's emancipation to one that looked to the "state" (which really had none of the true authority or powers of an actual state) to fulfill women's rights. In the process, many previously successful women's grassroots organizations were transformed into advocacy NGOs or came under the growing influence of NGO practices. As a result, these NGOs became important actors and acquired more power than their parent political parties.

The period from 1988 to 1994 witnessed a noticeable increase in feminist women's organizations in the form of NGOs. These new organizations included women's affairs centers in Nablus in 1988 and in Gaza in 1989. In Jerusalem, the Women's Study Center was founded in 1989, the Women's Center for Legal Aid and Counseling in 1991, and the Women's Affairs Technical Committee in 1991. The Women's Studies Program at Birzeit University was initiated in 1994 (Jad 2000, 44). The growing number of institutions propagated a new discourse on women and women's status—but within the context of a steady decline in women's mobilization and activism. An unpublished study of five women's mass organizations found that membership declined by 37 percent after 1993 and that new enrollment in 1996 did not exceed 3 percent, with most of it occurring (probably due to patronage) in the Fateh women's organization (ibid.).

While it is difficult to give an exact number of Palestinian NGOs (sources vary in their estimates, from 2,000 members in 1990 to 1,000 in 2006), it is safe to conclude that important changes in the landscape and composition of NGOs, as mentioned above, occurred after the signing of the Oslo Agreement in 1993 (Challand 2009, 68). The Oslo years were characterized by a turnover with the establishment of many new NGOs: 37.6 percent of NGOs active in 2001 were created after the signing of the agreement. There is no accurate estimate of the exact amount of funding received by this sector; for instance, estimates vary from $60 million to $240 million for the year 1996 alone (ibid.).

The largest newcomer on the scene, the Palestinian Authority, embarked on gaining bureaucratic power and capturing funds from the NGOs. The PA co-opted some of the activists who had moved to the NGO sector and simultaneously separated them from their grassroots political base. Other activists formed their own autonomous advocacy NGOs, which viewed the PA as an authority that threatened their autonomy and acted to control their funds. Within the women's movement, power was granted to a new elite working within civil society in advocacy NGOs or within the PA apparatuses.

Femocrats: Between Patronage and Feminism

Along with the rise in the numbers of NGOs, a new category of women came into its own in the post-Oslo period with the formation of the PA. This is the category of women referred to as "femocrats" (i.e., women who work in the state bureaucracy).[13] Palestinian "femocrats" are not necessarily feminist, nor are they "employed within state bureaucratic positions to work on advancing the position of women in the wider society through the development of equal opportunity and anti-discrimination" (Yeatman 1990, 65). Most Palestinian "femocrats," in particular those in high-ranking positions, are nominated through patronage relations and not for their feminist credentials. However, patronage per se does not necessarily mean that the women are antifeminist or that they will not do their best to represent other women. Thus, while some use the gender agenda and their political access to promote their own interests, others work to develop a gender agenda despite the numerous constraints facing the PA and their position within it. At times, as Goetz observes from her experience in Uganda, patronage has led to a situation whereby "high-profile appointments of women to senior civil service positions have significantly enhanced women's presence in the administration" (2003, 110).

The locus of femocrats within the Palestinian quasi-state apparatus was the Inter-Ministerial Committee for the Advancement of Women's Status (*lajnet al-tansiq al-wizaria lerafʿa makanat al-maraʾa*), until it was dissolved and replaced by the Ministry of Women's Affairs. IMCAW consisted of women in key positions in their respective ministries, mostly nominated by the president and assigned to mainstream gender issues (i.e., to integrate gender concerns in all policies, legislation, and programs) in their structures. Success in fund-raising and capacity building was seen as vital if women in IMCAW were to prove themselves as professionals; they attempted to imitate professional women in NGOs at the expense of their "old" image as militants. As the United Nations Development Fund for Women (UNIFEM) coordinator put it, "The members of IMCAW feel that they need lots of training on capacity building. They feel they lag behind the skills in the women's NGOs who all know how to fund-raise, how to formulate a strategy, how to manage and communicate, [while] they used to be mere freedom fighters. They did not need to fund-raise; they used to get funds through money collections and donations from the Arabs or the Palestinians in the diaspora" (Al-Yassir 2001).

Thus, NGO-ization set the model for the "old" militants and was their path to professionalization. Unfortunately, although it was assigned (in the Palestinian Development Plan, 1996–1998 [Palestinian Ministry of Cooperation and International Relations 1996]) the task of "developing" women and mainstreaming gender, IMCAW was not allotted resources. Lacking the means to develop and pursue an overall goal for development, IMCAW femocrats tended to focus on technicalities, such as how many workshops were needed to develop a mainstreaming plan. In so doing, they fell into the trap Goetz (1997) describes—that of focusing on processes and means rather than ends, resulting in a preoccupation with the minutiae of procedures at all levels rather than clarity or direction about goals. It is not surprising that the committee was heavily dependent on donor aid and working as an NGO (or, in this case, a GONGO, a governmental nongovernmental organization). This apparent oxymoron is explained by the fact that many "first ladies" within the government depend on donor aid and work, as do "independent" NGOs.

Essentially, the new NGOs shifted their priorities and roles from acting as service providers to their communities and as a political facade for their parties to becoming advocates of democratization and citizens' rights, in an attempt to define new boundaries between state and society. In their new role, they were portrayed and saw themselves as the voice of democratic, secular civil society. Whereas grassroots NGOs had worked to provide health, education, jobs, and child care for poorer communities, many of the newer NGOs turned to focus on donor-driven agendas such as good governance and violence against women at the expense of economic inequality. The so-called war on terror and the frenzied U.S. effort to (purportedly) "democratize" the Middle East have intensified the tendency of many donors to concentrate on issues of government administration rather than economic or social needs. All of this has meant a power shift within what must now be categorized as the secular Palestinian women's movement, tilting it toward a more highly educated, middle-income and professional class at the expense of a female cadre of rural or refugee backgrounds.

The composition of today's NGOs contributes to this tendency. The typical NGO now consists of a board of seven to twenty members and a highly qualified professional and administrative staff, generally few in number, depending on the number and character of projects. The practical decision-making power frequently lies not in the hands of the board but with the director, who has to answer to the funders—who are themselves international NGOs or foreign government bodies. The power of the director stems from the ability to raise funds; to be convincing, presentable, and competent; and to be able to deliver the well-written reports that the well-educated foreign donors require. Indeed, all administrative staff members are required to have highly professional skills. Sophisticated communication skills, including facility with English as the common language and use of modern technology, become vital, since donors employ and promote the use of communication methods such as media, workshops, and conferences and use modern communication equipment including fax machines, computers, and mobile phones. This reliance on globalized, rather than local, tools automatically limits the number and range of possible employees; and while it may not necessarily directly affect the relationship between an NGO and its local constituency, it often does.

As for the internal governance of NGOs, a survey of more than sixty Palestinian NGOs found that most of their employees do not participate in decision making, due to "their passivity or their lack of competence" (Shalabi 2001, 52). Nor do the target groups participate in decision or policy making. When NGO administrators were asked why this was so, they answered that since they were themselves part of this society and understood it, they were therefore qualified to decide about its needs (ibid., 152). In many women's NGOs, staff members have nothing to do with the general budget of their organization and do not know how it is distributed. According to Shalabi, the internal governance of the NGOs surveyed was "a mirror reflection of the Palestinian political system based on individual decision making, patronage and clientelism," and on a lack of rules organizing internal relations (ibid., 154).

In effect, since the typical structure of NGOs bars them from serving as mobilizing or organizing agents, however much they proliferate, they can neither sustain or nor expand a constituency nor tackle issues related to social, political, or economic rights on a macro or national level. A case in point is the effort by women's NGOs in 1998 to undertake a national initiative and establish the Model Parliament Project.

The Model Parliament Experiment and the Islamist Challenge

The project, entitled "Palestinian Model Parliament: Women and Legislation," was launched by a prominent West Bank women's NGO, the Women's Center for Legal Aid and Counseling (WCLAC), in 1998. It aimed to achieve a defined set of goals, including the endorsement of Palestinian legislation guaranteeing equality and human rights for Palestinian women, as well as women's participation in building a civil society based on justice and equality and on respect for human rights and the rule of law.

To launch a broad national debate in which all social groups in Palestinian society, whether male or female, would be targeted, the WCLAC invited individuals and institutions, including the religious establishment, activists in the Islamic movement, women's organizations, government bodies, various social groups, political parties, and Legislative Council members, to join the call for legal reform. All who accepted the invitation were considered members in the Model Parliament (Othman 1998, 62).

However, the WCLAC organizers were not attuned to the different contending discourses about Palestinian national identity and citizenship and were therefore totally unprepared for either the range or the intensity of political, social, and cultural sensitivities the project triggered. To many, it was not clear exactly what the Model Parliament Project entailed. Some saw it as an exercise to train the public and legislators on how to tackle women's rights through legislation and how to involve the public in participating in this discussion (Hammami and Johnson 1999). Others saw it as a consciousness-raising practice to make existing laws known to the broader public. Some others saw it as a litmus test to evaluate who is "with us" and who is "against us." What was clear was that there was no consistent view as to what should be the outcome of the "project" or "anticipation as to its results" (Siniora 2000, 2). The rationale for the project, as explained in the project brochure, changed over time. In particular, after the Islamists attacked the project as a clear imposition on the part of some "Westernized, donor-driven, Marxist feminists to change the law of shari'a for Muslims" (al-Huda Association 1998), the objective shifted to the more neutral and less polarizing one of realizing "freedom of expression."[14]

At this point, before continuing with the story of the Model Parliament, it is important to address the rise of what is sometimes called Muslim "religious fundamentalism." While there is a considerable volume of writing on contemporary Islamic movements (Hroub 1996, 2000; El-Hamad and Bargothi 1997; Abul-Omrein 2000), there has only been sketchy reference to their gender ideology, and very little attention has been paid to women activists themselves. Such an omission is surprising, particularly given the growing activism in Palestinian civil society of Islamist women, who are not considered by many feminists to be part of the women's movement.[15]

The increasing influence of Islamic movements in the Middle East is usually examined in the context of states' withdrawal from providing vital social and economic services to their citizens. This frame does not fit in the case of Palestine, where a sovereign nation-state has never existed. In the West Bank and Gaza, the socioeconomic and political transformations produced by the Israeli Occupation were important in promoting the Palestinian Islamists directly or indirectly. The Israeli Occupation and the Jordanian regime colluded to boost the Palestinian Islamic Resistance Movement, an offspring of the Muslim Brotherhood, in 1988, and it managed to build an impressive infrastructure of cultural, social, economic, and political institutions that proved crucial in sustaining the Islamic movement. The PA's lack of delivery on national rights came as Hamas emerged to contest the hegemonic role of the PLO over the Palestinian communities. Hamas constituted itself as an Islamic national movement representing the historical Palestinian demand for self-determination and the return of Palestinian refugees to their homeland through the mobilization and organization of the Palestinians in the West Bank and Gaza to resist the Israeli Occupation.

The "new" Islamists are different from those active during the British Mandate or during Jordanian rule. The old generation of Muslim Brothers came from the wealthy urban upper stratum; the new generation comes mainly from the peasant refugee population in the Gaza Strip. The older generation of founders, including Ahmed Yassine, Ibrahim Yazouri, Abdul Fatah Dokhan, and Mohammad Hassan Sahm'a, were schoolteachers and minor members of the clergy. The second generation, including Mahmoud Zahar, Abdul Aziz Rantissi, Salah Shihada, Eissa al-Nashar, Isma'il Abu Shanab, and Mossa Abu Marzouk, came from poor backgrounds in refugee camps and were trained as doctors, engineers, headmasters, and university teachers at Arab universities (Abul-Omrein 2000, 257; Al-Bargothi 2000, 57–59). Their supporters consisted mainly of students, especially from poor and conservative families, as well as clergy and professionals (Al-Bargothi 2000; Abul-Omrein 2000). Emulating the secular and leftist political groups and in reaction to them, the Islamists learned how to "adjust" their appeal to attract a wider constituency. As Islamist groups gained hegemony in civil society, other advocates lost out.

In December 1995 Hamas announced the establishment of the Islamic National Salvation Party. The Women's Action Department is one of thirteen departments in the party managing all aspects of activities and administration, ranging from public relations and cultural and political affairs to women's affairs. Unlike women's organizations in the secular national movement, the Women's Action Department of Hamas has been able to integrate women not into a separate section but fully into its political appendages, whether in the leadership or in its popular base.

The party and its women's department opened its doors to the "new Islamic woman" who is highly educated, outspoken, and modern. Modernity is reflected in the fact that these women are educated, professional, and politically active. The veil is seen as a signifier of modernity since it is different from "traditional dress." The "new Islamic dress" (long robe of plain color and a white or black head scarf) is seen as "different from the *thub* (traditional peasant woman's dress) which is used by our mothers and grandmothers. [Islamic dress] is different in its meanings; it is a unifying symbol to our followers and members. If I see a woman wearing it, I will immediately realize that she is *ukhot*[16] [a sister]. It indicates that we are educated and not like our mothers who are mostly illiterate. It gives us *heiba* [respect] as the dress of our ulema [religious clergy]. It is economic, simple, and modest" (Haroun and Salah 2000).

In this sense, Islamist dress is regarded as superior to the thub because it is a uniform of conviction, unlike the blind adherence to tradition that is presumed to explain clothing choices and other practices among the masses. Implicit in the Islamist veiling style is participation in a national social movement that lends the wearer a heightened sense of status, both moral (vis-à-vis secularists) and social (vis-à-vis women who cover instead of veiling). However, despite its political cachet, behind the social force of veiling, "one can discern the familiar principle of *himaya* (guidance and protection), by (and from) men" (White 2002, 223).

Unlike in some other Islamic parties, as in Turkey, for example, in which Islamist women, once married, lose their "voice" when they retreat to the security and seclusion of the patriarchal family (White 2002), the party and its women's department made available an important venue for a category of women who are highly educated (holding bachelor and higher degrees) and at the same time have limited access to a restricted male-dominated labor market. In order to facilitate this *damj* (integration) process, the party and its satellite societies run a massive web of kindergartens with a minimal charge in which poorer women and wives of political prisoners are exempted from paying any fees. Running kindergartens was a common task formerly undertaken by nationalist and secularist women's organizations and later abandoned. The vacuum left by these organizations was filled not by the PA when it was established in 1994 but by Islamist organizations. By running a system of kindergartens, the Islamists solved a major problem for working mothers and women's activists. However, it is important to note that the two women who managed to make it to the top level of the party were both unmarried. The work in the politburo, according to Amira and Youssra, "is intense, diversified, needs lots of time and strong characters" (Haroun and Salah 2000). The times set for political meetings were identified by many feminists as a hindrance to women's participation in political parties since these are usually set to the convenience of men rather than women (Waylen 1996). When asked about the time of their meetings and if they are suitable for the women, the veil was cited as a facilitator for late meeting hours. As they clarified, "We have certain days to discuss our general plans within the party. For these meetings, we choose collectively the best time for all of us, men and women. But, even if we have to be late sometimes, this does not pose a problem for us. . . . No one approaches us to do any harm. It is known that we work for the benefit of our people, and we are well respected for that" (Haroun and Salah 2000). In this case, the veil facilitates mobility for politically committed women and gives them the required validation for transcending the social taboos that might ordinarily restrict unmarried women from mobility during late hours. If the impetus to maintaining one's virtue is located in behavior, then behavioral signals become important markers of the inapproachability and inviolability of Islamist women.

The Women's Action Department employs various strategies and methods for reaching and recruiting women. They work face-to-face, building cells in refugee camps as entry points. Their task is facilitated by the presence of large numbers of political prisoners to whom they give special attention in their activities and in which they include their families. The department organizes a yearly campaign for political prisoners (who are now forgotten by almost all nationalist and secular women's organizations), in the form of demonstrations against the Israelis and the PA. The demonstrations against the latter take place because of their "lack of democracy and to oppose the continuous harassments against the party offices and journal alongside the arrest of its leaders" (Haroun and Salah 2000).[17] In the yearly plan the activities directed toward women combine both a national and a gender-specific agenda. The department targets the more educated women for recruitment in different types of programs. Cultural and educational activities are directed to women with higher education, while vocational education and material support target the poorer and less educated. It organizes many workshops (*dawrat*) in political socialization (*tathqif seyyassi*), very similar to the kind of programs conventionally offered by secular leftist (Marxist) women's organizations. A program called "women's encounter" (*al-multaqa al-nassawi*), aimed at linkage and mobilization (*al-tawassol wal taf'ieel*), targets women lawyers, writers, journalists and media experts, doctors, and accountants. In addition, there is an annual year-long course for women's cadre formation (*ie'adad kader*) that borrowed its organizational form from Marxist groups and that sometimes lasts for a year.[18] These types of programs are innovative in comparison to those of the nationalist and secularist women's organizations, which fail to target this category of women in such a systematic and sustained manner.

When asked if they use their power within the party to pressure their husbands to change their minds about their women's participation, the answer was negative. This reaction could be attributed to the contradictory values promoted by the Islamist Party: involvement versus motherhood, obedience to husbands, and the unity of the family.

As for specific women's issues, the department organizes a one-day women's conference annually, in which men and women participate by presenting papers on gender issues. The papers cover "hot topics" put on the agenda by other secular nationalist women's groups or treat specific problems that women face in their respective fields of activity, such as work, political life, and culture. Some of the workshops are directed at the male members of the department and focus on topics such as socialization and involve thorough discussion of sharia family law.

The attitude of the party and of Palestinian Islamist women concerning sharia is "modified" and ever evolving. It both challenges the discourse of the feminist NGOs, which is based on a liberal, individualistic notion of rights, and ignores the plight Palestinians face under Occupation, and the rather ambivalent Palestinian secularism that uses Islam as a source of legitimacy. It is important to note that the motivations behind the call to reform sharia are in essence a move to change the internal power relations between males and females within the family structure. Some male members are receptive to change and support men and women participating jointly in the same activities, which enhances the image of the party and its women as "modern," while they continue to object to significantly deeper and less "visible" changes within the family. According to Amira, "Some topics elicit fierce resistance from men, as in the discussion of shari'a, while other topics like mixing (male and female) are contested and some male members are provoked by the separation between the sexes in our activities" (Haroun and Salah 2000). As one male member of the party put it, "As a party keen for the development of women, we should abolish segregation in the Party" (Zeyyad 2000).

Support for mixing, however, is not shared by all Islamists, many of whom encourage segregation among students in the university, a position that suggests that the veil is not enough to transcend sexual barriers. In the end, Hamas's gender ideology, while supporting the "new Islamic woman" and thus potentially contradicting the common perception of the Palestinian woman as a fertile womb, does, like the secular nationalist ideology, emphasize the more accepted role of women in reproducing the nation. By "Islamizing" Palestine and "nationalizing" Islam, the Islamists have proved successful in forging a brand of nationalism to which Islam is integral and that constitutes a mobilizing force for the masses.

As time goes on, the strict gender agenda and moral system inherited from the Muslim Brotherhood continues to evolve in relation to the pressure exerted by Islamist women on their leaders and the level of empowerment these women achieve through their activism in the movement. The observation that "the text does not prohibit" was one that recurred throughout my interviews with women Islamists. What they meant was that religious texts are open-ended, making it possible for changing interpretations to forge for women a wider legitimate space in the public arena. Islamist women, while fully complicit in disseminating the movement's gender ideology, are the first to push its boundaries and stretch their public presence. Islamist women have managed to build impressive, well-organized constituencies among highly educated and professional women, at times using more temporal discourses based on sustainable development and women's rights, as well as new textual interpretations. The efforts of the Women's Action Department in the Salvation Party have opened a space for common ground with secular women, as they have fostered gender equality—and not merely complementarity—and more egalitarian social ideals, as they have "mainstreamed" gender issues into the politics of an Islamic party.

None of these developments could, however, prevent a veritable firestorm of debate and dissent—in addition to the secularists' confusion about the purpose of the project described earlier—from engulfing the WCLAC's Model Parliament Project. The Model Parliament elicited reactions covering the entire spectrum, both positive and negative. Probably the most serious involved a challenge from Islamist clergy, who questioned the legitimacy of such a debate being undertaken by women or the public or even by elected members of the existing Palestinian parliament, the Legislative Council. In other words, the ulema (religious clergy) were claiming the prerogative of being the sole agency authorized to rule in such matters. The most violent reaction came from Islamists who focused on delegitimizing women activists involved in the project as "inauthentic," as a marginal non-Muslim minority (i.e., Christian[19] or secular atheist), and calling it a Western-initiated and-funded ploy (al-Huda Association 1998, 4, 6). In the end, Islamic discourse gained clear hegemony, empowered by the failure of the PA to bring about national independence or social change, by the PA's weak legal structure, and by flagrant efforts on the part of the PA to marginalize not only the Islamists (Independent Task Force 1999; Kayed 1999) but *all* leftist parties and organizations.

As a result, some women activists had trouble resuming their networking and organizational efforts in poorer areas. Others, especially lawyers, had problems resuming their work with judges in sharia courts. Many had to explain or distance themselves from what had happened. In spite of all this, the project did achieve important gains, including articulating a general agreement among Palestinians that existing "personal status laws need serious consideration" (Siniora 2000, 6). It also showed that ordinary people could be involved in changing laws and legislation and convinced many that this should not be the task of legislators and experts only. The project allowed women to test their strengths and their weaknesses and to learn important lessons for better networking, mobilization, and organization. It also exposed the many contradictions in Palestinian nationalism and in its relation to religion (Hammami and Johnson 1999; Welchman 2003).

The generally hostile reaction to the Model Parliament Project caused deep anxiety among the different women's organizations. Some felt that they had been dragged into an overt confrontation with the Islamic movement at a time when they neither desired nor had planned for it. At the same time, they could not take a stand against the policy or the vision of WCLAC since many of them shared some WCLAC objectives, if not the organization's strategy for legal reform. Most important, the project left bitter feelings and a lack of trust among the different women's organizations. It also led to clearer polarization between women's NGOs and mass-based organizations. Far from creating a united women's front, the project led only to further fragmentation.

Demobilization of a Grassroots Organization: The Women's Committees for Social Work

Paralleling the rise of both the Islamist women's movement in Gaza and the new NGOs with their contingents of femocrats was the gradual *demobilization* of the grassroots organizations that had earlier played such a large role in both the nationalist movement and the building of consciousness around women's rights. The main grassroots women's organization was the Women's Committee for Social Work (WCSW), allied with Fateh. This was one of the women's committees, which were each connected to a political party and together had played such an important role during the first intifada. The WCSW, however, had a wider outreach than the women's organizations in the leftist parties. Like the Islamists, the WCSW targeted villages and refugee camps and managed to organize young educated women. One activist explained the reason for WCSW's popularity among rural and refugee women: "We use a simple language the people can understand; we give each one what he or she would like to hear. If they are religious, we use religious language; if they are leftist, we use leftist language. The most important thing was how to mobilize people to join the struggle, but for women, we paid special attention to providing services for them and their children. Women were lacking everything. In villages they have no services, no employment, and a striking level of poverty" (Azraq 2002). For women from Fateh, the gender agenda was understood to equate to fulfilling women's basic needs, that is, providing services, especially for poor women. Urban professional and academic women, for their part, were more inclined to join leftist organizations, seeing the WCSW as conservative and lacking a feminist vision.

With the establishment of the PA, many leaders of grassroots women's organizations faced a dilemma. If they joined the PA structure, they might lose the power base they had managed to build; if they didn't join the PA, they would leave the dividends of the process to the undeserving. It did not take long for almost all the women's leaders who supported the Oslo Accords to join the PA bureaucracy, but handling their new governmental posts while heading their nongovernmental organizations caused the latter to suffer. Uncertain about the durability of the PA and its institutions, women leaders did not want to take the risk of leaving their base to other leaders. The lack of internal elections made it easy for them to keep both posts, although the pressure on many of these leaders to prove themselves as professional femocrats meant they had little time for their own grassroots organizations. Rabiha Deyyab, for example, then head of the WCSW, was put under tremendous pressure to choose between that post or her position as general director in the Ministry of Youth and Sports; she had to fight to preserve both, "as men do" (2001). Thus, the women who had previously built the grassroots organizations were co-opted, and their organizations were paralyzed by a lack of democracy.

When many women's leftist organizations and NGOs started making claims on the "state" for women's rights, the WCSW felt at a loss. The following excerpt reveals the dilemma felt by many women activists in Fateh:

We in Fateh are not like women in the leftist organizations who raised the women's issues from the beginning of their work. We were more oriented to the national cause; we never dealt with or spoke about what should be the social status of women once we have a state; that was delayed until after liberation. When the PA was established we discovered our *matab* [impasse]. Now there is no national struggle; now it is a state-building era, and we have no vision about what we have to do. We thought of enlarging the Executive Committee of the WCSW; we thought of adding more highly educated professional women to help us to draw up a mission statement and manage our organization. We have great women militants who sacrificed a lot during the struggle, but they are not highly educated; they are not *motakhassissat* [professional]. We had very little money we needed to fund-raise for our organization. The PA did not help us financially, and we were obliged to register as an NGO to fund-raise for our own activities. We hoped that this might open new avenues and provide new contacts. (Azraq 2002)

As the WCSW oriented itself toward advocacy of women's rights, it became alienated from its previous vision and programs.

Meanwhile, events within Fateh were having a major effect on its women's organizations. Even before taking its place as the ruling party within the Palestinian Authority, Fateh had been subject to efforts on the part of the Palestinian leadership to control it. Efforts ranged from nominating students linked to the internal security apparatus for positions on university campuses to sabotaging party elections. Without elections, Fateh began to experience internal decay. The attempts of different groups, including returnees and supporters of the Oslo process, to build new power bases within Fateh led to further fragmentation. The main division was between those who supported the Oslo Agreement and those who opposed it. Fateh's internal divisions were mirrored in the WCSW, which took a position critical of Oslo and was close to a local leader who advocated the path of "struggle" and "resistance" against Israeli oppression.[20] The response of the PLO leadership was an attempt to dilute the old WCSW leadership by enlarging its membership. The addition of more women seemed on the face of it to be an attempt to increase representation of women in decision-making bodies, but in reality it was an attempt to control and weaken the grassroots organization. Original WCSW members criticized the newcomers as follows: "The women they added have no political awareness and no organizational experience; and they almost know nothing about the political organization of women. Many other members were more deserving to be in their place, but they were chosen to create patronage and not for any personal merit; they wanted to control Fateh locally by using women" (ibid.).

The new enlarged WCSC "elected" a new leadership of thirteen members, which did not include Rabiha Deyyab, then head of WCSW. Many women's complaints reached the PA president, who assigned the new incumbent the role of reorganizing women's participation in Fateh. This led to the creation of a new organizational body for women called the Women's Organization (*tanthim al-mar'a*). This new body was strongly contested by women activists in the WCSW. They perceived the change as a replacement of the militant activists who came mainly from villages and refugee camps by professional women who "never sacrificed their time and lives as we did." The women also charged that "they wanted to put all women in a small hall to fight each other. The WCSW is the women's organization of Fateh, so why create an- other body and this time isolated from its base? They just wanted to mar- ginalize us" (ibid.).[21]

The attempt to create a parallel women's organization ended as the second Palestinian intifada erupted in 2000, but by that time the largest Palestinian women's organization was already demoralized, divided, and losing its vision. At the time of this writing, the WCSW has still not solved its dilemma. The women in the organization are highly political: They know if they hire profes- sionals it might come at the expense of their own power to decide and might shift the organization in a direction over which they have no control. Yet at the same time they need professionals if they are to participate in the predominant lucrative trend toward NGO-ization.

Conclusion: What Hope in the Face of a Crippling Military Occupation?

The emergence of the PLO—a national secular leadership, especially after the Arab defeat of 1967—played an important role in consolidating Palestinian na- tional identity based on core elements of struggle, return, and sacrifice. The new construction of Palestinian nationalism constituted women in contradic- tory images: on the one hand, the traditional, sacrificing mother whose main role was to reproduce her nation by providing male fighters, and, on the other, the revolutionary militant who should join the struggle hand in hand with her brothers to liberate the nation. This contradictory construction was contested by women activists, who started to challenge the prevailing gender order by pressuring their organizations for more equitable policies and legislation to re- dress this inequality. The unstable political situations, however, in which the

Palestinians and their leaderships have existed since 1947, have always worked against any serious push by women for social change. Nevertheless, the "revolutionary" era in the diaspora and the Occupied Territories was an important phase in the development of the Palestinian women's movement during which women's activism was successful in bridging the gap between urban elite women, rural women, and refugees. This linkage was an important shift to broader organization and mobilization for women at the grassroots level and the recruitment of new women activists who, for the first time, did not come from middle-class backgrounds.

The Oslo Agreement and the emergence of the PA triggered an ephemeral process in which civil society organizations shifted from sustaining their community into claiming citizens' rights. This shift brought the professional urban elites back to the fore at the expense of the rural and refugee leadership. The merger between the structures of the PLO with those of the newly created Palestinian Authority led to the marginalization and fragmentation of all grassroots organizations and their elites. A process of NGO-ization supported by foreign funding, mainly Western, added to the fragmentation and demobilization of all social movements in general and of the national secular women's movement in particular. The vacuum was immediately filled by new forms of activism, new forms of nationalism, and a new gender ideology developed by men and women in the Islamist movement (see, for example, Jad 2005).

The obstacles in the way of the development of an aware gender mainstreaming in Palestine are now so enormous that international blueprints for women and development may simply be incapable of overcoming them. The blueprints, brought by international aid agencies and international women's movements, assume a situation of political normality and stability, the existence of a state with functioning structures, and a stable and well-defined civil society. Clearly, none of these exist in Palestine. The Palestinian women's movement in its secular form forged important ties with international and transnational women's movements through attending conferences and global communication media. Through these linkages, women activists gained important awareness about gender issues related to domestic violence and women's representation in public offices and acquired important knowledge on universal conventions.

From the 1990s onward, however, the effects of NGO-ization started to appear in the formulation of the national agenda geared so far to resist the Occupation. This position is credible since some of the main donors for Palestinian NGOs and activists in international women's movements insisted upon "correct political conditions" in an attempt to separate these organizations from politics.[22]

Many women activists became involved in projects to bring both Israeli and Palestinian women to "reconciliatory conferences" to build "peace and reconciliation." Most of these activities ignored the painful reality of the Occupation and its policies of land confiscation. These conferences may not have helped support the "peace process" but rather helped the intensification of the Occupation policies by covering them up and directing international attention to the endless "peace process" that never leads to real peace. But, again, it would be an oversimplification to perceive NGOs as passive recipients and donors as simply following or executing their governments' policies. It was argued that local NGOs, as well as international actors, have a space to negotiate their mutual relationships. Cohen and Comaroff, for example, state that NGOs "do not respond to a need, but negotiate relationships by convincing the other parties of the meaning of organizations, events and processes. . . . They act as brokers of meanings" (1976, 88, cited in Hilhorst 2003, 191). I would argue that, besides their ability to convince international donors of the vitality of their work, "peace activists" are equally involved in this process, driven by their own interests. The involvement in "peace process" activities by many NGOs, aside from getting them funding, supports the NGOs' claim to acquire more power and legitimacy. "Peace process" activism might constitute a power base for the NGO elite to reach decision-making positions whether in the PA or in the leadership of the Palestinian women's movements and other social movements.

The tendency of outside experts is to ignore the impact of structural and national instability and to pursue the implementation of externally designed projects of mainstreaming gender, despite the fact that the continuing military Occupation and confiscation of land in the West Bank and Gaza render useless most development mechanisms. The freeze in the expansion of the GUPW, for instance, is related not only to the power struggle between returnees and locals but also to the facts on the ground created by Oslo. When Salwa Abu Khadra, head of the GUPW and the EC, was faced with persistent criticisms about the lack of new elections in the GUPW, she stated:

> What prevent elections from happening are very real and problematic issues such as the scope and location of the election. The members in the diaspora cannot all come unless the Israelis grant them permits, and the Israelis don't accept that because of the shaky political situation. We cannot organize in the diaspora as an issue of principle; the Occupied Territories are now the center of the headquarters of the leadership. Also it will be very costly to bring big numbers of women representatives from the diaspora, and the Union coffers are empty. And even if they restrict the election to members

living in the homeland in Gaza and the West Bank, the members in Gaza cannot join because of the siege. (2001)

Thus, on top of the absence of gender-related policies on the part of the PA, the very real repression enacted daily by the occupying power has also stifled any attempts to define or promote citizenship or to make progress of any kind in the West Bank or Gaza. Most Palestinian resources are hostage to Israeli control and punitive actions (Hilal and Khan 2004). The infrastructure and most development projects of the nascent PA have been subject to ongoing, systematic destruction. The Separation Wall has cut off Palestinians from their own land and water resources, as well as from one another. Complete lack of control over land, sea, and airspace; the inability of Palestinians to travel from town to town even in the "PA-controlled" areas; continual raids, invasions, targeted assassinations, and killings—these and countless other aspects of the Israeli Occupation all make any kind of development impossible. Whatever the conflict and confusion within the PA and within the women's organizations, there is no denying that the Israeli military Occupation has been and remains a primary factor in the shaping and in the eventual demise of the Palestinian women's movements in the West Bank and Gaza.

In the end, while providing a forum in which to discuss democratization, human rights, and women's rights, the relatively new forms of Palestinian civil society have effectively weakened the capacity that Palestinian society previously possessed to organize and mobilize different groups, in particular women's groups aiming to combat the Occupation (Jad 2004). The extremity of the situation became undeniable in March 2002 when women leaders examined the possibility of pouring into the streets to stop the advance of the Israeli tanks reoccupying Palestinian cities. Their conclusion was simple but revealing: "We are not organized," they said (Khreishe 2002). While many scholars view the proliferation of NGOs in the Middle East as evidence of a vibrant civil society and as counterhegemonic to Islamist discourse (Norton 1993, 1995; Ibrahim 1995; Al-Sayyid 1993; Moghadam 1997), little work has been done to evaluate the impact of the proliferating NGOs on the empowerment of the different social groups they claim to represent, much less on their capacity as viable alternatives to Islamist groups. Nor are there attempts to verify whether NGOs in fact succeed in mobilizing or organizing different groups in pursuit of their rights. Indeed, few studies on the Middle East focus on how NGOs affect and interact with other forms of social organization—whether in the form of unions, political parties, or social movements involving students, women, or workers (Hanafi and Tabar 2002).

Ultimately, the transformation of Palestinian women's organizations from grassroots organizations capable of mass mobilization into NGOs was disempowering in that it weakened the mobilizing potential of secular feminist women's organizations and depoliticized their activism, leaving the Islamist women's movement as the main force contesting the previous hegemony of the secular women's movement. Reality contradicts the prevailing perception of women's secular feminist NGOs as modern and democratic "agents of civil society," whether in Palestine in particular or in the Middle East in general (Moghadam 1997, 25; Kandil 1995). It problematizes the unqualified and interchangeable use of the terms *NGO* and *social movement* in the Palestinian case or in the greater Middle East (Bishara 1996; Beydoun 2002; Bargouthi 1994; Chatty and Rabo 1997; Shalabi 2001). Meanwhile, the growing power of the Islamists has considerably complicated the possibility of forming a unifying agenda for combating the Occupation or achieving women's rights (Jad 2005). Despite the fact that they are seen by many of the secularists as undemocratic, "fundamentalist," and not part of a "true" civil society, the Islamists are now essentially carrying the cause of national struggle and national service, thereby further complicating the possibility of forming a unifying agenda for combating the Occupation or achieving women's rights.

Notes

1. In advertisements in Palestinian newspapers, it is common to read about collective community actions organized by youth groups, such as cleaning the streets, planting trees, painting walls, and so forth, followed by a little icon indicating the name of the donors who funded these projects. It is also noticeable that many of the NGO activities are held in fancy hotels, serving fancy food, distributing glossy material, and hiring "presentable" youth to help organize the event. All this has led to the gradual disappearance of the traditional image of the casual activist with the peasant accent and look.

2. The PLO was established in 1964 to contain most Palestinian political and military organizations with the exception of the Islamists. From 1964 to 1969 the organization was headed by the Palestinian moderate Ahmad Shoukiri. After the defeat of 1967, military resistance gained momentum and was empowered by military groups, with Yasir Arafat as the head of the organization from 1969.

3. This term appears to have been an Australian neologism invented to refer to a feminist bureaucrat; it is the equivalent of the Scandinavian term *state feminist*. The term originally referred to women who are employed within a state bureaucracy to work on advancing the position of women in the wider society through advancement of policies supportive of equal opportunity and antidiscrimination. This professionalization of feminism and its incorporation into the state administration have been significant points of tension for feminists who have tended to identify with a popular grassroots women's movement and who considered their ideological commitment to be uncompromised by either career advancement motives or by co-optation into agendas of a state that is still under male control. Femocrats are distinguished from women career public servants in nonfemocrat positions because the former occupy career positions that feminism has legitimated, such as women working to mainstream gender in the national bureaucracy. See Yeatman 1990, 65.

4. Since having a constitution is a sign of sovereignty, the Oslo Agreement allowed Palestinians to have what is called a Basic Law to organize governance during the interim period (1993–1999) and stipulated that it "might be extended until the implementation of the new constitution of the Palestinian State" (Article 106 of the Draft Basic Law, cited in G. Friedman 1999, 2).

5. Interview with the author Ramallah, April 9, 2001; the interviewee asked to remain anonymous.

6. Interview with the author Ramallah, April 9, 2001; the interviewee asked to remain anonymous.

7. One such example is the poem "Ahmed al-Za'atar," by the famous poet Mahmud Darwish, which was written after the 1976 attacks by the Syrian army on the Palestinian refugee camp Tel al-Za'atar during the Lebanese civil war.

8. In a local television (Phalastine) interview on December 18, 1999, in the West Bank town of Jericho, after a physical assault in Jericho's prison on M.P. Saleh Abdel-Jawad (also former minister of agriculture), General Al-Tirawi, head of the Palestinian Intelligence Service Office, declared, "We have two sacristans, the president and the flag."

9. I refer to it as "symbolic militarism" because when the Israeli troops invaded the PA area in April 2002, a national strategy for resistance, whether military or civil, was not on display. The political leadership denounced many local groups' or individuals' resistance actions as acts of "terror."

10. In Palestinian culture, it is common practice to give the name of the first male son to his parents. Thus, Abu Muhammad means the *father* of Muhammad. It is therefore an honorary nom du guerre. In 1997 Aisha was appointed to serve as the head of a local police station in Gaza but was later removed when a prisoner in her station escaped.

11. In the second intifada, many women's NGOs ran counseling programs for mothers and children so they could cope with the immense psychological stress of the Israeli violence.

12. Hamas issued many statements forbidding women from military activities since there are "enough men to continue the struggle." See Jad 2005.

13. In drawing on a similar situation in Africa, Amina Mama juxtaposes femocracy with feminism. In her view, feminism is defined as being the popular struggle of African women for their liberation from various forms of oppression, and "femocracy" is described as "an anti-democratic female power structure which claims to exist for the advancement of ordinary women, but is unable to do so because it is dominated by a small clique of women whose authority derives from their being married to powerful men, rather than from any actions or ideas of their own" (1995, 41). She questions whether "femocracy" can result in improvement of the status of ordinary women or be democratized, as well as whether state structures can act as vehicles for ordinary women's struggles or only serve the elite.

14. Many academics and women's rights supporters who tried to defend the Model Parliament used this argument. It was also used by the governor of Ramallah, who came to read a message of support for women's rights. The focus of the defense was the call for freedom of expression and women's right to speak freely.

15. I use the word *Islamists* to denote the supporters and militants of Islamic movements in Palestine. From the Islamists' point of view, there is hostility toward the use of the label "Islamic fundamentalism" as a foreign notion. I use *Islamic movement* to refer to a sociopolitical movement founded on an Islam defined as much in terms of political ideology as in terms of religion. This is the term that activists in the movement use to define themselves (Bassam Jarrar, one of the Islamist leaders in the West Bank, in Usher 1997, 336). I reserve the term *Islamist women* for those who belong to the Islamist movement and are actively engaged in the public sphere in promoting what Keddie has called "an Islamic state that would enforce at least some Islamic laws and customs" (1988, in Karam 1998, 16). Islamist women have only mobilized into a movement in Gaza, and there is little coordination between Islamist organizations in Gaza and the West Bank.

16. It is also worth noting that Fateh also used to call a woman member *ukhot* (sister), while in the leftist parties she is called *rafiqa* (comrade).

17. In 2001 the PA raided local party offices to confiscate all their equipment, documents, and computers and issued a rule to ban the party from all activities as well as to ban its journal,

al-Rissala. According to Amira (Haroun and Salah 2000), the party functions at a very low level only from its headquarters in Gaza City. At this moment, even though the party managed to obtain a ruling on March 21, 2003, from the highest court canceling the PA ruling 113/2003 that allowed the PA to put its hand on the budgets of thirty-nine Islamic societies, the PA refuses to implement the ruling and renewed its own budget-taking powers with ruling 40/2004 (http://www.Palestine-info.net).

18. The course contains topics related to more "modern" and "scientific" issues such as self-assertiveness, self-building, effective communication, political awareness, socialization, program designing, and collective picnics.

19. It happened that the lawyer who reviewed the laws and submitted her recommendations, which included a civil family law, as well as the head of the WCLAC and the project director, were all Christians.

20. Women were close to Marwan Barghouthi, a popular Fateh leader and PLC member who is currently serving several life sentences in an Israeli prison.

21. Khawla is an active member of Fateh and the WCSW from a refugee camp. Rabiha is from a poor village, as are most of women activists in the WCSW.

22. The head of USAID in Tel Aviv announced the intention to make further aid conditional on positive political developments. The formal statement made by the head of USAID, Larry Garber, announced that aid would stop if a declaration of independence were made by the Palestinian National Authority (Hanafi and Tabar 2002, 35). In 2003 the same organization circulated a form on all Palestinian NGO recipients of its funds to "certify" that they don't support "terrorism" through their activities.

12

The Women's Movement
and Feminism in Iran:
A Glocal Perspective

NAYEREH TOHIDI

Women's status and rights in contemporary Iran and thereby the trajectory of Iranian women's activism and feminist movements are paradoxical and complicated.[1] Many factors have shaped this contradictory status, including the patriarchal and patrimonial patterns in Iranian history and culture, be it secular or religious (Islamic), the state policy and state ideology, or the influential ideological or intellectual trends such as nationalism, socialism, Islamism, and more recently liberalism and a human rights framework. Another set of factors, of increased influence in more recent years, has to do with increased processes of globalization and the international currency of the discourses of human/women's rights spreading through transnational feminist activism and new communication technology such as the Internet and satellite TV. Increased globalization has intensified "glocal" dialectic, meaning the interplay of local-national factors with the global-international factors.

This chapter provides an overview of the current women's movement and feminism in Iran from a *glocal* perspective. First, a brief review of the historical background of this movement is presented. Then, to illustrate predominant characteristics of leading feminist activists in Iran, a glance is cast over two prominent women, Sedigheh Dowlatabadi and Shirin Ebadi, who represent different generations of Iranian feminisms. This is followed by a brief discussion on methodological and theoretical issues concerning the women's movement in Iran. Then the trajectory of women's activism after the 1979 Revolution and the ironic and paradoxical aspects of the emergence of a growing women's movement and feminist discourse under an Islamist state are discussed. Special attention is paid

IRAN

Human Development Index ranking: .759
Gender-Related Development Index value: .750
Gender Empowerment Measure value: .347

General

Type of government: Islamic Republic
Major ethnic groups: Persian (51%); Azeri (24%); Gilaki and Mazandarani (8%); Kurd
(7%); Arab (3%); other (7%)
Languages: Persian and Persian dialects (58%); Turkic and Turkic dialects (26%);
Kurdish (9%); Arabic (1%); other (6%)
Religions: Muslim (98%; Shi'a 89%, Sunni 9%); Zoroastrian, Jewish, Christian,
Baha'i (2%)

Demographics

Population, total (millions), 2005: 69.4
Annual growth rate (%), 2005–2015: 1.3
Total fertility (average number of births per woman): 2.1
Contraceptive prevalence (% of married women aged 15–49): 74
Maternal mortality ratio, adjusted (per 100,000 live births), 2000: 140

Women's Status

Date of women's suffrage: 1963
Life expectancy: M 68.7; F 71.8
Combined gross enrollment ratio for primary, secondary, and tertiary education
(female %), 2005: 73
Gross primary enrollment ratio: 122*
Gross secondary enrollment ratio: 78
Gross tertiary enrollment ratio: 25
Literacy (% age 15 and older): M 88; F 76.8

Political Representation of Women

Seats in parliament (% held by women): 4.1
Legislators, senior officials, and managers (% female): 16
Professional and technical workers (% female): 34
Women in government at ministerial level (% total): 6.7

Economics

Estimated earned income (PPP US$): M 11,363; F 4,475
Ratio of estimated female to male earned income: .39
Economic activity rate (% female): 38.6**
Women in adult labor force (% total): 35 (this figure obtained at the CEDAW Statis-
tical Database)

*Gross enrollment ratios in excess of 100% indicate that there are pupils or students outside
the theoretical age groups who are enrolled in that level of education.
**Estimates of economic activity range from 14% to 38%.

to transnational, diasporic, and international interplay with local-national factors such as state policies, oppressive laws, and patriarchal cultural traditions as well as socioeconomic and demographic changes.

Historical, Socioeconomic, and Political Contexts

The history of Iranian women's quest for equal rights and their collective actions for sociopolitical empowerment dates back to the late nineteenth and early twentieth centuries. In Iran, as in other parts of the world, the women's movement and feminist discourse are by-products of modernity and industrial capitalism. At the same time the women's movement, especially feminism, has provided a challenge to and a critique of the andocentric aspects of modernity. Modernity in Iran and in many other Middle Eastern countries has been associated with Western intrusion, imperialism, or colonialism, thus resulting in mixed feelings, resistance, and nationalistic anti-Western resentment among many women and men.

Feminism or women's quest for emancipation has often been perceived as an exogenous idea, a Western phenomenon associated with sexual license exported to penetrate the *dar ol-Islam* and the traditional family and thereby destroying the internal moral fabric of the entire society. Therefore, women activists aspiring for equal rights (who may or may not identify as feminist) have found themselves in a defensive position. They have usually tried to assure their community of their loyalty and patriotism. They have to also convince the elites that feminism has indigenous roots in Iranian history, is not incompatible with progressive understandings of Islamic tradition, or both (see, for instance, Kar and Lahidji 1372/1993 or Tavassoli 1382/2003). The women's movement in Iran, therefore, has been intertwined with nationalism. Feminists often have to carefully navigate between identity politics, a societal quest for "authenticity," and independence, on the one hand, and the aspiration for individual rights and universal values such as equality, human rights, freedom of choice, and democracy, on the other.

Patriarchal Consensus on Family Law. In their hundred-year history of collective activism, Iranian women have made remarkable achievements in the realms of education; economic productivity; scientific, literary, and artistic creativity; and sociopolitical participation. However, they have not succeeded in gaining equal rights in many areas, particularly in the family (marriage, divorce, and child custody). While many institutions in Iran, including the public education and judiciary systems, went through secularization during the process of modernization from the 1930s through the 1970s, personal status and family law remained strictly on the basis of sharia (Islamic law).

In Iran, as in many other Muslim-majority countries, egalitarian reforms in family law, whether by revising and reinterpreting sharia or by replacing it with secular law, have been painfully slow. This has been due to several complex reasons, the most important one being a patriarchal consensus (based on a tacit distribution of power) among the secular nationalist elite and religious Islamic elites or the clerics, or ulema. Laws governing women's roles in the public domain increasingly fall under the control of the secular modernizing state elites, whereas laws governing women in the family (and domestic gender relationships and personal status areas) remain under the control of the clergy and religious authorities.

But with the rise of Islamism and after the establishment of the theocratic state of the Islamic Republic (1979 to present), many of the laws and policies in both the public and domestic domains have come under the direct control of the clerics, who have furthered the degree of gender discrimination and male bias. A few significant progressive reforms made in family law in 1960s and '70s under the rubric of the Family Protection Law were repealed in 1980s, and family law and the penal code regressed to the way they were in the 1930s and '40s (Kar 2008). Due to women's objections, however, and also because no replacement legislation was passed, in practice the FPL remained the guide for answering questions not explicitly dealt with in sharia, hence a reversal of some of the initial regressions (see Mir-Hosseini 2002, 167, 187). The women's movement in Iran, therefore, has remained predominantly rights oriented—making its main target the discriminatory laws that reinforce violence, such as polygamy and stoning. The demand for changes in the law and the role of lawyers in almost all women's organizations have become more prominent than ever.

Two Illustrations. The complex and seemingly contradictory dynamics of the Iranian women's movements can be illustrated by the lives of two prominent Iranian women: Sedigheh Dowlatabadi (1882–1961) and Shirin Ebadi (1947–). Like most other influential Iranian feminists, they both had to navigate between the state-provided opportunities or obstacles; the daily prejudices of ordinary people against nontraditional women; the attacks instigated by the conservative clergy; the contradictory interests and priorities between the nationalist, socialist, and feminist movements; and the perils and promises of the international support and transnational feminist connections.

Dowlatabadi is one of the most respected and influential members of the first generation of feminists in Iran who pioneered the women's movement in this country. Her prolific and paradoxical personal and social life represents not only the construction of the "modern womanhood" in Iran but also how she herself contributed to this construction (see Najmabadi 1998). Her upbringing in a rather religious upper-middle-class family in a major city (Isfahan), a father and mother who encouraged daughters' as well as sons' education, and her approach to helping with "women's progress" through "educating, organizing and enlightening" constitute a pattern rather typical to many leading women activists that made up the first generation of Iranian feminists. She was a member of the executive committee of the Patriotic Women's League (Anjoman Nesvan Vatankhah), which was set up in 1922 by Mohtaram Eskandari, a Qajar princess who was married to Soleyman Eskandari, the prominent socialist leader (Paidar 1995, 95).[2] The PWL associated itself with the Socialist Party (1922–1932), yet one of its stated objectives was "to emphasize continuing respect for the laws and rituals of Islam" (Bamdad 1977, 64, cited in Paidar 1995, 96).

Sedigheh Dowlatabadi navigated between socialism, feminism, Islam, and nationalism in her evolving ideological tendencies and various activities in different organizations; as an individual journalist, educator, and founder of schools for girls; as one of the first representatives of Iranian women in international conferences on women in Europe (for instance, Paris in 1927 and Geneva in 1947); and as one of the first women to stop wearing the veil and adopt a modern Western style of dress. One of the main goals of the Isfahan Women's Partnership (Sherkat Khavatin Esfahan) that she had created was to encourage women not to buy foreign products but promote products made in Iran. Her edited journal *Zaban Zanan* (Women's Language) was banned because of her critical editorial against the prime minister of the time (Vossouq-ol-douleh) because of his signing of a loan contract with foreign banks that intellectuals deemed detrimental to Iran's national interests.

The present example of the continuous complexity and contradictions in feminist endeavors in Iran is Shirin Ebadi, one of the pioneering woman judges in Iran, a defense lawyer, and the first Iranian and the first Muslim woman to receive the Nobel Prize for Peace (2003). She was born in the city of Hamedan and raised in Tehran within a loving and cultured middle-class family. During her formative years, she was influenced by the nationalist movement headed by Mohammad Mossadegh, whose popular and democratically elected prime ministry ended in favor of the Shah through a coup in 1953 supported by British intelligence and the American CIA. At the same time, Ebadi is a member of the modern professional middle class, a stratum that benefited from and grew under the modernization policies of the Pahlavi Shahs. In 1975 she became the first woman in Iranian history to achieve chief judicial status. But after the 1979 Revolution and the establishment of the Islamic Republic of Iran (IRI), Ebadi and all other women judges in Iran were either dismissed or forced to resign. This was due to the new state's ideology and interpretation of Islam that viewed women to be too emotional, hence unsuitable for judgeship. Ebadi was demoted to a secretary position at the branch where she had previously presided. She and her female colleagues protested their demotions and were subsequently given a somewhat higher position as legal advisers. Ebadi was finally granted a license in 1992 to practice law, and as an attorney she used her law office as an advocacy center for civil and human rights. Through her writings and practice, Ebadi soon emerged as a leading promoter of human and civil rights, especially the rights of women and children in Iran (see, for example, Ebadi 2000). Along with a number of other activists and lawyers, Ebadi founded two important nongovernmental organizations (NGOs): the Society for Protecting the Rights of the Child, founded in 1994, and the Center for Defenders of Human Rights (CDHR), founded in 2001.

Since receiving the Nobel Prize for Peace, Ebadi has become very active at international levels and has helped expand the transnational connections of the Iranian women's movement. In 2006 Ebadi and five other Nobel Laureates for Peace established the Nobel Women Initiative: United for Equality and Peace with Justice, which is a high-profile transnational network aimed at shedding light on women's antiviolence activism in different parts of the world (see http://www.nobelwomensinitiative.org/).

Mehrangiz Manucherian (1906–2000), a leading lawyer preceding Ebadi; several other contemporary feminist lawyers such as Mehrangiz Kar, Farideh Gheirat, Zohreh Arzani, Shadi Sadr, and Nasrin Sotoudeh (to name just a few); and even some profeminist male lawyers such as Abdolkarim Lahidji, Abdolfattah Soltani, and Mohammad Dadkhah have played important roles in the shaping and framing of the women's rights movement and the broader civil and human rights movement in Iran. This is reflective of the great need for legal reforms and for the rule of law in Iran, hence the significance of lawyers' role in the process of democracy building. For example, during the 1990s, Ebadi was one of the lawyers, academics, and intellectuals who paved the way to the reform movement later manifested in the May 1997 landslide presidential election of the reformist Mohammad Khatami.

Ebadi, a self-identified Muslim feminist, has been a leading player in the contemporary women's movement and in defending feminists who face arrest and persecution. She has tied her courageous campaign for human rights (especially women's and children's rights) with a continuous respect for Islamic faith and repeated condemnation of any Western military attacks on Iran. She calls for separation of state and religion, and her Islamic identity has a secular and liberal orientation. Like Dowlatabadi and other pioneering feminists, Ebadi has been a target of the conservative clerical wrath, including threats and imprisonment.

The recent rise in the power of Islamist hard-liners and their increased attacks on feminist activists in Iran (more than fifty arrests in 2006–2008), especially the latest attacks on Shirin Ebadi and the closure of her founded CDHR,[3] signify times of extra hardship and new challenges for the women's movement in Iran. For the national and international observers of Iran, Ebadi has become a barometer of the status of human rights in general and women's rights in particular. If they can attack the home of such an internationally acclaimed Nobel Laureate and confiscate her computers and her clients' private files, this is tantamount to an attack on Iranian human rights and women's rights altogether. At the same time, this is indicative of the growth in the appeal of feminists such as Ebadi and the strength of their effectiveness as a social movement. Otherwise, the present government would not have perceived it as a challenge to its patriarchal ideology and policies and would not have branded it as a "threat to national security."

Before discussing the trajectory of the women's movement in Iran, some conceptual and theoretical clarification and definitions that make up the framework of this study are offered.

Theoretical and Conceptual Considerations

I make a distinction between "women in movement" and "women's movement."[4] "Women in movement" refers to women's participation and active role in various social movements such as anticolonial nationalist movements and class-based labor movements. The "women's movement," however, pertains to social movements in which women are the leading and primary players and women's empowerment and gender equality in legal rights and sociocultural opportunities are the predominant goals. Women's movements usually have a feminist orientation, even though many of their actors may not identify themselves as feminist. While some women's movements might have pursued a rather one-dimensional approach or upheld a strict school of feminism, many recent women's movements uphold various feminisms. The current feminist movement in Iran is for the most part eclectic and pragmatic, and many of the leading players recognize the intersectionality of gender, race, class, nationality, sexuality, and other bases of power, or the "matrices of domination" (Collins 1990).

My recent survey among leading Iranian women activists shows that many of them uphold an eclectic understanding of feminism, and many of the actions are organized around specific shared goals and intersectional concerns rather than ideological inclinations.[5] Urban, educated, middle-class women make up the predominant class and socioeconomic composition of the activists. Although the concerns of urban poor and working-class, rural, and ethnic minority women are occasionally addressed on various women's Web sites and in publications, and although special educational events are occasionally held in poor neighborhoods or small towns, the leading feminist groups have not yet succeeded in drawing a considerable number of rural or working-class women or women of ethnic or religious minorities into the movement.

However, some of the activists involved in the movement represent voices of women of diverse classes. Aliyeh Eghdam Doust, a fifty-seven-year-old activist from Fouman, a small town in northern Iran, for example, cogently indicates this reality. Sentenced to three years of imprisonment because of taking part in a peaceful demonstration in 2006, in a recent interview, given by cell phone from her jail in the Evin Prison, she said, "I am a woman, also a laborer, and also a teacher." She has a master's degree in Persian literature and for many years was a schoolteacher in a small town before being sacked because of her political activism. After that she worked for many years as an industrial laborer in an automobile factory (Mazda). She has experienced a painful unwanted abortion due to poverty and a painful divorce. She states that she has closely experienced the issues and concerns of women of different classes (see http://free-aliyeh.com/spip.php?article77; and in English, see http://free-aliyeh.com/spip.php?article58).

Rather than on economic and class-related issues, the current emphasis in the women's movement is on legal reform, "change for equality," and campaigns against discriminatory laws, policies, and traditional customs. Many feminists argue that discriminatory laws and practices (such as polygamy and men's privileged rights to divorce and child custody) reinforce violence and humiliation against women of all walks of life, and therefore should constitute the movement's priorities. They also point to other social movements that may and do address economic and working-class issues of women as well as men, but it is only the women's movement and feminists that focus on issues directly related to gender and sexuality.

The very notion of a "women's movement" in Iran is still a contested subject. The ruling conservative Islamists never acknowledge the existence of such a movement. They portray women's activism for equal rights as a "feminist deviation instigated under the Western influence,"[6] or as a disguise for the Zionist and American agenda toward "regime change" through a "velvet revolution." Thus, they react to it by smear campaigns, negative propaganda, arrest, and imprisonment (Tohidi 2008a).

Many of the moderate Islamic reformers and secular progressive Muslim intellectuals, however, express support for the demands of women and condemn the government's arrest and repression of women activists. Some of them, however, insist that there is no "women's movement" yet in Iran; rather, there are feminist activists.[7] Basing their arguments on some classic definitions and old theories of social movements, they point out that the current women activists lack a strong organizational structure capable of mobilizing a vast number of the populace, generating serious conflicts with the state, and bringing about political changes. Their arguments, however, seem unrealistic in light of the more recent public protests, networks of campaigns, and many arrests and conflicts between the women activists and the state organs. An increasing number of sociologists (men and women), however, have begun writing about the recent rise in feminism and the women's movement in Iran with enthusiasm, characterizing it as an "inspiring model" (see, for example, Alamdari 1387/2008) for other civil society movements or as a "definer of a true social movement" (see Mashayekhi 1387/2009; and Keshavarz 1387/2008).

An interesting alternative view in this regard has been presented by another sociologist, Asef Bayat, who defines the current women's activism in Iran as "a women's non-movement." He argues that in an authoritarian and repressive context such as that of Iran, "collective activities of a large number of women organized under strong leadership, with effective networks of solidarity, procedures of membership, mechanisms of framing, and communication and publicity—the types of movements that are associated with images of marches, banners, organizations, lobbying, and the like," are not feasible. Instead, as Bayat cogently stresses, women's activism through their presence in the public domains and their daily resistance to the state's ideology of seclusion and policies of sex segregation and forced veiling remains significant. To be a woman activist in the Iran of today means to be able to

> defy, resist, negotiate, or even circumvent gender discrimination—not necessarily by resorting to extraordinary and overarching "movements" identified by deliberate collective protest and informed by mobilization theory and strategy, but by being involved in daily practices of life, by working, engaging in sports, jogging, singing, or running for public offices. This involves deploying *the power of presence*, the assertion of collective will in spite of all odds, by refusing to exit, circumventing the constraints, and discovering new spaces of freedom to make oneself heard, seen, and felt. The effective power of these practices lies precisely in their ordinariness. (1997, 162)

Although the "power of presence" and the "ordinariness" of women's resistance constitute important aspects of women's agency in Iran, more so than in democratic countries,[8] I believe, Iranian women's activism in more recent years has actually evolved beyond "ordinariness." I would argue that many of the features of social movements mentioned by Bayat, especially those of the "new social movements" not addressed by him, do exist in the current collective women's activism in Iran. New social movements that emerged since the 1970s and 1980s in Europe, America, and other parts of the world around women's issues, feminism and sexuality, the environment, civil rights, and antiwar sentiment are categorically different from the movements in the past. Instead of labor movements engaged in class conflict, many present-day movements are engaged in sociocultural and political conflicts involving primarily middle-class people. According to the New Social Movements theory, participants in new social movements are motivated by postmaterial politics and newly created identities. It focuses on how culture influences and is influenced by social movements (see Larana, Johnston, and Gusfield 1994). Instead of formal organizational structure, new social movements are "segmentary" (have several, sometimes competing, organizations and groupings), "polycentric" (have multiple and sometimes competing leaders), and "reticulate" (are linked to each other through loose networks) (see Gerlach 1999). Theoretically, then, the current women's movement in Iran falls under the "new social movement" category.

Stages of the Women's Movement

The character of the women's movement in modern Iran—its demands, strategies, and tactics—has varied in accordance with varying socioeconomic developments, state policies, political trends, and cultural contexts at national and international levels. This history can be roughly divided into six periods. First was the era of Constitutional Revolution and constitutionalism (1905–1925), during which the first generation of women activists emerged mostly through their involvement in the proconstitutional and anticolonial activities. The first associations of women, usually semisecret, helped with women's literacy; demanded women's access to public education, hygiene, and vocational training; and criticized women's seclusion, polygamy, and domestic violence against women. Second, the era of modern nation building (1920s–1940s) was associated with increasing literacy and women's entrance at tertiary levels of higher education, expansion in women's associations and women's press, and the state-dictated mandatory unveiling of women and forced adoption of the Western dress code for men and women. Third, the era of nationalism (1940s–1960s) brought more women into the public and into political activism within both nationalist and socialist ideological and organizational frameworks. Many reform projects and egalitarian ideas concerning women's roles and status were brought into the public discourse, yet neither the nationalist nor the socialist parties could succeed in bringing about legislative reforms concerning women's suffrage or changes in family law. Fourth, the era of modernization (1960s–1970s) saw a growth in the social visibility of modern working and professional women in the rapid process of urbanization, positive legal reforms concerning women's suffrage and family law, but the subsequent erosion of women's autonomous associations along with increased state control and a top-down process of autocratic modernization without democratization. Fifth, the era of Islamist Revolution and Islamization (1978–1997) and, sixth, the era of post-Islamist reform and pragmatism, notwithstanding the latest backlash (1998–present),[9] are the latest stages that constitute the main periods discussed in this chapter.

Autocratic Modernization and the Rise of Islamism (1950s–1970s)

As the monarchy became increasingly autocratic in the years following the 1953 coup, all political and civil organizations, including women's associations, were banned or brought under state control. Women's activism around gender issues was confined to a single state-controlled Women's Organization of Iran (1963–1978) headed by Princess Ashraf, the twin sister of the Shah. This statization of the women's organizations and women's rights discourse produced contradictory results. On one hand, it facilitated certain reforms in family and personal status law that grassroots women activists had been pushing for several decades. On the other hand, because the Pahlavi state had lost its legitimacy due to the CIA-supported coup in 1953 and increased repression, the close association of women's rights with an autocratic and repressive state in the late 1960s and 1970s turned many people away from their earlier support for women's rights.

The uneven and autocratic modernization created a dual society. As middle-class "unveiled women" entered the public sphere in the growing urban centers, resentment and anxiety also grew among the urban poor, the traditionalist segments of society and their "veiled women," and conservative clerics. Intellectuals' support for women's rights and empowerment began to decline as well; many of them viewed the new "modern woman" sanctioned under the Pahlavi version of modernization and emancipation as nothing more than "westoxicated painted dolls" preoccupied with consumerism and materialism (Tohidi 1994).

The Shah's regime alienated both secular and Islamist forces. Given the weakness and lack of organization on the part of the secular democratic forces (in part due to systematic suppression by the infamous secret police, SAVAK), the Islamists, much stronger and better organized by the clerical organizational structures and financial resources, quickly gained the upper hand among those resisting the Shah. The Islamist discourse therefore prevailed over other discourses in the anti-imperialist and antimonarchy movement, hence the Islamic Revolution of 1978–1979.[10]

Millions of women took active part in the revolution and played important roles in different forms, including disseminating news, distributing leaflets, giving shelter to the wounded or the activists under attack, marching and demonstrating in the streets, and helping erect barricades against the police. Some women even took up arms and went underground as members of guerrilla organizations (Tohidi 1991).

The predominant image of the 1979 Revolution, including the one reflected in the Western media, highlighted protesting women covered in black chadors (all-encompassing veils), indicating the mobilization of many religious and traditional women behind Ayatollah Khomeini. Many secular, unveiled, and nontraditional women also felt compelled to wear a veil (either the chador or at least a head scarf) during those demonstrations, in order to signify solidarity and political opposition to the Shah's version of women's emancipation or his father's compulsory deveiling policies. However, the subsequent policy of mandatory veiling under Ayatollah Khomeini proved the perils and complications of donning veils for political purposes.

The rise of cultural nationalism and growing emphasis on Islamic identity during the 1970s pushed women's rights to the background. The Islamic Republic of Iran, in its initial stage of consolidation, put an end to the implementation of some of the progressive legal reforms that women had achieved since the Constitutional Revolution. These modern changes and reforms contributed to the emergence of a small but significant group of educated professional middle- and upper-middle-class women who did not easily succumb to the retrogressive trends in their rights and status.[11] Many of those who turned against the Shah's regime because of its dictatorship and loss of national legitimacy made up the core of the next stage of the women's movement against the theocratic authoritarianism that replaced the secular dictatorship of the monarchy.

Islamist State and Rise of Feminist Response (1980s–1990s)

The need for a feminist agenda became increasingly pressing when the new Islamic government began to take away some important parts of women's civil and personal rights: mandating the veil, increasing sex segregation, repealing reforms (the Family Protection Law of 1975) within family law, promoting polygamy and male unilateral right to divorce and child custody, promoting *sigheh* (temporary marriage), barring women judges from their practice, lowering the age of consent from eighteen to nine for girls and thirteen for boys, and establishing the sexist and violence-prone "Law of Retribution" (*qisas*).[12] These were among the most blatant sexist measures the new government pursued in the name of Islam. The government dismissed women's criticisms against such retrogressive moves and accused critics of being under the influence of either the West or the East, namely, the Soviet Union.

The first sign of an emerging Iranian feminist opposition to the new Islamist government and its retrogressive and sexist policies appeared on the national and global scenes during the International Women's Day (IWD) on March 8, 1979. For the first time in many women's lives, women organized independent mass demonstrations primarily for women's causes in line with a global feminist movement. Newly formed women's organizations such as the National Unity of Women (Etehad Melli Zanan), Association for Woman's Emancipation (Anjoman Rahai Zan), and Society for Awakening of Woman (Jamiát Bidari Zan) (though many were still politically affiliated with male-dominated political organizations) joined their forces together in order not only to celebrate the IWD but also to protest compulsory veiling and other newly announced discriminatory measures by the new Islamist government.[13] Thousands of women took to the streets and shouted, "We did not make revolution to go backward!" and "Freedom is neither Western nor Eastern, it is universal!"[14]

Other spontaneous demonstrations and sit-ins by women continued for the next week in front of the Ministry of Justice and the National Television Building, which had refused to broadcast the women's demonstrations; the University of Tehran; and the headquarters of two main secular leftist organizations (Fadaiyan Khalq and Mojahedin Khalq). A small group of veiled women waged a counterdemonstration demanding compulsory veiling for all women. Groups of zealot men armed with knives, clubs, and stones also attacked women demonstrators and caused many injuries. While the revolutionary guards passively watched the assaults, some male supporters tried to protect the unveiled protesters. The vigor and extent of outrage expressed by women protesters and the leniency in the nature of the provisional government of Mehdi Bazargan (a moderate Islamic nationalist) led to a temporary retreat by the Islamists. But women's resistance soon lost the momentum as the "hostage crisis" (1979–1981) and the Iraqi invasion of Iran resulted in a long and bloody Iran-Iraq war (1980–1988).

During the war, as wars usually do, the general atmosphere turned into a masculinist militarism of which only the Islamist and nationalist hard-liners could and did benefit. Soon gaining the upper hand in the state power organs, the Islamist hard-liners marginalized the Islamic moderates and repressed and banned all secular groups, including women's organizations. Activists fighting for the rights of ethnic and religious minorities, independent journalists, students, academics, newly formed labor councils, publishers, and progressive parties all became subjects of repression by the rapidly growing Islamist extremists who were after building a totalitarian system.

Concern over the control of women and sexuality has been central to the ideology, policy, and discourse of the ruling Islamists in Iran. During its formative years, the IRA deliberately presented sex segregation and mandatory veiling as the hallmarks of its cultural identity. The constitution, the sharia-based penal code, civil law, family code, and personal status all provide legal bases for a subordinate positioning of and unequal rights for women. In short, the law became a major basis of discrimination against women in Iran in areas such as inheritance; witness in the court; penal code, that is, the law of retribution or qisas (e.g., *diyeh*, that is, the blood money of a woman is half that of a man's); divorce; child custody; dowry (bride price, or *mahriyeh*); alimony; employment; and citizenship.

But women's lives and gender relations are not shaped by the law alone. The social dynamism of revolutionary and postrevolutionary Iran; the diversity and contradictions within Islamic thinkers, political groups, and state policies; and the increasing influence of globalization would not allow the years of silence, conformity, and demoralization to last very long. Thanks to a widespread resistance from all sides, especially women, the project for a totalitarian theocracy, including the idea of creating a uniformed "Islamist womanhood," has not succeeded in Iran.

Divergence of Islamic Gender Politics

The extremist policies of the radical Islamists soon caused opposition in various degrees and forms from all sides. A growing split in the outlook and policies between the hard-liners and moderates in the new ruling circles led to the resignation or marginalization of the latter. By the late 1980s and early 1990s, the following understandings of Islam or Islamic groups could be distinguished from each other on the basis of their gender ideology and views or attitudes toward democracy:

Traditionalist/conservative Islam is advocated mainly by traditionalist ulema and the traditional layers of popular classes, especially bazaar merchants. They insist on preservation of a patriarchal gender regime. They would like to confine women to the private domain and consider wifehood and motherhood to be the sole roles and obligations of women. Veiling is used as the main device for the maintenance of strict sex-based division of labor and segregated spaces. Traditionalists, however, are not necessarily political or after gaining the state power.

Liberal/modern or reform Islam is advocated by modern thinking ulema, new Islamic intellectuals (*naw-andishan dini*), and national-Islamic (*Melli-Mazhabi*) groups that are usually members of the modern, educated, and urban middle class. Many of them believe that "true Islam" is defined in its egalitarian ethics and is essentially just and compatible with human and women's rights and democratic polity. They apply rationalist and "dynamic" (*pouya*) *ijtihad* (reasoning) and "dynamic" *fiqh* (jurisprudence) versus "traditionalist" (*sunnati*) jurisprudence. Thereby, they reinterpret Islamic texts (especially the Quran) in the context of the twenty-first century's realities rather than those of fourteen hundred years ago on the Arabian Peninsula.[15] The advocates of reform or modernist/ liberal Islam gradually entertain egalitarian gender relations and feminist ideas. This is in part due to the influence of feminist critiques, growing women's movements, and modernist Muslim thinkers' eagerness to distance themselves from the conservative traditionalists and militant Islamists. The more progressive among them have embraced a growing number of Muslim feminist activists such as Shirin Ebadi, Shahla Sherkat, Nargess Mohamadi, and reformist women deputies such as Fatemeh Haghighatjoo, Elaheh Koolaee, Fatemeh Rakei, and Jamileh Kadivar who played active roles in legislative reforms in favor of women's rights during the fifth (1996–2000) and sixth Majlis (Parliament) (2000–2004).

Revolutionary Islamism or radical Islam has posed itself as a political alternative or solution for all of the social ills and gender-related "moral decadence" experienced in both traditionalist and modern systems. The Islamists' agenda with regard to gender issues is not always in line with the conservative traditionalists. In the specific context of an Iran where Islamists have seized state power, they have often pursued contradictory and instrumentalist gender policies. In order to appeal to a women constituency and counter the growing feminist appeal, the Islamist state has not shunned women's education and sociopolitical activism as long as those activities serve their state power. At the same time, the ruling Islamists have tried to implement sex segregation and reinforce sexual stereotypes in all spheres of life, from textbooks and the media to public buses and parks. By using the new "Islamic *hijab*"[16] as an identity marker, they try to keep their women's identity and behaviors distinct from the gender regimes and sexual mores promoted by secular Westernized modernists, liberals, socialists, and feminists.

Convergence of Women's Responses

During the years of war, socioeconomic hardship, repressive atmosphere, and intensive Islamization, secular women activists mainly engaged in small group studies, reflecting on what went wrong and what could be done. They became involved in feminist literary production, translation, research, and humanitarian work concerning those affected by war. Many Islamic women, too, began questioning and criticizing the oppressive policies, the male-biased and "unjust" laws that seemed to contradict the state promise of an "Islamic just society." For example, they printed open letters to the religious leaders about hardworking divorced women, left with no support or alimony because their husbands wanted to marry younger women. Or they would complain against paternal in-laws that take children away from widows who have lost their husbands to the war, since children legally belong to paternal grandparents in the absence of fathers.[17]

In the relatively more relaxed atmosphere of the postwar and post-Khomeini years of the 1990s under the presidency of Hashemi Rafsanjani (officially called the era of construction—*sazandegi*), the divergence of views and ideological and political splits among the Islamic forces became more clear. The political excesses, blatant discriminations, and socioeconomic failures of the Islamist extremists led to increasing disillusionment among men and especially women supporters. In the camp of the secular Left, too, the disintegration of the Soviet Union had moved many secular activists away from ideological absolutism.

The increasing factional differences within the state that came to open by the late 1990s and the growth of pragmatism among all sides of polity functioned as a sort of structural opportunity for many civil rights activists. Women activists would maneuver around mixed or contradictory messages or declarations made by various state authorities. They would test the limits by utilizing any ambiguities or contradictions within the legal, theological, or policy frameworks. For instance, many women in urban centers have gradually turned the initial strict Islamic hijab and state-mandated dress code into more relaxed, colorful, and diverse forms of fashion statement. Another example to be discussed later is the notion of "*rajol*" enshrined in the IRI constitution as a criterion for qualified presidential candidates. Utilization of the space created due to the electoral rivalries among the presidential candidates is another such example to be discussed later. In sum, specific shared concerns and available opportunities, rather than ideological agreements, have brought many women activists of diverse religious and secular backgrounds into a de facto collaboration.

Zanan magazine is an illustrative example of convergence between women activists from different ideological backgrounds. Its editor and founder, Shahla Sherkat, was a young radical Islamist during the Revolution. After the Revolution, she became editor of *Zan-e Ruz*, a state-controlled women's magazine, and grew increasingly disillusioned. In 1992 Sherkat broke away from the state-controlled publishing house, Keyhan, which did not allow her to take a feminist direction. She then founded *Zanan* (Women) as a new independent feminist magazine. She identified herself as a Muslim feminist when the word *feminism* was still taboo. She invited secular feminists of liberal, nationalist, and socialist tendencies to contribute. Mehrangiz Kar and Shirin Ebadi, two prominent feminist lawyers, and Shahla Lahidji, a prominent writer and publisher, were among a growing number of secular feminists who used *Zanan* as a relatively open and diverse forum for discussing gender issues.[18]

Later, even Iranian feminists active in the diaspora began contributing to *Zanan*. One of the first contributions from a well-known diaspora feminist was a long analytical report on the Fourth World Conference on Women in Beijing in 1995 that included a critical assessment of the role of Iranian NGOs and governmental delegations during the conference. This report helped break not only the secular versus Islamic divide but also the "inside-Iran versus outside-Iran" divide. Its critical tone, however, angered sectarian activists on both sides as well as the government authorities. Despite some initial opposition, such collaboration helped enhance the transnationalization of Iranian feminism (see Tohidi 1995 and for a different version, in English, Tohidi 1996). Among other sections, in a series of interviews with prominent intellectuals, *Zanan* took the male reformers to task on the significance of women's rights and their negligence of gender issues. *Zanan*, by far the most important and widely read feminist magazine in the Iranian history of the women's movement, was finally shut down in January 2008 by the government after publishing 140 issues and persevering through several previous threats for sixteen years (for more on *Zanan*, see Tohidi 2004a).

Islamic versus secular feminism: Divergence and convergence: To many observers of the women's movement in Iran, *Zanan* also represented "Islamic feminism," a feminist voice of Islamic reformation that is spreading in many Muslim-majority nations and among Muslim-minority or diaspora communities in the West. An illustrative example of this trend is "Sisters in Islam" in Malaysia, whose motto is "Justice, Democracy, and Equality" (see http://www.sistersinislam.org.my/).

But this trend has been the subject of confusion and controversy beginning with its very name, "Islamic feminism," and its definition. In the context of Iran, for example, two ideologically and politically opposite groups have expressed the strongest objection to this term and to any mixture of Islam and feminism. On the one hand are the right-wing conservative traditionalists and radical Islamists who adamantly oppose "Islamic feminism" because of their strong antifeminist views and feelings. On the other hand are some secularist feminists (especially among the Iranian diaspora) who hold strong anti-Islamic views and feelings. Both camps essentialize Islam and feminism and see the two as mutually exclusive, and hence the term *Islamic feminism* as an oxymoron.

Aside from these two hostile objections to "Islamic feminism" in the Iranian context, in other communities, too, some feelings of unease and concern have arisen among Muslim women activists and also among some scholars and professionals about the confusing and divisive implications that this new categorization—coined mainly by secular Western-based feminist scholars—may entail.[19] Theoretically or conceptually, a potential problem is a sort of orientalistic or essentialist Islamic determinism characterized by continually "foregrounding the Islamic spirit or influence as the regularly primary force in Middle Eastern societies, hence disregarding the complexities of social/political and economic transformations."[20]

Elsewhere, I have suggested using the term *Muslim feminist* or *Muslim feminism* in reference to those Muslims who see their faith as compatible with feminism. The term *Islamic feminism*, however, can be used in reference to analytical categorization in the field of feminist theology or feminist exegesis within the Islamic tradition.[21] Shirin Ebadi made a similar observation, saying, "If Islamic feminism means that a Muslim woman can also be a feminist and feminism and Islam (or Muslimhood) would not have to be incompatible, I can agree with it. But if it means that feminism in Muslim societies is somehow peculiar and essentially different from feminism in other societies so that it has to be always Islamic, I do not agree with such a concept. Similarly notions such as 'Islamic democracy' and 'Islamic human rights' are misleading; these are universal principles and values that need no relativistic adjectives" (interview with author, December 1999).

I have also suggested avoiding polarization or dichotomization of a "faith position" and a "secular position" with regard to commitment to women's rights. To set secular and Muslim (or Islamic) feminism in conflict can only benefit the reactionary patriarchal forces, be they of traditional or new Islamist patriarchy or secular modern patriarchy. To equate secular or modern with equality and feminism is as naive and misinformed as equating faith and religion with antimodernity and antifeminism. Not all Muslims are against equal rights for women and a secular state, and not all secular people are profeminism or in favor of women's equal rights (see Tohidi 2006, 2002b).

Societal Changes and the Post-Islamist Reform Era (1990s–2005)

A growing disillusionment with Islamist extremism and totalitarian policies helped the marginalized moderates and secular forces gain gradual strength. During the 1990s a widespread reform movement began to take shape among many former

Islamists and some ruling clerics as well as intellectuals and students. This ideological shift from Islamism to moderation and democracy manifested itself most visibly by the surprise victory of a moderate cleric, Seyyed Mohammad Khatami, in the presidential elections of 1996. The active support lent by women and youth (half of them female) played the key role in this upset victory.

The political shift toward moderation and pluralism facilitated the growth of women's activism and the rising feminist movement. But this could not have happened without a wide range of interconnected demographic and socioeconomic changes in recent decades, including rapid urbanization that intensified in the 1960s–1980s; a youth bulge (70 percent of the population is below age thirty); a rise in female literacy rates and educational attainment (as of 2005, more than 60 percent of university enrollment was female); a remarkable decrease in women's fertility rates; an overall improvement in women's health and life expectancy; increasing participation of women in economic activities, especially in the informal sector; changes in sexual attitudes (particularly an increase in delayed marriage); increased access to the media, news, and information thanks to new communication technology and globalization; and the ability to facilitate local-global interaction and growing awareness of alternatives to the state-propagated patriarchal Islamist discourse.[22]

Among the sociological paradoxes of Iran under an Islamist state is a rapid transformation of sexual mores and sexual identities that some scholars have branded a "sexual revolution" (see Mahdavi 2008; and Afary 2009). Ironically, Shii Islamic devices such as *mutá* or *sigheh* (temporary marriage) are occasionally used by members of the secular and nonconformist youth to cover their illicit sexual relationships that otherwise would face severe punishments (on sigheh practice in Iran, see Haeri 1989).

Women's Rising Activism and Feminist Intervention

Cultural Production. In addition to all these changes in society at large, women's expanding roles in cultural and artistic production have contributed to the rise of a new wave of feminist movement. Women writers and translators of both older and younger generations such as Simin Daneshvar, Shahrnoush Parsipour, Goli Taraqi, Zoya Pirzad, Lili Farhadpour, Monirou Ravanipour, Firouzeh Mohajer, and Farzaneh Taheri have written widely read works, including best-selling fiction and nonfiction (see Milani 1992). Filmmakers such as Manijeh Hekmat, Rakhshan Banietemad, Tahmineh Milani, and Pouran Derakhshandeh have produced internationally acclaimed and award-wining films, many with feminist messages. The number of women publishers and journalists also increased considerably. In addition to publishing houses owned and run by women, such as Roshangaran of Shahla Lahiji, Towsèh of Noushin Ahmadi Khorasani, and Shirazeh of Ziba Jalali, and women's press and periodicals such as *Zanan, Hoquq Zanan, Farzaneh, Zan, Jens Dovom,* and *Payam Hajar,* many women journalists such as Asiyeh Amini and Nooshabeh Amiri have worked within the conventional daily papers and raised gender issues from within the mainstream press. Many Web sites, online journals, and Web logs have replaced the banned print press of women.

Civil Society Building. In 1997 there were only 67 women NGOs; in 2005 this number reached to more than 480, a sevenfold growth. After the backlash under Mahmoud Ahmadinejad's presidency, however, the quantity and quality of the growing trend in civil and political activism have been declining. The number of women NGOs, for example has risen from 480 in 2005 to about 600 only. Women are engaged in various civil activities, including protection of the environment and promotion of sustainable development; establishment of local libraries, study groups, and cultural centers; awareness raising regarding AIDS and drug abuse; antiviolence training; protection of battered women; protection of children's rights, especially street children; improving living conditions of poor and working-class women; and provision of legal advice to abused women.[23]

Political Participation. In political society, too, women play a considerable role, both within and outside of state-approved boundaries at formal and informal levels. Due to the suppression of secular parties, all the 240 registered political parties or organizations (18 of them being women's groups) in today's Iran are the ones that have religious orientation or at least are willing to identify themselves religiously with an Islamic affix or suffix in their names, such as Hezb Mosharekat-e Islami (Islamic Participation Party). At the formal level, these registered political parties are broadly divided along the "reformist" and "conservative" spectrum. Some women activists work mainly within these formal and state-recognized political entities, while many others reach out beyond these boundaries and interact with secular or Islamic women who side with oppositional politics. While most feminists have maintained their independence from the repressive state, they have not shunned collaboration and coalition building with women's groups who work within the reformist Islamic frameworks or lobby the state organs such as the Majlis for legislative changes.

As mentioned earlier, during the presidential election of 1996, women's active support played a decisive role in the unexpected victory of Khatami, who ran under a reform platform and ruled from 1997 to 2005. Moreover, during the sixth (1998) and seventh (2003) parliamentary elections, 351 and 504 women, respectively, sat among the candidates (a considerable increase from

287 in the previous election) (see Baniyaghoob 1384/2005). Nevertheless, the number of women deputies in the Majlis has remained very low (4 to 5 percent), far below the world average (15 percent). Yet the quality and composition of women deputies in the sixth Majlis were encouraging. Due to their commitment to reform and women's rights and outspokenness, some of them (Fatemeh Haqiqatjou and Elaheh Koolaee, for example) were persecuted by judiciary power that represented the conservative hard-liners.

During the latest parliamentary election for the eighth Majlis in the winter of 2007, Islamist, conservative, and reformist women's groups formed separate coalitions among themselves. Despite their ideological and political differences, a common goal for all groups was to set a 30 percent quota on their respective parties' electoral lists.[24] But their attempts ended with failure, so much so that the number of women deputies in the eighth Majlis is even smaller than the previous ones (10 instead of 12).[25] In the seventh and eighth (the present) Majlis, women deputies have been overwhelmingly conservative and have done little in support of women's rights.

Lately, however, thanks to the impact of the growing women's movement and lobbying of some conservative as well as reformist women's groups, including a couple of the current conservative women deputies, a small yet significant legislative reform is under way. This reform, which has received the state and also supreme leader's blessing, pertains to inheritance rights of women that would expand a woman's proportion of inheritance to nonremovable (i.e., land) as well as removable properties of her husband. Furthermore, as will be discussed later, recently some of the conservative and Islamist women's groups joined a de facto coalition with reformist and secular feminist women to oppose a state-proposed Family Bill that aimed at facilitating polygyny and temporary marriage.

During the presidential election of 2001, 47 women nominated themselves as candidates for the presidency, and in the latest one (June 2005) almost 100 women did so. But the Guardian Council, a conservative body that vets the candidates and overrules the Majlis, did not approve of their candidacies without ever openly admitting that disqualification of all women candidates was due to their femaleness. This is related to a vague clause in the constitution that requires the head of the state to be a *rajol*, an Arabic word that can mean male or a politically experienced and knowledgeable person. Knowing this ambiguity and lack of consensus among the clerics about its meaning in this context, some reformist women activists, including Azam Taleghani, a prominent Islamic reformer, have kept nominating themselves in various presidential elections. This political game with the conservatives is in line with taking advantage of any possible space for raising women's political profile.

Not only at the parliamentary level, and not only in urban areas, but also in rural areas women have been gradually, slowly, but steadily taking part in social spheres, including political competitions. For example, in the first municipal elections in 1999, women made up 7.3 percent of candidates: 2,564 urban women and 4,688 rural women ran as candidates in the elections of city councils and village councils. What is more important is that many of these women actually got elected: 1,120 women were elected in different cities, winning one-third of the seats in major cities. In all central cities of the provinces, except for Ilam, Sanandaj, and Yasooj, women were elected as the primary members of the city councils, that is, they won the highest number of votes. In short, in 109 cities, 114 women won the most or the second-highest number of votes. In 176 cities at least 1 woman, in 48 cities 2 women, in 8 cities 3 women, and in 1 city 4 women became the primary elected members of the city councils. In a village of the Kahnuj region in Kerman, all primary and secondary elected members of the council were women.

Dialectic of State Policies and Women's Status. I give all these detailed numbers because I feel these indicate that Iranian society is not misogynistic, and it seems that many people in Iran are gradually getting ready to take women seriously and accept them in leading roles. But it is mainly the ruling Islamists and their supportive traditionalist strata that keep trying to hold women back by forceful sex segregation and by resisting legal reforms.

For instance, a quick comparison between the conservative governments preceding Khatami's presidency and the hard-liner government of Ahmadinejad that followed would demonstrate the importance of the dialectic between state policies and women's status concerning their freedom and mobility, the number of women NGOs, the nature of legislative reforms, the degree of restrictions and pressure on women's dress code and sex segregation, and the number of movies, books, newspapers, and magazines published by and about women. The increasing repression of political and civil activism, even spatial sociability of women; more strict censorship of the media, books, and arts; and the continuous filtering of Web sites under President Ahmadinejad have had dampening effects in all areas of women's social life.

At the same time, recent changes in gender roles and sexual mores, resistance and nonconformity among women and youth, and persistence of women's collective demands for change have been contributing to the widening of factional conflicts and differences of views on gender issues among the clerics and other ruling elites. Women activists in turn try to use the space created by such differences toward their cause whenever possible.

Below, a review of the ninth presidential election in 2005 is presented to illustrate the changing gender politics and the significance of women as a political constituency in light of the current women's rights activism in Iran.

The Race for Women's Votes

While women supported Khatami's candidacy during the seventh and eighth presidential elections, their demands remained within general terms such as "development of civil society" and "democracy and human rights." During the ninth election, however, many women, disappointed with the shortcomings and unfulfilled promises of Khatami, responded differently. In protest against the undemocratic intervention of the Guardian Council in disqualifying many candidates, especially all women candidates, some women's groups and prominent women activists such as Shirin Ebadi boycotted the ninth election. Other activists called for a national referendum for the election of a new constitutional assembly and the establishment of a secular and egalitarian constitution compatible with the Universal Declaration of Human Rights. Many others participated to support the reform candidate or relatively more moderate ones in order to prevent the victory of their hard-line rival, Ahmadinejad.

Despite varying views and strategy vis-à-vis the election, all activists agreed to take advantage of the relative openness of the political atmosphere of the election times and bring women's demands into the public debates by taking each candidate to task. While raising women's specific demands, women's groups challenged each candidate to come up with specific statements about their views on gender issues and specific plans for tackling gender-related problems (including interpretation of *rejal,* reform in women's civil rights, the question of compulsory hijab and freedom of choice, and women's participation in sociopolitical arenas). Some women's groups presented a list of their demands to their favorite candidate and entered into negotiation with them. The Women's Commission of the Participation Front of Islamic Iran (Jebheye Mosharekat Iran Eslami), for example, came up with a list of twenty-nine demands for Mostafa Moìn, the main candidate from the reform camp.

All the eight presidential candidates, conservative as well as reformists, felt compelled to address women's issues in their platforms, on their Internet sites, and in their campaign speeches. They also formed special "Women's Committees" in their campaign headquarters. Moìn went so far as to appoint a woman, Elaheh Koolaee, as his spokesperson, and his wife accompanied him during some of his campaign trips. Hashemi Rafsanjani, too, appeared in some public scenes along with his wife, unprecedented for a high-ranking cleric.

As *Zanan* magazine indicated in a headline, a unique aspect of the ninth presidential election was the "Men's Race over Women's Votes."[26] Deliberate efforts to appease women and attract their votes extended to the instrumental use (by Hashemi and Qalibaf) of some young pretty women, girls, and boys in "un-Islamic" dress and appearance in order to appeal to the young and to women, the two groups that proved to be important constituencies during Khatami's victory.

Many activist groups chose to address more systemic problems (see Shekarloo 2005). About 90 NGOs concentrating on women and gender issues, the environment, and education joined 350 prominent female writers, academics, lawyers, artists, activists, journalists, and 130 bloggers to call for a public protest against the breaches of women's rights in the Islamic Republic of Iran. The result was an unprecedented and unauthorized demonstration on June 12, 2005, just a couple weeks before the election.

In spite of intimidation, about 3,000 women gathered at five in the afternoon in front of the main gate of the University of Tehran. The protesters were determined, well organized, and keen on making their voices heard, both inside and outside Iran. Their slogans and their ending statement stressed the necessity for changing the constitution and reforming the legal system. They identified the present laws, based on sharia, as the main obstacle to achieving equality and the empowerment of women.

The security forces came in overwhelming numbers and tried to interfere, but the event was relatively peaceful, with no confirmed reports of arrest or serious injury. The organizers cleverly timed the protest for the peak of the presidential election campaign, a less repressive period when security forces would be reluctant to attack women before the eyes of the public.

Again due to certain glocal dynamics, Mahmoud Ahmadinejad, a hard-liner backed by conservatives, won a surprise victory. At the national-local level, the shortcomings of Khatami and the reform camp, especially the disappointment of the student movement when Khatami failed to defend them against violent attacks by the hard-liners, turned many away from active participation in the 2005 elections. The reform camp was badly divided and could not present a single candidate, and thus the breakup of the votes worked in favor of conservatives. At the international-global level, many factors worked against the reform candidates; the disastrous consequences of the invasion of Iraq, the intensification of the Israeli-Palestinian conflict, the designation of Iran by President Bush as part of the "axis of evil," and the threat of military attacks on Iran all further isolated the liberals and moderates in Iran and emboldened Islamist radicals such as Ahmadinejad.

As many suspected, the status of civil rights, human rights, and especially women's rights has deteriorated under the government of Ahmadinejad.

Though Ahmadinejad sought to soften his image on gender issues during the week before the runoff on June 24, 2005, even speaking against "sexist attitudes," his electoral base on the far Right has continually agitated for a harder line. His base is particularly offended by the looser standards of "Islamic dress" for women and the freer mixing of the sexes in public places that slowly developed over the two terms of President Khatami.

New Wave of the Women's Rights Movement

Despite the current backlash that is associated with an intensification of crackdown on personal, social, and political freedoms, especially on women activists, the latest trends in the women's movement, manifested also in a few issue-oriented campaigns, seem to reflect a post-Islamist and postideological pragmatic approach. Some feminist- or gender-focused NGOs continue to work around women's health; some are focused on environmental protection and sustainable development; some focus on domestic violence and provide abused and battered women with legal advice and references; and some engage primarily in antiwar activities.

Today, there are a handful of organized and focused collective campaigns that constitute important components of the current women's rights movement in Iran. The largest, most grassroots-oriented and influential one is the One Million Signatures Campaign to change discriminatory laws. A smaller yet more focused and regionally grounded one is the Stop Stoning Forever Campaign. Other campaigns of smaller scale include the Women for Equal Citizenship Campaign, Women's Access to Public Stadiums Campaign, National Women's Charter Campaign, and Mothers for Peace.[27] Due to the limits of this chapter, I will discuss only two of these campaigns, the one with the sharpest focus, the Stop Stoning Forever Campaign, and the one with a broader agenda and the largest and most influential grassroots supporters, the One Million Signatures Campaign.

The Stop Stoning Forever Campaign

The target of this campaign, stoning adulterers, is a practice that is globally perceived as the most repugnant part of the penal code in Iran. Although it is practiced rarely and may directly affect only a few people, perhaps five to seven women per year, its practice and legality have important violent and patriarchal implications. For one, it is based on the assumption that women's sexuality and male-female sexual relationships are to be punitively controlled by religious authorities rather than the mutual consent of two adults. Moreover, its public ritual of torturous killing (usually women) by community members would reinforce violence, cruelty, and misogyny at large. Therefore, the fight against stoning has broader significance that goes beyond protection of the human rights of a few adulterous people.

Although during the reform era the head of the judiciary had declared a moratorium on stoning, under the presidency of Ahmadinejad the practice resurfaced sporadically in different parts of Iran. In mid-2006 several lawyers, academics, and activists inside and outside Iran came together to form a campaign to stop stoning forever.[28] The state authorities usually deny the enforcement of this law, while the practice goes on in some small towns. Since it has not been outlawed, some local judges (who are members of the clergy) see it as their own prerogative to issue stoning sentences against adulterers (usually women and occasionally men, too). The campaigners then saw it necessary to first document the cases on the ground. In 2006 they succeeded in publicizing seven cases of imprisoned women and two of men pending stoning (see Vahdati 2006).

This campaign brought to the surface the differences of opinions and interpretations among the ulema (Islamic scholars and clergy) with regard to the question of stoning. Many argue that there is no Quranic injunction about stoning. Some clerics have codified this outdated and inhumane punishment as part of the sharia in the IRI penal code only on the basis of some dubious instances in the Hadith (sayings attributed to the Prophet Mohammad).

Stoning recently resurfaced as a "community punishment ritual" in the Kurdish province of Iraq but not in the Iraqi penal code. Actually, Iran and the Sudan are the only Muslim-majority countries that have stoning in their criminal codes.[29] Moderate jurists such as Ayatollah Yousef Sanei and Ayatollah Hussein Mousavi Tabrizi call for the stop of this practice for both theological and pragmatic modern-age considerations (see Alasti 2007).

More recently, for strategic reasons and due to increasing pressures, the activists involved in the campaign against stoning decided to further internationalize the operation of this campaign and move most of its efforts outside Iran. Specifically, it is now in conjunction with the transnational network of Women Living Under Muslim Laws (WLUML) that the Stop Stoning Forever campaign is continuing its efforts on the national and global levels.

The One Million Signatures Campaign

One of the recent feminist initiatives in Iran seeks "Change for Equality" (Taghyir Baray-e Barabary) through the collection of one million signatures to be presented to the parliament demanding changes to the present discriminatory laws.[30]

Named the "One Million Signatures Campaign to Change Discriminatory Laws," it evolved from two peaceful demonstrations demanding equal rights on June 12 in 2005 and in 2006. The police and plainclothes security forces violently attacked both, especially the second demonstration. This led some activists to question the costs and effects of holding street demonstrations under the hard-liners' government of Ahmadinejad. In fact, a number of activists had expressed reservation and objections to holding of the demonstration on June 12, 2006, while the one in 2005 had received much wider support. It was following some internal debates and tension over various strategies that the idea of the campaign was born.[31] The campaign was officially inaugurated during a seminar on August 27, 2006, in Tehran with the attendance of more than two hundred advocates of women's rights, including several prominent writers, lawyers (such as Simin Behbahani and Shirin Ebadi), journalists, and students.[32]

Fifty-four young and middle-aged women activists were the founding members of this campaign. Soon joined by hundreds of others, they have pursued a face-to-face and door-to-door educational strategy for collecting signatures from women and men at places that women usually gather—parks, public buses, metro trains, shops, schools, offices, hair salons, or simply at their homes. During such contacts, they distribute an instructive pamphlet about the biases in the present laws and the way discriminatory laws reinforce violence and harm the well-being of women, men, and family life.

This campaign was modeled after a similar campaign that was begun in 1992 by Moroccan women and produced progressive changes in family law in that country. Becoming inspired by Moroccan women and adopting a strategy from feminists in North Africa rather than Western Europe or North America is itself an interesting shift in the gaze of Iranian women activists. Neither the anti-West Islamism nor the secularist infatuation with the West—so prevalent in Iran of the previous eras—is common now. It seems that global feminism has gained rainbow colors and is perceived in a polycentric world rather than an Islamo-centric or Eurocentric world order.

As is evident from the writings of the activists in this campaign, unlike political parties, the women's movement neither has the intention of overthrowing the government nor wants to seize state power (see, for instance, Tahmasebi 2008). The campaign reaches beyond governments and aims at transforming the dominant patriarchal cultural patterns, attitudes, and socioeconomic and political relations to achieve greater equality. Thanks to the impact of this campaign and other pressures from different women's groups, there has been much more discussion among decision makers and religious leaders about the need to reform laws on women (ibid.).

Despite intimidation and arrests, this campaign has grown into a network of thousands of activists with branches in more than fifteen of the country's provinces. It gained recognition and respect among various political and civil society organizations, intellectuals, journalists, and even some moderate clerics. Two special committees, Men for Equality (Mardan baraye Barabari) and Mothers of the Campaign (Madaran-i Campaign), reflect the involvement of men, usually of the younger generation, and mothers, who are not necessarily activists as such.[33]

The campaign also mobilized support among Iranians abroad and gained increasing recognition and solidarity among transnational feminist networks and human rights organizations. The campaign and campaigners have become recipients of several international awards and recognitions. In 2008 the Olaf Palme Prize was awarded to Parvin Ardalan, one of the leading campaigners; another international human rights prize in Italy was awarded to Nasrin Sotoudeh, a defense lawyer of the Campaign; yet another one from Nuremberg, Germany, was awarded to Abdolfattah Soltani, a male defense lawyer (see http://www.campaign 4equality.info/spip.php?article3350 and http://www.campaign4equaly.info/spip .php?article3362). The Youth Organization of Amnesty International made a song posted on YouTube recognizing the efforts of the campaign. Two recent prizes that have been awarded to the campaign as a whole instead of any specific individual are the Simone de Beauvoir Prize from France (in 2008) (http://www .campaignforequality.info/english/spip.php?article436) and the Global Women's Rights Award from the United States by the Feminist Majority Foundation (http://www.feministschool.com/english/spip.php?article256 and http://change forequality-ca.org/English/obalWomensRightsAward.html). Such prestigious international awards by nongovernmental entities provide the women and civil rights activists in Iran with international recognition and moral support, also further strengthening transnational and global ties.

In addition to provinces in Iran, the campaign has branches in some other countries among the Iranian diaspora. Those with active Web sites include Kuwait, the United States (California), Germany, Cypress, England, Sweden, and Austria. The California branch, the first of its kind and one of the most active ones, has recently been on the news.[34] One of its student activists, Esha Momeni, was arrested in Iran on October 15, 2008, during her visit while preparing a video documentary on the campaign for her master's thesis. Though freed on bail after six weeks, she was banned from leaving Iran and returning to her studies in Northridge, California until August 11, 2009.

Despite its difficulties and shortcomings, this promising campaign contributes to feminist culture building, the configuration of a common identity among many activists, and consciousness raising about women's rights in society at large. It brought the debate over family law to the surface, and even some prominent clerical authorities have admitted that the old *fiqh* (jurisprudence) does not reflect the new realities of the twenty-first century and can be subject to reinterpretation and revision.

Large Coalition, Small Victory

Instead of listening and yielding to the legitimate demands of the women's campaigns, the government of hard-line president Mahmoud Ahmadinejad proposed a bill named, in Orwellian fashion, the "Family Protection Bill." If passed it would have threatened the stability, equilibrium, and mental health of families by reinforcing and facilitating polygamy, temporary marriage, and men's privileged position with regard to divorce" (Tohidi 2008a). Shirin Ebadi warned the authorities that she and her colleagues would stage a sit-in at the Majlis building should the bill be discussed on the Majlis floor. When it became clear that such a discussion was imminent, in an unprecedented action in the Islamic Republic of Iran, dozens of prominent women entered the Majlis building on August 31, 2008, and met with members of parliament and made compelling arguments against the bill, calling it the "Anti-Family Bill."

In addition to presenting a petition signed by more than three thousand activists and intellectuals, this diverse coalition of women's rights activists, which had gained the support of even some moderate clerics and politicians, persuaded a judicial commission to drop some of the most contested articles, and the parliament passed an amended version on September 9, 2008. This version maintains the present law that makes second marriage contingent upon the first wife's consent and does not attach any tax on the amount of dowry to be paid to the wife in case of divorce.

This small yet symbolically significant victory for women displayed the power in their unity around urgent issues and the effectiveness of building coalitions. It also brought Islamic and secular feminists together again around specific issues of common concern and demonstrated the effectiveness of combining different tactics that were used by various women's groups, including exerting pressure through media coverage, both printed and online media; petitioning and signature collecting; lobbying; distribution of educational brochures; a letter writing drive; a phone call drive to the Majlis representatives; and finally direct public and physical presence in the organs of power, face-to-face communication, peaceful confrontation, and the threat of a sit-in.

International and Diasporic Support

Many women activists in Iran are well aware of the global feminism and transnational feminist networks. Thanks to new communication technology, an increasing number of computer-savvy, highly educated, multilingual women activists are effectively employing the Internet and transnational space in the service of women's movements. Dissident secular feminists, women of ethnic and religious minorities, and the gender-egalitarian Islamic women reformers disillusioned with theocracy actively seek these international connections. They have engaged in cross-cultural dialogues at the regional and international levels. Many have traveled abroad to take part in workshops and gender-training sessions sponsored by UN agencies or academic institutes, human rights organizations, or international donor agencies. The UN-sponsored regional and international conferences and their outcomes, such as the Convention on the Elimination of All Forms of Discrimination Against Women (CEDAW), Nairobi's Forward Looking Strategies, and the Beijing Platform of Action, have played a significantly positive role in gender sensitization, legitimization of the women's rights movement, and development of women's NGOs.[35]

The UN Commission on the Status of Women, itself an outcome of global women's movements, has helped the engendering of state machinery in many countries, including Iran. As a UN member state, the IRI during the presidency of Hashemi Rafsanjani created an Office of Women's Affairs to report to and advise the president on gender policies and plans. The new elite professional and highly educated Islamic women who were well connected to state organs and the new bureaucracy have benefited from this machinery. Their active presence at international conferences and work to establish international connections are supposed to be in the service of public relations and diplomatic strengthening of the Islamic state, especially in regard to its gender image. Yet in the process of their own experience with sexist barriers and their contacts and dialogue with the international community, especially women's organizations and feminist discourse, they have come to be less ideological, relatively more open-minded, more pragmatic, and more conscious about women's rights.

The UN gender and development documents and criteria gave women activists a legitimate tool or a sort of blueprint and framework upon which they could argue for their issues and put pressure on state agencies to comply with the UN-demanded gender standards. Under Khatami's presidency, the functions of this office, now named the Office of Women's Participation, further expanded and emphasized women's participation in politics and civil society building. Encouraged by his call for "dialogue among civilizations," women

NGOs and those connected to government resources sought further international contacts at both intergovernmental and global civil society levels.

During the past thirty years, there have been ninety-seven Iranian women's groups outside Iran on four continents, in sixteen countries and twenty-six cities (see Navaeei 1999, 18). The diaspora women activists have contributed to the women's movement inside Iran at different levels, including political, informational, theoretical, technical, and organizational. The activities of diaspora Iranian women include raising international awareness, mobilizing international pressures against violations of women's rights in Iran, sending in literature and supplying women activists inside Iran with materials and scholarly works published abroad, doing research on women in Iran for translation and publication both in Iran and abroad, helping the women's press financially by distributing and selling copies among the immigrant communities abroad, and providing Iranian women's rights pioneers with international forums and transnational connections and visibility by inviting them to international academic conferences or activist meetings. One such forum is the Iranian Women's Studies Foundation, which has held annual conferences in Europe, Canada, and the United States.[36]

International Support: A Mixed Blessing?

It is important to note that the local-global interplay, diaspora intervention, and international support at times have hurt rather than helped the women's rights movement in Iran. The Iranian diaspora is politically divided. The majority of them tend to be secular, nationalist, highly educated, resourceful, and overall progressive. A small but rich and vocal segment, mostly concentrated in Southern California, is composed of Jewish or Muslim conservatives who follow a promonarchy right-wing politics and have been supportive of the neoconservative policies of the Bush administration. Nonprofessional right-wing secular conservative monarchists run a couple dozen satellite television channels based in Los Angeles. Their interventions in Iran's politics have been often based on a nostalgic and nonrealistic past and vindictive agitation instead of nourishing a democratic and egalitarian culture.

As pointed out in the beginning of this chapter, Iranian feminism had been intertwined with nationalism, and often women's rights have become stuck in the midst of political games and international rivalries. The present case in point is the continuous tension between the government of Iran and the Western governments, especially with the United States over the nuclear program of the IRI.

U.S. policy toward Iran and the continuous threat of military attack have further complicated the situation of all civil rights activists, particularly feminists. In 2003 the allocation of seventy-five million dollars in U.S. aid to Iranian civil rights organizations spurred the Iranian government to repress all voices of dissent. Any civil society organizations or individuals doing effective work toward democracy and human and women's rights have been accused of being agents in a U.S. plan for regime change.[37] While the hardliners and radical Islamists cast peaceful and transparent campaigns as national security threats, that charge is actually better applied to them. Their belligerent foreign policies have brought sanctions and economic hardship and created the danger of military attacks on Iran. As one of the activists talking against polygamy aptly put it, "How could my protest against my husband's right to bring a second wife into our home threaten my country's national security!?"[38]

Most arrested women activists have been charged with "endangering national security" or "contributing to the enemy's propaganda against the regime." Under such threats, most women's rights activists have been careful not to receive any donations or grants from international donors. This has deprived Iranian women's rights groups of international monetary resources available to women's groups in many countries. Even the international awards that have monetary values attached to them have become a source of tension and political divisions among the activists.[39] Unfortunately, some have developed an aversion to any financial help or even symbolic awards from Western agencies. But many others see this as yielding to the governmental pressures and contrary to their practical needs and interests.

Many activists have come to differentiate two issues in this regard. One concerns the liabilities of international support, that is, loss of local actors' control over their agendas. Dependency and other negative consequences of donor-driven agendas have been criticized in several other countries (see, for example, Kay 2004). The other issue is related to the current government's paranoid attitude toward any relationship with the "West." It is within the present hostility between the governments of Iran and the United States that women's establishing of international feminist networks backfires. This is an important issue, but it doesn't necessarily suggest that international movements and human rights agencies should not make support available. Rather, it raises the practical question of how Iranian feminists can make use of such resources without risking a backlash.

Many Iranian feminists feel they are caught in a double bind, trapped between what they see as the Islamist masculinist forces inside Iran and the secu-

lar imperial hegemonic forces in the West, for both of whom women's empowerment is the last concern (see Tohidi 2007b). Iranian women's rights activists
are keen about the experiences of women's postcolonial struggles around the
world as well as those of their own mothers and grandmothers in Iran. They have
resolved not to take a passive approach, one that relies on the support of the West
or promises of salvation through bombs and mortar shells. For example, they re-
sent the neo-cons' justification of their hegemonic policies in Iraq in the name
of saving women and men from existing human rights abuses.

Nor have women activists taken a defensive stance in favor of the ruling patriarchy in Iran because of its defiance of the West. Rather, they are taking
practical steps toward democracy and equal rights, demarcating the women's
movement from both the native Islamist and Western imperial patriarchies.
Likewise, many women's groups make de facto alliances with other civil rights
groups and reformist parties, especially student movements. At the same time,
many are keen on retaining their autonomy and not pinning their hopes on national political groups and parties that give attention to women and their issues
only at election time or during political turmoil.

Conclusion

The women's movement in Iran is learning to be more creative and flexible in
employing different strategies. Despite personality frictions, ideological divergence, and differences in strategy and tactics, they often converge in practice
to collaborate over common goals. They are becoming increasingly more informed of the current trends within global feminisms, especially the mechanisms, tools, and machineries created through the UN gender projects and
conventions such as CEDAW (see Tohidi 2008b). Due to the vetting power of
the conservative Guardian Council, the attempts made by the reformist
deputies in the sixth Majlis to ratify CEDAW did not succeed. However, most
women activists, including some Islamic as well as secular ones, have been
framing their demands within the CEDAW framework.[40]

Nevertheless, due to increased repression and lack of access to the mainstream media, the strong potential of the movement has not been actualized.
Like most typical feminist women's movements, it is predominantly made up
of the urban middle class in major cities. The movement has a long way to go
to reach various classes and ethnic or religious minorities among the wider populace in small towns, provinces, and rural areas.

In today's increasingly globalized world system, feminists and women activists in many countries have been using at least three groups of strategies to

empower women and bring about egalitarian changes: women's policy machinery within state institutions, building an issue advocacy network outside of formal institutions, and developing women's movement practices that are aimed at cultural production, consciousness raising, and knowledge creation (see Ferree 2006). The repressive and authoritarian state in Iran has made it very difficult for Iranian feminists to utilize all these strategies effectively. Yet whenever such spaces become available due to changes and contradictions within the political system (as under Khatami's presidency), women activists can and have utilized such structural opportunities.

Islamism, as a totalitarian state ideology, has resulted in a prevalent aversion toward any ideological absolutism among intellectuals, feminists included. A pragmatic, social, or liberal democratic human rights framework has become the common denomination for collaboration and coalition building. Aside from some who still fight for an abstract utopian society based on certain ideologies, many tend to work for concrete changes toward improvement of the rights and living conditions of all citizens regardless of their gender, ethnicity, sexual orientation, and ideological stand.

Most women activists too have adopted nonconfrontational, nonideological, nonsectarian, and reform-oriented strategies. Deploying the "power of presence," they have entered into a strategic engagement not only with the state and ruling elite but also with society at large. They engage the political reformers inside and outside the government, the intelligentsia, the media, the law and lawmakers in the parliament, the clerics, other social institutions, and ordinary people. This engagement takes various forms and tactics, constructive criticisms within as well as outside of the framework of the existing laws and Islamic sharia toward revision, reinterpretation, and reform as well as deconstruction and subversion. Their desire to stay away from both elitism and populism and also keep moving ahead pragmatically in the face of increasing repression under the hard-liners' government of Ahmadinejad has proved a most challenging task. Nevertheless, the Iranian women's rights movement has remained potentially vigorous and actually defiant. It has maintained its homegrown roots and independence both despite and because of all the national and international pulls and pushes.

One hopes that the current cold war in U.S.-Iran relations will end with the change of administration in the U.S. government and that a shift toward moderation inside Iran's polity will revive civil society organizations, especially women's movements in Iran. This requires a better understanding of and appreciation for the tense and conflicted yet dialogical, glocal, creative, and pragmatic syncretism of our increasingly globalized and diversified societies.

Postscript

While this book was going to press, the Iranian society began facing a new up-heaval. Conflicts within the leadership and between the people and the state came to the fore during and after the tenth presidential election in June 2009, of which Ahmadinejad was declared the winner by a wide margin. Iranian women figured prominently both in pre- and in postelection political processes. They played an active and visible role in the large preelection rallies and in the massive street protests that followed the vote, as opposition candidates and their supporters raised accusations of wholesale fraud in the official results and declared it an "electoral coup."

The international media, largely unaware of the brewing women's movement in Iran, were surprised to see women marching in the demonstrations in large numbers and braving the violent response by security forces, dramatically illus-trating the clash between a changing society and an increasingly repressive gov-ernment. The women's prominent and impressive role in the current uprising for democracy, however, turned out to be a strong confirmation of the main pre-cept of this chapter, that is, that the women's rights movement has become a major agent of change, democratization, and modernity in present-day Iran.

Based on an analytical review of the one hundred years of women's rights activism in Iran, especially during the past thirty years under an Islamist regime as presented in this chapter, the massive participation of women in the latest protests is not only not surprising but also an expected and refreshing feature. The main characteristics of women's participation in the current movement in-dicate some continuity but also important changes from those in the 1979 Rev-olution. This time, gender consciousness and demands for women's rights constitute an important component of the broader social movement for change.

Though mostly young and urban middle class, women from all walks of life took part in both electoral campaigns and the protests against the fraudulent re-sults. Some, covered in the traditional black chadors, seem to be devotedly reli-gious, while many others appeared in colorful scarves and secular and modern fashions. Unlike the government-orchestrated demonstrations we were used to seeing in the past thirty years, the latest demonstrations are not sex segregated. Women are marching not behind men but alongside men or even in the forefront.

The nightly cries of "Allah-o-Akbar" (God is great) and "Death to the Dic-tator" on the rooftops are similar to those during the 1978–1979 Revolution. Unlike then, however, the current movement is non-Islamist, nonsectarian, nonideological, and nonviolent. Neither the revolutionary Islamism nor the rev-olutionary Marxist-Leninism of the guerrilla movements of 1970s Iran makes up the predominant framework of the current movement. While a populist, religious fundamentalist (Islamist), and anti-imperialist discourse led by Ayatollah Khomeini was predominant in Iran in the 1970s, today a post-Islamist, democratic, and predominantly secular discourse based on human rights and civil rights makes up the main framework of the current movement.

Elections in Iran are neither free nor fair. People are allowed to choose only among a few candidates that have passed the screening process and been vetted by an unelected body called the Guardian Council.[41] It was only a few months before the elections that the overall mood shifted from political apathy and hopelessness to a sense of hope for change, and thus vast mobilization to participate in voting. This was mainly due to the progressive platforms for change presented by the two reformist front-runners, Mir-Hossein Mousavi and Mehdi Karrubi. What distinguished the reform candidates from the incumbent president, Ahmadinejad, was their promises to stop his onslaught on civil rights and to improve the rights of women and religious and ethnic minorities, to mend the mismanaged economy (marked by 25 percent inflation, rising unemployment, and soaring prices), and to change the hostile and confrontational foreign policy that has resulted in UN resolutions against Iran, economic sanctions, increasing militarization, isolation, the threat of military attacks and war, and thus an overall sense of insecurity.

Among women activists, too, it took a while to overcome the widespread hesitance to engage in the electoral process, especially by those who had lost all hope for political reform and trust in any of the candidates. About three months before election day, however, an increasing number of feminists and women's groups decided to take advantage of the relative openness of the political atmosphere and rendered an active feminist intervention in the process. They formed a diverse coalition called the Convergence of Women (Hamgarayee Zanan) that represented forty-two women's groups and seven hundred individual activists in order to press the presidential candidates on two specific sets of women's demands: ratification of CEDAW and revision of four specific articles (19, 20, 21, and 115) in the constitution that enshrine gender-based discrimination.[42] This was a demand-centered (motalebeh-mehvar) coalition that did not endorse any particular candidate. Rather, it put each candidate on the spot to address women's issues and respond to the demands specified by the coalition.

Through their publications; appearances in the media, at street rallies, on the campaign trails, and in press conferences; interviews with the candidates; and networking and mobilization by an effective utilization of new communication technology (SMS and email via cell phone and the Internet), the coalition members were able to bring women's issues to the surface. Meanwhile, a film made by a prominent feminist director, Rakhshan Banietemad, put all these efforts together in one documentary, including revealing interviews with the presidential candidates along with their wives on women's issues, in which all but Ahmadinejad had agreed to participate.

Change in the gender politics of the tenth presidential elections in 2009 was more visible than the ones during the ninth in 2005. For one, both candidates promised to address women's demands raised by the coalition and also include woman ministers in their cabinets, should they get elected. The front-runner candidate, Mousavi, was usually accompanied by his wife, Zahra Rahnavard, holding each other's hands, a bold and unprecedented act in the Iranian sex-segregated political culture. She is a prominent Muslim feminist; a highly accomplished academic, writer, and artist; and the first woman to become a university president in Iran. Her academic stature, strong personality, outspokenness about human and women's rights, and colorful head scarf were among the traits that added to the appeal of this couple as a promising choice for change.

The other reform candidate, Karrubi, also carried a more woman-friendly campaign than the one in the previous election. Though he is a clergyman, his campaign team—composed of some respected reformers—included a prominent woman activist, Jamila Kadivar, as the spokesperson of his campaign headquarters. His wife, a strong professional woman, was also actively involved in his campaign management. The conservative candidate, Mohsen Rezai, too was seen accompanied by his wife in several campaign rallies. Even Ahmadinejad felt compelled to bring his wife along in public during one of his campaign occasions.

In short, both in symbolism and content, the tenth presidential elections signified considerable progress in gender politics, and this was due to the years of consciousness raising, cultural reconstruction, struggles, campaigns (especially the One Million Signatures Campaign), and feminist interventions that women coalitions carried out slowly but consistently, especially in the past ten to fifteen years. The prevalence of artistic images, songs, and poetry, especially the choice of the color green as the unifying symbol of the reform camp, gave a "feminine" ambiance to the electoral campaign that soon turned into a growing green movement for change in which the youth, especially young women, play a critical role.

In the vote's aftermath, millions of marchers, flashing victory signs (instead of clenching fists), carry green-colored banners with a simple and modest yet profound slogan: "Where is my vote?" which signifies a prevalent keenness in civil and political rights. The color green signifies certain symbolism not only rooted in the national Islamic as well as secular pre-Islamic mythology and poetry of Iran but also in the global color of peace, nonviolence, and environmental protection. Even the first icon and martyr of the current civil rights movement is a woman: Neda Agha-Soltan, who was gunned down by the government-controlled militia while peacefully demonstrating. Her death was captured by a cell phone camera for all the world's eyes to see, inspiring more demonstrations and the outrage that followed. [43]

Despite increasing violent suppression, around 4,000 arrests, and the dead numbering in the seventies (according to official figures), the green movement so far is still less masculinist and less violent than the one in 1978–1979. A new women's group, Mourning Mothers (Madaran-e Azadar), has emerged, initiated by mothers who lost their sons or daughters during the prodemocracy demonstrations.[44] For instance, Parvin Fahimi, mother of the second popular icon of this movement, Sohrab Arabi, a nineteen-year-old student who was killed while in the security forces' custody, is among the leading figures of this new group. In order to commiserate and commemorate the martyrs and keep the spirit of resistance high, they hold rallies for an hour in certain public parks every Saturday while wearing black. Several seasonal activists of the One Million Signatures campaign are also among the organizers of Mournful Mothers. Shirin Ebadi has called on mothers in other parts of the world to set similar rallies on a weekly basis as a show of global solidarity with Iranian women.

Women's rights advocates, similar to their counterparts in other civil and human rights struggles, now face an increasingly brutal suppression by the growingly unpopular and illegitimate government led by a military-clerical alliance. The main subject of discussion among the Iranian women activists at present is how to continue a feminist intervention in the current democracy movement in order to influence its path toward a nonviolent, inclusive, and egalitarian future. This is a daunting struggle yet exciting and inspiring challenge from which global feminisms can learn many new lessons.

Notes

1. I am grateful to Nikki Keddie and Amrita Basu for their very helpful comments on an earlier draft of this chapter. Part of this work was supported by the Keddie-Balzan Fellowship at UCLA awarded to me during 2005–2006.

2. For more on the history and politics of the women's movement in Iran, see Sanasarian 1982; Milani 1992; Beck and Neshat 2004; Moghissi 1996; Moghadam 1993; Afary 1996; Mir-Hosseini 2002; Hoodfar 1999; Afshar 1998; and Sedghi 2007.

3. See reports on these attacks on December 27, 2008, and January 1, 2009 at http://feminist school.ws/english/spip.php?article210 and http://www.changeforequality.info/english/spip.php? article432.

4. I found Rowbotham's categorization in this regard helpful (1992).

5. Some of the information is drawn from the findings of an open-ended long questionnaire carried out among fifty-seven leading activists inside Iran during 2006–2007. This survey aimed to document a sociological portrayal of the primary actors in the current women's movement in Iran. This chapter is a small part of a larger book project in progress that draws from findings of this survey as well as years of conceptual work and empirical research, including

participant observation, interviews, and content analysis of feminist literatures and actions in Iran.

6. Even the supreme leader, Ayatollah Khamenei, has on a few occasions warned "Muslim sisters" against the danger of feminism. See Tohidi 2002a.

7. A series of interviews with some prominent male and female scholars about the question of whether there is a women's movement in Iran appeared in several issues of the magazine *Zanan*.

8. Such "dailyness" or "ordinariness" of women's activism is not unique to Iran. A prominent American feminist has discussed the significance of the dailyness of women's activism and feminist practice in the American context. See Aptheker 1989.

9. This chronological division is very similar to the one presented by Parvin Paidar in her seminal book *Women and the Political Process in Twentieth-Century Iran* (1995).

10. There is a rich body of studies on the reasons that led to the Islamization of the 1979 revolution in Iran. See, for instance, Keddie 2003 and Abrahamian 1982.

11. For the role of the new middle class created during the modernization era and its impact on women's resistance under the IRI, see various chapters in the book *In the Eye of the Storm: Women in Post-Revolutionary Iran*, ed. Mahnaz Afkhami and Erika Friedl (1994). See also Esfandiari 1997.

12. To review gender-related articles of this premodern and tribal body of law, see the appendix to Tohidi 1991, 261–265.

13. For information on these and other women's organizations formed during the revolutionary years and banned right after the establishment of the Islamist state, see *In the Shadow of Islam: The Women's Movement in Iran*, ed. Azar Tabari and Nahid Yeganeh (1982), 203–230.

14. Actually, the commemoration of the IWD has gained a symbolic significance for the women's movement in Iran because of both signifying an international solidarity with global feminisms and establishing a day of their own within a secular and nonstate framework. See Shojaee 2009.

15. A good example of such modern progressive and egalitarian Islamic thinkers (some even among clerics) who play a critical role from within an Islamic framework in the process of democratization and secularization of Iran is Hassan Yousefi Eshkevari. A mid-rank cleric, Eshkevari was condemned to death in December 2000 for "apostasy" and "war against Islam." One of the reasons that led to such a harsh sentence was his declaration that there is no Quranic injunction about covering women's hair. The sentence was later commuted to five years in prison, and he was also defrocked. See Mir-Hosseini and Tapper 2006.

16. Many Islamists in Iran, unlike traditionalists, have come to accept a new "Islamic *hijab*" in place of the all-encompassing black chador. This new Islamic hijab constitutes a dark color (gray, black, brown, or dark-blue) long overcoat, pants, and large scarf that would cover the hair completely. This dress code is more mobile and practical than the chador, which keeps a woman's hands busy holding it tight.

17. For more on these examples, see Hoodfar 1999, 32–34.

18. For Kar's own account on how, as a secular feminist, she became engaged in collaborative projects with "Islamic feminists," see Kar 2001.

19. See, for instance, the article in the *Middle East Women's Studies Review* (Winter–Spring 2001): 1–3, by Omaima Abou-Bakr, who raises a number of interesting points about the notion of "Islamic feminism." For further discussion on this, see Tohidi 2006. See also Tohidi 2002b.

20. Quoted from Hoda El-Sadda by Abou-Bakr in her article in the *Middle East Women's Studies Review* (Winter–Spring 2001).

21. For a somewhat different approach to the naming and articulation of "Islamic feminism," see Badran 2001.

22. "According to official statistics, the number of Internet users increased from 250 in 1994 to 4 million in 2006 and the number of blogs from just 1 in 2001 to more than 65,000 today" (Kian-Thiébaut 2009, 55).

23. Examples include the Women's Cultural Center led by Noushin Ahmadi Khorasani, Mansoureh Shojaee, and others; the Training Center for Women NGOs led by Mahboubeh Abbasqoli-Zadeh; the Raahi Center led by Shadi Sadr; and the Association of Health Advocates led by Rezvan Moghadam.

24. The question of a parliamentary quota for women (introduced by a few reformist women) has not generated a successful public debate. Some research conducted by my colleagues (Homa Hoodfar and Shadi Sadr in Iran) indicate that women see the reform of family law to be more significant than having quotas for women in the parliament or having a woman president. Among the political parties, the Islamic Participation Party, which is the largest party among the modernist reformers, has established a 30 percent quota. This has been due to active women reformers within this party such as Elaheh Koolaee, Farideh Macshini, Shahindokht Molaverdi, and Fakhrolsadat Mohtashamipour.

25. This declining trend is due to several factors, including the rejection of women candidates by the Guardian Council and also a lower turnout of voters in more recent elections because of increasing disillusionment about electoral integrity and also poor performance of the conservative women deputies in the increasingly conservative Majlis.

26. See *Zanan* 14, no. 121 (Khordad 1384/June 2005): cover page, 2.

27. For an extensive and informative documentation of five of these campaigns, see Terman forthcoming.

28. See reports about this campaign at http://www.meydaan.org/english/default.aspx and http://www.meydaan.org/petition.aspx?cid=46&pid=9.

29. For an extensive documentation on the campaign against stoning, see Terman forthcoming.

30. Visit their Web sites at http://w.changefoualy.info/english/, http://femschool.info/english/spip .php?rubrique3, http://femschool.info/campaign/, and http://www.campaign4equality.info/spip.php? rubrique9.

31. Part of these internal debates was published in *Zanan* magazine, nos. 133–134 (June–July 2006).

32. For a detailed description and analysis on the birth of the campaign and the related issues and concerns, see the book by one of its leading founders, Noushin Ahmadi Khorasani (1386/2007).

33. Visit the Web site of Men for Equality, http://forequality.wordpress.com/. On feminist men, see, for instance, "Babak Ahmadi der mosahebeh ba weblog Mardan Baraye Barabary: Der kooshesh baraye azadi digary ast ke azadi man tahaqoq miyabad" (Babak Ahmadi in an interview with the blog of Men for Equality: "It is in the quest for others' freedom that my freedom can actualize," October 14, 2008, http://forequality.wordpress.com/2008/10/14/babakahmadi/).

34. Visit their Web site at http://changeforequality-ca.org/english.php and http://changefor equality-ca.org/.

35. For a detailed case study of the impact of the UN-sponsored women's conferences and other activities and resolutions on the course of feminism and women's rights in today's Iran, see Tohidi 2002a.

36. For more discussion on this, see Ghorashi 2007.

37. For example, in 2007 the office of Rahi (a center that offered legal advice to abused and violated women) was shut down in Tehran under the pretext of its receiving grants from Hivos.

38. Quoted from Shirin Ebadi during one of her media appearances in May 2007.

39. The latest case in point is the monetary value attached to the Simon de Beauvoir prize (30 thousand Euros), which caused heated debates among the campaigners, who finally decided to not accept the money but only the prize for its symbolic value.

40. For a discussion on the debate over CEDAW in the sixth Majlis, see Tohidi 2003.

41. The Guardian Council is composed of six clerics appointed by the unelected supreme leader and six jurists selected by the head of the judiciary for approval by the Majlis. The council also has veto power over bills passed by the elected parliament.

42. For information on this coalition, see http://www.feministschool.com/spip.php?article2461.

43. For more gender analysis on postelection events, see http://www.juancole.com/2009/09ohidi-women-and-presidential-elections.html.

44. Visit their Web site at http://www.mournfulmothers.blogfa.com/.

13

Intersecting Oppressions: Rethinking Women's Movements in the United States

JULIE AJINKYA

In 2007 Senator Hillary Clinton announced her bid for the U.S. presidency. Amid a generally conservative political climate that claimed the United States had become a "postfeminist" society where the women's movement of the 1960s and 1970s had already won equal opportunity for women, vocal feminists heralded Clinton's candidacy as a desperately needed boost of energy for the ailing women's movement. Women were predicted to unite in a voting bloc that would nominate Clinton as the Democratic Party's presidential nominee in 2008. As the primary race kicked off, however, another viable candidate announced his bid not even a month later—Senator Barack Obama, a young black freshman senator from Chicago. As young women and women of color moved to support Obama in overwhelming percentages, feminist Clinton supporters argued that in abandoning the first viable female candidate for president, they were abandoning feminism itself. There was an immediate spike in the discussion of Second Wave versus Third Wave feminism in newspapers, magazines, and blogs, trying to explain why women were aligning with either candidate. In February 2008 an article entitled "Feminists for Clinton" was posted on the well-followed political blog the Huffington Post, documenting 264 prominent U.S. feminists' support for Clinton's candidacy. The discussion board erupted between Clinton and Obama supporters (Stansell 2008):

> I support Hillary. The media bias has been [about] Obama the savior and Hillary the bad one. I have never bought into the Obama hype. I supposed

---

UNITED STATES

Human Development Index ranking: .951
Gender-Related Development Index value: .937
Gender Empowerment Measure value: .762

General

Type of government: Federal Republic
Major ethnic groups: White (79.7%); Black (12.9%); Asian (4.4%); American and Alaskan Native (1%)
Languages: English; Spanish
Religions: Protestant (51.3%); Roman Catholic (23.9%); Mormon (1.7%); Jewish (1.7%); other or none (21.4%)
Date of independence: 1776
Former colonial power: Britain

Demographics

Population, total (millions), 2005: 299.8
Annual growth rate (%), 2005–2015: .9
Total fertility (average number of births per woman): 2.0
Contraceptive prevalence (% of married women aged 15–49): 76
Maternal mortality ratio, adjusted (per 100,000 live births), 2000: 11

Women's Status

Date of women's suffrage: 1920
Life expectancy: M 75.2; F 80.4
Combined gross enrollment ratio for primary, secondary, and tertiary education (female %), 2005: 98
Gross primary enrollment ratio: 99
Gross secondary enrollment ratio: 95
Gross tertiary enrollment ratio: 97
Literacy (% age 15 and older): M 99; F 99

Political Representation of Women

Seats in parliament (% held by women): 16.3
Legislators, senior officials, and managers (% female): 42
Professional and technical workers (% female): 56
Women in government at ministerial level (% total): 14.3

Economics

Estimated earned income (PPP US$): M 40,000; F 25,005
Ratio of estimated female to male earned income: .63
Economic activity rate (% female): 59.6
Women in adult labor force (% total): 46 (this figure obtained at the CEDAW Statistical Database)

that is because I don't live in la la land. I live in reality. I'm not an impressional [sic] youth. I'm a 39 yr old mother who is excited about Hillary being president.—(Clinton supporter)

As a woman of a generation that had to fight hard to make things a bit easier for the current generation, I really fear that our younger women have no idea what is at work here. What we are seeing here is an example of a highly competent woman of substance having to work twice as hard to convince people she is as good as a mediocre man with a golden tongue of vapid chanting hollow messages.—(Clinton supporter)

As a long-time feminist, I will not allow anyone to bully me into supporting someone whom I don't think is the best choice as the Democratic nominee—based solely on her sex. America is at a crossroads—we can have a decent president (Hillary Clinton), a disastrous president (John McCain) or an extraordinary president—Barack Obama, a man with enormous vision, more legislative experience than Hillary Clinton, and most importantly, a modern thinker who understands how to unite us as a nation, as opposed to polarizing us further.—(Obama supporter)

According to you, us women who vote for Obama are sell-outs to the cause of feminism. And that's the biggest lie coming from the Clinton camp. As a woman, I have no qualms about voting for Obama and still feeling like I'm supporting women. People accuse Obama of misogyny, but that couldn't be further from the truth. Obama is a product of all of the women in his life. Raised by a single mother. A father of two daughters. A husband of a strong, working mother in Michelle Obama. He is no stranger to the cause of feminism, and has benefited from it. Stop guilting women into voting for Clinton. This is identity politics at its worst.—(Obama supporter)

Women continued arguments like these for pages upon pages in response to articles posted online about the candidates and feminism. Obama supporters were accused of taking women's struggles in the 1960s and '70s for granted, and Clinton supporters were accused of prioritizing gender above race in identity politics. Attacks across generations often cited references to the *feminist waves*—an approach used in women's studies that describes U.S. feminism as occurring in three sequential periods: the *First Wave* imparts the struggle for suffrage; the *Second Wave* refers to the struggle for social, economic, and political equality; and the *Third Wave* focuses on the intersection of different nongender identities (e.g. race, class, sexuality, and so on) with gender itself (Baumgardner and Richards 2000; Garrison 2000). "Second Wave feminists" assumed that younger feminists voted for Obama because they took their predecessors' struggles during the 1960s–

1970s for granted, and "Third Wave feminists" argued that women who supported Clinton over Obama believed in an exclusive version of feminism that only applied to white middle-class straight women.

This chapter takes its cue from the election controversy concerning divisions within U.S. feminism to argue that this "wave approach" obscures important political divisions beyond age and cohort; this approach misleadingly suggests a homogenous group of feminists within each wave, thinking about women's rights in the same way during each given time period, and it misrepresents the extent of diversity within U.S. feminism. If we are truly interested in the development of feminism in the United States we should explore these time periods for similar tensions within themselves that divided feminists and different women's organizations. This chapter makes the argument that one such division that repeatedly appeared in women's activism was the relationship that feminists pursued with the state. While liberal organizations and movements saw the state as an ally and believed in institutional reform, radical organizations believed in finding alternative solutions to the state and pursued community-oriented strategies to fight discrimination. Although this classification continues to describe a major rift in feminist discourse today, women's activism—through issue-based campaigns and organizations—negotiates a more complicated relationship with the state, at times lobbying for institutional or legislative reform, while also protesting the policies that it contests. I will conclude with a discussion of the electoral controversy that began this chapter, in order to demonstrate how this election's attention to *intersectional feminism* might encourage feminists to start bridging their differences.

What is the relationship between feminism and women's movements in the United States? While feminism is a political theory that discursively liberates women from gender-based oppression, women's movements mobilize women behind an action agenda, aimed at procuring some level of tangible change in women's situations. This distinction suggests that feminism does not necessarily lead to the mobilization of women's movements but that women's movements must necessarily incorporate, at a bare minimum, the fundamental feminist conviction that the oppressive circumstances that women face derive from their gender identity, even if it is in combination with other identities. In other words, a welfare rights movement that mobilizes women is considered a women's movement if it acknowledges in its raison d'être that women experience welfare and its reform differently from men; it can, and must, emphasize class-based oppression as well, but its interaction with gender-based oppression must play a definitive role, even if the movement itself does not necessarily designate itself as *feminist*. Likewise, this understanding of women's movements excludes certain women's mobilizations, such as women from the religious Right, if they derive their political beliefs from a larger movement that does not challenge gender inequality. Such women are not feminist, nor do they constitute a women's movement, because they do not struggle against gender-based oppression; they merely form an interest group of the larger political movement (e.g., religious fundamentalism) itself. While the growth of women *in* such movements is an interesting topic that warrants further research in U.S. politics, it is beyond the scope of this chapter.

The group of women who are traditionally referred to as "Third Wave feminists" should more accurately be understood as those feminists who use *intersectionality theory* to a greater extent, as an epistemological tool that connects those women who experience interlocking oppressions at the crossroads of their gender, race, class, citizenship, sexuality, and other identities. Intersectionality theory originated in the scholarship of Kimberle Crenshaw in the late 1980s and was popularized by Patricia Collins's work in the 1990s, but there is evidence of intersectionality in women's activism dating back to abolition in the nineteenth century. Crenshaw introduces the concept of intersectionality to caution against the essentialization of gender as an exclusive category in women's identities; instead, women's multiple identities are posited to intersect and interact, describing women's experiences more thoroughly than attention to any one discrete identity might accomplish (see Crenshaw 1989).[1] She argues that an analysis of discrimination that tries to categorize women's experience along single-axis oppressions loses sight of the multidimensional nature of women's identities: "Consider an analogy to traffic in an intersection, coming and going in all four directions. Discrimination, like traffic through an intersection, may flow in one direction, and it may flow in another. If an accident happens, in an intersection, it can be caused by cars traveling from any number of directions and, sometimes, from all of them. Similarly, if a Black woman is harmed because she is in the intersection, her injury could result from sex discrimination or race discrimination" (1989, 139).

Collins (2000) expands on Crenshaw's understanding of intersectionality by describing how individuals are socially located in the middle of crosscutting systems of oppression and how these systems form mutually constructing features of social organization. While there has been appreciation of women as multidimensional characters throughout American history, an intersectional epistemology failed to substantively develop until the 1980s and has now shifted to a position of prominence in contemporary American feminism.

Looking at intersectionality in this epistemological way, as a *form of knowledge* itself, helps us understand how this concept enables feminism to make sense of women's different locations in society. While intersectionality theory broadly describes oppression coming from multiple directions, its particular application in contemporary feminism takes this analysis one step further and connects those women who belong to groups that have been historically conceptualized as second-class citizens: blacks as slaves, the poor as the voiceless majority, immigrants as foreigners, lesbians as deviants, and so on; these women join together with the understanding that they cannot turn to the state as a solution—as other feminists have in the past—because the state is, for them, a part of the problem.

That said, the extent to which the state is still framed as a potential ally versus an irreconcilable force outlines important divisions within feminist discourse and women's movements in the United States today. These contemporary divisions are reminiscent of divisions within feminist women's movements in the 1960s and '70s that also derived from women activists' different interpretations of the state. Initially, the *liberal* branch of feminism was born out of frustration with sexism in institutional reform and developed as an ideology based on the individualist assumption that women were capable of accomplishing everything men could and that legal reform was the way to remove institutional discrimination that limited their opportunities. Meanwhile, for those feminists who disagreed with institutional reform as the ultimate strategy to win women's rights, the *radical* branch of feminism emerged as an ideology that focused on patriarchy as the systemic oppressive force that violated women's rights and called for a radical realteration of society's order, including gender roles in the public and private spheres (Rosen 2000; Roth 2004).

As Mary Katzenstein (1998) argues in her analysis of feminism in the military and church, the legacy of liberal feminism led to the institutionalization of women's movements that work for reform from *within* the establishment. Liberal feminism's efforts during the 1960s and '70s accomplished a certain degree of legislative and judicial validation for feminism, and many women are now found launching their own egalitarian campaigns for better benefits or against sexual harassment within their own organizations, instead of turning to help from "outsider" women's movements. In this sense, liberal feminism still believes that institutional reform is the answer to gender discrimination, instead of overtly challenging systemic gender relations that curb the percentage of both men in secretarial roles and women in executive positions.

Radical feminism was also reincarnated in the contemporary phase of feminism, but it went through a more fundamental shift in disposition than liberal feminism did. While radical feminism continues to disagree with a state-centric approach, its focus on patriarchy as *the* oppressive force has now shifted to *state systems* perpetuating not only patriarchy but racism, classism, nativism, and heterosexism as well. As will be explained in greater detail below, this critical disagreement in seeing the state as ally or adversary shaped the politics of the 1960s and '70s and has continued to affect the development of feminist consciousness today.

This chapter outlines the development of these divisions within phases of feminism and women's activism, countering the traditional "wave approach" in women's studies, and highlights the strengths and weaknesses of contemporary feminism's intersectional approach. In doing so, I conclude with a set of key questions intersectional feminists might address in order to translate their discursive contributions into an action agenda.

The Early Years, 1848–1920

The conflict between gender and race as intersecting oppressions can be traced back to the inception of the women's movement, as suffragist leaders such as Susan B. Anthony and Elizabeth Cady Stanton actually began their activist careers as female abolitionists. Ultimately, however, sexism in the abolitionist movement that refused to consider women's leadership or input drove these women to fight for women's representation and found the suffragist movement. Excluded from both feminist organizations and antislavery organizations that were run by either white women or black men, black women found themselves stranded at the crossroads of their identities and started their own organizations, including the Manhattan Abolition Society and the Colored Female Anti-Slavery Society (see Dicker 2008). Though early women's rights activists at this time used abolitionists' human rights rhetoric on the black male slave and analogously applied it to women, it was most often framed as a question of rights for both white women and black men, with no mention of black women's rights. Black women were instead forced to choose their allegiance to either black rights or women's rights. In fact, though the period is often marked by the leadership of three white abolitionist women, Anthony, Stanton, and Lucy Stone, the hostility directed toward the efforts of the most prominent black women's rights leader, Sojourner Truth, in highlighting the plight of black women slaves, revealed that they expected gender to trump race politics; against this backdrop, women's rights grew to mean white women's rights.

Because of this narrow understanding of feminism as the liberation of *white women*, this phase thwarted the development of intersectional feminist analysis. Certain accomplishments were made along the way to suffrage, such as the Married Women's Property Act of 1860, but the main victory that effectively brought an end to this period of women's activism is the ratification of the Nineteenth

Amendment to the Constitution of the United States, granting (white) women the right to vote in 1920. Besides winning this right for white women, the other lasting legacy that this period would leave on women's activism was the marginalization of those women not considered to inhabit the mainstream of America.

The Middle Years, 1960s–1970s

The second period of feminism emerged out of the disillusionment of women activists with both institutional reform in the 1960s and the more radical New Left and civil rights movements. These liberal feminists were looking to build a relationship with the state beyond the voting rights that their predecessors had won in the early 1900s; now they were looking to actually insert women into the state and pursue reform from within. The central liberal-feminist organization, the National Organization for Women (NOW), was founded in 1966 by professional women who sat on state commissions on the status of women, after their proposal for the new Equal Employment Opportunity Commission to take sex discrimination as seriously as racial discrimination was turned down. These women had been activists with political interest groups and unions, among other institutions, prior to the founding of NOW, so they retained their institutionalization and established a branch of feminism that believed women could be equal to men without altering the fundamental structure of society, as long as legal roadblocks (such as employment discrimination) were removed along the way.

Meanwhile, other women who were active in the New Left and civil rights movements were growing frustrated with having their activist potential stymied by their male peers. While these male activists allegedly fought against injustice and discrimination, it became clear to women—who were still expected to take notes and make coffee at movement meetings as secretaries, cook and clean at home while bearing children as wives and mothers, and stay quiet while setting organizational agendas—that it was the forms of injustice and discrimination that *men* experienced on the grounds of race or class but not manifestations that they, as women, endured because of their gender. What progress could women make simply by joining organizations, or working within the state, if women were still relegated to menial tasks once inside?

Women who grew frustrated with both these gender relations in the private and public spheres and the state-centric focus of liberal feminist organizations that fought for institutional reform generated their own version of feminism: *radical* feminism. This branch employed consciousness raising (CR) as its main strategy of empowering women to realize that "the personal is political"—prioritizing an agenda that challenged systemic gender norms in society and women's personal lives, instead of focusing on institutional reform. Women gathered in small groups for these CR sessions and shared life stories, asking deeply personal questions about why things were ordered in their lives the way they were (e.g., why were women sequestered in the kitchen, while men worked outdoors?). The sessions were meant to help women understand that they were not alone in their house arrest under strict gender roles. In Rosen's interviews with participants of such sessions, one woman gives an account of watching another woman in the group "get it": "I'll never forget one night, this marvelous woman. She was very blunt, very outspoken; she was talking about how while she grew up, she wasn't the stereotypical feminine type, and how this caused her a lot of grief. Then she said, 'I realized that it was ok to be a strong woman.' Suddenly there was complete silence, followed by shouts of agreement. It was a very exciting moment. People were getting it, right there, in that meeting" (2000).

These sessions, however, were mainly composed of white middle-class women, which was a reflection of the composition of radical feminism itself. Different groups of women objected to this branch for different reasons. Black women thought that CR sessions that talked about women's dreams to work outside of the home and spend less time with their families were endlessly alienating, because a large majority of black women already worked outside the home to meet expenses and they *wanted* more time at home with their families; they also wanted to discuss the intersecting oppressive forces of race, class, and gender in their experiences. Socialist feminists objected to radical feminists' claims that patriarchy was the fundamental oppressive force with which all women contended, and instead argued that it was capitalism to blame for a class structure that oppressed women. Queer women argued that radical feminists were essentializing the role of gender and that gay women's experiences fell outside of the traditional gender role dynamic.

In essence, because of both feminist branches' failure to consider diversity in women's experiences, marginalized women began forming their own organizations, such as the National Black Feminist Organization in 1973, the National Alliance of Black Feminists in 1976, the Freedom Socialist Party in 1966, and the Radicalesbians in 1970. These groups varied according to the issues and identities they prioritized but retained focus on their own axes of oppression. They experimented with temporary coalitional work from time to time, working on issue-based campaigns such as violence against women, but after these campaigns were over, the groups went back to their original corners and stayed distinct from one another—often addressed as "minority groups" by the dominant white middle-class straight majority, but rarely finding any other similarities in the struggles they faced.

Violence Against Women

The issue of violence against women is an instructive example of coalition politics during the Second Wave of American feminism. The issue of rape, for example, was a juncture in women's activism that temporarily bridged divisions among feminist liberals and radicals, whites and blacks. It seems logical that radical feminists were among the first paying attention to the issue, using CR techniques to encourage women to speak out about the violence they experienced. In order to make the personal experience of rape a political issue for women to rally behind, "speak-outs" linked episodes of rape (and sexual assault more broadly defined) to systemic problems of male dominance.

Though the strategies of radical and liberal feminists diverged during this period, their political positions merged on the topic of sexual assault. Radical feminists, usually disdainful of electoral and legal reform, put their reservations aside and listened to the concerns of rape victims, who complained of feeling victimized a second time by the criminal justice system after reporting their claims; reforming police behavior required cooperation with the institutionalized strategies of liberal feminism. Liberal feminists took advantage of the CR technique's ability to facilitate massive awareness-raising campaigns. Together, radical and liberal feminists united behind reframing rape as an example of violence—not passion—and efforts to make the postrape experience the least traumatic for the victim possible (Gillmore 2008).

Black feminists, particularly in Washington, D.C., challenged the white leadership of rape crisis centers in black-dominated areas like the nation's capital and insisted that rape was also a consequence of poverty and racism (Bavacqua 2008). In this way, antiviolence campaigns birthed coalitions across class and race, but these coalitions proved difficult to sustain as organizations retreated to their separate spheres after temporary alliances. Breines (2006) describes a notable episode of cooperation between black and white feminists toward the end of the Second Wave. She recounts the murders of twelve black women in predominantly black Boston neighborhoods that encouraged cross-racial cooperation among local feminists in the formation of the Coalition for Women's Safety in 1979. Activist women united behind anger toward the police and media; they criticized these institutions for systemically perpetuating attitudes toward black women that made these crimes possible. They were accused of painting the black victims as prostitutes and using prejudice against such women to excuse their responsibility to solve the crimes. In response to sexism in their racial communities, black women turned to explicitly feminist groups and saw that white women were interested in serving as allies; the coalition proved hard to maintain beyond this single-focus campaign, though, and the alliance eventually dissolved.

The politics of the antirape movement were closely aligned with those of the shelter movement, another widespread women's movement against violence, but one that had a far more entangled relationship with the state. The shelter movement in the United States emerged from a consciousness-raising group in Minnesota that started their own crisis telephone hotline to assist women, even taking victims into their own homes until they could find support elsewhere. Eventually, this grassroots network raised enough funds to purchase their own house for battered women, and thus was born the mainstream women's shelter movement in 1974 (Elman 2003). The tangible services that shelters provided drew increased attention from both the state and growing numbers of women in need, until shelters finally turned to the state for funding and increasingly became *institutionalized* with professional staff in an effort to expand their services and *depoliticized* as the state imposed rules and process. Ironically, as funding poured in, services had to download assistance measures onto localities and streamline their provisions to adhere to austerity measures dictated by the government. Shelters lost their grassroots base as staff was forced to worry about grants, efficiency, and "clientele," similar to state social service agencies. These temporary coalitions between liberal and radical feminists failed to translate into more sustainable alliances, because as the state became more involved, radical feminists grew fearful of co-optation.

The divisions within women of color had also become apparent during the rise of the women's shelter movements in the 1970s, when mainstream battered women's shelters were unable to provide services to immigrant women in particular. These shelters failed to provide translation services and could not manage cultural sensitivities regarding violence, divorce, and dietary restrictions. South Asian activists, for example, found women from their own community leaving shelters to return to their abusers instead of remaining in shelters where they felt discrimination from other women. These activists turned around and founded their own organizations and shelters, facing the same intersection of discrimination from men in their community who believed they were "corrupted" by American radical feminist ideas and banned them from cultural gatherings, as well as discrimination from the women in the mainstream shelter movement. Similar to black and Latina feminists who were starting their own organizations during this period, Asians forged their own intersectional alternative as well. Groups such as Manavi and Sakhi were eventually born in the 1980s, providing counseling, shelter services, and legal support to South Asian victims of domestic violence (Das Dasgupta 2007). Feminists outside of the mainstream were preoccupied with finding spaces for their own distinct intersections, but the political land-scape still lacked any serious attempt at articulating the commonality these groups all shared under an intersectional framework.

Women's Economic Inequality

Women's activism around economic inequality was divided between two main agendas: inequality between men and women in the workplace and inequality between the growing numbers of women on welfare and society at large. Liberal feminist groups dominated the first front, and successfully won the Equal Pay Act of 1963 and sexual discrimination provisions in the Civil Rights Act of 1964. Their campaigns' focus on institutional reform and the white-collar world, however, effectively alienated working-class women, who were more concerned with the systemic factors of poverty on the second front.

Women in poverty found a home in welfare activist organizations, as opposed to mainstream liberal and radical feminist organizations that still neglected discussions over race and class. Because the majority of welfare recipients were women, welfare rights consequently became framed as "poor women's rights." White and black women on welfare also formed organizations parallel to one another, coming together in city or statewide coalitions, such as the Welfare Rights Coalition in Baltimore and the City-Wide Coordinating Committee of Welfare Rights Groups in New York. One of the most prominent groups of this time, the National Welfare Rights Organization, was founded in 1967 and led by committees made up of welfare recipients who were mostly black women; the NWRO protested cutbacks in federal assistance to poor families and their disproportionate effects on women and children.

The welfare rights movement made several key gains in defending poor people's rights during this time. Chief among them were the campaigns for fair hearings from caseworkers, better recognition for their roles as mothers, and school clothing for their children; these activists' roles as mothers proved to be an important mobilizing tool and common ground for these coalitions with women across race. The issue-based nature of this movement allowed women to organize in greater numbers against the deprivation they all faced, instead of the abstract articulation of gender equality and structural reform that often alienated those dealing with the daily pressures of living in poverty; at the same time, this focus on institutional reform, in terms of benefits and wages, meant that this subset of radical feminists compromised their stance on avoiding state-centric campaigns. Initially, this compromise was understood as a needed trade-off to accomplish policy improvements, but as the state grew more receptive to reform advocacy, the welfare rights movement feared the same co-optation to which the antiviolence movements had fallen prey.

However, the heavy involvement of the state was not to last. In the 1980s an overinflated economy, the oil crisis, the deficit, and the election of a conservative regime under Ronald Reagan led to a fundamental reconfiguration of state institutions. Katzenstein (2003) argues that this reconfiguration hardly affected the ability of privileged women to hold on to the institution-based associational politics they had developed as insiders, but it severely limited the ability of poor women to organize and defend their own interests. This class bifurcation undid the hard work of the activists in the welfare rights movement; they had come close to establishing welfare as an entitlement and had temporarily won legislative reforms that suggested poor women would be included in the nation's citizenry. Now, increased privatization and delegating federal obligations to the state level pushed poor women back to the margins, while co-opting middle-class liberal feminist efforts.

Women's Political Representation

As is clear by now, liberal feminism was primarily focused on working through legislative and electoral avenues to accomplish its own understanding of gender equality. A series of legislative reforms were implemented during the 1960s, including President Kennedy's President's Commission on the Status of Women in 1961, the Equal Pay Act of 1963, the 1964 Civil Rights Act and its sexual discrimination protections in Title VII, and President Johnson's Executive Order 11375 in 1967, which imposed affirmative action measures on employment receiving federal funds. By 1971 it was clear that liberal feminists had begun to take political parties seriously with the founding of the National Women's Political Caucus (NWPC). The multipartisan caucus was founded with the primary purpose of promoting women into elected and appointed office at local, state, and national levels of government. They pledged to support female candidates financially, as well as to provide them with strategic assistance and campaign training workshops. Candidates were chosen according to prochoice platforms, which explained why the majority of candidates supported by the caucus hailed from the Democratic Party, in spite of its multipartisan mission.

In spite of the NWPC's efforts at increasing the number of women in public office, the actual levels of representation changed little over the next two decades. Beckwith's analysis (2003) shows that the percentage of women in the House of Representatives in 1974 was 4.4 percent of all House members, while in 1994 it had risen to only 11 percent. Liberal feminists, however, tried to take advantage of the federalist structure of the U.S. government and focused on winning seats for women at the statehouse level, which proved more successful. The same analysis shows an increase from 8.1 percent of total state house legislature women's representation to a more significant 20.6 percent in 1995. The impact of this increase in representation on women's policy concerns is still unclear. For example, this increase at the state level corresponded to the offloading of welfare policy management and shelter services from state responsibility to nonprofit provisions; if the increase in women's representation presumably served the best interests of women, one would think that the shelters' petitions, to both the state and the private sector, for more funding to meet their expanding clientele would have been answered favorably by the state legislature—and it was not.

In the 1980s more organizations emerged to work on promoting women's representation, including liberal women of color organizations such as the National Political Congress of Black Women, founded by the first black woman, Rep. Shirley Chisholm, to be elected to the House of Representatives in 1968. Chisholm had also been a key founder of the NWPC in the early 1970s, but believed that an organization focused on promoting black women in politics was necessary after her experiences with sexism and racism serving in Congress; she founded the NPCBW (which would later become the National Congress of Black Women) after leaving office in 1983. Two years later, in 1985, another group concerned with women's representation was founded called EMILY's List; in response to the realization that democratic women were not receiving the financial support necessary for a viable campaign, female supporters came together to start the organization on the principle that "early money is like yeast" and to fund-raise for prochoice Democratic women to get elected into office. While these organizations prioritized getting more women into public office, radical feminist groups such as the Combahee River Collective of Radical Women still saw a great deal of work to be done on grassroots issues in their communities and felt electing women to office put the cart before the horse. There was no indication that simply electing women to office would necessarily translate into better outcomes for women's interests—especially for women from communities that felt ignored by the liberal feminist agenda.

While radical feminists did not pursue political representation, they did participate in a scheme initiated by liberal feminist congresswomen in 1977: the National Women's Conference, an effort funded and authorized by Congress, to bring feminists from all over the country together in Houston to discuss the status of women and issues of concern to them. Support for the conference was primarily provided by liberal feminist organizations such as the National

Women's Political Caucus, Women's Action Alliance, Federally Employed Women, and National Organization for Women.

In spite of these initial indications that the conference might be yet another manifestation of the now well-established division between liberal and radical feminists, as well as further divisions based on race, ethnicity, class, sexuality, and other identities, the conference was a marked success in terms of diverse attendance: not only were a quarter of the attendants women from minority racial communities, but there were also women from numerous ethnicities, all sexualities, variations in socioeconomic status, and even representation from the right-wing opposition (National Commission on the Observance of International Women's Year 1978). At least temporarily, these diverse groups crossed the liberal and radical feminist divide in order to see if the conference could bridge their differences. Five million dollars allocated to the project by Congress enabled women to hold state conferences leading up to the national gathering, in order to elect its 2000 representatives with representative privileges. This funding also included travel support for the delegates to attend the conference in Houston, regardless of socioeconomic standing.

The chief purpose of the conference was to bring these diverse groups of women together to discuss and vote on the twenty-six planks of the National Plan of Action for Women devised by the state conventions. A close reading of the plan's planks, however, demonstrates the continued marginalization of women outside of the mainstream liberal feminism establishment. The practice of only discussing the concerns of nonwhite non-middle-class gay women in auxiliary caucuses such as the "Minority Women Plank" and "Sexual Preference Plank," and not in the large-issue planks such as the "Education Plank" or "Employment Plank," further strengthened the construction of the *default* woman as white, middle class, and straight. In this sense, the diversity of women's identities was treated as an additive concept, instead of an intersectional concept that would also question the intersection of the mainstream woman's gender identity with her white race, middle-class status, or straight sexuality.

For example, the issue of forced sterilization in communities of color was not included in planks concerning violence against women, which was an issue primarily dealt with under the "Battered Women Plank" or the "Rape Plank"—both planks addressed violence only as it pertained to wife battery in the home or sexual assault at the individual level. The "Sexual Preferences Plank" also detailed employment discrimination concerns that were neglected under the "Employment Plank," which discussed discrimination only as it pertained to women as a homogenous group of employees, in terms of equal pay, merit promotion principles, and upward mobility. The majority plank lacked any

discussion of the different obstacles faced by lesbian women when even ap-
plying for said jobs.

In spite of these discrepancies between minority caucus groups' planks and
the mainstream-issue planks, minority communities made two main advances
through this conference. First, for the first time, a number of women had the
(federally funded) opportunity to come together with the sisters of their respective communities and discuss the problems they were facing in person.
Second, from this point onward, instead of expressing minority women's identities as though they were isolated from one another, more women from these
communities came together under the umbrella identification of "women of
color," which would give rise to more intersectional analysis in the future. The
"Minority Caucus" brought women from different racial and ethnic communities together to discuss the commonality of their experiences with what they
called "double discrimination." The conference report explained:

> For the first time, minority women—many of whom had been in the lead-
> ership of the women's movement precisely because of their greater political
> understanding of discrimination—were present in such a critical mass that
> they were able to define their own needs as well as to declare their stake in
> each women's issue. They were also able to make the media aware of their
> importance and to forge their own internal networks and coalitions in a way
> that was far reaching, inclusive, and an historic "first" for their communities,
> for women and men. (ibid.)

By creating the *permanent category* of "women of color," in which women
from different racial and ethnic communities could claim membership, these
feminists were, interestingly, addressing the idea of intersectionality without
ever explicitly mentioning it. While the discussion of double discrimination was
limited to race and ethnicity at this conference, other identities eventually ap-
propriated its analytical traction to forge new coalitions of feminists who felt
marginalized—most prominently those who felt marginalized by the liberal
feminist agenda of institutional reform, an alliance with the state that had left
them behind.

Intersectional analysis was emerging elsewhere around the same time as the
conference. Women who had become disillusioned with the liberal feminism of
the National Black Feminist Organization, for example, had left in 1974 and
founded the Combahee River Collective, a black feminist lesbian organization
that was symbolically named after the guerrilla action led by Harriet Tubman
in 1863 to free 750 slaves at the site of the Combahee River in South Carolina.

Committed to the analysis of interlocking oppressions that shaped the conditions of members' lives, the collective released an important statement in 1977—the same year as the NWC, which they did not attend—that outlined why the concepts of identity politics and intersectionality were vital to understanding the multiple oppressions their members experienced. In their own words, they were "actively committed to struggling against racial, sexual, heterosexual, and class oppression and see as [their] particular task the development of integrated analysis and practice based upon the fact that the major systems of oppression are interlocking." The collective also made clear that the white women's movement had dealt with race, class, and sexuality diversity in only superficial ways; it argued that the main onus was on white women to put more effort into understanding the multiple oppressions that nonwhite women faced: "One issue that is of major concern to us and that we have begun to publicly address is racism in the white women's movement . . . eliminating racism in the white women's movement is by definition work for white women to do, but we will continue to speak to and demand accountability on this issue" (Combahee River Collective 1986). Advocating this position, it would be hard for one to imagine the collective's approval of the NWC's caucus approach to intersecting oppressions—the absence of white women in minority discussions, for example, absolved the former of the accountability that Combahee demanded.

Around this time, the term *women of color* was used more frequently by feminists who started to see commonality in their interlocking oppressions. Frustrated by the same superficial treatment with which their experiences with racism, classism, and, in some cases, homophobia were met by mainstream liberal and radical feminism of the 1960s and '70s, some of the first women to bring attention to these ideas were writers and artists such as Audre Lorde, Cherríe Moraga, bell hooks, Barbara Smith, Beverly Smith, and Merle Woo; among numerous others, they were published in a volume of critical essays, poetry, and fiction entitled *This Bridge Called My Back: Writings by Radical Women of Color*. These women presumably felt liberated from organizational politics and used their personal, expressive art forms to communicate these ideas to the general public.

The Later Years, 1990–Today

In 1991 a young black woman named Anita Hill testified at a Senate confirmation hearing regarding the sexual harassment she received as an employee at the Equal Employment Opportunity Commission. The alleged harasser was Clarence Thomas, a black man who had served as the chair of the EEOC and was under consideration to replace Justice Thurgood Marshall, the first African American to be appointed to the Supreme Court bench. Feminists across the liberal and radical divide became increasingly invested in how the courtroom drama played out, waiting to see how the most senior legal institutions in the country treated sexual harassment.

The liberal branch of feminism from the 1960s and '70s had consolidated in 1983 into the National Council of Women's Organizations (NCWO), a coalition of the predominant liberal national organizations at the time that met in Washington, D.C., to discuss public policy agendas and their persistent commitment to legislative reform. Member groups such as NOW objected to Thomas's nomination even before Hill's allegations were unveiled, in response to his position on abortion rights, but the sexual harassment allegations reinvigorated their stance; they argued that Hill was being treated unfairly by the all-male judiciary committee and that sex discrimination was still rampant in the U.S. workforce. Meanwhile, male leaders in the black community argued that the all *white* male committee was unduly grilling Thomas because of his race. Black women were once again caught between their gender and their race, reminiscent of the intersectional conflicts from the 1960s and '70s.

In 1992 Rebecca Walker, the daughter of renowned black feminist Alice Walker, wrote a groundbreaking essay in *Ms.* magazine entitled "Becoming the Third Wave," in which she outlined her frustrations over the hearings, bemoaning the fact that young women felt estranged from their mothers' generation and found few other feminist options. She declared that she was not a "post-feminist feminist" as young women had been portrayed by the conservative backlash in the media that claimed feminism was dead; instead, she claimed that she, and others her age, were its "Third Wave."

It was this introduction to "Third Wave" language that misleadingly implied homogeneity in two groups: the young Walker's peers and their "Second Wave" predecessors. In reality, it was older black feminists who felt alienated enough by their mostly white liberal feminist peers and their male black peers to initiate an effort in 1991 called African-American Women in Defense of Ourselves. This group even managed to gather more than 1,600 signatures for a statement against Thomas's confirmation that appeared in the *New York Times* (B. Smith 2000). So while the "Third Wave" traditionally refers to young contemporary feminists, it should instead refer to those women, regardless of age or generation, who address the importance of intersectional feminism. Heywood and Drake explain the "Third Wave agenda": "A third wave goal that comes directly out of learning from these histories and working among these traditions is the development of modes of thinking that can come to terms with the multiple, constantly shifting bases of oppression in relation to the multiple, interpenetrating axes of identity, and the creation of a coalition politics based on these understandings—understandings that acknowledge the existence of oppression, even though it is not fashionable to say so" (1997, 3).

A number of key feminist anthologies that met these requirements began appearing in the 1990s, such as *Listen Up: Voices from the Next Feminist Generation* and *Colonize This! Young Women of Color on Today's Feminism*, but the young authors credited their feminist consciousness to writers such as Lorde, hooks, Anzaldua, Moraga, and countless other feminists who belonged to the age cohort before them. To call these older women "Third Wave feminists" discredits their important contributions in the 1960s and '70s, and incorrectly assumes that their feminist consciousness sequentially followed the feminism of white middle-class straight feminists from the same time period (Roth 2004).

As feminism experienced these discursive developments, the political climate of the 1980s ushered in important changes in the state. After Ronald Reagan took office in 1981, the new conservative government began to roll back a number of accomplishments that Second Wave feminism had accomplished, including allowing more restrictive conditions on abortions, cutbacks in welfare allowances to single mothers, and less oversight against sexual discrimination in the workplace. Meanwhile, civil society witnessed a growth in conservative women's groups as well; the NWC had not only served as organizing grounds for women of the Left but had also given conservative women the same opportunities to come together and give birth to the New Right. Even the 1990s, under the Clinton administration, failed to usher in any relief for women from communities who were feeling the backlash against affirmative action, welfare policies, and the tightening of immigration control under Democratic and Republican administrations.

For its part, liberal feminism had also gone through a major metamorphosis. While organizations had consolidated into the NWCO, their legislative victories from the 1960s and '70s had successfully multiplied the presence of women in the workplace. As Mary Katzenstein (1998) argues in her analysis of women's activism, feminism became so institutionalized that women argued for their own interests from *within* even the least-likely institutions (such as the military and the church), instead of turning to outside women's organizations for support. At the same time, liberal feminism joined other political causes in a surge toward NGO-ization, as various causes prioritized their professionalization in response to the reconfigured state. Former radical groups, in contrast, retreated from the political scene, abandoning their CR sessions and finding refuge in university collectives. As radical feminists negotiated with campus administrations to change sexist organizational culture, and liberal groups continued to bargain with the state, it became conventional for women's activists to negotiate with authorities to accomplish their feminist goals. In this new era of intersectional women's activism, however, there is less emphasis on the state as a potential partner in negotiations; instead, new women's organizations, such as INCITE, CodePink, and the Third Wave Foundation, place alternatives to state power at the center of their feminist analysis. These alternatives include organizing direct action and protests against state domestic and foreign policy, establishing alternative funding sources for like-minded organizations, training women in self-defense, and holding workshops and political art shows to educate the public and encourage resistance against the state-perpetuated violence against their communities.

Violence Against Women and Women's Economic Inequality

The capacity of antiviolence organizations that emerged during the 1960s and '70s to serve women from communities outside of that mainstream severely diminished over the next few decades. Not only were shelters poorly equipped to manage women who spoke languages other than English or handle special dietary restrictions, but they also failed to address violence against women of color in all of its forms—not just wife battery or domestic violence but the more systemic forms of violence that women outside the mainstream suffered at the hands of the *state*.

The debate around the Violence Against Women Act, passed in 1994, illustrated these tensions. The act, which had been championed by liberal feminist groups such as NOW, provided $1.6 billion in government funds to strengthen the prosecution of crimes perpetrated against women, increased pretrial detention periods for the accused, and allowed women civil redress for unprosecuted cases. Women of color, however, criticized the act's focus on harsher penalties for perpetrators of violence, which called for thousands more police on *their* streets; women of color saw these measures as only protecting those women whose racial and socioeconomic communities were not already targeted by an oppressive criminal justice apparatus. At the same time, the problems of violence that still existed in these communities could not be ignored. In order to address violence against *all* women, they argued, the country needed a more comprehensive plan that focused on community health and safety, without persecuting poor communities of color.

In 2000 women of color from across the country who were frustrated with the efforts of racial justice, social justice, *and* antiviolence organizations' inability to address the overlapping oppressions they faced organized a conference called "The Color of Violence: Violence Against Women of Color" in order to shift the analysis around violence against women to place marginalized women of color at its center (Smith et al. 2006). This conference intended to reclaim the issue of violence and bring women outside the mainstream together in a sustainable coalition with one another for the first time. The conference drew so much attention in its planning stages that the organizers received calls begging for them to choose a larger venue so that more women could attend. In the end more than 2,000 women made it to the conference, while 2,000 others had to be turned away. The energy driving these women to come together in person for the first time and forge new coalitions while drafting an agenda to fight violence against women resembled the spirit behind the National Women's Conference in Houston in 1977, in spite of two major differences.

The first major point of departure from the conference in 1977 was this conference's position toward the state. Angela Davis opened up the conference with a powerful keynote address that outlined the obstacles that women of color, lesbians, and low-income women faced in their struggle against violence and how the state played a particular role in this. She argued, "Given the racist and patriarchal patterns of the state, it is difficult to envision the state as the holder of solutions to the problem of violence against women. However, as the anti-violence movement has been institutionalized and professionalized, the state plays an increasingly dominant role in how we conceptualize and create strategies to minimize violence against women. One of the major tasks of this conference, and of the anti-violence movement as a whole, is to address this contradiction, especially as it presents itself to poor communities of color" (2000, 4).

Women who claimed membership to a group that was treated as second-class citizens by the state, such as blacks, immigrants, the poor, Native Americans, or homosexuals, all had experience with institutional discrimination. Davis argued that it was inconceivable for women from these groups to place their faith in a system that had historically failed them. The perception of the state as an ally in 1977's conference shifted toward seeing the state as a main adversary in the violence this group of women experienced.

The second main point of departure was the shift in strategy away from legislative reform toward grassroots organizing. At the conference in 2000, there was a session called "Depoliticization of the Anti-Violence Movement" where activists came together to criticize the institutionalization and professionalization of the antiviolence movement. During that session speakers recounted stories of the federal government's interference in and co-optation of antiviolence organizations' work, implicitly arguing that liberal feminism had failed to recognize the state's role in violence against women. They also discussed how the depoliticization of the antiviolence movement broke leaders' connections with their communities and even led to the perpetuation of cultural stereotypes and structures that ultimately oppress those same communities—an example was given where leaders of a domestic violence organization were photographed at their annual meeting on Maui wearing plastic skirts, a cultural misappropriation of Hawaiian dress.

Conference organizers decided to found a new organization that would replace institutionalized, apolitical social service models with grassroots organizing against violence in women's communities, called INCITE! Women of Color Against Violence. This organization aimed to change feminist discourse and activism in the United States by communicating that all oppression is connected—for example, by linking the oppression that women of color experience inside the United States with that experienced by "third world women" outside the United States. Radical feminist writers from the 1980s even called themselves "third world women," reappropriating the term to emphasize how they were considered second-class citizens in their own country and deriving lessons from women's movements against violence in developing countries (Lorde 2002).

While scholars rightfully criticize some U.S. women's organizations for not being critical enough of how their country's policies affect women in other parts of the world, arguments that categorically discount all women's organizations' activism inaccurately homogenize feminism in the same manner as the wave approach (for example, see Tripp 2006). Groups like INCITE! and CodePink are consistently critical of U.S. foreign policy's impact on women abroad, particularly its militarization and trade policies that disproportionately harm women. Granted, they are not the predominant women's organizations called to government hearings on women's issues, nor does the media wait with baited anticipation to see which presidential candidate they endorse, but to overlook their activism would be akin to ignoring the Combahee River Collective's contributions in prior decades.

At the INCITE! conference, for example, Anannya Bhattacharjee, a prominent advocate for immigrants and workers' rights, drew connections between immigrant women, women of color, and transnational factors. She described the common vulnerability to the state that women of color share transnationally, as well as how globalization has intensified the push-pull economic factors between countries, making immigrant women particularly vulnerable on either end of that migration: "Immigration laws privilege the entry of highly skilled professionals and their families. A poor immigrant worker faces two options, starve with the children in her home country, or near permanent separation from her children as she migrates to the US to work without legal papers" (2000).

The second INCITE! conference was held in 2002 and built on the first conference's discussion of transnational intersecting oppressions by extending the analysis to themes of global peace and justice, connecting feminist issues with the aftermath of 9/11. Julia Sudbury, an academic activist, claimed her allegiance to communities of color all around the world, arguing that it was important to broaden the concept of violence such that it included not just personal violence such as rape or domestic violence but also state violence such as the "military, border patrols, the police, prisons, the Immigration and Naturalization Service, the bombing of Vieques in naval exercises in Puerto Rico, the bombing of Iraq and Afghanistan, and the violence occurring in Colombia, Chile, and Palestine, all of which are funded by the U.S." (Mantilla 2005). Another activist, Katherine Acey, spoke of her multiple identities as an Arab American socialist working-class lesbian feminist; she cited the example of lesbians and gay groups protesting the fact that a bomb was dropped over Afghanistan after 9/11 with the words "Hijack this, fags" scrawled on its side.

The same year a group of feminists concerned with the U.S. war in Afghanistan and its impending invasion of Iraq founded CodePink, a grassroots organization that fights to stop existing U.S. wars, prevent new wars, and reallocate government spending to health care, education, green jobs, and other "life-affirming activities" (CodePink n.d.). CodePink not only runs campaigns that bring attention to the impact of U.S. policies on women in Iraq, Iran, Pakistan, Sudan, and other countries where conflict disproportionately affects women but also uses a feminist perspective to protest brutality broadly speaking, such as efforts to close down Guantanamo Bay.

Similarly, the third INCITE! conference in 2005 centered on U.S. foreign policy and discursively connected women's experiences in the United States to women in Iraq, Afghanistan, and Palestine. And, for the first time, Arab American women were given notable consideration as belonging to a community of color in the United States. Nevertheless, women activists acknowledged that Arab American women are still grossly misrepresented *within* groups of women of color, citing examples of activists' inclination to "save Arab women" who wear *hijab*. In the same way, campaigns that addressed women's issues abroad were sometimes complicated and controversial. The Feminist Majority Foundation, for example, campaigned since 1996 against the Taliban's treatment of women in Afghanistan, but it fell on deaf ears in the U.S. government. But when the Bush administration needed public support to start its war in 2001, officials courted the FMF, co-opted its language on women's rights in the region, and started selling the war as an effort to fight violence against women abroad (Faludi 2007). INCITE! duly criticized the FMF's uncritical support of this military aggression, arguing that U.S. policies abroad were not a simple solution to the predicament of women under the Taliban. If the state had helped create the problem, in pushing the Taliban to power in Afghanistan, how could it also be seen as the solution?

Women's Political Representation

Liberal feminists, conversely, still take great interest in the state, particularly through electoral politics. While organizations such as EMILY's List and the National Congress of Black Women continue to promote women's entering public office, nongovernmental organizations also form political action committees (PACs) to endorse political candidates without endangering the parent organization's tax status. Various liberal women's organizations made statements during the primary race mentioned at the beginning of this chapter, releasing documents such as candidate "report cards" on women's rights, or voting records on women's issues. Clinton, an iconic feminist lawyer from the 1970s, wife of former president Bill Clinton, and the current senator from New York, and Obama, a community organizer, lawyer, and freshman senator from Illinois, both competed for women's votes by courting large women's organizations, such as the NCWO and the National Abortion and Reproductive Rights Action League (NARAL).[2] Early predictions in the campaign made infamous claims that white women, as the largest demographic in the Democratic Party at 44 percent, could rally behind Clinton and that she needed only a little additional help from another voting bloc to usher her into the convention as the party's nominee.[3] Instead, the primary season turned into a battleground for divisions within contemporary feminism, with a particular focus on black women's support because they resided at the intersection of Clinton's gender and Obama's race.

Different demographics aligned themselves with one candidate over the other. CIRCLE, a nonpartisan research center that studies youth civic engagement, showed that 60 percent of the youth vote favored Obama, while 38 percent favored Clinton. Age demographics even influenced a population that was otherwise split between the two candidates—white college-educated voters above forty-five years of age preferred Clinton, while those under forty-five chose Obama (Frankovic 2008). Pundit discourse imposed these age discrepancies onto the women's vote, suggesting that the Second and Third Waves of feminism clashed over the two candidates and ignoring that these age divisions were not restricted to women. Some feminists were, indeed, split between the two candidates, but viewing these divisions through the lens of age or cohort obscures the nature of the disagreement between different types of feminists.

These divisions surfaced mainly over the importance of reproductive rights. Liberal feminist Martha Burk authored an online essay entitled "Why Hillary Is the Right Choice for Women" (2008), with the joint support of nine other prominent feminists. She argued that Clinton's leadership in protecting women's reproductive health made her the best candidate for feminists, as though reproductive health was the sole concern for this group. Feminist journalist Laura Flanders (2008) immediately challenged Burk's endorsement and argued that Clinton believed in "different womanhoods." She criticized Clinton's affirmative stance on U.S. policies that harmed women outside of the United States, such as trade policies that created a global sweatshop economy and laws that marginalized certain women within the United States, such as those that banned marriage between lesbian women. While Clinton feminists believed that their candidate's record on reproductive rights made her the best candidate for women, Flanders suggested they were not concerned with their candidate's record on issues that affected *other* women.

In January 2008, after Obama emerged victorious in the first caucus contest held in Iowa and black women started supporting him at an overwhelming 78 percent, prominent liberal feminist Gloria Steinem (2008) wrote an opinion editorial in the *New York Times*, arguing that Obama could not have accomplished what he had if he'd been a woman, because "gender is probably the most restricting force in American life." She went on to argue that race and sex are interdependent and must both be dealt with together, but the position that gender ought to trump racial identification in the minds of voters rang clear in her analysis—for example, she posited a hypothetical where a black woman who has all of Obama's credentials could never be as viable as Obama himself. Not once does she posit the same hypothetical for Clinton, replacing her whiteness with membership in a black racial group.

Kimberle Crenshaw argued against Steinem in the media and highlighted intersectional feminism that considered both race and gender in this election. She argued that the long history of division between feminists—particularly across race, and *not* generation—had resurfaced. Not only were black women voters expected to prioritize their gender identity at the expense of their racial membership, but white female Clinton supporters ignored the intersectional impact that Hillary's race had on her candidacy: "You cannot deny that whiteness is playing a role in this every bit as much as gender is . . . basically the feminists who are making this argument are doing what we've been concerned they've been doing for a long time—they're not acknowledging that race is playing a role in elevating Hillary as much as they claim race has played on the other side . . . we don't have agreement, I don't think, on how difficult the rhetoric [is] making life for those of us who want to organize as women of color and who are feminists" (Crenshaw 2008, n.p.).

A younger black feminist scholar, Melissa Harris-Lacewell, also took issue with Steinem's portrayal of gender in the election. In a news program Harris-Lacewell argued that Steinem's position on gender in the race alienated black women's intersectional experience: "[What Steinem is] trying to do there is [bring] black women into a coalition around questions of gender and asking us to ignore the ways in which race and gender intersect. This is actually a standard problem of second-wave feminism, which, although there have been . . . forty years, actually, of African American women pushing back against this, [they] have really failed to think about the ways in which trying to appropriate black women's lives' experience in that way is really offensive, actually" (*Democracy Now* 2008).

When Steinem tried to clarify that she believed both race and gender were important identities and needed to work in "coalition" with one another, Harris-Lacewell argued that mere coalition work would not be enough: "I do agree . . . that we ought to be in coalition. But I think we've got to be in coalition on fair grounds. Part of what, again, has been sort of an anxiety for African American women feminists like myself is that we're often asked to join up with white women's feminism, but only on their own terms, as long as we sort of remain silent about the ways in which our gender, our class, our sexual identity . . . intersect, as long as we can be quiet about those things and join onto a single agenda" (ibid.).

Harris-Lacewell argued that Steinem's proposed coalition work reminded her of the superficial coalition work from the 1960s and '70s that produced minority caucuses instead of sustainable alliances. This particular election did, however, encourage some feminists to make amends over their interpretation of the state as friend or foe. While radical groups such as INCITE! still refrained from endorsing a candidate, other intersectional feminists, such as Rebecca Walker, spoke out in this election because of its ability to encourage intersectional discourse around race and gender. In essence, the possibility of the country's first female president or its first black president lured women into the electoral arena who would most likely have abstained from another conventional election between two white male candidates.

The candidates themselves essentially refrained from such intersectional discourse, speaking to individual demographics (particularly age, gender, and race) that fell in their respective camps. While individual feminists and pundits continued to argue about the "women's vote," as Hillary won only slightly above a majority of her party's primary turnout, everyone waited to see where women's organizations would fall. Institutional feminist organizations overwhelmingly endorsed Clinton. When a prominent group called the National Abortion and Reproductive Rights Action League Pro-Choice America became the first feminist organization to endorse Obama in May 2007, other liberal feminist groups made their disapproval publicly known.

The founder of EMILY's List, Ellen Malcolm, went on record as finding NARAL's endorsement "tremendously disrespectful of Sen. Clinton" in spite of the fact that Obama had a strong record on choice issues (Goldstein 2008). After Obama won the party nomination, rounds of media speculation suggested that large numbers of Clinton supporters would defect from their party to the Republican candidate, Senator John McCain (Dickerson 2008; Rubin 2008; "Clinton supporters" 2008). Though early polls reported close to 30 percent of Clinton supporters pledging to switch party allegiance on election day, these worries were unsubstantiated as a sweeping majority supported Obama in the end.[4] Ultimately, large numbers of feminist Clinton supporters turned to fundraising and canvassing for Obama, as his policy positions fell in line with feminist policy positions much more than McCain's did. Liberal feminist groups, such as NOW-PAC, even switched their public endorsement from an earlier Clinton endorsement in March 2007 to Obama in September 2008 (National Organization of Women 2008).

In the end, while disagreement persisted among feminists over the reasons to support either candidate, these divisions challenged traditional assumptions about the roles age, race, and institutionalization played in feminist discourse; the focus on intersectional feminism and common oppressions revealed the complicated, often hidden, history of women's activism and its relationship with the state. The binary of state as friend or foe has lost resonance in the feminist community. Instead, women activists pursue a more constructive, mixed strategy that outlines the state as the actor that has legislative influence over women's conditions; at the same time, some groups rightfully continue to critically analyze the state's role in perpetuating systemic violence against particular communities. Ultimately, the viability of a black male feminist candidate in the 2008 presidential election paradoxically encouraged radical feminists to rethink their position on state-centric approaches, while also digging up historical grievances between the branches of feminism that traditionally dissuaded radical feminists from seeing the state as a solution in the first place. Alice Walker, for example, publicly endorsed Obama in this election: "I feel we desperately need people in leadership who have more of an idea of the real world than any of the people we've had before" ("Writer Alice Walker" 2008).

Conclusion

This chapter has attempted to illustrate the historic levels of diversity in U.S. feminism and women's movements that the traditional "wave approach" tends to bury in obscurity. While there have been three established periods of feminism in U.S. history, describing them as waves implies a misleading sense of sequence. In reality, there were parallel associations that worked on similar issue-based campaigns such as violence against women or economic inequality, and there were parallel divisions that highlighted the extent to which women's movements' relationship with the state differed. Ultimately, to tell the story of U.S. feminism properly, we must stop thinking of feminism in age cohorts, and continue to explore how gender intersects with other identities, namely, those of race, class, citizenship, and sexuality.

While the recent presidential election drew the public's attention to multiple identities and overlapping oppressions, future research on intersectional feminism should consider the following set of questions. First, whereas the election encouraged a surge of discourse focused on the intersection between race and gender, it is critical to address the intersection between gender and other identities as well. For example, how do feminists and women's organizations make sense of political candidates' positions on same-sex marriage, U.S. foreign policy, workers' rights, or welfare reform? Intersectional feminist discourse and activism have been especially weak on women in poverty; only connecting race and class introduces poor women of color into the discussion. Though socialist feminists argue that capitalism is at fault for the oppression of women, intersectional feminists largely disapprove of their sole focus on class exploitation and encourage a broader interpretation of oppressive forces. In practice, however, women's movements do not seem to advocate for working-class women who do not come from communities of color, with liberal feminist groups focusing on sexual harassment and equal-pay campaigns for middle-class women in white-collar jobs or groups such as INCITE! organizing mothers of color on welfare.

Second, what does intersectional feminist theory mean for women's movements broadly? While political theorists outline the normative dimensions of overlapping oppressions, movement theorists should consider the ramifications intersectional feminism poses for coalition politics. What are the benefits and drawbacks of organizational coalitions that temporarily align according to common-issue campaigns but then dissolve back to individual corners after victory or defeat? Do intersectional feminists propose forming new permanent organizations that unite groups experiencing overlapping oppressions, *instead* of temporary coalitions and alliances? How would these organizations manage internal hierarchical politics and avoid ranking oppressions during agenda-setting sessions?

Finally, how do intersectional feminists intend to translate their revolutionary discourse into an action agenda? For example, INCITE! calls for an "alternative" to the state, focusing on community-centered solutions, but it is thus far unclear what this alternative model would really look like. Would communities really be able to completely replace state paradigms of policing and corrections, or would communities be expected to advocate for state models that incorporate more communities' input? Could CodePink's example of alliance politics with the peace and justice movement against U.S. wars abroad be held as an exemplar of translating intersectional discourse into action? At present, it seems that direct action against current state policies must be accompanied by constructive alternative suggestions. For example, INCITE! runs community radio shows that educate the public on violence against their communities, as well as self-defense training seminars; advocating for state funding for these programs runs the risk of co-optation, as other women's movements experienced in the past, but also sends the message that the state believes these programs are important in a broader sense—instead of pitting state solutions diametrically opposite to community solutions, a hybrid between the two seems promising. CodePink almost operates as a watchdog group, maintaining a stance critical of U.S. domestic and foreign policy and protesting in public to demand government transparency—another action strategy that tries to transform the state instead of rendering it obsolete or useless.

Despite these questions that remain regarding the future of intersectional feminism, it should at least be clear that feminism is alive and well in the United States. In fact, feminists could use the media's fascination over the recent split in women's votes to inject feminism even deeper into the public's vernacular. A recent radio news program invited Farah Jasmine Griffin (a professor of English and comparative literature and African American studies at Columbia University), Carol Jenkins (a former broadcaster and president of the Women's Media Center in New York City), and Eleanor Smeal (president of the Feminist Majority Foundation) to discuss the lasting legacy of this election on women's rights, feminism, and political participation:

> [This election] inspired people to get involved that haven't been involved. And so women all over this country volunteered hours and hours, they went to states, they did things they never thought they could do. . . . This is the most progressive platform a major party has passed for women's issues and for civil

rights issues. But for women, it's in every section of [Obama's] platform.—Eleanor Smeal

What has happened with Hillary's candidacy, and with that sexism in the media, is that the genie is out of the bottle. Women will no longer, ever, go back to that sort of complacent stage where they weren't paying attention and weren't active.—Carol Jenkins

I think the most disturbing trend was our continued use of black and women, as if black women didn't fit into one or the other. . . . One had to be black or one had to be a woman . . . I also think one of the problems faced by black women was the sense that in choosing . . . Obama, that they were voting against their interest as women . . . there's still a great deal of work to do. But I think that all of the women, the women that I know, the women that I worked with over the years, have been committed to coming together, especially at this moment.—Dr. Farah Jasmine Griffin

We have to be—when this is over, we have to be together. And I think we will be, but there were a lot of unkind things said, and a lot of people stopped talking to each other, but I think that increasingly, we're beginning to get beyond that.—Carol Jenkins

These women represent a microcosm of the diversity we find in contemporary U.S. feminism; they vary by race, class, candidate endorsement, and age—to name just a few. While they all acknowledge that wounds must still heal and a great deal of work lies ahead, one thing is clear—U.S. feminism is most certainly not "dead," and the 2008 presidential election made it more of a household concept than ever before.

Notes

1. In "Mapping the Margins" (1991), Crenshaw explains intersectionality in more detail: "[I] consider intersectionality a provisional concept linking contemporary politics with postmodern theory. In mapping the intersections of race and gender, the concept does engage dominant assumptions that race and gender are essentially separate categories. By tracing the categories to their intersections, I hope to suggest a methodology that will ultimately disrupt the tendencies to see race and gender as exclusive or separable."

2. Author's interview with a senior political strategist who wishes to remain anonymous; this strategist first worked on Clinton's campaign for the presidency and then transitioned to Obama's team (August 1, 2008).

3. See washingtonpost.com online discussion hosted by feminist writer Linda Hirschman, http://www.washingtonpost.com/wp-dyn/content/discussion/2008/02/29/DI200802290 2857.html.

4. For poll predictions, see Gallup Polling 2008. Interestingly, the same poll reports that 19 percent of Obama supporters would vote for McCain in a Clinton versus McCain race, which was left out of reports discussing women switching party allegiance.

Selected Bibliography

Abrahamian, Ervand. 1982. *Iran between two revolutions*. Princeton: Princeton University Press.

Abubikirova, N. I., T. A. Klimenkova, E. V. Kotchkina, M. A. Regentova, and T. G. Troinova. 1998. *Spravochnik: Zhenskie nepravitel'stvennye organizatsii rossii i SNG* [Directory: Women's NGOs in Russia and the CIS]. Moscow: Women's Information Network.

Abu Khadra, Salwa [head of the General Union of Palestinian Women, General Command]. 2001. Interview with Islah Jad, Ramallah, July 11.

Abul-Omrein, Khaled. 2000. *Hamas: Harakat al-moqawameh al-islameyya fi falastine* [Hamas: The Islamic resistance movement in Palestine]. Cairo: Marqaz al-Hadara al-'Arabeyya (the Arab Civilisation Center).

ActionAid. n.d. "Rotten fruit: Tesco profits as women workers pay a high price." http://www.wfp.org.za.

Afary, Janet. 1996. *The Iranian Constitutional Revolution, 1906–1911: Grassroots democracy, social democracy, and the origin of feminism*. New York: Columbia University Press.

———. 2009. *Sexual politics in modern Iran*. Cambridge: Cambridge University Press.

Afkhami, Mahnaz, and Erika Friedl, eds. 1994. *Eye of the storm: Women in post-revolutionary Iran*. London: I. B. Tauris.

Afshar, Haleh. 1998. *Islam and feminisms: An Iranian case study*. New York: Macmillan.

Agarwal, Bina. 1997. "Bargaining and gender relations: Within and beyond the household." *Feminist Economics* 2, no. 1: 1–50.

Agnes, Flavia. 1994. "Women's movement in a secular framework: Redefining the agendas." *Economic and Political Weekly*, May 7, 1123–1128. Reprinted in *Women's studies: A reader*, ed. Mary E. John, 501–508. New Delhi: Penguin Books India, 2008.

Ahmadi Khorasani, Noushin. 1386/2007. "Jonbesh yek million emza: Ravayati az daroun" [The One Million Signatures movement: A narrative from inside]. http://www.femschool.info/campaign/spip.php?article86.

Aidi, Guo. 2009. "Nuganbu yanchi tuixiu tiaokuan bei shanchu" [Elimination of clauses on extension of retirement of women executives]. China Women's New Daily. http://news.xinhuanet.com/legal/2009-05/05-content_11313716.htm.

Aivazova, Svetlana. 1998. *Russkie zhenshchiny v labarinte ravnopraviia* [Russian women in the labyrinth of equal rights]. Moscow: RIK Rusanova.

———. 2000. "Zhenshchina i vlast': Liubov' bez vzaimnosti" [Women and political power: Unrequited love]. *Zhenshchina Plius* 1.

Alamdari, Kazem. 1387/2008. "Jonbesh yek-million emza, ulgouyi bara-ye jamèh madani dar Iran." 10 Farvardin/March. http://www.femschool.info/campaign/spip.php?article210.

Alarcón, Norma. 1990. "The theoretical subjects of this bridge called my back and Anglo-American feminism." In *Making FACES/MAKING Soul: Haciendo caras*, ed. Gloria Anzaldúa. San Francisco: Aunt Lute.

Alasti, Sanaz. 2007. "Comparative study of stoning punishments in the religions of Islam and Judaism." *Justice Policy Journal* 4, no. 1 (Spring).

Alexander, M. Jacqui, and Chandra Talpade Mohanty, eds. 1997. *Feminist genealogies, colonial legacies, democratic futures.* New York and London: Routledge.

Alvarez, Carmen. 2000. "Cosmovisión maya y feminismos: ¿Caminos que se unen?" In *La encrucijada de las identidades, mujeres feminismos y mayanismos en diálogo,* ed. Aura Estela Cumes and Ana Silvia Monzón, 19–31. Guatemala City: Serviprensa.

Alvarez, Sonia E. 1990. *Engendering democracy in Brazil: Women's movements in transition politics.* Princeton: Princeton University Press.

———. 1994. "La (trans)formación del (los) feminism(s) y la política de gênero em la democratización del Brasil." In *Mujeres y participación política,* ed. Magdalena Leon. Avances y desafios em América Latina. Bogotá: Tercer Mundo.

———. 1998a. "Advocating feminism: The Latin American feminist NGO boom." Conference made at the Latin American Studies Program, Mount Holyoke College, on May 2, 1998. http://www.mtholyoke.edu/acad/latam/schomburgmoreno/alvarez.html.

———. 1998b. "Latin American feminisms 'go global': Trends of the 1990s and challenges for the new millennium." In *Cultures of politics/politics of cultures: Revisioning Latin American social movements,* ed. Sonia E. Alvarez, Evelina Dagnino, and Arturo Escobar. Boulder: Westview Press.

———. 2000. "Translating the global: Effects of transnational organizing on local feminist discourses and practices in Latin America." *Meridians: Feminism, Race, Transnationalism* 1, no. 1 (Autumn): 30–31.

Alvarez, Sonia E., Nalu Faria, and Miriam Nobre. 2004. "Another (also feminist) world is possible: Constructing transnational spaces and global alternatives from the movements." In *The world social forum: Challenging empires,* ed. Jai Sen, Anita Anand, Arturo Escobar, and P. Waterman, 199–206. New Delhi: Viveka.

Alvarez, Sonia E., Elisabeth J. Friedman, Ericka Beckman, Maylei Blackwell, Norma Chinchilla, Nathalie Lebon, Marissa Navarro, and Marcela Ríos Tobar. 2003. "Encountering Latin American and Caribbean feminisms." *Signs: Journal of Women in Culture and Society* 28, no. 2: 537–579.

AMB—ARTICULAÇÃO de mulheres brasileiras. 2004. *Articulando a luta feminista nas políticas públicas.* Recife: [s.n.]. (Texto para discussão.)

American Anthropological Association. 1947. "Statement on human rights." *American Anthropologist* 49: 539–543.

Amin, Samir. 1989. *Eurocentrism.* Trans. Russel Moore. New York: Monthly Review Press.

Antrobus, Peggy. 2004. *The global women's movement: Origins, issues, and strategies.* London: Zed Books.

Aptheker, Bettina. 1989. *Tapestries of life: Women's work, women's consciousness, and the meaning of daily life.* Amherst: University of Massachusetts Press.

Araújo, Clara. 2003. "Quotas for Women in the Brazilian Legislative System." Paper presented at the International IDEA Workshop, "The Implementation of Quotas: Latin American Experiences," Lima, Peru, February 23–24.

Arendt, Hannah. 1958. *Human Condition.* Chicago: University of Chicago Press.

Artía Rodríguez, Patricia. 2001. "Desatar las voces, construir las utopías: La coordinadora nacional de mujeres indígenas en Oaxaca." Master's thesis, CIESAS, Mexico City.

"Article 7—Public and Political Life." 2006. Chap. 5 of *Second and Third Alternative Report on CEDAW.* Delhi: NAWO.

Ash, T. Garton. 1999. "Letter from Warsaw: 'Helena's kitchen.'" *New Yorker,* February 15, 32.

Ashwin, Sarah. 2006a. "Dealing with devastation in Russia: Men and women compared." In *Adapting to Russia's new labor market gender and employment strategy,* ed. Sarah Ashwin, 1–31. London: RoutledgeCurzon.

———. 2006b. "The post-Soviet gender order: Imperatives and implications." In *Adapting to Russia's new labor market gender and employment strategy,* ed. Sarah Ashwin, 32–56. London: RoutledgeCurzon.

Aston, Elaine, and Sue-Ellen Case, eds. 2007. *Staging international feminisms.* New York: Palgrave Macmillan.

Attwood, Lynne. 1997. "'She was asking for it': Rape and domestic violence against women." In *Post-Soviet women: From the Baltic to Central Asia,* ed. Mary Buckley, 99–118. Cambridge: Cambridge University Press.

Austin, J. L. 1962. *How to do things with words.* Cambridge: Harvard University Press.

Azraq, Khawla [Fateh activist]. 2002. Interview with Islah Jad, Beirut, December 22.

Babb, Florence E. 2003. "Out in Nicaragua: Local and transnational desires after the revolution." *Cultural Anthropology* 18, no. 3: 304–328.

Badran, Margot. 2001. "Understanding Islam, Islamism, and Islamic feminism." *Journal of Women's History* 13, no. 1 (Spring): 47–52.

Bal, Vineeta, Vani Subramanian, and Saheli Laxmi Murthy. n.d. "Contraceptive research: Is there a gender neutral approach?" Reprinted in *Women's Studies: A Reader,* ed. Mary E. John, 371–380. New Delhi: Penguin Books India, 2008.

Baldez, Lisa. 2002. *Why women protest: Women's movements in Chile.* Cambridge: Cambridge University Press.

———. 2004. "Elected bodies: Gender quotas for female legislative candidates in Mexico." *Legislative Studies Quarterly* 29, no. 2: 231–258.

Bamdad, Badr ol-Moluk. 1977. *Darkness into light: Women's emancipation in Iran.* Ed. and trans. F. R. C. Bagley. New York: Exposition Press.

Banaszak, Lee Ann, ed. 2006. *The U.S. women's movement in global perspective.* Lanham, MD: Rowman and Littlefield.

Banaszak, Lee Ann, Karen Beckwith, and Dieter Rucht. 2003. *Women's movements facing the reconfigured state.* Cambridge: Cambridge University Press.

Banerjee, Paula. 2008. "Communities, gender, and the border: A legal narrative on India's North East." In *Challenging the rule(s) of law: Colonialism, criminology, and human rights in India,* ed. Kalpana Kannabiran and Ranbir Singh, 257–280. New Delhi: Sage.

Baniyaghoob, Zhila. 1384/2005. "Zanan der dowran-e riyasat jomhouri-ye Mohammad Khatami" [Women during the presidency of Mohammad Khatami]. *Gooya News,* 3 Shahrivar.

al-Bargothi, Eyyad. 2000. *Al-islam al-seyassi fi falastine: Ma wara al-seyassa* [Political Islam in Palestine: Beyond politics]. Jerusalem: Jerusalem Media and Communication Center.

Bargouthi, Mustafa. 1994. "Monazamat al-mojtama' al-madani wa dawreha fil-marhala al-moqbela" [Civil society organizations and their role in the coming era]. Paper presented at the conference "The Future of the Palestinian Civil Society," Birzeit University, May 13–15.

Barlett, Katharine T. 1990. "Feminist legal methods." *Harvard Law Review* 103, no. 4 (February).

Barnes, T. 1991. "Differential class experiences amongst African women in colonial Harare, Zimbabwe, 1935–1970." Paper presented at the Women and Gender Conference, University of Natal.

———. 1999. *We women worked so hard: Gender, urbanisation, and social reproduction in colonial Harare, Zimbabwe, 1930–1956.* Portsmouth: Heinemann.

Barton, Carol. 2004. "Global women's movements at a crossroads: Seeking definition, new alliances, and greater impact." *Socialism and Democracy* 18, no. 1 (January–June).

Bartra, Eli, ed. 2002. *Feminismo en México: Ayer y hoy.* Mexico City: Universidad Autónoma Metropolitana, México DF.

Baskakova, Marina. 2000. "Gender aspects of pension reform in Russia." In *Making the transition work for women in Europe and Central Asia,* ed. Marina Lazreg. World Bank Discussion Paper no. 411. Washington, DC: World Bank.

Basu, Amrita, ed. 1992. *Two faces of protest: Contrasting modes of women's activism in India.* New Delhi: Oxford University Press.

———. 1995. *The challenge of local feminisms: Women's movements in global perspective.* Boulder: Westview Press, 1995.

———. 2005a. "Transnational feminism revisited." *Feminist Africa,* no. 5: 90–95.

———. 2005b. "Women, political parties, and social movements in South Asia." Occasional Paper 5. Geneva: UNRISD.

Batliwala, Srilatha. 2007. "Putting power back into empowerment." Open Democracy News Analysis, July 30. http://www.opendemocracy.net/node/34195/pdf.

Baumgardner, Jennifer, and Amy Richards. 2000. *Manifesta: Young women, feminism, and the future.* New York: Farrar, Straus, and Giroux.

Bavacqua, Maria. 2008. "Reconsidering violence against women: Coalition politics in the antirape movement." In *Feminist coalitions: Historical perspectives on Second-Wave feminism in the United States,* ed. Stephanie Gillmore, 163–177. Urbana: University of Illinois Press.

Bayat, Asaf. 1997. February. *Street Politics: Poor People's Movements in Iran.* New York: Columbia University Press.

Baxi, Pratiksha. 2006. "Habeas corpus in the realm of love: Litigating marriages of choice in India." *Australian Feminist Law Journal* 25: 59–78.

Baxi, Pratiksha, Shirin M. Rai, and Shaheen Sardar Ali. 2006. "Legacies of common law: 'Crimes of honour' in India and Pakistan." *Third World Quarterly* 27, no. 7: 1239–1253.

Baxi, Upendra. 2005. "The Gujarat catastrophe: Notes on reading politics as democidal rape culture." In *The violence of normal times: Essays on women's lived realities,* ed. Kalpana Kannabiran. New Delhi: Women Unlimited in association with Kali for Women.

Bayard De Volo, Lorraine. 2003. "Analyzing politics and change in women's organizations." *International Feminist Journal of Politics* 5, no. 1 (March).

Bayat, Asef. 2007. "A women's non-movement: What it means to be a woman activist in an Islamic state." *Comparative Studies of South Asia, Africa, and the Middle East* 27, no. 1.

Beck, Lois, and Guity Neshat, eds. 2004. *Women in Iran: From 1800 to the Islamic republic.* Urbana: University of Illinois Press.

Beckwith, Karen. 2003. "The gendering ways of states: Women's representation and state reconfiguration in France, Great Britain, and the United States." In *Women's movements facing the reconfigured state,* ed. Lee Ann Banaszak, Karen Beckwith, and Dieter Rucht. Cambridge and New York: Cambridge University Press.

Bedi, Kiran. 2003. "Women *sarpanches* as rubber stamps." *Chandigarh Tribune,* online ed., November 23.

Benson, Koni. 2008. "Sokhula Sonke: A social movement union led by women." Unpublished report for the International Labour Research and Information Group.

Berquó, Elza. 2002. "Perfil demográfico das chefias femininas no Brasil." *Gênero, democracia e sociedade brasileira* 34, no. 1 (August): 243–265.

Berrío Palomo, Lina Rosa. 2008. "Sembrando sueños, creando utopías: Liderazgos femeninos indígenas en Colombia y México." In *Etnografías e historias de resistencia: Mujeres indígenas, procesos organizativos y nuevas identidades políticas,* ed. Rosalva Aída Hernández, 181–217. Mexico City: Publicaciones de la Casa Chata CIESAS/PUEG-UNAM.

Beydoun, Aza S. 2002. *Nissa wa jam'eyyat: Libnaneyat bayna insaf el-that wa khedmat al-ghayr* [Women and societies: Lebanese women between self-assertion and caring for the others]. Beirut: Dar el-Nahar.

Bhattacharya, Ananya. 2000. "Second Plenary Session." In *Color of violence: Violence Against Women of Color conference summary.* Minneapolis: INCITE! Women of Color Against Violence.

Bishara, Azmi. 1996. *Mossahama fi nakd al mujtam'a al madani* [A contribution to the critique of civil society]. Ramallah: Muwatin (the Palestinian Institute for the Study of Democracy).

Blizzard, Sarah Marie. 2006. "Women's roles in the 1994 Rwanda genocide and the empowerment of women in the aftermath." http://etd.gatech.edu/theses/available/etd-07062006-212615/unrestricted/blizzard_sarah_m_200608_mast.pdf.

Bobo, K. A., J. Kendall, and S. Max. 2001. *Organizing for social change: A manual for activists.* 3rd ed. Cabin John, MD: Seven Locks Press.

Bolpress. 2006. "Evo dijo que la instancia sería borrada de la estructura del Ejecutivo." January 20. http://www.bolpress.com/.

Bond-Stewart, K. 1987. *Independence is not only for one sex.* Harare: Zimbabwe Publishing House.

Boswell, Barbara. 2003. "Locating gender and women's studies teaching and research programs at African universities: Survey results." Unpublished report, prepared for the African Gender Institute, University of Cape Town.

Breines, Winifred. 2006. *The trouble between us: An uneasy history of white and black women in the feminist movement.* Oxford and New York: Oxford University Press.

Bridger, Sue, Rebecca Kay, and Kathryn Pinnick. 1996. *No more heroines? Russia, women, and the market.* London: Routledge.

Brzeziecki, A., and Mateusz Fik. 2003. "Zagwarantowac zagwarantowane." *Tygodnik Powszechny,* no. 5 (February 2). http://www.tygodnik.com.pl/numer/279505/brzeziecki.html.

Bu, Wei. 2005. "Organizing against ecomestic violence: Exploring the use of a popular theatre troupe as alternative media in rural China." In *China history and society: Women and gender in Chinese studies,* ed. Nicola Spakowski and Cecilia Milwertz, 48–63.

Buckley, Mary. 1989. *Women and ideology in the Soviet Union.* Toronto: Harvester Wheatsheaf.

Budlender, Debbie. 2007. "Where is the money to address gender based violence?" Unpublished report prepared for the Centre for the Study of Violence and Reconciliation Gender Based Violence Program.

Bunch, Charlotte. 1990. "Women's rights as human rights: Toward a revision of human rights." *Human Rights Quarterly* 12: 486–498.

Bunting, Helen. 2007. "Chile's Bachelet signs bill to promote women's participation in politics." *Santiago Times,* October 30. http://www.santiagotimes.cl/santiagotimes/.

Burk, Martha. 2008. "Why Hillary is the right choice for women." *Huffington Post,* February 3. http://www.huffingtonpost.com/martha-burk/why-hillary-is-the-right-_b_84718.html.

Butler, Judith. 2001. *El género en disputa: El feminismo y la subversión de la identidad.* Mexico City: Paidós/PUEG-UNAM.

Cai, Yiping, Wang Zheng, and Du Fangqi, eds. 1999. *Engendering the study of history.*

Carneiro, Sueli. 1999. "Black women's identity in Brazil." In *Race in contemporary Brazil: From indifference to inequality,* ed. Rebecca Reichmann. University Park: Pennsylvania State University Press.

Castañeda, Jorge G. 2006. "Latin America's left turn." *Foreign Affairs* 85, no. 3: 28–43.

Causes of farmer suicides in Maharashtra: An enquiry; Final report submitted to the Mumbai High Court, March 15, 2005. 2005. Tuljapur, India: Tata Institute of Social Sciences, Rural Campus.

CEDAW. 2007. *Concluding comments of the Committee on the Elimination of Discrimination Against Women: India.* 37th sess., January 15–February 2. http://www.un.org/womenwatch/daw/cedaw/cedaw37/concludingcommentsAU/India_Advance%20unedited.pdf.

César de Oliveira, Glaucira [political liaison and directorate member, Cfemea]. 2002. Interview with Elisabeth Friedman, Brasilia, Brazil, August 1.

Chakrabarty, Dipesh. 2000. *Provincializing Europe: Post-colonial thought and historical difference.* Princeton: Princeton University Press.

Chakravarti, Uma. 1989. "Whatever happened to the Vedic Dasi? Orientalism, nationalism, and a script for the past." In *Recasting women: Essays in colonial history,* ed. Kumkum Sangari and Sudesh Vaid. New Delhi: Kali for Women.

Challand, Benoit. 2009. *Palestinian civil society: Foreign donors and the power to promote and exclude.* London and New York: Routledge.

Chatty, Dawn, and Annika Rabo. 1997. *Organizing women: Formal and informal women's groups in the Middle East.* Oxford: Berg.

Cherkassov, Gleb. 2000. "Partii-autsaidergy" [Outsider parties]. In *Rossiia v izbiratel'nom tsikle 1999–2000 godov* [Russia in the electoral cycle of 1999–2000], ed. Michael McFaul, Nikolai Petrov, and A. Ryabov. Moscow: Moscow Carnegie Center.

Chernenkaia, Irina [former executive director of the Syostri Center for Victims of Sexual Assault]. 1999. Interview with Lisa McIntosh Sundstrom, Moscow, April 5.

China Project Group. 2004. "Enhance gender mainstreaming capacity and improve gender equality in employment policies" [Tigao shehui xingbei zhuliuhu nengli zhidao shouce]. Beijing: China Society Press.

Chinchilla, Norma S. 1993. "Women's movements in the Americas: Feminism's Second Wave." *NACLA Report on the Americas* 27, no. 1: 17–23.

Chow, Esther Ngan-ling, Naihua Zhang, and Jinling Wang. 2004. "Promising and contested fields: Women's studies and sociology of women/gender in contemporary China." *Gender and Society* 18, no. 2: 161–188.

Chowdhry, Prem. 2007. *Contentious marriages, eloping couples: Gender, caste, and patriarchy in northern India.* New Delhi: Oxford University Press.

Christensen, Hilda Romer, Beatrice Halsaa, and Aino Saarinen, eds. 2004. *Crossing borders: Remapping women's movements at the turn of the 21st century.* Odense: University Press of Southern Denmark.

"Clinton supporters turn to McCain." 2008. NPR, June 10. http://www.npr.org/templates/story/story.php?storyId=91356785.

CodePink. n.d. Mission statement. http://www.codepink4peace.org/article.php?list=type&type=3.

Collier, George. 1994. *Basta! Land and the Zapatista rebellion in Chiapas.* Oakland: Food First Books.

Collins, Patricia. 2000. *Black feminist thought: Knowledge, consciousness, and the politics of empowerment.* New York: Routledge.

Collins, Patricia Hill. 1990. *Black feminist theory.* Boston: Unwind Hyman.

Comaletzin. 1999. "Documento de Presentación de la Organización Comaletzin." Manuscript. Puebla.

Combahee River Collective. 1986. *The Combahee River Collective statement: Black feminist organizing in the 1970s and 1980s.* Lanham, MD, and New York: Kitchen Table, Women of Color Press.

Conway, Janet. 2007. "Transnational feminisms and the World Social Forum: Encounters and transformations in anti-globalization spaces." *Journal of International Women's Studies* 8, no. 3: 49–70.

Coordinadora de la Mujer, Católicas por el Derecho a Decidir, Oficina Jurídica de la Mujer, and CLADEM Bolivia. 2007. *Aportes y complementaciones al cuestionario presentado por el gobierno boliviano ante el Comité de la CEDAW.* http://www.iwraw-ap.org/resources/pdf/40_shadow_reports/Bolivia_SR.pdf.

Cornwall, Andrea, and Vera Schatten Coelho, eds. 2006. *Spaces for change? The politics of citizen participation in new democratic arenas.* London: Zed Books.

Costa, Ana Alice Alcantara. 2005. "O movimento feminista no Brasil: Dinâmicas de uma intervenção política." *Gênero* 5, no. 2: 9–36.

———. 2008. "Women and politics: The Brazil paradox." Open Democracy, November 3, 2008. http://www.opendemocracy.net/article/5050/political_representation_brazil.

Costa, Ana Alice Alcantara, and Cecilia M. B. Sardenberg. 1994. "Teoria e praxis feministas nas ciências e na academia: Os núcleos da mulher nas universidades Brasileiras." In "Anais do Simpósio Internacional, 'Formação, Pesquisa e Edição Feministas nas Universidades.'" Special issue, *Revista Estudos Feministas* (Rio de Janeiro, CIEC/ECO/UFRJ): 387–400.

———, eds. 2002. *Feminismo, ciência e tecnologia.* Salvador, Bahia: REDOR, NEIM.

Craske, Nikki. 2000. *Continuing the challenge: The contemporary Latin American women's movements.* Research Paper 23. Liverpool: Institute of Latin American Studies, University of Liverpool.

Crenshaw, Kimberle. 1989. "Demarginalizing the intersection of race and sex." *University of Chicago Legal Forum* 139.

———. 1991. "Mapping the margins: Intersectionality, identity politics, and violence against women of color." *Stanford Law Review* 43, no. 6.

———. 2008. "Should Clinton or Obama be first?" NPR radio transcript, March 11. http://www.npr.org/templates/transcript/transcript.php?storyId=88099579.

Crisis in Zimbabwe Coalition. 2003. December. Statement on the Occasion of the Commonwealth Heads of Government. Harare: Crisis in Zimbabwe Coalition. http://www.kubatana.net/docs/hr/crisis_orgviol_mar_030328.pdf.

Cumbre de Mujeres Indígenas de las Américas. 2003. *Memoria de la primera cumbre de mujeres indígenas de América.* Mexico City: Fundación Rigoberta Menchú Tum.

"Curtain Falls on World Conference on UN Year of Women." 1975. *People's Daily,* July 4, 6.

Daly, Mary. 1978. *Gyn/ecology: The metaethics of radical feminism.* New York: Beacon Press.

Darwish, Mahmoud. 2002. "A State of Siege." http://www.arabworldbooks.com/Literature/poetry4.html.

Das, Rahul. 2003. "Women *sarpanches* asserting their authority." *Chandigarh Tribune,* November 28.

Das, Ranendra Kumar, and Veena Das. 2005. *The interface between mental health and reproductive health of women among the urban poor in Delhi.* Trivandrum: Achutha Menon Centre for Health Science Studies, Sree Chitra Tirunal Institute for Medical Sciences and Technology.

Dasgupta, Shamita. 2007. *Body evidence: Intimate violence against South Asian women in America.* New Brunswick: Rutgers University Press.

Davin, Delia. 1976. *Woman-work: Women and the party in revolutionary China.* Oxford: Clarendon Press.

Davis, Angela. 2000. "The color of violence against women." *Colorlines* 3, no. 3 (September 30).

Del Campo, Esther. 2005. "Women and politics in Latin America: Perspectives and limits of the institutional aspects of women's political representation." *Social Forces* 83, no. 4: 1697–1726.

Democracy Now. 2008. "Race and gender in presidential politics: A debate between Gloria Steinem and Melissa Harris-Lacewell." January 14. http://www.democracynow.org/2008/1/14/race_and_gender_in_presidential_politics.

Desai, Manisha. 2005. "Transnationalism: The face of feminist politics post-Beijing." *International Social Science Journal* (October).

De Sousa Santos, Boaventura. 1997. "Una concepción multicultural de los derechos humanos." *Revista Memoria* (July): 41–53.

———. 1998. *La globalización del derecho: Los nuevos caminos de la regulación y la emancipación.* Bogota: ILSA/Universidad Nacional de Colombia.

Devi, Dr. Rama, cf. P. Sainath. 2004. "How the better half dies." *India Together*, August.

Deyyab, Rabiha [head of the union of Palestinian Woman for Social Work and general director in the Ministry of Youth and Sports]. 2001. Interview with Islah Jad, Ramallah, July 11.

Dhagamwar, Vasudha. 2005. "'The shoe fitted me and I wore it . . .': Women and traditional justice systems." In *The violence of normal times: Essays on women's lived realities*, ed. Kalpana Kannabiran, 46–66. New Delhi: Women Unlimited.

Diani, Mario. 2000. "The concept of social movement." In *Readings in contemporary sociology*, ed. Kate Nash, 155–176. Malden, MA: Blackwell.

Dicker, Rory. 2008. *A history of U.S. feminisms.* Berkeley: Seal Press.

Dickerson, John. 2008. "The great snipe hunt of 2008." Slate, June 13. http://www.slate.com/id/2193470/pagenum/2.

Dollarhide, M., and I. Bouabid. 2004. "License to kill in the name of honor, religion, and tradition." http://www.voices-unabridged.org/article.php?id_article=45&numero=1.

Domanski, H. 2002. "Nagle oko i fakty." *Res Publica*, January.

Dongxiao Liu. 2006. "When do national movements adopt or reject international agendas? A comparative analysis of the Chinese and Indian women's movements." *American Sociological Review* 71, no. 6: 921–942.

Draper, Melissa. 2006. "Women and the mud ceiling." Democracy Center blog, October 3. http://www.democracyctr.org/blog/2006/10/bolivian-women-and-mud-ceiling.html.

Du, Fangqin. 1993. "Qianyan." Introduction to *Zhongguo funu yu fazhan: Diwei, jiankong, jiuye* [Chinese women and development: Status, health, and employment], ed. Women's Studies Center of the Tianjin Normal University, 1–10. Zhengzhou: Henan People's Press.

———. 2000. "Yunming yu shiming: Gaoxiao funu yanjiu zhongxin de licheng he qianjin" [Opportunities and mission: Paths and prospects of women's studies centers in university]. *Baokan fuyin ziliao: funu yanjiu* (reprinted materials from newspapers and journals, Women's Studies) 3: 16–20.

———. 2001. "Wo de funu yanjiu licheng" [My road to women's studies]. In *Shen lin "qi" jing* [In "wonder" land], ed. Li Xiaojiang et al., 171–194. Nanjing: Jiangsu People's Press.

———. 2005. "Developing women's studies at universities in China: Research, curriculum, and institution." *Asian Journal of Women's Studies* 11, no. 4.

Du, Fangqin, and Jun Wang. 2008. "Zhongguo funu/xingbie yanjiu sanshi nian: Lilun yu shijian, 1979–2008" [Discipline building of women's/gender studies in China in the past three decades, 1979–2008]. In *Zhongguo funu yanjiu fazhen baogao* [Report on the development of women's education in China], ed. Linxi Zhang. Beijing: Social Sciences Documentary Materials Publishing House.

Du Plessix Gray, Francine. 1989. *Soviet women: Walking the tightrope.* Toronto: Doubleday.

Durán, Lydia Alpizar, Noel D. Payne, and Anahi Russo, eds. 2007. *Building feminist movements and organizations: Global perspectives.* New York: Palgrave Macmillan.

Durham, Eunice. 1986. "A pesquisa antropológica com populações urbanas: Problemas e perspectivas." In *A aventura antropológica,* ed. R. Cardoso. Rio de Janeiro: Paz e Terra.

Dworkin, Ronald. 1996. *Freedom's law: The moral reading of the American Constitution.* Cambridge: Harvard University Press.

Dyukova, Natalia. 1998. "Istoriia sozdaniia feministskogo dvizheniia v nachale 80-kh godov" [History of formation of the feminist movement in the early 1980s]. Paper presented at the conference "Society and Totalitarianism: First Half of the 1980s," St. Petersburg.

Ebadi, Shirin. 2000. *History and documentation of human rights in Iran.* Trans. Nazila Fathi. New York: Bibliotheca Persica Press.

El-Hamad, Jawad, and Eyyad al-Bargothi. 1997. *Derassa fi fikr harakat al-moqawamah al-islameyya hamas* (A Study in the Political Ideology of the Islamic Resistance Movement, Hamas 1987–1996). Amman: Middle East Study Centre.

Elliott, Carolyn, ed. 2008. *Global empowerment of women: Responses to globalization and politicized religions.* New York: Routledge.

Elman, Amy R. 2003. "Refuge in reconfigured states: Shelter movements in the United States, Britain, and Sweden." In *Women's movements facing the reconfigured state,* ed. Lee Ann Banaszak, Karen Beckwith, and Dieter Rucht, 94–113. Cambridge and New York: Cambridge University Press.

"Em 2007, governo pagou 67, 32% do Orçamento Mulher." 2008. *Jornal Fêmea* 155. http://www.cfemea.org.br/jornalfemea/pesquisa.asp.

Engle, Karen. 2001. "From skepticism to embrace: Human rights and the American Anthropological Association." *Human Rights Quarterly* 23: 536–560.

Engle Merry, Sally. 2003. "Human rights law and the demonization of culture (and anthropology along the way)." *Polar: Political and Legal Anthropology Review* 26, no. 1: 55–77.

Enloe, Cynthia. 2000. *Maneuvers: The international politics of militarizing women's lives.* Berkeley and Los Angeles: University of California Press.

———. 2004. *The curious feminist: Searching for women in an age of empire.* Berkeley and Los Angeles: University of California Press.

Ershova, Elena [coordinator of the Consortium of Women's Nongovernmental Organizations]. 1998. Interview with Lisa McIntosh Sundstrom, Moscow, July 21.

Eschle, Catherine. 2001. *Global democracy movements, social movements, and feminism.* Boulder: Westview Press.

Escobar-Lemmon, Maria, and Michelle Taylor-Robinson. 2005. "Women ministers in Latin American government: When, where, and why?" *American Journal of Political Science* 49, no. 4: 829–844.

Esfandiari, Haleh. 1997. *Reconstructed lives: Women and Iran's Islamic revolution.* Washington, DC: Woodrow Wilson Center.

Espina, Gioconda. 2000. "Sudden awakening in Venezuela: Venezuelan women active in placing controversial issues in parliament." *LOLApress* 13: 62. http://giocondaespina.com.ve/GIOCONDA/mvenezolanas.php?itemmmvv=33.

———. 2007. "Beyond polarization: Organized Venezuelan women promote their 'minimum agenda.'" *NACLA Report on the Americas* 40, no. 2: 20–24.

———. 2008. "Creado el Meamujer." *El Siglo*, April 2. http://giocondaespina.com.ve/GIOCONDA/mvenezolanas.php?itemmmvv=33.

Espinoza Damián, Gisela. 2009. *Cuatro vertientes del feminismo en Mexico: Diversidad de rutas y cruces de caminos.* Mexico City: Colección Teoría y Análisis, Universidad Autónoma Metropolitana, Unidad Xochimilco, Division de Ciencias Sociales.

Espinoza Damián, Gisela, and Alma Sánchez. 1992. *También somos protagonistas de la historia de México.* Cuadernos Para La Mujer, Serie Pensamientos y Lucha, no. 7. Morelia, Michoacán: Equipo de Mujeres en Acción Solidaria/Centro Michoacano de Investigación y Formación Vasco de Quiroga.

Espinoza, Gisela y Lorena Paz Paredes. 1988. "Pioneras del feminismo en los sectores populares. La experiencia de CIDHAL 1977–1995." Documento mecanografiado.

Essig, Laurie. 1999. *Queer in Russia: A story of sex, self, and the other.* Durham: Duke University Press.

Estrada, Daniela. 2007. "Chile: High-profile trial opens dialogue on domestic violence." Global Information Network, May 9. http://www.globalinfo.org/.

Evans, Alfred B. 2005. "Vladimir Putin's design for civil society." In *Russian civil society: A critical assessment*, ed. Alfred B. Evans, Laura A. Henry, and Lisa McIntosh Sundstrom. Armonk, NY: M. E. Sharpe.

———. 2008. "The first steps of Russia's public chamber: Representation or coordination?" *Demokratizatsiya* 16, no. 4: 345–362.

Faludi, Susan. 2007. *Terror dream: Fear and fantasy in post 9-11 America.* New York: Metropolitan Books.

Farthing, Linda. 2007. "Everything is up for discussion: A 40th anniversary conversation with Silvia Rivera Cusicanqui." *NACLA Report on the Americas* 40, no. 4: 4–9.

Fernandes, Sujatha. 2007a. "Barrio women and popular politics in Chávez's Venezuela." *Latin American Politics and Society* 49, no. 3: 97–127.

———. 2007b. "The gender agenda of the pink tide in Latin America." Zmag.org, October 7. http://www.zmag.org/content/showarticle.cfm?ItemID=13958.

Fernandez, Bina, and N. B. Gomathy. 2005. "Voicing the invisible: Violence faced by lesbian women in India." In *The violence of normal times: Essays on women's lived realities*, ed. Kalpana Kannabiran, 224–265. New Delhi: Women Unlimited.

Ferree, Myra Max. 2006. "Globalization and feminism: Opportunities and obstacles for activism in the global arena." In *Global feminism*, ed. Myra Max Ferree and Aili Mari Tripp. New York: New York University Press.

Ferree, Myra Max, and Beth B. Hess. 2000. *Controversy and coalition: The new feminist movement across four decades of change.* 3rd ed. New York and London: Routledge.

Ferree, Myra Max, and Aili Marie Tripp, eds. 2006. *Global feminism: Transnational women's activism, organizing, and human rights.* New York: New York University Press.

Ferree, Myra Max, and Patricia Yancey, eds. 1995. *Feminist organizations: Harvest of the new women's movement; Women in the political economy.* Philadelphia: Temple University Press.

"Finding women's security in the 21st century: A gendered perspective." 2002. Panel presentation and discussion organized by the National Council for Research on Women, New York, February 21.

Flanders, Laura. 2008. "Which womanhood does Clinton defend?" AlterNet, February 5. http://www.alternet.org/reproductivejustice/76020/.

Fleischmann, Ellen. 2003. *The nation and its "new" women: The Palestinian women's movement, 1920–1948.* Berkeley and Los Angeles: University of California Press.

Flood, Merielle. 1994. "Changing gender relations in Zinacantán, México." *Research in Economic Anthropology* 15.

Forbes, Geraldine. 2003. "Reflections on South Asian women's/gender history: Past and future." *Journal of Colonialism and Colonial History* 4, no. 1.

Franceschet, Susan. 2003. "'State feminism' and women's movements: The impact of Chile's *servicio nacional de la mujer* on women's activism." *Latin American Research Review* 38, no. 1: 9–40.

Frankovic, Kathy. 2008. "Age gap may start younger than thought." CBS News, April 25. http://www.cbsnews.com/stories/2008/04/25/opinion/pollpositions/main4045033.shtml?source=search _story.

Fraser, Nancy. 2003. "Rethinking recognition: Overcoming displacement and reification politics." In *Recognition struggles and social movements: Contested identities, agency, and power*, ed. Barbara Hobson. Cambridge: Cambridge University Press.

Freeman, Jo. 1999. "On the origins of social movements." In *Waves of protest: Social movements since the sixties*, ed. Jo Freeman and Victoria Johnson, 7–24. Lanham, MD: Rowman and Littlefield.

Freyermuth, Graciela, and Mariana Fernández. 1995. "Migration, organization, and identity: The case of a women's group from San Cristóbal las Casas." *Signs* 20, no. 4 (Summer): 25–40.

Friedman, Elisabeth J. 1995. "Women's human rights: The emergence of a movement." In *Women's rights, human rights: International feminist perspectives*, ed. Julie Peters and Andrea Wolper, 18–35. New York: Routledge.

———. 1998. "Paradoxes of gendered political opportunity in the Venezuelan transition to democracy." *Latin American Research Review* 33, no. 3: 87–135.

———. 2000. *Unfinished transitions: Women and the gendered development of democracy in Venezuela, 1936–1996*. University Park: Pennsylvania State University Press.

Friedman, Gil. 1999. *The Palestinian Draft Basic Law: Prospects and potentials*. Jerusalem: Palestinian Independent Commission for Citizen's Rights.

Friedman-Rudovsky, Jean. 2007. "Abortion under siege in Latin America." *Time*, August 9. http://www.time.com/time/world/article/0,8599,1651307,00.html.

Fuszara, M. 2000. *The new gender contract in Poland*. SOCO/IWM Working Papers. Vienna: SOCO/IWM.

———. 2006. "Udzial Kobiet we wladzy." Warsaw: Kobiety w polityce. http://www.cpk.org.pl/ images/artykuly/attach_82.pdf.

Gabriel Xiquín, Calixta. 2004. "Liderazgo de las Mujeres Mayas en las Leyendas y Mitologías según su Cosmovisión." Manuscript, Guatemala City.

Gaidzanwa, R. 1992. *The ideology of domesticity and the struggles of women workers: The case of Zimbabwe*. Zimbabwe: Institute of Social Studies.

Gallup Polling. 2008. March 26. http://www.gallup.com/poll/105691/McCain-vs-Obama-28-Clinton -Backers-McCain.aspx.

Gandhi, N., and N. Shah. 1991. *The issues at stake: Theory and practice in the contemporary women's movement in India*. New Delhi: Kali for Women.

Gao, Xiaoxian. 2000. "Minjian funu zuzhi de minzhuhua jianshe" [Democratic construction of women's popular organizations]. *China Women's News*. http://www.westwomen.org/jigou/ 2007/1024/article_57.html.

———. 2001a. "Strategies and space: A case study of the Shaanxi Association for Women and Family." In *Chinese women organizing cadres, feminists, Muslims, queers*, ed. Ping-Chun Hsiung, Maria Jaschok, and Cecilia Milwertz, 193–208. Oxford: Berg.

———. 2001b. "Zhongguo minjian funu zuzhi de kongjian he celue" [Space and strategies for Chinese popular women's organizations]. In *Shen lin "qi" jing* [In "wonder" land], ed. Li Xiaojiang et al., 215–236. Nanjing: Jiangsu People's Press.

———. 2009a. "Cong heyang moushi dao shaanxi moushi: Tuidong nongcun funu canxuan canzheng de shijian yu sikao: Jianlun dangdai zhongfuo funu yundong de celue yu tedian" [From Heyang Model to Shaanxi Model: Practices and reflection on advancing rural women's participation in election and governance]. Paper presented at the First International Conference on Gender Studies in China, Shanghai, June 26–29.

————. 2009b. *Shiwu nian, women zou dao le nali.* [Where are we after 15 years].

Gao Xiaoxian, Jiang Po, and Wang Guohong. 2002. "Tudong Shehui Xingbei yu fazhan bentuhua de nuli" [Efforts in promoting indigenization of gender and development in China]. In *Shehui Xingbei yu fazhan zai zhongguo: Huigu yu zhanwang* [Gender and development in China: Looking back and forward], 1–20. Xian: Shaanxi People's Publishing House.

Garrison, E. K. 2000. "U.S. feminism—grrrl style! Youth (sub)cultures and the technologics of the Third Wave." *Feminist Studies* 26, no. 1: 141–170.

Garza, Ana María, and Sonia Toledo. 2004. "Mujeres, agrarismo y militancia: Chiapas en la década de los ochenta." In *Tejiendo historias: Tierra, género y poder en Chiapas*, ed. Maya Lorena Pérez Ruíz. Mexico City: CONACULTA-INAH.

Garza Caligaris, Anna María. 2002. *Género, interlegalidad y conflicto en San Pedro Chenalhó.* Mexico City: PROIMMSE, UNAM / IEI, UNACH.

Gerlach, Luther. 1999. "The structure of social movements: Environmental activism and its opponents." In *Waves of protest: Social movements since the sixties*, ed. Jo Freeman and Victoria Johnson. Lanham, MD: Rowman and Littlefield.

Ghai, Anita. 2008. "A disabled feminism?" In *Women's studies in India: A reader*, ed. Mary E. John. New Delhi: Penguin Books India.

Ghorashi, Haleh. 2007. "Iranian women's voices across borders." In *Women, feminism, and fundamentalism*, ed. Ireen Dubel and Karen Vintges, 82–95. Amsterdam: Humanistics University Press.

Ghosh, Jayati. 2006a. "Nutrition concerns." September 11. http://www.macroscan.com/cur/sep06/cur110906Nutrition_Concerns.htm.

————. 2006b. "Rent a womb: An Indian expert." *Deccan Chronicle*, November 11.

Gillmore, Stephanie. 2008. *Feminist coalitions: Historical perspectives on Second-Wave feminism in the United States.* Urbana: University of Illinois Press.

Goetz, Anne Marie, ed. 1997. *Getting institutions right for women in development.* London: Zed Books.

————. 2003. "Women's political effectiveness: A conceptual framework." In *No shortcuts to power: African women in politics and policy making*, ed. Anne Marie Goetz and Shireen Haseem. London: Zed Books.

Goldfarb, Jeffrey C. 1997. "Why is there no feminism after communism?" *Social Research* 64, no. 2: 235–257.

Goldstein, Dana. 2008. "Feminist groups prepare to back Obama." *American Prospect*, June 17. http://www.prospect.org/cs/articles?article=feminist_groups_prepare_to_back_obama.

Gondolf, Edward. 1997. "Spousal homicide in Russia versus the United States: Preliminary findings and implications." *Journal of Family Violence* 12, no. 1.

Govender, Pregs. 2007. *Love and courage: A story of insubordination.* Johannesburg: Jacana.

Government of India. 1974. *Towards equality.* New Delhi: Government of India.

Graff, Agnieszka. 1999. "Patriarchat po seksmisji." *Gazeta Wyborcza*, June 19–20.

Groenewald, Yolandi. 2008. "New land act like apartheid." October 23. http://www.mg.co.za/article/2008-10-23.

Grupo de Mujeres Mayas Kaqla. 2000. *Algunos colores del arco iris: Realidad de las mujeres Mayas.* Discussion paper. Guatemala City: La Palabra y el Sentir de las Mujeres Mayas de Kaqla.

Gu, Xiulian. 2001. "Renqing xingshi, mingque renwu, nuli kaichuang fulian jiaoyu peixun gongzuo de xin jumian" [Have a clear view of the situation, make clear the tasks, strive to open up a new prospect for Women's Federation's work in education and training]. *Zhongguo fuyun* [Chinese Women's Movement] 9: 9–15.

Guo Aidi. 2009. "Nuganbu yanchi tuixiu' tiaokuan bei shanchu" [Elimination of clauses on extension of retirement age of women cadres]. Xinhua Net. http://news.xinhuanet.com/legal/2009-05/05/content_11313716.htm.

Guha, Ranajit. 1983. *Elementary aspects of peasant insurgency in colonial India.* Delhi: Oxford University Press.

Haas, Leisl. 2007. "The rules of the game: Feminist policymaking in Chile." *Política* 46: 199–225.

Habermas, J. 1996. *The structural transformation of the public sphere.* Cambridge: MIT Press.

Haeri, Shahla. 1989. *Law of desire: Temporary marriage in Shi'i Iran.* Syracuse: Syracuse University Press.

Hahner, June Edith. 1990. *Emancipating the female sex: The struggle for women's rights in Brazil, 1850–1940.* Durham: Duke University Press.

Hammami, Rema, and Penny Johnson. 1999. "Equality with a difference: Gender and citizenship in transitional Palestine." *Social Politics: International Studies in Gender, State, and Society* 6: 314–343.

Hanafi, Sari, and Linda Tabar. 2002. "NGOs, elite formation, and the second intifada." *Between the Lines* (Jerusalem) 2, no. 18 (October): 31–37. http://www.between-lines.org.

Haroun, Amira, and Youssra Salah [Women's Action Department, Islamic Khalas Party]. 2000. Interview with Islah Jad, Gaza, October 1–2.

Harriss-White, Barbara. 1999. "Gender cleansing: The paradox of development and deteriorating female life chances in Tamil Nadu." In *Signposts: Gender issues in post-independence India*, ed. Rajeswari Sunder Rajan, 124–153. New Delhi: Kali for Women.

Hassim, Shireen. 2003. The gender pact and democratic consolidation: Institutionalising gender equality in the South African state." *Feminist Studies* 29: 3.

———. 2005. "Terms of engagement: South African challenges." *Feminist Africa* 5.

———. 2006. *Women's organizations and democracy in South Africa: Contesting authority.* Madison: Wisconsin University Press.

Haussman, Melissa, and Birgit Sauer, eds. 2007. *Gendering the state in the age of globalization: Women's movements and state feminism in postindustrial democracies.* Lanham, MD: Rowman and Littlefield.

Hautzinger, Sarah J. 2007. *Violence in the city of women: Police and batterers in Bahia, Brazil.* Berkeley and Los Angeles: University of California Press.

Hawthorne, Susan, and Bronwyn Winter, eds. 2003. *September 11, 2001: Global feminist perspectives.* Vancouver: Raincoast Books.

Hellman, J. A. 1992. "The study of new social movements in Latin America." In *Latin America and the question of autonomy in the making of social movements in Latin America*, ed. S. Alvarez and A. Escobar. Boulder: Westview Press.

Henderson, Sarah. 1998. "Importing civil society: Western funding and the women's movement in Russia." Paper presented at the annual meeting of the American Political Science Association, Boston.

———. 2003. *Building democracy in contemporary Russia: Western support for grassroots organizations.* Ithaca: Cornell University Press.

———. 2008. "Shaping civic advocacy: International and domestic policies towards Russia's NGO sector." Paper presented at the conference of the Canadian Political Science Association, Vancouver, BC.

Hernández, Daisy, and Bushra Rehman, eds. 2002. *Colonize this! Young women of color on today's feminism.* New York: Seal Press.

Hernández Castillo, Rosalva Aída. 1994. "Reinventing tradition: The women's law." *Akwe:Kon: A Journal of Indigenous Issues* 2, no. 2: 67–70.

———. 1996. "From the community to the women's state convention." In *The explosion of communities in Chiapas,* ed. June Nash, 20–52. Copenhagen: International Working Group for Indigenous Affairs (IWGIA).

———. 2002. "Indigenous law and identity politics in México: Indigenous men's and women's perspective for a multicultural nation." *Political and Legal Anthropology Review* 25, no. 1: 90–110.

———. 2006a. "Between feminist ethnocentricity and ethnic essentialism: The Zapatistas' demands and the national indigenous women's movement." In *Dissident women: Gender and cultural politics in Chiapas*, ed. Shannon Speed, R. Aída Hernández Castillo, and Lynn Stephen, 57–75. Austin: University of Texas Press.

————. 2006b. "Fratricidal war or ethnocidal strategy? Women's experience with political violence in Chiapas." In *Engaged observer: Anthropology, advocacy, and activism,* ed. Victoria Sanford and Asale Angel-Ajani, 149–170. New Brunswick: Rutgers University Press.

————. 2007. "State and gender violence: Backlashes on women's human rights in Mexico." Fray Bartolomé de las Casas Lecture, Latin American Studies Center, University of Oregon, April.

————. 2008. *Etnografías e historias de resistencia: Mujeres indígenas, procesos organizativos y nuevas identidades políticas.* Mexico City: Publicaciones de la Casa Chata CIESAS/PUEG-UNAM.

He Xiaopei. 2001. "Chinese queer (*tongzhi*) women organizing in the 1990s." In *Chinese women organizing cadres, feminists, Muslims, queers,* ed. Ping-Chun Hsiung, Maria Jaschok, and Cecilia Milwertz, 41–59. Oxford: Berg.

Heywood, Leslie, and Jennifer Drake, eds. 1997. *Third Wave agenda: Being feminist, doing feminism.* Minneapolis: University of Minnesota Press.

Hilal, Jamil. 1999. *Al-mojtam' al-falastini wa iskaleyat al-dimocrateya* [Palestinian society and democracy problems]. Nablus: Center for Palestine Research and Studies.

Hilal, Jamil, and Mushtaq H. Khan. 2004. "State-society relationships, rent-seeking, and the nature of the PNA quasi-state." In *State formation in Palestine,* ed. Mushtaq Khan, George Giacaman, and Inge Amundsen. London: Routledge.

Hilhorst, Dorothea. 2003. *The real world of NGOs: Discourses, diversity, and development.* London: Zed Books.

Hirschkind, Charles, and Saba Mahmood. 2002. "Feminism, the Taliban, and politics of counter-insurgency." *Anthropological Quarterly* 75, no. 2 (Spring): 339–354.

Holland, Dorothy, Gretchen Fox, and Vinci Daro. 2008. "Social movements and collective identity: A decentered, dialogic view." In "Meaning-making in social movements." Special issue, *Anthropological Quarterly* 81, no. 1 (Winter): 95–126.

Holmgren, Beth. 1995. "Bug inspectors and beauty queens: The problems of translating feminism into Russian." In *Postcommunism and the body politic,* ed. Ellen E. Berry. New York: New York University Press.

Honderich, Ted. 1989. *Violence for equality: Inquiries in political philosophy.* London and New York: Routledge.

Hoodfar, Homa. 1999. "The women's movement in Iran." *WLUML* (Winter).

Howell, Jude. 1997. "Post-Beijing reflections: Creating ripples but not waves in China." *Women Studies International Forum,* 20, no. 2: 235–252.

Howell, Jude, and Diane Mulligan, eds. 2005. *Gender and civil society: Transcending boundaries.* London: Routledge.

Hroub, Khalid. 2000. *Hamas Political Thought and Practices.* Beirut: Institute of Palestine Studies.

————. 1996. "Obstacles to Democratisation in the Middle East." *Contention 14*: 81–106.

Hsiung, Ping-chun, and Yuk-lin Renita Wong. 1998. "*Jie Gui*—connecting the tracks: Chinese women's activism surrounding the 1995 World Conference on Women in Beijing." *Gender and History* 10, no. 3: 470–497.

Htun, Mala. 2003. *Sex and the state: Abortion, divorce, and the family under Latin American dictatorships and democracies.* Cambridge: Cambridge University Press.

al-Huda Association. 1998. *Al-mara' al-falestenyya wa mo'amrat al-'al-a'maneyyat* [Palestinian woman and the plot of secular women]. al-Bireh: al-Huda Association.

Hull, Gloria T., Patricia Bell Scott, and Barbara Smith, eds. 1982. *All the women are white, all the blacks are men, but some of us are brave: Black women's studies.* New York: Feminist Press.

Human Rights Watch. 1997. *Russia—too little, too late: State response to violence against women.* New York: Human Rights Watch.

Hunter, Wendy, and Timothy Power. 2007. "Rewarding Lula: Executive power, social policy, and the Brazilian elections of 2006." *Latin American Politics and Society* 49, no. 1: 1–30.

IBGE. 2003. *Síntese de indicadores sociais.* Rio de Janeiro: IBGE (Instituto Brasileiro de Geografia e Estatística).

Ibrahim, Sa'd Eddin, ed. 1993. *Al-mujtama' al-madani wal tahawol al-dimoqrati fil watan al-'arabi* [Civil society and democratic transformation in the Arab world]. Annual report. Cairo: Markaz Ibn Khaldoun.

———. 1995. "Civil society and prospects of democratisation in the Arab world." In *Civil society in the Middle East*, ed. Augustus R. Norton. Vol. 1. Leiden: E. J. Brill.

INAMUJER. 2008. "Puntos de Encuentro con INAMUJER." August 1. http://www.inamujer.gob.ve/index.php?option=com_content&task=view&id=21&Itemid=44.

INCITE! Women of Color Against Violence. 2000. *Color of violence: Violence against women.* Conference summary. Minneapolis: INCITE! Women of Color Against Violence.

———. 2006. *Color of violence: The INCITE! anthology.* Cambridge: South End Press.

Independent Task Force. 1999. *Strengthening Palestinian public institutions: Council on Foreign Relations.* Prepared by Yazid Sayiegh and Khalil Shaqaqi, June 28. http://www.cfr.org.

Inglehart, Ronald, Miguel Basáñez, and Alejandro Menéndez Moreno. 1998. *Human values and beliefs, a cross-cultural sourcebook: Political, religious, sexual, and economic norms in 43 societies; Findings from the 1990–1993 world values survey.* Ann Arbor: University of Michigan Press.

International Initiative for Justice. 2003. *Threatened existence: A feminist analysis of the genocide in Gujarat.* Mumbai: International Initiative for Justice.

Inter-Parliamentary Union. 2008a. "Women in national parliaments." April 7. http://www.ipu.org/wmn-e/classif-arc.htm.

———. 2008b. "Women in national parliaments, situation as of 25 January 1998." April 7. http://www.ipu.org/wmn-e/arc/world250198.htm.

Islamic Resistance Movement. 1996. *The practices of the self-rule authority against the Palestinian civil society.* May 20. Document distributed by Hamas.

Jackson, Cecile, and R. Pearson, eds. 1998. *Feminist visions of development: Gender analysis and policy.* London: Routledge.

Jad, Islah, 1990. "From salons to the popular committees: Palestinian women, 1919–1989." In *Intifada: Palestine at the crossroads,* ed. Jamal R. Nassar and Roger Heacock. New York: Praeger.

———. 2000. *Palestinian women: A status report—women and politics.* Palestine: Birzeit University, Women's Studies Institute.

———. 2004. "The 'NGOisation' of the Arab women's movement." In *Repositioning feminisms in development,* ed. Andrea Cornwall, Elizabeth Harrison, and Ann Whitehead. Sussex: Sussex University Press; *IDS Bulletin* 35, no. 4 (October).

———. 2005. "Islamist women of Hamas: A new women's movement?" In *On shifting ground: Muslim women in a global era,* ed. Fereshteh Nouraie-Simone. New York: Feminist Press.

Jad, Islah, et al. 2003. "Qiraah nassaweyya lemosswadat al dosstor al-falastini" [A feminist reading for the draft of the Palestinian Constitution]. *Review of Women's Studies* (Birzeit University) 1, no. 1: 8–12.

Jad, Islah, Penny Johnson, and Rita Giacaman. 2000. "Gender and citizenship under the Palestinian Authority." In *Gender and citizenship in the Middle East,* ed. Suad Joseph. Syracuse: Syracuse University Press.

Jahangir, Asma, and Hina Jilani. 1990. *A divine sanction? The Hudood Ordinance.* Lahore: Sang-e-Meel Publications.

Jamal, Amina. 2005. "Transnational feminism as critical practice." *Meridians: Feminism, Race, and Transnationalism* 5, no. 2: 57–82.

James, Joy, and T. Denean Sharpley-Whiting, eds. 2000. *The black feminist reader.* Malden, MA: Blackwell.

Jäppinen, Maija. 2008. "Tensions between familialism and feminism: A case study of a crisis centre for women in Udmurtia." Paper presented at the annual meeting of the American Association for the Advancement of Slavic Studies, Philadelphia, November.

Jaquette, Jane S., ed. 1989. *The women's movement in Latin America: Feminism and the transition of democracy.* Boston: Unwin Hill Hyman.

————, ed. 1991. *The women's movement in Latin America: Feminism and the transition to democracy.* Boulder: Westview Press.

Jaquette, Jane S., and Sharon L. Wolchik, eds. 1998. *Women and democracy: Latin America and central and Eastern Europe.* Baltimore: Johns Hopkins University Press.

Jeffery, Patricia, and Amrita Basu, eds. 1998. *Appropriating gender: Women's activism and politicized religion in South Asia.* New York: Routledge; New Delhi: Kali for Women.

Jeffreys, Sheila. 2002. "Trafficking in women versus prostitution: A false distinction." Keynote address, Townsville International Women's Conference, James Cook University, Australia, July 3–7.

Jiang, Yongping. 2007. "Shehui xingbie yu gonggong zhengce yanjiu zongshu" [Overview on gender and public policy]. In *Zhongguo Funu Yanjiu Nianjian (2001–2005),* ed. Quanguo Fulian Funu Yanjiusuo, 59–68. Beijing: Shehui Kexue Wenxian Chubanshe.

Jiang, Yongping, and Tang Binyao. 2007. "Funu yu jingji yanjiu zongshu" [Overview on women and economic research]. In *Zhongguo Funu Yanjiu Nianjian (2001–2005),* ed. Quanguo Fulian Funu Yanjiusuo, 98–108. Beijing: Shehui Kexue Wenxian Chubanshe.

JMCC [Jerusalem Media and Communication Center, Palestine]. 2000a. *Palestine: Report* (February 23).

————. 2000b. *Report* (May 24).

————. 2000c. *Report* (June 14).

John, Mary E., ed. 2008. *Women's studies: A reader.* New Delhi: Penguin Books India.

Johnson, Janet Elise. 2007. "Contesting violence, contesting gender: Crisis centers encountering local government in Barnaul, Russia." In *Living gender after communism,* ed. Janet Elise Johnson and Jean C. Robinson, 40–59. Bloomington: Indiana University Press.

————. 2008. "The plight of women's crisis centers in Putin's Russia." Paper prepared at the annual meeting of the American Association for the Advancement of Slavic Studies, Philadelphia, November.

————. 2009. *Gender violence in Russia: The politics of feminist intervention.* Bloomington: Indiana University Press.

Johnson, Janet Elise, and Jean C. Robinson. 2007. "Living gender." In *Living gender after communism,* ed. Janet Elise Johnson and Jean C. Robinson, 1–21. Bloomington: Indiana University Press.

Jurna, Irina. 1995. "Women in Russia: Building a movement." In *From basic needs to basic rights: Women's claim to human rights,* ed. Margaret Schuler. Washington, DC: Women Law and Development International.

Kabeer, Naila. 1998. *Realidades trastocadas: Las jerarquías de género en el pensamiento de desarrollo.* Mexico City: Ed. Paidos-PUEG-UNAM.

Kampwirth, Karen. 2008. "Neither left nor right: Sandinismo in the anti-feminist era." *NACLA Report on the Americas* 41, no. 1: 30–43.

Kampwirth, Karen, and Victória Gonzalez. 2001. Introduction to *Radical women in Latin America: Left and right,* ed. Karen Kampwirth and Victória Gonzalez, 1–28. University Park: Pennsylvania State University Press.

Kandil, Amani. 1995. *Civil society in the Arab world.* Washington, DC: Civicus.

Kannabiran, Kalpana. 2005. Introduction to *The violence of normal times: Essays on women's lived realities,* ed. Kalpana Kannabiran. New Delhi: Women Unlimited.

————. 2006. "A cartography of resistance: The national federation of *dalit* women." In *The situated politics of belonging,* ed. Nira Yuval Davis, Kalpana Kannabiran, and Ulrike Vieten. London: Sage.

————. 2008a. "Sexual assault and the law." In *Challenging the rule(s) of law: Colonialism, criminology, and human rights in India,* ed. Kalpana Kannabiran and Ranbir Singh. New Delhi: Sage.

————. 2008b. "Violence and women's lifeworlds." *Journal of the National Human Rights Commission* (December 10).

Kannabiran, Kalpana, and Ekta. 2006. "Article 7: political and public life." In *Second and Third Alternative Report on CEDAW*, 53–60. Delhi: National Alliance of Women.

Kannabiran, Kalpana, and Vasanth Kannabiran. 1997. "Looking at ourselves: The women's movement in Hyderabad." In *Feminist genealogies, colonial legacies, democratic futures*, ed. M. Jacqui Alexander and Chandra Talpade Mohanty. New York and London: Routledge.

Kannabiran, Kalpana, and Ritu Menon, eds. 2007. *From Mathura to Manorama: Resisting violence against women in India.* New Delhi: Women Unlimited and International Centre for Ethnic Studies.

Kannabiran, Vasanth, Volga, and Kalpana Kannabiran. 2004. "Women's rights and Naxalite groups." *Economic and Political Weekly*, November 6, 4874–4877.

Kar, Mehrangiz. 2001. "Women's strategies in Iran from the 1979 revolution to 1999." In *Globalization, religion, and gender: The politics of women's rights in Catholic and Muslim contexts*, ed. Jane Bayes and Nayereh Tohidi, 177–202. New York: Palgrave.

———. 2008. "Discrimination against women under Iranian law." *Gozar* (Freedom House) (December 8).

Kar, Mehrangiz, and Shahla Lahidji. 1372/1993. *Shenakht-e hovviyat-e zan-e irani dar gostareh-ye pish-tarikh va tarikh.* Tehran: Roshangaran.

Karam, Azza M. 1998. *Women, Islamisms, and the state: Contemporary feminisms in Egypt?* London: Macmillan.

Katzenstein, Mary Fainsod. 1998. *Faithful and fearless: Moving feminist protest inside the church and the military.* Princeton: Princeton University Press.

———. 2003. "Redividing citizens—divided feminisms: The reconfigured U.S. state and women's citizenship." In *Women's movements facing the reconfigured state,* ed. Lee Ann Banaszak, Karen Beckwith, and Dieter Rucht, 203–218. Cambridge and New York: Cambridge University Press.

Katzenstein, Mary Fainsod, and Carol McClurg Mueller. 1987. *The women's movements of the United States and Western Europe: Consciousness, political opportunity, and public policy.* Philadelphia: Temple University Press.

Kay, Rebecca. 2004. "Meeting the challenge together? Russian grassroots women's organizations and the shortcomings of Western aid." In *Post-Soviet women encountering transition,* ed. Kathleen Kuehnast and Carol Nechemias, 241–261. Washington, DC: Woodrow Wilson Center Press.

Kayed, Aziz. 1999. *Takrir hawl tadakhol al-salaheyyat fi mo'assat al-solta al-wataneyya al-falastineyya* [A report on the overlapping of authority in the Palestinian National Authority]. Ramallah: Palestinian Independent Commission for Citizen's Rights.

Keck, Margaret E., and Kathryn Sikkink, eds. 1998. *Activists beyond borders: Advocacy networks in international politics.* Ithaca: Cornell University Press.

Keddie, Nikki. 2003. *Modern Iran: Roots and results of revolution.* New Haven: Yale University Press.

Kedzie, Christopher [program officer, Ford Foundation]. 1999. Interview with Lisa McIntosh Sundstrom, Moscow, March 29.

Kemp, A., et al. 1995. "The dawning of a new day: New South African feminisms." In *The challenge of local feminisms,* ed. Amrita Basu. Boulder: Westview Press.

Keshavarz, Nahid. 1387/2008. "Kampaign yek million emza be masabeh jonbesh-e ejtemayi." 15 Ordibehesht/April. http://femschool.info/spip.php?article550.

Khan, Omar Asghar. 1985. "Political and economic aspects of Islamisation." In *Islam, politics, and the state: The Pakistan experience*, ed. Asghar Khan, 127–163. London: Zed Books.

Khanday, Zamrooda. 2005. *Negotiating reproductive health needs in a conflict situation in the Kashmir Valley.* Trivandrum: Sree Chitra Tirunal Institute for Medical Sciences and Technology.

Khotkina, Zoya [senior research affiliate and former codirector, Moscow Center for Gender Studies]. 1999. Interview with Lisa McIntosh Sundstrom, Moscow, March 27.

Khreishe, Amal [head of the Palestinian Working Woman's Society for Development]. 2002. Telephone interview with Islah Jad, March 29.

Kian-Thiébaut, Azadeh. 2009. "Social change, the women's rights movement, and the role of Islam." *Middle East Institute Viewpoints: The Iranian Revolution at 30* (January 29).

Kishwar, Madhu. 1984. "Bondage: Women and fundamental rights." *PUCL Bulletin* 4, no. 2: 2-84.

Kondratowicz, Ewa. 2001. *Szminka na Sztandarze.* Warsaw: Sic!

Kotiswaran, Prabha. n.d. "Preparing for civil disobedience: Indian sex workers and the law." http://www.altlawforum.org.

Kozina, Irina, and Elena Zhidkova. 2006. "Sex segregation and discrimination in the new Russian labour market." In *Adapting to Russia's new labor market gender and employment strategy,* 57–86. London: RoutledgeCurzon.

Kozol, Wendy, and Wendy Hesford, eds. 2005. *Just advocacy? Women's human rights, transnational feminisms, and the politics of representation.* New Brunswick: Rutgers University Press.

Krook, Mona. "Quota laws for women in politics: Implications for feminist practice." *Social Politics, 15* (3): 345–368.

Kuehnast, Kathleen, and Carol Nechemias. 2004. "Introduction: Women navigating change in post-Soviet currents." In *Post-Soviet women encountering transition: Nation building, economic survival, and civic activism,* ed. Kathleen Kuehnast and Carol Nechemias, 1–20. Washington, DC: Woodrow Wilson Center Press; Baltimore: Johns Hopkins University Press.

Kurzman, Charles. 2008. "A feminist generation in Iran?" *Iranian Studies* 41, no. 3 (June): 297–321.

Lala fanjiabao xiangmu [Anti-domestic Violence Project for Lesbians and Bisexual Women]. http://dv.tongyulala.org/.

Lamas, Marta. 1986. "La antropología feminista y la categoría de género." *Nueva Antropología* 8, no 30: 173–222.

———. 1992. "El movimiento feminista en la década de los ochenta." In *Crisis y sujetos sociales en México,* ed. Enrique de la Garza. Mexico City: UNAM/Miguel Angel Porrúa, México DF.

Lamas, Marta, Alicia Martínez, María Luisa Tarrés, and Esperanza Tuñon. 1995. "Building bridges: The growth of popular feminism in Mexico." In *The challenge of local feminisms,* ed. Amrita Basu. Boulder: Westview Press.

Lapidus, Gail Warshofsky. 1978. *Women in Soviet society: Equality, development, and social change.* Berkeley and Los Angeles: University of California Press.

Larana, Enrique, Hank Johnston, and Joseph Gusfield. 1994. *New social movements: From ideology to identity.* Philadelphia: Temple University Press.

Lau, Jaiven Ana. 2002. "El nuevo movimiento feminista Mexicano a fines del milenio." In *Feminismo en México: Ayer y hoy,* ed. Eli Bartra. Mexico City: Universidad Autónoma Metropolitana.

Lavinas, L. 1996. "As Mulheres No Universo Da Pobreza: O Caso Brasileiro." In *Estudos Feministas,* Vol. 4, No. 2, 464–479.

Lebon, Nathalie. 1997. "Volunteer and professionalized activism in the São Paulo women's movement." Paper prepared for presentation at the 1997 meeting of the Latin American Studies Association, Guadalajara, Mexico, April 17–19.

Lee, Peggy. 2008. "Hate crimes against LGBTI in South Africa: Homophobic violence as patriarchal social control." Unpublished report prepared for the Triangle Project, July.

Levina, Yelizaveta. 2001. "Rewriting the labor code." *Russia Journal* 7 (November).

Lewis, D. 2007. "Feminism and the radical imagination." *Agenda* 72: 18–31.

Liang, Jun. 2001. "Cong xiaojia zouxiang dajia" [From small family to the large family]. In *Shen lin "qi" jing* [In "wonder" land], ed. Li Xiaojiang et al., 63–82. Nanjing: Jiangsu People's Press.

Li, Hongtao. 2005. "Intervention and counseling strategies for men's domestic violence against women in Beijing." In *China history and society: Women and gender in Chinese studies,* ed. Nicola Spakowski and Cecilia Milwertz, 64–73.

Lin, Zhibin. 2008. "Chinese women and poverty alleviation: Reflections and prospects for the future." *Chinese Sociology and Anthropology* 40, no. 4 (Summer): 27–37.

Li, Suwen. 1975. "Geguo funu yao zhengqu jiefang bixu jinxing fan di fan zhi fan ba douzheng" [To win liberation women of all countries must carry out the struggle against imperialism, colonialism, and hegaminism]. *People's Daily,* June 24, 5.

Li, Xiaoyun, and Wang Yihuan. 2007. "Nongcun funu yanjiu zongshu" [Overview of research on rural women]. In *Zhongguo funu yanjiu nianjian (2001 2005),* ed. Quanguo Fulian Funu Yanjiusuo, Beijing: Shehui Kexue Wenxian Chubanshe.

Liu, Bohong. 2009a. "Jiang xingbei pingdeng leiru lifa guocheng" [Incorporating gender equality into the process of law making]. In *Xingbei pingdeng yu falu gaige* [Gender equality and law reform], ed. Huang Lei, 21–33. Beijing: China Social Sciences Press.

———. 2009b. "Lianheguo tuijin xingbei pingdeng de sange zhongyao wenshu he woguo zhixiang qingkuang" [Three important UN documents to promote gender equality and their implementation in our country]. In *Tamen yanzhong de xingbei wenti* [Gender issues in their eyes], ed. Tan Lin and Meng Xianfan, 179–194. Beijing: Social Sciences Documents Publishing House.

Liu, Dongxiao. 2006. "When do national movements adopt or reject international agendas? A comparative analysis of the Chinese and Indian women's movements." *American Sociological Review* 71, no. 6 (December): 921–942.

Liu, Wenming. 2007. "Funu yu zongjiao yanjiu zongshu" [Overview on women and religion]. In *Zhongguo Funu Yanjiu Nianjian (2001–2005)*, ed. Quanguo Fulian Funu Yanjiusuo, 171–179. Shehui Kexue Wenxian Chubanshe.

Llanos, Beatriz, and Kristen Sample. 2008. *30 years of democracy: Riding the wave? Women's political participation in Latin America.* Peru: International Institute for Democracy and Electoral Assistance.

Lobo, Elizabete Souza. 1987. Mulheres, feminismo e novas práticas sociais. *Revista de Ciências Sociais* (Porto Alegre) 1, no. 2.

Lorde, Audre. 1984. "An open letter to Mary Daly." In *Sister outsider: Essays and speeches by Audre Lorde,* 66–71. Freedom, CA: Crossing Press.

———. 2002. "The master's tools will never dismantle the master's house." In *This bridge called my back: Writings by radical women of color,* ed. Cherríe L. Moraga and Gloria E. Anzaldúa, 98–101. Berkeley: Third Woman Press.

Lovera, Sara, and Nellys Palomo. [1997] 1999. *Las alzadas.* Mexico City: Centro de Información de la Mujer, A.C./Convergencia Socialista, Agrupación Política Nacional.

Luciak, Ilja A. 2001. *After the revolution: Gender and democracy in El Salvador, Nicaragua, and Guatemala.* Baltimore: Johns Hopkins University Press.

Lycklama à Nijeholt, Geertje, Virginia Vargas, and Saskia Wieringa, eds. 1998. *Women's movements and public policy in Europe, Latin America, and the Caribbean.* New York: Garland.

Lyon, Tania Rands. 2007. "Housewife fantasies, family realities in the new Russia." *In living gender after communism,* ed. Janet Elise Johnson and Jean C. Robinson, 25–39. Bloomington: Indiana University Press.

Macaulay, Fiona. 2006. "Judicialising and (de)criminalising domestic violence in Latin America." *Social Policy and Society* 5, no. 1: 103–114.

MacDonald, Laura. 2002. "Globalization and social movements." *International Feminist Journal of Politics* 4, no. 2 (August).

Mackie, Vera. 2001. "The language of globalization, transnationality, and feminism." *International Feminist Journal of Politics* 3, no. 2 (August).

Magallón, Carmen. 1988. "La participación de las mujeres en las organizaciones campesinas: Algunas limitaciones." In *Las mujeres en el campo,* ed. Josefina Aranda. Oaxaca: Instituto de Investigaciones Sociológicas.

Maghassib, Aisha Abu [Fateh member and ex-militant]. 2001. Interview with Islah Jad, Cairo, July 11.

Maharaj, Irma. 2008. Interview with Elaine Salo, Saartjie Baartman Centre, Cape Town, November 3,

Mahdavi, Pardis. 2008. *Passionate uprisings: Iran's sexual revolution.* Stanford: Stanford University Press.

Mama, Amina. 1995. "Feminism or femocracy? State feminism and democratisation in Nigeria." *Africa Development/Afrique et Développement* 20: 37–58.

———. 1999. "Dissenting daughters? Gender politics and civil society in a militarized state." *CODESRIA Bulletin,* nos. 3–4.

Mani, Lata. 1998. *Contentious traditions: The debate on sati in colonial India.* Berkeley and Los Angeles: University of California Press.

Mantilla, Karla. 2005. "Off our backs." Paper presented at INCITE! Third Color of Violence Conference, New Orleans. http://www.incite-national.org/media/docs/6256_cov3-offourbacks-mayjune2005.pdf.

Manuh, T. 1993. "Women, the state, and society under the PNDC." In *Ghana under PNDC rule*, ed. Gyimah-Boadi. Senegal: CODESRIA.

Ma Qiusha. 2006. *Non-governmental organizations in contemporary China: Paving the way to civil society?* New York: Routledge.

Marcos, Sylvia. 1997. "Mujeres indígenas: Notas sobre un feminismo naciente." *Cuadernos Feministas* 1, no. 2.

———. 1999. "La *Otra* Mujer: Una propuesta de reflexión para el VIII Congreso Feminista Latinoamericano y del Caribe." *Cuadernos Feministas* 2, no. 9.

Marody, M. 1993. "Why am I not a feminist?" *Social Research* 60, no. 4 (Winter).

Marsiaj, Juan P. 2006. "Expanding human rights: The Brazilian gay, lesbian, and travesti movement and the struggle against homophobic discrimination." Paper presented at the Twenty-sixth Latin American Studies Association Congress, San Juan, Puerto Rico.

Martins, Alaerte L., and Lígia C. Mendonça, eds. 2005. "Aborto: Mortes Previsíveis e Evitáveis; Dossiê Aborto Inseguro." http://www.redesaude.org.br/dossies/assets/docs/revista)05.pdf.

Mashayekhi, Mehrdad. 1387/2009. "Iranian women placing the social movement in its proper place." 17 Esfand/February. http://www.femschool.infspip.php?article2235.

Matynia, Elzbieta. 1994. "Women after communism: A bitter freedom." *Social Research* (Summer).

———. 1995. "Finding a voice: Women in postcommunist central Europe." In *The challenge of local feminism: Women's movements in global perspective*, ed. Amrita Basu. Boulder: Westview Press.

———. 1998. "Reluctant feminism; or, Are we listening?" Manuscript prepared for a conference in Ann Arbor, Michigan, April.

———. 2001. "The lost treasure of Solidarity." *Social Research* 68 (Winter).

———. 2009. *Performative democracy.* Boulder: Paradigm.

Mazur, Amy, ed. 2001. *State feminism, women's movements, and job training policy in the global economy: Making democracies work.* New York: Routledge.

McCallum, Cecilia. 2007. "Women out of place? A micro-historical perspective on the black feminist movement in Salvador da Bahia, Brazil." *Journal of Latin American Studies* 39: 55–80.

McFadden, P. 2002. "Becoming postcolonial: African women changing the meaning of citizenship." Paper presented at a conference at Queens University, Canada.

"MDC launch sets stage for bruising battle." 1999. *Financial Gazette,* September 16.

Medical Research Council. 2005. "Health systems trust health statistics." http://www.hst.org.za/healthstats/147/data.

Meintjies-Moakes, Ingrid. 2008. "Women AIDS activists' experiences as leaders in the Treatment Action Campaign, 2005–2007." Bachelor's thesis, University of Cape Town.

Mejía Flores, Susana. 2008. "Los derechos de las mujeres nahuas de Cuetzalan: La construcción de un feminismo indígena desde la necesidad." In *Etnografías e historias de resistencia: Mujeres indígenas, procesos organizativos y nuevas identidades políticas*, ed. Rosalva Aída Hernández, 453–503. Mexico City: Publicaciones de la Casa Chata CIESAS/PUEG-UNAM.

Menon, Ritu. 2007. "Alternative forms of protest." In *From Mathura to Manorama: Resisting violence against women in India*, ed. Kalpana Kannabiran and Ritu Menon. New Delhi: Women Unlimited and International Centre for Ethnic Studies.

Metelska, A., and E. Nowakowska, eds. 1992. *Gdzie Diabet nie moze . . .* Warsaw: BGW.

Meyer, David S., and Debra C. Minkoff. 2004. "Conceptualizing political opportunity." *Social Forces* 82, no. 4 (June): 1457–1492.

Mezentseva, Elena. 2004. "'Outsiders' in the labour market: Russian men and women facing new realities." In *Russia: Continuity and change*, ed. Gerald Hinteregger and Hans-Georg Heinrich, 311–338. New York: Springer.

Miguel, Luis F. 2008. "Political representation and gender in Brazil: Quotas for women and their impact." *Bulletin of Latin American Research* 27, no. 2: 197–214.

Milani, Farzaneh. 1992. *Veils and words: The emerging voices of Iranian women writers.* Syracuse: Syracuse University Press.

Millán Moncayo, Margara. 2008. "Nuevos espacios, nuevas actoras: Neozapatismo y su significado para las mujeres indígenas." In *Etnografías e historias de resistencia: Mujeres indígenas, procesos organizativos y nuevas identidades políticas,* ed. Rosalva Aída Hernández, 217–249. Mexico City: Publicaciones de la Casa Chata CIESAS/PUEG-UNAM.

Millán, René. 1996. "La Reforma Del Estado: Reflexiones Sobre la Política Social." *Las políticas sociales de México en los años noventa.* ed. Rosalba Casas Guerrero. Universidad Nacional Autónoma de México, 145–234

Miller, Francesca. 1991. *Latin American women and the search for social justice.* Lebanon, NH: University Press of New England.

Milwertz, Cecilia. 2002. *Beijing women organizing for change: The formation of a social movement wave.* Copenhagen: NIAS Press.

———. 2003. "Activism against domestic violence in the People's Republic of China." *Violence Against Women* 9, no. 6 (June): 630–654.

"Minister Jaruga-Nowacka o Swoich Planach." 2002. *Gazeta Wyborcza,* January 24.

Minoo, Moallem. 2006. "Feminist scholarship and the internationalization of women's studies." *Feminist Studies* 32, no. 2 (Summer).

Minow, Martha. 1990. *Making all the difference.* Ithaca: Cornell University Press.

Mir-Hosseini, Ziba. 2002. "Negotiating the politics of gender in Iran: An ethnography of a documentary." In *The new Iranian cinema,* ed. Richard Tapper. London: I. B. Tauris.

Mir-Hosseini, Ziba, and Richard Tapper. 2006. *Islam and democracy in Iran: Eshkevari and the quest for reform.* London: I. B. Tauris.

Misra, Nirja, Shobhita Rajan, and Kavita Srivastava. 1993. "The gang rape of Bhanwri: Response of state, WDP, and women's groups." Paper presented at the Sixth National Conference on Women's Studies, Mysore.

Mitchell, Timothy. 1991. "The limits of the state: Beyond statist approaches and their critics." *American Political Science Review* 85, no. 1 (1991): 77–94.

Mody, Perveez. 2008. *The intimate state: Love marriage and the law in Delhi.* New Delhi: Routledge.

Mogannam, Matiel. 1937. *The Arab woman.* London: Herbert Joseph.

Moghadam, Valentine. 1993. *Modernizing women: Gender and social change in the Middle East.* Boulder: Lynne Rienner.

———. 1997. *Women, work, and economic reform in the Middle East and North Africa.* Boulder: Lynne Rienner.

———. 2000. "Transnational feminist networks: Collective action in an era of globalization." *International Sociology* 15, no. 1 (March).

———. 2005. *Globalizing women: Transnational feminist networks.* Baltimore: Johns Hopkins University Press.

Moghissi, Haideh. 1996. *Populism and feminism in Iran: Women's struggle in a male-defined revolutionary movement.* New York: St. Martin's Press.

Mohanty, Chandra Talpade. 1991. "Under Western eyes: Feminist scholarship and colonial discourses." In *Third world women and the politics of feminism,* ed. Chandra Mohanty, Ann Russo, and Lourdes Torres. Bloomington: Indiana University Press.

Molyneux, Maxine. 1985a. "Mobilisation without emancipation? Women's interests, the state, and revolution in Nicaragua." In *New social movements and the state in Latin America,* ed. D. Slater, 233–259. Amsterdam: CEDLA.

———. 1985b. "Mobilization without emancipation? Women's interests, the state, and revolution in Nicaragua." *Feminist Studies* 11, no. 2 (Summer): 227–254.

———. 1986. "Mobilization without emancipation." In *Transition and development: Problems of third world socialism,* ed. R. Fagen et al. New York: Monthly Review Press.

———. 1998a. "Analyzing women's movements." *Development and Change,* no. 29.

―――. 1998b. "Analyzing women's movements." In *Feminist visions of development: Gender analysis and policy*, ed. Cecile Jackson and Ruth Pearson. London: Routledge.

―――. 2001. *Women's movements in international perspective: Latin America and beyond*. London: Palgrave.

―――. 2003. *Movimientos de mujeres en América Latina: Estudio teórico comparado*. Madrid: Colección Feminismos Ediciones Cátedra.

Molyneux, Maxine, and Shahra Razavi, eds. 2002. *Gender justice, development, and rights*. Oxford: Oxford University Press.

Monasterios, Karin. 2007. "Bolivian women's organizations in the MAS era." *NACLA Report on the Americas* 40, no. 2: 33–37.

Mongrovejo, Norma. 2000. *Un amor que se atrevio a decir su nombre: La lucha de las lesbianas y su relacion con los movimientos homosexual y feminista en America Latina*. Mexico: Plaza y Valdes Editores/CDHAL.

Montecinos, Verónica. 2001. "Feminists and technocrats in the democratization of Latin America: A prolegomenon." *International Journal of Politics, Culture, and Society* 15, no. 1 (September): 175–199. http://www.kluweronline.com/issn/0891-4486.

Moraga, Cherríe L., and Gloria E. Anzaldúa, eds. 2002. *This bridge called my back: Writings by radical women of color*. Berkeley: Third Woman Press.

Moser, Annalise. 2004. "Happy heterogeneity? Feminism, development, and the grassroots women's movement in Peru." *Feminist Studies* 30, no. 1: 211–239.

Moser, Robert G. 2001. "The effects of electoral systems on women's representation in post-communist states." *Electoral Studies* 20, no. 3: 353–369.

Motsei, Mmatshilo. 2007. *The kanga and the kangaroo court: Reflections on the rape trial of Jacob Zuma*. Cape Town: Jacana.

Movimiento de Integración y Liberación Homosexual. 2008. *VI informe anual: Derechos humanos minorías sexuales Chilenas (Hechos 2007)*. Santiago, Chile: Movilh.

"M.P. government declares Section 144 in Khargone to prevent public hearing by NCW: Women of 4 Narmada dams hold public hearing sans NCW chairwoman." 2004. NBA press release, December 6.

Mujeres y Asamblea Constituyente. 2007. "Quienes Somos." November 27. http://www.mujeres constituyentes.org/quienes_somos.php.

Mumtaz, Khawar. 1998. "Political participation: Women in national legislatures in Pakistan." In *Shaping women's lives: Laws, practices, and strategies in Pakistan*, ed. Farida Shaheed, Sohail Akbar Warraich, Cassandra Balchin, and Aisha Gazdar, 319–369. Lahore: Shirkat Gah.

Mumtaz, Khawar, and Samiya K. Mumtaz. Forthcoming. *Women's participation in the Punjab peasant movement: From community rights to women's rights?*

Mumtaz, Khawar, and Farida Shaheed. 1987. *Two steps forward, one step back? Women of Pakistan*. London: Zed Books; Lahore: Vanguard.

Naihua, Zhang, with Wu Xu. 1995. "Discovering the positive within the negative: The women's movement in a changing China." In *The challenge of local feminisms: Women's movements in global perspective*, ed. Amrita Basu, 25–57. Boulder: Westview Press.

Najmabadi, Afsaneh. 1998. Introduction to *Sedighe dowlatabadi: Nameh-ha, neveshteh-ha ve yad-ha* [Letters, writings, and remembrances], ed. Mahdokht Sanati and Afsaneh Najmabadi, 3: 659–682. New York: Midland Press.

Naples, Nancy A., and Manisha Desai, eds. 2002. *Women's activism and globalization: Linking local struggles and transnational politics*. New York: Routledge.

Narayan, Uma, and Sandra Harding, eds. 2000. *Decentering the center: Philosophy for a multicultural, postcolonial, and feminist world*. Bloomington: Indiana University Press.

Nash, June. 1993. "Mayan household production in the modern world." In *The impact of global exchange on Middle American artisans*, ed. June Nash. Albany: State University of New York Press.

National Commission on the Observance of International Women's Year. 1978. *The spirit of Houston: The first National Women's Conference*. Washington, DC: U.S. Government Printing Office.

National Organization for Women. 2008. "National Organization for Women PAC endorses Obama-Biden." September 16. http://www.now.org/press/09-08/09-16.html.

Navaeei, Shahin. 1999. *Avaye Zan*, nos. 38–39 (Winter).

Nemenyi, Maria. 2001. "The social construction of women's roles in Hungary." *Replika* 1.

Newell, Andrew, and Barry Reilly. 1996. "The gender wage gap in Russia: Some empirical evidence." *Labour Economics* 3, no. 10: 337–356.

NGO Coordinating Committee for Beijing +5. 2000. *Pakistan NGO review: Beijing +5*. Lahore: Shirkat Gah.

Nkomo, Boshadi. 2000. "New customary marriages act sees women as equal partner." http://www.afro.com.

Nogueira, Rogério. 2005. *O Preceito de Diversidade e a Composição da Força de Trabalho no Setor Público*. Brasília: Universidade de Brasília, OPAS.

Noonan, Norma Corigliano, and Carol Nechemias, eds. 2001. *Encyclopedia of Russian women's movements*. Westport, CT: Greenwood Press.

Norton, Augustus Richard. 1993. "The future of civil society in the Middle East." *Middle East Journal* 47, no. 2 (Spring): 205–216.

———, ed. 1995. *Civil society in the Middle East*. Vols. 1-2. Leiden: E. J. Brill.

NotiEMAIL. 2006. "Diputada cree viceministerio Género es 'retroceso' para mujeres." October 2. http://bolivia.notiemail.com/.

Nussbaum, Martha C. 2004. "Sex equality, liberty, and privacy: A comparative approach to the feminist critique." In *India's living constitution: Ideas, practices, controversies*, ed. Zoya Hasan, E. Sridharan, and R. Sudarshan. Delhi: Permanent Black.

Office on the Status of Women. n.d. "South Africa's national policy framework for women's empowerment and gender equality." http://www.womensnet.org.za/free-tags/office-status-women.

Okin, Susan Moller. 1999. *Is multiculturalism bad for women?* Princeton: Princeton University Press.

Omvedt, Gail. 2008. *Seeking Begumpura: The social vision of anticaste intellectuals*. New Delhi: Navayana.

172nd report of the Law Commission of India on reform of rape laws. 2000. Delhi: Law Commission of India.

"Orissa: Probing starvation deaths." 2002. *Economic and Political Weekly*, August 24, 3477.

Osava, Mario. 2007. "Brazil: Turning women's rights into reality." *Inter-Press Service*, August 16.

Othman, Zeyad. 1998. "Al-barlaman al-sowary, al-marah wal tashri' bayna al-tajdeed wal qawlaba" [The model parliament: Women and legislation between renewal and preservation]. *Al-seyassa al-falastineyya* [Palestinian Politics] 19.

Outsjhoorn, Joyce, and Johanna Kantola, eds. 2007. *Changing state feminism*. New York: Palgrave Macmillan.

Paidar, Parvin. 1995. *Women and the political process in twentieth-century Iran*. Cambridge: Cambridge University Press.

Palestine Media Centre. 2005. "Al-markaz al-falastini lil i'lam, qassamyyon wa qassameyyat" [Male and female *qassamis*]. August 18. http://www.palestineinfo.com/arabic/palestoday/reports/report2005/qassameyoon.htm.

Palestinian Ministry of Cooperation and International Relations. 1996. *Palestinian Development Plan (PDP), 1996–1998*. Ramallah: Palestinian Ministry of Cooperation and International Relations.

Pecheny, Mario. 2003. "Sexual orientation, AIDS, and human rights in Argentina: The paradox of social advance amid health crisis." In *Struggles for social rights in Latin America*, ed. Susan E. Eckstein and Timothy P. Wickham-Crowley, 253–270. New York: Routledge.

Penn, Shana. 2001. "The great debate: When feminism hit the headlines, Poland hit the roof." *Ms.*, January.

———. 2005. *Solidarity's secret: The women who defeated communism in Poland*. Ann Arbor: University of Michigan Press.

Peteet, Julie. 1991. *Gender in crisis: Women and the Palestinian resistance movement.* New York: Columbia University Press.

Phillips, Anne. 1991. *Engendering democracy.* Philadelphia: University of Pennsylvania Press.

———. 2002. "Does feminism need a conception of civil society?" In *Alternative conceptions of civil society,* ed. Simone Chambers and Will Kymlicka, 71–89. Ethikon Series in Comparative Ethics. Princeton: Princeton University Press.

Picheta, Sophie. 2008. "Brazilian president calls homophobia a 'perverse disease.'" Pink News, June 11. http://www.pinknews.co.uk/.

Pinto, Célia Regina Jardim. 2003. *Uma história do feminismo no Brasil.* São Paulo: Editora Fundação Perseu Abramo.

Pitanguy, Jacqueline. 2002. "Bridging the local and the global: Feminism in Brazil and the international human rights agenda." *Social Research* (Fall). http://findarticles.com/p/articles/mi_m2267/is_3_69/ai_94227142.

Potapova, Anna [executive director, ANNA]. 1999. Interview with Lisa McIntosh Sundstrom, Moscow, May 12.

Power, Margaret. 2001. "Defending dictatorship: Conservative women in Pinochet's Chile and the 1988 plebiscite." In *Radical women in Latin America: Left and right,* ed. Karen Kampwirth and Victória Gonzalez, 299–324. University Park: Pennsylvania State University Press.

"Predvybornye spiski partii" [Preelection party lists]. n.d. http://www.kreml.org/topics/160523714.

Qadeer, Imrana. 1998. "Reproductive health: A public health perspective." *Economic and Political Weekly,* October 10, 2675–2684. Reprinted in *Women's studies: A reader,* ed. Mary E. John, 381–387. New Delhi: Penguin Books India, 2008.

Qunta, Christine. 1987. *Women in southern Africa.* Johannesburg: Skotaville Publishers.

Rafidi, Tami [Fateh activist]. 2001. Interview with Islah Jad, Ramallah, July 3.

Rai, Shirin. 1996. "Women and the state in the third world: Some issues for debate." In *Women and the state: International perspectives,* ed. S. Rai and G. Lievesley. London: Taylor Francis.

———. 2002. *Class, caste, and gender: Women in parliament in India.* Stockholm: International IDEA. Available at http://www.idea.int.

———. 2004. "Gendering global governance." *International Feminist Journal of Politics* 6, no. 4 (December).

Rai, Shirin, and Geraldine Lievesley, eds. 1996. *Women and the state: International perspectives.* London: Taylor and Francis.

Rai, Shirin, and Georgina Waylen, eds. 2008. *Global governance: Feminist perspectives.* New York: Palgrave Macmillan.

Rajan, Rajeswari Sunder. 2002. *The scandal of the state: Women, law, and citizenship in postcolonial India.* New Delhi: Permanent Black.

Rakowski, Cathy. 2006. "Developing power: How women transformed international development / The global women's movements: Origins, issues, and strategies." *Rural Sociology* 71, no. 2 (June).

Ramamirthammal, Muvalur. 2003. *Web of deceit: Devadasi reform in colonial India.* Trans. and ed. Kalpana Kannabiran and Vasanth Kannabiran. New Delhi: Kali for Women.

Rathgeber, Eva M. 1990. "WID, WAD, GAD: Trends in research and practice." *Journal of Development Areas* 24 (July).

Ratnamala, M. 1979. "Adimanavi." *Nutana.*

———. 2008. "Women and forced migration." Trans. Kalpana Kannabiran from Telugu audio recording. Lecture delivered at the Workshop on Forced Migration organized jointly by the Asmita Resource Centre for Women and the Calcutta Research Group, Hyderabad, February 22–24. 2008.

Ray, Raka. 1999. *Fields of protest: Women's movements in India.* Minneapolis: University of Minnesota Press.

Razavi, Shahra. 2000. *Women in contemporary democratization.* Occasional Paper no. 4. Geneva: UNRISD.

Rede Feminista de Saúde. 2008. "Eleições sem retrocesso: Un desafio para o feminismo brasileiro." CFEMEA, July 26. http://www.cfemea.org.br/temasedados/imprimir_detalhes.asp?IDTemasDados=151.

Reis, Vilma. 2007. "Black Brazilian women and the Lula administration." *NACLA Report on the Americas* 40, no. 2: 38–41.

"Report on lesbian meeting: National Conference on Women's Movements in India, Tirupati, 1994." 2007. In *Sexualities*, ed. Nivedita Menon. New Delhi: Women Unlimited in association with Kali for Women.

"Resolution on Section 377: Annual conference of the Indian Association of Women's Studies, Goa, 2005." 2007. In *Sexualities*, ed. Nivedita Menon. New Delhi: Women Unlimited in association with Kali for Women.

Ribeiro, Matilde 1995. "Mulheres Negras Brasileiras: De Bertioga à Beijing." *Revista Estudos Feministas* 3, no. 2: 446–457.

Ricciutelli, Luciana, Angela Miles, and Margaret McFadden, eds. 2004. *Feminist politics, activism, and vision: Local and global challenges.* New York: Palgrave Macmillan.

Richter, James. 2002. "Promoting civil society? Democracy assistance and Russian women's organizations." *Problems of Post-Communism* 48, no. 1: 30–41.

Ríos Tobar, M. 2007. "Chilean feminism and social democracy from the democratic transition to Bachelet." *NACLA Report on the Americas* 40, no. 2: 25–29.

Rompiendo el Silencio. 2008. "Partido Socialista apoyaría Ley de Unión Civil." March 16. http://www.rompiendoelsilencio.cl/.

Rosen, Ruth. 2000. *The world split open: How the modern women's movement changed America.* New York: Viking.

Roth, Benita. 2004. *Separate roads to feminism: Black, Chicana, and white feminist movements in America's Second Wave.* Cambridge: Cambridge University Press.

Rovira Sancho, Guiomar. 1997. *Mujeres de maíz.* Mexico City: Era.

Rowbotham, Sheila. 1992. *Women in movement: Feminism and social action.* London: Routledge.

Rowley, Michelle. 2006. "Rising tide: Gender equality and cultural change around the world / A critical rewriting of global political economy: Integrating reproductive, productive, and virtual economies." *Journal of Women in Culture and Society* 31, no. 2 (Winter).

Rubin, Jeffery W. 2004. "Meanings and mobilisations: A cultural politics approach to social movements and states." *Latin American Research Review* 39, no. 3 (October).

Rubin, Jennifer. 2008. "McCain's play for Clinton's women." *New York Observer*, May 30. http://www.observer.com/2008/mccains-play-clintons-women.

Russia Profile. n.d. Political parties and movements. http://www.russiaprofile.org/resources/political.

Saartjie Baartman Centre. 2007. *Annual report.* Manenberg, South Africa: Saartjie Baartman Centre.

Sainath, P. 2002. "Clouds of despair: The poor and the permanent 'drought.'" *The Hindu*, August 11.

Salmenniemi, Suvi. 2003. "Democracy without women? The Russian parliamentary elections and gender equality." http://www.balticdata.info/russia/elections/russia_elections_suvi.htm.

Salo, Elaine. 2005. "Multiple targets, mixing strategies: Complicating feminist analysis of contemporary South African women's movements." *Feminist Africa* 5.

Sanasarian, Eliz. 1982. *The women's rights movement in Iran: Mutiny, appeasement, and repression from 1900 to Khomeini.* New York: Praeger.

Sánchez, Martha. 2005. *La doble mirada: Luchas y experiencias de las mujeres indígenas de América Latina.* Mexico City: UNIFEM/ILSB.

Sanghatana, Stree Shakti. 1989. *We were making history: Women in the Telangana armed struggle.* New Delhi: Kali for Women.

SANPERI. 2008. *The position of women workers in wine and deciduous fruit value chains.* Stellenbosch: Women on Farms Project.

Santos, Cecilia M. 2007. "Transnational legal activism and the state: Reflections on cases against Brazil in the Inter-American Commission on Human Rights." *Sur-International Journal on Human Rights* 7, no. 4: 29–59.

Sardenberg, Cecilia M. B. 2004. "With a little help from our friends: 'Global' incentives and 'local' challenges to feminist politics in Brazil." *IDS Bulletin* 35, no. 4 (October): 125–129.

———. 2007a. "Negotiating culture in the promotion of gender equality and women's empowerment in Latin America." Background paper elaborated for UNFPA's *2008 World Annual Report.*

———. 2007b. "The right to abortion: Briefing from Brazil." Open Democracy, October 26. http://www.opendemocracy.net/article/5050/how_feminists_make_progress.

Sardenberg, Cecilia M. B., and Ana Alice Alcantara Costa. 1994. "Feminismos, feministas e movimentos sociais." In *Mulher e Relações de Gênero,* ed. M. Brandão and M. Clara Binghemer, 81–114. São Paulo: Ed. Loyola

Sarkar, Tanika. 1999. "Pragmatics of the Hindu Right: Politics of women's organisations." *Economic and Political Weekly,* July 31, 2159–2166.

———. 2002. "Semiotics of terror: Muslim women and children in Hindu Rashtra." *Economic and Political Weekly* 37, no. 28.

Sassen, Saskia. 2002. "Finding women's security in the 21st century: A gendered perspective." Panel presentation and discussion organized by the National Council for Research on Women, New York, February 21.

Savelis, Peter M. 2007. "How new is Bachelet's Chile?" *Current History* 106.

al-Sayyid, Mustapha K. 1993. "A 'civil society' in Egypt?" *Middle East Journal* 47, no. 2 (Spring): 228–242.

Sawer, Marian. 2007. 'The Fall of the Femocrat." In *Changing State Feminism,* ed. Joyce Outshoorn and Johanna Kantola, 20–40. New York: Palgrave Macmillan.

Schatral, Susanne. 2007. "Stop violence: Framing strategies of Russian women's NGOs." In *Movements, migrants, marginalisation: Challenges of societal and political participation in Eastern Europe and the enlarged EU,* ed. Sabine Fischer, Heiko Pleines, and Hans-Henning Schroder, 43–56. Stuttgart: Ibidem-Verlag.

Schevchenko, Iulia. 2002. "Who cares about women's problems? Female legislators in the 1995 and 1999 Russian state Dumas." *Europe-Asia Studies* 54, no. 8: 1201–1222.

Schild, Verónica. 1998. "New subjects of rights? Women's movements and the construction of citizenship in the 'new democracies.'" In *Cultures of politics/politics of cultures: Revisioning Latin American social movements,* ed. Sonia E. Alvarez, Evelina Dagnino, and Arturo Escobar, 93–117. Boulder: Westview Press.

Schmidt, E. 1992. *Peasants, traders, and wives: Shona women in the history of Zimbabwe, 1870–1939.* Portsmouth: Heinemann.

Schulz, Helena Lindholm. 1999. *The reconstruction of Palestinian nationalism: Between revolution and statehood.* Manchester: Manchester University Press.

Scott, Eryn. 1995. "Differences and intersections between feminism in Africa and feminism in North America." *South African Feminist Review* 1, no. 2 (December).

Second and Third Alternative Report on CEDAW. 2006. Delhi: National Alliance of Women.

Sedghi, Hamideh. 2007. *Women and politics in Iran: Veiling, unveiling, and reveiling.* New York: Cambridge University Press.

Shaheed, Farida. 1994. "Controlled or autonomous-identity and the experience of the network: Women living under Muslim laws." *Signs: Journal of Women in Culture and Society* 19, no. 4: 997–1019.

———. 1999. "Constructing identities: Culture, women's agency, and the Muslim world." *International Social Science Journal* 51, no. 1 (March): 61–73.

Shaheed, Farida, and Neelum Hussain. 2007. *Interrogating the norms: Women challenging violence in an adversarial state.* Colombo: ICES.

Shaheed, Farida, and Aisha L. F. Shaheed. 2005. *Great ancestors—women asserting rights in Muslim contexts: A book of narratives.* Lahore: Shirkat Gah.

Shalabi, Yasser. 2001. "Al-ta'thirat al-dawleya 'ala tahdid ro'aa al-monathmat ghayr al-hokomeyya al-felastineyya wa-adwareha" [International and local impacts on the visions and roles of Palestinian NGOs]. Master's thesis, Birzeit University.

Shekarloo, Mahsa. 2005. "Iranian women take on the constitution." Middle East Report Online, July 21. http://middleeastdesk.org/article.php?id=208.

Shinde, Tarabai. [1882] 1994. "A comparison between women and men: An essay to show who's really wicked and immoral, women or men?" In *A comparison between women and men: Tarabai Shinde and the critique of gender relations in colonial India*, ed. Rosalind O'Hanlon, 73–134. New Delhi: Oxford University Press.

Shisana, O., Rehle, T., Simbayi, L., Parker, W., Zuma, K., Bhana, A., Connolly, C., Jooste, S., and Pillay, V. eds. 2005. *South African National HIV Prevalence, HIV Incidence, Behaviour and Communication Survey*. Cape Town: Human Science Research Council Press.

Shojaee, Mansoureh. 2009. "The history of International Women's Day in Iran." March. http://www.feministschool.com/english/spip.php?article253.

Shu-Mei, Shih, and Sylvia Marcos. 2005. "Conversation on feminist imperialism and the politics of difference." In *Dialogue and difference: Feminisms challenge globalization*, ed. Marguerite Waller and Sylvia Marcos, 143–163. New York: Palgrave Macmillan.

Sierra, María Teresa. 2004. "Diálogos y prácticas interculturales: Derechos humanos, derechos de las mujeres y políticas de identidad." In *Desacatos*, nos. 15–16: 126–148.

Sierra, María Teresa, and Rosalva Aída Hernández. 2005. "Repensar los derechos colectivos desde el género: Aportes de las mujeres indígenas al debate de la autonomía." In *La doble mirada: Luchas y experiencias de las mujeres indígenas de América Latina*, ed. Martha Sánchez. México City: DF, UNIFEM/ILSB.

Siklova, Jirina. 1996. "Different region, different women: Why feminism isn't success." Special English-language issue of *Replika: Hungarian Social Science Journal* 1.

Simpson, Peggy. 2001. "In Poland women run the largest news organization." *Nieman Reports* (Winter).

Sinelnikov, Andrei. 1998. "Russia: Inside the broken cell." Family Violence Prevention Fund. http://www.fvpf.org/global/gf_russia.html.

Siniora, Randa. 2000. "Lobbying for a Palestinian family law: The experience of the Palestinian model parliament; Women and legislation." Paper presented to the International Conference on Islamic Family Law in the Middle East and North Africa: Theory, Practice, and the Chances of Reform, Amman, Jordan, June 24–25.

Šmejkalová, Jirina. 1996. "On the road: Smuggling feminism across the post–Iron Curtain." Special English-language issue of *Replika: Hungarian Social Science Journal* 1.

Smith, Andrea, Beth Richie, Julia Sudbury, and Janelle White. 2006. Introduction to *Color of Violence: The INCITE! Anthology*. Cambridge: South End Press.

Smith, Bonnie, ed. 2000. *Global feminism since 1945*. New York: Routledge.

Smith, Lois M., and Alfred Padula. 1996. *Sex and revolution: Women in socialist Cuba*. Oxford: Oxford University Press.

Snitow, Ann. 1993. "The church wins, women lose." *Nation*, April 26.

———. 1997. "Response." In *Transitions, environments, translations: Feminism in international politics*, ed. J. Scott et al. New York and London: Routledge.

Soares, Gilberta, and Cecilia Sardenberg. 2008. "Campaigning for the right to legal and safe abortions in Brazil." *IDS Bulletin* 39, no. 3 (July): 55–61.

Soares, Vera, Ana Alice Costa, Cristina Buarque, Denise Dora, and Wania Sant'Anna. 1995. "Brazilian feminisms and women's movements: A two-way street." In *The challenge of local feminisms: Women's movements in global perspective*, ed. Amrita Basu. Boulder: Westview Press.

Sonke Gender Justice Network. 2007. "South Africa country report." http://www.genderjustice.org.za.

Sopronenko, Igor. 2008. *Twenty years forward? The contents and discontents of modern Russian feminism*. Produced by Beth Holmgren.

Spakowski, Nicola. 2000. "The internationalization of China's women's studies." *Berliner China-Hefte* 20: 79–100.

Speed, Shannon, and Jane Collier. 2000. "Limiting indigenous autonomy in Chiapas, Mexico: The state government's use of human rights." *Human Rights Quarterly* 22, no. 4 (November): 877–905.

Sperling, Carrie. 2006. "Mother of atrocities: Pauline Nyiramasuhuko's role in the Rwandan genocide." *Fordham Urban Law Journal* (January 1). http://www.accessmylibrary.com/coms2/summary _0286-15844560_ITM.

Sperling, Valerie. 1999. *Organizing women in contemporary Russia: Engendering transition.* Cambridge: Cambridge University Press.

———. 2005. "The fair sex in an unfair system: The gendered effects of Putin's political reforms." Program on New Approaches to Research and Security in Eurasia (PONARS), Policy Memo No. 398 (December). http://csis.org/files/media/csis/pubs/pm_0398.pdf.

———. 2006. "Women's organizations: Institutionalized interest groups or vulnerable dissidents?" In *Russian civil society: A critical assessment,* ed. Alfred B. Evans, Laura A. Henry, and Lisa McIntosh Sundstrom, 161–177. Armonk, NY: M. E. Sharpe.

Sperling, Valerie, Myra Max Ferree, and Barbara Risman. 2001. "Constructing global feminism: Transnational advocacy networks and Russian women's activism." *Signs* 26, no. 4: 1155–1186.

SPM. 2008. *II Plano Nacional de Políticas para as Mulheres.* Brasilia: Governo do Brasil, Secretaria Especial de Políticas para mulheres.

Springer, Kimberly. 2005. *Living for the revolution: Black feminist organizations, 1968–1980.* Durham: Duke University Press.

Stammers, Neil. 1991. "Social movements and the social construction of human rights." *Human Rights Quarterly* 21, no. 4.

Stansell, Christine. 2008. "Feminists for Clinton." *Huffington Post,* February 15. http://www .huffingtonpost.com/christine-stansell/feminists-for-clinton_b_86929.html.

Staunton, I. 1990. *Mothers of the revolution.* Harare: Baobab Books.

Steinem, Gloria. 2008. "Women are never front-runners." *New York Times,* January 28.

Steinmetz, George. 1999. *State/culture: State-formation after the cultural turn.* Ithaca: Cornell University Press.

Sternbach, Nancy S., Marysa Navarro-Aranguren, Patricia Chuchryk, and Sonia E. Alvarez. 1992. "Feminisms in Latin America: From Bogota to San Bernardo." *Signs* 17, no. 2: 393–434.

Stetson, Dorothy McBride, ed. 2001. *Abortion politics, women's movements, and the democratic state: A comparative study of state feminism.* New York: Oxford University Press.

Stetson, Dorothy McBride, and Amy Mazur, eds. 1995. *Comparative state feminism.* Thousand Oaks, CA: Sage.

Stevenson, Linda S. 2007. "Fragmented feminisms and disillusion with democracy: Social movement downswings, inadequate institutions, and alliances under construction in Latin America." *Latin America Research Review* 42, no. 3 (October).

Stickley, Andrew, Irina Timofeeva, and Par Spären. 2008. "Risk factors for intimate partner violence against women in St. Petersburg, Russia." *Violence Against Women* 14, no. 4.

Sugimoto, L. 2005. "Uma Mulher Morre a Cada Três Minutos." *Jornal da Unicamp* (Salda de Imprensa) 305 (October 10–17). http://www.unicamp.br/unicamp/unicamp_hoje/ju/outubro2005/ ju305pag04html.

Sundstrom, Lisa McIntosh. 2001. "Strength from without? Transnational actors and NGO development in Russia." Ph.D. diss., Stanford University.

———. 2003. "Limits to global civil society: Gaps between Western donors and Russian NGOs." In *Global civil society and its limits,* ed. Gordon Laxer and Sandra Halperin, 146–165. London: Palgrave.

———. 2005. "Foreign assistance, international norms, and NGO development: Lessons from the Russian campaign." *International Organization* 59, no. 2: 419–449.

———. 2006. *Funding civil society: Foreign assistance and NGO development in Russia.* Stanford: Stanford University Press.

Suttner, Raymond. 2007. "The Jacob Zuma rape trial: Power and African National Congress masculinities." Unpublished seminar paper delivered at University of Stellenbosch History Department, May 29.

Szacki, Jerzy. 1995. *Liberalism after communism*. Budapest: CEU Press.

Tabari, Azar, and Nahid Yeganeh, eds. 1982. *In the shadow of Islam: The women's movement in Iran*. London: Zed Books.

TAC. 2007a. *Annual report, 2006/2007*. Cape Town: TAC.

———. 2007b. "Poor PMCT program: ALP letter on behalf of TAC to minister of health." October 1. http://www.tac.org.za/xommunity/node/2136.

———. n.d. "About TAC." http://www.tac.org.za.

Tahmasebi, Sussan. 2008. "Answers to your most frequently asked questions about the campaign." February 24. http://www.changeforequality.info/english/spip.php?article226.

Tamale, S. 1999. *When hens begin to crow: Gender and parliamentary politics in contemporary Uganda*. Kampala: Fountain Publishers.

Tan, Lin, Wu Jing, and Li Yan-ni. 2005. "Jiang funu/shehui xingbei yanjun naru zhongguo shehui yanjiu de zhuliu" [Mainstreaming women/gender studies into China's social sciences research]. *Funu yanjiu luncong* [Collection of Women's Studies] 69: 96–100.

Tarazi, Rema [head of the General Union of Palestinian Women, West Bank Branch]. 2001. Interview with Islah Jad, Ramallah, April 9.

Tarrow, Sidney. 1994. *Power in movement: Social movements, collective action, and politics*. Cambridge: Cambridge University Press.

———. 2005. *The new transnational activism*. New York: Cambridge University Press.

Tavassoli, Nahid. 1382/2003. "Nov-garayi dini va zan" [Modernist religiosity and woman]. In *Chera khawb-e zan chap ast?* by Nahid Tavassoli. Tehran: Nashr Qatreh.

Tedlock, Dennis. 1979. "The Analogical Tradition and the Emergence of a Dialogical Anthropology," *Journal of Anthropological Research* 35:387–400.

Terman, Rochelle. Forthcoming. "The contemporary Iranian women's rights movement."

Thayer, Millie. 2001. "Transnational feminism: Reading Joan Scott in the Brazilian Sertão." *Ethnography* 2, no. 2: 243–271.

Tilly, Charles. 1995. *Popular contention in Britain, 1758–1834*. Cambridge: Harvard University Press.

———. 2003. *The politics of collective violence*. Cambridge: Cambridge University Press.

Tohidi, Nayereh. 1991. "Gender and Islamic fundamentalism: Feminist politics in Iran." In *Third world women and the politics of feminism*, ed. Chandra Mohanty, Ann Russo, and Lourdes Torres. Bloomington: Indiana University Press.

———. 1994. "Modernization, Islamization, and gender in Iran." In *Gender and national identity: Women and politics in Muslim societies*, ed. Valentine Moghadam, 110–147. London and Karachi: Zed Books and Oxford University Press.

———. 1995. "The Fourth World Conference of Women in Beijing and the Iranian delegation." *Zanan* (Tehran), no. 25 (September).

———. 1996. "'Fundamentalist' backlash and Muslim women in the Beijing conference." *Canadian Women Studies* 16 (Summer): 3.

———. 2002a. "The international connections of the women's movement in Iran, 1979–2000." In *Iran and the surrounding world: Interaction in culture and cultural politics*, ed. Nikki Keddie and Rudi Matthee, 205–231. Seattle: University of Washington Press.

———. 2002b. "Islamic feminism: Perils and promises." *Middle East Women's Studies Review* 16, nos. 3–4 (Fall–Winter): 13–27. http://www.amews.org/review/reviewarticles/tohidi.ht.

———. 2003. "Women's rights in the Muslim world: The universal-particular interplay." *Hawwa Journal on Women in the Middle East and Islamic World* 1, no. 2: 152–188.

———. 2004a. *Encyclopedia of the modern Middle East and North Africa*, ed. Philip Matter, 4: 2423–2424. 2nd ed. Detroit: Macmillan Reference USA.

———. 2004b. "Women, building civil society, and democratization in post-Soviet Azerbaijan." In *Post-Soviet women encountering transition*, ed. Kathleen Kuehnast and Carol Nechemias, 149–171. Washington, DC: Woodrow Wilson Center Press and the John Hopkins University Press.

————. 2006. "'Islamic feminism': Women negotiating modernity and patriarchy in Iran." In *The Blackwell companion of contemporary Islamic thought*, ed. Ibrahim Abu-Rabi, 624–643. Oxford: Blackwell.

————. 2007a. "Muslim feminism and Islamic reformation." In *Feminist theologies: Legacy and prospect*, ed. Rosemary Radford Ruether. Minneapolis: Fortress Press.

————. 2007b. "The women's movement in Iran facing a double blackmail" [Grogan-giri-ye doganeh harekat-e zanan]. August 6. http://www.roozonline.com/archives/2007/08/006680.php.

————. 2008a. "Iran's women's rights activists are being smeared." September 17. http://www.womensenews.org/article.cfm/dyn/aid/3743. Reprinted in http://www.femschool.org/english/spip.php?article149.

————. 2008b. "Ta'amol mahali-jahani feminism dar jonbesh-e zanan-e Iran" [The local-global intersection of feminism in the women's movement in Iran]. http://feministschl.net/spip.php?article1660.

————. 2009. "Women and the presidential elections: Iran's new political culture." http://www.juancole.com/2009/09/tohidi-women-and-presidential-elections.html.

Toledo, Sonia, and Anna María Garza. 2006. "Gender and stereotypes in the social movements in Chiapas." In *Dissident women: Gender and cultural politics in Chiapas*, ed. Shannon Speed, R. Aída Hernández Castillo, and Lynn Stephen, 57–75. Austin: University of Texas Press.

Toor, Sadia. 1997. "The state fundamentalism and civil society." In *Engendering the nation-state*, ed. Neelum Hussain, Samiya Mumtaz, and Rubina Saigol. Vol. 1. Lahore: Simorgh.

Transparency International. 2001. "Global corruption report, 2001." http://www.globalcorruption report.org.

Trevizo, Dolores. 2006. "Between Zapata and Che: A comparison of social movement success and failure in Mexico." *Social Science History* 30, no. 2 (Summer): 197–229.

Trinh, Min-ha. 1988. *Woman, native, other: Writing postcoloniality and feminism*. Bloomington: Indiana University Press.

Tripp, Aili. 2006. "The evolution of transnational feminisms." In *Global feminism: Transnational women's activism, organizing, and human rights*, 51–75. New York: New York University Press.

True, Jacqui. 2008. "Global accountability and transnational networks: The women leader's network and Asia Pacific economic cooperation." *Pacific Review* 21, no. 1 (March).

Tsikata, D. 1999. "Gender equality and the state in Ghana: Some issues of policy and practice." In *Engendering African social sciences*, ed. A. Imam et al. Senegal: CODESRIA.

Tsutsui, Kiyoteru. 2006. "Redressing past human rights violations: Global dimensions of contemporary social movements." *Social Forces* 85, no. 1 (September).

Tuñón, Esperanza. 1997. *Mujeres en escena: De la tramoya al protagonismo (1982–1994)*. Mexico City: Programa de Estudios de Género.

"Tusk: Find More Women." 2009. *Gazeta Wyborcza*, August 25. http://wyborcza.pl/1,86871, 6961181,Tusk_Find_More_Women.html.

UNDP. 1999. *Human Development Report, 1999*. http://hdr.undp.org/en/reports/.

————. 2007. *Human Development Report, 2007*. http://hdr.undp.org/en/reports/.

United Nations. 1991. *Resolutions and decisions of the Economic and Social Council, 1990*.

U.S. Congress. 1975. House. Committee on Government Operations. *National Women's Conference: Hearing before a subcommittee of the Committee on Government Operations*. 94th Cong., 1st sess., H.R. 8903. Washington, DC: U.S. Government Printing Office.

Usher, Graham. 1997. "What kind of nation? The rise of Hamas in the Occupied Territories." In *Political Islam: Essays from Middle East report*, ed. Joel Beinin and Joe Stork. Berkeley and Los Angeles: University of California Press.

Vahdati, Soheila. 2006. "Women victims of stoning: Interview with Asiyeh Amini." Meydaan-e Zanan, September 5. http://meydaan.net/English/showarticle.aspx?arid=40&cid=46.

VAMP [Veshya Anyaya Mukti Parishad] and Sangram. 2007. "A statement of women in prostitution." In *Sexualities*, ed. Nivedita Menon, 325–328. New Delhi: Women Unlimited in association with Kali for Women.

Vannoy, Dana, Natalia Rimashevskaya, Lisa Cubbins, Marina Malysheva, Elena Meshterkina, and Marina Pisklakova. 1999. *Marriages in Russia: Couples during the economic transition.* Westport, CT: Praeger.

Vargas, Virginia. 1992. "The feminist movement in Latin America: Between hope and disenchantment." *Development and Change* 23, no. 3: 195–214.

———. 2003. "Feminism, globalization, and the global justice and solidarity movement." *Cultural Studies* 17, no. 6: 905–920.

———. 2006. "Advocacy or counter-power?" In *Pause for thought: Lessons learnt and ways forward for women's human rights advocacy.* GEO/ICAE [Gender and Education Office of the International Council for Adult Education] and REPEM [Red de Educación Popular entre Mujeres de América Latina y el Caribe].

VeneKlasen, Lisa, and Valerie Miller. 2002. *A new weave of power, people, and politics: The action guide for advocacy and citizen participation.* United Kingdom: Practical Action, 2002.

Vetten, Lisa. 2007. "Violence against women in South Africa." In *State of the nation: South Africa, 2007,* ed. Sakhela Bulungu et al. Pretoria: HSRC Press.

Vickers, Jill. 2006. "Bringing nations in: Some methodological and conceptual issues in connecting feminisms with nationhood and nationalisms." *International Feminist Journal of Politics* 8, no. 1 (March).

Villela, Wilza Vieira. 2001. "Expanding women's access to abortion: The Brazilian experience." In *Advocating for abortion access: Eleven country studies,* ed. B. Klugman and D. Budlender, 87–108. Johannesburg: University of Witwatersrand.

Volbrecht, G. 1986. "Feminism or Marxism?" Unpublished paper delivered at the Association for Sociology in Southern Africa.

Volga, Vasanth Kannabiran, and Kalpana Kannabiran. 2001. *Mahilavaranam/Womanscape.* Secunderabad, India: Asmita.

———. 2005a. "Peace and irresponsibility." *Economic and Political Weekly,* March 26, 1310–1312.

———. 2005b. "Reflections on the peace process in Andhra Pradesh." *Economic and Political Weekly,* February 12, 610–612.

Voronina, Olga. 1993. "Zhenshchina i sotsializm: Opyt feministskogo analiza" [Woman and socialism: The experience of feminist analysis]. In *Feminizm: Vostok, zapad, rossiia* [Feminism: East, West, Russia], ed. M. T. Stepaniants. Moscow: Nauka.

Vyasulu, Poornima, and Vinod Vyasulu. 1999. "Women in Panchayati Raj: Grass roots democracy in Malgudi." *Economic and Political Weekly,* December 25.

Waler, Marguerite, and Sylvia Marcos, eds. 2005. *Dialogue and difference: Feminisms challenge globalization.* New York: Palgrave Macmillan.

Walter, Lynn, ed. 2001. *Women's rights: A global view.* Westport, CT: Greenwood Press.

Wang Libing, Gong Zun, and Cheng Tingting. 2007. "Nucunguan Caizheng Zhizheng de guocheng, tedian, hekunnan fenxi" [Analyzing the process of Nucungun's political participation, administrative experiences, unique attributes and difficulties]. *Nongcun Jingji* [Rural Economy] 10. http://www.nongjianv.org/web/Html/njnczhyizh/2008-11/20/1120155014.html.

Wang, Zheng. 2006. "Dilemma of Inside Agitators: Chinese State Feminists in 1957." *China Quarterly* 188:913–932.

Wang, Zheng. 1997. "Maoism, feminism, and the UN Conference on Women: Women's studies research in contemporary China." *Journal of Women's History* 8, no. 4: 126–143.

Waters, Elizabeth. 1989. "In the shadow of the Comintern: The communist women's movement, 1920–1943." In *Promissory notes: Women in the transition to socialism,* ed. Sonia Krucks, Rayna Rapp, and Marilyn B. Young, 9–56. New York: Monthly Review Press.

———. 1993. "The emergence of a women's movement." In *Gender politics and post-communism: Reflections from Eastern Europe and the former Soviet Union,* ed. Nanette Funk and Carol McClurg Mueller, 287–302. New York: Routledge.

Waters, Elizabeth, and Anastasia Posadskaya. 1995. "Democracy without women is no democracy: Women's struggles in post-communist Russia." In *The challenge of local feminisms: Women's movements in global perspective,* ed. Amrita Basu. Boulder: Westview Press.

Watson, Joy. 2008. "Equal opportunities in decision-making: Facilitating the increase of women in public office." Unpublished paper prepared for the 50/50 Campaign, Equal Representation and Participation of Women by 2015.

Watson, Peggy. 1997. "(Anti)feminism after communism." In *Who's afraid of feminism?* ed. A. Oakley and J. Mitchell. London: Penguin.

Watson, P. 1998. *Determined to act: The first 15 years of the Women's Action Group, 1983–1998.* Harare: WAG.

Waylen, Georgina. 1994. "Women and democratization: Conceptualizing gender relations in transition politics." *World Politics* 46, no. 3: 327–354.

———. 1996. *Gender in third world politics.* Buckingham: Open University Press.

Wee, Vivienne, and Farida Shaheed. 2007. "Indigenous feminisms: Resistance to culturally embedded patriarchies." Paper presented at the conference "Reclaiming Feminism: Gender and Neo-liberalism." Brighton, Sussex, July 9–10. Organized by the Institute of Development Studies, University of Sussex, with the University of London.

Welchman, Lynn. 2003. "In the interim: Civil society, the shari'a judiciary, and Palestinian personal status law in the transitional period." *Islamic Law and Society* 10, no. 1: 34–69.

Weldon, S. Laurel. 2002. *Violence against women: Protest, policy, and the problem of women.* Pittsburgh: University of Pittsburgh Press.

White, Jenny. 2002. *Islamist mobilisation in Turkey: A study in vernacular politics.* Seattle: University of Washington Press.

"Women brave violence to say no." 2000. *Standard*, March 26.

Women on Farms. n.d. "Building women's leadership." http://www.wfp.org.za.

Women's Coalition. 2001. *The Women's Charter: Shortened version.* Harare: Bardwell.

"Women's groups oppose ban on dance-bars: Women's groups in Mumbai and all over India, 2005." 2005. *Saheli Newsletter,* January–April. Reprinted in *Sexualities,* ed. Nivedita Menon, 295–297. New Delhi: Women Unlimited in association with Kali for Women, 2007.

Womensnet. 2008. "1 in 9 campaign event." http://www.womensnet.org.za/1-9-campaign-event.

Wong Yuenling, ed. 1995. *Reflections and resonance: Stories of Chinese women involved in international preparatory activities for the 1995 NGO Forum on Women.* Beijing: Ford Foundation.

Woodhull, Winnie. 2003. "Global feminisms/transnational political economies: Third world cultural production." *Journal of International Women's Studies* (April).

"Writer Alice Walker endorses Barack Obama." 2008. May 16. http://technorati.com/videos/youtube.com%2Fwatch%3Fv%3DW3-9gq_htUo.

Xiaolan, Bao, and Wu Xu. 2001. "Feminist collaboration between diaspora and China." In *Chinese women organizing cadres, feminists, Muslims, queers,* ed. Ping-Chun Hsiung, Maria Jaschok, and Cecilia Milwertz, 79–99. Oxford: Berg.

al-Yassir, 'Alya [UNIFEM]. 2001. Interview with Islah Jad, Ramallah, June 25.

Yeatman, Anna. 1990. *Bureaucrats, technocrats, femocrats: Essays on the contemporary Australian state.* Sydney: Allen and Unwin.

Yi, Ying. 2000. "Dangdai zhongguo funu yanjiu zuzhi chutan" [Preliminary review of women's studies organizations in modern China]. *Funu yanjiu luncong* [Collection of Women's Studies] 2: 34–38.

Young, Iris Marion. 1989. "Polity and group difference: A critique of the ideal of universal citizenship." *Ethics* 99: 250–274.

Youssef, 'Itaf [ex-militant and now editor for *Sawt al-Nissa* newspaper, WATC]. 2001. Interview with Islah Jad, Ramallah, July 3.

Yuval-Davis, Nira. 2006. "Human/women's rights and feminist transversal politics." In *Transnational feminisms: Women's global activism and human rights,* ed. Myra Max Ferree and Aili Mari Tripp. New York: New York University Press.

Zabelina, Tatiana. 2002. *Rossiia: Nasilie v sem'e—nasilie v obshchestve* [Russia: Violence in the family—violence in society]. Moscow: UNIFEM, UNFPA.

Zetkin, Klara. 1934. *Lenin on the woman question.* New York: International Publishers.

Zeyyad [Islamic Khalas Party]. 2000. Interview with Islah Jad, Gaza, October 3.

Zhang, Naihua, with Wu Xu. 1995. "Discovering the positive within the negative: The women's movement in a changing China." In *The challenge of local feminisms: Women's movements in global perspective,* ed. Amrita Basu, 25–57. Boulder: Westview Press.

Zia, Shahla, and Farzana Bari. 1999. *Baseline report on women's participation in political and public life in Pakistan.* Islamabad: Aurat Foundation and Pattan.

Zuidberg, L., P. McFadden, and H. Chigudu. 2004. "The role of women's organisations in civil society building in Zimbabwe." Country report, Zimbabwe for CFA Program Evaluation. ICCO, HIVOS, and CORDAID.

About the Contributors

Julie Ajinkya is a Ph.D. candidate in Government at Cornell University. Prior to entering graduate school, she worked as a community organizer at the Institute for Policy Studies in Washington, D.C. Her research focuses on intersectional identity politics, immigration, and feminism, with particular attention to the role that Muslim women play in generating a "new" Muslim identity in the West. She received her B.A. in Political Science from Amherst College and her M.A. in Government from Cornell University.

Amrita Basu is the Paino Professor of Political Science and Women's and Gender Studies at Amherst College. She is the editor of *The Challenge of Local Feminisms: Women's Movements in Global Perspective* (1995) and the author of *Two Faces of Protest: Women's Activism in Contemporary India* (1992). She has edited or coedited four other books and numerous articles on women's activism and religious nationalism in India.

Ana Alice A. Costa holds a Ph.D. in Political Sociology from UNAM, the Autonomous University of Mexico, in Mexico City. She has been active in the Brazilian and Mexican feminist movements since the late 1970s. A member of the Faculty of Philosophy and Human Sciences of the Federal University of Bahia (UFBA) in Salvador, Bahia, Brazil, since 1982, she was one of the founders of UFBA's Nucleus of Interdisciplinary Studies on Women (NEIM/UFBA), and director from 1999 to 2004. She is currently coordinator of the M.A. and Ph.D. Programs on Interdisciplinary Studies on Women, Gender, and Feminism at NEIM/UFBA. She has published several articles and books on feminist studies in Brazil.

Shereen Essof is a feminist activist who worked at the Zimbabwe Women's Resource Centre and Network in Harare for close to six years, first as a research, networking, and advocacy program officer, then as a project coordinator. During that time she was involved in setting up a number of initiatives including the Women and Land Lobby Group and the Women's Coalition on the Constitution. She is now based at the African Gender Institute, University of Cape Town, South Africa, where she worked as a project assistant. She was an editorial member on *Feminist Africa* and has published in the areas of feminism, women's movements, and social movement organizing. Her first coedited collection on social movements in South Africa is forthcoming from UNISA Press. While in Cape Town she has been active in struggles for basic services, particularly with the Water for All Coalition and in opposing the outsourcing of services through the University of Cape Town's Workers Support Committee. A founding member of Building Women's Activism, she is currently working on her doctoral degree.

Elisabeth Jay Friedman is an associate professor of politics and chair of Latin American Studies at the University of San Francisco (USF). She is also a coordinator of the USF Global Women's Rights Forum. She has written two books, *Unfinished Transitions: Women and the Gendered Development of Democracy in Venezuela, 1936–1996* (2000) and *Sovereignty, Democracy and Global Civil Society: State-Society Relations at UN World Conferences* (with Kathryn Hochstetler and Ann Marie Clark, 2005). She has published articles on women's organizing in Latin America and globally in the *International Feminist Journal of Politics*; *Latin American Politics & Society*; *Media, Culture, & Society*; *Signs*; *Women & Politics*; and *Women's Studies International Quarterly*. She was guest editor for the *NACLA Report on the Americas'* March 2007 issue "How Pink Is the Pink Tide: Feminist and LGBT Activists Challenge the Left." Her current research focuses on the diffusion of gender-based and sexual rights in Latin America as well as the impact of information and communication technologies on gender-based organizing in the region.

Rosalva Aída Hernández Castillo earned her doctorate in anthropology from Stanford University and is now a professor and senior researcher at the Center for Research and Advanced Studies in Social Anthropology in Mexico City. One of her projects involves exploring opportunities for reshaping power through indigenous women's collective organization and daily resistance. She has worked extensively on exploring plural identities in Chiapas as well as the human rights of Guatemalan refugees in Mexico. She is the author of *Histories and Stories from Chiapas: Border Identities in Southern Mexico* (UT Press 2001), also published in Spanish *as La Otra Frontera: Identidades Múltiples en el Chiapas Postcolonial* (2001), and is coeditor of *Descolonizando el Feminismo, Teorías y Prácticas desde los Márgenes* (Catedra 2008); *Dissident Women: Gen-*

der and Cultural Politics in Chiapas (UT Press 2006); *El Estado y los indígenas en tiempos del PAN: neoindigenismo, identidad y legalidad* (Porrúa 2004); *Mayan Lives, Mayan Utopias: The Indigenous Peoples of Chiapas and the Zapatista Rebellion* (Rowman & Littlefield 2003); *The Other Word: Women and Violence in Chiapas Before and After Acteal* (IWGIA 2001); and other books.

Ping-Chun Hsiung is an associate professor in the Department of Sociology at the University of Toronto. Her research areas are: family and social change in Chinese societies, feminist epistemology and methodology, gender issues in comparative perspective, and the women's movement and community organizing in China.

Islah Jad is an assistant professor of Gender and Development at Birzeit University and the cofounder of the Birzeit University Women's Studies Institute and of the Women's Affairs Technical Committee, a national coalition for women. She has published many works on Palestinian and Arab women's political participation. She also coauthored the *Arab Human Development Report* (2005).

Kalpana Kannabiran heads the Chityala Ailamma Centre for Interdisciplinary Research at Asmita Resource Centre for Women, Secunderabad. A longtime activist in the feminist movement in India, she was formerly professor of sociology at NALSAR University of Law, Hyderabad, India, and a member of the Expert Group on the Equal Opportunity Commission, Government of India, 2007–2008. She was chair of Women in Society of the International Sociological Association from 2002–2006 and general secretary of the Indian Association for Women's Studies from 1998–2000. She received the Rockefeller Humanist in Residence Fellowship at Hunter College, CUNY 1992–1993, and in 2003 the VKRV Rao Award for Social Science Research in social aspects of law from the Indian Council for Social Science Research. A frequent contributor to the Economic and Political Weekly, she has most recently co-edited *Challenging the Rule(s) of Law: Essays on Colonialism, Criminology and Human Rights* (2008).

Elzbieta Matynia is associate professor of Sociology and Liberal Studies, New School for Social Research. Born in Poland, she studied literature, sociology, and philosophy at Warsaw University, and did postdoctoral studies at the Graduate Faculty of the New School for Social Research. She is director of the Transregional Center for Democratic Studies at the New School for Social Research, which conducts study programs and facilitates research projects in

East & Central Europe, Sub-Saharan Africa, and Latin America. The author of *Performative Democracy* (2009) and *Social Science in Transition: The Case of Central Europe* (2002), she edited *Grappling with Democracy* (1996), and has written numerous essays on social and political transformations. She is also the editor-in-chief of the *International Journal of Politics, Culture, and Society.*

Elaine Salo is the director of the Institute for Women's and Gender Studies at University of Pretoria. She has a Ph.D. in Anthropology from Emory University, USA. Her research interests include feminist theorizing and women's movements in African contexts, and gender, sexuality, and identity in peripheral urban spaces of Southern African cities. Recent publications include *Glamour, Glitz and Girls: The Meanings of Femininity in High School;* "Matric Ball Culture" (with Bianca Davids) in the book *The Prize and The Price, Shaping Sexualities in South Africa,* edited by Melissa Steyn and Miki Van Zyl (2009); and "Women in the Academy" in *Gender Activism in Contemporary South Africa,* edited by Greg Ruiters 2008.

Cecilia M. B. Sardenberg is a Brazilian feminist who holds a Ph.D. in Anthropology from Boston University. She has been a member of the Faculty of Philosophy and Human Sciences of the Federal University of Bahia (UFBA) in Salvador, Bahia, Brazil, since 1982. She was one of the "founding mothers" of UFBA's Nucleus of Interdisciplinary Studies on Women (NEIM/UFBA), and is currently its director. She teaches feminist theory at the newly created Master's and Ph.D. Programs on Interdisciplinary Studies on Women, Gender, and Feminism at NEIM/UFBA. She has worked in the area of gender and development in Brazil, both as a practitioner and as a researcher, and has published several articles in Brazil and abroad on feminist and gender studies. She is the convener for the Latin American Hub in the Pathways of Women's Empowerment Research Program Consortium.

Farida Shaheed, a sociologist and human rights activist, is deputy director of the multicountry research consortium *Women's Empowerment in Muslim Contexts: Gender, Poverty and Democratisation from the Inside* and director of research in Shirkat Gah Women's Resource Centre (Lahore, Pakistan). Decades of combining women-focused research, policy advocacy, and grassroots work have led her to focus both her writings and her activism on the complex forces at play in the interface of women, culture, identity, and governance and state, in South Asia and Muslim contexts, particularly in Pakistan. She is a founding member of the Women's Action Forum, the platform that led the movement for women's rights during the 1977–1988 military dictatorship of General Zia-ul-Haq. Awards include the Second Annual Award for Women's Human Rights (1997) and the Prime Minister's Award (1989) for her coauthored book *Two Steps Forward, One Step Back? Women of Pakistan.*

Lisa McIntosh Sundstrom is an assistant professor of Political Science at the University of British Columbia. Her major areas of research include Russian women's and human rights organizations, democratization, and foreign assistance. Recent publications include *Funding Civil Society: Foreign Assistance and NGO Development in Russia* (2006), *Russian Civil Society: A Critical Assessment* (2005, coedited with Alfred B. Evans Jr. and Laura A. Henry), "Foreign Assistance, International Norms and NGO Development: Lessons from the Russian Campaign" (2005), and "Women's NGOs in Russia: Struggling from the Margins" (2002). She has published recently on the comparative politics of climate policy and Russia's ratification and implementation of the Kyoto Protocol in a special issue of *Global Environmental Politics* (2007).

Nayereh Tohidi is professor and chair of the Gender and Women's Studies Department at California State University, Northridge, and a research associate at the Center for Near Eastern Studies at UCLA, where she has been coordinating the Bilingual Lecture Series on Iran since 2003. A native of Iran, Tohidi earned her B.S. (with Honors) from the University of Tehran in Psychology and Sociology and her M.A. and Ph.D. from the University of Illinois at Urbana-Champaign. Her teaching and research areas include sociology of gender, religion (Islam), ethnicity, and democracy in the Middle East and post-Soviet Central Eurasia, especially Iran and Azerbaijan Republic. She is the recipient of fellowships and research awards, including a year of Fulbright lectureship and research at the Academy of Sciences of the Soviet Republic of Azerbaijan; postdoctoral fellowships at Harvard University, Stanford University, and the Kennan Institute of the Woodrow Wilson International Center for Scholars; and the Keddie-Balzan Fellowship at the Center for Near Eastern Studies at UCLA. She was editor or author of *Globalization, Gender and Religion: The Politics of Women's Rights in Catholic and Muslim Contexts*; *Women in Muslim Societies: Diversity within Unity;* and *Feminism, Democracy and Islamism in Iran.*

Naihua Zhang is an associate professor of Sociology at Florida Atlantic University in the United States. She researches and publishes in the areas of sociology of development and social movements, in particular the contemporary women's movement and women's organizations in China.

Index